UNIVERSAL MINORITY RIGHTS

Universal Minority Rights

A Commentary on the Jurisprudence of International Courts and Treaty Bodies

Edited by

MARC WELLER

OXFORD
UNIVERSITY PRESS

OXFORD
UNIVERSITY PRESS

Great Clarendon Street, Oxford OX2 6DP

Oxford University Press is a department of the University of Oxford.
It furthers the University's objective of excellence in research, scholarship,
and education by publishing worldwide in

Oxford New York

Auckland Cape Town Dar es Salaam Hong Kong Karachi
Kuala Lumpur Madrid Melbourne Mexico City Nairobi
New Delhi Shanghai Taipei Toronto

With offices in

Argentina Austria Brazil Chile Czech Republic France Greece
Guatemala Hungary Italy Japan Poland Portugal Singapore
South Korea Switzerland Thailand Turkey Ukraine Vietnam

Oxford is a registered trade mark of Oxford University Press
in the UK and in certain other countries

Published in the United States
by Oxford University Press Inc., New York

First published 2007

British Library Cataloguing in Publication Data
Data available

Library of Congress Cataloging in Publication Data
Data available

Typeset by Newgen Imaging Systems (P) Ltd., Chennai, India
Printed in Great Britain
on acid-free paper by
Biddles Ltd., King's Lynn

ISBN 978–0–19–920851–7

1 3 5 7 9 10 8 6 4 2

This volume, published under the auspices of the European Centre for Minority Issues and the Centre of International Constitutional Studies, University of Cambridge, is dedicated to Professor Sir Elihu Lauterpacht QC, CBE

Preface

Governments have remained hesitant in giving concrete shape to minority rights. In universal human rights law only a single provision of the International Covenant on Civil and Political Rights specifically addresses minorities. There has been no movement seeking to convert the UN Declaration on the Rights of Persons Belonging to National or Ethnic, Religious and Linguistic Minorities (UNGA Resolution 47/135) into a binding legal standard. Regionally, only Europe has progressed to a binding treaty on minority rights, the European Framework Convention for the Protection of National Minorities. Still, the latter has been cast in general terms, leaving states a wide margin of appreciation in its implementation. Moreover, the Convention was removed from the ambit of the European Court of Human Rights. Instead an Advisory Committee and thus a weaker system of monitoring was established.

In practice, however, the situation is somewhat less grim. Minority rights have graduated from a political commitment to an uncontested part of the body of international human rights law. In the first commentary on *The Rights of Minorities,* published in the series of Oxford Commentaries on International Law, we set out to demonstrate the status of minority rights in the European human rights regime. Through a very detailed analysis of the implementation practice of the Framework Convention and the activities of the Advisory Committee, we explored the substance of the general commitments enshrined in the Convention. We hope to have shown thereby that the rights in question are indeed treated as legal obligations properly so-called, and that state practice has significantly advanced the interpretation of these rights.

This volume is an extension of the first commentary and should be considered its complement. In this volume, we have assembled and assessed the implementation practice of human rights bodies worldwide. Admittedly, none of these bodies has been set up with the specific aim of addressing minority rights issues and they cannot draw on many, sometimes any, binding legal standards in this matter. Nevertheless, we hope to demonstrate that there is an emerging universal jurisprudence on minority rights, drawing on the corpus of general human rights.

In addition to this overall goal, we strive to advance the understanding of the application of human rights in relation to minorities in general and their application to issues of particular relevance to minorities. Accordingly, each section of the commentary is designed so as to offer both a scholarly and a practice-oriented assessment of the law on the issue under investigation.

Finally, we aspire to add momentum to the idea of a convention on minority rights as part of universal international law. The time has been ripe for the transformation of the UN Declaration into a binding standard for some time. This commentary may suggest that in this area practice is sufficiently mature to warrant codification or progressive development.

In addition to the contributors to this volume, we have many individuals to thank. First of all, we are greatly indebted to the Volkswagen Foundation, which allowed us to launch this process and to generate the first commentary. Furthermore, we are pleased to acknowledge the support of the German Ministry of Foreign Affairs. With the financial support of the Ministry, we generated a comprehensive Digest of Minority Rights Jurisprudence, now published by the Council of Europe Press which can also be accessed electronically through the ECMI website, www.ecmi.de. This Digest, on which the authors of this volume have heavily drawn, was prepared by Ms Alcidia Moucheboeuf with her typical energy and efficiency. Moreover at ECMI, a number of individuals supported this project further, including in particular Ms Colleen French, Ms Adriana Nikolova, Ms Heu Yee Leung, Ms Marnie Lloyd, Mr Josee Lavoie, and Mr Matthew Ward. It was brought to its conclusion with the highly professional assistance of Mr Vladislav Michalcik and, more recently, Ms Janina Dill and Ms Katherine Nobbs, who also compiled the tables of treaties and cases and the index. Sub-editorial work was performed by Jude Chillman.

Once again, we have special reason to acknowledge gratefully the very efficient and kind processing of the volume by Oxford University Press, in particular on the part of John Louth and Alex Flach.

Marc Weller
Flensburg, July 2007

Contents

Table of Cases

AFRICAN COMMISSION ON HUMAN AND PEOPLES' RIGHTS (ACHPR)

EUROPEAN COMMISSION ON HUMAN RIGHTS (ECommHR)

EUROPEAN COURT OF HUMAN RIGHTS (ECtHR)

EUROPEAN COURT OF JUSTICE (ECJ)

INTER-AMERICAN COURT OF HUMAN RIGHTS (Inter-Am CtHR)

PERMANENT COURT OF INTERNATIONAL JUSTICE (PCIJ)

INTERNATIONAL COURT OF JUSTICE (ICJ)

UNITED NATONS COMMITTEE AGAINST TORTURE (CAT/C)

UNITED NATIONS ECONOMIC AND SOCIAL COUNCIL (ECOSOC)

UNITED NATIONS COMMITTEE ON ECONOMIC, SOCIAL AND CULTURAL RIGHTS (CESCR/C)

UNITED NATIONS COMMITTEE ON THE ELIMINATION OF DISCRIMINATION AGAINST WOMEN (CEDAW/C)

UNITED NATIONS COMMITTEE ON THE ELIMINATION OF RACIAL DISCRIMINATION (CERD/C)

UNITED NATIONS HUMAN RIGHTS COMMITTEE (HRC)

SOUTH AFRICA

UNITED KINGDOM

Table of International Instruments, National Legislation and Implementation Bodies

Selected Abbreviations

(I)CCPR	(International) Covenant on Civil and Political Rights
(I)CESCR	(International) Covenant on Economic, Social and Cultural Rights
(UN)HRC	(United Nations) Human Rights Committee
ACFC	Advisory Committee under the Framework Convention
ACHR	American Convention on Human Rights
AfrCh	African Charter on Human and Peoples' Rights
AfrCommHPR/ ACHPR	African Commission on Human and Peoples' Rights
CAHMIN	Ad Hoc Committee for the Protection of National Minorities
CAT	Convention against Torture
CAT/C	Committee against Torture
CEDAW	Convention on the Elimination of Discrimination against Women
CEDAW/C	Committee on the Elimination of All Forms of Discrimination against Women
CERD	Committee on the Elimination of Racial Discrimination
CERD/C	Committee on the Elimination of All Forms of Racial Discrimination
CESCR/C	Committee on Economic, Social and Cultural Rights
CMW	Convention on Migrant Workers
CRC	Convention on the Rights of the Child
CSCE	Conference on Security and Cooperation in Europe
EC	European Communities
ECHR	European Convention on Human Rights and Fundamental Freedoms
EChRML	European Charter for Regional or Minority Languages
ECJ	European Court of Justice
ECommHR	European Commission on Human Rights
ECOSOC	UN Economic and Social Council

ECPT	European Convention for the Prevention of Torture
ECRI	European Commission against Racism and Intolerance
ECtHR	European Court of Human Rights
EPZ	Export Processing Zone
EU	European Union
FCNM	Framework Convention for the Protection of National Minorities
IACHR	Inter-American Commission on Human Rights
ICRMW	Protection of the Rights of All Migrant Workers and their Families
IGO	Inter-governmental organization
ILO	International Labour Organization
Inter-AmCtHR	Inter-American Court of Human Rights
NGO	Non-governmental organization
OAS	Organization of American States
OAU	Organization of African Unity, today African Union
OSCE	Organization for Security and Cooperation in Europe
PCIJ	Permanent Court of International Justice
PKK	Partiya Karkerên Kurdistan / Kurdistan Workers' Party
RAF	Red Army Faction
TEC	Treaty of the European Community (Treaty of Rome)
TRNC	Turkish Republic of North Cyprus
UDHR	Universal Declaration of Human Rights
UN	United Nations
UN Decl. Min.	UN Declaration of the Rights of Persons Belonging to National or Ethnic, Religious and Linguistic Minorities
UNGA	United Nations General Assembly
UNESCO	United Nations Educational, Scientific and Cultural Organization
UNFICYP	United Nations Peacekeeping Force in Cyprus
UNRISD	United Nations Research Institute for Social Development

Notes on Contributors

Asbjørn Eide is the former Director and present Senior Fellow of the Norwegian Institute of Human Rights. He is the former secretary-general of the International Peace Research Institute in Oslo, and the author of numerous books and articles on peace and conflict issues and human rights. He is the President of the Advisory Committee of the Framework Convention for the Protection of National Minorities. He has been a member since 1981 of the United Nations Sub-commission on Prevention of Discrimination and Protection of Minorities, and was the Chair of the United Nations Working Group on the Rights of Minorities until 2004. He also served as a Special Rapporteur on the right to food as a human right.

Lauri Hannikainen is Professor of International Law at the University of Turku (Abo) in Finland, and Senior Researcher and Acting Director at the Northern Institute for Environmental and Minority Law, University of Lapland, Finland. He is a member of the European Commission against Racism and Intolerance at the Council of Europe.

Hurst Hannum is a Professor of International Law, teaching courses in international organizations, international human rights law, peacekeeping, and nationalism and ethnicity at Tufts University, Fletcher School of Law and Diplomacy. Professor Hannum has served as counsel in cases before the European and Inter-American Commissions on Human Rights and the United Nations; he has also been a member of the boards of several international human rights organizations. He has written about and/or participated in meetings concerned with minority rights generally, as well as particular situations in the Russian Federation (Tatarstan and Chechnya), Cyprus, Turkey, Northern Ireland, South Tyrol, India, Sri Lanka, East Timor, Sudan, Georgia (South Ossetia and Abkhazia), Greenland, the Balkans, Tibet, and US dependent territories. He also serves as a consultant to the United Nations negotiations on East Timor. At present, he is also a Sir YK Pao Professor of Public Law at Faculty of Law, University of Hong Kong.

Kristin Henrard is Senior Lecturer at the University of Groningen where she teaches human rights, refugee law, and constitutional law. She studied Law at the Catholic University of Leuven, Belgium, with special focus on human rights and international law. She graduated magna cum laude in 1994 and obtained an LLM degree at Harvard Law School in 1995 during which she further specialized in human rights and humanitarian law. Between 1995 and 1999 she conducted doctoral research and took her doctorate at the Catholic University of Leuven. During these years she also worked at the Constitutional Court of South Africa as researcher for Judge Kriegler and monitored the South African constitutional negotiations in 1996 for the Flemish Government. Furthermore, Kristin Henrard is Managing Editor of the Netherlands International Law Review; a member of the international advisory board of the Global Review of Ethnopolitics; Chair of a working group on the political participation of minorities (ethnic autonomy); and Country Specialist on South Africa for Amnesty International–Dutch Section.

Geoff Gilbert is a Professor in the Department of Law and the Human Rights Centre at the University of Essex in the United Kingdom. He has published widely in the field and he is the Editor-in-Chief of the International Journal of Refugee Law. He was Director of the Human Rights Centre's OSCE Project that received funding from the Foreign and Commonwealth Office. He has been an academic contributor to the UN Working Group on Minorities and prepared reports for it.

Zdenka Machnyikova is a legal expert specializing in the protection of minorities under international law and the relationship between human rights and conflict prevention. She was until recently Senior Legal Adviser to the OSCE High Commissioner on National Minorities. In her work with the OSCE she has analysed and evaluated legislation and provided advice regarding policy, law, and practice affecting minority rights and inter-ethnic relations in many European countries. Among other OSCE work in this field, she participated in elaboration of the *Oslo Recommendations regarding the Linguistic Rights of National Minorities* (1998), the *Lund Recommendations on Effective Participation of National Minorities in Public Life* (1999), and the *Warsaw Guidelines to Assist National Minority Participation in the Electoral Process* (2001). Prior to her employment with the OSCE she worked as Legal Adviser in the International Law Department of the Czech Ministry of Foreign Affairs. She is also a member of the Conflict Prevention Working Group of the Canadian Peacebuilding Coordinating Committee.

Sally Holt is a Research Fellow at the Centre for International Cooperation and Study at the University of Bradford. She previously worked as a Legal Officer for the OSCE High Commissioner on National Minorities. Her main research interests relate to the OSCE, security, conflict prevention, human rights, and the protection of minorities. Her work to date has focused mainly on the linguistic, educational, and participatory rights of minorities, as well as on matters of citizenship and integration related to minorities in the OSCE region.

Fernand de Varennes is a Senior Lecturer at Murdoch University School of Law, Perth, Australia. He has published widely on language rights, indigenous peoples and minority rights, international law, and ethnic conflicts. He is also a former Director at the Asia-Pacific Centre for Human Rights and the Prevention of Ethnic Conflict and the founding Editor-in-Chief of the Asia-Pacific Journal on Human Rights and the Law. He is recognized as one of the world's leading legal experts on language rights. He is Senior (Non-Resident) Research Associate at the European Centre for Minority Issues in Flensburg, Germany.

Patrick Thornberry is a Professor of International Law at Keele University in the United Kingdom, and has published widely in the field of public international law and human rights, specializing in the rights of minorities and indigenous peoples, and racial discrimination, including *Indigenous Peoples and Human Rights* (2002) and *Minority Rights in Europe* (2004). He is currently a member of the UN Committee on the Elimination of Racial Discrimination and has chaired the Minority Rights Group and maintains links with a range of NGOs and organizations of indigenous peoples.

Rainer Hofmann is Professor of Public Law and Public International Law at the University of Frankfurt, Germany; Co-Director of the Merton Centre for European Integration and International Economic Order; the former President of the Advisory Committee of the Council of Europe Framework Convention for the Protection of National Minorities; a Member of the Board of the European Centre for Minority Issues, Flensburg; and a member of the academic advisory board on international law to the German Foreign Ministry. He has published extensively in the field of human and minority rights.

Halida Nasic is currently working as an Associate Human Rights Officer at the Special Procedure Branch of the Office of the High Commissioner for Human Rights. Before, she worked as a Researcher at the International Law Department at Frankfurt University, an independent consultant conducting human rights training programmes as an expert for the Council of Europe, the International Organization for Migration, as well as non-governmental organizations, including Human Rights Internet. She was Programme Officer for the OSCE Mission to Kosovo from 2004 to 2005, and Research Associate of the OSCE Mission to Macedonia and Bosnia and Herzegovina from 2003 to 2004. Ms Nasic holds a Master of Political Science (MA) from Stockholm University, Sweden, and a European Master on Human Rights and Democratization (EMA) from the European Inter-university Centre for Human Rights and Democratization in Venice, Italy.

Margot Salomon is a Lecturer at the Centre for the Study of Human Rights and Department of Law, London School of Economics and Political Science. She serves as Legal Advisor to the United Nations High-Level Task Force on the Right to Development and has recently been appointed to the Committee on the Rights of Indigenous Peoples of the International Law Association. Margot regularly trains UK Foreign Office officials in minority rights, and prior to joining the LSE in 2004 she represented the NGO Minority Rights Group International to the UN and the African Commission on Human and Peoples' Rights. Margot holds a PhD in International Law from the LSE and an LLM from University College London. Her research interests include world poverty and human rights: external state obligations, human rights and international organizations, and the interface between human rights and economic development, with forthcoming research addressing the human rights dimensions of climate change. Recent publications include: *Global Responsibility for Human Rights: World Poverty and the Development of International Law* (Oxford University Press, 2007); 'International Economic Governance and Human Rights Accountability' in M. E. Salomon, A. Tostensen, and W. Vandenhole (eds), *Casting the Net Wider: Human Rights, Development and New Duty-Bearers* (Intersentia, 2007).

Marc Weller is the Director of the European Centre of Minority Issues in Flensburg, Germany. His writings mainly focus on conflict management, issues of international law and minority rights. He has acted as legal adviser to several governments and organizations, and as a member of international peace processes. Dr Weller is also a Reader in International Law at the University of Cambridge and a Fellow of the Lauterpacht Research Centre for International Law and Hughes Hall. He is also Director of the Carnegie Project on Resolving Self-determination Disputes through Complex Power-sharing and of the Cambridge Rockefeller Project on Restoring an International Consensus of the Rules Governing the Use of Force. He is also the editor of the companion volume to this Commentary, *The Rights of Minorities* (Oxford University Press, 2005).

INTRODUCTION: MECHANISMS FOR SUPERVISION AND REMEDIAL ACTION

Asbjørn Eide

I. International Institutions and their Forms of Jurisprudence

This commentary on the jurisprudence of international courts and treaty bodies concerning universal minority rights provides a unique insight into the achievements made in the evolution of international cooperation for human rights in general and minority rights in particular. 'Jurisprudence' broadly speaking refers to descriptions and analyses of the practice of institutions interpreting and applying law. The focus in this book is on the practice of international institutions interpreting and applying human rights law with specific attention to minority protection and the rights of persons belonging to minorities. This introduction provides a brief review of the evolution of such institutions and a systematic categorisation of those institutions that now exist.[1]

[1] Among different publications dealing with international institutions for the protection of human rights, three need special mention here: G. Alfredsson, J. Grimheden, B. Ramcharan & A. de Zayas (eds.) *International Human Rights Monitoring Mechanisms: Essays in Honour of Jakob Th. Möller* (The Hague: Kluwer Law International, 2001). It provides a broad and comprehensive overview (980 pages). Specifically on UN institutions: see P. Alston, *The United Nations and Human Rights. A Critical Appraisal* (Oxford: Oxford University Press 1992/ Clarendon Paperbacks 1995). Specifically for minority rights: ECMI and the Council of Europe Publishing, *Mechanisms for the*

The Framework Convention for the Protection of National Minorities (FCNM) Article 1 states that protection of minorities, and of the rights of persons belonging to minorities, forms an integral part of the international protection of human rights, and as such falls within the scope of international cooperation. A similar consideration with universal scope is reflected in the preamble to the United Nations Declaration on the Rights of Persons belonging to National or Ethnic, Cultural and Linguistic Minorities, which emphasizes that the promotion and realization of the rights of persons belonging to minorities would contribute to the strengthening of friendship and cooperation among peoples and states, and that the United Nations has an important role to play regarding the protection of minorities.

Minority protection, as an integral part of human rights, is now generally recognized to fall within the scope of international cooperation. But international cooperation requires multilateral institutions to guide, coordinate and implement the commitments of cooperation. Promotion and protection of universal human rights, including minority protection, is a prime example where international cooperation is required, but for many governments also difficult: at home, governments are affected by, and also often represent, the dominant groups in society and their interests; what the international community demands from them is to ensure equality for all together with a recognition and promotion of the identity also of the weaker and politically less influential groups in society. To cooperate internationally for such purposes may run counter to short-range interests of many governments, and it takes a long-range perspective on future stability in society to understand and recognize that such cooperation is beneficial to the state.

It is therefore not surprising that the evolution of the international mechanisms for cooperation in supervision and control has at times met reluctance and opposition, with states seeing the mechanisms as international interference in what, under the traditional international law of coexistence, was treated purely as internal affairs.

Nevertheless, a wide array of mechanisms has been developed since the establishment of the United Nations, and mainly during the last 50–60 years. Controversies are still surrounding them; the abolition at the United Nations in 2006 of the Commission on Human Rights, and its replacement by the Human Rights Council, is to a large extent a result of the controversies surrounding the development and use of mechanisms in the human rights field.

Implementation of Minority Rights, 2004. A large number of other books deals with institutions in the context of the broader description and analysis of substantive human rights, among them the important volume by Thornberry and Estebanéz (2004) mentioned in footnote 10 below.

A somewhat less turbulent evolution of international mechanisms has occurred in Europe, initially covering mainly Western and Southern Europe, but now including all European countries from Ireland in the West to the Russian Federation and Azerbaijan in the East (Byelorussia and the Central Asian former republics of the Soviet Union are not yet included). The specific focus on the protection of minorities, however, has been a very recent addition, going back to the adoption of the FCNM in 1994 and its entry into force in 1998. As will be seen in this book, the European Commission and the European Court on Human Rights had earlier already adopted decisions of importance for minority protection, applying the individual rights in the European Convention on Human Rights and Fundamental Freedoms in conjunction with its article on non-discrimination in Article 14.

A parallel development occurred also in the Americas beginning with the adoption of the American Declaration of 1948, which led to the establishment of the Inter-American Commission on Human Rights, and later through the American Convention on Human Rights of 1969 to the establishment in 1978 of the Inter-American Court. A fundamental weakness of the latter is that neither the United States nor Canada is a party to the Convention, which deprives the Inter-American Court of the possibility to deal with complaints about alleged violations by those countries. The United States signed the Convention in 1977, under the presidency of Jimmy Carter, but ratification has not followed; Canada has not even signed it. The issue of minorities has not been prominent in the inter-American setting, except for the issue of indigenous peoples and their rights.

More recently, the Organization of African Unity and its successor, the African Union, have developed comparable mechanisms, mainly with a basis in the African Charter on Human and Peoples' Rights. The main agency is the African Commission on Human and Peoples' Rights. An additional protocol has been adopted and has now entered into force providing for the establishment of an African Court on Human and Peoples' Rights. The Court has not yet been established. The term 'peoples' rights' in the African setting, as used in the African Charter mentioned above, can be understood to refer to minorities and indigenous peoples.

Some of the presently existing institutions have been created on the basis of specific treaties, others on the basis of the inherent power of the organizations that created them and using declarations as a basis for their work. The institutions operate in a variety of different ways, with different compositions, mandates and procedures. Taken together, the institutions and their procedures are frequently called 'mechanisms'.

The purpose of this introduction is to provide an overview of these mechanisms, the institutions and their procedures, with a focus on mechanisms to supervise or control national implementation of and compliance with international human rights standards including minority rights. Particular reference will be made to mechanisms concerning human rights in general and minority rights in particular. The presentation is done through two steps: first, a cursory review is given of the main stages in the evolution of mechanisms, reflecting the increasing level of international cooperation regionally and globally; second, there is a brief presentation and categorisation of the mechanisms that now exist. It will be concluded by some reflections on the functions and relative usefulness of the different mechanisms.

A. Historical Stages in the Evolution of International Mechanisms

1. Before the United Nations

International law of cooperation is a relatively recent development. Classic international law, better described as interstate law, was based on the system of entirely sovereign states recognizing no authority above them. It was a horizontal legal order of state coexistence with a minimal scope for international agencies. The content of the law addressed almost exclusively the relations between states, such as recognition of states and governments, borders at land and at sea, diplomatic relations, treaty-making, issues relating to the conduct of war. Internal relations between the state and its own inhabitants were exclusively matters of internal affairs and of national law, and were not a subject of international cooperation.

This was the basic structure of international law from the end of the Napoleonic wars and with some modifications lasting until World War II. For most of that time it included only a limited range of political entities or states—the so-called 'civilized states', most of them Christian. Turkey had been included at the time of the Crimean war in the 1850s, and Japan after the Japan/Russia war at the beginning of the 20th century.

The first (and limited) inroad into the traditional structure of international law was made by the League of Nations, established after the devastations of the First World War and intended to help build more comprehensive mechanisms for cooperation. The League of Nations was established 'to promote international cooperation and to achieve international peace and security'. It was the first effort to develop international cooperation on issues of political importance, and to move from the pattern of international conferences and congresses of the past to organized cooperation with a secretariat and regular meetings. The scope of cooperation under the League was much more limited, however, than the one which many years later (in 1945) was set for the United Nations.

The League did not have human rights as part of its concerns, but it did have a rudimentary minority regime. Far from elaborating a universal law on minorities, the minority arrangements under the League applied only to some states in Central and Eastern Europe. These were based on minority treaties relating to Poland, to the Kingdom of Serbs, Croats and Slovenes, and to Czechoslovakia, Romania and Greece; on minority commitments made by Austria, Bulgaria, Hungary and Turkey in peace treaties; and on unilateral commitments made by Albania, Lithuania, Latvia and Estonia. One non-European country, Iraq, also made a unilateral commitment in regard to its Kurdish minority. These arrangements gave rise to a petition system which could be used by the minorities concerned, which was quite a revolutionary step in giving individuals or groups legal standing at the international level. The practice which was developed within the League of Nations in this regard provided some lessons that could be drawn upon by the United Nations many years later.

The Permanent Court of International Justice (PCIJ) was established under Article XIV of the Covenant of the League of Nations intended to contribute to the peaceful settlement of international disputes. Only states or the League itself could initiate proceedings before the Court. The PCIJ was also authorized to offer advisory opinions on any dispute or question referred to the Court by the League of Nations Council. The PCIJ under the League played an important role, and rendered a number of important decisions in the minority area. Cases could not be brought to the PCIJ by individuals or groups, but only by states or the League itself. The origin of the case could, however, be a petition to the Council of the League which was then taken forward to the PCIJ by a state or the League.

The cooperation between states envisaged by the League of Nations was not sustained for more than a decade. The League performed a useful role during the 1920s, but was gradually weakened due in part to the impact of the Russian revolution, which implied that two conflicting economic and political systems were confronting each other, and particularly due to the intensification of nationalist confrontations during the 1930s. The League collapsed with the beginning of World War II.

2. Under the United Nations

The horrendous cruelty before, and during, World War II motivated the international community to take a giant step in transforming international law from coexistence to cooperation including the area of human rights. Under the Charter's Article 1(3), one of the main purposes set for the United Nations is to 'achieve international cooperation in solving international problems of an economic, social, cultural, or humanitarian character, and in promoting and encouraging respect for human rights and for fundamental freedoms for all without distinction as to race, sex, language, or religion.'

The founding states of the UN were initially reluctant with regard to minority rights. Some thought these could be protected through individual rights. There were also fears that protection and promotion of separate minority identity could hamper the effort to ensure equality for all on an individual basis, and that it could lead to internal conflict and tensions. Nevertheless, uneasiness about the plight of minorities was sufficiently strong to make the United Nations General Assembly state that it could not remain indifferent to their fate. It was therefore decided to establish a separate expert body, the Sub-Commission on Prevention of Discrimination and Protection of Minorities[2], to deal with that issue.

Another feature of the UN was the inclusion in the Charter of the principle of self-determination for peoples. The implications were not initially fully recognized but, through the subsequent process of decolonization, it led to a vast overhaul of the international state system and thereby of international law itself. A generation after the adoption of the UN Charter the number of member states had tripled. International law thereby covered a much more comprehensive set of states representing several different cultural traditions or civilizations. While this led to a much more inclusive international legal order, one of its consequences was the difficulty of ensuring support throughout its broad membership for the values on which the United Nations was initially built.

When the United Nations started operating, there was initially much enthusiasm for effective cooperation in the area of human rights, and it was assumed that protection of minorities would be safeguarded if human rights were fully respected. Not only did the Charter set the promotion and protection of human rights as one of its main purposes, but it also provided explicitly for the establishment of the Commission on Human Rights.

The growth of international cooperation envisaged by the UN Charter was set back for nearly half a century by the eruption of the Cold War, which can be dated to the coup in Praha in 1948, and which ended only with the fall of the Berlin Wall in 1989.

[2] A more detailed review is found in Eide, 'The Non-Inclusion of Minority Rights' in G. Alfredsson and A. Eide (eds.), *The Universal Declaration of Human Rights: A Common Standard of Achievements* (The Hague, Martinus Nijhoff, 1999), 655–75.

The first priority of the Commission was to set the standards for human rights. As a forum for drafting universal standards the Commission functioned admirably in spite of the increasingly adverse circumstances. Over a period of 16 months it drafted the Universal Declaration, and then proceeded to draft the two main covenants, which were finished from the side of the Commission in 1954. The reasons why it took another 12 years for the covenants to be adopted by the General Assembly are to be found in the Cold War, and the arrival of a large number of new members with their own preoccupations.

3. Dealing with Communications about Violations

While the Commission was expeditious in its drafting of substantive standards, it was much more hesitant concerning the mechanisms that could be used in the protection of human rights. From its very first year of operations in 1946, the United Nations was flooded with 'communications' containing allegations, with a demand for some kind of reaction or redress. These communications ended up in the Commission.

It might have been argued that the reference in the UN Charter to cooperation for the promotion and protection of human rights could have been a sufficient basis for the Commission to respond to such communications. Indeed, on 31 January 1947, the representative of India proposed that every human being should have the right of access to the United Nations, without risk of reprisal, wherever there is an actual or threatened infringement of human rights, and that the Security Council should be seized of all alleged violations of human rights, investigate them and enforce redress within the framework of the United Nations.[3]

This was not the view of the majority of the Commission, however.[4] It was argued that without a more specific legal basis for action than the vague terms of the Charter, it was impossible for the United Nations to act. From 1947, the United Nations Commission on Human Rights declared itself devoid of competence to deal with communications about alleged violations of human rights. In its first report to ECOSOC, the Commission stated: 'The Commission recognizes that it has no power to take any action in regard to any complaints concerning human rights'.[5]

[3] E/CN.4/11.

[4] A detailed review of the discussions concerning communications or petitions is found in J. Møller, 'The Right of Petition' in Alfredsson and Eide (eds.), *Universal Declaration of Human Rights, supra*, n. 2, 613–53.

[5] E/259, Chapter V, para. 22 (dated 11 February 1947).

The prevailing thinking was therefore that the United Nations and its Commission on Human Rights could not use its inherent powers under the Charter to take action in regard to violations. The next question, therefore, was what kind of mechanisms should be established to monitor and supervise the implementation of the substantive standards which were under preparation.

During the initial planning of what was then called the International Bill of Human Rights, many proposals were made for the inclusion of a right of petition for individuals or groups, but they were initially not accepted. It was agreed first to concentrate on the Universal Declaration of Human Rights, which should not include implementation mechanisms, and then move to the adoption of one or more human rights covenants which should include implementation measures.

Unfortunately, at an early stage in this process, the spirit of cooperation was replaced by the frozen coexistence between the two antagonistic groups of states, West and East, locked into the Cold War. Their conflicting approaches to human rights made it difficult to draw the institutional and procedural consequences of the intended cooperation in the field of human rights.

The Commission remained obstinate for two decades in its rejection of any power to act regarding complaints of violations, claiming that it had no legal basis to do so. This attitude started to change only in the late 1960s, and then mainly due to pressure from the developing countries, mostly the new members from Africa and Asia. The Trusteeship Council, based on Article 87(c) of the UN Charter, had for several years had an effective petition system. During the second part of the 1960s there was growing concern with human rights violations in southern Africa, meaning apartheid South Africa and in its mandated territory South West Africa (now Namibia), Rhodesia (now Zimbabwe), and the Portuguese colonies (now Mozambique, Angola, Guinea-Bissau and Sao Tome and Principe). The first outcome was to establish a group under the Commission to monitor and report on human rights violations in the racist and colonial regimes of southern Africa, but the enabling resolution was broader, opening up the investigation of gross and systematic violations wherever they may occur.[6]

This led to the establishment of two procedures, named after the number of the resolution by the ECOSOC which authorized these procedures: The '1235' procedure and the '1503' procedure. The first provides a basis for an annual public debate within the Commission focusing on gross violations of

[6] For details of the beginning of this evolution see Alston, *United Nations and Human Rights*, *supra*, n. 1, 143–80.

human rights, which can lead to adoption of resolutions relating to particular countries, including decisions to investigate in more detail the situation in that country and to apply pressure for change. This may include the appointment of special rapporteurs to produce, for a specified number of years, an annual report on the human rights situation in that country. The 1503 procedure provides a mechanism by which the Commission could examine, and possibly act on, communications about violations submitted by individuals and non-governmental organisations, provided the Commission found that the violations, if proven, revealed a gross and systematic pattern of violations. It did not provide for a specific finding in regard to the alleged violation reported, nor did it provide a remedy for the victim, but the procedure was used to assist the Commission to identify situations involving 'a consistent pattern of gross and reliably attested violations' (the formulation used in resolution 1503).

This process was confidential in all stages until, and if, the Commission decided to make it public. It was deeply flawed by political manipulation which made the choice of countries found to engage in such violations rather arbitrary. Nevertheless, the two procedures paved the ground for the development of what came to be known as the 'special procedures' of the United Nations.

These special procedures of investigation and reporting are generally divided into 'country rapporteur' procedures and thematic procedures. While a number of country rapporteurs were appointed already in the 1970s, starting with the case of Chile after the Pinochet coup and the human rights situation in the Palestinian territories occupied by Israel after the 1967 war, the thematic mechanisms started only in the 1980s. The first among them was the working group on enforced disappearances, whose adoption was strongly influenced by the practices of the Argentinean military during its 'dirty war' against its opponents in the country, but the phenomenon of enforced disappearances was more widespread both in the Americas and other places under authoritarian regimes or during internal conflicts, such as in Sri Lanka.

The number of thematic mechanisms has increased substantially over the last quarter century and now covers some economic and social rights as well as some civil and political rights. The main content of the mechanisms is to collect evidence on the violations or compliance with particular human rights standards. There are thematic mechanisms on extralegal execution (violations of the right to life), torture, freedom of religion and belief, and on the independence of judges and lawyers. Regarding economic and social rights there are rapporteurs on the violations of or non-compliance with the right to food, the right to housing, the right to health, and the right to education. While most of those mechanisms may have a bearing on the protection of minorities, since violations are often directed against minorities (and judges and lawyers are sometimes biased against particular minorities), some thematic mechanisms are of particular importance for minorities: the Special Rapporteur on contemporary forms of racism, racial discrimination, xenophobia and related intolerance, first appointed in 1993, the Special Rapporteur on the situation of human rights and fundamental freedoms of indigenous peoples, first appointed in 2001, and the Independent Expert on minority issues, first appointed in 2005. The mandates of the two last mechanisms, which are further described below, are presently held by Rodolfo Stavenhagen from Mexico (on indigenous peoples) and Ms. Gay McDougall from the United States (on minorities).

4. Developing Monitoring Mechanisms and Quasi-judicial Complaint Mechanisms

At the United Nations, treaty-based arrangements started with the adoption of the International Convention on the Elimination of All Forms of Racial Discrimination (CERD) in 1965. It was drafted in record time in 1993–1994. It provided for the establishment of the Committee on the Elimination of Racial Discrimination (CERD/C) (Article 8), which has the authority to monitor the implementation of the convention on the basis of periodical reporting by states (Article 9) as well as to deal with complaints by a state party against another state party (Article 11), and to receive and consider communications from individuals claiming to be a victim of a violation by a state party, but only if that state has declared that it accepts the competence of the Committee to deal with such complaints (Article 14). It is therefore a so-called optional arrangement. The convention had 170 state parties in March 2006; of these, 40 had made the declaration under Article 14 which allows for individual complaints.

A similar arrangement was made regarding the International Covenant on Civil and Political Rights, which was adopted in 1966 and entered into force in 1976. It provides for an expert monitoring body, called the Human Rights Committee. It is mandated to monitor the implementation of the Covenant on the basis of periodic reporting by states (Article 40), to consider communications by a state party claiming that another state party is not fulfilling its obligations, provided that both state parties have declared that they recognize the competence of the Committee to consider such communications (Articles 41 and 42), and to receive and consider communications from individuals under the Optional Protocol, provided that the individual is subject to the jurisdiction of the state addressed, and that the latter has recognized the competence of the Committee by ratifying the Optional Protocol. Article 27 CCPR deals with rights of persons belonging to minorities, and has given rise to a number of cases concerning minorities under the Optional Protocol. The optional arrangement for individual complaints under CERD Article 14 has not been widely ratified and is rarely used. An optional protocol to CEDAW (Convention on the Elimination of Discrimination against Women) providing a similar procedure for communications was adopted in 1999.

In 1982, the Convention against Torture and other Cruel, Inhuman and Degrading Treatment or Punishment was adopted, which provides an option for any state party to declare that it recognizes the competence of the Committee against Torture to receive complaints by states that another state violates its obligations under that convention (Article 21), and a similar option regarding communications from or on behalf of individuals who claim to be victims of violations of the convention (Article 22). Both are further discussed below.

A proposal is pending for the drafting and adoption of a similar Optional Protocol to the Covenant on Economic, Social and Cultural Rights. The new Human Rights Council decided in June 2006 to start the drafting of the protocol.

5. Regional Developments: Europe

At the regional level regimes for cooperation in the field of human rights were developing from the 1950s. This was done in Western Europe through the Council of Europe, and in the Americas through the Organization of American States, later also in Africa (through the Organization of African Unity, now the African Union).

Under the European Convention on Human Rights and Fundamental Freedoms (ECHR) adopted in 1950, the European Human Rights Commission was set up, and provisions were made for the establishment of the European Court of Human Rights, which was established in 1959. The initial commitment was only to make obligatory the state-to-state complaint system. There was still hesitance regarding a right of individuals to make complaints, which therefore was initially made an optional arrangement, applicable only to states which accepted the competence of the Commission to receive such complaints. The complaint could only go to the Commission, not to the Court even after its establishment in 1959. The role of the Commission was limited—its main task was to filter admissible complaints from the large mass that was considered inadmissible, and with those that were admissible, to seek to obtain a friendly settlement based on the rights contained in the ECHR.

When friendly settlements were not possible, the Commission could either take the case to the Court or express its views on the case and transmit it to the political organ, the Committee of Ministers, which could make the final decision. Individuals could not bring their cases to the European Court; only the Commission and states could initiate proceedings there.

A major overhaul of the system was made in 1998 through the entry into force of Protocol eleven to the ECHR. The old Court was replaced with a new and quite different court. Individuals were given the right to bring claims about violations of the ECHR directly to the European Court, provided they had exhausted domestic remedies. The European Commission on Human Rights was abolished.

A number of initiatives have been made in the Council of Europe to promote and strengthen cooperation for the protection of minorities, but no significant results were obtained until the dramatic years of 1990–1993 when extensive, violent ethnic conflicts erupted in the Balkans and in the trans-Caucasus region. The Parliamentary Assembly, in its resolution 1201 (1993), presented a proposal for an additional protocol to the European Convention on Human Rights and Fundamental Freedoms. Had it been adopted it would have meant that the rights of (persons belonging to) minorities set out in that protocol would have fallen within the jurisdiction of the European Court of Human Rights, in regard to countries that ratified the protocol. The proposal was not accepted by the Committee of Ministers. Instead, it called for the adoption of a separate convention not linked to the jurisdiction of the court, and in 1994 the Council of Europe adopted the Framework Convention for the Protection of National Minorities (FCNM). It entered into force and has, in 2006, 38 state parties out of the total of 46 members of the Council of Europe.

6. Regional Developments in the Americas and in Africa

The Organization of American States adopted its American Declaration on the Rights and Duties of States in May 1948, six months before the Universal Declaration was adopted by the United Nations. The OAS established a Commission on Human Rights to review developments on the basis of the American Declaration, but no court was provided for until the adoption of the American Convention on Human Rights in 1969; it entered into force in 1978.

In Africa, the Organization of African Unity adopted, in 1981, the African Charter on Human and Peoples' Rights, which entered into force in 1986. An African Commission was established to monitor the implementation of the Convention. In 1998 a Protocol was adopted envisaging the establishment of an African Court on Human and Peoples' Rights. The Protocol establishing the African court entered into force on January 1, 2004 upon its ratification by 15 member states, but the statute of the court has not yet (July 2006) been promulgated and a seat for the court has yet to be determined.

B. Existing Mechanisms: A Systemic Survey

Looking back on developments since the introduction of human rights into international law in 1945, we can see that a wide array of mechanisms has been established. Application at the international level of human rights, including minority rights, takes several forms, and has evolved over the last six decades in an interplay between the development of institutions and procedures in the context of a growing acceptance that human rights and minority rights are legitimate areas of international cooperation. The result is a great variety of mechanisms. Below follows an analytical survey of the main mechanisms used within international organisations, with special attention to those that are relevant for minority protection. The concern here is with multilateral mechanisms only. States do also address such issues in their bilateral relations. Minority issues are in some cases included in bilateral treaties. These will not be dealt with here.

1. Political versus Legal Mechanisms, Charter-based and Treaty-based

A systematic survey requires categorisation. The most general distinction is between 'political' and 'legal' mechanisms. At the United Nations this corresponds, broadly speaking, to the distinction between 'Charter-based' and 'treaty-based' mechanisms, which can also be used to explain the difference between the two.

A treaty-based mechanism is one which is provided for in a specific treaty, and where the main outlines of its mandate and procedure are set out. A Charter-based mechanism, in UN parlance, is a mechanism established on the basis of what is considered to be the inherent power of the organization under the UN Charter. More generally, therefore, 'political' mechanisms are those that are not provided for in a treaty, but established based on the inherent power of the organization, usually through a resolution by a competent body, which also sets out the statute or mandate for the institution and some general procedural guidelines. The mechanisms are established by the relevant body through a vote or by consensus, and as such are not dependent on consent by the individual state—they are not subject to ratification or accession, and can be applied in relation to all states members of the organization.

The operation of a treaty-based (legal) mechanism in relation to a particular state is based on the consent given by that state, through ratification or accession to the treaty or—where applicable—through a declaration by that state to accept an additional and optional competence of the relevant international body, such as the (first) optional protocol to the Covenant on Civil and Political Rights. It is called a legal mechanism because of its express basis in a treaty to which the state gives its consent.

2. Political Mechanisms: Working Groups and 'Special Procedures' at the United Nations

Under the United Nations Sub-Commission on the Prevention of Discrimination and Protection of Human Rights, two working groups of special relevance for this book have been set up. One deals with the rights of minorities, the other with the situation of indigenous peoples. Their agenda is broad and their procedures fall somewhat outside the scope of this preface.

The (now defunct) Commission on Human Rights developed a range of 'special procedures' beginning in the late 1960s. Though there is some uncertainty whether or not these will be rationalized after the abolition in 2006 of the Commission on Human Rights and its replacement by the Human Rights Council, it is likely that the main elements of the system will be maintained. The 'special procedures' fall into two categories: country-specific procedures and thematic procedures.

The country-specific procedures have their basis in two different resolutions by the UN Economic and Social Council, the '1235' procedure and the '1503' procedure. The former authorizes a public debate within the Human Rights Commission on the human rights situation in any country, the latter is based on communications from aggrieved individuals or groups of individuals or by non-governmental organizations, claiming, on the basis of particular actions or events, that a gross and systematic violation of human rights is taking place in the country concerned.[7] The process is confidential unless the Commission on Human Rights decides to adopt its views on the matter in public. Both of these procedures may lead to the appointment of a special rapporteur (appointed by the Chairman of the Commission after consultation with the regional groups) or a special representative (appointed by the UN Secretary-General). The rapporteur or representative is requested to collect information on the human rights

[7] For more details, see Alston, *United Nations and Human Rights*, *supra*, n. 1, 155–73.

situation in the country, if possible visiting the country (which can only be done with the consent of the government concerned), and to report annually to the Commission and sometimes also to the Third Committee of the General Assembly of the United Nations. The purpose of these reports is to focus attention on human rights violations. Country rapporteurs are generally only appointed in relation to countries which have a bad human rights record, and which are not prepared for a bona fide cooperation with the UN significantly to improve the situation. Through the reports, it is hoped to increase the pressure on these governments to alter their policies in regard to the human rights issues involved.

Several of the country rapporteurs deal with states where there are serious violations of minority rights. As an illustration the case of Sudan can be mentioned, which for most of the time since 1994 has been the subject of a country rapporteur. It was established by the Commission on Human Rights resolution 1993/60 with the mandate to establish direct contact with the government and with the people of the Sudan, and to investigate and report to the Commission on the situation of human rights in the Sudan, including any progress made there towards the full restoration of human rights, and compliance with international human rights instruments and international humanitarian law. The rapporteur was requested to seek and receive credible and reliable information from governments, non-governmental organizations and any other parties who have knowledge of these matters. The government of the Sudan was called upon to extend its full and unreserved cooperation, and to assist the Special Rapporteur in the discharge of his mandate and, to this end, to take all necessary steps to ensure that the Special Rapporteur had free and unlimited access to any person in the Sudan whom he wished to meet. In the resolution, the government of Sudan was requested to comply with applicable international human rights instruments, in particular the International Covenants on Human Rights and the Convention on the Elimination of All Forms of Racial Discrimination, to which the Sudan is a party, and to ensure that all individuals in its territory and subject to its jurisdiction, including members of all religious and ethnic groups, enjoy fully the rights recognized in these instruments.

There is considerable opposition by targeted governments to the appointment of country rapporteurs, since such an appointment implies that the country is placed on a 'black list'. If the intended target state has significant influence within the UN it usually manages to prevent a majority vote to set up a country rapporteur.

Therefore the mechanism of country rapporteurs was complemented with a thematic use in 1980/1981. The immediate background was the gross violations committed by the military regime in Argentina in the late 1970s and early 1980s, and the ability of the Argentinean regime to prevent a majority vote. The most severe violation at that time were enforced disappearances, many of which consisted of murder, by government agents, of the persons described as disappeared. It was therefore decided to appoint a special working group to investigate the problem of disappearances, not only in Argentina but wherever it might occur. This made it easier to have the resolution adopted, and the first thematic mechanism was established. The procedure consists of: the collection of allegations from anywhere in the world that somebody has forcibly been made to disappear, followed by correspondence with the state to seek to have the matter clarified. When there is not a satisfactory explanation by the government, the information about the enforced disappearance is included in the annual report of the Working Group on Disappearances, which until now has been examined and discussed in the Commission on Human Rights, a procedure which from now on will have to be taken over by the UN Human Rights Council.

Since then, a considerable number of thematic rapporteurs, special representatives or independent experts have been appointed to deal with particular human rights or minority rights issues. Two of these should be particularly mentioned here. The first is the United Nations Independent Expert on minority issues (presently Ms Gay McDougall from the United States) was appointed in 2005 on the basis of Human Rights Commission resolution 2005/79, with the mandate (*a*) to promote the implementation of the Declaration on the Rights of Persons Belonging to National or Ethnic, Religious and Linguistic Minorities, including through consultations with Governments, taking into account existing international standards and national legislation concerning minorities; (*b*) to identify best practices and possibilities for technical cooperation by the Office of the United Nations High Commissioner for Human Rights at the request of Governments; (*c*) to apply a gender perspective in his or her work; (*d*) to cooperate closely, while avoiding duplication, with existing relevant United Nations bodies, mandates, mechanisms as well as regional organizations; and (*e*) to take into account the views of non-governmental organizations on matters pertaining to his or her mandate. The independent expert is requested to submit annual reports on her activities to the Commission, including recommendations for effective strategies for the better implementation of the rights of persons belonging to minorities. In carrying out her mandate, the independent expert is required to receive information from diverse sources including states, expert bodies, United Nations agencies, regional and other inter-governmental organizations, NGOs and other civil society organizations.

Based on such information, she communicates with states concerning implementation of the Declaration on the Rights of Minorities, and requests further consultation and information relating to good practices on minority issues. She is also requested to undertake, at the invitation of governments, country visits to further constructive consultation, observe relevant programmes and policies, register concerns, and identify areas for cooperation. She studies the national legislation, policy, regulatory frameworks and institutions and practices, in seeking to promote the effective implementation of the Declaration on the Rights of Minorities.

The second example of a thematic rapporteur is the office of *the Special Rapporteur on the situation of human rights and fundamental freedoms of indigenous peoples,* established by Commission on Human Rights resolution 2001/57. The office is held by Rodolfo Stavenhagen from Mexico. His functions are set out in the enabling resolution as follows:

> (*a*) to gather, request, receive and exchange information and communications from all relevant sources, including Governments, indigenous people themselves and their communities and organizations, on violations of their human rights and fundamental freedoms; (*b*) to formulate recommendations and proposals on appropriate measures and activities to prevent and remedy violations of the human rights and fundamental freedoms of indigenous people; (*c*) to work in close relation with other special rapporteurs, special representatives, working groups and independent experts of the Commission on Human Rights and of the Sub-Commission on the Promotion and Protection of Human Rights, taking into account the request of the Commission contained in resolution 1993/30.

The rapporteur is invited to take into account a gender perspective while carrying out her/his mandate, paying special attention to discrimination against indigenous women. He shall also pay special attention to violations of the human rights and fundamental freedoms of indigenous children. Furthermore, in terms of institutional cooperation, he shall take into account all the recommendations of the Working Group on Indigenous Populations of the Sub-Commission on the Promotion and Protection of Human Rights, and of the Permanent Forum on Indigenous Issues relevant to her/his mandate.

As do all other rapporteurs, he provides an annual report to the Commission on Human Rights (in the future, the Human Rights Council).

3. Regional Political Mechanisms

Political mechanisms (here understood in the sense that they are not provided for in particular treaties) are used also at the regional level. Two of those functioning in Europe will be briefly mentioned here.

The Organization for Security and Cooperation in Europe (at that time: Conference on Security and Co-operation in Europe, CSCE) established, in 1992, the office of the High Commissioner on National Minorities. Its creation was decided by the participating states in the Conference on Security and Co-operation in Europe in Helsinki in 1992, and contained in the Helsinki Summit Declaration. The High Commissioner is intended to be an instrument of conflict prevention at the earliest possible stage, by providing 'early warning' and 'early action' with regard to tensions involving national minority issues which in the judgement of the High Commissioner, have the potential to develop into a conflict within the OSCE area, affecting peace, stability or relations between participating states, requiring the attention of, and action by, the OSCE. The High Commissioner works on the basis of OSCE principles (in particular the so-called 'Copenhagen document' adopted at the CSCE meeting on the human dimension, in 1990). He is required to work in confidence and independently of all parties directly involved in the tensions. He is barred from considering national minority issues in situations involving organized acts of terrorism. He does not deal with individual complaints except as a source of information to address more systematic issues facing minorities.

Another example is a body set up under the Council of Europe, the European Commission against Racism and Intolerance (ECRI). It was set up by Committee of Ministers resolution (2002) 8 as a body of the Council of Europe entrusted with the task of combating racism, racial discrimination, xenophobia, anti-Semitism and intolerance in greater Europe. This is done from the perspective of the protection of human rights, in the light of the European Convention on Human Rights, its additional protocols and related case law.

Its mandate is to review member states' legislation, policies and other measures to combat racism, xenophobia, anti-Semitism and intolerance, and their effectiveness; to propose further action at local, national and European level; to formulate general policy recommendations to member states, and to study international legal instruments applicable in the matter with a view to their reinforcement where appropriate.

ECRI carries out country visits and produces country-specific reports which are submitted to the Council of Europe.

4. Treaty-based Mechanisms

The two most commonly known forms of treaty-based mechanism are monitoring/dialogue, and complaint procedures. The *monitoring/dialogue* procedures are based on a system of periodic reporting by states describing their implementation of, and compliance with, international human rights/minority rights commitments undertaken by the state concerned, followed by an examination of those reports by a monitoring body which pursues a dialogue with the state concerning achievements and shortcomings in that implementation and compliance. The *complaint* procedure starts with complaints from a victim, or from someone acting on behalf of victims, seeking a finding by a competent institution that a violation of a human right has taken place, usually also requesting some redress for the violation.

A third treaty-based mechanism is that of inquiry. The UN Committee against Torture and the Committee on the Elimination of Discrimination Against Women may, on their own initiative, initiate inquiries if they have received reliable information containing well-founded indications of serious or systematic violations of the conventions by a state party. Inquiries may only be undertaken with respect to state parties who have recognized the competence of the relevant Committee in this regard. Article 20 of the Convention Against Torture, and Articles 8 to 10 of the Optional Protocol to CEDAW set out the basic procedure for the relevant Committee to undertake urgent inquiries. Under the Optional Protocol to the Convention against Torture adopted in 2002, a Sub-Committee on Prevention under the Committee against Torture is mandated to visit places of detention inside state parties, and the state parties are obliged to accept such visits.[8] The CEDAW procedure, which is provided for in the Optional Protocol to the CEDAW convention, specifically authorizes visits to the territory of the state under consideration, when warranted and with the state's consent.

A strong basis for inquiries is found in the European Convention for the Prevention of Torture and Inhuman or Degrading Treatment or Punishment, which in Article 1 mandates the committee to visit any place within the jurisdiction of state parties where persons are deprived of their liberty by a public authority, and every state party is obliged to permit such visits. After each visit, the Committee shall draw up a report on the facts found during the visit, taking account of any observations which may have been submitted by the party concerned. The report shall be confidential unless the state party requests its publication (Article 11), but the Committee shall prepare annually a general report on its activities (Article 12).

[8] The Optional Protocol to the Convention against Torture is not in force at the time of writing (July 2006).

5. Monitoring/Dialogue Procedures

The monitoring/dialogue procedures are based on the duty of states to present periodic reports on the implementation of treaties to which they are party, and to submit to an examination of those reports by specifically appointed supervisory bodies. At the United Nations, state parties have to provide reports under the International Covenant on Civil and Political Rights (CCPR) Article 40, the International Covenant on Economic, Social and Cultural Rights (CESCR) Article 16, the Convention on the Elimination of All Forms of Racial Discrimination (CERD) Article 9, the Convention on the Elimination of Discrimination against Women (CEDAW) Article 18, the Convention against Torture (CAT) Article 19, and the International Convention on the Protection of the Rights of All Migrant Workers and their Families (CMW) Article 73.

At the European level, state parties have to submit periodic reports under the European Framework Convention for the Protection of National Minorities (FCNM) Article 25, the European Charter on Regional and Minority Languages Article 15, the European Social Charter Articles 21 and 22, and others.

The content of the state reports varies according to the content of the convention, but in general, they shall provide information on legislative, judicial, administrative and other measures which the state has adopted and which give effect to the obligations they have made under the convention.

The state reports should also provide information on factors and difficulties they have encountered affecting the degree of fulfilment of their obligations. The supervising body examines the reports, taking into account information from other sources, including the so-called 'shadow reports' prepared by non-governmental organizations.

At the United Nations, the supervising body invites representatives of each reporting state for a further dialogue on the implementation of its convention, based on the state report and other information available to the supervisory body. Under the European Framework Convention on National Minorities, the Advisory Committee has developed a practice of visiting the country itself for discussions with representatives of the different relevant branches of government, the national human rights institutions, representatives of the minorities and non-governmental organizations.

The outcome of the monitoring at the United Nations takes the form of a set of concluding observations, consisting of appreciation of positive steps taken, critical comments on persisting shortcomings, and a set of recommendations for further action. At the next stage of the reporting the state party will be asked what it has done to follow up on those recommendations. All relevant documents, including the state report and the concluding observations, are publicly available. The outcome of the monitoring by the Advisory Committee on the Framework Convention is the preparation of a comprehensive opinion including comments, positive and critical, regarding the implementation of each article under the Convention, and a set of recommendations where required. The opinion is transmitted to the European Committee of Ministers which in due time adopts its own resolution, largely based on the recommendations by the ACFC. The state report and the opinion of the ACFC are made public at the latest when the Council of Ministers has adopted its resolution.

6. *Quasi-judicial Mechanisms of Complaint Procedures at the United Nations*

Four of the United Nations human rights treaty bodies (HRC, CERD/C, CAT/C and CEDAW/C) may, under certain circumstances, consider individual complaints or communications from individuals. The HRC may consider individual communications relating to state parties to the First Optional Protocol to the CCPR. The CEDAW may consider individual communications relating to state parties to the Optional Protocol to CEDAW. The CAT Committee may consider individual communications relating to state parties that have made the necessary declaration under Article 22 of CAT, under which a state party to CAT may declare that it recognizes the competence of the Committee to receive, and consider, communications from, or on behalf of, individuals subject to its jurisdiction who claim to be victims of a violation by a state party of the provisions of the Convention. The CERD may consider individual communications relating to state parties who have made the necessary declaration under Article 14 of CERD. The Convention on Migrant Workers also contains provision for allowing individual communications to be considered by the CMW.

The best known, and most widely used, mechanism is under the (first) Optional Protocol to the CCPR, under which a state party to that Covenant which ratifies or accedes to the Optional Protocol recognizes the competence of the Committee to receive, and consider communications from, individuals subject to its jurisdiction who claim to be victims of a violation by that state party of any of the rights set forth in the Covenant (Article 1).

Individuals within that state who claim that any of their rights enumerated in the Covenant have been violated, and who have exhausted all available domestic remedies, may submit a written communication to the Committee for consideration (Article 2).

The complaint must therefore satisfy the mentioned admissibility criteria: that the complainant is subject to the jurisdiction of that state, that the complainant asserts that he or she is a victim (hence, the complaint cannot be made on behalf of others, except as an authorized representative of the alleged victim), and she or he must be a victim of a violation of the rights contained in that Covenant. Furthermore, the Committee shall consider inadmissible any communication which is anonymous, or which it considers to be an abuse of the right of submission of such communications or to be incompatible with the provisions of the Covenant (Article 3).

The procedure is purely written and not very elaborate. When receiving a communication from alleged victims, the Human Rights Committee first examines its admissibility. If it is found admissible, the state party against which the complaint is made is required to submit to the Committee 'explanations or statements clarifying the matter and the remedy, if any, which may have been taken'. At the end of the procedure, the Committee adopts its views, which in many cases are that a violation has taken place, and makes a recommendation as to the remedy that should be made. These views are not legally binding. The Human Rights Committee, and the other committees which are empowered under these optional arrangements to deal with individual complaints, are not courts. Even so, the application and interpretation of the provisions of the relevant conventions have generated considerable case law and thus produced an important jurisprudence.

7. Judicial Bodies in the Regional Systems

From a legal perspective, the most advanced institution for the protection of human rights is the European Court of Human Rights. All members of the Council of Europe are parties to the European Convention on Human Rights (ECHR), and the jurisdiction of the Court now extends to all parties to the convention. Cases may be brought by any European country against any other European country[9] under ECHR Article 33, and cases may also be brought by any person, non-governmental organisation or group of individuals claiming to be the victim of a violation by any European state of the rights set forth in ECHR and the Protocols to it. A substantial caseload now exists which has resulted in very elaborate jurisprudence of the Court.

[9] Excluding Byelorussia, which is not a member of the Council of Europe.

There are important admissibility criteria to be taken into account. One of them is that all domestic remedies must have been exhausted before the case can be processed by the European Court. More importantly for the subject of the present book is that the Court can only deal with claims that there has been a violation of a right contained in the ECHR or one of its protocols. The ECHR does not mention minority rights as such, except for Article 14 which states that 'the enjoyment of the rights and freedoms set forth in this Convention shall be secured without discrimination on any ground, such as... association with a national minority.' This is not an independent right, but accessory to rights set out in ECHR Articles 2 to 14 and in the Protocols.

Nevertheless, the jurisdiction of the Court can be, and has been, very important for minorities. Many of the rights set out in the Convention are of great significance for persons belonging to minorities, among others the right to respect for private and family life (Article 8), freedom of thought, conscience and religion including the right to manifest one's own religion (Article 9), freedom of expression (Article 10) which includes expression in one's own language, freedom of assembly and association (Article 11), which includes the right of any minority to form their own associations, irrespective of whether the government has recognized them as a minority or not. Violations of these rights against persons belonging to minorities have often been found without reference to Article 14. Of considerable importance is the new Protocol 12, under which 'the enjoyment of any right set forth by law shall be secured without any discrimination on any ground such as... association with a national minority.' This considerably extends the protection against discrimination, in that it covers 'any right set forth by law', including any national law in the country concerned.

Thornberry and Estebanez[10] have examined the relevance of the ECHR to, and the practice of the European Court of Human Rights on, issues pertaining to minorities such as existence, pluralism and self-definition; self-determination; the norm of non-discrimination; identity issues including promotion of identity, language, education, participation, religion and property; the question of loyalty; and on the position of minorities in the implementation of the convention, the '*locus standi*'. Minorities as groups do not have rights under ECHR, but individual members can act jointly if each of them can claim to be a victim.

[10] In Patrick Thornberry and María Amor Martín Estébanez, *Minority Rights in Europe*, (Strasbourg, 2004), ch. 1.

Fernand de Varennes has discussed the use of the European Court to protect various rights of minorities, mentioning in particular issues such as the existence and recognition of minorities, freedom in the use of minority languages in a number of different contexts as well as positive obligations of the state with regard to minority language, the registration and operation of minority organisations, and the respect of minority culture or lifestyle.[11]

As previously noted, the American Court on Human Rights was established when the American Convention on Human Rights entered into force in 1978, and it has already had considerable significance particularly for indigenous peoples. A protocol to the African Charter on Human and Peoples' Rights providing for the establishment of the African Court on Human and Peoples' Rights entered into force in 2004, but the court has not yet been set up and its statute has not yet been adopted. Once it starts its operations it may have considerable significance for minorities in Africa.

8. A Brief Note on the International Criminal Court and the Yugoslav and Rwanda Tribunals

The evolution of institutions applying international criminal law is likely to have considerable significance for minorities and generate important jurisprudence in this field. The jurisdiction of the International Criminal Court covers genocide, crimes against humanity, and serious violations of humanitarian law. Such crimes are often directed against minorities—the Holocaust against Jews and Roma/Gypsies before and during World War II being the prime but not the only example—the Rwanda genocide against Tutsis and the ethnic cleansing against different groups in the former Yugoslavia are more current examples. The practice of these institutions has already generated some jurisprudence, and more is forthcoming, including on principles of criminal responsibility in the dealings by authorities with their minorities during times of conflict.

II. Reflections on the Functions and Usefulness of the Different Mechanisms

A comprehensive assessment of the mechanisms is beyond the scope of this brief introduction, but a few points can be made.

[11] Fernand de Varennes, 'Using the European Court of Human Rights to Protect the Rights of Minorities', in M. Weller and A.H.E. Morawa (eds.), *Mechanisms for the Implementation of Minority Rights* (Strasbourg, 2004), ch. 4.

The first observation is that there has been a gradual development towards more binding or constraining mechanisms. The development has been stronger at the regional level than the global, and more robust in Europe than in the Americas (where the United States and Canada have kept themselves aloof from the American Convention) and in Africa which has not yet established the Court envisaged in a protocol which is already in force.

The second observation is that different mechanisms still exist, side by side, and are likely to do so for a considerable time. There are political and legal mechanisms, and both of them are likely to continue to have their uses. The legal mechanisms are helpful in regard to countries which generally are supportive of human rights, and are willing effectively to submit to international supervision and/or adjudication. Some states ratify international instruments, but do not effectively submit to their implementation. This can be shown in their low record of reporting or in reports which are practically devoid of content. It has happened that some countries have used their ratification of conventions as an argument against being subjected to political mechanisms such as country rapporteurs, while at the same time abstaining from an effective dialogue under the convention. Political mechanisms can be useful in increasing the pressure on states which are reluctant to cooperate in the implementation of human rights and minority rights.

The third observation concerns the coexistence of two different legal mechanisms, the monitoring/supervising mechanism based on state reports, and the judicial or quasi-judicial procedures relating to claims about specific violations. In the United Nations these two coexist with regard to the same set of rights: under CCPR, under CERD, under CEDAW and under CAT; in the future also under the migrant worker convention (CMW). In Europe, it is different: civil and political rights are not subject to state reporting but to the complaint procedure under the European Human Rights Court; social rights are subject to a reporting/monitoring process, but with some scope for collective complaints; and minority rights under the FCNM are subject solely to monitoring and dialogue through the supervisory body. As noted, however, many minority concerns are covered by the individual rights set out in the ECHR, and there is to some extent a parallel process of individual complaints before the Court and of monitoring/dialogue before the ACNM.

This leads to the fourth observation: monitoring/dialogue under reporting procedures and complaint procedures have different functions, each of which is useful in its own right. The role of a court is to determine whether a violation has taken place in a concrete and specific context. Clearly its decision in a specific case can be precedent for the understanding of the minimum that states have to fulfil in order not to be held to have violated their obligations, but each case is specific and does not necessarily provide much insight into more general questions of implementation.

In contrast, the monitoring bodies, working on the basis of state reports and other relevant information, are not required or even entitled to adopt decisions whether violations have been committed in specific cases. Their role is to encourage states to pursue an optimal implementation of the relevant convention, which may include recommendations for changes in laws and in administrative and other practices.

It is possible that a decision by a court can weaken the position of the monitoring body in regard to the recommendation of optimal policies, when the court finds in a specific case that a particular action does not constitute a violation, while the monitoring body generally has recommended avoidance of such actions. To illustrate: in the context of the right of persons belonging to minorities to return after periods of conflict, the Advisory Committee argued against the termination of protected tenancies due to the temporary absence of Serbs in Croatia. A specific case of termination was dealt with by the European Court of Human Rights (*Blečić v. Croatia,* 2004)[12] which found that there had been no violation. Under the very specific circumstances of that case, the decision was justified, but as an expression of a general policy it was very unfortunate.

The lesson to be drawn from this and other cases is to underscore the difference between monitoring which focuses on optimal policies for the implementation of international commitments and the use of specific court cases as precedence for more general questions. It is important to keep these different roles in mind when analysing the jurisprudence of the different international institutions dealing, directly and indirectly, with issues affecting minorities and their rights.

[12] *Blečič v. Croatia*, 2004. Judgment of 29 July 2004, ECtHR App No. 59532/00 [2004] ECHR 397.

LEGAL NATURE OF MINORITY RIGHTS AS PART OF HUMAN RIGHTS, LIMITATIONS, DEROGATIONS, RESERVATIONS, AND INTERPRETATIVE STATEMENTS

Lauri Hannikainen

I. Minority Rights as Human Rights

The 1966 Covenant on Civil and Political Rights (CCPR) is one of the most important international human rights conventions. It is the universal counterpart of two respectable regional conventions, namely the European Convention on Human Rights (ECHR) and American Convention on Human Rights (ACHR). Article 27 of the Covenant provides minority rights as follows:

> In those States in which ethnic, religious or linguistic minorities exist, persons belonging to such minorities shall not be denied the right, in community with the other members of their group, to enjoy their own culture, to profess and practise their own religion, or to use their own language.

Thus, Article 27 provides for three human/minority rights. The Human Rights Committee (HRC) which is the international monitoring organ of the

Covenant explains the essence of the Article in its General Comment, stating that it 'establishes and recognizes a right which is conferred on individuals belonging to minority groups and which is distinct from, and additional to all the other rights which, as individuals in common with everyone else, [they] are already entitled to enjoy under the Covenant'.[1] The Optional Protocol of the CCPR provides for the right of persons, who consider that their rights under the Covenant have been violated and that they have not got redress before national authorities, to make complaints (communications) to the HRC. The Committee in many of its reports on complaints referring to Article 27 has recognized the legal character of the rights included in Article 27.

The Framework Convention for the Protection of National Minorities (FCNM), applicable in Europe, is the most notable convention dedicated solely to minority rights. It states in Article 1 that the protection of national minorities, and of the rights and freedoms of persons belonging to those minorities, forms an integral part of the international protection of human rights. However, it should be noted that the states parties are under no obligation to ensure the direct applicability of the substantive provisions of the Convention before their administrative and judicial authorities. That means that the rights provided in the Convention are not justiciable. The emphasis is placed upon the protection of persons belonging to national minorities by the ratifying states.[2] The Explanatory Report on the FCNM which was adopted by the Ad Hoc Committee for the Protection of National Minorities (CAHMIN) at the same time as the FCNM points out that the protection of minority rights does not fall within the reserved domain of states.[3]

The Declaration on the Rights of Persons belonging to National or Ethnic, Religious or Linguistic Minorities, adopted by the UN General Assembly by consensus in 1992, follows the basic philosophy of Article 27 of the CCPR. However, as a non-binding declaration it is not meant to provide any justiciable rights to persons belonging to minorities.[4]

What kinds of conclusions can be drawn from the above instruments and their commentaries? The HRC's General Comment speaks of individuals' rights in Article 27 which are distinct from, and additional to, all the other rights belonging to every individual under the Covenant. The terms 'distinct'

[1] Human Rights Committee, General Comment No. 23 (50) in 1994 , Art. 27, GAOR, Forty-ninth Session, Supplement No. 40 (A/49/40), annex V, para. 1.

[2] See two articles in M. Weller (ed.), *The Rights of Minorities in Europe: A Commentary on the European Convention for the Protection of National Minorities* (Oxford 2005): Rainer Hofmann, 'The Framework Convention for the Protection of National Minorities: An Introduction', 1–24, at 5; and Hans-Joachim Heintze, 'Article 1', 77–96, at 88 and 96.

[3] FCNM, Collected texts, 22.

[4] GA res. 47/135.

and 'additional' could mean that minority rights are a category separate from (and additional to) general human rights or that they belong to the body of universal human rights as an additional sub-category. Both views have gained support. Scheinin argues that minority rights should neither be reduced to the principles of equality and non-discrimination nor seen as a separate or an additional category of human rights, either. 'Rather, minority rights as a sub-category of human rights should be seen as a form of added protection to universal human rights, deemed necessary in order to secure human rights to persons in a minority situation.' Addressing minority rights as something separate from general human rights easily leads to the subordination of minority rights to politics.[5] A state, referring to its sovereignty, could say that, of course, we recognize and respect human rights but, instead, we do not agree with the category of minority rights. There are states such as France which argue that all citizens are equal with all general human rights and that this is enough.

In international jurisprudence the case *Hopu and Bessert v. France* before the HRC is of particular interest.[6] Two indigenous Polynesians complained that they were the lawful owners of a land tract in Nuuroa, Tahiti, on which French Polynesian authorities had started the construction of a hotel. The hotel was being constructed on a traditional burial ground of the indigenous inhabitants of Tahiti and at a fishing lagoon still used by some 30 families for their subsistence. The authors of the complaint claimed violations of, *inter alia*, their right to enjoy their culture and their private and family life.

The HRC had a number of limitations when it started to deliberate the case. Since there is no property clause in the CCPR, the HRC could not consider whether the authors were right in their claim of being the lawful owners of the land. Another limitation was that France has made a reservation to Article 27 which excludes the article from the sphere of its obligations under the Covenant. The majority of the HRC accepted France's reservation. This means that the HRC could not directly use the right to culture of the Polynesian minority as the criterion. The Committee concentrated on the notions of privacy and family which are included in Articles 17 and 23 of the Covenant and reasoned in the following manner:

> The Committee observes that the objectives of the Covenant require that the term 'family' be given a broad interpretation so as to include all those comprising the

[5] Martin Scheinin, 'Minority rights: additional or added protection? ', in M. Begrsmo (ed.), *Human Rights and Criminal Justice for the Downtrodden: Essays in Honour of Asbjørn Eide* (Leiden: Boston, 2003), 487–504.

[6] *Francis Hopu and Tepoaitu Bessert v. France* (Communication No. 549/1993, UN Doc. CCPR/C/60/D/549/1993/Rev. 1. (1997).

family as understood in the society in question. It follows that cultural traditions should be taken into account when defining the term 'family' in a specific situation. It transpires from the authors' claims that they consider the relationship to their ancestors to be an essential element of their identity and plays an important role in their family life. This has not been challenged by the State party; nor has the State party contested the argument that the burial grounds in question plays an important role in the authors' history, culture and life.... The Committee considers that the authors' failure to establish a direct kinship link cannot be held against them in the circumstances of the communication, where the burial grounds in question predate the arrival of European settlers and are recognized as including the forbears of the present Polynesian inhabitants of Tahiti. The Committee therefore concludes that the construction of a hotel complex on the authors' ancestral burial grounds did interfere with their right to family and privacy. The State party duly took into account the importance of the burial grounds for the authors, when it decided to lease the site for the building of a hotel complex.

Thus, the Committee referred to the right to identity, and to cultural traditions, in its assessment of the contents of the rights to family and privacy of the indigenous complainants. The Committee recognized the interdependence of human rights; a minority person's right to family and privacy involved also the rights to identity and culture. The link between human rights and minority rights is evident.

Let us have a closer look at different minority rights beyond Article 27 of the CCPR. The prohibition of discrimination and the right not to be discriminated against is provided in many human rights conventions. The right to freedom of conscience and religion is guaranteed in different human rights conventions, including Article 18 of the CCPR, Article 9 of the ECHR and Article 12 of the ACHR. The right to culture is guaranteed in Article 15 of the Covenant on Economic, Social and Cultural Rights in the form of the right to take part in cultural life. The right to use a minority language is less protected in general human rights conventions, but certainly the right to freedom of expression offers protection. The right of association which is well guaranteed in a number of human rights conventions is important for the participatory rights of minorities. The right to identity is not specifically guaranteed in general human rights conventions, but it is one of the underlying concepts behind the entire body of human rights and its different traits are present in many provisions.[7] The ACHR stipulates in Article 5 that every person has the right to have his physical, mental or moral integrity respected.

[7] See Yvonne M. Donders, *Towards a Right to Cultural Identity* (Intersentia, Antwerpen—Oxford—New York, 2002).

Regarding the fundamental right to existence, the 1948 Convention on the Prevention and Punishment of the Crime of Genocide endeavours to guarantee it.

The ECHR does not contain any provision recognizing minority rights with the exception of Article 14 which prohibits discrimination on many grounds relevant for minorities, including race, language, religion, national or social origin and association with a national minority. The prohibition of discrimination is strengthened by Additional Protocol 12 of 2000. If articles other than that on non-discrimination were interpreted in a minority-insensitive way, persons belonging to minorities would factually enjoy weaker human rights than persons belonging to the majority population.

One may conclude that minority rights are legal rights, a part of the general body of human rights, and add a further element of specificity in relation to minority communities and individuals. If minority rights were understood as a category separate from, and additional to, general human rights, this would mean that persons belonging to minorities would have more human rights than other persons.[8] It is better to understand minority rights as a specific sub-category in the body of general human rights with the purpose of ensuring the de facto equality of minorities with the majority and/or the survival of minorities (if the persons belonging to a minority want to save the group's separate identity). These minority rights may contain supportive features, such as affirmative action or special protection to ensure de facto equality or even mild special rights to ensure the survival of a minority.[9] The recognition of such phenomena is based on the evident fact that the minority in question is not able to take advantage of the existing body of general human rights to a sufficient extent. However, since affirmative action and special rights may raise negative feelings towards minorities among the majority population, and should be resorted to with caution, it is important, as the *Hopu and Bessert v. France* case evidences, to interpret all human rights provisions in a minority-sensitive way—in recognition of the interdependence of human rights.

II. Limitations of Minority Rights

A number of human rights conventions specify that limitations are permissible to a number of their articles, and also specify the grounds for limitations. On

[8] Scheinin, *ibid.*, 489–94.

[9] See Kristian Myntti, 'The Prevention of Discrimination v. Protection of Minorities: With Particular Reference to "Special Measures"', *Baltic Yearbook of Human Rights*, 2 (2002), 199–226.

the other hand, many human rights conventions do not address the question of limitations at all.

From the perspective of this article, the most interesting human rights conventions are the CCPR, ECHR and ACHR which in several of their articles contain provisions on the right to make limitations. However, it should be pointed out at once that Article 27 of the CCPR does not contain any provision on the right of states to make limitations. On the other hand, the FCNM addresses the question of limitations in general terms in Article 19, permitting only such limitations as are provided for in international legal instruments, in particular the ECHR, in so far as they are relevant to the rights and freedoms flowing from the said principles.[10] This provision is quite vague and there is no relevant specification available in the practice of the international monitoring organs of the FCNM. However, when (below) the case law of the ECtHR is explained, it is good to keep in mind that it may have a bearing on the FCNM.

The CCPR, ECHR and ACHR take similar approaches to limitations, but their provisions are not identical. Since the ECHR has most jurisprudence on limitations, let us pay it special attention.

Why are limitations permitted to human rights provisions, especially to the provisions on freedom rights? Freedom rights as such are very broad; take the right to freedom of expression as an example. To start with, it is without limits; however, this would be harmful for society and for other persons. The most common grounds of limitation permitted by human rights conventions are national security, public order/safety, health, morals and the rights of other persons, and quite often also the prevention of crime.

There is jurisprudence on the limitation grounds specified in human rights conventions, in particular in the ECHR, relevant for minority rights, but there are also many cases where limitations have been made on other grounds. To give examples, the HRC has taken a stand on the rights of a person belonging to a given minority vis-à-vis the minority as a whole. If the individual has lost the case, the ground has been the whole minority's interest and that cannot be simply reduced to the ground of 'rights of others'. Another example: if a number of wandering Roma families start to use a given piece of land as their camping ground with the claim that the authorities have not provided enough camping sites, and refer to the right to freedom of movement and to respect for family life, their claim is more likely to succeed if the site is located on publicly owned land in the countryside, quite far from urban areas than in a city near to

[10] For an analysis of Art. 19, see Lauri Hannikainen, 'Article 19', in M. Weller (ed.), *The Rights of Minorities in Europe, supra*, n. 2, 519–34.

its centre. If the claim is turned down, the ground may be public order/safety, but the ground may also be the will of the authorities to use that piece of land for other purposes.

Since Article 27 of the CCPR does not provide for limitations, the HRC's analysis quite naturally has taken a different approach to disputes. Most of its individual cases on Article 27 have dealt with either the rights of an individual person or group of persons vis-à-vis an indigenous (minority) people as a whole, or complaints by indigenous persons that state-authorized economic activities in their traditional lands infringe their right to culture. In most of those cases the bigger party, the respondent state (and on its side in some cases the indigenous people concerned as a whole) has emerged as winner.[11] However, to report on a different outcome, in the *Sandra Lovelace v. Canada* case the HRC upheld (indigenous) Lovelace's right to return to her home reserve because of the right to enjoy her native culture. Her return could not be characterized as harmful to the community; the rights of others were not unduly restricted.[12]

One more case should be reported from the HRC. In *Apirana Mahuika et al. v. New Zealand*,[13] the applicants who belonged to a numerical minority within the indigenous Maori people lost their case because the Committee recognized the right of the numerical majority to negotiate a settlement for the Maori people with the government in fishery matters. Their reference to their right to culture did not match, in the opinion of the Committee, the advantages of the fishery settlement for the indigenous people as a whole.

A. Cases before the European Court of Human Rights

In the ECHR the most notable provisions on limitations are in the Articles providing for the rights to freedoms of thought, conscience and religion (9), of expression (10), of assembly and association (11), and of movement (Protocol No. 4, Article 2), as well as the right to respect for privacy, family unity, home and correspondence (8). In particular, Article 10, (on freedom of expression) includes a long list of permissible limitation grounds.

[11] See Patrick Thornberry, *Indigenous Peoples and Human Rights* (Manchester University Press, Manchester, 2002), 116–81.

[12] Communication No. 24/1977, UN Doc. CCPR/C/OP/1 (1985). Another example is the case of *Chief Bernard Ominayak and the Lubicon Lake Band v. Canada* in which the HRC unequivocally concluded that the State of Alberta had authorized excessive exploitation of the natural resources of the territory of the Lubicon Lake Band and thus violated the rights to culture of the members of the Band. See Communication No. 167/1984, UN Doc. CCPR/C/33/D/167/1984 (1990).

[13] Communication No. 547/1993, UN Doc. CCPR/C/70/D/547/1993 (2000).

The limitations are exceptions to these freedom rights. It is a general principle of international law that exceptions to the main rule are to be interpreted narrowly, and this is the line applied by the European Court.[14] The limitations must 1) be prescribed by law, 2) have a legitimate aim, 3) be necessary in democratic society, and 4) respect the principle of proportionality. The Court has interpreted these requirements in great detail; however, it has permitted states a certain margin of appreciation whose extent varies in different cases between broad and narrow.

There is quite a rich jurisprudence on several aspects of minority rights by the European Court. However, the fact that the ECHR lacks any specific provisions on minority rights, and has had until recently only a fairly weak prohibition of discrimination, has set limits on the handling by the Court of complaints of applicants who belong to a minority. Gilbert concludes that the ECHR is not designed to protect minority rights, and it is open to the Court in any particular case where the applicant refers to minority rights to state that the claim is 'manifestly ill-founded'.[15] On the other hand, a positive point is that the Convention does not deny the right of groups to claim their rights under the ECHR if they prove to be victims in their own right.[16]

There may be situations in which a state can claim to have compelling grounds to interfere with limitations to minority affairs. One is the application by a minority of old-fashioned patriarchal practices which substantially limit the individual human rights guaranteed by a convention. However, in international jurisprudence such cases have been fairly rare.[17] Another example is a conflict situation where a territorial minority rebels against the state and makes a claim of secession and national independence. The state can then have ample grounds to prescribe limitations on the grounds of national security and territorial integrity. There are many cases in the ECtHR's jurisprudence reminiscent of this second example but where the state has partially overreacted, eg the relationship between Turkey and the non-recognized Kurdish minority. The government has reacted forcefully, not only against armed uprising by certain Kurdish guerilla organizations, but also has resorted to ruthless terrorist-type force against the civilian population. In addition, it has overreacted against speeches and writings calling for recognition of the Kurdish minority.

[14] See Robert Jennings and Arthur Watts, *Oppenheim's International Law*, Vol. I, 9th edn (Longman, London, 1992), 421; Jukka Viljanen, *The European Court of Human Rights as a Developer of the General Doctrines of Human Rights Law*, (Tampere University, Tampere, 2003), Part III, 165–331.

[15] Geoff Gilbert, 'The Burgeoning Minority Rights Jurisprudence of the European Court of Human Rights', *Human Rights Quarterly*, 24 (2002), 780.

[16] *Ibid.*, 740.

[17] See *Sandra Lovelace v. Canada*, (Communication No. 24/1977, UN Doc. A/36/40, 30 July 1981).

Among other minority-related cases before the European Court there have been cases on the registration of associations formed by persons and groups which regard their group as a minority; freedom of expression; discrimination; educational rights; religious groups and their institutions (several on the appointment of the leader of an institution of a minority religion by the authorities); participatory rights; the way of life of persons belonging to a minority (Roma) in the context of the right to respect for one's family life and home.[18] However, not all these cases have addressed the question of limitations. When limitations have been on the agenda, there have been cases, on the one hand, to the detriment of claimed minority interests and, on the other hand, for their protection.

In the practice of the European Court some cases concerning the rights to freedom of association and of expression of members belonging to minorities are especially relevant in this context, also some judgments on Article 8. Many cases on the freedom of expression deal with expressions in support of the rights of the Kurdish people in Turkey which the Turkish government and courts have regarded as a threat to the national unity and territorial integrity of Turkey. The European Court has found violations in many of those cases.[19]

1. Cases relating to the Limitation of the Freedom of Association by Minority Entities

Some cases on the freedom of association are of particular interest. In *Sidiropoulos and others v. Greece* and *Metropolitan Church of Bessarabia and others v. Moldova* the European Court found violations of the freedom of association. In *Sidiropoulos*[20] the applicants belonged to an association called 'Home of Macedonian Civilization'. At issue was the fact that the Greek authorities refused to register the group on the grounds that they caused a threat to the territorial unity and national security of Greece. The government interpreted the inclusion of the word 'Macedonian' in their name as a sign of wanting to identify the Greek region of Macedonia with the neighbouring state of the 'Former Yugoslavian Republic of Macedonia', and as favouring the annexation of Greek Macedonia to this neighbouring state. The association claimed that it represented a territorial entity of the Macedonian minority in Greece, and

[18] See *ibid.*, 737–80; Sia Spiliopoulou Åkermark, 'The Limits of Pluralism—Recent Jurisprudence of the European Court of Human Rights with Regard to Minorities: Does the Prohibition of Discrimination Add Anything?', *Journal on Ethnopolitics and Minority Issues in Europe (JEMIE)*, 3 (2002).

[19] See C. Ovey and R. White (eds.), *Jacobs and White: The European Convention on Human Rights*, 3rd edn, (Oxford, 2003), 281–2.

[20] Appl. No 26695/95, 10 July 1998, Merits.

spoke for the rights of this suppressed minority. Admittedly the name of the association is quite grandiose—Home of Macedonian Civilization. One could submit that the neighbouring FYR Macedonia may want to claim this 'Home' as part of its own territory. However, the European Court did not find evidence to the effect that the association formed a threat to Greece: its declared aim was to assert minority consciousness and to preserve and develop the traditions and culture of this minority.

In the *Metropolitan Church* case[21] the authors established a regional autonomous Orthodox church in Bessarabia, Moldova, attached to the patriarchate of Bucharest. The founding document of the church emphasized its non-political and Moldovan character, and was recognized by all Orthodox patriarchates with the exception of the patriarchate of Moscow. The Moldovan government claimed that the establishment of this church nurtured conflicts not only between Orthodox churches, but also threatened state relations, risking the independence and territorial integrity of the young Republic of Moldova vis-à-vis Russia and Ukraine. According to the government, the members of this new church could be full and active members in the existing Metropolitan Church of Moldova as there was no difference, from a religious point of view, between the two. A claim was also made that this church's activities would foster nationalistic tendencies with negative consequences for the political and social situation in Moldova. The European Court was not convinced by these arguments, however. It noted that the denial of recognition and registration had prevented the new church from defending its interest, and that only formal recognition could give it sufficient legal standing. According to the Court, when the authorities recognized other liturgical associations, they did not apply the criteria which they used in refusing to recognize the aspiring church.

On the other hand, in *Gorzelik and others v. Poland* the European Court accepted the denial of the right of one minority association.[22] The applicant organization was the Union of People of Silesia, whose aim was to awaken and strengthen the national consciousness of Silesians, restore Silesian culture, and protect the ethnic rights of persons of Silesian nationality. One paragraph of the founding document stated that the Union was an organization of the Silesian national minority. In highlighting this passage, the Polish government was able to prove to the European Court that the registration of the Union would mean the recognition of the Silesian ethnic group as a national minority. While Polish law grants specific rights to national minorities, even

[21] Appl. No 45701/99, 13 December 2001, Merits.

[22] Appl. No 44158/98, 20 December 2001.

the Union admitted that it was not seeking the formal recognition as a national minority with the aim of benefiting from privileges for minorities granted by Polish law. The government stated that if the Union agreed to delete or alter the term 'national minority' in its founding document, it would be registered without difficulty, but the Union refused to do this. The European Court supported the government's argument and found that with slight modification of its founding document, the Union could secure registration. Since it refused a reasonable compromise, the Court found no violation of Article 11.

Only two of the three cases discussed deal with entities that could be regarded as national minorities, the cases of *Sidiropoulos* and *Gorzelik*. The third case *Metropolitan Church,* can also be of value in the assessment of the extent of legal limitations to the right of freedom of association of national minorities, however.

Stankov and the United Macedonian Organisation Illinden v. Bulgaria before the ECtHR combines the right of association and autonomy claims by a territorial minority. According to the ECtHR, the fact that a group of persons calls for autonomy or even requests secession—thus demanding fundamental constitutional and territorial changes—cannot automatically justify a prohibition of its assemblies. Demanding territorial changes in speeches and demonstrations does not automatically amount to a threat to the country's territorial integrity and national security.[23] It would be different if violent action were resorted to in order to enforce the claim.

2. Roma Cases Relating to the Limitations of the Right to Respect for Family Life and Home

There have been a number of cases before the ECtHR on the right to respect for family life and home concerning Gypsy/Roma families in the United Kingdom according to Article 8. The Court identified a conflict between this right and the interests of the community (the rights of other persons) in the form of public authorities' powers to issue planning permission. The Court's main criterion was whether the interference with the applicant's claimed right was 'necessary in a democratic society'.

Let us concentrate on *Chapman v. United Kingdom*.[24] The applicant was a Gypsy/Roma who since her birth had constantly travelled in the Hertfordshire area. When she married, she and her husband continued to live in caravans. They had four children. The family used to stop for as long as possible on

[23] Appl. No 29221/95 and 29225/95, 21 October 2001, Merits.
[24] Appl. No 27238/95, 18 January 2001, Merits.

temporary or unofficial sites when the husband found work as a landscape gardener. They were constantly moved from place to place by the authorities. Their children's education was constantly interrupted because they had to move about. To stabilize the situation the applicant bought a piece of land in 1985 with the intention of living on it in a mobile home, but the authorities refused her application for planning permission, and when the family did not move away they were twice fined. The family felt that it was compelled to return to a nomadic life. Again they were constantly moved from one place to another by the authorities. This effectively prevented the possibility of the children having an education.

The applicant complained, *inter alia*, against infringement of her right to respect for family life and home in the traditional Gypsy lifestyle. The Court, which, by the way, examined the development of minority rights in contemporary international instruments and texts beyond the ECHR,[25] recognized that the vulnerable position of Gypsies as a minority meant that some special consideration should be given to their needs and their different lifestyle, both in the relevant regulatory planning framework, and in reaching decisions in particular cases. To this extent, there is a positive obligation imposed on states by virtue of Article 8 to facilitate the Gypsy way of life. This sounds promising for the applicant but the Court went on to say that Article 8 does not in its terms recognize a right to be provided with a home; nor does any of the jurisprudence of the Court acknowledge such a right. There are unfortunately in the contracting states many persons who have no home. Whether the state provides funds to enable everyone to have a home is a matter for political not judicial decision. Where a dwelling has been established without the planning permission which is needed under national law, there is a conflict of interest between the right of the individual under Article 8, and the right of others in the community to environmental protection. It is highly relevant whether or not the home was established lawfully—in this case it was established unlawfully. There were strong environmental reasons for the refusal of planning permission, and the applicant's personal circumstances had been taken into account in the decision-making process. The Court was not persuaded that there were no alternatives available to the applicant. The conclusion was that Article 8 had not been violated by the United Kingdom. The same was the outcome in some other Gypsy cases.

[25] Among them was the FCNM and the 2000 Report on the situation of Roma and Sinti in the OSCE area by the High Commissioner on National Minorities of the OSCE. The Commissioner's recommendations included a recommendation that in view of the extreme insecurity many Roma experience in respect of housing, governments should endeavour to regularize the legal status of Roma who now live in circumstances of unsettled legality.

The Court's judgment was far from unanimous—the vote was ten to seven. The joint dissenting opinion of those seven judges pointed out that there were also four other cases before the Court dealing with problems similar to the *Chapman* case. All these cases disclosed elements of hardship and pressure on a vulnerable group. The long-term failure of authorities to make effective provision for Gypsies in their planning policies was evident. There was a significant shortfall of official, lawful sites available for Gypsies in the country as a whole. They were not welcome on private residential sites which were, in any event, prohibitively expensive. Recognition had been given domestically to the difficulties through the 'toleration' of some unlawful Gypsy sites. The planning authorities themselves recognized that the only practicable options open to Gypsies were local authority-owned sites or privately owned Gypsy sites. It was not a question of Gypsies imposing particular preferences as to location and facilities without realistic reference to their own resources. The options open to them were, as in this case, severely limited, if they existed at all. The dissenters also pointed out that in this case the applicant had a home, in her caravan on her land, but was prevented from settling there.

The dissenters were of the opinion that the majority was interpreting the criterion 'interference necessary in a democratic society' incorrectly. United Kingdom legislation and policies have long recognized the objective of providing for Gypsies' special needs, but in practice environmental considerations were given stronger consideration. 'Our view that Article 8 . . . imposes a positive obligation on the authorities to ensure that Gypsies have a practical and effective opportunity to enjoy their right to respect for their home and their private and family life, in accordance with their traditional lifestyle, is not a startling innovation.'

It can be submitted that the Court applied Article 8 in the *Chapman* case in a minority-insensitive way.[26]

3. Turkish Cases relating to Limitations to the Right to Freedom of Expression

In the second part of the 1990s and the early years of the twenty-first century the ECtHR has had before it a high number of applications made against Turkey. Most of them are connected to the territorial Kurdish rebellion in south-east Turkey and to the efforts of the state, in the name of national unity, to suppress

[26] In a later case dealing with the rights under Art. 8 by a Roma family to live in a local site meant for Roma living, *Connors v. United Kingdom* (Appl. No 66746/01, 27 August 2004, Merits), the ECHR found violation of Art. 8 by the state, but the significance of the judgment is diminished by the Court's reasoning of finding a violation: the eviction of the applicant and his family from the local authority site was not attended by the requisite procedural safeguards. The decision was made in a summary process.

Kurdish claims. A violent struggle has been waged since 1984 in south-east Turkey between separatist Kurdish militants, and Turkish military forces. The ruthless struggle resulted in an estimated 20,000–30,000 deaths, as well as massive displacements, human rights violations and abuses, upheavals and grave economic consequences. Both parties engaged in armed and terrorist-type actions against civilians. However, the armed struggle began to calm down at the end of the 1990s and has virtually come to its end. The situation in 2005 is quite peaceful. The claims for secession of Turkish Kurdistan have diminished.

The Turkish state has taken a stringent attitude to minority questions. Certain non-Muslim religious (and linguistic and ethnic) minorities were given recognition in the 1923 Lausanne Treaty; they are at present tiny minorities. The ethnic Kurdish group makes up some 10–20 per cent of the population of Turkey. They are Muslims by religion, and are regarded by the state as individual Turkish citizens on the basis of equality. However, the Kurds have their own language, the use of which was subjected to many substantial restrictions, including the ban on using it in mass media or teaching it at school. In recent years these restrictions have been somewhat eased, but not fully revoked.[27]

The European Commission against Racism and Intolerance (ECRI) has expressed disagreement with the Turkish policy of attempting to resolve issues of ethnic differences by denying expressions of difference. A more open attitude towards cultural and linguistic plurality within Turkey might contribute to resolving some of the problems faced by the country, by allowing more space for non-violent public, as well as private, expression of cultural and ethnic identity.[28]

Many applications before the ECtHR deal with Article 2 (on the right to life), Article 3 (on the prohibition of torture, inhuman treatment etc.), and Article 6 (on the judicial guarantees for persons accused of having committed a crime). However, these judgments of the Court do not disclose significant minority-specific statements.[29]

Instead, the applications against violations of Article 10 (on the right to freedom of expression) are of interest. As was mentioned above, this Article

[27] See the country reports on Turkey by the European Commission against Racism and Intolerance, in 1999 and 2001; the first round report became public on 9 November 1999 and the second report on 3 July 2001. These texts can be found in <www.ecri.coe>.

[28] *Ibid.*

[29] See Manoj Kumar Sinha, 'New Dimensions to the European Convention on Human Rights in the Light of Turkish Cases', *Indian Journal of International Law,* 40 (2000), 728–68, at 728–58.

contains a long list of lawful grounds to limit this right. In the context of the applications against Turkey, of special relevance among permissible grounds of limitation were national security, territorial integrity, public safety, and prevention of disorder or crime. The applicants have been either Kurds or other persons supporting the Kurdish cause who were sentenced by courts because of criminal utterances. Even though for many years south-east Turkey was under 'public emergency', the public emergency provision in the ECHR, Article 15, has not been on the agenda before the ECtHR.

The European Court in its jurisprudence supported a widespread right to freedom of expression. It has stringently applied the test of whether a given limitation is to be regarded as necessary in a democratic society. However, in Turkish cases there have been calls for the use of violence, and that clearly was a matter of national security and public safety. The Court's basic distinction in the Turkish cases between violation and non-violation of Article 10 by Turkey has been whether the author had incited or encouraged the use of violence or not.[30] The Court has shown understanding towards Turkey if the statements under consideration included support of the armed struggle by the Kurdish People's Party (PKK); for example, in the words of the Court in *Sürek v. Turkey (No.1)* the author's letters published in a newspaper 'amounted to an appeal to bloody revenge by stirring up base emotions and hardening already embedded prejudices', and in the context of the ongoing conflict in south-east Turkey 'the message which is communicated to the reader is that recourse to violence is a necessary and justified measure of self-defence in the face of the aggressor'. The Court did not give protection to such statements.[31]

On the other hand, if a person supported the right of the Kurdish group to minority rights, and to express Kurdish political aspirations, the Court has found a violation of Article 10 by Turkey. The same applies to a call to the state to end state terrorism against the Kurdish people, as well as to references to Kurdistan or critical remarks about the fundamental values the Turkish state is founded on.

In individual cases the drawing of the distinction between violation and non-violation has sometimes been complicated. In *Zana v. Turkey* the author, a former mayor of Diyarbakir, stated in an interview which was published in a major national newspaper that he supported the PKK's efforts of national liberation, but was not in favour of massacres; the author labelled the PKK's

[30] See Iain Cameron, *National Security and the European Convention on Human Rights* (The Hague, 2000), 385–94.

[31] Appl. No 26682/95, 8 July 1999, Merits.

killing of women and children as mistakes. The Court by a vote of 12–8 rejected the application. As relevant factors the majority took the facts that Mr Zana was a public figure, and that the situation at the time of the statement was one of 'extreme tension'. The dissenting opinion of seven judges pointed out that Mr Zana, who was an activist of the Kurdish cause since the 1960s, was not a member of the PKK and had consistently spoken against violence. Nor were they convinced that the position of Mr Zana as the former mayor of the most important city in south-east Turkey had any great significance.[32]

On the other hand, even though the applicant in *Karatas v. Turkey* had used in his poems extremely aggressive language which could be taken as inspiring the Kurdish people to armed resistance, the Court regarded his use of words as consistent with Article 10. The majority of judges took into account that the applicant had expressed himself through the medium of poetry using metaphorical language, and the publication had a small audience only. The minority disagreed: the language used was far from metaphorical, it was direct and clear.[33]

The general line of the ECtHR in the Turkish cases on Article 10 is quite understandable. To use the right to freedom of expression for incitement or encouragement of the use of violence is against democratic principles. Even if a government took undemocratic measures against a minority, the ECHR under its present wording cannot give a green light to the encouragement of violence, other than strictly defensive use of violence against aggressive use of violence by the authorities against non-violent civilian persons. The PKK's use of violence was not strictly defensive in character.

However, one can note that in a number of cases there were dissenting opinions. The Court may not have been successful in its argumentation in some individual cases.

4. *Cases relating to the Right to Freedom of Religion*

Under Article 9 of the ECHR, the right to freedom of thought, conscience and religion includes the freedom, either alone or in community with others, and in public or private, to manifest religion in worship, teaching, practice and observance. Limitations necessary in a democratic society, in the interests of public safety, for the protection of public order, health or morals, and for the protection of the rights of others are permissible.

In several cases against Greece the ECtHR has stated as a matter of principle that in a democratic society, in which several religions coexist within

[32] Appl. No 18954/91, 25 November 1997, Merits.
[33] Appl. No 23168/94, 8 July 1999, Merits.

one and the same population, it may be necessary to place restrictions on this freedom in order to reconcile the interests of the various groups, and ensure that everyone's beliefs are respected. However, this may not be done in a dictatorial way which foremostly favours the authorities. The case of *Serif v. Greece* may serve as the example of those cases; it deals with a Muslim religious community. Following the death of one of the Muslim religious leaders of Thrace, the Mufti of Rodopi, the State appointed a mufti *ad interim*, whom the President of the Republic later confirmed in the post. Two independent Muslim members of Parliament requested that the State organize elections for the post of Mufti of Rodopi and Mufti of Xanthi, as provided by law. Having received no reply, they decided to organize elections themselves. The applicant in the case, Mr Serif, was elected Mufti of Rodopi by those attending prayers at the mosques on a particular day. However, in the meantime, a legislative decree modifying the manner of selecting muftis had been adopted and was later validated retroactively by Parliament. Selection became a matter for the authorities to decide—no more elections. Mr Serif was convicted of unlawful action—of usurping the functions of a minister of a 'known religion', and of publicly wearing the robes of such a minister without being entitled to do so.

The ECtHR showed very little tolerance towards the modified law. True, the interference pursued a legitimate aim, namely to protect public order, but it was not necessary in a democratic society. Punishing a person for the mere fact that he acted as religious leader of a group that willingly followed him could hardly be consistent with the demands of religious pluralism. The Court did not identify in the behaviour of Mr Serif factors that would have been causing disturbance or friction between religious factions or groups. Greece had violated Article 9.[34]

B. Conclusions

The international case law on limitations of minority rights does not give any comprehensive picture on how to draw a line between lawful and unlawful limitations. This outcome is to be expected, since Article 27 of the CCPR does not contain anything on the limitation question, and the ECHR does not contain specific articles on minority rights. However, the jurisprudence of the ECtHR has produced a number of valuable statements. The strict general

[34] Appl. No 38178/97, 14 December 1999, Merits. The other cases are *Agga v. Greece*, (Appl. No 50776/99 and 52912/99); *Manoussakis v. Greece*, (Appl. No 18748/91); *Kokkinakis v. Greece*, (Appl. No 14307/88).

criteria applied by the Court have given protection to minorities and persons belonging to minorities, but it cannot be said that the Court would be a protector of minority rights. The outcome is still quite sporadic.

III. Derogations

The term 'derogation' in human rights instruments means limitations of human rights during public emergency—a state derogates from its human rights obligations. In emergency circumstances, a state is temporarily excused from a number of its human rights obligations for the purpose of restoring and maintaining order. The regulation and administration of derogations shall contribute to early resolution of the crisis. Derogations are permissible only to the extent that they are 'strictly required by the exigencies of the situation'. When the actual crisis is solved, the derogations shall be terminated and human rights be restored in full.

During a public emergency, a state may, under the CCPR (Article 4), the ECHR (Article 15) and the ACHR (Article 27), derogate from a number of its human rights obligations, but not from all of them. Each convention pronounces a list of human rights which cannot be subjected to derogations even during public emergencies. Those human rights can be considered to have absolute character. However, the minority rights included in Article 27 of the CCPR are not on the list of absolute rights. When in 2001 the Human Rights Committee adopted its General Comment on the interpretation of the public emergency article of the CCPR, Article 4, the Committee through its interpretation extended the list of non-derogable rights but did not include minority rights in its list.[35]

Each of these three conventions includes one article on public emergency. Those articles are not identical, but they have many similarities. Article 4(1) of the CCPR spells out the criteria for derogation as follows:

> In time of public emergency which threatens the life of the nation and the existence of which is officially proclaimed, the State Parties to the present Covenant may take measures derogating from their obligations under the present Covenant to the extent strictly required by the exigencies of the situation, provided that such measures are not inconsistent with their other obligations under international law and do not

[35] General Comment No. 29 (72), Art. 4, adopted by the Human Rights Committee at its 1950th meeting on 24 July 2001, UN Doc. CCPR/C/21/Rev.1/Add.11.

involve discrimination solely on the ground of race, colour, sex, language, religion or social origin.

In the quoted provision the stipulation on discrimination is relevant for ethnic, linguistic and religious minorities; it gives minimum protection to minorities and to persons belonging to them. In Article 4(2) on non-derogable human rights one should take note of Article 16 according to which everyone should have the right to recognition everywhere as a person before the law, and of Article 18 which recognizes the right of everyone to freedom of thought, conscience and religion. It should be pointed out, however, that Article 18 permits the limitation of freedom to manifest one's religion or beliefs *even in normal circumstances* on the grounds of public safety, order, health, or morals or the fundamental rights and freedoms of others, making the scope of this non-derogable right quite narrow. In comparison, the ECHR's shorter list on non-derogable rights includes none of the provisions discussed in this paragraph.

It should be added that certainly the prohibition of genocide is of absolute character and safeguards basic protection to minorities.[36]

There is no international jurisprudence on derogation (and its limits) from human rights obligations during public emergency which would address derogation from minority rights. The ECtHR has not discussed the armed conflict between the Kurdish rebels and the Turkish armed forces in south-east Turkey in terms of Article 15 on public emergency, but in terms of other Articles. Article 15 could have been discussed if the applicants had referred to it, because a violent interethnic conflict in a state can well qualify as a legitimate public emergency enabling the government to restrict various rights (especially freedom rights) with the effect that these derogations might substantially reduce the right of persons belonging to the involved minority to their culture, religion and language.[37]

[36] Packer considers that the prohibition of genocide and the prohibition of discrimination in accordance with Art. 4 of the CCPR are of absolute character and cannot be derogated at all; the prohibition of discrimination also covers the prohibition on advocacy or hatred or incitement to such discrimination and violence. See John Packer, 'United Nations Protection of Minorities in Time of Public Emergency: The Hard-Core of Minority Rights', in *Non-Derogable Rights and States of Emergency*, gen. ed. Daniel Prémont (Etablissements Émile Bruylant, Brussels 1996), 501–20. See also Lauri Hannikainen, 'Peremptory Norms (Jus Cogens)' in *International Law: Historical Development, Criteria, Present Status* (Helsinki, 1998), 456–89.

[37] It should be emphasized that derogations during public emergency can be temporary only and after the termination of the emergency the restricted human rights have to be restored in full. However, in a severe conflict the public emergency may last for several years.

IV. Reservations

The CCPR does not contain any provisions on reservations. Many ratifying states have made reservations to this Covenant. Thus, the criterion pronounced by the 1969 Vienna Convention on the Law of Treaties in Article 19 for (multilateral) treaties not addressing the question of reservations at all is applicable: reservations are permissible, but only as far they are not incompatible with the object and purpose of the treaty.

There are reservations made to Article 27. One is made by France in short terms without further explanation: it is the view of France that its constitution and other legislation fully guarantee human rights to everyone living in France. The HRC recognized the reservation by France in the *Hopu and Bessert v. France* case (see section 1 above). The Committee examined the case in terms of some other articles without addressing in any depth France's reservation.

Article 23(3) of the Covenant stipulates that no marriage shall be entered into without the free and full consent of the intending spouses. The United Kingdom in a reservation to this provision stated that it reserves the right to postpone its application to a small number of customary marriages in the Solomon Islands. Thus, the United Kingdom gave protection to traditional marriages by an ethnic minority group.

The HRC gave a General Comment on the right to make reservations to the CCPR in 1994. According to it, reservations must be specific and transparent. They shall not be general, but must refer to a particular provision of the Covenant and indicate in precise terms its scope in relation thereto.[38] The same basic approach is shared by the ECHR in Article 64 which permits reservations to the Convention but prohibits those of a general character. Indeed, reservations with a wide scope are of the character of being incompatible with the object and purpose of a treaty.

There are no cases of interest in international jurisprudence concerning reservations to treaty provisions on minority rights apart from the above mentioned *Hopu* case.[39]

The criterion spelled out in Article 19 of the Vienna Convention on the Law of Treaties is applicable also to the FCNM which contains no provision on reservations. Since the Convention does not give any kind of definition of

[38] General Comment No. 24 (52) of 2 November 1994, UN Doc. CCPR/C/21/Rev.1/Add.6.

[39] See, however, the case *Loizidou v. Turkey* before the ECtHR, preliminary objections in ECHR 1995, Ser. A 310, and Application no. 15318/89; the date of the judgment was 18 December 1996. The case dealt with Turkey's declaration excluding the applicability of the ECHR to Turkey in Northern Cyprus.

a 'national minority', a number of states parties have made reservations—or interpretative declarations—regarding their understanding of this term and the scope of its applicability to themselves.[40] To give an example, Switzerland declared that in Switzerland national minorities are groups of individuals numerically inferior to the rest of the population, their members are Swiss nationals, they have long-standing, firm and lasting ties with Switzerland and are guided by their will to safeguard their specific characteristics. Like Switzerland several states point out that persons belonging to national minorities have to be their nationals. Several states named those groups which they regard as national minorities within their jurisdiction. For example, Denmark notified that the only national minority in the sense of the FCNM is the German minority in Southern Jutland.

The Advisory Committee was not satisfied with the grounds given by Denmark to limit the applicability of the Convention to the German minority only. It noted that the Faroese, Greenlanders and Roma had long-standing historical ties to Denmark. Thus, Denmark's approach was incompatible with the Convention. The Advisory Committee advised Denmark to consult with concerned parties and re-examine the scope of application of the FCNM.[41]

The Danish government disagreed with the Advisory Committee. Since neither the FCNM nor general international law contained a definition of 'national minority', it was left to states to determine the content of the notion through actual practice.[42] However, the Committee of Ministers of the Council of Europe sided with the Advisory Committee with the statement that the personal scope of application of the FCNM merited further consideration by the government of Denmark in consultation with those concerned.[43]

The statements of the Advisory Committee and of the Committee of Ministers imply that Denmark had made a questionable reservation and should reconsider the matter in the light of those monitoring organs' views.

[40] The texts of the interpretative declarations and reservations to the FCNM can be found from the Treaty Office of the Council of Europe in its home page http://conventions.coe.int. See also Jochen A. Frowein and Roland Bank, 'The Effect of Member States' Declarations Defining "National Minorities" upon Signature or Ratification of the Council of Europe's Framework Convention', *Zeitschrift für ausländisches öffentliches Recht und Völkerrecht*, (1999), 649–76.

[41] Advisory Committee Opinion on Denmark, ACFC/INF/OP/I (2001) 005, 1999, para. 39. See also the Committee's second opinion on Denmark, ACFC/INF/OP/II (2004) 005, paras. 12–17.

[42] Comments of the Government of Denmark on the Opinion of the Advisory Committee on the Implementation of the FCNM in Denmark, GVT/COM/INF/OP/I (2001) 005, 2001.

[43] Resolution ResCMN (2001) 2, adopted 31 October 2001.

It is not for individual states to decide unilaterally on the definition of international legal terms. In the context of the FCNM the essential notion of 'national minority' shall be defined by the ratifying states together with the international monitoring organs of the Convention.[44] International practice has shown that in the course of time the views of international monitoring or supervisory organs have become decisive.

It has been the line of the Advisory Committee to call upon states not to emphasize the division between recognized national minorities and non-recognized minority groups but to include information, even if less, on the latter groups as well. Some states in their interpretative declarations have shared this view and indicated that also non-recognized minority groups enjoy many of the rights stipulated in the FCNM.[45]

[44] For an analysis, see Hans-Joachim Heintze, 'Article 3', in M. Weller (ed.), *The Rights of Minorities in Europe, supra,* n. 2, 107–37, at 111–18.

[45] For example, Germany and Latvia. Estonia has done so in practice, see Advisory Committee Second Opinion on Estonia, ACFC/INF/OP/II (2005) 001.

THE CONCEPT AND DEFINITION OF MINORITIES

Hurst Hannum

I. Introduction

The rights of particular classes or groups of people may be protected for a number of reasons. In some instances, special rights or protections may be achieved by the powerful, eg, trade unions in a strong bargaining position or wealthy elites with sufficient access and money to influence policymakers. In other cases, a political or other decision-making system may seek to reflect categories of people rather than simply one-person, one-vote, as exemplified by proportional representation in elections or the tripartite structure of the International Labour Organization. In the human rights context, however, particular protections are most often developed for the relatively weak, poor, or powerless, who are unable to protect their own rights and interests through exercising their own political or economic strength.

Of course, one of the most basic elements of both early and contemporary human rights law is non-discrimination; the United Nations Charter identifies non-discrimination based on race, sex, language, or religion as the touchstone of all human rights, even though the drafters of the Charter in 1945 were unable to articulate what these other rights might be. The Universal Declaration of Human Rights refers to equality or non-discrimination in Articles 1, 2, 6, 7, 10, 16, and 21. The two Covenants reiterate the prohibition of discrimination in identical terms in Articles 2 and 3.

But the principle of non-discrimination is not inconsistent with the recognition that particularly vulnerable categories of people may need to be singled out for protection by the international community, and more specific norms have been developed to complement the general norms found in the Universal Declaration of Human Rights. Among these categories are workers, refugees, women, prisoners and other detainees, indigenous peoples, children, disabled persons, and migrant workers; prohibitions against discrimination on the basis of race and religion have also been adopted.

Another of these vulnerable categories is the subject of the present book: a particular kind of minority, which is distinguished by ethnic, religious, linguistic, cultural, or 'national' characteristics. Although ethnic and other minorities have historically suffered from discrimination and repression, they were not among the vulnerable groups with whose rights the international community was concerned in the post-1945 era until very recently. In light of the attention paid to minorities in the period from 1919 until the outbreak of World War II, as well as the proliferation of human rights norms since 1945, this failure to develop international norms to protect minorities seems incongruous. What accounts for the world's reluctance to address this particular issue or protect these particularly vulnerable groups?

First, the concept of 'minorities' does not fit easily within the theoretical paradigm of the state, at least as the state has been defined in the individual social contract theory of Western democracies or the class-based precepts of Marxism. Under these two views, the state is seen as a collection of shifting coalitions founded either on individual self-interest or the economic interests of classes; neither takes account of ethnic, religious, or linguistic ties.

Similarly, the heterogeneity of states in the contemporary world runs counter to the theory of the nation-state as it developed in the nineteenth century. Both older and more recently independent states have largely accepted the rhetoric of 'one people, one state', with little concern for the strong national or cultural ties that exist below the level of the often artificial 'sovereign' state and its people. As a result, 'nation-building' in the 1960s and 1970s (more accurately described as state-building) rarely included respect for diversity among its goals, and few states adopted constitutional or other provisions which recognized that minorities might need special protection.

Third, there is a fundamental fear on the part of *all* countries, and especially newer states, that the recognition of minority rights may encourage fragmentation or separatism, thus undermining national unity and the requirements of national development. Despite the fact that international law has insisted that minorities have no right of self-determination, and has never defined a legal right to secession, states fear that recognizing differences among ethnic communities or any form of 'group' rights might make it impossible to forge a larger, multi-cultural unity which encompasses all of the state's citizens.

Fourth, as implied above, some believe that recognition of particular groups runs counter to the philosophical underpinning of human rights, ie, that there are certain rights that belong to each of us simply because we are human. In this view, while individuals may possess rights that are relevant to the expression of ethnic or cultural identity (eg, freedom of religion, language, expression, and association), it would be a mistake to define rights based on shared group characteristics, such as language or religion.

Finally, one must recognize the unpleasant fact that widespread discrimination and intolerance based on religion, ethnicity, and cultural practices continue to exist, and minority rights are unlikely to be taken seriously in such an environment. This intolerance exists in all regions of the world and in states at all stages of economic development. It may be fanned by dictators and democrats alike to serve narrow political interests or identify convenient scapegoats. Without entering into a discussion of whether intolerance is inherent in the human species, it seems clear that prejudice and fear of 'the other' often are present even prior to the violent exploitation of those fears by 'ethnic entrepreneurs' who can arise from within both majority and minority populations.

II. Historical Understandings of Minorities

Most early empires considered at least religious minorities worthy of recognition, if only for the purpose of exercising indirect control over subject populations, where religion and politics were often intertwined.[1] The millet system developed under the Ottoman empire allowed religious communities a degree

[1] An excellent historical survey of minority rights is James B. Muldoon, 'The Development of Group Rights,' in Jay A. Sigler (ed.), *Minority rights, a Comparative Analysis* (Westport and London, 1983), 31–66.

of personal and cultural autonomy, although it has been observed that millets were 'the solution devised by a government that did not know what nationality meant and, therefore, was unfamiliar with the majority-minority concept.'[2] The development of autonomous, religious-based communities also was consistent with Quranic injunctions of tolerance for other religions, and large non-Muslim communities continued to flourish throughout the Ottoman empire.[3] Defining such minorities was not difficult, as only certain religions were considered worthy of special protection; the rest were, at best, tolerated or, at worst, persecuted.

In Europe, international protection of minorities can be traced to the 1648 Treaty of Westphalia, under the terms of which the parties agreed to respect the rights of certain religious minorities within their jurisdiction. However, given the historical congruence of religious and secular authority prior to this period, such agreements could just as easily be seen as recognizing the power of certain political groups rather than guaranteeing religious rights per se. There was no definitional problem, because the particular groups were identified by name; there was no intention to extend rights to minorities generally.[4]

In the nineteenth century, the development of nationalism in Europe was based on the theory that political power was best exercised by groups that shared ethnic or linguistic ties. 'Nations' sought to establish a separate political identity, whether by incorporating peoples spread over many countries (Germany, Italy) or by demanding greater political power for groups within existing empires (Greece, Hungary, Serbia, Poland, the Baltic states, and others). These political transformations were most often based on real or presumed linguistic affinity, but concern with the protection of linguistic, religious, or other minorities seemed to end as soon as new political frontiers were created.[5]

[2] Peter F. Sugar, *Southeastern Europe under Ottoman Rule, 1354–1804* (Seattle, 1977), 274.

[3] Cf., eg, Farooq Hassan, *The Concept of State and Law in Islam* (Lanham, MD, and London, 1981) 45–6, 225–41. Christians and Jews, as monotheistic 'people of the Book', occupy a special position in an Islamic state, and it is on this basis that the millets were allowed to develop their own culture and civil administration. *Ibid.*, 45.

[4] It might also be noted that only three (Arts. 28, 49, and 77) of the treaty's 128 Articles deal with the free exercise of religion; guarantees are extended to those of the 'confession of Augsberg', the 'Reformed' Protestants, and Catholics.

[5] Among the many works that trace the development of nationalism, see Benedict Anderson, *Imagined Communities* (London and New York, rev. edn 1991); John Breuilly, *Nationalism and the State* (Chicago, 2nd edn, 1993); Rogers Brubaker, *Citizenship and Nationhood in France and Germany* (Cambridge, MA, 1992); Partha Chatterjee, *Nationalist Thought and the Colonial World* (London, 1986); Walker Connor, *Ethnonationalism, The Quest for Understanding* (Princeton, 1993); Alexander J. Motyl (ed.), *Encyclopedia of Nationalism* (San Diego, 2001); Thomas Hylland Eriksen, *Ethnicity and Nationalism, Anthropological Perspectives* (London, 1993); Ernest Gellner,

Even after the consolidation and rearrangement of much of Europe during the nineteenth century, many ethno-linguistic populations remained outside the country of their kinfolk. The destruction of the Austro-Hungarian and Ottoman empires in the wake of World War I resulted in a European map that did a significantly better job of correlating languages and states, but it remained far from perfect. In partial compensation for their disappointed political aspirations, those regions that did not achieve independence as a result of the frontier changes were granted a degree of cultural protection—although, again, the motivation of the international community was driven more by the desire to ensure political stability than to recognize new rights per se.

This protection was achieved through adoption of the so-called Minority Treaties at the end of World War I and their monitoring by the League of Nations.[6] These treaties, all of which were adopted in 1919 or soon thereafter, fell into three categories, although the substantive protections included in each were similar.[7] The first group of treaties included those imposed upon the defeated states of Austria, Hungary, Bulgaria, and Turkey. The second included either new states created out of the dissolution of the Ottoman Empire or states whose boundaries were altered, at least in part to respond to the demands of ethnic or linguistic groups; in this category were Czechoslovakia, Greece, Poland, Romania, and Yugoslavia. Finally, special provisions relating to minorities were included in the international regimes established in Danzig, the Memel Territory, and Upper Silesia. The provisions of the various treaties obviously applied only to certain states, and those protected were persons within one of these states who differed from the majority population by race, language, or religion; many were German-speakers in non-German-speaking states. Some treaties identified the specific groups to be protected by name.[8]

Nations and Nationalism (Cornell, 1983); Liah Greenfeld, *Nationalism* (Cambridge, MA, 1992); Adrian Hastings, *The Construction of Nationhood* (Cambridge, 1997); E.J. Hobsbawm, *Nations and Nationalism Since 1780* (Cambridge, 2nd edn, 1992); Harold R. Isaacs, *Idols of the Tribe* (Cambridge, MA, 1975); Elie Kedourie, *Nationalism* (London, 4th edn, 1993); Anthony D. Smith, *The Ethnic Origins of Nations* (London, 1988); *id.*, *National Identity* (Reno, 1991).

[6] Perhaps the best and most detailed treatment of the adoption and implementation of the treaties is C.A. Macartney, *National States and National Minorities* (London, 1934), 212–423; also see United Nations, *Study on the Rights of Persons Belonging to Ethnic, Religious and Linguistic Minorities* (F. Capotorti, Special Rapporteur), E/CN.4/Sub.2/384/Rev.1 (1979) (Capotorti Study), 16–26; Patrick Thornberry, *International Law and the Rights of Minorities* (Oxford, 1991), 38–52.

[7] The unilateral declarations to guarantee minority rights made by states before the League of Nations might be considered a fourth category. See Capotorti Study, 18.

[8] These groups included Jews; the Valachs of Pindus; the monastic communities of Mount Athos; Moslems in Albania, Greece, and the Serb-Croat-Slovene Kingdom (later Yugoslavia); the Czeckler and Saxon communities in Transylvania, Romania; and the Ruthenes in Czechoslovakia. See Information Section, League of Nations Secretariat, *The League of Nations and the Protection*

Proposals were made to extend protections to minorities more generally, and Germany indicated its willingness to protect minorities within its territory in a manner equivalent to the protections enjoyed by German-speakers in other states. However, the League's rapporteur on minorities probably reflected the majority view of countries not subject to the League's minority regime when he concluded:

> [T]he mere co-existence of groups of persons forming collective entities, racially different, under the territory and within the jurisdiction of a State, is not sufficient to create the obligation to recognise the existence in that State, side by side with the majority of its population, of a minority requiring a protection entrusted to the League of Nations. In order that a minority, according to the meaning of the present treaties, should exist, it must be the product of struggles, going back for centuries, or perhaps for shorter periods, between certain nationalities, and of the transference of certain territories from one sovereignty to another through successive historic phases[.][9]

Here we have perhaps one of the first attempts (although no doubt a thorough search of the League archives would turn up others), albeit in a negative way, to define minorities protected under international law: while racial, linguistic, or religious difference were a necessary condition, minority rights were to be recognized only in the context of historical 'struggles' between groups which involved territorial changes. In addition, citizenship also was thought to be necessary for a person to claim minority status, since minorities had a duty to be 'loyal fellow-citizens'.[10]

One of the major advances of this period was the legitimization of *international* interest in minority rights, by giving the League of Nations a supervisory role in monitoring the treaties.[11] In many instances, the Permanent Court of International Justice (PCIJ) was given jurisdiction over minority disputes or issues affecting the interpretation of the minorities treaties, although the definition of minorities arose in only a few cases. Among the judgments and

of Minorities of Race, Language and Religion (Geneva, rev. edn 1927), 24–6. See generally Inis L. Claude, Jr., *National Minorities* (Cambridge, MA, 1955), 17–28; Oscar I. Janowsky, *Nationalities and National Minorities* (New York, 1945), 112–15; Macartney, 273–94, 502–6 (text of the Polish Minorities Treaty); Capotorti Study, 18–19; UN Sub-Commission on Prevention of Discrimination and Protection of Minorities, *Treaties and International Instruments concerning the Protection of Minorities 1919–1951*, UN Doc. E/CN.4/Sub.2/133 (1951), paras. 2–12.

[9] Remarks of Mr. de Mello Franco of Brazil, quoted in *The League of Nations and the Protection of Minorities*, 19.

[10] Resolution of the League Assembly adopted in 1922 and quoted in *ibid.*, 26.

[11] See generally Macartney, 308–69; Capotorti Study, 20–4; Louis B. Sohn and Thomas Buergenthal, *International Protection of Human Rights* (Indianapolis, 1973), 213–306.

advisory opinions of the PCIJ concerned with minority issues, four considered definitional questions in some detail and are worthy of attention.[12]

In the *Acquisition of Polish Nationality* case,[13] the Court noted that minorities need not necessarily be nationals of the state concerned, referring to Article 2 of the Polish Minorities Treaty, which prohibits discrimination on the basis of, *inter alia*, 'nationality'.[14] Thus, 'the term "minority" seems to include inhabitants who differ from the population in race, language or religion, that is to say, amongst others, inhabitants of this territory of non-Polish origin, whether they are Polish nationals or not.'[15] In a subsequent case, however, the Court in interpreting the same treaty distinguished between 'minorities in the broad sense and minorities in the narrow sense'.[16] The former—non-nationals—enjoy certain protections, such as freedom of religion, while the latter—minorities who are nationals of the state concerned—enjoy additional rights with respect to civil and political matters and education.[17] In both cases, of course, reference must be had to the terms of the treaty at issue, and the Court did not purport to address the broader question of what is a minority.

In *Rights of Minorities in Upper Silesia (Minority Schools)*, the Court admitted that there might be some doubt as to just who belonged to a minority: 'Such an uncertainty might for example exist, as regards language, where either a person does not speak literary German or literary Polish, or where he knows and makes use of several languages, and, as regards race, in the case of mixed marriages.'[18] While the Court rejected the notion that belonging to a minority could be defined purely as a question of the intention of an individual, it nonetheless confirmed that a declaration of minority status by an individual could not be questioned by the authorities, a practice which was specifically prohibited in the German-Polish convention at issue in the case.

[12] See, eg, *German Settlers in Poland*, Ad. Op. of 10 September 1923; *Rights of Minorities in Upper Silesia* (Minority Schools); *Access to German Minority Schools in Upper Silesia*, Ad. Op. of 15 May 1931; *Interpretation of the Statute of Memel*, Judgment of 11 August 1932; *Minority Schools in Albania*, Ad. Op. of 6 April 1935; *Consistency of Certain Danzig Legislative Decrees with the Constitution of the Free City*, Ad. Op. of 4 December 1935.

[13] PCIJ, Ad. Op. of 15 September 1923.

[14] Treaty Between the Principal Allied and Associated Powers and Poland, signed 28 June 1919, 112 Great Britain T.S. 232, Art. 2.

[15] *Supra*, n. 13, 14–15.

[16] *Treatment of Polish Nationals and Other Persons of Polish Origin or Speech in the Danzig Territory*, Ad. Op. of 4 February 1932, 39.

[17] *Ibid.*

[18] PCIJ, Judgment of 26 April 1928, 34.

The most apposite precedent for present purposes is the *Greco-Bulgarian 'Communities'* case,[19] in which the PCIJ was called upon to define a 'community' as that term was used in a 1920 treaty between Greece and Bulgaria concerning reciprocal voluntary emigration, the purpose of which was 'to eliminate or reduce in the Balkans the centres of irredentist agitation which... have been so often the cause of lamentable incidents or serious conflicts....'[20] The treaty was designed both to encourage reciprocal emigration, and to minimize any economic or property loss that might result from emigration. One of the questions that arose was whether such property included not only individual property but also the property of communities which had been dissolved due to emigration.

With little discussion, the Court equated 'communities' with minorities and defined a community as:

> a group of persons living in a given country or locality, having a race, religion, language and traditions of their own and united by this identity of race, religion, language and traditions in a sentiment of solidarity, with a view to preserving their traditions, maintaining their form of worship, ensuring the instruction and upbringing of their children in accordance with the spirit and traditions of their race and rendering mutual assistance to each other...
>
> .... [E]verything leads to the conclusion that the Convention regards the conception of a 'community' from the point of view of this exclusively minority character which it has had for centuries past in the East...[21]

The Court also concluded that whether a community existed was a question of fact, not of law, and that the national law of the state concerned was not determinative.[22]

III. Post-1945 Definitions

The preparation of a definition [of minority] capable of being universally accepted has always proved a task of such difficulty and complexity that neither the experts in this field nor the organs of the international agencies have been able to accomplish it to date.[23] (1979)

[19] PCIJ, Ad. Op. of 31 July 1930.

[20] *Ibid.*, 19.

[21] *Ibid.*, 21–2. This definition was cited with approval in the *Minority Schools in Albania* case, *supra*, n. 12, 11.

[22] *Ibid.*, 22.

[23] Capotorti Study, para. 20.

As to what constitutes a minority, there seems only to be general agreement that there is no generally agreed definition.[24] (1991)

[C]onsideration of issues involving minorities has featured persistent conceptual and terminological confusion in the social sciences, humanities and law.[25] (1999)

"Minority" is an ambiguous term, potentially definable through an endless combination of interacting variables like religion, language, ethnicity, race, culture, physical characteristics and a variety of other traits.[26] (2000)

The scope of application of the Framework Convention [on National Minorities] remains probably the most complicated and politically sensitive issue related to its implementation.[27] (2004)

The international search for an internationally accepted definition of the terms "minority" and "national minority" has not been very successful up to now.[28] (2005)

Despite the above quotes, the picture is not quite as bleak as it appears. The combination of factors referred to by the PCIJ in the *Greco-Bulgarian 'Communities'* case—objective differences of 'race, religion, language and traditions' from the majority population plus a subjective 'sentiment of solidarity, with a view to preserving their traditions'—has been retained in most post-1945 attempts to define a minority. However, the key word remains 'attempts'—no legally binding international instrument contains a definition of 'minority', and the few instruments that have been adopted since 1945 might not have been agreed upon if it had been necessary to first reach consensus on a definition.[29]

There is no reference to minorities in the Universal Declaration of Human Rights; a separate section of the resolution adopting the declaration merely noted that 'it was difficult to adopt a uniform solution for this complex and delicate question [of minorities], which had special aspects in each State in which it arose.'[30] It was not until 1966 that the Covenant on Civil and Political Rights was opened for signature and ratification; it included Article 27, which

[24] Thornberry, *supra*, n. 6, 164.

[25] John Packer, 'Problems in Defining Minorities', in D. Fottrell and B. Bowring (eds.), *Minority and Group Rights in the New Millennium* (The Hague, Boston, London, 1999), 223–73, at 223.

[26] Javaid Rehman, *The Weaknesses in the International Protection of Minority Rights* (The Hague, London, Boston, 2000), 14.

[27] Boriss Cilevič, 'The Framework Convention within the context of the Council of Europe', in Council of Europe, *Filling the Frame: Five years of monitoring the European Framework Convention for the Protection of National Minorities* (Strasbourg, 2004), 28–37, at 30.

[28] Rianne M. Letschert, *The Impact of Minority Rights Mechanisms* (The Hague, 2005), 27.

[29] A list of UN studies and discussions which address the question of a definition of 'minority' may be found in UN Sub-Commission on Prevention of Discrimination and Protection of Minorities, Note by the Secretary-General, UN Doc. E/CN.4/Sub.2/1984/31 (1984).

[30] GA Res. 217C (III) (1948).

formulated rather minimal protections for members of minorities in cultural, religious, and linguistic matters. Article 27 is discussed in greater detail below, but no definition was included in its text.

The UN Sub-Commission on Prevention of Discrimination and Protection of Minorities (renamed the Sub-Commission on the Promotion and Protection of Human Rights in 1999) considered the issue of defining minorities at various stages in its history, and one of the most influential studies (and definitions) was concluded under the Sub-Commission's auspices. That study, by Italian jurist Francesco Capotorti, arrived at the following definition:

> A group numerically inferior to the rest of the population of a State, in a non-dominant position, whose members—being nationals of the State—possess ethnic, religious or linguistic characteristics differing from those of the rest of the population and show, if only implicitly, a sense of solidarity, directed towards preserving their culture, traditions, religion or language.[31]

While Capotorti specifically limited this definition to the context of Article 27 of the Covenant, which had come into force two years before the study was completed, it has remained the model for most of the definitions that followed. The parallels to the PCIJ's definition in the *Greco-Bulgarian 'Communities'* case are clear.

Yugoslavia submitted a draft declaration on the rights of minorities to the Commission on Human Rights in 1979, initiating a process that would eventually lead to adoption of a declaration by the General Assembly over a decade later, which is discussed below. In 1984, as part of this process, the Commission requested the Sub-Commission to explore again the issue of defining 'minority'. After surveying various national and international precedents, Sub-Commission member Jules Deschênes submitted the following definition to the Sub-Commission, which did not differ substantially from that proposed in the earlier Capotorti report:

> A group of citizens of a State, constituting a numerical minority and in non-dominant position in that State, endowed with ethnic, religious or linguistic characteristics which differ from those of the majority of the population, having a sense of solidarity with one another, motivated, if only implicitly, by a collective will to survive and whose aim is to achieve equality with the majority in fact and in law.[32]

[31] United Nations, *Study on the Rights of Persons Belonging to Ethnic, Religious and Linguistic Minorities*, UN Doc. E/CN.4/Sub.2/384/Rev.1 (1979), para. 568 (republished by the UN as UN Sales No. E/91/XIV/2 (1991)).

[32] UN Sub-Commission on the Promotion and Protection of Human Rights, *Proposal concerning a definition of the term 'minority' submitted by Mr. Jules Deschênes*, UN Doc. E/CN.4/Sub.2/1985/31 & Corr.1 (1985), 30.

The Sub-Commission did not formally adopt or approve the definition, which was simply forwarded on to the Commission. In 1986, the Commission's Working Group on the Minorities Declaration decided to postpone further discussion of definitional questions, and there is no definition included in the declaration as it was finally adopted in 1992.[33]

Article 27 of the Covenant on Civil and Political Rights refers only to 'ethnic, religious or linguistic' minorities. Instruments adopted by the Conference on Security and Cooperation in Europe and the Council of Europe, on the other hand, refer only to 'national' minorities.[34] The 1992 UN Declaration has the theoretically broadest scope, encompassing persons belonging to 'national or ethnic, religious and linguistic minorities'; the Declaration also refers to protecting 'cultural' identity.

The only definition of 'national minority' included in any formal text is that proposed in 1993 by the Parliamentary Assembly of the Council of Europe, in its recommended (but not adopted) additional protocol to the European Convention on Human Rights:

> [T]he expression "national minority" refers to a group of persons in a State who:
> (a) reside on the territory of that State and are citizens thereof;
> (b) maintain longstanding, firm and lasting ties with that State;
> (c) display distinctive ethnic, cultural, religious or linguistic characteristics;
> (d) are sufficiently representative, although smaller in number than the rest of the population of that State or of a region of that State;
> (e) are motivated by a concern to preserve together that which constitutes their common identity, including their culture, their traditions, their religion or their language.[35]

After a survey of the relevant texts, one of the most comprehensive recent examinations of the definition of minority concludes that:

> the definitions elaborated, even though they show slight differences, reflect the conviction that the term 'minority' means a group historically rooted in the territory of a State and whose specific ethno-cultural features (with the respective claims of

[33] Declaration on the Rights of Persons Belonging to National or Ethnic, Religious and Linguistic Minorities, adopted by the UN GA on 18 December 1992, GA Res. 47/135.

[34] See, eg, the Final Act of the Conference on Security and Cooperation in Europe, adopted on 1 August 1975, reprinted in 14 ILM 1292 (1975) (CSCE Final Act), 6; Second Conference on the Human Dimension of the CSCE, 5 June – 29 July, Document of the Copenhagen Meeting of the Conference on the Human Dimension of the CSCE, Copenhagen 1990 (CSCE Copenhagen Document), paras. 30–40; Framework Convention for the Protection of National Minorities, adopted on 1 February 1995, entered into force on 1 February 1998, ETS No. 157 (FCNM).

[35] Proposal for an additional protocol to the Convention for the Protection of Human Rights and Fundamental Freedoms, Parliamentary Assembly of the Council of Europe, Recommendation 1201 (1993), 44th Sess., 22nd Sitting, 1 February 1993, Art. 1.

protection) markedly distinguish it from the rest of the population of the State; the effect is also to 'orient' the permanent social and political links of its members with the State as manifested by citizenship.[36]

IV. Recent Jurisprudence and Views

A. Human Rights Committee

As noted above, the Covenant on Civil and Political Rights remains the only legally binding instrument of global application that includes a provision that directly sets forth minority rights. The Human Rights Committee oversees implementation of the Covenant through its examination of states' periodic reports, the adoption of 'views' on individual cases submitted under the First Optional Protocol, and the adoption of 'General Comments' that address both procedural requirements and substantive issues.

It was not until 1994, two years after the GA Declaration, that the committee was able to reach sufficient consensus to adopt a General Comment on Article 27.[37] The committee addresses definitional issues only indirectly, first observing in a cursory manner that 'it is not relevant to determine the degree of permanence that the term 'exist' connotes'.[38] The committee goes on to adopt the expansive view that Article 27 applies to everyone belonging to one of the named categories of minorities and present within a country, including 'migrant workers or even visitors'.[39] Finally, with respect to definitional issues, the committee offers its opinion that members of minorities need not be citizens of the state concerned, extrapolating from the general obligation in Article 2(1) to guarantee Covenant rights to all individuals within a state's territory and subject to its jurisdiction.[40]

The committee's General Comment contains no reference to relevant *travaux préparatoires* of the Covenant to support its conclusions, and there is no further attempt to clarify which groups fall within or outside the scope of Article 27. If one does examine the meaning of minority at the time that the Covenant was being drafted, however, the conclusions are quite different. For example,

[36] Gaetano Pentassuglia, *Defining 'Minority' in International Law: A Critical Appraisal* (Rovaniemi, 2nd rev. edn, 2000), 10. Also see *id.*, *Minorities in International Law* (Strasbourg, 2002), 55–75.

[37] HRC, General Comment No. 23, UN Doc. CCPR/C/21/Rev.1/Add.5 (1994).

[38] *Ibid.*, para. 5.2.

[39] *Ibid.*

[40] *Ibid.*, para. 5.1.

the Annotations on the text of the draft of the International Covenants on Human Rights, prepared by the Secretary-General for the General Assembly in 1955, state, 'It was agreed that the article should cover only separate or distinct groups, well-defined and long-established on the territory of a State'.[41] A well-respected treatise on minority rights published prior to the committee's General Comment concluded that 'aliens are prima facie excluded' from the scope of Article 27.[42] '[T]he General Comment is perhaps best interpreted as representing the personal views of committee members rather than an authoritative interpretation of the text of the Covenant.'[43]

The opinions of the Human Rights Committee certainly deserve serious consideration, but the committee is not given the authority under the Covenant to interpret its provisions in a manner that is legally binding on states. It is clear that, deliberating several decades after the Covenant was drafted, the committee attempted to formulate a more contemporary version of minority rights than that contained in the Covenant itself. However, it does not appear that this expansive approach has been adopted by state parties to the Covenant in their reports to the committee.[44] As Pentassuglia concludes, 'however captivating, [the arguments of the committee for an extensive notion of minority] . . . do not appear entirely persuasive.'[45]

The committee has adopted a number of 'views' concerning Article 27 in the context of individual applications filed pursuant to the First Optional Protocol to the Covenant. Many of these applications have been from indigenous peoples asserting their right to self-determination under Article 1 of the Covenant, but the committee has consistently rejected these arguments and has held that it is impermissible to raise 'peoples' rights set forth in Article 1 under the individual application mechanism of the Optional Protocol.[46] Nonetheless, the

[41] UN Doc. A/2929 (1955), para. 184. Additional references to the Commission's discussions may be found in M. J. Bossuyt (ed.), *Guide to the* 'Travaux Préparatoires' *of the International Covenant on Civil and Political Rights* (Dordrecht, 1987), 494.

[42] Thornberry, *supra*, n. 6, 171. Also see Pentassuglia, *supra*, n. 36, 28–31, at 30: 'The Committee does not succeed in explaining why one should equate the idea of a "historical-permanency-citizenship" scheme with the idea of a "non-permanent or occasional residence-non-citizenship" scheme.... In the absence of clarifications, the scope of application of Article 27 could be interpreted so extensively that it may jeopardise its credibility as the expression of an international minimum standard.'

[43] Hurst Hannum, 'New Minority Rights for the Twenty-First Century', in Y. Danieli, E. Stamatopoulou, and C. J. Dias (eds.), *The Universal Declaration of Human Rights: Fifty Years and Beyond* (Amityville, 1999), 163–73, at 169.

[44] See generally Pentassuglia, *supra*, n. 36, 18–36.

[45] *Ibid.*, 18.

[46] See, e.g., HRC, Communication No. 167/1984, *Chief Bernard Ominayak and the Lubicon Lake Band v. Canada*, view of 26 March 1990, [1990] Annual Report 1, 5, para. 13.3.

committee has addressed the merits of a number of indigenous cases, examining them under Article 27.[47]

The applicants were clearly indigenous, and no question of definition arose; neither the Committee nor the respondent government questioned the applicability of Article 27. In one case, however, the committee did address definitional issues, although its discussion of the scope of Article 27 was limited to the facts of the case.

Ballantyne et al. v. Canada[48] challenged legislation in Quebec that, *inter alia*, prohibited the use of any language other than French in commercial signs. The applicants asserted rights under Article 27, thus raising the question of whether English-speakers within the province of Quebec were a 'minority' within the meaning of that article. While the committee found that the restrictions in question violated the right to freedom of expression under Article 19 of the Covenant, it rejected the applicants' claims under Article 27:

> [T]he minorities referred to in article 27 are minorities within . . . a state, and not minorities within any province. A group may constitute a majority in a province but still be a minority in a State and thus be entitled to the benefits of article 27. English speaking citizens of Canada cannot be considered a linguistic minority.[49]

A number of separate opinions were written by individual committee members, some of which touched on the definitional question. One member rather unhelpfully offered the opinion that 'the issue of what constitutes a minority in a State must be decided on a case by case basis, due regard being given to the particular circumstances of each case.'[50] Four other members disagreed with the majority's approach of interpreting the term 'minorities' in Article 27 'solely on the basis of the number of members of the group in question in the State party.'[51]

> The criteria for determining what is a minority in a State (in the sense of article 27) have not yet been considered by the Committee, and do not need to be foreclosed by a decision in the present matter . . . . The history of the protection of minorities in international law shows that the question of definition has been difficult and controversial and that many different criteria have been proposed . . . .

[47] See, e.g., the cases concerning indigenous people collected in R. Hanski and M. Scheinin (eds.), *Leading Cases of the Human Rights Committee* (Turku/Åbo, 2003), 375–99.

[48] HRC, Communications Nos. 359/1989 and 385/1989, views of 31 March 1993, [1993] Annual Report, vol. 2, 91.

[49] *Ibid.*, para. 11.2.

[50] *Ibid.*, Individual opinion submitted by Mr. Bertil Wennergreen (concurring).

[51] Individual opinion submitted by Ms. Elizabeth Evatt, co-signed by Mr. Nisuke Ando, Mr. Marco Tulio Bruini Celli and Mr. Vojin Dimitrijevic (concurring and elaborating).

To take a narrow view of the meaning of minorities in article 27 could have the result that a State party would have no obligation under the Covenant to ensure that a minority in an autonomous province had the protection of article 27 where it was not clear that the group in question was a minority in the State considered as a whole entity.[52]

This specific issue was not addressed in the committee's General Comment on Article 27, which was adopted the following year and is discussed above.

B. Working Group on Minorities of the Sub-Commission on the Promotion and Protection of Human Rights

Following the adoption of the UN Declaration on minorities in 1992, a Working Group on Minorities was created as a subsidiary body of the Sub-Commission on the Promotion and Protection of Human Rights. The working group adopted a broad, flexible approach to its work, and, after an early unsuccessful attempt, has not subsequently attempted to define 'minority'.[53] In many ways, the working group has considered itself a forum in which dialogue can be pursued, rather than even wa quasi-legal body whose task is to identify the rights to which minorities are entitled.[54]

The group's chairman, Asbjørn Eide, did author a relatively detailed commentary on the declaration, which ultimately was approved by the working group as representing the views of the group.[55] The commentary avoids dealing directly with the issue of definition, although it does offer observations on the scope of application of the declaration. It offers the opinion that 'citizenship as such should not be a distinguishing criterion which excludes some persons or groups from enjoying minority rights under the Declaration'.[56] However,

[52] *Ibid.*

[53] The working group discussed definitions and categories during its first four sessions, but the debates did not lead to any consensus. See the annual reports of the working group, E/CN.4/Sub.2/1996/2 (1995) (1st session), paras. 76–90; E/CN.4/Sub.2/1996/28 (1996) (2nd session), paras. 131–174; E/CN.4/Sub.2/1997/18 (1997) (3rd session), paras. 99–104. Working group member Stanislav Chernichenko submitted a working paper on a definition of minorities, which included a seven-article 'working definition' that retained a requirement that persons be permanently resident in a state although not necessarily citizens of that state; however, the working paper was not acted upon by the working group. See E/CN.4/Sub.2/AC.5/1996/WP.1 (1996). A related paper prepared a few years later by Mr. Bengoa on the existence and recognition of minorities likewise led to no further agreement on a definition. See E/CN.4/Sub.2/AC.5/2000/WP.2 (2000).

[54] This approach was outlined in a paper by the working group's first chairman, Asbjørn Eide, 'Report on the Possible Ways and Means of Facilitating the Peaceful and Constructive Solution of Problems Involving Minorities', E/CN.4/Sub.2/1993/34 (1993).

[55] See UN Doc. E/CN.4/Sub.2/AC.5/2005/2 (2005).

[56] *Ibid.*, para. 10.

it then goes on to suggest that different kinds of minorities might have different rights; in particular, '[t]hose who have been established for a long time on the territory may have stronger rights than those who have recently arrived.'[57] This would seem to implicitly reject the approach of the Human Rights Committee, although, like the committee, the working group has no formal authority to interpret the document on which its mandate is based, ie, the 1992 GA Declaration.

With respect to the kinds of minorities referred to in the Declaration, the commentary notes that '[t]here is hardly any national minority, however defined, that is not also an ethnic or linguistic minority,' although the reverse is not necessarily true (ie, a group that might not be considered to be a national minority under the European instruments that use this term might nonetheless constitute an ethnic, religious, or linguistic minority).[58]

C. European Framework Convention on National Minorities

As already noted, the Framework Convention (FCNM) does not itself define the 'national minorities' to which it applies. The Explanatory Report attached to the FCNM when it was adopted notes: 'It was decided to adopt a pragmatic approach, based on the recognition that at this stage, it is impossible to arrive at a definition capable of mustering general support of all Council of Europe member States.'[59] However, a number of state parties to the FCNM have attached declarations to their instruments of ratification or accession that either identify the particular minorities to which the convention will apply or define the term national minorities. As direct examples of state practice, any common features of such declarations should constitute relatively persuasive evidence of the meaning of 'national minority.'

Those countries offering a definition are Austria, Estonia, Latvia, Luxembourg, Poland, and Switzerland. Austria defines 'national minorities' as 'those groups which come within the scope of application of the [Austrian] Law on Ethnic Groups . . . and which live and traditionally have had their home in parts of the territory of the Republic of Austria and which are composed of Austrian citizens with non-German mother tongues and with their own ethnic cultures'.[60] Estonia considers minorities to be Estonian citizens

[57] *Ibid.*

[58] *Ibid.*, paras. 6, 8.

[59] FCNM, Explanatory Report, para. 12, at http://conventions.coe.int/Treaty/en/Reports/Html/157.htm.

[60] Declaration of 31 March 1998, at http://conventions.coe.int/Treaty/Commun/ListeDeclarations.asp?NT=157&CM=&DF=&CL=ENG&VL=1.

who 'reside on the territory of Estonia; maintain longstanding, firm and lasting ties with Estonia; are distinct from Estonians on the basis of their ethnic, cultural, religious or linguistic characteristics; are motivated by a concern to preserve together their cultural traditions, their religion or their language, which constitute the basis of their common identity.'[61] Luxembourg provides more succinctly that a national minority is 'a group of people settled for numerous generations on its [Luxembourg's] territory, having the Luxembourg nationality and having kept distinctive characteristics in an ethnic and linguistic way.'[62] Latvia, Poland, and Switzerland offer similar definitions; all include citizenship as a necessary criterion for membership in a national minority.

A number of other states (Denmark, Germany, Netherlands, Slovenia, Sweden, and the former Yugoslav Republic of Macedonia) simply identify the specific groups to which the Convention will apply, each of which is consistent with the definitions set forth above. Liechtenstein, Luxembourg, and Malta declare that there are no national minorities within their respective territories.

The Advisory Committee established to monitor implementation of the FCNM has not attempted to adopt a formal definition of national minorities. Some of its comments would seem to suggest that its 'pragmatic' approach might go beyond groups traditionally considered to be national minorities, eg, its attention to the condition of foreigners and asylum-seekers in Liechtenstein. 'The Advisory Committee thus attaches importance to promotion by the authorities of a spirit of tolerance and mutual respect between all persons living on the territory of Liechtenstein. In this context, it is important that the Liechtenstein authorities try to remedy any possible integration difficulties certain groups may encounter because of their religious and cultural differences from the majority population.'[63] The second opinion on Liechtenstein considers racism, intolerance, and discrimination issues and 'welcomes the fact that Liechtenstein has included information in its State Report on measures taken to improve the integration of foreign nationals and prevent racism and discrimination, even though the Government does not consider these groups as national minorities.'[64]

[61] Declaration of 6 January 1997, *ibid.*

[62] Declaration of 18 July 1995, *ibid.*

[63] Advisory Committee on the FCNM, Opinion on Liechtenstein, adopted on 30 November 2000, para. 15, ACFC/INF/OP/I(2001)003.

[64] Advisory Committee on the FCNM, Second Opinion on Liechtenstein, adopted on 1 October 2004, para. 10, ACFC/INF/OP/II(2004)001.

In a general comment in response to an initiative of the Council of Europe's Parliamentary Assembly, the Advisory Committee stated:

In the Advisory Committee's opinion, the Framework Convention is not an instrument that operates on an 'all-or-nothing' basis. Even if a group is covered by the Framework Convention, it does not necessarily follow that all of the Convention's articles apply to the persons belonging to that minority. Similarly, if a minority is not covered by the majority of the provisions in the Framework Convention, that does not necessarily mean that none of the provisions is relevant to the members of that group. The Advisory Committee believes that a nuanced, article-by-article approach to the 'definition' question is not only fully in line with the text of the Framework Convention but is actually dictated by it. This flexibility in the implementation of the Framework Convention could be made more difficult by including a definition in a legally binding European instrument.[65]

Reflecting a continuing unwillingness to examine the issue of defining national minorities, the Committee of Ministers of the Council of Europe observed with respect to the same Parliamentary Assembly proposal:

With regard to the proposal for an additional protocol to the European Convention on Human Rights concerning the rights of national minorities, which would include the definition of national minority contained in Assembly Recommendation 1201(1993) [set forth above], the Committee of Ministers considers that it is somewhat premature to reopen the debate on this project. The Committee of Ministers would stress in this connection that, when Protocol No.12 to the European Convention on Human Rights comes into force, any discrimination against a member of a national minority, including discrimination based on association with such a minority, will be covered by the general prohibition on discrimination.[66]

V. Proposals for Expanding the Definition

There can be little doubt that most states and the majority of commentators today retain a concept of minority that includes the subjective and objective components described by the PCIJ and reiterated by Capotorti and others.

[65] Opinion of the Advisory Committee on the Framework Convention for the Protection of National Minorities adopted on 14 September 2001 on Parliamentary Assembly Recommendation 1492 (2001) on the rights of national minorities, para. 17, at http://www.coe.int/t/e/human%5Frights/minorities/2.%5Fframework%5Fconvention%5F%28monitoring%29/2.%5FMonitoring%5Fmechanism/4._Opinions_of_the_Advisory_Committee/2._Other_opinions/ACFC%20Opinion%20on%20Rec%201492%20E.asp#TopOfPage.

[66] Decision of the CoE Committee of Ministers, 799th meeting, 13 June 2002, Item 4.2.

There is certainly nothing in the various international instruments themselves that would suggest that such a definition is inappropriate or outmoded, but some commentators have suggested that a broader definition is now either required or desirable. The expansive interpretation by the Human Rights Committee of Article 27 of the Covenant on Civil and Political Rights is but one example.

Proponents of broadening the definition seem to have two primary motivations. The first stems from a universalist, liberal understanding of human rights that sees minority rights as situated firmly in the context of a body of law that ascribes rights to individuals merely because they are human. The limitation of minority rights to groups that are defined by ethnicity, religion, language, culture, citizenship status, or permanence on the territory of a state appears to these observers as anachronistic and unnecessarily limiting.

The second motivation is more pragmatic. The traditional definition of minorities is rejected either because it might omit groups that need protection or simply because waiting for consensus on any definition would prevent progress on developing substantive rights. Coincidentally, this approach is often adopted by international bodies for which a strict definition might result in a limitation on their mandate as they interpret it; thus, the Human Rights Committee wants to include tourists within Article 27, and the Advisory Committee wants to address broader issues of tolerance and non-discrimination under the FCNM.

A. The Liberal Human Rights Approach

One of the proponents of the first approach (many others could be cited) is John Packer, a former senior legal adviser to the OSCE's High Commissioner on National Minorities. Packer would reject all of the traditional limitations that define the 'minorities' who are the beneficiaries of special rights, in favour of a 'contractarian associational' definition:

> Notwithstanding the specificities of each...situation, the essence of 'minority' remains the same: it is the stuff of *belonging*—a matter of association—which is socially contracted according to reciprocal subjectivities, the contractual elements of which are observable and objectifiable. From the perspective of human rights philosophy and law, a good definition of 'minority' must emphasize freedom of choice.... [I]t is both consistent and workable to define a minority as 'a group of people who freely associate for an established purpose where their shared desire differs from that expressed by the majority rule.'[67]

[67] Packer, *supra*, n. 25, 271–2.

In essence, the argument is that both liberal human rights theory and sociological reality render a focus on particular kinds of minorities untenable and even discriminatory in the modern world. Why should ethnic, religious, linguistic, and national groups be privileged over those with a different sexual orientation,[68] the disabled, and other groups whose non-dominant or even marginal position in society is analogous to that of traditional minorities?

One answer, of course, is that many of these other groups (eg, women, children, refugees, displaced persons, migrant workers, persons with disabilities) have benefitted from international attention and instruments directed at their particular situations. In fact, it is precisely the traditional minorities who were largely ignored until the last decade of the twentieth century, although some of their concerns were addressed in the process of developing individual human rights norms related to expression, association, religion, culture, and education. In any event, while the expansive concept of minority advanced by Packer finds echoes in some other commentators, it has yet to be endorsed by any state or international body.

B. The Pragmatic Approach

There is little contribution that pragmatism can make to the search for a definition of minority, for its essence consists of a desire to avoid defining the concept. As stated in a Council of Europe report, 'The delimitation of beneficiaries [of minority rights] has been a major stumbling block for international standard-setting activities . . . In light of these and other difficulties, it is probably worthwhile to look for an alternative to a comprehensive and globally applicable defnition.'[69]

When analyzing the value of such an approach, however, it is important to keep in mind the purpose of bodies that choose deliberate obfuscation or generality, rather than a clear definition. If the primary purpose is conflict prevention, for example, then disputes between any two groups might be relevant, not only conflicts between groups one of which might be identified as a traditional minority; a definition might unnecessarily limit the oportunities for mediation. If the purpose is to identify 'best practices' in the field of decision-making and participation in a pluralist state, then minority 'rights' may be less relevant than political theories of devolution and power-sharing. If

[68] See, eg, Eric Heinze, 'The Construction and Contingency of the Minority Concept', in D. Fottrell and B. Bowring (eds.), *Minority and Group Rights in the New Millennium* (The Hague, Boston, London, 1999), 25–74.

[69] CoE, *7th International Colloquy on the European Convention on Human Rights*, 30 May–2 June, Report on 'Equality and non-discrimination: minority rights' (Strasbourg, 1990).

the purpose is to engage states in a dialogue that might contribute to minimizing discrimination and increasing tolerance, formal definitions may be less important than expanding the framework for that dialogue. Of course, even if one adopts the more traditional definition of minority, such a norm would not in any respect prevent a state from adopting both a broader definition of groups that should be protected and providing a more extensive set of rights to such groups.

Even if the international community were to reach consensus on a binding definition of minority, the extraordinarily diverse circumstances in which minorities find themselves necessarily require a flexible or pragmatic identification of what *rights* they enjoy—as opposed to what political, social, or economic measures might be taken to further related goals, such as the peaceful resolution of disputes, the reduction of social tensions, or a more equitable distribution of societal resources. It is not coincidental that many of the 'rights' identified in documents such as the GA Declaration and the European Framework Convention are circumscribed by terms such as 'encourage.... effectively.... where appropriate.... favourable'[70] or 'where necessary... adequate measures... take due account of the specific conditions... where [a] request responds to a real need.... as far as possible.'[71] Thus, to a certain extent, pragmatism must prevail.[72]

C. Individual versus Group Rights

The question of whether 'minority rights' are essentially group rights or individual rights may be of theoretical interest, but the practical implications of the debate are more difficult to discern. For example, Article 27 of the Covenant and all other intergovernmental instruments relating to minorities apply formally only to 'persons belonging to' minorities, although Article 1 of the UN Declaration does oblige states to protect 'the existence and... identity of minorities within their respective territories', not just individual members of minorities.

[70] These words appear in the UN declaration.

[71] These phrases are from the FCNM.

[72] One might note that the matching of rights to particular situations may be necessary even in the context of individual rights. The concept of 'progressive realisation' of rights is fundamental to the Covenant on Economic, Social and Cultural Rights, but civil and political rights also may be determined with reference to a particular context. For example, one would not expect the judicial system in Sweden to match that in Cameroon, nor does freedom of expression have the same meaning in different social and cultural contexts. These variations are often subsumed under the principle of granting a 'margin of discretion' to national authorities; while this principle may be abused, it does not in and of itself undermine the rights concerned.

The very concept of a 'minority' implies a community or group, and the reference in international instruments to the rights of 'persons' should be understood primarily as a jurisdictional rather than a substantive limitation. For example, if rights were accorded only to minority groups *qua* groups, difficult questions might arise as to who was entitled to represent the minority and what persons should be considered to be members of the minority. Far simpler (and more supportive of the underlying rights) is the individually oriented approach of the Covenant and other documents, which enable any aggrieved member of a minority to complain about alleged violations of his or her rights, which, in any event, can only be exercised with others. While this issue remains theoretically divisive (the 'individual' versus 'collective' debate was for many years a constant in debates about the rights of indigenous peoples, for example), it is not generally raised as an impediment against or an argument for adopting a more precise definition of minority.

Similar observations might apply to distinctions among the various categories of minorities identified in international texts, ie, national, ethnic, religious, linguistic, and cultural minorities. No jurisprudence or governmental commentary has focused on these differences, with the exception of attempts to define national minorities (discussed above). Nonetheless, this is an issue that may deserve greater attention, and it may offer a way of reconciling expansive versus restrictive definitions.

It seems indisputable that the category of 'national minority' has acquired a connotation (at least within Europe) of a long-settled group with historical ties to a particular territory; citizenship of the state in which they live is often considered to be an essential element of this category as well, although this may simply be a different reflection of the need to be a permanent member of the society in which one lives.[73] Linguistic or religious minorities, on the other hand, might be more easily understood as encompassing relatively recent arrivals in a country (although the extension of minority rights to tourists, as suggested by the Human Rights Committee, goes too far).

Having identified national minorities as possibly distinct, however, international law has not thus far formally ascribed different or greater rights to national as opposed to other kinds of minorities. Perhaps the most salient difference among different kinds of minorities is their degree of territorial concentration or dispersion. Thus, there may be a difference in the rights that can be effectively exercised by geographically concentrated minorities, on one hand, and minorities whose members are dispersed throughout the state, on

[73] This concept is discussed in particular by Pentassuglia, *supra*, n. 36, 19–28.

the other hand; this difference does not depend on whether a particular group is categorized as a national, religious, ethnic, or other minority.[74]

VI. Conclusions

It should be recognized first that definitional questions are important only if they carry with them legal or political consequences. In the case of minorities, emerging international norms would obviously benefit groups which fall within their scope, while they would be unavailable to groups considered to be only political, regional, or social groups. However, there are also some potentially negative consequences to being classified as a minority; for example, 'minorities' do not enjoy any right to self-determination, while 'peoples' do enjoy that right.[75]

Although the rights of ethnic, religious, linguistic, and national minorities have been the subject of international legal instruments for centuries, it should not be surprising that none has thus far included a definition of minorities in general. This is explained primarily by historical reasons. In an era before the universal application of either minority rights or human rights, minorities that became the subject of international legal agreements were defined, implicitly or explicitly, by the terms of those agreements. It has been only after the proclamation and acceptance of the idea of universal human rights norms that the question of a globally applicable definition of minorities arose.

Neither the substance nor scope of rights can always be determined in advance, no matter how detailed the instrument in which they are proclaimed. For most human rights, it is only the substance of the right that needs to be articulated over time; there seems little doubt, for example, that the customary international law norm against 'torture or inhuman or degrading treatment or punishment' will evolve as various international monitoring bodies analyze the concept, and as states adjust their practices to correspond with their interpretation of the norm. For minorities, however, both the substance of their rights and the issue of who is entitled to exercise those rights have developed at the same time. Many of the rights that decades ago were enjoyed *only* by

[74] See, eg, the discussion of territorially concentrated and dispersed groups in OSCE High Commissioner on National Minorities, *Lund Recommendations on the Effective Participation of National Minorities in Public Life,* September 1999.

[75] See, eg, HRC, General Comment No. 23, para. 3.1 ('The Covenant draws a distinction between the right to self-determination and the rights protected under Article 27. The former is expressed to be a right belonging to peoples.... Article 27, on the other hand, relates to rights conferred on individuals as such'.)

certain minorities are now available to everyone, as freedom of religion, language, and cultural expression have been extended to all individuals. At the same time, however, the traditional content of minority rights is expanding into much more problematic territory, particularly in terms of 'effective participation' in economic, cultural, and especially political life. While states may be willing to adopt a broad definition of those minorities entitled to cultural or linguistic protection, expanding special participatory political rights to groups defined too broadly threatens both the stability of the state and the notion of one-person, one-vote democracy.

International law is still made by states, not by scholars or philosophers (although the latter no doubt contribute to the progressive development of the law). The great majority of states appear to define minorities to whom they owe legal obligations (as opposed to minorities whose demands may be satisfied simply because it is politically expedient to do so) as reflecting the traditional PCIJ/Capotorti concept of groups that share certain objective characteristics, combined with a subjective understanding of themselves as a group or community that desires to develop and perpetuate those attributes that define them, ie, language, religion, and culture.[76] As persuasively argued by Pentassuglia: 'The Capotorti definition (as well as the other definitions substantially inspired by it) reflects a basic convergence of views historically consolidated. It seems difficult to believe that any change in the general outlook has actually occurred.'[77]

Other groups or individuals wishing to protect particular interests or characteristics may do so under both general human rights law and under more detailed instruments, such as those adopted to protect the rights of children, women, prisoners, migrants, and many other groups. When those interests reflect a desire to preserve linguistic, religious, or cultural identities, it is likely that such groups will be deemed to fall within the scope of linguistic, religious, or cultural minorities. Where they do not, the rights of such groups and individuals may be equally well protected under 'ordinary' human rights norms, as the Human Rights Committee found in the *Ballantyne* case.

Particularly where the assertion of rights requires positive acts on the part of the state (whether through the expenditure of funds or other means) or where

[76] It is difficult to imagine a community whose sole distinction is that it is ethnically different from the dominant society, although it shares with that society all of the attributes of language, religion, and culture (the distinction between Tutsi and Hutu in Rwanda and Burundi may be close). Any demand for separate treatment intended solely to recognize and maintain such ethnic distinctions would seem more akin to *apartheid* than to contemporary understandings of human rights.

[77] Pentassuglia, *supra*, n. 36, 49.

the rights asserted encompass newly formulated demands for effective participation, states are likely to continue to insist that their obligations extend only to long-established, relatively permanent, and perhaps historically identifiable minorities. While most states link this criterion to that of citizenship, it is permanency rather than status that is often the real issue.[78]

Every individual and group is entitled to benefit from the norms of non-discrimination and equality that are fundamental to modern conceptions of human rights. However, the rights of groups identified by states for over a century as deserving particular protection or consideration—protection for their religious, linguistic, and cultural identity—will be undermined if all socially disadvantaged groups are lumped together as 'minorities'. Racism and discrimination can be combatted without asserting that every situation in which they appear implicates 'minority' rights. Responding to intolerance and discrimination is necessary no matter what the grounds for the discrimination, but confusing the equality of all with the particular (and particularly sensitive) equality needs of certain ethno-cultural-linguistic-religious groups serves no one well.

Few human rights are absolute, and the rights of minority and non-minority individuals must usually be balanced against the legitimate rights and interests of the majority in a democratic society. That balance may be struck differently in different contexts; like other rights, minority rights merely set a floor for minority protection, not a ceiling that would prevent a state from adopting an expansive definition of minorities and their rights. The fact that a traditional—some would say restrictive—definition of minority continues to prevail in international law need not deter those who wish to expand its scope. As of today, however, the scope of application of minority rights properly understood is limited to those ethnic, religious, linguistic, and national communities who have a relatively permanent presence within the territory of a state, who have not opted to remain apart from it (by refusing citizenship where it is readily available), and who desire to maintain the characteristics that define them.

[78] While human rights law recognizes a right to nationality, it does not recognize the right to any particular nationality. If a state deliberately seeks to prevent well-established groups of people from obtaining citizenship, non-citizen status should not undermine otherwise applicable rights. Where citizenship is available but, for whatever reason, is voluntarily declined, the citizenship criterion may not be an unreasonable prerequisite for the enjoyment of certain minority rights.

NON-DISCRIMINATION AND FULL AND EFFECTIVE EQUALITY

Kristin Henrard

I. Introduction

A. Relevance of Non-discrimination for Minority Communities

It is generally (albeit not unanimously) accepted that an adequate system of minority protection is constructed on two pillars, the first of which concerns non-discrimination in combination with individual human rights of special relevance for minorities, the second consisting of minority-specific standards aimed at protecting and promoting the right to identity of minorities. In light of this, it is not surprising that the prohibition of discrimination is often called the *conditio sine qua non* for an adequate minority protection.[1]

At the same time, it should be underlined that substantive or real, full equality is the ultimate goal of minority protection, while the right to identity of minorities is another foundational principle of minority protection. Hence, it is important to assess to what extent (the interpretation of) the first pillar achieves substantive equality and protects and promotes the right to identity of minorities.

The relevance of non-discrimination for minorities and minority protection cannot be denied, as was abundantly clear in the view of the Human Rights Committee (HRC) in *Waldman v. Canada*. The case concerns a preference given to Roman Catholic schools compared to schools for other religious minorities as regards funding by the provincial government. According to the HRC this amounted to a violation of the prohibition of discrimination (Article 26 CCPR). In addition to showing the contribution of the prohibition of discrimination to the achievement of typical minority concerns and claims, this view also clarified that one is just as much a victim of discrimination when the advantaged group is a comparable minority as when the advantaged group is a majority.[2]

However, the actual level of protection for members belonging to minorities flowing from this prohibition depends on how it is being interpreted (see below for an enumeration of relevant aspects).

B. Survey of Legal Standards

When comparing the non-discrimination provisions in conventions, it is evident that there is no uniform description of what amounts to discrimination. Nevertheless, it is equally obvious that the definitions are very similar and differ mainly as to the detail with which they are drafted. In this regard reference can already be made to General Comment No. 18 of the Human Rights Committee, which acknowledges that the CCPR does not define the concept of discrimination, nor indicates what constitutes discrimination, but then continues to provide a definition on the basis of the definitions found in CERD and CEDAW.[3]

[1] K. Henrard, *Devising an Adequate System of Minority Protection: Individual Human Rights, Minority Rights and the Right to Self-Determination* (The Hague, 2000), 8–11. See also S. Fredman, 'Introduction', in S. Fredman (ed.), *Discrimination and Human Rights: The Case of Racism* (Oxford, 2001), 23.

[2] S. Joseph, J. Schultz and M. Castan, *The International Covenant on Civil and Political Rights: Cases, Materials and Commentary* (Oxford, 2004), 681.

[3] HRC, General Comment No. 18, Non-Discrimination, paras. 6–7.

Nevertheless, this apparent 'consistency' in descriptions of the phenomenon 'discrimination' hides a variety of intricate conceptual problems and lingering uncertainties, as will be outlined under section 1C and developed under section 2 below.

One striking difference in the formulation of the non-discrimination provisions concerns the scope of the prohibition of discrimination. Sometimes the provision is 'parasitic' in the sense that the prohibition of discrimination only applies in relation to the other substantive rights of the Convention. Discrimination in relation to a right which does not feature in the Convention would simply not be covered. In contrast, an autonomous prohibition of discrimination would have a general, all-encompassing nature and would apply to discriminations in any domain or field of law.

In a judgment of 17 October 2005 the Inter-American Court of Human Rights has confirmed the extensive reach of the general prohibition of discrimination. The Court's ruling in *Yean and Bosico v. Dominican Republic* marks the first time that an international human rights tribunal has unequivocally upheld the international prohibition on racial discrimination in access to nationality. The Court underlined that even though states maintain the sovereign right to regulate nationality, states' discretion is limited by international human rights standards, and more particularly by the prohibition of discrimination (on the basis of race). In granting nationality, states must abstain from producing and enforcing regulations that are discriminatory on their face or that have discriminatory effects on different groups within a population.[4] In any event, it is widely agreed that the prohibition of discrimination does not require identical treatment, in other words, not every differentiation amounts to a prohibited discrimination.[5]

Related to that and by way of a starting point, it can be put forward that a differentiation of treatment would amount to a prohibited discrimination when, and in so far as, there would not be a reasonable and objective justification for this differentiation.[6] Over time, there have been several refinements to this understanding of the concept 'discrimination' (see below).

[4] See also HRC, *Borzov v. Estonia* (Communication No. 1136/2002, 26 July 2004), para 7.4, where the Committee also indicates implicitly that the grant of citizenship is not totally within the exercise of a state party's sovereign powers in the sense that a certain refusal of a grant of citizenship could amount to a violation of the prohibition of discrimination, more specifically if there would not be 'objective and reasonable grounds' for the refusal.

[5] HRC, General Comment No. 18, para 8 and 13.

[6] HRC, General Comment No. 18, para 13.

Here, I only want to give a broad outline of the distinctive provisions and their respective 'coverage'. The more in-depth discussion can be found in section 2.

1. The Two General UN Human Rights Covenants of 1966: The International Covenant on Civil and Political Rights (CCPR) and the International Covenant on Economic, Social and Cultural Rights (CESCR)

The CCPR contains various non-discrimination provisions, more specifically Articles 2, 3 and 26. While Articles 2 and 26 consider multiple grounds of prohibited discrimination, Article 3 focuses on equal rights for men and women, and thus concerns only the gender dimension.[7] While Article 2 is limited to the enjoyment of the rights in the CCPR, Article 26 has a general reach.[8] An Article of the CCPR which is also relevant is Article 20, paragraph 2[9] which obliges states to prohibit, by law, any advocacy of national, racial or religious hatred which constitutes incitement to discrimination.[10] Finally, Article 24 contains a non-discrimination provision in relation to children and their right to be protected as minors.[11]

The CESCR on the other hand only has one Article on non-discrimination, Article 2 which is more or less a copy of the prohibition of discrimination in Article 2 CCPR. However, it should be noted that in Article 2 CCPR, the word 'discrimination' does not feature—only the word 'distinction'. Nevertheless, it is obvious, and also is clear in General Comment No. 18 (paragraph 1 and following), that the HRC understands 'distinction' as 'discrimination'.

Article 3 reveals special attention for gender discrimination and a strong concern to achieve real, substantive equality between men and women (Article 3, paragraph 3) with seemingly far-reaching positive obligations.[12]

Even though Article 26 contains a general prohibition of discrimination, and hence has an extensive scope of application, the quasi jurisprudence of the HRC has revealed that this scope is not limitless. *Isabel Hoyos y Martinez de Irujo v. Spain* is a case in point, and concerns a complaint about the hereditary rules in relation to titles of nobility in Spain. It should be highlighted though that this

[7] Article 23, para 4 CCPR is also relevant in this respect as it concerns the equality of rights of spouses.

[8] HRC, General Comment No. 18, para. 12.

[9] See HRC, General Comment No. 18, para. 2.

[10] See also pp. 160–71 in this book on the freedom of expression.

[11] HRC, General Comment No. 18, para. 5.

[12] See also HRC, General Comment No. 28 on equality of rights between men and women.

decision is a controversial one, which is also reflected by the fact that there are three dissenting opinions.

The majority of the Committee concludes that the complaint is inadmissible. The Committee starts by underlining that:

> [A]rticle 26 of the Covenant is a free-standing provision which prohibits all discrimination in any sphere regulated by a State Party to the Covenant. However, the Committee considers that article 26 cannot be invoked in support of claiming a hereditary title of nobility, an institution that due to its indivisible and exclusive nature, lies outside the underlying values behind the principles of equality before the law and non-discrimination protected by article 26.[13]

This line of thinking can be contrasted with the position of one of the dissenters, who correctly points out that:

> although the right to titles of nobility is not a human right protected by the Covenant, as the State party rightly contends, the legislation of States parties must not deviate from article 26. It is true that as the Committee has pointed out in its jurisprudence, a different treatment based on arguments, including sex, of relevance to the purposes of article 26 does not constitute prohibited discrimination provided that it is based on reasonable and objective criteria. However, the establishment of the superiority of men over women, which is tantamount to saying that women are inferior to men, in matters of succession to titles of nobility governed by Spanish law and implemented by its courts, would not only deviate from such criteria but would be going to the opposite extreme. While States are allowed to grant legal protection to their historical traditions and institutions, they must do so in conformity with the requirements of article 26 of the Covenant. . . .
>
> In ruling legally that a particular honour should be granted principally to men and only accessorily to women, the State party is taking a discriminatory position vis-à-vis women of noble families that cannot be justified by reference to historical traditions or historical rights or any other grounds.[14]

It would be interesting to see how the Committee would come out if similar rules in minority communities were at issue. As the discussion of certain general comments of the HRC will show, there are indications that the Committee would come out differently.

[13] HRC, *Isabel Hoyos y Martinez de Irujo v. Spain* (Communication 1008/2001, 30 March 2004), para 6.5. See also the similar case of *Mercedes Carrion Barcaiztegui v. Spain* (Communication 1019/2001, 30 March 2004), para. 6.4.

[14] HRC, *Isabel Hoyos y Martinez de Irujo v. Spain* (Communication 1008/2001, 30 March 2004), dissenting opinion by Committee member Hipolito Solari-Yrigoyen.

In order to give a solid first impression of the scope of the prohibition of discrimination in the CCPR, reference should be made here to General Comment No. 31 on the Nature of the General Legal Obligation imposed on States Parties to the Covenant. As will be elaborated upon below, this General Comment clarifies and emphasizes the possible indirect horizontal effect of the rights in the Covenant, including the prohibition of discrimination, through the positive obligations of states to protect the covenant rights of individuals under their jurisdiction against acts committed by private persons. General Comment No. 28 also adds to this (more specifically) that states should be particularly vigilant as regards cultural or religious practices within minority communities that might affect the rights of women.[15]

Finally, even though General Comment No. 18 on non-discrimination does not refer to Article 27 on the rights of persons belonging to ethnic, religious or linguistic minorities, General Comment No. 23 on Article 27 highlights (in paragraph 4) that the prohibition of discrimination in Articles 2 and 26 also benefits persons belonging to minorities.[16] More importantly, General Comment No. 23 gives a clear indication of the relationship between minority-specific, special measures in terms of Article 27 and the prohibition of discrimination. After pointing out that states might, on the basis of Article 27, have a positive obligation to take special measures to protect the identity of a minority, the HRC emphasizes that 'such positive measures must respect the provisions of Articles 2, paragraph 1 and 26 of the Covenant both as regards the treatment between different minorities and the treatment between the persons belonging to them and the remaining part of the population. However, as long as those measures are aimed at correcting conditions which prevent or impair the enjoyment of the rights guaranteed under Article 27, they may constitute a legitimate differentiation under the Covenant, provided that they are based on reasonable and objective criteria.'[17]

So far, it is clear that the prohibition of discrimination constitutes the outer limit of the special minority measures (without stating that the prohibition of discrimination itself would imply an obligation to adopt these special measures or an obligation to differentiate).

[15] HRC, General Comment No. 28, para. 32. See also under CEDAW.

[16] See also UN Declaration on the Rights of Persons belonging to National or Ethnic, Religious and Linguistic Minorities, Art. 4, 1.

[17] HRC, General Comment No. 23, para. 6.2.

2. CERD

In regard to both CERD and CEDAW, it should be emphasized that these conventions are special in two respects in comparison with the other provisions discussed here. On the one hand, these conventions are narrow in that they focus on one particular ground of differentiation. On the other hand and because these conventions are exclusively focused on the elimination of discrimination (on these specific grounds), they contain multiple specifications and considerable detail. CERD/C for example explicitly urges states to eradicate forms of racial segregation (Article 3) and hate speech (Article 4). Article 5 contains a non-exhaustive enumeration of rights the contracting parties should promote ie, the equal enjoyment of, amongst others: the freedom of religion, the right to security of the person (protection against bodily harm), the right to adequate housing and education as well as access to public facilities like restaurants and hotels.

In any event, the prohibition of racial discrimination, which is being furthered by CERD, is particularly relevant for minorities because of its broad interpretation of racial discrimination and thus also of 'race'.[18]

It should also be emphasized that CERD is one of the few international instruments which explicitly addresses affirmative action. Furthermore, CERD has an unusual positive stance in this regard in that it even contains an obligation to take such measures (in certain circumstances).

3. CEDAW

There are at least two reasons why the Convention on the Elimination of All Forms of Discrimination against Women should not be left out of an overview of the jurisprudence on equality. First of all, as will become clear throughout the assessments below, the prohibition of gender discrimination tends to be one of the grounds, if not the ground, about which most case law has been developed. In other words, the development of various clarifications and 'technical refinements' in regard to the equality principle have emerged in this case law. Secondly, and particularly relevant from a minority protection perspective, one can ask oneself the question whether and to what extent the prohibition of gender discrimination (as expounded in CEDAW) implies limits on the enjoyment of one's own religion and culture (from the side of the male members of the relevant community). This relates again to the extent to which the prohibition of gender discrimination obliges states to interfere in the relationships between private parties (see below).

[18] See Article 1 CERD and see below.

4. European Convention for the Protection of Human Rights and Fundamental Freedoms (ECHR)

The text of the Convention itself contains one provision with a prohibition of discrimination, more specifically Article 14. One of the typical features of this provision is that it contains a parasitic provision in that the prohibition of discrimination only applies in so far as it is related to one of the Convention rights. The lack of a general prohibition of discrimination has given rise to ample criticism, *inter alia* by academics concerned about minority protection. In the meantime, additional Protocol 12 has come into effect (since 1 April 2005) adding a general prohibition of discrimination to the ECHR. However, it should be emphasised that so far the European Court of Human Rights has not yet pronounced a judgment in terms of this Protocol. Consequently, the only document that can be drawn upon for further clarification is the Explanatory Memorandum to the Protocol and the jurisprudence which will be discussed in this chapter will thus all be based on Article 14 ECHR. It is expected that the principles developed so far in relation to the prohibition of discrimination will be followed as well in relation to the Additional Protocol 12, with the exception of course of the case law related to the non-autonomous character of Article 14.

In the latter respect, it needs to be highlighted that the Court has nuanced the rigidity of this requirement. The starting point remains and it has been amply underlined by the Court that Article 14:

> has no independent existence since it has effect solely in relation to 'the enjoyment of the rights and freedoms' safeguarded by those provisions. Although the application of Article does not necessarily presuppose a breach of these provisions—and to this extent it is autonomous—there can be no room for its application unless the facts at issue fall within the ambit of one or more of the latter.[19]

The Court has tended to interpret this requirement loosely, in the sense that it rather easily accepts that the facts of a case fall within the ambit of one of the substantive provisions. Nevertheless, it is obvious that the ambit of the prohibition of discrimination remained restricted.

5. Framework Convention for the Protection of National Minorities (FCNM)

In view of the fact that the supervisory mechanism of the FCNM is limited to periodic state reporting and a review of these reports, there is no (quasi) jurisprudence to be analysed. While the actual supervisory practice that has unfolded thus far has exceeded expectations, the analysis of the principles that

[19] ECtHR, *Cha'are Shalom ve Tsedek v. France* (27 June 2000), para. 29.

can be deduced from the opinions of the Advisory Committee[20] simply does not lend itself to the development of advanced principles in terms of a model of review for the prohibition of discrimination and the like.

It should be highlighted that Article 4 FCNM contains, in addition to a prohibition of discrimination in paragraph 1, also an obligation in paragraph 2 to adopt 'special' differential measures aimed at the realization of full, or real, substantive equality. In contrast to CERD and CEDAW, the 'special' measures here are not necessarily temporary, in the sense that as long as they are required in order to achieve full equality they can endure (see below). In other words, the focus here is not exclusively on redressing disadvantages from the past but could also include some kind of institutionalized measures. It should be highlighted though that this obligation to adopt 'special' measures is not seen as a dimension of the prohibition of discrimination, but rather as an 'additional' principle.[21]

The third paragraph goes on to state that measures adopted in accordance with paragraph 2 shall not be considered an act of discrimination. As will be further explained below, this qualification does not seem in line with the generally accepted criteria to distinguish a legitimate differentiation from discrimination because it only seems to require a certain legitimate goal (full equality) without any reference to proportionality. The Explanatory Report, however, 'adds' that these 'special' measures should be 'adequate', that is in line with the proportionality principle, in order not to violate the prohibition of discrimination.[22]

Before going on to discuss the standards developed within a different European organization, reference should be made to the excellent work of the European Commission against Racism and Intolerance (ECRI), another organ of the Council of Europe. While the ECRI's mandate does not include a quasi judicial component, it has developed several General Recommendations of relevance to a study of the equality principle.

6. EU Standards[23]

While the achievement of equality now has taken up a quite central place in the European Union's agenda, this has not always been the case. Indeed, EC

[20] As is developed in Asbjørn Elide's chapter on minority rights implementation, above, while the ultimate responsibility for the supervision of the FCNM lies with the Committee of Ministers (CoM) of the Council of Europe, de facto the Advisory Committee of independent experts (ACFC) determines the outcome (the actual content of the resolutions of the CoM).

[21] See also G. Alfredsson, 'Article 4', in M. Weller (ed.), *The Rights of Minorities: A Commentary on the European Framework Convention for the Protection of National Minorities* (Cambridge, 2005), 145–6.

[22] Framework Convention for the Protection of National Minorities and Explanatory Report (Council of Europe Press, 1995), para. 9.

[23] For a nice overview of the development of EU law and policy in respect of the prohibition of discrimination: M. Bell, *Anti-Discrimination Law and the European Union* (Oxford, 2002).

law initially only set out to prohibit discrimination on the basis of nationality (limited to the nationality of other member states, as related to its aim to achieve the internal market) and the prohibition of discrimination on the basis of gender. The interpretation of the European Court of Justice provided important additional clarifications about the exact scope, reach and implications of these prohibitions, as well as the provisions of the various directives (especially in relation to the prohibition of gender discrimination), which elaborated upon these Treaty provisions.[24]

Even though these grounds of prohibited discrimination are not directly relevant for minority protection purposes, the development of both the jurisprudential principles and the clarifications in the directives are considered important parameters also outside the scope of EC law (eg in relation to the concept of 'indirect discrimination' and to the legitimacy of affirmative action, which are both of special relevance to minorities).

In any event the Treaty of Amsterdam, and more specifically the inclusion of Article 132 entailed a tremendous broadening and strengthening of the principle of equality within EC law. Not only was equality between men and women introduced as one of the tasks and activities of the Community, but, and this is especially relevant for the focus of this book, the EC was also given competence to combat discrimination based on racial or ethnic origin, religion or belief, disability, age and sexual orientation. Obviously both 'racial or ethnic origin' and 'religion or belief' are grounds of special relevance to minorities. Two directives were adopted relatively quickly after the coming into force of the Treaty of Amsterdam, one of which is entirely devoted to racial discrimination,[25] while the other addresses *inter alia* discrimination on the basis of religion.[26]

Various characteristics of the Race Directive even seemed to indicate that the protection against racial discrimination would be strongest and hence at the top of the EU's equality hierarchy. First of all, the Race Directive has several characteristics in common with the Framework Directive which ostensibly

[24] See below for further information on these directives and the jurisprudence of the ECJ. See also the relevant chapters in Bell, *supra*, n. 23 and *inter alia* C. Barnard, 'The Changing Scope of the Fundamental Principle of Equality?', *McGill Law Journal*, 46 (2001), 958–9.

[25] EC, Council Directive 2000/43 of 29 June 2000 implementing the principle of equal treatment between persons irrespective of racial or ethnic origin [2000] OJ L 303/16 (hereinafter Race Directive). For an excellent assessment of the Race Directive and its contribution to minority protection see G. Von Toggenburg, 'The Race Directive: A New Dimension in the Fight against Ethnic Discrimination in Europe', *European Yearbook of Minority Issues* (2003), 321–44.

[26] EC, Council Directive 2000/78 of 27 November 2000, establishing a general framework for equal treatment in employment and occupation [2000] OJ L 303/16 (hereinafter Framework Directive).

indicate that the EU is serious about achieving an effective protection against discrimination,[27] *inter alia* the new and broader definition of indirect discrimination, the reversal of the burden of proof in civil cases and the emphasis on effective remedies. In addition, the Race Directive also has an unusually broad field of application touching on areas at the outer limits of Community competence (like social protection and social advantages, education and especially access to and supply of goods and services which are available to the public, including housing), and introduces the obligation on the part of the member states to establish a national body for the promotion of equal treatment of all persons without discrimination on the basis of racial or ethnic origin.

In any event, the possible impact of the Race Directive should be put in perspective in that it can only 'reach' as far as the field of the EU's competences. It has in other words no application in those domains that remain within the exclusive jurisdiction of the states.

It should also be highlighted that since the Race Directive, two directives have been adopted in regard to the prohibition of gender discrimination which ostensibly set out to upgrade the protection against gender discrimination to (more or less) the same level as that of racial discrimination.[28]

7. African Charter on Human and Peoples' Rights (AfrCh)

The African Charter contains two provisions of relevance to the equality principle, more specifically, Article 2 and Article 3. Article 2 is actually similar to Article 2 CCPR in the sense that it covers an open enumeration of grounds of prohibited discrimination, and only applies to the enjoyment of the rights in the convention. The grounds of prohibited discrimination enumerated include 'ethnic group', which is not that common (even though it tends to be covered implicitly under 'race' and would fall in any event under the open category 'other status').

Article 3 ensures that every individual shall be equal before the law and be entitled to equal protection of the law. In so far as these dimensions of the equality principle feature in international conventions, they seem to be enumerated as

[27] For a further elaboration, see below.

[28] Directive 2002/73/EC of the European Parliament and of the Council of 23 September 2002 amending Council Directive 76/207/EEC on the implementation of the principle of equal treatment for men and women as regards access to employment, vocational training and promotion, and working conditions also takes up the extended definition of indirect discrimination, includes various provisions aimed at making the protection against gender discrimination effective and obliges member states to set up a national equality body. Council Directive 2004/113/EC of 13 December 2004 implementing the principle of equal treatment between men and women in the access to and supply of goods and services, extends the field of operation of gender discrimination so as to bring it in line with the field of operation of the prohibition of racial discrimination.

something additional to the prohibition of discrimination, without giving any further indication about the way these dimensions would be (inter)related.

8. American Convention on Human Rights (ACHR)

The ACHR contains one provision on non-discrimination which is at the same time very concise and very broad in scope. Article 24 reads: 'All persons are equal before the law. Consequently, they are entitled, without discrimination, to equal protection of the law.'

As there is no enumeration at all of the prohibited grounds of discrimination, any possible ground would seem to do. However, as will be developed below, the provisions that have a list of enumerated grounds while ending on an open category do not cover any type of differentiation. Arguably, similar considerations would apply here.

Article 24 is special in that it appears to establish an explicit causal link between equality before the law, non-discrimination and equal protection of the law, while these dimensions are normally enumerated next to each other as if they were not so related.[29]

C. Delineation of Content: Overview of Specific Issues to be Considered

While the concept of 'equality' is rather meagre on the one hand as it is merely relative, always presupposing some kind of comparison (and thus does not have a specific content),[30] it is very rich on the other hand, because it has many different (albeit interrelated) dimensions (discrimination, affirmative action, equality before the law, equal protection of the law etc.).[31]

From the perspective of minorities the absence of a substantive underpinning is particularly problematic as this absence actually means that a claim of equal treatment does not necessarily have to be met by the extension of a benefit to the relatively underprivileged individual (often the members of minorities) which would imply a levelling up or equalizing at a high point. Indeed, a claim of equal treatment can just as easily be met by removing a benefit from the relatively privileged group, and equalizing the parties at the lower point (levelling down).[32]

[29] See above and see HRC, General Comment No. 18, para. 1 which uses the following connectors between these expressions: 'not only', 'as well' and 'but also'.

[30] Fredman, *supra*, n. 1, 18.

[31] See also HRC, General Comment No. 18, para. 1.

[32] See also S. Fredman, 'Beyond the Dichotomy of Formal and Substantive Equality: Towards a New Definition of Equal Rights', in I. Boerefijn et al. (eds.), *Temporary Special Measures* (Antwerp, 2003), 113.

In relation to the comparative component of the equality principle, it should also be outlined that this is anything but straightforward. There is no such thing as pure equality in the sense that two objects are always different in some way or another.[33] The question then is what are, in a particular context, relevant differences? Unfortunately exactly this aspect is entirely underdeveloped in the (quasi)jurisprudence, in the sense that the supervisory organs do not even appear to try to develop relevant criteria in this respect.

The richness of the equality principle also lies in the fact that there are several distinctive conceptions of equality, which entail different ways of defining and understanding the dimensions enumerated above. An important distinction needs to be made between formal equality (or equality as consistency), which sets out to treat everybody in exactly the same way on the one hand, and substantive, or real or full equality on the other hand. Full equality acknowledges differences in starting positions which might necessitate differential treatment in order to reach real, effective equality. The latter, namely the need to treat individuals differently in order to obtain substantive equal treatment is coined 'the paradox of the equality principle'. The latter was already nicely captured by Aristotle who argued that likes should be treated alike, while different things should be treated differently to the extent of the inequality. It was already highlighted above that minorities aim to obtain substantive equal treatment in comparison with the rest of the population. Nevertheless, the demand that 'like should be treated alike' is also rather important and positive from a minority perspective in that it tackles formal exclusionary rules.

Another important distinction that should be made is between policies aimed at equal opportunities and those aimed at equal results/outcome.[34] The equal opportunities approach takes into account the need for differential treatment to some extent in order to achieve substantive equality. The effects of past or on-going discrimination need to be countered in order to level the playing field and equalize the starting point for the various competitors. This might necessitate special measures for the disadvantaged group.

Equality of results or outcome goes beyond the equalization of the starting point, which it considers insufficient and hence ineffective to obtain real, substantive equality, and focuses on the outcome and actual equality of results. The use of quotas and targets forms part and parcel of this approach.[35] It

[33] E. Holmes, 'Anti-Discrimination Rights Without Equality', *The Modern Law Review*, 68 (2005), 179.

[34] Fredman, *supra*, n. 32, 110–11, and 113–15.

[35] Fredman argues that even equality of outcome is not adequate and sufficient as mere quantifiable change might only partially reflect qualitative change; the latter would also be reached by

may be obvious that this approach is most controversial because it seems to contradict the principle of equal treatment (on an individual basis). The more the preference rules or quota are used in a strict and rigid way, and the less the relative qualifications of the candidates come into play, the more controversial they become.[36] However, it should be pointed out that the 'equal opportunities approach' also has its problems. Indeed, this approach is actually deceptively simple.[37] How to ensure that previously disadvantaged persons have a genuinely equal chance of satisfying the criteria for access to a particular social good is (often) not self-evident. The envisaged measures should go far enough in that they should critically assess existing standards and criteria in order to take full account of these unequal starting positions, while also providing additional training and education to make up for some of the 'under-qualifications' due to the past disadvantage.

The analysis of case law will focus on the prohibition of discrimination (being the central component of the first pillar of an adequate system of minority protection), while including affirmative action and more specifically the interrelation of non-discrimination and affirmative action. Throughout the analysis the underlying theme is the extent to which certain mechanisms contribute (or not) to substantive equality, being the ultimate goal of minority protection.

The following issues should be considered in a jurisprudence overview regarding the prohibition of discrimination (and the equality principle). A first relevant question is: what is the model of review developed in order to assess complaints of discrimination? This is related to the fact that not every differentiation amounts to a prohibited discrimination. This in turn requires one to look at the fact whether an open or a closed system of possible justifications (for a differential treatment) is used. A second point to be considered is the grounds of prohibited discrimination that are explicitly taken up in non-discrimination provisions. An important related point concerns the different levels of scrutiny that are adopted by the supervisory organs in relation to the distinctive grounds of discrimination. When different levels of scrutiny are indeed developed, it is important to assess whether the supervisory body concerned uses a symmetrical or an asymmetrical approach. Thirdly, and taking up substantive equality as the overarching theme of minority protection, it should be investigated whether, and to what extent, the prohibition of discrimination

'equality as transformation', through its focus on institutional structures (Fredman, *supra*, n. 32, 115).

[36] Fredman, *supra*, n. 1, 19.

[37] Fredman, *supra*, n. 1, 20–1.

furthers substantive equality. This arguably depends (*inter alia*) on the extent to which the supervisory body recognizes indirect discrimination and an obligation to differentiate (as a possible second dimension of the prohibition of discrimination), and also on the evaluation of affirmative action measures (in relation to the prohibition of discrimination). A fourth theme that needs to be addressed concerns questions related to the burden of proof demanded by the supervisory organs in relation to claims of discrimination. Finally, and in view of the pervasiveness of discrimination against minorities, it is also important to assess to what extent the prohibition of discrimination would impose positive obligations on states to eradicate 'private' discrimination.

II. Analysis of Case Law

The analysis will not always include references to all (relevant) supervisory bodies, but will select each time those that have made the most important contributions in relation to a specific point. This also implies that the order in which the bodies are discussed is not always going to be the same, and will not necessarily go from global to regional bodies.[38]

A. Model of Review in Relation to Complaints of Discrimination

Since not every differentiation amounts to a prohibited discrimination, it is important to analyse how supervisory bodies determine whether a particular differentiation is legitimate or not.[39]

It can be deduced from the (quasi) jurisprudence of several supervisory organs[40] that they use a two-step model of review.[41] The first step amounts to some kind of preliminary hurdle that needs to be taken, and which basically sets out to determine whether or not there is a differentiation that merits a justification test, whether there is in other words a prima facie case of discrimination.

[38] The analysis of the relevant jurisprudence of the ECHR draws heavily on the equality chapter of the *Handbook on Human Rights* (Mensenrechten vanuit Internationaal en Nationaal Perspectief (Boom, 2006) and several case notes from ECHR cases in 2004–2006.

[39] *Infra* for the extension of the prohibition of discrimination, which would also include an obligation to differentiate in relation to substantively different matters (ECtHR, *Thlimmenos v. Greece*).

[40] For a more extensive elaboration on the three major components of the model of review, see Gerards, *Rechterlijke Toetsing aan het Gelijkheidbeginsel* (The Hague, 2002), 100–2.

[41] The model of review can be found to some extent at least, in the global, regional and national equality jurisprudence.

This often (but by no means always) is said to require, in addition to the establishment of a differential treatment,[42] that this differential treatment concerns comparable situations.

Subsequently, the assessment is made whether this differential treatment amounts to a prohibited discrimination or not.[43] Even though the (quasi) case law does not use these terms, these steps can be coined 'review hurdle' and 'justification phase'. It should also be highlighted that these respective steps do not (necessarily) take the same form nor are equally visible.

Before proceeding with further elaboration of this model of review it needs to be pointed out that the African Commission on Human Rights (AfrCommHPR) so far has not really picked up on this model.[44] In most of its cases, the Commission notes that someone has been singled out for disadvantaged treatment on the basis of ethnic origin (without clarifying what type of proof is adduced and thus also without providing indications about the requisite standard of proof), and concludes then that Article 2 of the African Charter is violated.[45] Although one could argue that this stance of the African Commission could reflect the fact that differential treatment on the basis of ethnic origin would in principle never be justifiable (reflecting heightened scrutiny), it would be vastly preferable if the Commission would state this explicity and use some kind of model of review. In any event, in *Purohit and another v. the Gambia* the African Commission's reasoning in concluding that there had been a violation of Article 2 was similarly (over) concise while it did not concern the ground of 'ethnicity' but of 'wealth'.[46]

[42] Note however also the adaptation that needs to be made in relation to the second dimension of the prohibition of discrimination, requiring differential treatment of situations that are not comparable.

[43] For an extensive analysis of the use and development of this model of review by the European Court of Human Rights, and the European Court of Justice, see Gerards, *Rechterlijke Toetsing, supra*, n. 40, 120–64 and 236–306. Also the Committee on the Elimination of Racial Discrimination acknowledges that only once a prima facie case of discrimination has been established by the claimant, the duty rests on the respondent state to offer the required justifications (CERD/C, General Comment No. 3 on Discrimination against Non-citizens, para. 24).

[44] In its views as regards *Legal Resources Foundation v. Zambia* (2001, AHRLR 84 (ACHPR 2001), 92–94, paras 63–71) the African Commission on Human and Peoples' Rights is leaning towards some kind of (more) explicit model of review but this is not in line with the model explained above in the sense that the African Commission 'simply' uses the principles regarding a legitimate limitation on the exercise of human rights, while being confused about the relation between 'limitation' and 'justification'.

[45] *Amnesty International v. Zambia* (2000) AHRLR 325 (ACHPR 1999), 331; *Organisation Mondiale Contre la Torture and Others v. Rwanda* (2000) AHRLR 282 (ACHPR 1996), 285; *Union Interafricaine des Droits de l'Homme* (2000) AHRLR 18 (ACHPR 1997) 20–21.

[46] The Commission noted that only persons charged with capital offences are entitled to legal assistance and argued that 'the category of persons that would be detained as voluntary or

The absence of reasoning along a certain model of review (as can be deduced from the practice of the ECtHR , the Inter-American Court and various treaty bodies) is remarkable because the African Commission is supposed to rely on appropriate and relevant international and regional human rights instruments, principles and standards when interpreting and applying the African Charter.[47]

The 'review hurdle' that needs to be passed is developed primarily in relation to direct discrimination. The jurisprudence of the most prominent bodies with the power to pronounce legally binding judgments (ECtHR and ECJ) emphasizes the use of a comparability test (requiring the proof of a differential treatment of persons[48] that are comparable in relation to the norm making the differential treatment),[49] and the HRC often seems to use this test also.[50] However, this test is often not actually used[51] or is replaced by a disadvantage test.[52] The latter test requires the proof of a differential treatment which results in considerable disadvantage for the claimant. Whether the disadvantage is serious enough will depend on the exact circumstances of the case.

It is to some extent obvious that only a differential treatment of sufficiently comparable cases is reviewed under the justification test, as is nicely expressed in the saying that one should not compare apples with lemons.[53] The comparability test should furthermore only refer to similarities that are relevant in relation to the alleged discrimination. All persons are indeed comparable in

involuntary patients under the LDA are likely to be people picked up from the streets or people from poor backgrounds. In cases such as this, the African Commission believes that the general provision in law that would permit legal claims by anybody injured by another person's act can only be available to the wealthy and those that can afford the services of private counsel. Clearly the situation presented above fails to meet the standards of anti-discrimination and equal protection of the law laid down under the provisions of articles 2 and 3 of the African Charter *(Purohit and another v. Gambia* (2003) AHRLR (ACHPR 2003), 103–104, paras. 53–54).

47 Articles 60–61 AfrCh.

48 *Contra* ECtHR, *Gerger v. Turkey* (8 July 1999), para. 69, which concerned a distinction between different types of crimes.

49 If according to the Court there is no differential treatment of comparable persons, the Court concludes that there is no problematic type of differential treatment and hence no violation of Article 14.

50 For an overview of various examples where the HRC has used this test, see W. Vandenhole, *Non-Discrimination and Equality in the View of the UN Human Rights Treaty Bodies* (Antwerp, 2005), 45–6.

51 *Inter alia* ECtHR, *Inze v. Austria* (28 October 1987).

52 *Inter alia* ECtHR, *Elsholz v. Germany* (13 July 2000), paras. 59–61.

53 This has become even more pronounced in the more recent line of jurisprudence in which it is clarified that the prohibition of discrimination is not only relevant for the unequal treatment of persons in comparable positions but also for an equal treatment of persons in incomparable (sufficiently different) situations (see *infra* on the Thlimmenos judgment of the ECtHR).

many ways, while also not comparable in many other ways or from many other perspectives.[54]

It can be pointed out though that the use of the comparability test is not always that positive or desirable. This is more specifically the case when it is noted that the differential treatment concerns situations that are said not to be comparable. This assessment would imply that at no point will it be evaluated whether or not this differential treatment is at all proportionate (an important component of the justification test).[55] Another critical point that can be made in regard to the comparability judgment is that it cannot be purely objective. Consequently, it can easily be used in order to avoid the justification phase (for example because this would deal with very sensitive questions in society). This explains the aversion of various academics to a separate comparability test by way of 'hurdle of review',[56] the argument being that these comparability issues should be taken on board in the justification test.[57] Nevertheless, it is difficult to deny that comparability issues cannot be totally neglected, as also flows from the fact that the prohibition of discrimination can be violated when there is NO differential treatment of situations which are not comparable, without reasonable and objective justification. This obligation to differentiate, as flowing from the prohibition of discrimination, simply contains the reverse situation and hence would require a proof of the absence of differential treatment of not comparable situations.

In any event, Gerards has amply shown that while both the ECtHR and the ECJ in theory use a comparability test, this test is not used consistently. More particularly, the ECtHR does not tend to use this test when it concerns a differential treatment on one of the suspect grounds triggering heightened scrutiny (see below). Even in regard to non-suspect classifications the EtCHR often leaves this out.[58] It is equally evident that the ECJ does not use it in relation to the manifold cases on indirect discrimination it is confronted with. In any event, as will be elaborated upon below, indirect discrimination does necessitate certain changes to the model of review because of the specific nature of this type of discrimination.

[54] Gerards, *Rechterlijke Toesting, supra*, n. 40, 58–66; G. Goederteir, 'Verbod van Discriminatie', in J. Vande Lanotte & Y. Haeck (eds.), *Handboek EVRM (Deel 2: Artikelsgewijze commentaar, volume II)* (Antwerp, 2005), 162–5.

[55] Gerards, *Rechterlijke Toetsing, supra*, n. 40, 346.

[56] J. H. Gerards, 'Gelijke Behandeling en het EVRM', *NJCM Bulletin* (2004), 189–90; A. E. Morawa, 'The Evolving Human Rights to Equality', *European Yearbook of Minority Issues* (2003), 163–6.

[57] O. de Schutter, *The Prohibition of Discrimination under the European Human Rights Law: Relevance for EU Racial and Employment Equality Directives* (Brussels, 2005), 14.

[58] Gerards, *Rechterlijke Toetsing, supra*, n. 40, 211–12.

In contrast to the African Commission which so far has not established a clear model of review for discrimination complaints,[59] the Inter-American Court takes note of the jurisprudence of the ECtHR, and follows its jurisprudence (albeit not in identical words or format). The Inter-American Court uses the comparability test but without clearly distinguishing it as a preliminary question to the actual justification test. According to the Inter-American Court, 'there would be no discrimination in differences in treatment of individuals by a state when the classifications selected are based on substantial factual differences *and* (my emphasis) there exists a reasonable relationship of proportionality between these differences and the aims of the legal rule under review'.[60]

When comparing the justification test used by the various supervisory organs, it emerges that this is broadly similar and tends to demand a reasonable and objective justification[61] for the differential treatment. Some supervisory bodies break this requirement down in sub-criteria.

The European Court of Human Rights in any event has a long line of established jurisprudence (since the *Belgian Linguistics* case) in which it indicates that a difference of treatment only amounts to a prohibited discrimination if it has no objective and reasonable justification, that is, if it does not pursue 'a legitimate aim' or if there is not a 'reasonable relationship of proportionality between the means employed and the aim sought to be realised'.[62]

In regard to the requirement of a legitimate aim, it should be highlighted that in contrast to the doctrine of legitimate limitations, Article 14 does not contain a limitative enumeration of possible legitimate aims.[63] At first the Court did not make use of its jurisdiction to impose substantive requirements as to the type of aim that was invoked by states. While there is still no clear line of jurisprudence in this regard,[64] the ECtHR has put forward certain

[59] See *inter alia* AfrCommHPR, *Federation Internationale des Ligues de droits de l'homme v. Angola*, para. 18; AfrCommHPR , *Legal Resources Foundation v. Zambia*, para. 52; AfrCommHPR, *Organisation Mondiale Contre la Torture v. Rwanda*, para. 22.

[60] Inter-AmCtHR, Proposed Amendments to the Naturalization Provisions of the Constitution of Costa Rica, para. 57. It should be noted that it explicitly refers to the ECtHR's line of jurisprudence in this respect in the preceding para. (56).

[61] Until 2005 the CESCR/C had never explicitly stated that distinctions made on the basis of objective and reasonable criteria did not amount to discrimination (Vandenhole, UN *Human Rights Treaty Bodies, supra*, n. 50, 63). However in its General Comment no 16 on the Equal Rights of Men and Women to the Enjoyment of all Economic, Social and Cultural Rights, the Committee explicitly included the criterion of objective justification (para 12).

[62] *Inter alia* ECtHR, *Belgian Linguistic* case (23 July 1968), para. 10; ECtHR, *Abdulaziz, Cabales and Balkandali v. UK* (28 May 1985), para. 72.

[63] Goedertier, *Verbod van discriminatie, supra*, n. 54, 170.

[64] Gerards, *Gelijke Behandeling, supra*, n. 56, 194.

substantive requirements in certain judgments.[65] What can be put forward as a general requirement is that the aim of the differential treatment should not be prohibited by the European Convention and its basic values. In other words, the aim should be reconcilable with the foundational principles of the democratic society. In any event, this component of the justification test in itself is seldom a problem to the extent that the Court sometimes does not even address it.[66]

The required relationship between the differentiation and the legitimate aim pursued, however, does receive a lot of attention and has elicited several further clarifications by the Court. The Court has emphasized that the distinction made should be pertinent and adequate or relevant to the achievement of the legitimate aim. Even though this requirement of pertinence is often distinguished from the proportionality test, these are closely interwoven. When the legitimate aim is not sufficiently related to the differential treatment, the measure complained of will not pass the proportionality test either. On the other hand, a pertinent distinction is not necessarily a proportional one. In other words, the pertinence of the distinction is a necessary condition of the proportionality of the distinction (in relation to the legitimate aim).[67]

The proportionality test clearly refers back to the legitimate aim and adds some demands to the required relationship between the differentiation made and the legitimate aim this differentiation has to serve. This test undoubtedly is the one that has the strongest impact in the sense that the particular strictness demanded in terms of proportionality in a particular case tends to determine the outcome (the decision whether or not the prohibition of discrimination is violated).

The proportionality test in the broad sense can be further broken down into at least two components.[68] First of all proportionality requires there to be a reasonable relationship between the legitimate aim on the one hand and the differential treatment (and the underlying interests which it interferes with) on the other. In other words, the differential treatment should not go beyond what is strictly necessary in order to achieve the goal.[69] This first component is also called the proportionality test in the narrow sense. A more specific aspect

[65] *Inter alia* ECtHR, *Buchen v. Czechia* (26 November 2002), para. 75 (demand of objectivity of the aim); ECtHR, *L and V v. Austria* (9 January 2003), para. 52 (requirement that the aim is not related to prejudices of any kind).

[66] Gerards, *Gelijke Behandeling, supra*, n. 56, 193.

[67] Goedertier, *Verbod van discriminatie, supra*, n. 54, 175.

[68] Gerards, *Rechterlijke Toetsing, supra*, n. 40, 102.

[69] ECtHR, *Karner v Austria* (24 July 2003), para. 41.

of the proportionality test concerns the subsidiarity test. This test implies an investigation of whether there are no alternatives which can achieve the desired legitimate aim while implying less of an interference with the right to equal treatment.

The proportionality test also plays an important, even central, role in the doctrine on the legitimate limitations of human rights (generally). In the case law of the ECtHR, the presence of this proportionality test implies the grant of a certain margin of appreciation to the contracting states. It is exactly the extent of this margin of appreciation in a particular case which determines (more or less) the outcome. Traditionally, the contracting states tend to get a rather broad margin of appreciation,[70] which has provoked the justifiable criticism that the supervision by the Court is too deferential to the contracting states, with the danger of a reduced level of protection.[71] In this respect, the development of heightened scrutiny (and a reduced margin of appreciation) as regards certain 'suspect' grounds is to be welcomed, especially as these concern typical minority characteristics such as religion and race (see below). It is clear that it is important to identify the factors which determine the extent of this margin of appreciation. In relation to the prohibition of discrimination, the ECtHR seems to rely most heavily on the presence or absence of a European consensus about the special reprehensibility of a certain ground of distinction.[72]

While it is no longer required (in terms of the non-autonomous nature of Article 14) that the right, in combination with which Article 14 is invoked, is also violated in itself,[73] another restrictive feature of the ECtHR's jurisprudence concerns the tendency of the Court no longer to investigate the discrimination complaint (or at least not to develop any further argumentation in this regard) after it has made its conclusion on the violation of the treaty right in itself. A good example of this 'practice' can be found in the case of *Cha'are Shalom ve Tsedek v. France*, where the European Court of Human Rights stipulates:[74]

> The Court notes that the facts of the present case fall within the ambit of Article 9 of the Convention (see paragraph 74 above) and that therefore Article 14 is applicable.

[70] See also Morawa, *The Evolving Right to Equality, supra*, n. 56, 168–71; D. de Prins, S. Sottiaux, & J. Vrielink, *Handboek Discriminatierecht* (Antwerp, 2005), 23–5.

[71] O. De Schutter, 'Observations: Le Droit au Mode de Vie Tsigane devant la Cour Européenne des Droits de l'Homme', *Revue Trimestrielle des Droits de l'Homme* (1997), 89–90. See also R. Eissen, 'Le Principe de Proportionalité dans la Jurisprudence de la Cour Européenne des Droits de l'Homme', in L.E Pettiti et al (eds.), *La Convention Européenne des Droits de l'Homme: Commentaire Article par Article* (Paris, 1995), 80.

[72] Gerards, *Gelijke Behandeling*..., 186.

[73] ECtHR *Belgian Linguistics Case*, para. 9.

[74] ECtHR, *Cha-are Shalom ve Tsedek v. France* (27 June 2000), para. 87.

However, in the light of its findings in paragraph 83 above concerning the limited effect of the measure complained of, findings which led the Court to conclude that there had been no interference with the applicant association's freedom to manifest its religion, the Court considers that the difference of treatment which resulted from the measure was limited in scope. It further observes that, for the reasons set out in paragraph 84, in so far as there was a difference of treatment, it pursued a legitimate aim, and that there was 'a reasonable relationship of proportionality between the means employed and the aim sought to be realised' (see, among other authorities, the Marckx v. Belgium judgment of 13 June 1979, Series A no. 31, p. 16, § 33). Such difference of treatment as there was therefore had an objective and reasonable justification within the meaning of the Court's consistent case-law.

At first sight this practice seems justified from a point of view of 'judicial economy', especially if the issue complained about in terms of Article 14, is exactly the same as the one in terms of the convention right in itself.[75] The Court tends to indicate that it will nevertheless review the complaint in terms of Article 14 in so far as 'a clear inequality of treatment in the enjoyment of the right in question' forms a fundamental aspect of the case. However, this is an extremely vague criterion, and this approach of the European Court is often criticized as another confirmation of the overall reluctance of the Court to find a violation of the prohibition of discrimination.[76]

The ECJ[77] uses a similar justification model, and investigates whether the differentiation pursues a legitimate aim and whether the differentiation is proportionate to the legitimate aim pursued. In relation to the determination of a legitimate aim the ECJ has clarified that the aim cannot be inherently discriminatory (which seems a very evident requirement), and the goal pursued by the differentiation should not reflect altogether too general assessments as regards a certain group.

In relation to the proportionality test, it should be underlined that this depends on the level of scrutiny adopted (see also below). In contrast to the ECHR, where the base line is a marginal review or a low reasonableness test as regards the relation between differential treatment and legitimate aim,[78] the ECJ developed its jurisprudence mainly in relation to the two singled-out grounds of prohibited discrimination of nationality and gender, which tend

[75] ECtHR, *Lustig-Prean and Beckett v. United Kingdom*, 27 September 1999, para. 109.

[76] D. J. Harris, M. O'Boyle and C. Warbrick, *Law of the European Convention on Human Rights* (London, 1999), 469; P. Van Dijk and G. J. H. Van Hoof, *Theory and Practice of the European Convention on Human Rights* (The Hague, 1998), 593.

[77] Gerards, *Rechterlijke Toetsing, supra*, n. 40, 352–7.

[78] But see below on levels of scrutiny.

to engender a high level of scrutiny (while certain circumstances could lead to a reduced level of scrutiny).[79] It should be noted though that since the Treaty of Amsterdam several new problematic grounds of differentiation were added, entailing a variety of levels of scrutiny (see below).

As was mentioned before, the Inter-American Court is guided by the jurisprudence of the ECtHR in this respect. Without following the exact formulation used by the ECtHR, the Inter-American Court refers to the requirement of a legitimate aim (for the difference in treatment), and a reasonable relationship of proportionality between these differences and the legitimate aim. The Inter-American Court adds in this respect that 'these aims may not be unjust or unreasonable, that is, they may not be arbitrary, capricious, despotic or in conflict with the essential oneness and dignity of human kind', and also that the difference in treatment 'does not lead to situations which are contrary to justice, to reason or to the nature of things'.[80]

At the global level, the HRC is the only UN treaty body which has developed a certain theoretical model in relation to the prohibition of discrimination. While the HRC does not use the terms legitimate aim and proportionality, it does investigate whether the distinction is objective and reasonable, the latter implying proportionality considerations.[81] In its General Comment No. 18[82] and its quasi case law the Committee emphasizes that the prohibition against discrimination does not make all differences of treatment discriminatory since a 'differentiation based on reasonable and objective criteria does not amount to a prohibited discrimination'.[83] The General Comment does explicitly add that the aim of the differentiation is to achieve a purpose which is legitimate under the covenant (which is actually also subsumed under the requirement of 'reasonable and objective criteria' for a differentiation).

A study of the practice of the HRC (both in terms of quasi jurisprudence and concluding observations in relation to periodic reporting) reveals that while initially the requirements of legitimate aim and proportionality were not explicit, they do feature in more recent 'views' and concluding observations.[84]

[79] Gerards, *Rechterlijke Toetsing, supra*, n. 40, 358–62.

[80] Inter-AmCtHR, Proposed Amendments to the Naturalization Provisions of the Constitution of Costa Rica, para. 57.

[81] HRC, *Lahcen BM Oulajin and Mohammed Kaiss v. Netherlands*, Communication 406/1990 and 426/1990, 23 October 1992, para. 7.4; HRC, *Sister Immaculate Joseph and 80 teaching sisters of the Holy Cross of the Roder of Saint Francisco in Menzinger v. Sri Lanka*, Communication 1249/2004, 21 October 2005, para. 7.4.

[82] HRC, General Comment No. 18, para 13.

[83] R. Hanski & M. Scheinin, *Leading Cases of the Human Rights Committee* (Abo, 2003), 326.

[84] Vandenhole, *UN Human Rights Treaty Bodies, supra*, n. 50, 54–5.

Furthermore, this practice also shows that the assessment of whether the distinction is reasonable depends on several factors like the nature of the right to which the discrimination is attached,[85] and the ground of discrimination (see also below concerning levels of scrutiny).[86]

Open and Closed Systems of Available Justifications for Differential Treatment

While most international conventions work with an open model for possible justifications for differential treatment, the general criteria of which have been developed immediately above, the European Union and some national legislation (like the Dutch General Act on Equal Treatment) work with a closed system.

Typical for the provisions on non-discrimination in the EU legal system is the distinction which is operated between direct and indirect discrimination (see further). Only for cases of indirect discrimination is the generally framed justification possibility followed. In regard to direct discrimination there are only a limited number of possible justification grounds, which are explicitly enumerated. Actually this can be considered as a kind of additional hurdle in the sense that the requirement of 'legitimate aim' is narrowed down. The jurisprudence of the Court has indeed demonstrated that the proportionality requirement also needs to be respected in order to justify instances of direct discrimination.

B. Grounds of Discrimination

The following two sections of this chapter are closely interrelated. Here the focus will be on the kind of grounds of differentiation/classification that are included in, or at least covered by, the respective international provisions, and on the definition of the grounds most relevant from a minority perspective. The subsequent part will then continue with the study and analysis of the different levels of scrutiny that have been developed in relation to certain grounds of classification, as well as the intrinsically related question of whether or not the supervisory body adopts a symmetrical or asymmetrical approach in this regard.

A first distinction that needs to be made is between open and closed systems in relation to the grounds of discrimination included in a certain provision. Most regional instruments have an open enumeration of prohibited grounds of discrimination, ending with a catch-all provision like 'or other status'. At

[85] *Ibid.*, 49. [86] *Ibid.*, 44–5.

EU level, however, the list of grounds of discrimination covered by the EU's non-discrimination law is closed. This has to be understood against the background of the EU's main (and still predominant) focus, namely economic integration. The original two grounds of discrimination, namely nationality and gender, were clearly linked to concerns regarding the creation and success of the internal market.[87] The addition of five additional grounds by the Treaty of Amsterdam (Article 13) reflects a shift in the EU towards more social policy.[88] Nevertheless, Article 13 is clearly limited to the grounds explicitly enumerated and does not broaden the field of competence of the EC beyond these grounds. The Charter of Fundamental Rights adds, in its non-discrimination provision, various other grounds of prohibited discrimination, further underscoring that equality is now being considered a value in its own right (and not just a means to economic ends). Grounds in Article 21 of the Charter that are additional to those in Article 13 TEC concern 'social origin, genetic features, language, political or any other opinion, membership of a national minority, property, birth', two of which are of special relevance for minority protection, namely language and membership of a national minority. It has to be kept in mind though that the Charter at the same time indicates that it does not imply an extension of the competences of the Union.[89] It remains to be seen how the ECJ will deal with this apparent contradiction once the successor to the Constitution of the EU (including Chapter 2 containing the Charter of Fundamental Rights) comes into effect.

Furthermore, at regional level, reference should also be made to the recent Protocol on women's rights, to the AfrCh, which also concerns non-discrimination but only on the ground of gender.[90]

At UN level there are, in addition to the general human rights conventions, CCPR and CESCR, issue-specific conventions that focus on the prohibition of discrimination on a single ground, namely race (CERD) and gender (CEDAW).

While there are differences between the grounds that are explicitly enumerated in the open models, the following are usually present, and are of special relevance to minorities: race, and religion or belief. Others, that are equally

[87] *Inter alia* Barnard, *The Changing Scope, supra*, n. 24, 958.

[88] *Inter alia* Bell, *Anti-Discrimintion Law, supra*, n. 23, 16–17.

[89] Article 51(2) Charter. See also Barnard, *The Changing Scope, supra*, n. 24, 965.

[90] The Protocol to the African Charter on Human and Peoples' Rights on the Rights of Women in Africa was adopted by the 2nd Ordinary Session of the Assembly of the Union, Maputo, CAB/LEG/66.6 (13 September 2000); reprinted in *Afr. Hum. Rts. L.J.*, 1, 40, and entered into force November 25, 2005.

relevant but do not feature in the majority of conventions are language (CCPR and CESCR), and association with a national minority (ECHR). While ethnic origin or ethnicity and colour are also not consistently present, they are largely understood as being encompassed by the concept 'race' (see below). One might argue that it does not really matter, because open models are open and have a catch-all expression, like 'or other status' which would cover those that are not mentioned. However, it seems that the grounds that are enumerated are more strongly protected (heightened scrutiny), at least by several of the supervisory organs.[91] The underlying reason why grounds are explicitly enumerated is that they concern criteria which are clearly of no relevance to merit or social value, while some of them are innate.[92]

The fact that Article 14 ECHR includes as a ground of prohibited discrimination 'association with a national minority' seemed to reflect, right from the start, a concern that the contracting states should not neglect the minority issue. Nevertheless, traditionally the ECtHR was rather restrictive in its assessment of claims put forward by members of minorities.[93] Apparently, its explicit enumeration as a prohibited ground of discrimination added little extra protection. In any event, several of the other enumerated grounds, like religion and race, cover minority identity features. In the recent case *D.H. and others v. Czech Republic,* the Court chose to ignore the fact that the claimants had, in addition to race and ethnic origin, also invoked 'association with a national minority'. Furthermore, when the Court does take this ground up explicitly it does not clarify it in any way,[94] which can also be related to the fact that it often does not offer additional arguments having found that a certain matter amounted to a violation of a convention right in itself. Be that as it may, it does not augur well for a possible recognition of this ground as engendering heightened scrutiny.

A final remark that should be made in regard to the so-called open system of prohibited discrimination, is that it is not totally open-ended and limitless. The European Court of Human Rights has highlighted in some of its judgments that in order to be relevant from the perspective of Article 14, the

[91] Vandenhole, *UN Human Rights Treaty Bodies, supra*, n. 50, 183 (in relation to the HRC). However, this analysis clearly does not apply to the European Court of Human Rights as that has attached heightened scrutiny to grounds that are not explicitly enumerated, like sexual orientation, while no heightened scrutiny has been adopted in relation to several of the enumerated grounds.

[92] See also *infra* on the underlying reasons why certain grounds merit heightened scrutiny.

[93] *Inter alia* A. Fenet, 'Europe et les Minorités', in A. Fenet et al (ed.), *Le Droit et les Minorités: Analyses et Textes* (Bruxelles, 1995), 97, 102; Gilbert, 'The Legal Protection Accorded to Minority Groups in Europe', *N.YB.I.L.* (1992) 90.

[94] ECtHR, *Ozgür Gündum v. Turkey* (16 March 2000), para. 75.

distinction should be made in terms of one or more personal characteristics.[95] The Court has emphasized for example in its decision on (in)admissibility in the case of *Hasan Sanli and Fatma Erol v. Turkey* that:

article 14 is not concerned with all differences of treatment but only with differences having as their basis or reason a personal characteristic ('status') by which persons or group of persons are distinguishable from each other.[96]

The complaint concerned a piece of legislation that distinguished between various kinds of misdemeanors in relation to the possibility of having the pre-trial detention being reviewed by a judge. According to the Court this distinction could never amount to a discrimination in terms of the Convention.

The quasi-jurisprudence of the HRC also reveals that the 'or other status' is not a boundless category.[97] The HRC has not indicated that certain types of characteristics would not be relevant in terms of the prohibition of discrimination, but the relevance of a distinction presumably varies according to the right at issue. The HRC has for example not refused to consider the place of residence within a state,[98] or family responsibility[99] as relevant grounds. However, according to the HRC a distinction between 'different categories of civil servants for the availability of a special widow's pension would not be based on any of the relevant characteristics enumerated in Article 26, nor amount to other status in the sense of this article'.[100] Unfortunately, the Committee does not provide any further argument as to why this would not be the case. In any event, it immediately adds that the differentiation 'does not disclose a lack of reasonableness and objectivity',[101] again without further explanation.

Interestingly, Schultz points out that there are indications that the issue of 'other status' grounds is now being subsumed by the issue of reasonableness (and thus addressed in the justification phase).[102]

[95] Gerards, *Gelijke Behandeling, supra*, n. 56, 183.

[96] ECtHR, *Hasan Şanli and Fatma Erol v. Turkey* (17 October 2000), para. 5–6.

[97] In *Kavanagh v. Ireland* the HRC seemed even to indicate that it would not be necessary to identify any specific basis for a differentiation, since 'the Committee took the view that the executive's decision to put the author on trial before a special court, was as such a violation of article 26 in the absence of proper justification' (Hanski and Scheinin, *Leading Cases, supra*, n. 83, 328). However, this has not developed into a line of jurisprudence.

[98] HRC, *Lindgren et al v. Sweden* (Communication No. 298-9/77).

[99] See *inter alia* HRC, Concluding Observations on Hong Kong (1996), para. 13.

[100] HRC, *GJ Jongenburger-Veerman v. Netherlands* (Communication 1238/2004, 1 November 2005), para. 7.2.

[101] *Ibid.*

[102] Joseph, Schultz & Castan, *Cases, Materials and Commentary, supra*, n. 2, 693.

Grounds of Special Relevance to Minorities: Further Conceptual Clarification

It has already been indicated above that the ground 'association with a national minority' in the ECtHR does not seem to have contributed in any significant way to minority protection.

In addition to some remarks on the potential of the prohibited grounds of discrimination of 'language' and 'religion' special attention shall be given here to the relationship between race and language, race and religion and race and nationality, in view of the fact that 'race' tends to trigger heightened scrutiny (as is reflected in the number of single issue instruments focusing on this ground of differentiation).

(a) Language

The CCPR is one of the few international documents which explicitly includes 'language' as a prohibited ground of discrimination. Two particularly relevant cases in this regard are *Diergaardt v. Namibia* and *Ballantyne et al v. Canada*. In *Ballantyne*[103] the signage law in the province of Quebec, prohibiting public commercials in English, did not amount to discrimination on the basis of language because it would affect the French and the English companies equally. This concerns a general rule which is neutral on its face, but which has a disproportionate impact on English companies because they arguably want to reach English speaking clientele more than French. The HRC seems at this stage (still) unsympathetic to ideas concerning indirect discrimination (see below).

In *Diergaardt*[104] the HRC qualified the instruction of the Namibian government to public servants not to communicate in Afrikaans either orally or in writing (even when they would be able to do so) as being targeted towards Afrikaners, and thus in violation of the prohibition of discrimination. If the HRC had followed the *Ballantyne* line it would have argued that this instruction would equally affect persons who are not Afrikaners (but who are able to speak Afrikaans).

However, one can remark that the HRC fails to take into account that English is now the only official language of Namibia, and that Afrikaans is now at the same level as the (other) indigenous languages. The instruction can thus be understood as having as its goal the eradication of a lingering and now unjustified advantage for Afrikaans speakers in comparison to the speakers of indigenous languages.[105]

103 HRC, *Ballantyne, Davidson and McIntyre* (Communication No. 359/1989, 13 March 1993).

104 HRC, *Diergaardt et al v. Namibia* (Communication No. 760/1996, 25 July 2000).

105 See also A. E. Morawa, *Minority Languages and Public Administration: A Comment on Issues Raised in Diergaardt et al v. Namibia* (ECMI Working Paper 16, October 2002).

(b) Religion

So far, the HRC has not concluded in many individual communications that there has been a violation of the prohibition of discrimination on the basis of religion. For example, the obligation to wear protective head gear for construction workers or motorcycle riders does not amount to discrimination on the basis of religion in regard to Sikhs (who cannot wear their turban when having to wear such head gear). Obviously this requirement serves a legitimate purpose and does not seem to be disproportionate.[106] *Waldman v. Canada,* however, concerned a complaint by a Jewish father about the exclusive provision of public funding in the province of Ontario (Canada) for private Roman Catholic schools, while other religious minority schools were not funded at all. Regarding the alleged violation of Article 26 the Committee observes—in line with the steady jurisprudence of the ECtHR in this respect—that 'the Covenant does not oblige States parties to fund schools which are established on a religious basis. However, if a State party chooses to provide public funding to religious schools, it should make this funding available without discrimination.[107] According to the Committee, there are no reasonable and objective criteria to justify the differential treatment between the Roman Catholic faith and the author's religious denomination. Hence it concluded that Waldman's rights under Article 26 were violated.

In regard to the prohibited ground of discrimination 'race', it should be highlighted that CERD includes under racial discrimination, discrimination on the basis of race, colour, descent, and national or ethnic origin. Arguably this implies that 'race' is interpreted as encompassing 'colour, descent and national or ethnic origin'. The Committee on the Elimination of All Forms of Racial Discrimination has in its practice, especially in relation to concluding observations to periodic state reports, also addressed issues pertaining to *language*. It has for example urged states to maintain the possibility of the various ethnic groups receiving instruction in their own languages[108] as well as of using their mother tongue in private and in public.[109] Similarly the CERD/C has indicated that in terms of the Convention specific legislation may be required on the status of languages.[110] Also in its views it is obvious that CERD is of the

[106] See also HRC, *Singh Bhinder v. Canada* (Communication No. 208/186, 9 November 1989), para. 6.2.

[107] HRC, *Waldman v. Canada* (Communication No. 694/1996, 3 November 1999), para. 10.6.

[108] UN Doc. CERD/C/304, Add.51, para. 13 (Armenia); UN Doc.CERD/C/304/Add.46, para. 13 (Netherlands).

[109] UN Doc.CERD/C/304/Add.38, para. 15 (Macedonia).

[110] UN Doc.CERD/C/65/CO/3, para. 12 (Kazakstan).

opinion that language requirements for employment could amount to racial discrimination, to the extent that there would not be a reasonable and objective justification for these requirements.[111]

It is equally obvious that 'race' and 'religion' intersect and overlap,[112] giving rise to several borderline cases, especially since 9/11 and the rise of Islamophobia.[113] In this respect it should be highlighted that ECRI took the firm stance that racism should include issues of religious discrimination in its 2000 General Policy Recommendation on combating intolerance and discrimination against Muslims.[114]

Similarly, it is widely understood that there is a considerable overlap between minority ethnic communities and foreigners or non-nationals.[115] In other words, differential treatment on the basis of *nationality* could possibly hide a differential treatment on the basis of race, which could be revealed by a disproportionate impact on a racial (or ethnic) group. This underscores again the importance of the concept 'indirect discrimination' (see below). Nevertheless, both CERD (Article 1, paragraph 2) and the EU's Race Directive (Article 3, paragraph 2) explicitly exclude differentiation on the basis of nationality from the scope of the prohibition of racial discrimination. However, it should be highlighted that in its General Recommendation No. 25 of 2004 on discrimination against non-citizens, CERD/C drastically reduces the permissibility of differential treatment on the basis of nationality.[116] It is highlighted that Article 1, paragraph 2 should not undermine the basic prohibition of racial discrimination, which indirectly acknowledges the link with indirect discrimination on the basis of race.[117]

In other words, the emphasis now seems to be on the equal enjoyment of human rights and 'apart from the right to participate in elections, to vote and stand for elections—rights which are mentioned as such by the Committee as allowing for confinement to citizens—differentiation between citizens and non citizens with regard to human rights is no longer permissible'.[118]

[111] CERD, *Emir Sefic v. Denmark* (Communication 032/2003), para. 7.2.

[112] M. Bell, 'Setting Standards in the Fight against Racism: a Comparison of the EU and the Council of Europe', in J. Niessen and I. Chopin (eds.), *The Development of Legal Instruments to Combat Racism in a Diverse Europe* (Dordrecht, 2004), 219.

[113] P. Thornberry, 'Confronting Racial Discrimination: A CERD Perspective', *Human Rights Law Review*, 5 (2005), 259.

[114] ECRI General Policy Recommendation No. 5, CRI (2000) 21.

[115] *Inter alia* Bell, *Setting Standards, supra*, n. 112, 218–19.

[116] Vandenhole, *UN Human Rights Treaty Bodies, supra*, n. 50, 91.

[117] CERD/C, General Recommendation No. 25, para. 2.

[118] Vandenhole, *UN Human Rights Treaty Bodies, supra*, n. 50, 91. See also CERD/C General Recommendation No. 25, para. 3.

This position can also be seen to be reflected in the supervisory practice of other bodies, albeit to different degrees. The CESCR/C, like CERD/C allows for differentiation on the basis of nationality. While the Committee has not taken an explicit position on this theme in general, it has highlighted in its General Comment on Education and Water that nationality should not be the basis of differentiation.[119] Arguably this could indicate a similar development as in CERD, to only accept a differentiation on the basis of nationality in very limited circumstances. This in turn would reflect that increasingly 'nationality' is considered to be a suspect class, receiving heightened scrutiny.

The HRC seems to take an even stricter stance in the sense that its starting point is that 'nationality' is a prohibited ground of discrimination (full stop). The HRC underlines that the relevant circumstances in each case should be carefully reviewed to determine whether a differentiation on the basis of nationality is objective and reasonable. It seems rather critical towards the justifications offered for such differentiation. For example in *Karakurt v. Austria* nationality was not held to constitute an objective and reasonable ground for differentiation in relation to the capacity to stand for election for a works council. The Committee underlined that this exclusion on the basis of nationality is especially unreasonable in view of the fact that it concerned a person who had been granted the right to work in the country concerned, while the right to stand for elections to a work council can be considered a close and natural incident of employment.[120] Similarly, the HRC has underlined in a string of cases that when a state party is itself responsible for the departure of a person from its territory while that person seeks refuge in another country where a new citizenship is obtained, 'it would be incompatible with the Covenant to require the author to satisfy the condition of... citizenship for the restitution of his property or alternatively for compensation.'[121] Finally, also the practice of the CRC/C reveals that nationality is explicitly recognized as a prohibited ground of discrimination. It is, however not that obvious whether 'nationality' is subsumed under one of the enumerated grounds or under the open ground 'other status'.

[119] UN Doc. HRI/GEN/1/Rev. 7, General Comment No. 13 (1999), The Right to Education, para. 30 and 34; UN Doc. HRI/GEN/1/Rev.7, General Comment No 15 (2002), The Right to Water, para. 16(f).

[120] HRC, *Karakurt v. Austria* (Communication 965/00), para. 8.4.

[121] HRC, *Kriz v. Czech Republic* (Communication 1054/2002, 1 November 2005), para. 7.3. See also HRC, *Adam v. Czech Republic* (Communication No. 586/1994, 23 July 1996), para. 12.6; HRC, *Blazek v. Czech Republic* (Communication 857/1999), para 5.8; HRC, *Marik v. Czech Republic* (Communication 945/2000), para. 6.4.

The ground of ethnic origin features prominently in the framework of CERD and the Committee pays specific attention to problems of minorities in terms of this ground of differentiation. Strikingly, CERD/C even draws conclusions concerning the definition of minorities, which should not be too restrictive. In terms of this ground the Committee also pays specific attention to the scope of language requirements in relation to employment, particularly in the private sector.[122] This seems to indicate that there is not only a close relationship between race and language, but also between ethnic origin and language. The Committee also encourages the state parties to ensure education and teaching in the mother tongue of minorities.[123]

C. Different Levels of Scrutiny (Margin of Appreciation—Proportionality Test of Justification)

The level of scrutiny adopted by a supervisory organ is extremely important as it determines the effective protection provided in terms of the provision concerned. Arguably the level of scrutiny is inversely related to the margin of appreciation granted to states, which in turn is first of all related to the proportionality principle (as part of the justification phase). Nevertheless, it can be argued that the level of scrutiny is also determined by the burden of proof, and the distribution of this burden of proof. As will become clear below, the supervisory bodies as yet do not have (highly) developed doctrines in relation to the burden of proof, let alone of the kind that it would be explicitly related to the level of scrutiny.

The focus here will be on whether, and to what extent, one can distinguish different levels of scrutiny as related to the proportionality test, in relation to the distinctive grounds of differentiation. First of all the relevance of different levels of scrutiny is highlighted for open and closed systems (of grounds of prohibited discrimination). Secondly, some of the underlying factors explaining why certain grounds receive heightened scrutiny are enumerated. Subsequently, the case law of the supervisory bodies is reviewed in this respect, while some attention is also given to different modes along which certain grounds (of classification) receive heightened scrutiny.

Different levels of scrutiny seem especially relevant for systems with open grounds of differentiation, as they provide some structure within the broad range of grounds covered (which is *in se* present in closed models). Nevertheless, also for closed models these different levels of scrutiny are important, especially

[122] CERD/C, Concluding Observations on Estonia, A/57/18, para. 356.
[123] CERD/C, Concluding observations on Ukraine, A/56/18, para. 376.

in relation to the concept of indirect discrimination which can bring differentiation on other grounds within the field of application of a ground triggering heightened scrutiny.[124]

Several reasons have been put forward why certain grounds of differentiation would be suspect, triggering heightened scrutiny. Criteria that feature generally in these accounts are that suspect classes concern immutable characteristics or characteristics that are inherent to one's ego. Classes are also suspect when they refer to a group which has historically suffered from unjustifiable discrimination and therefore is especially vulnerable to such treatment.[125]

While heightened scrutiny can be discovered by studying the (quasi) case law of the supervisory bodies, for systems with closed models of grounds of classification like in EC law, important deductions can already be made on the basis of provisions themselves and the 'exceptions' they provide for the prohibition of differentiation. Arguably, when in terms of EC law there are very few 'exceptions' to the prohibition to differentiate (direct discrimination) on a particular ground, this points towards a suspect class with heightened scrutiny.

It should also be pointed out that some of the enumerated grounds of prohibited differentiation are considered in much more detail in the sense that the implications of the prohibition of discrimination on these grounds is specified and elaborated upon in a greater number of specific areas of law. In this respect, one could refer to the multiple General Recommendations by CERD/C and CEDAW/C, each time reflecting specific problematic and/or sensitive areas/issues for the 'groups' concerned. In regard to CEDAW the following General Recommendations should be noted: General Recommendations No. 12 (1989) and 19 (1992) on violence against women, General Recommendation No. 23 (1997) on women in political and public life, and General Recommendation No. 24 (1999) on women and health. Also CERD/C has elaborated several General Recommendations that are quite telling as to specific 'sensitive' or problematic issues, like General Recommendations on racial segregation (No. 19), and recently on the prevention of racial discrimination in the administration of justice and functioning of the criminal justice system (No. 31).

Arguably this higher degree of elaboration and specification provides an indication of the higher level of scrutiny, which is adopted in regard to differentiation on these grounds.

[124] E. Holmes, 'Anti-Discrimination Rights without Equality', *The Modern Law Review*, 68 (2005), 184.

[125] *Inter alia* Joseph, Schultz and Castan, *Cases, Materials and Commentary, supra*, n. 2, 693.

While the HRC is not keen on the use of the doctrine of the margin of appreciation, its supervisory practice has revealed that different levels of scrutiny are adopted.[126] It has been pointed out in this respect that the 'HRC probably views certain grounds of distinction as inherently more suspect and deserving of greater scrutiny than other grounds'.[127] It can be argued that all the enumerated grounds and some others like nationality, sexuality, age or disability would receive a higher level of scrutiny. Others point out that differentiations on the basis of 'other status' are almost never considered to be a prohibited discrimination by the HRC, except in certain cases concerning a differentiation on the basis of nationality.[128] In particular, the grounds of race and gender seem to be considered 'suspect' classifications by the HRC.[129]

The HRC does not often use language which clearly indicates that the justification test is done with heightened scrutiny. However, in *Muller and Engelhard v. Namibia*[130] the Committee underlines (in a case concerning differentiation on the basis of gender), that :

> A differentiation based on reasonable and objective criteria does not amount to prohibited discrimination within the meaning of article 26. A different treatment based on *one of the specific grounds enumerated in article 26*, clause 2 of the Covenant, however, places a *heavy burden* on the the State party to explain the reason for the differentiation.

In most cases the Committee is not explicit in that way. Nevertheless the views make it abundantly clear that the Committee considers differentiation on certain grounds hardly ever acceptable.[131] In this regard it is instructive to compare the assessments by the HRC in *Waldman v. Canada* and *Blom v. Sweden*.[132] The HRC obviously has less difficulty accepting that the distinction between private and public schools in regard to state funding is objective and reasonable.

The jurisprudence of the European Court on Human Rights has made it clear that several grounds of differentiation are considered to be suspect.

[126] Joseph, Schultz and Castan, *Cases, Materials and Commentary, supra*, n. 2, 693.

[127] J. Bair, *The International Covenant on Civil and Political Rights and its (First) Optional Protocol* (Berlin) 117; Joseph, Schultz and Castan, *Cases, Materials and Commentary, supra*, n. 2, 693; Vandenhole, *UN Human Rights Treaty Bodies, supra*, n. 50, 113.

[128] *Inter alia* HRC, *Gueye v. France* (Communication No. 196/85); HRC, *Foin v. France* (Communication 666/1995); HRC, *Maille v. France* (Communication No. 689/1996).

[129] Vandenhole, *UN Human Rights Treaty Bodies, supra*, n. 50, 113.

[130] HRC, *Muller and Engelhard v. Namibia* (Communication No. 919/00), para. 6.7.

[131] See in relation to religion HRC, *Waldman v. Canada* (Communication No. 694/96), paras 10.5 and 10.6 and in relation to gender HRC, *Broeks v. Netherlands* (Communication No. 172/84).

[132] HRC, *Blom v. Sweden* (Communication No. 191/85).

It should be acknowledged that the Court has not yet developed general criteria to identify 'suspect' classes. It is rather a question of deduction, based on the level of scrutiny adopted in relation to a particular ground of differentiation.

The jurisprudence in relation to the grounds that have enjoyed for some time the status of 'suspect ground of differentiation', namely gender, illegitimate birth, religion, nationality and sexual orientation,[133] shows that the Court usually expresses a heightened level of scrutiny by requiring that the defending state puts forward 'very weighty reasons' for the differentiation concerned. This test implies that the Court screens not only the 'legitimate aims' for sufficient seriousness, but also uses a stricter proportionality test. Sometimes the Court uses a heightened scrutiny while adopting a different formula. In a case concerning differentiation on the basis of gender, *Van Raalte v. Netherlands* (21 February 1997) the Court found that 'compelling reasons have been adduced to justify a difference in treatment [between men and women]'.[134] The judgment in *Hoffmann v. Austria* (23 June 1993) is also particularly instructive (in light of the determination whether 'race' is a suspect class) as it is considered to be the basic judgment clarifying that 'religion' is a suspect class, while it uses an alternative formulation. Moreover this formulation also features in the case, which is now considered to have established that 'race' is a suspect class. In *Hoffmann*, the Court put forward that 'a distinction based essentially on a difference in treatment based on religion alone is not acceptable'.[135] Arguably, this statement clearly indicates that 'religion' is hardly ever considered to be a legitimate ground of differentiation, hence indicating its 'suspect' nature and a concomitant very high level of scrutiny.

It is already indicated above that the ground 'association with a national minority' is not so far considered to be a suspect class, while 'religion' obviously qualifies as such. It should be highlighted though that for a long time the jurisprudence of the Court did not give a clear answer to the question whether 'race' was indeed a suspect class.[136] It was only in the recent case of *Timishev v. Russia* that the Court adopted an unequivocal point of view, which arguably builds on the pointers that were already available in older case law, like *Nachova v. Bulgaria* and *Moldovan v. Roumenia*.[137] In *Timishev*, the

[133] De Prins, Sottiaux & Vrielink, *Handboek Discriminatierecht, supra*, n. 70, 26–35.

[134] ECtHR, *Van Raalte v. Netherlands* (21 February 1997), paras. 41–42.

[135] ECtHR, *Hoffmann v. Austria* (23 June 1993), para. 36.

[136] Van Dijk & Van Hoof, *Theory and Practice, supra*, n. 76, 728.

[137] ECtHR, *Nachova v. Bulgaria* (26 February 2004 and GC 6 July 2005), and ECtHR, *Moldovan v. Romania* (12 July 2005).

Court underlines that 'no difference in treatment which is based exclusively or to a decisive extent on a person's ethnic origin is capable of being objectively justified in a contemporary democratic society built on the principles of pluralism and respect for different cultures'.[138] The Court seems to be going a step further than in the *Hoffmann* case by indicating that no justification would be good enough to justify a differentiation on the basis of race. Nevertheless, it is generally accepted that it is unlikely that the Court would want to add a further distinction within the suspect classes of so-called super suspect classes.[139] The formulation used seems rather to express (or confirm) that a distinction on this ground is reviewed very critically and is indeed 'suspect'. When the Court adopts a high level of scrutiny, this usually results in a finding of violation of the prohibition of discrimination because of a lack of a reasonable and objective justification for the differential treatment.[140]

In several previous cases there were already (clear) indications that 'race' is such a suspect class. For example, the European Commission on Human Rights held in 1970, in the *East African Asians* case (10 October 1970), that a distsinction on the basis of race could, in certain circumstances, amount to 'degrading treatment' in terms of Article 3 ECHR. It should be emphasized that degrading treatment is absolutely prohibited and that no justification is good enough in this respect. Arguably this qualification implies that differentiation on the basis of 'race' (at least in certain circumstances) triggers heightened scrutiny. This line of thought was furthermore confirmed by the Court itself in the judgment of *Cyprus v. Turkey* (10 May 2001)[141] as well as in the more recent case of *Moldovan et al v. Roumenia* (12 July 2005), concerning a violent outburst against a group of Roma inhabitants of a village during which their houses and possessions were destroyed.

Be that as it may, in terms of Article 14 the Court for a long time did not give incontestable signals as to the suspect status of 'race' as a ground of differentiation. The first signals arguably can be dated back to the two judgments in the case of *Nachova v. Bulgaria.*

In the first judgment of 26 February 2004 several pronouncements of the Chamber seemed to indicate that 'race' is a suspect class. One of the most important signals in this respect was the unusually victim-oriented attitude in relation to the burden of proof and the related distribution of the burden of

[138] ECtHR, *Timishev v. Russia* (13 December 2005), para. 58.

[139] De Prins, Sottiaux & Vrielink, *Handboek Discriminatierecht, supra*, n. 70, 31; Gerards, *Rechterlijke Toetsing, supra*, n. 40, 204.

[140] Gerards, *Rechterlijke Toetsing, supra*, n. 40, 161.

[141] ECtHR, *Cyprus v. Turkey* (10 May 2001), paras. 308–310.

proof (the so-called reversal of the burden of proof). However, several other statements seem to point to an emerging heightened scrutiny for differentiation on the basis of race, like the reference to the special duty of the government to eradicate racially inspired violence[142] as well as the reference to 'the need to reassert continuously society's condemnation of racism and ethnic hatred'.[143] Even though the Grand Chamber[144] did not follow the Chamber in relation to the distribution of the burden of proof, it did repeat explicitly the special duty on the part of national authorities to speak out against, and to eradicate, racism and ethnic intolerance in society.[145] The Grand Chamber also qualifies racial violence as 'a particular affront to human dignity'.[146] Arguably, such pronouncements do give the impression that the Court dedicates special attention to differentiation on the basis of race.

While similar statements were taken up in *Timishev v. Russia*[147] the Court also adopted clearly a very high level of scrutiny when evaluating the proportionality of the differential treatment complained of. The latter case thus provides a strong basis to argue that the Court considers 'race' and 'ethnic origin' (which it used interchangeably) as suspect classes, deserving heightened scrutiny.

A Symmetrical Versus an Asymmetrical Approach to Non-discrimination

It is only relevant to speak of a symmetrical or asymmetrical approach in relation to non-discrimination in so far as the supervisory body concerned adopts different levels of scrutiny. A symmetrical approach implies that no matter what the goal or underlying reason for the differential treatment of a suspect class, such a differentiation will always be scrutinized strictly. However, it can be argued that while strict scrutiny is appropriate in relation to forms of so-called invidious discrimination, this is not the case for differentiations that have as their aim the redress of previous disadvantages (affirmative action being the prototypical example), and hence contribute to the achievement of real or substantive equality. In other words a symmetrical approach augurs negatively for the legitimacy of affirmative action measures (across the board). An asymmetrical approach does take into account the underlying rationales of

142 ECtHR, *Nachova v. Bulgaria* (26 February 2004), para. 155.
143 ECtHR, *Nachova v. Bulgaria*, para. 157.
144 ECtHR (Grand Chamber), *Nachova v. Bulgaria* (6 July 2005).
145 Grand Chamber, *Nachova v. Bulgaria*, para. 145, 160–4.
146 Grand Chamber, *Nachova v. Bulgaria*, para. 145.
147 ECHR, *Timishev v. Russia*, para. 56.

the differential treatment, and would not use heightened scrutiny in regard to a differentiation on the basis of a suspect class when this differentiation would have a positive (substantive equality) aim.

As will become clear in relation to the discussion of the case law concerning affirmative action, both the ECtHR and the ECJ exhibit rather symmetrical approaches. On the other hand, the issue-specific conventions like CEDAW and CERD seem much more open towards affirmative action, and hence would rather veer towards an asymmetrical approach. This is especially clear in relation to CEDAW[148] in the sense that even the title of the Convention shows that it is asymmetric since it is targeted to redress discrimination against women,[149] and expressly seeks to benefit women.[150] Furthermore, CEDAW/C acknowledges this asymmetric approach explicitly in its General Recommendation on Temporary Special Measures where it points out that the:

> convention goes beyond the concept of discrimination used in many national and international legal standards and norms. While such standards and norms prohibit discrimination on the ground of sex and protect both men and women from treatment based on arbitrary, unfair and/or unjustifiable distinctions, the Convention focuses on discrimination against women, emphasizing that women have suffered and continue to suffer from various forms of discrimination because they are women.[151]

D. Discrimination and Full, Substantive Equality

In view of the critical importance of substantive equality for minorities, it is important to assess more carefully to what extent the prohibition of discrimination contributes to the realization of full, substantive equality.

It is generally understood, and was elaborated upon above in relation to the models of review, that not every differentiation amounts to a prohibited discrimination. Be that as it may, it should be emphasized that not all concepts of non-discrimination are equally 'open' towards substantive equality considerations. Traditionally, the jurisprudence of international supervisory bodies, like the European Court on Human Rights, revealed (in this respect) a focus on formal equality, as was demonstrated *inter alia* by the *Belgian Linguistics*

[148] *Inter alia* UN Doc.CRC/C/15/Add.135, para. 25 (UK–overseas territories).

[149] By contrast, the CRC/C seems in regard to sex discrimination more symmetrical than CEDAW and the other UN Treaty bodies, as it has rather systematically also paid attention to 'gender bias faced by boys' (Vandenhole, *UN Human Rights Treaty Bodies, supra*, n. 50, 164).

[150] Fredman, *Beyond the Dichotomy, supra*, n. 32, 116.

[151] CEDAW, General Recommendation No. 25 on Temporary Special Measures, para. 5.

case.[152] The base line is that everybody is treated in exactly the same way, or in a formally equal way. In order for a differential treatment to be acceptable, cogent arguments need to be put forward. Nevertheless, it is possible to identify three developments which entail important nuances, to the extent that these developments come through in a more pronounced way; these are the acceptance of indirect discrimination, of an obligation to differentiate in terms of the prohibition of discrimination, and of affirmative action.

1. Nuance 1: Indirect Discrimination

Following a description of the notion 'indirect discrimination', certain remarks are in order in relation to the assessment whether and to what extent 'indirect discrimination' is taken on board by supervisory bodies. Arguably two different steps can be identified here. Thirdly and most importantly the (quasi) jurisprudence of various supervisory bodies is reviewed and analysed, particularly in light of the two 'steps' identified.

A wide variety of definitions of 'indirect discrimination' exist. The following two definitions (one in a book on the CCPR and the other in a book on EC law in regard to indirect discrimination) indicate that there is broad agreement on the core understanding of this concept. According to Schultz et al 'indirect discrimination occurs when a practice, rule, requirement, or condition is neutral on its face, but impacts disproportionately upon particular groups'.[153] Tobler's definition equally points to the issues of the use of a 'neutral criterion' having a 'disproportionate impact' when she describes indirect discrimination as referring to the use of 'seemingly neutral differentiation criteria with a disproportionate impact or effect upon certain groups, protected by an explicit prohibition of discrimination'.[154] This description of indirect discrimination already reveals that the focus is on the effects (of a disproportionate nature) of a measure or policy, irrespective of the intention behind it. It should be kept in mind though that indirect discrimination can also be intentional, in the sense that a particular group is targeted while hiding it through the use of an, at first sight, neutral criterion. Tobler highlights furthermore that proof of the intention could be important in order to counter the 'justification' (see below) invoked by the defendant state.[155]

[152] ECtHR., *Belgian Linguistics Case* (23 July 1968). See also its assessment in K. Henrard, *Devising an Adequate System of Minority Protection: Individual Human Rights, Minority Rights and the Right to Self Determination* (The Hague, 2000), 119–21.

[153] Joseph, Schultz and Castan, *Cases, Materials and Commentary, supra*, n. 2, 694.

[154] C. Tobler, *Indirect Discrimination: A Case Study into the Development of the Legal Concept of Indirect Discrimination under EC Law* (Antwerp, 2005), 57.

[155] *Ibid.*, 58.

There are arguably two related reasons why indirect discrimination is relevant for minorities and adequate minority protection. First of all, and this is inherent in the description of the phenomenon, the prohibition of indirect discrimination reflects a concern for the underlying reality or, better, for the actual effect of certain policies and rules. When the effects of an, at first sight, neutral rule are disproportional, in the sense that it has a disparate negative impact on a particular group without reasonable and objective justification, this would be illegitimate. In other words, prohibiting such indirect discrimination tends to contribute to the realization of full or real equality, of crucial importance for minorities. The prohibition of indirect discrimination tends to further the accommodation of diversity, by revealing that apparently neutral criteria de facto favour the dominant culture.[156]

A second reason why this prohibition of indirect discrimination is important is because of the inherent group focus it has, as also transpires in the above description.

When assessing the extent to which supervisory bodies 'take on board' indirect discrimination, two steps or elements can be identified. A preliminary question concerns the acknowledgement of the concept 'indirect discrimination', or in other words the recognition of the possible indirect nature of discrimination. Secondly, the specific nature of 'indirect discrimination' seems to require certain adaptations to the model of review as developed above. There is an ongoing debate about whether in relation to indirect discrimination the justification phase concerns 'justification proper' or rather causation.[157]

In regard to the first point, the analysis below will show that so far the record is still disappointing, in the sense that several supervisory bodies are anything but straightforward about their position in regard to indirect discrimination. Furthermore, even the jurisdictional bodies with an extensive body of case law on indirect discrimination, like the ECJ, have not yet worked out an appropriately tailored model of review for indirect discrimination.

After a prima facie case of indirect discrimination has been established by the claimant, the defendant state can first of all try to refute the causation, but if that does not work, there is still the possibility of justification, where proportionality principles play a vital role. In other words, the specific nature of indirect discrimination seems to entail a double possibility for the respondent state to counter the allegations of indirect discrimination.[158] When trying to

[156] Fredman, *Introduction, supra*, n. 1, 24.

[157] Tobler, *Indirect Discrimination, supra*, n. 154, 69.

[158] *Ibid.*, 258.

put this in terms of the review model developed above, it would be tempting to argue that the refutation of the causation would happen in the first phase (the establishment of a prima facie case), however this would cut through the related distribution of the burden of proof, as this is for the claimant in the first phase, while the respondent state has the burden of proof in the second phase (justification). Alternatively it can also be pointed out that merely the refutation of causation should not be the end of the matter in the sense that otherwise the model of review would not recognize the particular disadvantage suffered by the group disparately affected by the contested measure.[159]

As the following analysis will highlight, the operation of a model of review in relation to indirect discrimination remains unclear.

When considering the UN Treaty Bodies, the record is very uneven. The supervisory practice of the HRC was for a long time far from straightforward, and lacking consistency in regard to the acceptance of the idea of 'indirect discrimination'.[160] This is peculiar in view of the fact that its General Comment No. 18 on non-discrimination takes over the definition of discrimination as it is found in CERD and CEDAW, including the reference to 'purpose or effect'.[161] It should be pointed out that the words 'or effect' have been generally understood as implying an opening towards indirect discrimination.[162]

On the negative side, one can point to several cases in which the HRC does not take into account the discriminatory effects of relevant legislation, and focuses on the formally neutral application of the laws. This arguably amounts to a denial of the core concept of indirect discrimination.

A good example of the HRC's inconsistent approach to the concept of indirect discrimination can be detected when contrasting the two cases of special relevance for linguistic minorities which have already been mentioned before, namely *Ballantyne et al v. Canada* and *Diergaardt v. Namibia.* In the *Ballantyne* decision the HRC totally disregarded the fact that the prohibition of outdoor advertising in languages other then French would have a disproportionate impact on English traders in the province of Quebec, which is predominantly French. The Committee focused on the fact that the rule would apply equally to both French and English speaking traders.[163] However in the

159 *Ibid.*, 258.

160 Scott Davidson, 'Equality and Non-discrimination', in A. Conte, S. Davidson and R. Burchill (eds.), *Defining Civil and Political Rights* (Ashgate, 2004), 167; Joseph, Schultz and Castan, *Cases, Materials and Commentary, supra*, n. 2, 696.

161 Joseph, Schultz and Castan, *Cases, Materials and Commentary, supra*, n. 2, 694.

162 *Ibid.*, 694.

163 HRC, *Ballantyne et al v. Canada*, para. 11.5.

Diergaardt decision, the HRC found a violation of Article 26 CCPR because the prohibition to civil servants not to use Afrikaans in communications, over the phone or in writing, would have a deleterious impact on Afrikaans speakers even though,[164] in this case, the measure applied to everyone irrespective of ethnic background. In other words while in the *Ballantyne* decision the HRC was oblivious to the indirectly discriminatory impact of a measure, it took into account concerns about indirect discrimination in the *Diergaardt* decision.

The HRC seems to have fully acknowledged the phenomenon of (and the prohibition of) indirect discrimination only relatively recently,[165] more particularly in the *Althammer v. Austria*[166] and *Derksen v. the Netherlands*[167] decisions. Both decisions reveal a clear acknowledgement of the concept of 'indirect discrimination'. While the Committee starts by remarking that a certain measure is neutral on its face and does not have any intention to discriminate, it goes on to conclude that this measure nevertheless results in discrimination because of its exclusive or disproportionate adverse effects on a certain category of persons. Interesting here is that the HRC seems to use exactly the same model of review as in cases of direct discrimination and seeks to establish whether or not the 'distinction' (which must refer back to the disproportionate impact) is based on 'reasonable and objective criteria'. There does not seem to be confusion on the causation issue.

Both CERD/C and CEDAW/C take, from the beginning, a very positive stance in regard to 'indirect discrimination'. CERD/C acknowledges explicitly in its General Recommendation No. 14 on the definition of the concept 'racial discrimination', referring back to Article 1 CERD:

> In seeking to determine whether an action has an *effect contrary* to the Convention, it will look to see whether that action has an *unjustifiable disparate impact* upon a group distinguished by race, colour, descent, or national or ethnic origin[168] (emphasis added)

This clearly amounts to an acknowledgement that the inclusion of 'effect' in addition to 'purpose' in the definition in Article 1 is meant to refer to the phenomenon of 'indirect discrimination'. Similarly, CEDAW/C underscores

[164] HRC, *Diergaardt v. Namibia*, para. 10.10.

[165] Since 2002 the CESC/C has also explicitly referred to covert forms of discrimination, while its General Comment No. 16 (2005) includes in para. 13 an explicit definition of indirect discrimination, in line with the more general understanding of this concept: 'indirect discrimination occurs when a law, policy or program does not appear to be discriminatory on its face, but has a discriminatory effect when implemented'.

[166] HRC, *Althammer v. Austria* (Communication No. 998/2001), para. 10.2.

[167] HRC, *Derksen v. Netherlands* (Communication No. 976/2001), para. 9.3.

[168] CERD/C, General Recommendation No. 14, para. 2.

in relation to the extensive definition in Article 1 of the Convention that the prohibition includes both direct and indirect discrimination, by public as well as private actors.[169]

The supervisory practice of CERD/C confirms this acknowledgement of the concept of indirect discrimination. The Committee tends to address concerns of indirect discrimination directly,[170] and regularly makes statements in this regard which are of specific relevance to minorities. In its concluding observations regarding Denmark for example, it stated that 'the reported prohibition of the use of the mother tongue in some of these establishments may, though aimed at facilitating integration, lead to indirect discrimination against minorities'.[171]

However, CERD/C does seem to struggle with the appropriate model of review. In certain views it seems to confine the justification phase to a check of the causation, that is, whether the disproportionate impact on a specific category is really related to a prohibited ground of discrimination, without any further reference to justification in the sense that the 'distinction' should be based on objective and reasonable criteria.[172]

At the regional level, the case law of the two European courts is especially instructive, albeit not equally 'open' towards indirect discrimination. The ECJ has undeniably the most elaborate case law in this regard. While initially the entire concept of 'indirect discrimination' was developed by the ECJ, it was subsequently taken up in several directives and further refined (also by the subsequent case law of the ECJ) in the process.

It is important to highlight from the beginning that while the case law of the ECJ used to demand the production of statistical evidence showing actual differential impact, the 2000 directives indicate that this is no longer necessary and, in any event, not demanded by EU law. In terms of EC law it now suffices that there is a risk that certain neutral rules may operate to the particular detriment of a certain group.[173] Even though there were judgments in which the Court acknowledged in substance 'indirect discrimination',[174] the two

169 Vandenhole, *UN Human Rights Treaty Bodies, supra*, n. 50, 71.

170 *Ibid.*, 42.

171 CERD/C/60/CO/5, para. 12.

172 CERD/C, *R et al v. Slovakia* (Communication 031/2003, 7 March 2003), para. 10.4 (acknowledgement of the concept) and para. 10.5 (review model).

173 This approach conforms to the ECJ's approach in regard to free movement of persons, as reflected in *O'Flynn v. Adjudication Officer*, C-237/94 [1996] ECR I-2617, para. 18.

174 See also Case C 96/80 *Jenkins* (31 March 1981). See also Tobler, *Indirect Discrimination, supra*, n. 154, 108 and 140–5.

landmark decisions are *Bilka*[175] (in regard to gender) and *Sotgiu*[176] (in relation to nationality). The latter actually contained the first general description of the phenomenon of indirect discrimination, highlighting the need for a predominant (not an exclusive) disadvantage.[177]

The case law of the ECJ has acknowledged many times that the concept of indirect discrimination is vital for the effective protection against discrimination. Nevertheless, it is equally essential for this effective protection that the standards applicable with regard to the objective justification of indirect discrimination are clearly spelled out and consistently used.[178] However, the case law thus far is anything but specific with regard to the elements, and the modalities, of the justification test.[179]

In any event, as has already been pointed out, in regard to direct differentiations on the grounds covered by EC law, this is only legitimate in so far as there is an explicit legislative provision providing the legal basis for this. In contrast to this closed system in regard to direct discrimination, for indirect discrimination an open justification model is used, requiring an 'objective justification'.[180]

While *Bilka* is considered to be the landmark case on objective justification for indirect sex discrimination in relation to employers, *Rinner-Kuhn* is regarded as the landmark case in relation to indirect sex discrimination in state legislation. The tripartite tests developed by the ECJ are quite similar in both cases. First of all, both require that there must be an objective factor unrelated to the prohibited discriminatory ground. Secondly, an employer has to be able to demonstrate a genuine need on his part, while the public authorities must prove that the measure pursues a necessary aim of its social policy. The third requirement is again common to both, and demands that the measure must be suitable and necessary to attain the aim pursued.[181] Arguably, one can translate the above requirements in terms of the objective justification test for direct discrimination in the sense that the first and second would be related to the 'legitimate aim' requirement, while the third would refer to the proportionality requirement. Hence, it seems that the ECJ conceives the justification for indirect discrimination as indeed a 'proper' justification test with a specific

175 Case C 170/84, *Bilka-Kaufhaus* (13 May 1986).
176 Case C 152/73, *Sotgiu* (12 February 1974).
177 Tobler, *Indirect Discrimination, supra*, n. 154, 110.
178 *Ibid.*, 239.
179 *Ibid.*
180 *Ibid.*, 183.
181 *Ibid.*, 194–5.

focus, which can be explained by the 'indirect nature' of the discrimination. It should be noted that in regard to indirect discrimination on the basis of gender it is possible to distinguish a third test for the objective justification, and that is the very diluted test for social security legislation (with differential standards for part-time workers) which the Court used in *Nolte*[182] and *Megner and Scheffel*.[183] Although the Court started with the standard test for objective justification in regard to legislation, it went on to qualify this, underlining that in regard to social policy member states have a broad margin of appreciation and can choose the measures capable of achieving the aim of their social and employment policy. The Court concluded that 'in exercising its competence, the national legislature was reasonably entitled to consider that the legislation in question was necessary in order to achieve its aim'.[184] Arguably this test of 'reasonableness' is markedly weaker than the more stringent test put forward in *Rinner-Kuhn*.[185] In any event, in this case the justification test for indirect discrimination can be considered as one of 'justification proper'.

The landmark case in regard to indirect discrimination on the basis of nationality, *O'Flynn*, furthermore demonstrated that the justification test here is largely similar to the one in relation to gender.[186]

While the Burden of Proof Directive (in relation to gender discrimination), the 2000 directives (of special relevance for minority protection in so far as they have regard to the classification grounds of 'race' and 'religion'), and the subsequent directives in relation to gender discrimination add further refinements, the basic structure and principles remain the same.

The Burden of Proof Directive was the first legislative instrument to contain a definition of indirect discrimination.[187] This directive followed the ECJ case law in relation to indirect discrimination in that the 'disparate impact' component required proof of actual disparity, while this 'disparity' would have to concern a 'disadvantage of a substantially higher level'.[188] In regard to the justification phase, the directive seems to deviate from ECJ case law by mentioning first the proportionality requirement, and only later the 'legitimate aim' one, as if these were unrelated demands.[189]

182 Case C-317/93 *Nolte v. Landesverscherungsanstalt Hannover* [1995] ECR I-4625.

183 Case C-444/93 *Megner and Scheffel v. Innungskrankenkasse Vorderpfalz* [1995] ECR I-4741.

184 See also Case C-280/94 *Posthum van Dame* [1996] ECR I-179.

185 C. Barnard and B. Hepple, 'Indirect Discrimination: Interpreting Seymour-Smith', *Cambridge Law Journal* 58, (1999), 399, 409.

186 Case C 237/94, *O'Flynn* (23 May 1996), para. 19.

187 Tobler, *Indirect Discrimination, supra*, n. 154, 279.

188 *Ibid.*, 283–4.

189 *Ibid.*, 280.

The Race Directive introduces several further refinements in regard to 'indirect discrimination', while still confirming the general standards identified above. Similar comments can be made in relation to the Framework Directive and the revised second Equal Treatment Directive (gender).[190] In regard to the justification phase, the requirements follow the general pattern of the case law concerning indirect discrimination on the basis of gender.[191] Most of these refinements actually improve the position of the victims of indirect discrimination by making it easier to establish a prima facie case.

First of all, the level of disparate impact required has been lowered in that there is no longer a reference to specific proportions. It suffices that it concerns a 'particular disadvantage'. Furthermore, and this is really remarkable progress, it is no longer necessary to prove that this disadvantage has actually occurred. It suffices that the measure is of such a nature that it *would* put a certain group at a disadvantage. While this seems to negate the need for statistical evidence in terms of EC law, the directive still allows national legislation to require statistical evidence. This is unfortunate, especially in regard to indirect discrimination on the basis of race or religion as it is very difficult (because very sensitive) to collect statistical data on these grounds.[192]

The case law of the ECtHR demonstrates a totally different baseline attitude towards indirect discrimination, namely one of extreme reluctance. While the ECtHR now seems to have overcome that phase, it is still struggling with the appropriate model of review to the extent that it seems to continue to question the concept of indirect discrimination.

An important point of critique in relation to the traditional jurisprudence of the ECtHR in terms of Article 14 concerned the attitude towards indirect discrimination, which also revealed that states' interests tend to predominate in the weighing process. Indeed, the broad margin of appreciation of states granted by the Court, in combination with its refusal to review legislation *in abstracto* in individual complaints, often implied an avoidance of the issue of indirect discrimination.

The Court's reluctance to even accept the notion of indirect discrimination was very visible in *Abdulaziz, Cabales and Balkandali*.[193] The Court's reasoning in that case demonstrated that it would be virtually impossible to rely successfully on indirect discrimination since it classified as irrelevant the disparate impact on certain groups (because of their typical characteristics) of, at first

[190] *Ibid.*, 286.
[191] *Ibid.*, 288.
[192] *Ibid.*, 287.
[193] ECtHR, *Abdulaziz, Cabales and Balkandali*, Series A no 94, para. 85.

sight, neutral rules.[194] The Court tended to give the strong impression that it was not prepared to investigate thoroughly whether a certain measure could indirectly have discriminatory effects because it neglected the broader context determining the position of the people concerned when assessing the alleged discriminatory treatment.[195] The latter is particularly problematic in cases of systemic discrimination, as is the case in regard to minorities like the Roma.[196] It was only in May 2001, that the Court explicitly acknowledged that 'where a general policy or measure has disproportionately prejudicial effects on a particular group, it is not excluded that this may be considered as discriminatory notwithstanding that it is not specifically aimed or directed at that group'.[197] The 'founding' cases all concerned the claim that the activities of the security services in the conflict in Northern Ireland entailed a disproportionately high number of deaths in one particular religious group, which would amount to a violation of Article 14 in combination with Article 9. This principle has also been (*inter alia*) repeated in cases concerning the Roma. Although this acknowledgement is to be welcomed, its importance should not be overrated as the Court immediately adds: '[h]owever, even though statistically it appears that the majority of people shot by the security forces were from the Catholic or nationalist community, the *Court does not consider that statistics can in themselves disclose a practice which could be classified as discriminatory* within the meaning of Article 14'.[198] It is obvious that the Court seems to require a heavy burden of proof, while not identifying what exactly that should be.

The admissibility decision in *Hoogendijk v. Netherlands* (6 January 2005) contains various potentially important shifts in reasoning in relation to the phenomenon of 'indirect discrimination' which need to be discussed (even though the case itself does not concern minorities). First of all the Court indicated in regard to the use of statistical evidence 'although statistics are *not automatically* sufficient for disclosing a practice which could be classified as discriminatory under article 14'. This seems to express a more positive attitude in relation to this type of evidence as it is no longer ruled out that statistical

[194] See also J. H. Gerards, *Rechtelijke Toetsing, supra*, n. 40, 114.

[195] De Schutte, *Le Droit au Mode de la Vie Tsigane, supra*, n. 71, 79–85.

[196] ECtHR, *Buckley v. UK* (25 September 1996) is a paradigmatic case of this restrictive attitude of the Court as regards claims by Gypsies. See also de Schutter, *Le Droit au Mode de la Vie Tsigane, supra*, n. 71, 84–5.

[197] ECtHR, *Kelly v. UK* (4 May 2001), para 148; ECtHR, *Hugh Jordan v. UK* (4 May 2001), para. 154; ECtHR, *McShane v. UK* (28 May 2002), para. 135.

[198] ECtHR, *Nachova v. Bulgaria* (26 February 2004), para. 167.

evidence would do in order to establish a 'prima facie' case.[199] It is also in this case that the Court attempts to devise a model to assess complaints of indirect discrimination, by indicating that 'where an applicant is able to show, on the basis of undisputed official statistics, the existence of a *prima facie indication* that a specific rule—although formulated in a neutral manner—in fact affects a clearly higher percentage of women than men, it is for the respondent government to show that this is the result of objective factors unrelated to any discrimination on the ground of sex'. After this first level of 'justification' (which can be translated in terms of causation), if this were not successful, the state could still prevent a finding of discrimination by putting forward a 'reasonable and objective justification'. While the Court seemed critical at the first level of justification (not accepting that there would be objective grounds unrelated to discrimination that could explain the disparate impact), it is rather easy-going (on the state) in its assessment of the 'objective and reasonable justification' in that it follows the arguments of the government without much ado.

The next 'indirect discrimination' case was eagerly awaited in expectation of further clarifications of the Court's stance in *Hoogendijk*. However, the Court's judgment in *D.H. et al v. Czech Republic* anything but lived up to these expectations. This case concerns the pervasive problem of Roma children being side-lined to special schools for mentally retarded children in several Eastern European countries, *in casu* the Czech Republic. The Court in several respects seems to go back on the 'promise' in *Hoogendij*k.[200] First of all it seems to question again the whole idea of 'indirect discrimination', by putting so much emphasis on the importance of 'intent',[201] while the 'major strength of the concept of indirect discrimination lies in its denial of the relevance of any discriminatory intent as a prerequisite for bringing a successful claim'.[202] Moreover, the Court does not confirm its positive stance regarding 'convincing official statistics' and rather goes back to its old formulation that statistics in themselves are not sufficient. However, in the following reasoning, it is not clear whether it has nevertheless accepted them as prima facie proof of discrimination because it does not use a clear assessment model. The Court does not talk about 'reasonable, objective justification', while making statements

[199] See also A. Hendriks, 'Noot bij Hoogendijk t Nederland (EHRM, 6 January 2005)', *NJCM Bulletin* (2005), 452.

[200] See also K. Henrard, 'Noot bij D.H. en overige t. Tsjechië' (EHRM, 7 February 2006), *ECHR* 2006/43, 392–3.

[201] ECtHR, *D.H et al v. Czech Republic* (7 February 2006), para. 48, 52, 53.

[202] T. Loenen, 'Indirect Discrimination: Oscillating between Containment and Revolution', in T. Loenen & P. R. Rodriguez (eds.), *Non-Discrimination Law: Comparative Perspectives* (Martinus Nijhoff, 1999), 201; Tobler, *Indirect Discrimination, supra*, n. 154, 114.

about the margin of appreciation,[203] which is actually only relevant in the framework of the proportionality component of the justification test.[204]

It may be clear that this case has left more questions than it answered. Hence the de facto acknowledgement of, and protection against, indirect discrimination is still unclear.[205]

The above analysis demonstrates that there are great divergencies between the way in which the distinctive supervisory organs deal with the phenomenon of 'indirect discrimination'.

2. *Nuance 2: Obligation to Differentiate (as the Second Dimension of the Prohibition of Discrimination)*

An obligation to differentiate in terms of the demands of equality can be traced back to Aristotle's formula that unequal or different things should be treated differently to the extent of the difference. The underlying vision of equality is clearly substantive equality. To the extent that more recently such an obligation to differentiate is being identified in terms of non-discrimination, this development would equally imply an opening towards substantive or real, full equality.

It is important to realize that this type of differential measure is not necessarily temporary (in contrast to affirmative action measures).[206] In view of the need for enduring differential treatment in order to protect and promote the separate identity of minorities, this jurisprudential line is especially relevant for minorities, for example in relation to language rights in communications with public authorities.

The following analysis will furthermore clarify the close links and interrelation between this rationale and the one underlying both indirect discrimination and affirmative action.[207]

[203] ECtHR, *D.H.et al v. Czech Republic*, para. 47.

[204] K. Henrard, *Mensenrechten vanuit Internationaal en Nationaal Perspectief* (Boom, 2006), 185–6, 227.

[205] Nevertheless, the Court still seems rather hesitant to make use of the indirect discrimination concept. In *Podkolzina v. Latvia* (more fully discussed *infra*), the Court did not even look into the possible violation of Article 14, while a key issue of the case concerned harsh language requirements in Latvian electoral legislation with their possible discriminatory indirect effects. This is the more regrettable since such language requirements are at the heart of the problem *vis-à-vis* linguistic minorities. See also A. Spiliopoulou-Akermark, *Justifications of Minority Protection in International Law* (London, 1997), 6.

[206] M. Freeman, 'Temporary Special Measures: How Long is Temporary and What is Special?', in I. Boerefijn et al (eds), *Temporary Special Measures* (Antwerp, 2003), 100.

[207] See Fredman, *Introduction, supra*, n. 1, 32–6 who discusses the question 'when a state is required to differentiate between groups' entirely through the prism of indirect discrimination or disproportionate/disparate impact.

The supervisory organ which has developed this so-called second dimension of the prohibition of discrimination most explicitly is the ECtHR. The so-called founding case is *Thlimmenos v. Greece* of 6 April 2000. The Court significantly expanded its non-discrimination jurisprudence in favour of substantive equality by acknowledging that:

> The Court has so far considered that the right under Article 14 not to be discriminated against in the enjoyment of the rights guaranteed under the Convention is violated when States treat differently persons in analogous situations without providing an objective and reasonable justification... However, the Court considers that this is not the only facet of the prohibition of discrimination in Article 14. The right not to be discriminated against in the enjoyment of the rights guaranteed under the Convention is *also violated when States without an objective and reasonable justification fail to treat differently persons whose situations are significantly different*.[208] (emphasis added)

In other words, the prohibition of discrimination can, in certain circumstances, entail an obligation for states to treat persons differently 'whose situations are significantly different'. Depending on how far the Court would be willing to stretch this rationale, it could be the basis for the recognition of positive obligations on the state to adopt certain special minority rights, attuned to the specific needs and position of the members of the minority concerned. In this regard, it seems necessary to examine subsequent cases in which the Court has used the '*Thlimmenos* rationale' and to what effect. In this particular case, the Court agreed that someone who is convicted for being a conscientious objector, exercising his freedom to manifest his religion, could not be treated the same as someone who had committed another type of offence unrelated to the exercise of fundamental rights.

However, in so far as the Court has used the *Thlimmenos* rationale in other cases related to (ethnic or national) minorities, the results have been rather modest. The Court is clearly very careful to 'impose' exceptions to the application of general norms, when it is not related to the exercise of the freedom to manifest one's religion. *Chapman v. UK* might have established the important rule that states have a positive obligation to facilitate the Gypsy way of life (in terms of Article 8 ECHR, see below), but the Court was not willing to follow the argument of the claimant that applying general planning regulations and policies to Roma failed to accommodate their particular needs arising from their tradition of living and travelling in caravans.[209] The Court simply referred back to its reasoning in terms of Article 8 (see below) to justify

[208] ECtHR, *Thlimmenos v. Greece*, para. 44.
[209] ECtHR, *Chapman v. UK*, para. 127.

its conclusion that treating Roma the same as other people in this respect had an objective and reasonable justification.[210]

In *Nachova v. Bulgaria* the Court did establish the principle, which has been confirmed many times since,[211] that state authorities have a special duty 'to take all reasonable steps to unmask any racist motive and to establish whether or not ethnic hatred or prejudice may have played a role in the events':

> The Court considers that when investigating violent incidents and, in particular, deaths at the hands of State agents, State authorities have the additional duty to take all reasonable steps to unmask any racist motive and to establish whether or not ethnic hatred or prejudice may have played a role in the events. Failing to do so and treating racially induced violence and brutality on an equal footing with cases that have no racist overtones would be to turn a blind eye to the specific nature of acts that are particularly destructive of fundamental rights. A failure to make a distinction in the way in which situations that are essentially different are handled may constitute unjustified treatment irreconcilable with Article 14 of the Convention.[212]

It seems that the Court, in line with its rather restrictive attitude in relation to Article 14 complaints (see above, the model of review), and in line with its tendency to allow states an (extensive) margin of appreciation,[213] has easily accepted that the justification offered for the absence of differential treatment in specific cases is reasonable and objective. This has manifested itself clearly in *Chapman v. UK*[214] where the Court held in regard to the complaint that the UK should have treated the claims of the Roma wanting to live in caravans differently:

> Having regard to its findings above under Article 8 of the Convention that any interference with the applicant's rights was proportionate to the legitimate aim of preservation of the environment, the Court concludes that there has been no discrimination contrary to Article 14 of the Convention. While discrimination may arise where States without an objective and reasonable justification fail to treat differently persons whose situations are significantly different (see *Thlimmenos v. Greece* [GC], no. 34369/97, § 44, ECHR 2000-IV), the Court does not find, in the circumstances of this case, any lack of objective and reasonable justification for the measures taken against the applicant.

[210] ECtHR, *Chapman v. UK*, para. 129.

[211] *Inter alia*, ECtHR, *Bekos & Koutropoulos v. Greece* (13 December 2005), para. 73; ECtHR, *Ognyanova and Choban v. Bulgaria* (23 February 2006), para. 148.

[212] ECtHR, *Nachova v. Bulgaria* (26 February 2004), para. 158.

[213] For a more extensive analysis see the article I wrote to be published in a book *Synergies in Minority Protection* (eds. K. Henrard and R. Dunbar, Cambridge 2006). See also ECtHR, *Pretty v. UK*, para. 89.

[214] ECtHR, *Chapman v. UK*, para. 129.

In the recent *D.H. et al v. Czech Republic* judgment two of the judges made comments in regard to the *Thlimmenos* rationale in their separate opinions. Even though these were not addressed by the majority judgment, they at least give an indication about how certain judges in the Court think about it, and how they perceive the jurisprudence in this regard as it has developed until now. Judge Cabral emphasized in his dissenting opinion that '[t]hese pupils who, for various reasons—whether cultural, linguistic or other—find it difficult to pursue a normal school education should be entitled to expect the State to take positive measures to compensate for their handicap and to afford them a means of resuming the normal curriculum'.[215] Judge Costa remarked in his concurring opinion that:

> As for *positive* discrimination—which, in the present case, would have entailed increased resources for special schools to avoid the risk of their becoming, if not educational "ghettos", then at least "dead ends" where pupils remain until they reach the minimum school-leaving age, it seems to me that up till now this Court has refused to consider it a State obligation (see, with respect to Article 8, *Chapman v. the United Kingdom*, judgment of 18 January 2001 [Grand Chamber], ECHR 2001-1). On this point, the judgments cited by Judge Cabral Barreto (*Thlimmenos v. Greece* and *Posti and Rahko v. Finland*) do not, in my view, entail any criticism of States that fail to engage in positive discrimination (nor does he suggest that they do).[216]

The Human Rights Committee has not developed this second dimension of the prohibition of discrimination as such, but has identified positive state obligations to adopt special measures (and thus differential treatment) through its typology of state obligations. More specifically, the obligation to facilitate (as a subcategory of the obligation to fulfil) has induced the HRC several times to make recommendations to take positive measures especially with regard to minorities (and women). These positive measures could consist in (additional) training or education in order to enhance employment and higher education possibilities.[217]

To some extent this obligation to adopt differential measures is closely related to an obligation to adopt affirmative action measures. In this respect reference can be made to General Comment No. 18 on non-discrimination as paragraph 10 explicitly takes up a requirement to take affirmative action which would flow from the equality principle:

> the principle of equality sometimes requires States parties to take affirmative action in order to diminish or eliminate conditions which cause or help to perpetuate discrimination prohibited by the Covenant

215 Dissenting opinion of Judge Cabral in *D.H. et al v. Czech Republic*, para. 2.
216 Concurring opinion of Judge Costa in *D.H. et al v. Czech Republic*, para. 7.
217 Vandenhole, *UN Human Rights Treaty Bodies, supra*, n. 50, 219.

In other words, an obligation to take affirmative action measures, as well as other 'special' measures (not necessarily temporary backward-looking measures), could be argued to be inherent in the prohibition of discrimination, in the sense that a failure to take such measures 'to elevate such groups to a level of equality with other members of society could be regarded as the perpetuation of systematic discrimination and thus states would not be complying with their obligation to ensure equal and effective protection against discrimination as required by Article 26'.[218]

The CESCR/C seems to have a similar take on the prohibition of discrimination in Article 2 CESCR, in the sense that the Committee has indicated that the state obligations to facilitate (the prohibition of discrimination) would require them to adopt measures to ensure equal opportunities. Furthermore, the Committee has highlighted the obligation to ensure equal opportunities for minorities, including Roma, in several fields but especially in relation to employment, housing, health and education.[219]

Both in terms of CEDAW and CERD, the supervisory Committees mainly identify an obligation to adopt differential treatment in terms of an obligation to adopt affirmative action measures[220] (as can be found explicitly in Article 2(1) 1 CERD and is said to be inherent in CEDAW, see below). This has led to the criticism that CERD does not contain a safeguard against assimilationist policies because the approach of the convention would be integrationist at best, not providing for structural, institutional measures in addition to the temporary affirmative action ones.[221] Nevertheless, it should be underscored that the Committee seems to have taken on board the broader international law developments recognizing that minorities have a right to own an identity which should be protected, maintained and promoted. CERD/C has even put forward that:

> Governments should be sensitive towards the rights of persons belonging to ethnic groups, particularly their right to lead lives of dignity, to preserve their culture . . . Governments should consider, within their respective constitutional frameworks, vesting persons belonging to ethnic or linguistic groups . . . where

[218] S. Davidson, 'Equality and Non-Descrimination', in R. Burchill, S. Davidson, and A. Conte, *Defining Civil and Political Rights: The Jurisprudence of the United Nations Human Rights Committee* (Ashgate Publishing Ltd, 2004), 161–83.

[219] Vandenhole, *UN Human Rights Treaty Bodies, supra*, n. 50, 234.

[220] H. B. Schöpp-Schilling, 'Reflections on a General Recommendation on Article 4(1) of the Convention on the Elimination of all Forms of Discrimination Against Women', in I. Boerefijn et al (ed.), *Temporary Special Measures* (Antwerp, 2003), 28.

[221] K. Boyle and A. Baldaccini, 'A Critical Evaluation of Human Rights Approaches to Cases of Racism', in S. Fredman (ed.), *Discrimintion and Human Rights: The Case of Racism* (Oxford, 2001), 158.

appropriate, with the right to engage in activities which are particularly relevant to the preservation of the identity of such persons or groups.[222]

This has been taken up and further refined in General Recommendation 30 on Discrimination against non-citizens, where the CERD/C underlined that contracting states should ensure the preservation of the culture and the cultural identity of these racial groups (of non-citizens).[223] In this light the previous references to suggestions by CERD/C to adopt language laws etc. should be recalled.

This reasoning would seem to be in line with at least an encouragement (if not the establishment of a clear obligation) to adopt special, 'differentiating' measures (see immediately above) in order to abide by the prohibition of racial discrimination, being the focal point of CERD.

The text of CEDAW seems to allow for 'temporary special measures' without really containing an obligation for states to adopt such measures. Nevertheless it has been argued persuasively that Article 4(1) CEDAW would imply an obligation to adopt 'temporary special measures' aimed at real, substantive equality.[224] Indeed, the overall goal of CEDAW is to eliminate discrimination against women and the practical elimination of direct and indirect discrimination might well require the use of temporary special measures.[225]

Importantly, the obligations to take special measures aimed at realizing substantive equality are not restricted to 'temporary measures'. CEDAW underlines in this respect that 'it is not enough to guarantee women treatment that is identical to that of men. Rather, biological as well as socially and culturally constructed differences between women and men must be taken into account. Under certain circumstances, non-identical treatment of women and men will be required in order to address such differences'.[226]

In a subsequent General Recommendation on Article 4, paragraph 1 CEDAW clearly emphasizes that

state parties should clearly distinguish between temporary special measures taken under article 4, paragraph 1 to accelerate the achievement of a concrete goal for women of de facto or substantive equality, and other general social policies adopted to

[222] CERD, General Recommendation No. 21: The Right to Self-Determination (1996), para. 5.

[223] CERD, General Recommendation No. 30, para. 37.

[224] R. Cook, 'Obligations to Adopt Temporary Special Measures under the Convention on the Elimination of All Forms of Discrimination against Women', in I. Boerefijn (ed.), *Temporary Special Measures* (Antwerp, 2003), 129.

[225] *Ibid.*, 134.

[226] CEDAW, General Comment 25 on Article 4, para. 1 on temporary special measures, para. 8. See also *ibid.*, para. 11.

improve the situation of women and the girl child. Not all measures that potentially are, or will be, favourable to women are temporary special measures. The provision of general conditions in order to guarantee the civil, political, economic, social and cultural rights of women and the girl child, designed to ensure for them a life of dignity and non-discrimination, cannot be called temporary special measures.[227]

This arguably hints at an obligation to take differential measures for women in order to abide by the prohibition of discrimination. While this is not directly relevant for the focus of this volume, namely minority protection, the equality principle elaborated in terms of gender arguably has a broader scope of application.

3. Nuance 3: Affirmative Action

Even though there is a set definition of the concept 'affirmative action', it tends to concern temporary measures aimed at redressing historical disadvantages of a particular group. This description reveals not only that affirmative action has an inherent 'group focus' but also that it is ultimately aimed at realizing substantive or real equality.

Alternative concepts or synonyms include 'temporary special measures' or just 'special measures',[228] 'positive discrimination', and 'reverse discrimination'.

As most debate in relation to affirmative action centres on its legitimacy or its acceptability, it should be underlined that affirmative action measures must always comply with the principle of non-discrimination.[229] The HRC practice clearly reflects that 'as with other distinctions, the permissibility of affirmative action measures is judged by reference to the "reasonable and objective" test'.[230] In other words, affirmative action measures should serve a legitimate aim and be proportional to that aim. While the legitimate aim of affirmative action measures seems a given, namely to contribute to the achievement of substantive equality, there is still the additional need for the measures

[227] CEDAW, General Comment No. 25, para. 19.

[228] Ch. McCrudden, 'International and Legal Norms Regarding National Legal Remedies for Racial Equality', in S. Fredman (ed.), *Discrimination and Human Rights: the Case of Racism* (Oxford, 2001), 277.

[229] M. Bossuyt, 'The Concept and Practice of Affirmative Action', in I. Boerefijn et al (eds), *Temporary Special Measures* (Antwerp, 2003), 66 and 73: 'affirmative action to ensure full equality is not always legitimate. Affirmative action should not be interpreted as justifying any distinction based on any ground with respect to any right merely because the object of the distinction is to improve the situation of disadvantaged individuals or groups. Affirmative action is no exception to the principle of non-discrimination. Rather, it is the principle of non-discrimination that establishes limits to each affirmative action'.

[230] Joseph, Schultz and Castan, *Cases, Materials and Commentary, supra*, n. 2, 731.

concerned to be proportional. The proportionality principle arguably underlies the requirement that affirmative action measures should be temporary.

When the prohibition of discrimination determines the outer limits of legitimate affirmative action measures, it is obvious that one should discuss the acceptability of affirmative action in relation to the theory on non-discrimination, developed above. This would first of all require a consideration of the appropriate level of scrutiny which is inherently related to the question whether the supervisory body concerned adopts a symmetrical or an asymmetrical approach in this respect. In this regard it should be highlighted that affirmative measures are most often developed in regard to groups that are distinguished on the basis of a 'suspect' class, like race or ethnicity. A related interpretation and evaluation point is that affirmative action should not be qualified as an exception to the equality principle, but as an application of the principle of substantive equality.[231] The latter qualification would obviate the need to interpret the legitimacy of the measure restrictively. As the following analysis will show though, several supervisory bodies underscore that affirmative action is a negation of the individual right to equal treatment.

In this respect it is important to distinguish between different kinds of 'affirmative action' measures, which can be formulated in terms of the distinction between an equal opportunities approach versus an equal results approach, the latter concerning the 'stronger' and consequently also the more controversial forms.[232] When one takes the 'equal opportunities approach' one could define affirmative action measures as:

> time limited positive measures intended to enhance opportunities for historically and systematically disadvantaged groups, with a view to bringing group members into the mainstream of political, economic, social, cultural and civil life.[233]

Especially in relation to the 'equality of results' approach the danger of inadequate qualifications is often highlighted. In this respect CEDAW/C correctly points out that while this is relevant to some extent, it should not be forgotten that the required qualifications might in themselves have hidden discriminatory features. It emphasizes in this respect that 'questions of qualifications and merit, in particular in the area of employment in the public and private sectors,

[231] See *inter alia* CEDAW, General Comment No. 23 on public and political life, para. 15; CEDAW, General Recommendation No. 25 on temporary special measures, paras. 13–14.

[232] Bossuyt highlighted in his UN report on affirmative action that 'affirmative preference is particularly controversial because someone's gender or ethnicity etc. will be taken into account in the granting or withholding of social goods' (Bossuyt, *The Concept and Practice of Affirmative Action*, *supra*, n. 229, 67).

[233] Cook, 'Obligations', *supra*, n. 224, 119.

need to be reviewed carefully for... bias as they are normatively and culturally determined'.[234]

More generally, it can be said that CEDAW/C seems to embrace the stronger forms of affirmative action, by emphasizing that 'equality of results is the logical corollary of de facto or substantive equality'. This approach is also reflected in the statement that 'pursuit of the goal of substantive equality also calls for an effective strategy aimed at overcoming under-representation of women and a redistribution of resources and power between men and women'.[235]

While there is no explicit provision in the CCPR, the HRC clearly accepts the legitimacy of affirmative action, since it even points to an obligation to adopt such measures in certain circumstances.[236] General Comment No. 18, paragraph 10 stipulates that:

> the principle of equality sometimes requires States parties to take affirmative action in order to diminish or eliminate conditions which cause or help to perpetuate discrimination prohibited by the Covenant.[237]

The practice of the HRC furthermore clarifies that affirmative action measures need to be temporary, in the sense that they would only be acceptable as long as they are necessary to correct discrimination in fact. Arguably this refers back to the fact that the prohibition of discrimination constitutes the limit on affirmative action measures.[238]

The views of the HRC in *Jacobs v. Belgium* of 7 July 2004[239] also clearly indicate that the Committee is rather open to affirmative action measures, in the sense that it highlights that the goal of affirmative action is substantive equality and hence is not an exception to the equality principle.[240] These

[234] CEDAW, General Recommendation No. 25, para. 23.

[235] CEDAW, General Recommendation No. 25, paras. 8–9.

[236] Schultz et al highlight that: 'The HRC has confirmed that affirmative action is certainly permissible under the Covenant, and may have indicated that, in certain circumstances, it is mandatory for States to take such action.' Joseph, Schultz and Castan, *Cases, Materials and Commentary, supra*, n. 2, 738.

[237] In this respect, reference should also be made to General Comments No. 4 and No. 28 on Article 3 since these indicate (in respectively paras. 2 and 3) that the principle of non-discrimination in all three articles of the CCPR 'requires not only measures of protection but also affirmative action designed to ensure the positive enjoyment of rights'.

[238] See also the statement in HRC's General Comment No. 23 on Article 27 CCPR where it underscores that the obligation to take positive measures to protect the identity of a minority (in Article 27) is limited by the prohibition of non-discrimination, in the sense that the special measures a state would adopt in terms of Article 27 would have to comply with the proportionality principle, in addition to pursuing a legitimate goal.

[239] HRC, *Jacobs v. Belgium* (Communication 943/2000, 7 July 2004).

[240] HRC, *Jacobs v. Belgium*, para. 9.3 : 'states may take measures in order to ensure that the law guarantees to women the rights (contained in Article 25 ICCPR) on equal terms with men'.

views furthermore confirm that the HRC sees affirmative action and non-discrimination as intrinsically related in the sense that the latter constitutes the limits for justifiable affirmative action. According to the HRC relevant factors necessary in order to assess whether or not the affirmative action measures are objectively and reasonably justifiable (and proportional) are: the establishment of an under-representation of women in the public service, the fact that the preference for women only applies to 30 per cent of the entire category of positions (non justices to the High Council of Justice), and the fact that the respective qualifications of candidates were not irrelevant.[241] These factors all seem related to the proportionality principle underlying the need for an objective and reasonable justification.

It should be emphasized that the HRC even seems rather permissive in relation to one of the most sensitive affirmative action measures, more specifically the use of quotas. This is not only visible in some of its views, but also in its Concluding Observations. In the above quoted case *Jacobs v. Belgium,* the HRC found that the imposition of a gender quota for appointment to the High Council of Justice, whereby at least four out of eleven appointees had to belong to each sex, was not disproportionate in that particular case.[242] Similarly its Concluding Observations on India (1998) explicitly accepted the use of quotas for improving the representation of women and people belonging to the scheduled castes.[243]

The supervisory practice of CESCR/C also reveals that the Committee not only allows affirmative action measures in so far as they abide by the principle of non-discrimination,[244] but in certain circumstances even considers them obligatory. In its 2005 General Comment on Women the CESCR/C makes a statement pointing to an obligation to adopt affirmative action measures ('temporary special measures') in order to achieve real, substantive equality. Despite the focus of the General Comment this particular statement was not limited to gender issues as it reads: 'temporary special measures may sometime be needed in order to bring disadvantaged or marginalized groups of persons to the same substantive level as others'.[245] Similarly, in its General Comment on Discrimination against Roma the obligation to take special measures for this disadvantaged group is underlined. At the same time it is clear though that this is not an absolute obligation of result in the sense that the contracting

[241] HRC, *Jacobs v. Belgium*, paras. 9.4–9.5
[242] *Ibid.*, 13.11.
[243] *Ibid.*, 10.
[244] CESCR/C, General Comment No. 5 on 'Temporary special measures', para. 32.
[245] UN Doc. E/C.12/2005/3, General Comment No. 16 (2005), para. 15.

states are urged to take measures in order to realize an 'equality of opportunities' (and not equality of results) *inter alia* in regard to participation in public life.

In regard to both CERD/C and CEDAW/C it should be underlined that whereas both conventions and related supervisory practice are open towards affirmative action[246] measures, this would exclude permanent measures.[247]

Article 4 CEDAW seems to allow affirmative action measures in order to further the goal of substantive or real equality.[248] CEDAW/C does not qualify affirmative action as an exception to the equality principle, but as an application thereof. The Committee also considers the prohibition of discrimination as the inherent limit to justifiable affirmative action measures.[249] Furthermore, while the Convention does not identify an obligation to adopt affirmative action, the practice of the Committee seems to indicate that it can still be argued that the adoption of such measures would be obligatory if they can be shown to be necessary and appropriate in order to accelerate the achievement of the overall, or a specific goal of, women's de facto or substantive equality.[250]

The text of CERD is even more explicit about its acceptance of affirmative action measures in so far as these measures abide by the prohibition of discrimination.[251] The related criteria are spelled out more explicitly in the practice of the Committee. The goal or legitimate aim should be the 'acceleration of de facto equality'. The proportionality considerations are further specified in the requirements that measures should be temporary (they should not lead to the maintenance of separate standards and temporary special measures should be discontinued when objectives of equality of opportunity have been achieved).

In relation to the evaluation of the use of quotas, the practice of CERD/C is not very illuminating,[252] while CEDAW/C seems particularly permissive. In its concluding observations it has often not only recommended affirmative action measures,[253] but even advocated the use of quotas to achieve gender

[246] J. Swiebel, 'What Could the EU Learn from the CEDAW Convention?', in I. Boerefijn et al (eds.), *Temporary Special Measures* (Antwerp, 2003), 52.

[247] UN Doc E/C.12/2005/3, General Comment No. 16 (2005), para. 15.

[248] CEDAW/C, General Recommendation No. 25 (2004), para. 14.

[249] Vandenhole, *UN Human Rights Treaty Bodies, supra*, n. 50, 265.

[250] CEDAW/C, General Recommendation No. 25, para. 24.

[251] Thornberry, *Confronting Racial Discrimination, supra*, n. 113, 256.

[252] K. Boyle and A. Baldaccini, 'A Critical Evaluation of International Human Rights Approaches to Racism', in S. Fredman (ed.), *Discrimination and Human Rights: The Case of Racism* (Oxford, 2001) 157.

[253] For a more detailed overview of instances in which the Committee on the Elimination of Discrimination against Women has called on states to adopt affirmative action measures, see Vandenhole, *UN Human Rights Treaty Bodies, supra*, n. 50, 267–71.

balance in public and political bodies.[254] The Committee also clearly promotes equality of results, and not merely equality of opportunities. In this respect it is telling that General Comment No. 23 seems to indicate that the Committee considers equality of results as the logical corollary of substantive equality.[255]

The rather restrictive approach of the ECJ in relation to affirmative action measures has been amply assessed, even in relation to 'legislative' provisions that seemed to take a more lenient approach. This restrictive approach can also be related to a symmetrical approach to non-discrimination.[256] As is still reflected in the case law of the ECJ, affirmative action measures are seen as exceptions to the principle of formal equal treatment, and hence restrictively interpreted, despite the opening clause in Article 2(4) of the Equal Treatment Directive 76/207. The most relevant case law in this respect is found in *Kalanke* and *Marschall* (confirmed by *Badeck*). The Court ruled that the affirmative action measure at hand in *Kalanke v. Hansestadt Bremen* was illegitimate because it automatically gave priority to women when they were as equally qualified as men.[257] In *Marschall v. Land Nordrhein Westfalen* the Court added an important qualification by indicating that a state law that gave preference to a woman in a tiebreak situation is acceptable as long as an apparently equally qualified man was considered on his individual merits.[258] In other words, quotas are only acceptable in so far as they contain some kind of 'savings' clause.

It should be highlighted that since the Amsterdam Treaty the TEC has a formulation which acknowledges the aim of affirmative action as being full, substantive equality (Article 141(4) TEC).[259] This formulation has been taken up in the two directives of 2000. Article 5 of the Race Directive stipulates: 'with a view to ensuring full equality in practice, the principle of equal treatment shall not prevent any Member State from maintaining or adopting specific measures to prevent or compensate for disadvantages linked to racial or ethnic origin' (see also Article 7(1) Framework Directive and Directive 2002/73/EC).

It is quite obvious though that there is no obligation to take affirmative measures (in contrast to CEDAW or CERD).[260] This also applies to the opening made towards affirmative action in relation to gender in the Charter of

[254] CEDAW/C, General Comment No. 23, para. 29.
[255] Schöpp-Schilling, *Reflections, supra*, n. 220, 27.
[256] Barnard, *Changing Scope, supra*, n. 24, 960.
[257] C-450/93, [1995] ECR I-3051.
[258] C-409/95, [1997] ECR I-6363, paras 29–30.
[259] Swiebel, *What Could the EU Learn, supra*, n. 246, 55.
[260] *Ibid.*, 58.

Fundamental Rights: 'The principle of equality shall not prevent the maintenance or adoption of measures providing for specific advantages in favour of the under-represented sex.' This formulation is to be welcomed though because it provides for a more enduring kind of 'special measures' as well, hence acknowledging that affirmative action and its inherently temporary nature are not sufficient to reach full and true equality. It should be noted though that the Court has indicated in *Abrahamsson v. Fogelqvist* that the new formulation of the affirmative action clause does not make it assess affirmative action measures more asymmetrically, and thus more leniently. The ECJ ruled that a national rule which gave automatic priority to a person of the under-represented sex who had qualifications which were adequate, but inferior in minor respects to those of the person who would otherwise have been appointed, failed to satisfy the requirements of Article 141(4) TEC.

It remains to be seen whether the Court is going to hold on to this line of reasoning or may be induced to take a more accommodating approach in relation to affirmative action in terms of race or ethnic origin, because of the different social context.

The European Court on Human Rights, on the other hand, has not taken a clear, explicit position on this matter because it has not yet been confronted with a 'real' case of affirmative action.[261] Nevertheless, it did have to rule in two cases on measures which entailed treatment which benefited women, while excluding men: *Petrovic v. Austria*[262] (parental leave allowance only for women), and *Van Raalte v. Netherlands*[263] (only women over 45 could be exempted from paying a children-related levy). In the initial establishment of the appropriate level of scrutiny the Court seems to favour the symmetrical approach (with all its pernicious consequences for affirmative action measures).[264] In *Petrovic* though it took into account that as regards the question of parental leave allowance there was no common European standard yet, which de facto reduced the level of scrutiny, enabling the Court to conclude that Article 14 was not violated. This is to be welcomed to the extent that it reveals that the levels of scrutiny for certain grounds of differentiation are not rigid, but can be modulated by other considerations.[265] While this seems to suggest that the Court could shift towards a more asymmetrical approach, this has not yet materialized.

261 de Prins, Sottiaux & Vrielink, *Handboek Discriminatierecht, supra*, n. 70, 38.

262 ECtHR, *Petrovic v. Austria* (27 March 1989).

263 ECtHR, *Van Raalte v. Netherlands* (21 February 1997).

264 Gerards, *Rechterlijke Toetsing, supra*, n. 40, 202.

265 *Ibid.*, 210.

It can be concluded that in relation to affirmative action, the supervisory organs have demonstrated rather divergent attitudes and approaches. Arguably, the position of supervisory organs that have the power to pronounce binding legal judgments is more careful and restrained than those of other bodies.

E. Burden of Proof and Distribution of the Burden of Proof

While the requirements as to the proof of alleged discrimination are obviously essential to determine the effectiveness of the protection against discrimination, this matter is not explicitly dealt with in international instruments. Both the burden of proof and the distribution of this burden of proof have been developed in the case law of the supervisory bodies.

It has already been indicated above in relation to the model of review that the distribution of proof is inherently related to the two-step process identified there. As soon as the claimant has established a prima facie case of discrimination, the burden of proof (that the differentiation at issue does not amount to a prohibited discrimination) shifts to the respondent state.[266] Obviously, it is important to be able to identify criteria to determine when a 'prima facie' case of discrimination has been made out. One argument that can already be put forward is that arguably in a case of an alleged discrimination on a suspect ground, the heightened scrutiny should also be reflected in the required burden of proof, and more specifically in reduced demands in relation to a prima facie case of discrimination.

The subsequent analysis will reveal once again that the (regional) courts have taken a much more explicit, and elaborated, stance in relation to the burden of proof than the UN Treaty Bodies. The CERD/C does seem to acknowledge the two-step review model which implies that once the claimant has established a 'prima facie case' of discrimination, the burden of proof shifts to the state (which has to prove the distinction is based on objective and reasonable grounds).[267] However, there are no further indications to be found in relation to the burden of proof, let alone the distribution of the burden of proof. The HRC seems to require that there be 'sufficient evidence' to substantiate the communication, but again there are no more concrete guidelines to be distilled as to what this would imply.[268]

[266] Gold, 'Towards a Unified Theory of the Law of Employment Discrimination', *Berkeley Journal of Employment and Labor Law*, (2001).

[267] CERD/C, General Comment No. 30 on Discrimination against non-citizens, para. 24.

[268] Joseph, Schultz and Castan, *Cases, Materials and Commentary, supra*, n. 2, 22.

The Directives of the EU in 2000 both provide explicitly for a reversal of the burden of proof in civil cases, in a way that takes up the principles in this regard as developed in the Burden of Proof Directive concerning gender discrimination (Directive 97/80, Articles 3 and 4):

> when persons who consider themselves wronged because the principle of equal treatment has not been applied to them establish, before a court or other competent authority, facts from which it may be presumed that there has been direct or indirect discrimination, it shall be for the respondent to prove that there has been no breach of the principle of equal treatment.[269]

In light of the theory above in terms of 'prima facie case', the provisions in EC law concerning the reversal of the burden of proof are actually not that special or amazing. Nevertheless, the explicit provisions in this regard are important as they signal a clear willingness to alleviate the problems to prove a case on the side of victims of discrimination, who tend to be in a vulnerable position anyway. As will be elaborated upon below, the jurisprudence of the ECtHR has not been similarly forthcoming.

In regard to the ECtHR, there is a long history of criticism about the general 'standard of proof' required by the Court, namely proof 'beyond reasonable doubt'. This would be too demanding and hence not appropriate for cases about human rights violations.[270]

The Court has from the beginning nuanced this standard by indicating that 'proof may follow from the co-existence of sufficiently strong, clear and concordant inferences or of similar unrebutted presumptions of fact', while it often underlined that this standard of proof would be less demanding than the one in criminal cases.

The Court has furthermore taken into account the problems of obtaining the required proof by adjusting the distribution of proof in favour of the claimant. Typical examples here would be deaths of persons in police custody.[271] Sometimes the Court considers that the surrounding circumstances are so suspect that it concludes there has been a violation of a provision because the state has not dispelled all serious doubts about a possible violation.[272] Even though the Court in these circumstances talks about a 'reversal of the burden

[269] Race Directive, Article 8; Framework Directive, Article 10.

[270] It should be highlighted that this criticism does not only come from NGOs and other external sources but has also been voiced by individual judges of the Court, like Judge Bonello in *Veznedaroglu v. Turkey* (11 April 2000), para. 12; Judge Loucaides in regard to *Hasan Ilhan v. Turkey* (9 November 2004).

[271] ECtHR, *Salman v. Turkey* (27 June 2000), para. 97.

[272] ECtHR, *Conka v. België* (5 February 2002), para. 61.

of proof',[273] it seems more correct to speak in terms of 'distribution of the burden of proof' as the Court did explicitly in *Timishev v. Russia*.[274]

While several adjustments to the required standard of proof have been made, the base line remains the 'beyond reasonable doubt' standard. It still seems to be the case that the standard used de facto often leads to disappointing results. It is furthermore far from clear in what circumstances the Court will proceed to a relaxation of the standard of proof. However, this is essential for legal certainty and procedural balance among the parties.

The Court, in the Grand Chamber, did give a few factors that are relevant to determine the exact distribution of the burden of proof in *Nachova v. Bulgaria*, a case concerning an allegedly racial killing of two Roma by the Bulgarian police. While the Chamber had concluded that the claimants could benefit from a 'reversal of the burden of proof', the Grand Chamber indicated that while such a reversal is not ruled out in cases of alleged racial discrimination, more would be required before this 'reversal' would be triggered. Arguably, the Grand Chamber did not agree with the assessment of the Chamber that the claimants had made out a prima facie case of discrimination (after which the burden of proof shifts to the respondent state). The ECtHR Grand Chamber seems to acknowledge that whether or not a prima facie case has been made out will depend on the specific circumstances each time. Nevertheless it does provide a few criteria, more specifically the 'specificity of the facts, the nature of the allegations made, and the Convention right at stake'.[275] While this clarification should be welcomed, it has to be put in perspective since the Court has not dealt explicitly with these criteria. It may be obvious that these general criteria in themselves provide anything but a clear prediction for concrete decisions of the Court. An explicit application of the criteria to a concrete *casus* would have been very welcome.

It is, for example, far from obvious what is meant by the 'nature of the allegations'. This could refer to the gravity of the interference as this is a well-known parameter in the doctrine of legitimate limitations to human rights.[276] Very adverse decisions in relation to fundamental interests would seem to warrant a relaxation of the burden of proof to be borne by the claimant. In cases concerning discrimination, this 'nature of the allegations' could be related to the presence of 'suspect grounds' of differentiation. In this respect, one could

[273] ECtHR, *Nachova v. Turkey* (26 February 2004), para. 169.

[274] ECtHR (Grand Chamber), *Timishev v. Russia*, para. 39. See also ECtHR (Grand Chamber), *Nachova v. Bulgaria* (6 February 2006), para. 147.

[275] ECtHR (GC), *Nachova v. Bulgaria*, para. 147.

[276] J. Vande Lanotte & Y. Haeck, *Handboek EVRM: Algemene Beginselen* (Antwerp, 2005), 144–7.

refer to the statement by the Court itself that racial discrimination constitutes a 'particular affront to human dignity'.[277]

The 'convention right at stake' in turn raises the question whether the prohibition of discrimination could count as such, in view of the accessory character of Article 14 ECHR. The coming into force of the twelfth Additional Protocol and its general prohibition of discrimination seems to open this possibility. Finally, the criterion 'specificity of the facts' raises more questions than it answers. Does this refer to the available proof, the quantum of the ultimate uncertainty about the exact facts of the case (who bears the risk in case of insufficient or inconclusive proof?)? Even though the Court took up these criteria in the more recent case *Timishev v. Russia*, again it did not apply the criteria to the facts of the case and hence did not provide further clarifications.

Specific Nature of Indirect Discrimination: Additional Problem

It has already been highlighted above that the specific nature of indirect discrimination poses particular problems in this regard. The question is more particularly whether statistical evidence should be required to establish a prima facie case of indirect discrimination, and if so, what differential impact would need to be revealed?

While the position of the ECtHR is far from resolved, the HRC's views have not yet clarified this particular matter. Similarly, the CERD/C has indicated that 'indirect discrimination can only be demonstrated circumstantially', without however providing further specifications.[278]

The most recent EU directives on the prohibition of discrimination make a quantum leap in allowing also hypothetical cases of indirect discrimination, but further case law is required in order to be able to assess the actual impact of this new position, especially because the directives still allow national legal systems to require statistical evidence.

F. Positive State Obligations and Private Discrimination?

It is obvious that an effective protection against discrimination implies that there is also adequate protection against private forms of discrimination or discrimination by private actors (and not only public officials). When looking

[277] ECtHR (Grand Chamber), *Nachova v. Bulgaria*, para. 145. See in this respect also the judgments in which the Court has held that in certain circumstances racial discrimination amounts to a degrading treatment absolutely prohibited by Article 3 ECHR: ECommHR, *East African Asians v. UK* (3 EHRR 76, 1973), para. 207; ECtHR, *Cyprus v. Turkey* (10 May 2001), paras. 308–310.

[278] CERD/C, *R et al v. Slovakia* (Communication 031/2003, 7 March 2005), para. 10.4.

at a more general typology of state obligations,[279] three types are broadly distinguished, namely the obligation to respect, to protect and to fulfil.

In regard to the question posed here, the obligation to 'protect' seems most relevant since this would impose an obligation on the state to make sure that the right (*in casu* prohibition of discrimination) is also ensured in relations between private persons, or private instances more generally. In other words, the obligation to 'protect' would imply an obligation to eradicate, prevent and punish discriminatory acts between private persons.[280] When one accepts this type of positive state obligation, the more important and difficult question is how far this obligation would reach.[281]

In addition, the obligation to fulfil, in its various sub-dimensions, namely the obligation to facilitate, to promote and to provide, would also seem to reach the private sphere.[282] The related measures would, for example, be related to the assurance that private associations do not discriminate in their membership policies or that private companies do not discriminate against minorities (eg Roma) in their recruiting policies.[283] Again, it is clear that this would not be an obligation of result, so the question would again be to delimit the exact scope of this obligation. Similar assessments can be made in terms of the 'obligation to promote'. While it is not an obligation of result, and in any event would be more of a long-term goal, there still would be a positive obligation to change the attitudes of persons, and to promote tolerance among racial or ethnic groups which would ultimately contribute to the prevention of discrimination in the purely private sphere.[284]

At the global level, it seems that while the HRC is willing to go rather far, the text of the two issue-specific conventions (CEDAW and CERD) goes even further. Arguably this is typical for instruments that are issue-specific in the sense that they are less inclined to balance the demands in terms of the prohibition of discrimination with the demands in terms of other fundamental rights. It should be remembered though that, even though state obligations to eradicate private discrimination may seem to go far, the prohibition of discrimination does not entail a prohibition of all distinctions or differentiations.

[279] While this typology was developed in relation to second generation rights, they are now considered to be more generally applicable to all human rights (of all generations).

[280] Vandenhole, *UN Human Rights Treaty Bodies, supra*, n. 50, 187. See also Fredman, who refers to a trend to impose positive duties to promote equality on private employers as on public authorities (Fredman, *Introduction, supra*, n. 1, 26).

[281] Fredman, *Introduction, supra*, n. 1, 29.

[282] The obligation to provide is related to affirmative action, and hence Article 1(4) and 2(2) CERD and Article 4(1) CEDAW.

[283] CERD/C, General Recommendation No. 24: Article 1, para. 1(descent), paras. jj, kk and ll.

[284] See also Vandenhole, *UN Human Rights Treaty Bodies, supra*, n. 50, 204–5.

In terms of the CCPR, it has been suggested that the Article 2 duty to 'ensure all rights to all persons without distinction... seems to indicate that there would be a positive obligation to eradicate private discrimination'.[285] General Comment No. 28, focusing on equality of rights between men and women (Article 3) bears this out where it refers to an obligation to take 'all steps necessary... to put an end to discriminatory actions both in the public and the private sector'.[286] The subsequent paragraph builds on this understanding when it points out that 'state parties should ensure that traditional, historical, religious or cultural attitudes are not used to justify violations of women's rights to equality before the law and to equal enjoyment of all Covenant rights'. Further down, the General Comment is even more specific when it points to an obligation to implement all necessary measures in order to eliminate discrimination against women, in all fields, for example by prohibiting discrimination by private actors in areas such as employment, education, political activities, and the provision of accommodation, goods and services.[287]

Three remarks need to be made in regard to the possible scope of this positive obligation. First, even though this statement is made in a General Comment focusing on gender discrimination, it arguably has broader application. This is also buttressed by the fact that the latter paragraph of the General Comment actually refers to an obligation on the basis of Article 26 CCPR with its extensive scope of application. Similarly, this General Comment points out that despite the fact that Article 2(1) is primarily an obligation on states without direct horizontal effect as a matter of international law:

> the positive obligations on States Parties to ensure Covenant rights will only be fully discharged if individuals are protected by the State, not just against violations of Covenant rights by its agents, but also against acts committed by private persons or entitities that would impair the enjoyment of Covenant rights in so far as they are amenable to application between private persons or entities. There may be circumstances in which a failure to ensure Covenant rights as required by article 2 would give rise to violations by States Parties of those rights, as a result of States Parties permitting or failing to take appropriate measures or to exercise due diligence to prevent, punish, investigate or redress the harm caused by such acts by private persons or entities.[288]

The following two remarks, though, add nuance to this seemingly far-reaching positive state obligation.

[285] Joseph, Schultz and Castan, *Cases, Materials and Commentary, supra*, n. 2, 732.
[286] HRC, General Comment No. 28, para. 4.
[287] HRC, General Comment No. 28, para. 31.
[288] HRC, General Comment No. 28, para. 8.

Secondly, it should be highlighted that this positive state obligation to meddle in the private sphere is modulated in the sense that it would only apply in certain circumstances ('there may be circumstances'). In this respect, it should be highlighted that several commentators have argued that an obligation to protect from discrimination by private parties would not be comprehensive.[289]

Thirdly, and despite the formulation of paragraph 5 (see above), there are indications that this state obligation to eradicate private discrimination would not reach into the purely private sphere. This is borne out by the view in *Nahlik v. Austria* in which the HRC put forward that:

> The Committee observes that under articles 2 and 26 of the Covenant the State Party is under an obligation to ensure that all individuals within its territory and subject to its jurisdiction are free from discrimination, and consequently the courts of States Parties are under an obligation to protect individuals against discrimination, whether this occurs within the public sphere or among private parties in the quasi-public sector of, for example, employment.[290]

In other words, this particular positive obligation seems to be limited to the quasi public sector. However, it is not entirely clear where the line is drawn, and there will undoubtedly be a considerable grey zone.

In this regard, it should also be highlighted that General Comment No. 28 also indicates that the prohibition of gender discrimination would limit the minority-specific rights in terms of Article 27 CCPR:

> The rights which persons belonging to minorities enjoy under article 27 of the Covenant in respect of their language, culture and religion do not authorize any State, *group or person* to violate the right to equal enjoyment by women of any Covenant rights, including the right to equal protection of the law.[291]

Arguably, this would reach into the purely private sphere.

Nevertheless, the HRC does not always formulate this obligation as a clear, strong obligation on states but sometimes 'recommends' that states curb discrimination in the private sphere, for example by putting in place comprehensive anti-discrimination legislation regulating the private sphere.[292]

Overall, it has been pointed out that 'compared to the attention CERD has paid to private discrimination in its concluding observations, the HRC seems

[289] Vandenhole, *UN Human Rights Treaty Bodies, supra*, n. 50, 214.
[290] HRC, *Nahlik v. Austria* (Communication No. 608/95), para. 8.2.
[291] HRC, General Comment No. 28, para. 32.
[292] UN Doc. CCPR/C79/Add.104, para. 23 (Chile).

to be much more hesitant in systematically addressing states' obligation to protect against discrimination by third parties'.[293]

The CESCR/C also acknowledges that states would have a duty to protect against private discrimination, particularly in relation to race (and gender).[294] Similarly, it has indicated the need to take legislative measures, *inter alia* for the protection of Roma,[295] and to penalize certain forms of racial discrimination.[296] There are no further indications though that clarify how far this positive obligation would reach.

In regard to CERD, Fredman and Thornberry have highlighted that Article 2(1)(d) contains a clear obligation to redress private discrimination,[297] or to protect against private discrimination,[298] since it imposes an obligation on states to 'prohibit and bring to an end, by all appropriate means, including legislation as required by circumstances, race discrimination by any persons, groups or organization'. This obligation is reinforced by the provisions in *inter alia* Articles 4 and 5 (pertaining to employment and housing).

Nevertheless, it does not seem to be all that clear-cut (and far-reaching).[299] This provision, as well as several examples of rights enumerated in Article 5, reveal that CERD is meant to also reach at least some private activities. The supervising committee has specified in its General Comment No. 20 (on non-discriminatory implementation of rights and freedoms) that '*to the extent that private institutions influence the exercise of rights or the availability of opportunities*, the State Party must ensure that the result has neither the purpose nor the effect of creating or perpetuating racial discrimination' (emphasis added).[300] The wording of this General Comment makes clear that the Convention does not impose such positive obligation to prevent and eradicate private discrimination in a comprehensive way that would reach every interaction between private persons. The state obligations in terms of race do seem to have repercussions for employment in private enterprises, for housing provided by

293 Vandenhole, *UN Human Rights Treaty Bodies, supra*, n. 50, 217.

294 *Inter alia* UN Doc. E/C.12/1/Add.73, para. 9 (Croatia).

295 UN Doc. E/C.12/1/Add.58, para. 30 (China: Hong Kong).

296 *Inter alia* U N Doc. E/C.12/1/Add.54, para. 21(Belgium).

297 Fredman, *Introduction, supra*, n. 1, 192–3; Thornberry, *Confronting Racial Discrimination, supra*, n. 113, 251.

298 Fredman, *Introduction, supra*, n. 1, 196.

299 See also the concluding observations of CRC/C, which took the position that states have an obligation to outlaw racial discrimination by private persons in education and employment. While this doctrine is not as elaborated as in terms of CERD, it is unlikely that this would imply a strict obligation of result.

300 CERD/C, General Recommendation No. 20 (1996), para. 5. See also CERD/C, General Recommendation No. 27 on discrimination against Roma, paras. 31–32.

private owners or admission to private clubs. In *Miroslav Lacko v. Slovakia* the CERD/C underscored that the state parties should have in place legislation expressly prohibiting non-discrimination in access to public premises, like restaurants.[301] Still the determination of the exact reach of the Convention in regard to private actors is far from finalized.[302]

It would seem though that this positive obligation would have implications for national criminal law provisions, in the sense that 'CERD contains specific provisions that make it mandatory for a state to criminalize racial discrimination'.[303] In this respect, reference can also be made to Article 4(b) which obliges state parties to declare illegal, and prohibit, organizations which promote and incite racial discrimination. Similarly, CERD contains an explicit obligation on the state to criminalize hate speech. In its views in the *Jewish Community of Oslo v. Norway* the Committee agrees with the complainants that the national legislation did not protect sufficiently against hate speech.[304] Arguably this implies that the state did not abide by its obligation to counter private discrimination adequately in this respect.

Both the text and the supervisory practice in terms of CEDAW seems to go (even) further and require states to address outright private discrimination in the personal sphere. Article 2 paragraph 1(e) CEDAW obliges state parties to take all appropriate measures to eliminate discrimination against women by any person, organization or enterprise. It has been argued in this respect that: '[a]rticle 2 thus imposes accountability on the state party for action by the private sector, private organizations or political parties.'[305]

The supervising Committee has confirmed and emphasized this seemingly far-reaching obligation to counter private discrimination in its General Recommendations. General Comment No. 19 on violence against women acknowledges that the definition of discrimination includes gender-based violence, and also takes up this state obligation to act against private forms of discrimination, at least in certain circumstances.[306] As is confirmed in

[301] CERD/C, *Miroslav Lacko v. Slovakia*, para. 3.4.

[302] Boyle and Baldaccini, *A Critical Evaluation of, supra*, n. 252, 159.

[303] Vandenhole, *UN Human Rights Treaty Bodies, supra*, n. 50, 43.

[304] CERD/C, *The Jewish Community of Oslo v. Norway* (Communication 30/2003, 15 August 2005), paras. 10.1–12.

[305] Vandenhole, *UN Human Rights Treaty Bodies, supra*, n. 50, 246. CEDAW's General Comment No. 23 on public and political life seems to limit this obligation to take appropriate measures to counter private discrimination to activities of 'organizations like political parties' (para. 42), but this focus on the latter type of organization could also be explained by the specific subject matter of this particular General Comment.

[306] CEDAW/C, General Comment No. 19, para. 9.

CEDAW/C's views in *A.T. v. Hungary*, General Recommendation No. 19 addresses the question of whether state parties can be held accountable for the conduct of non-state actors in stating that:

> discrimination under the Convention is not restricted to action by or on behalf of Governments . . . under general international law and specific human rights covenants, States may also be responsible for private acts if they fail to act with due diligence to prevent violations of rights or to investigate and punish acts of violence.[307]

In this view the Committee gives an indication of relevant factors to be taken into account when evaluating when, in a specific case, the state has sufficiently prevented violence against women. States should adopt specific legislation to combat domestic violence, and sexual harassment; and there should be protection or exclusion orders available, and shelters should exist, for the immediate protection of women victims of domestic violence.[308]

Similar far-reaching positive state obligations to eradicate private forms of discrimination can be found in General Recommendation No. 23 (1997) on Political and Public life, which explicitly states that:

> state parties are under an obligation to take all appropriate measures, including the enactment of appropriate legislation that complies with their Constitution, to ensure that organizations such as political parties and trade unions, which may not be subject directly to obligations under the Convention, do not discriminate against women and respect the principles contained in articles 7 and 8.[309]

While there is clearly an obligation on states to prevent, and protect women from, gender discrimination by private actors, this is arguably not an absolute obligation, leaving open the question of its exact scope and reach.

Similarly, in its General Recommendation No. 25 CEDAW/C underscores that state parties are under an 'obligation . . . to ensure that there is no direct or indirect discrimination against women . . . committed by . . . private individuals—in the public as well as the private spheres'.[310] The same document also refers to a state obligation to take measures to 'accelerate the modification of cultural practices and stereotypical attitudes and behaviour that discriminate against or are disadvantageous for women'.[311] This obviously sets out to reach deep into the private domain and interactions between private individuals. Bayefski emphasizes in this respect that the practice under this

[307] CEDAW/C, *AT v. Hungary*, (Communication 2/2003, 26 January 2005), para. 9.2.
[308] *Ibid.*, para. 9.3.
[309] CEDAW/C, General Comment No. 25, para. 42.
[310] CEDAW/C, General Recommendation No. 25, para. 7.
[311] *Ibid.*, para. 38.

convention has revealed that obligations on the part of the state 'extend to inhibiting private actors from interfering with rights, actors such as husbands, partners or employers'.[312] However, it is not clear how far this obligation would reach in specific circumstances: it seems unlikely that it would be a strict obligation of result.

In terms of the ECHR and the jurisprudence of the Court, it is not really clear whether (and to what extent) there would be a positive obligation on states to eradicate private forms of discrimination. While the existence of such positive obligations could be argued, in line with similar developments in relation to other articles of the Convention, so far the Court has never explicitly deduced such positive obligations from Article 14. This can be related to the generally broad margin of appreciation allowed to states in regard to the prohibition of discrimination. On the other hand, in relation to those grounds of discrimination that are considered to be 'suspect', it cannot be excluded that in the future the Court will indeed identify positive state obligations to eradicate discrimination on these grounds in the private sphere also.[313] The twelfth Additional Protocol was not intended to impose a general positive obligation to this effect.[314] Nevertheless, the Explanatory Report clarifies that this could be the case in specific circumstances, since 'a failure to provide protection from discrimination in [private] relations may be so clear-cut and grave that it might engage clearly the responsibility of the State and then Article 1 of the Protocol could come into play'.[315] It will be interesting to see throughout the development of jurisprudence in this regard, where the line will be drawn.

III. Conclusion

The starting points in relation to minority protection on the one hand and the prohibition of non-discrimination and the equality principle on the other hand are that substantive equality (as opposed to mere formal equality) is an essential goal of minority protection while the prohibition of discrimination is a *conditio sine qua non* for adequate minority protection. This already makes clear that it is important to analyze how the prohibition of discrimination is being interpreted and applied by the supervisory organs. In this respect the

[312] AF Bayefski, 'CEDAW: Threat to or Enhancement of Human Rights?', *ASIL Proceedings* (2000), 197. See also Vandenhole, *UN Human Rights Treaty Bodies, supra*, n. 50, 79.

[313] Goedertier, *Verbod van discriminatie, supra*, n. 54, 146–8.

[314] Explanatory Report to the 12th AP, nr 24.

[315] *Ibid.*, no. 26.

previous discussion has clarified that the practice of several bodies has revealed openings towards substantive equality in regard to indirect discrimination, the obligation to adopt special measures, and the approach towards affirmative action measures. Furthermore, classifications on the basis of typical minority identity features like race, ethnicity and religion, have often received heightened scrutiny, enhancing the effective protection against discrimination on these grounds. Similarly, the approach taken by the supervisory bodies in regard to the required burden of proof for the claimant, and the related distribution of proof, has engendered certain developments amounting to enhanced levels of actual protection against discrimination. Finally, the reach of the state obligation to eradicate private forms of discrimination is also important to evaluate the effective levels of protection against discrimination and also in this respect, various extensions have been identified.

Nevertheless, it is equally clear that these positive developments have not been equally strong or consistent for all supervisory organs. First of all, it should be remembered that few supervisory bodies have the power to pronounce legally binding judgments. Secondly, the above analysis has revealed that there are great divergencies as to the degree of sophistication (of the equality law) reached. In any event, neither the most advanced systems nor those which result in legally binding judgments are necessarily the most protective in regard to discrimination. In this regard it should be highlighted that the issue-specific conventions, like CEDAW and CERD, while not having very sophisticated doctrines in terms of equality and non-discrimination, nor the power to pronounce legally binding judgments, tend to be more victim-oriented, and most demanding in relation to state obligations in terms of the prohibition of discrimination and the equality principle. Be that as it may, it is difficult to deny that there are across the board on-going developments mostly tending towards higher levels of protection against discrimination. However, there are lingering problematic stances in regard to the concept of indirect discrimination (by the ECtHR), the acceptability of affirmative action (especially for the ECJ), and the establishment of the distribution of the burden of proof.

In this sense, a lot remains to be done.

EXPRESSION, ASSEMBLY, ASSOCIATION

Geoff Gilbert

I. General Introduction

Classically, international human rights law protects the individual. As such, minority rights are rights for persons belonging to minority groups rather than the minority itself. Nevertheless, the right to freedom of expression, that is, the 'freedom to hold opinions without interference and to seek, receive and impart information and ideas through any media and regardless of frontiers',[1] is almost wholly redundant unless one can make use of it in relation to some other person. Thus, it allows members of linguistic minorities to use their own language when communicating with each other.[2] Equally, freedom of peaceful assembly is somewhat pointless if exercised alone. Most significantly for minorities, freedom of association is a right for individuals to act in community with each

[1] Article 19, Universal Declaration of Human Rights, 1948.

[2] How far it allows for use of one's mother tongue in all public situations, such as when seeking services from state administrative authorities, is not clear—see below.

other. Some would argue that minority rights are, in fact, no more than the joint exercise of human rights by individuals acting in association with each other.[3] It is, however, the contention of this chapter that the international law pertaining to minority rights is more than the sum total of the rights of the persons belonging to the minority group.

II. Content of the Rights

A. Historical and Theoretical Background of the Rights and Delineation of the Content

1. Freedom of Expression

Freedom of expression is fundamental to the exercise and enjoyment of many other rights,[4] and it is not surprising that it can be found in domestic documents dating back to the seventeenth century.[5] Moreover, the Minorities Treaties concluded after World War I,[6] designed to protect persons belonging to minority groups in the newly created states of Central and Eastern Europe and the Balkans, contained clauses that guaranteed elements of freedom of expression:

> Article 7.... No restriction shall be imposed on the free use by any Czecho-Slovak national of any language in private intercourse, in commerce, in religion, in the press or publications of any kind, or at public meetings.[7]

[3] See generally, Nigel S. Rodley, 'Conceptual Problems in the Protection of Minorities—International Legal Developments', *HRQ*, 17 (1995), 48–71 and J. Packer, 'On the Definition of Minorities', in J. Packer and K. Myntti, *The Protection of Ethnic and Linguistic Minorities in Europe* (Turku/Åbo, 1993), 23–65 at 58.

[4] The United Nations General Assembly Resolution 59(I), 1946, declared it to be 'a fundamental human right and a touchstone of all other freedoms to which the United Nations is consecrated'. Cited by Lauri Hannikainen and Kristian Myntti 'Article 19', in A. Eide, G. Alfredsson et al (eds.), *The Universal Declaration of Human Rights: A Commentary* (Oslo, 1992), 273–85 at 274.

[5] See the English Bill of Rights of 1688, 1 Will. & Mar. sess.2, c.2.

> 'Freedom of speech—That the freedome of speech and debates or proceedings in Parlyament ought not to be impeached or questioned in any court or place out of Parlyament.'

> See also, the United States Bill of Rights, First Amendment, 1791.

> 'Congress shall make no law respecting an establishment of religion, or prohibiting the free exercise thereof; or abridging the freedom of speech, or of the press; or the right of the people peaceably to assemble, and to petition the government for a redress of grievances.'

[6] See, for example, the Treaty of Versailles with respect to Poland (UKTS 8 (1919), Cmd 223); the Treaty of St Germain with Czechoslovakia, 1919 (UKTS 20 (1919), Cmd 479); the Treaty of St Germain with the Serb Croat-Slovene state, 1919 (UKTS 17 (1919), Cmd 461); and the Treaty of Trianon with Hungary, 1920 (UKTS 10 (1920), Cmd 896). For a full list, see the Commission on Human Rights, Study of the Legal Validity of the Undertakings Concerning Minorities, E/CN.4/367, 7 April 1950, Geneva, at pp. 2–3.

[7] Treaty of St Germain, *supra,* n. 6.

The first universal statement relating to freedom of expression is found in Article 19 of the Universal Declaration of Human Rights, 1948:

> Article 19—Everyone has the right to freedom of opinion and expression: this right includes freedom to hold opinions without interference and to seek, receive and impart information and ideas through any media and regardless of frontiers.

It is designed to promote a free flow of information without any hindrances. For the purposes of this analysis, however, it is important that the right is seen to entail a requirement that the communication might be in the mother tongue of a member of the minority group. Equally, that receiving and imparting information and ideas should take place regardless of frontiers—in the case of minority groups, they should have free access to information and ideas from any kin-state.

2. *Freedom of Assembly*

Freedom of assembly is one of the other fundamental political rights. The first thing to note is that apart from the African Charter on Human and Peoples' Rights, all international instruments require that it be exercised peacefully. It is often found in the same article as freedom of association,[8] but it is equally closely associated with freedom of expression. Like expression, though, it is not limited to political activities, and freedom of peaceful assembly is relevant to any group of individuals who need to come together for a purpose, such as exercising their freedom of religion. Its roots in the protection of Trade Unions are but part of a much broader guarantee of rights for the individual in community with others. From the outset, freedom of assembly has included the idea that the assembled group could march and demonstrate, especially when read with the right to freedom of expression.

3. *Freedom of Association*

While assembly and association are very closely related rights, in the area of minority rights association has a much more substantive role to play. In the absence of a minority rights provision in any international or regional human rights convention,[9] freedom of association has fundamental

[8] Article 20 of the Universal Declaration of Human Rights, 1948.

> Article 20 1. Everyone has the right to freedom of peaceful assembly and association. Cf. Articles 21 and 22 of the International Covenant on Civil and Political Rights.

[9] Article 27 of the International Covenant on Civil and Political Rights is a right for persons belonging to minorities, not for the minority group:

> 'In those States in which ethnic, religious or linguistic minorities exist, *persons belonging to such minorities* shall not be denied the right, in community with the other members of their group, to

importance for the minority group. Vis-à-vis the state, individuals can use their freedom of association in order to preserve and protect the group. Under the WWI Minorities Treaties, the Permanent Court of International Justice addressed the identity of community issue in the *Greco-Bulgarian Communities* case.

[A community] is a group of persons living in a given country or locality having a race, religion, language and tradition of their own[10] and *united by this identity of race, religion, language and tradition in a sentiment of solidarity*, with a view to preserving their traditions, maintaining their form of worship, ensuring the instruction and upbringing of their children in accordance with the spirit and tradition of their race and rendering mutual assistance to each other.[11]

The Minorities Treaties themselves were all in a similar format and contained a clause that provided an equitable share of public funds for minorities where there was 'a considerable proportion' of the minority population in the town or district.[12] Thus, effective freedom of association has been seen as central from the outset of international minority group protection. Subsequently, the non-legally binding Copenhagen Document[13] of the then Conference on Security and Cooperation in Europe[14] was to make freedom of association the lynchpin of the guarantees for national minorities.

Paragraph *(32)* To belong to a national minority is a matter of a person's individual choice and no disadvantage may arise from the exercise of such choice.

Persons belonging to national minorities have the right freely to express, preserve and develop their ethnic, cultural, linguistic or religious identity and to maintain and develop their culture in all its aspects, free of any attempts at assimilation against their will. In particular, they have the right

(32.1)–to use freely their mother tongue in private as well as in public;

(32.2)–to establish and maintain their own educational, cultural and religious institutions, organizations or associations, which can seek voluntary financial and other contributions as well as public assistance, in conformity with national legislation;

enjoy their own culture, to profess and practise their own religion, or to use their own language.' (emphasis added).

10 The list is disjunctive.

11 PCIJ, Series B, Nos 17, 19, 21, 22 & 33 (emphasis added).

12 eg Article 9 of the Treaty of St Germain with Czecho-Slovakia, *supra*, n. 6.

13 OSCE (CHD) Copenhagen Document, 11 HRLJ 232 (1990), and Buergenthal, 'A New Public Order for Europe', *HRLJ*, 11 (1990), 217.

14 Now Organization for Security and Cooperation in Europe.

(32.3)–to profess and practise their religion, including the acquisition, possession and use of religious materials, and to conduct religious educational activities in their mother tongue;

(32.4)–to establish and maintain unimpeded contacts among themselves within their country as well as contacts across frontiers with citizens of other States with whom they share a common ethnic or national origin, cultural heritage or religious beliefs;

(32.5)–to disseminate, have access to and exchange information in their mother tongue;

(32.6)–to establish and maintain organizations or associations within their country and to participate in international non-governmental organizations.

Persons belonging to national minorities can exercise and enjoy their rights individually as well as in community with other members of their group. No disadvantage may arise for a person belonging to a national minority on account of the exercise or non-exercise of any such rights.

There cannot be a minority group without the right of persons belonging to the minority group to associate freely. Implicit in that idea, of course, is that every member is free not to associate—the preservation of the minority group is a voluntary act and everyone has the right not to belong. Indeed, the above raises the parallel issues of non-assimilation of the minority group by the majority, of persons belonging to the group being able to leave it,[15] and of voluntary assimilation into the majority by those who do wish to shed their minority status.

B. Analysis of the Existence of the Rights in Different Regional and International Documents

1. *Freedom of Expression*

As one might expect for such a fundamental right, freedom of expression is found in all international and regional human rights treaties and in very similar format.[16] Nevertheless, there are subtle differences. The foundational document, the Universal Declaration, as discussed above, talks of freedom of opinion and expression in Article 19. Article 19 of the International Covenant

[15] For instance, it should be possible for a member of a particular religious minority to convert to another faith or simply deny their faith without any adverse consequences in relation to the minority group other than that they are no longer members.

[16] See Article 19 UDHR, Article 19 CCPR, Article 9 ACHPR, Article 13 ACHR, Article 10 ECHR. Moreover, given that the UDHR is not a legally binding document, it is worth also including Paras. 32.1, 32.4, 32.5, 33, and 34 of the Copenhagen Document.

on Civil and Political Rights separates opinion and expression into different sub-paragraphs. More significantly, Article 19.3 imposes duties on those claiming freedom of expression:

3. The exercise of the rights provided for in paragraph 2 of this article carries with it special duties and responsibilities. It may therefore be subject to certain restrictions, but these shall only be such as are provided by law and are necessary:

(a) For respect of the rights or reputations of others;
(b) For the protection of national security or of public order (*ordre public*), or of public health or morals.[17]

While the content of the restriction is understandable, the potential for states to limit the rights of persons belonging to minorities to freedom of expression is clearly present, and treaty bodies need to be vigilant so as to apply this limitation restrictively.[18] Equally though, it would allow the state to limit freedom of expression in the interest of the rights or reputation of persons belonging to minorities or where it would be in in the interests of public order. While only

[17] See also Article 29 of the UDHR.

[18] See Human Rights Committee, General Comment 10, Article 19 (Nineteenth session, 1983), Compilation of General Comments and General Recommendations Adopted by Human Rights Treaty Bodies, UN Doc. HRI/GEN/1/Rev.1 at 11 (1994), para. 4.

> 4. Paragraph 3 expressly stresses that the exercise of the right to freedom of expression carries with it special duties and responsibilities and for this reason certain restrictions on the right are permitted which may relate either to the interests of other persons or to those of the community as a whole. However, when a State party imposes certain restrictions on the exercise of freedom of expression, these may not put in jeopardy the right itself. Paragraph 3 lays down conditions and it is only subject to these conditions that restrictions may be imposed: the restrictions must be 'provided by law'; they may only be imposed for one of the purposes set out in subparagraphs (a) and (b) of paragraph 3; and they must be justified as being 'necessary' for that State party for one of those purposes.

Under the similarly phrased Article 10 ECHR, see, for example, *Arslan v. Turkey* 23462/94; *Baskaya & Okçuoglu v. Turkey* 23536 & 24408/94; *Ceylan v. Turkey* 23556/94; *Erdogdu & Ince v. Turkey* 25067 & 25068/94; *Gerger v. Turkey* 24919/94; *Karatas v. Turkey* 23168/94; *Okçuoglu v. Turkey* 24246/94; *Polat v. Turkey* 23500/94; *Sürek & Özdemir v. Turkey* 23927 & 24277/94; *Sürek v. Turkey (No. 1)* 26682/95; *Sürek v. Turkey (No. 2)* 24122/94; *Sürek v. Turkey (No. 3)* 24735/94; & *Sürek v. Turkey (No. 4)* 242762/94: (Grand Chamber), all 8 July 1999. See also, *Marsali v. Turkey* 40077/98, ECtHR (Second Chamber), 9 November 2004; *Mehdi Zana v. Turkey* 26982/95, ECtHR (Second Chamber), 6 April 2004; *Sener v. Turkey* 26680/95, ECtHR (Third Chamber), 18 July 2000; *Özler v. Turkey* 25753/94, ECtHR (Third Chamber), 11 July 2002 (Friendly Settlement); Committee of Ministers, *Resolution ResDH(2006)79, Execution of the judgments of the European Court of Human Rights delivered between 8/07/1999 and 27/09/2005 in 32 cases against Turkey concerning freedom of expression following convictions under former Article 8 of the Law against Terrorism No. 3713*, 20 December 2006; Committee of Ministers, *Resolution CM/ResDH(2007)20, concerning the judgments of the European Court of Human Rights delivered between 11 July 2002 and 2 October 2003 (Friendly settlements) in 6 cases against Turkey (see Appendix) relating to freedom of expression*, 28 February 2007.

individuals can bring complaints under the first Optional Protocol, the individual can represent the group.[19]

In addition, Article 20 CCPR has more than usual significance for freedom of expression with respect to minority groups. It provides in sub-paragraph 2 that '[any] advocacy of national, racial or religious hatred that constitutes incitement to discrimination, hostility or violence shall be prohibited by law'. As such, states have an obligation to outlaw hate speech against minority groups and their members, although it need not be criminalized, merely prohibited. The link with Article 26 CCPR and freedom from discrimination also needs to be noted.[20]

Turning to the regional conventions, Article 9.2 of the African Charter on Human and Peoples' Rights contains unfortunate wording. The right to express and disseminate opinions has to be 'within the law'. For the right to be effective, such law must be 'necessary for respect of the rights or reputations of others, [or] for the protection of national security or of public order (*ordre public*), or of public health or morals', to borrow the language of the CCPR.[21] The American Convention on Human Rights, referring in Article 13 to freedom of thought and expression, goes on to provide that there can be no prior censorship, only subsequent liability. Furthermore, Article 13.5 takes the ideas found in Articles 20.2 and 26 CCPR and obliges states to make the activities punishable offences.[22] Article 14 grants victims of inaccuracies a right of reply: since Article 44 permits groups of persons to lodge petitions with the Inter-American Commission of Human Rights, Articles 13 and 14

[19] See *Chief Bernard Ominayak and the Lubicon Lake Band v. Canada*, Communication No. 167/1984, UN Doc. CCPR/C/38/D/167/1984 (1990) at paras. 13.3 and 13.4.

[20] Article 26:

> All persons are equal before the law and are entitled without any discrimination to the equal protection of the law. In this respect, the law shall prohibit any discrimination and guarantee to all persons equal and effective protection against discrimination on any ground such as race, colour, sex, language, religion, political or other opinion, national or social origin, property, birth or other status.

See generally, Karl Josef Partsch, 'Freedom of Conscience and Expression, and Political Freedoms', in Louis Henkin (ed.), *The International Bill of Rights* (New York, 1981), 207–45, at 228–30.

[21] See *Media Rights Agenda, Constitutional Rights Project, Media Rights Agenda and Constitutional Rights Project vs Nigeria*, Comm. No. 105/93, 128/94,130/94, 152/96, not dated, at paras. 66 *et seq.*, discussed below.

[22] Article 13:

> 5. Any propaganda for war and any advocacy of national, racial, or religious hatred that constitute incitements to lawless violence or to any other similar action against any person or group of persons on any grounds including those of race, colour, religion, language, or national origin shall be considered as offences punishable by law.

can be utilized by minority groups in the Americas. Finally, Article 10 of the European Convention for the Protection of Human Rights and Fundamental Freedoms establishes freedom of expression in the following terms:

Article 10—Freedom of expression

1 Everyone has the right to freedom of expression. This right shall include freedom to hold opinions and to receive and impart information and ideas without interference by public authority and regardless of frontiers. This article shall not prevent States from requiring the licensing of broadcasting, television or cinema enterprises.

2 The exercise of these freedoms, since it carries with it duties and responsibilities, may be subject to such formalities, conditions, restrictions or penalties as are prescribed by law and are necessary in a democratic society, in the interests of national security, territorial integrity or public safety, for the prevention of disorder or crime, for the protection of health or morals, for the protection of the reputation or rights of others, for preventing the disclosure of information received in confidence, or for maintaining the authority and impartiality of the judiciary.

The limitations on the right set out in sub-paragraph 2 are the most extensive among the various conventions, but equally need to be recognized as an exhaustive list that must be interpreted restrictively. Moreover, there is extensive Strasbourg jurisprudence relating to the implementation of Article 10.

Beyond the human rights machinery, the Council of Europe's Parliamentary Assembly promulgated Recommendation 1589, Freedom of expression in the media in Europe, in 2003. That sets out in Paragraph 17(vi) that member states, where appropriate, ought 'to abolish restrictions on the establishment and functioning of private media broadcasting in minority languages'. The Kampala Declaration on Intellectual Freedom and Social Responsibility[23] of 1990 has general relevance to the freedom of expression of academics and intellectuals in Africa. Again as regards hortatory documents, Article 19, the international NGO on freedom of expression, amongst others, produced the Johannesburg Principles in 1995.[24] Of interest are Principle 4[25] dealing

[23] Arising out of a symposium on the topic, 29 November 1990—http://www1.umn.edu/humanrts/africa/KAMDOK.htm.

[24] The Johannesburg Principles on National Security, Freedom of Expression and Access to Information, Annex to UN Doc. E/CN.4/1996/39 (1996), submitted to the Commission of Human Rights by the UN special rapporteur on the promotion and protection of the right to freedom of opinion and expression. The Principles were adopted on 1 October 1995 by a group of experts in international law, national security, and human rights convened by Article 19, the International Centre Against Censorship, in collaboration with the Centre for Applied Legal Studies of the University of the Witwatersrand, in Johannesburg.

[25] Principle 4 Prohibition of Discrimination: In no case may a restriction on freedom of expression or information, including on the ground of national security, involve discrimination based on

with non-discrimination, Principle 7[26] on what does not constitute a threat to national security, a ground often cited to limit freedom of expression, Principle 10[27] that requires the state to take measures to prevent interference by third parties, and particularly Principle 9[28] that covers expression in the language of a national minority.

2. *Freedom of Assembly*

Article 20 UDHR provides for the right to freedom of peaceful assembly. The International Covenant on Civil and Political Rights speaks of the right of peaceful assembly being 'recognized' in Article 21. The language suggests that the right already existed under customary international law prior to its inclusion in the Covenant.[29] Article 21 does, however, make it clear that the exercise of the right can be limited.[30] The regional instruments reflect similar themes,[31] although Article 11 of the African Charter does not include the word 'peaceful'.

race, colour, sex, language, religion, political or other opinion, national or social origin, nationality, property, birth or other status.

[26] Principle 7 Protected Expression: (a) Subject to Principles 15 and 16, the peaceful exercise of the right to freedom of expression shall not be considered a threat to national security or subjected to any restrictions or penalties. Expression which shall not constitute a threat to national security includes, but is not limited to, expression that: (i) Advocates non-violent change of government policy or the Government itself.

[27] Principle 10 Unlawful Interference With Expression by Third Parties: Governments are obliged to take reasonable measures to prevent private groups or individuals from interfering unlawfully with the peaceful exercise of freedom of expression, even where the expression is critical of the government or its policies. In particular, governments are obliged to condemn unlawful actions aimed at silencing freedom of expression, and to investigate and bring to justice those responsible.

[28] Principle 9 Use of a Minority or Other Language: Expression, whether written or oral, can never be prohibited on the ground that it is in a particular language, especially the language of a national minority.

[29] See also, Article 27:

> In those States in which ethnic, religious or linguistic minorities exist, persons belonging to such minorities *shall not be denied the right*, in community with the other members of their group, to enjoy their own culture, to profess and practise their own religion, or to use their own language. (emphasis added)

[30] Article 21:

> … No restrictions may be placed on the exercise of this right other than those imposed in conformity with the law and which are necessary in a democratic society in the interests of national security or public safety, public order (*ordre public*), the protection of public health or morals or the protection of the rights and freedoms of others.

[31] Article 11 ACHPR, Article 15 ACHR, and Article 11 ECHR.

3. *Freedom of Association*

The ideas underpinning freedom of association come out of the protection of trade unions. Since trade unionists were amongst the first to be persecuted in Nazi Germany, it is not surprising that the post-war human rights movement should seek to protect freedom of assembly. The International Labour Organization implicitly acknowledged that there were organizations other than those for workers and employers in member states in Convention No. 87 Concerning Freedom of Association and Protection of the Right to Organize, 1948.[32] ILO Convention No. 98 Concerning the Application of the Right to Organize and to Bargain Collectively, 1949,[33] is imbued with the idea that organizations should be free from state control, an issue that is important for minority groups as well as trade unions and employers' organizations. The UDHR provides that everyone has the right to freedom of association and freedom from compulsory membership of an association. Article 22 CCPR is explicitly broader than mere membership of trade unions, since that particular aspect of the right is set out as but one example.[34]

The regional instruments also extend freedom of association beyond trade unions. Article 10 of the African Charter of Human and Peoples' Rights is, though, open to restrictive application by states: 'Every individual shall have the right to free association *provided that he abides by the law*' (emphasis added). As with the other instruments, such laws ought to be necessary in a democratic society.[35] Article16 of the American Convention provides a non-exhaustive list of reasons for associating that would cover minority groups.

[32] 68 UNTS 17, entered into force July 4, 1950.

Article 8:

1. In exercising the rights provided for in this Convention workers and employers and their respective organisations, like other persons or organised collectivities, shall respect the law of the land.
2. The law of the land shall not be such as to impair, nor shall it be so applied as to impair, the guarantees provided for in this Convention.

[33] 96 UNTS 257, entered into force July 18, 1951.

[34] Sub-para. 3 makes explicit reference to parallel ILO obligations. See also, Article 8 of the CESCR that also deals with the right to form trades unions.

[35] See for example, Article 11 ECHR:

1 Everyone has the right to freedom of peaceful assembly and to freedom of association with others, including the right to form and to join trade unions for the protection of his interests.

2 No restrictions shall be placed on the exercise of these rights other than such as are prescribed by law and are necessary in a democratic society in the interests of national security or public safety, for the prevention of disorder or crime, for the protection of health or morals or for the protection of the rights and freedoms of others. This article shall not prevent the imposition of lawful restrictions on the exercise of these rights by members of the armed forces, of the police or of the administration of the State.

Article 16. Freedom of Association

1. Everyone has the right to associate freely for ideological, religious, political, economic, labour, social, cultural, sports, or other purposes.

C. State Duties

In relation to all three rights, in so far as they relate to minority groups, the various international conventions impose both negative and positive duties. As the jurisprudence makes clear, not only must the state refrain from interfering in the individual's enjoyment of the rights to freedom of expression, assembly, and association, except to the extent permitted by the relevant provision, it also has positive obligations to ensure that those rights can be exercised by individuals, even if this requires it to regulate the behaviour of others.[36] For instance, the right to assemble and to march may entail restricting those who would seek to prevent the march or demonstration.[37]

III. Analysis of Case Law

It would never be possible to place any analysis of the case law from so many different treaty bodies, and over such a long time period, particularly in the case of the European Court of Human Rights and the former European Commission of Human Rights, into clearly defined 'boxes'. It is the nature of case law that it ebbs and flows, and that it is susceptible to analysis only on its own terms, not with respect to so many different parameters: treaty, region,

See *Media Rights Agenda, Constitutional Rights Project, Media Rights Agenda and Constitutional Rights Project vs Nigeria*, Comm. No. 105/93, 128/94,130/94, 152/96, not dated, para. 66, discussed below.

[36] See *Ozgür Gündem v. Turkey* 23144/93, ECtHR (Grand Chamber) 16 March 2000, at para. 43.

[37] See *Plattform 'Ärtze für das Leben' v. Austria* Series A, vol. 139:

> 30. In its decision of 17 October 1985 on admissibility, the Commission dealt at length with the question whether Article 11 . . . impliedly required the State to protect demonstrations from those wishing to interfere with or disrupt them. It answered this question in the affirmative.
> 31. The Court does not have to develop a general theory of the positive obligations which may flow from the Convention, but before ruling on the arguability of the applicant association's claim it has to give an interpretation of Article 11 . . . .
> 32. . . . Genuine, effective freedom of peaceful assembly cannot, therefore, be reduced to a mere duty on the part of the State not to interfere: a purely negative conception would not be compatible with the object and purpose of Article 11 . . . . Like Article 8 . . . , Article 11 . . . sometimes requires positive measures to be taken, even in the sphere of relations between individuals, if need be . . . .

See also, *UMO Ilinden and Ivanov v. Bulgaria* 44079/98, ECtHR (First Chamber) 20 October 2005, at para. 115.

nature of the body. Trends and developments can be discerned and individual decisions or approaches can be critiqued, but ultimately it is an analysis of principles that bodies may use in reaching their conclusions that can be produced.

A. Freedom of Expression

1. Content of the Right

Freedom of expression is very broad, including speech, newspapers, magazines, books, academic monographs, poetry, radio, television, video, advertising, and works of art.[38]

2. An Essential Aspect of Democracy

The various treaty bodies have stated that freedom of expression is essential. According to the African Commission of Human Rights in *Amnesty International v. Zambia*:

> 54. (...) This provision of the Charter [right to express and disseminate opinions: Art. 9(2)] reflects the fact that freedom of expression is a fundamental human right, essential to an individual's personal development, political consciousness and participation in the public affairs of his country.[39]

It reiterated this view in *Media Rights Agenda, Constitutional Rights Project, Media Rights Agenda and Constitutional Rights Project v. Nigeria*:

> 54. This Article [Art. 9] reflects the fact that freedom of expression is a basic human right, vital to an individual's personal development, his political consciousness, and participation in the conduct of public affairs in his country.[40]

The European Court of Human Rights reached a similar conclusion in *Arslan v. Turkey*:

> 44.... Freedom of expression constitutes one of the essential foundations of a democratic society and one of the basic conditions for its progress and for each individual's self-fulfilment.[41]

[38] Although it does not include defacing road signs written in the national language rather than the language of the region—*G.B. v. France* Communication No. 348/1989, UN Doc. CCPR/C/43/D/348/1989 (1991): '5.2 The Committee observes that the defacing of roadsigns does not raise any issues under article 19'.

More abstractly, membership of a political party can be an exercise of one's freedom of expression. In *Vogt v. Germany*, 17851/91, ECtHR, 26 September 1995, it was held that dismissing someone for membership of the Communist Party violated his Art. 10 rights.

[39] Comm. No. 212/98, not dated, at para. 54.

[40] Comm. No. 105/93, 128/94,130/94, 152/96, not dated.

[41] 23462/94, ECtHR (Grand Chamber), 8 July 1999.

The Court expanded on this with respect to the central role of the press in *Ozgür Gündem v. Turkey*:

58. As these cases also concern measures against newspaper publications, they must equally be seen in the light of the essential role played by the press for ensuring the proper functioning of democracy (see, among many other authorities, the *Lingens v Austria* judgment of 8 July 1986, Series A no. 103, p. 26, § 41, and *Fressoz and Roire v France* [GC], 29183/95, § 45, ECHR 1999-I). While the press must not overstep the bounds set, *inter alia*, for the protection of the vital interests of the State, such as the protection of national security or territorial integrity against the threat of violence or the prevention of disorder or crime, it is nevertheless incumbent on the press to convey information and ideas on political issues, even divisive ones. Not only has the press the task of imparting such information and ideas; the public has a right to receive them. Freedom of the press affords the public one of the best means of discovering and forming an opinion of the ideas and attitudes of political leaders (see the *Lingens* judgment cited above, p. 26, §§ 41–42).[42]

Given that effective participation by minority groups is essential for true democracy in a multiethnic state, freedom of expression in its fullest extent is part of that process of representative inclusion.

A further element with respect to democracy is that freedom of expression must allow for strong criticism of the government. Again, *Ozgür Gündem* sets out the basic position (para. 60): 'The authorities of a democratic State must tolerate criticism, even if it may be regarded as provocative or insulting'.[43] Furthermore, the language used can be strong and even offensive. Paragraph 49 of *Handyside v. United Kingdom*[44] laid down the parameters:

The Court's supervisory functions oblige it to pay the utmost attention to the principles characterising a 'democratic society'. Freedom of expression constitutes one of the essential foundations of such a society, one of the basic conditions for its progress and for the development of every man. Subject to paragraph 2 of Article 10 . . . , *it is*

[42] 23144/93, ECtHR (Grand Chamber) 16 March 2000, at para. 58.

[43] See also, *Yazar, Karatas, Aksoy and the People's Labour Party v. Turkey* 22723/93, 22724/93, 22725/93, ECtHR, 9 April 2002.

59. . . . The Court reiterates in this connection that the limits of permissible criticism are wider with regard to the Government than in relation to a private citizen. In a democratic system the actions or omissions of the Government must be subject to the close scrutiny not only of the legislative and judicial authorities but also of the press and public opinion.

[44] Series A, Vol. 24, 1976. See also, *Arslan*

44. . . . Subject to paragraph 2 of Article 10, it is applicable not only to 'information' or 'ideas' that are favourably received or regarded as inoffensive or as a matter of indifference, but also to those that offend, shock or disturb. Such are the demands of that pluralism, tolerance and broadmindedness without which there is no 'democratic society'.

applicable not only to 'information' or 'ideas' that are favourably received or regarded as inoffensive or as a matter of indifference, but also to those that offend, shock or disturb the State or any sector of the population. Such are the demands of that pluralism, tolerance and broadmindedness without which there is no 'democratic society'. This means, amongst other things, that every 'formality', 'condition', 'restriction' or 'penalty' imposed in this sphere must be proportionate to the legitimate aim pursued. (emphasis added)

The Court has reiterated on several occasions that there cannot be democracy without pluralism.[45] That pluralism may well reflect a bitter history of division between the majority and the minority population.

[The author] asserts that the 'resistance' of the Kurdish people at Silopi announced the 'joyful news of the day when they would tear down the fortress of violence of Turkish chauvinism.... It is obvious that this was not a 'neutral' description of historical facts and that through his book the applicant intended to criticise the action of the Turkish authorities in the south-east of the country and to encourage the population concerned to oppose it. Furthermore, the undeniable virulence of the style confers a certain amount of vehemence to this criticism.

The European Court of Human Rights has recognized that freedom of expression is very important for politicians.[46] Combining the ideas that freedom of expression is fundamental to democracy and that strong language can be used to express ideas with freedom of assembly and association under Article 11 ECHR, the Court has given opposition political parties broad protection for their expression:

37. The Court reiterates that notwithstanding its autonomous role and particular sphere of application, Article 11 must also be considered in the light of Article 10. The protection of opinions and the freedom to express them is one of the objectives of the freedoms of assembly and association as enshrined in Article 11.... As the Court has

[45] *Affaire Refah Partisi (Parti de la Prospérité) et autres c. Turquie*, 41340/98, 41342/98, 41343/98, 41344/98, (Third Chamber), 31 July 2001, at para. 89; *Socialist Party v. Turkey*, ECtHR, 20/1997/804/1007, 25 May 1998, at para. 41; *Yazar, Karatas, Aksoy and the People's Labour Party v. Turkey* 22723/93, 22724/93, 22725/93, ECtHR, 9 April 2002, para. 46.

[46] See *Selim Sadak and Others v. Turkey*, 25144/94, 26149-26154/95, 27100/95, ECtHR, 16 June 2002:

34. The Court has already held that '(w)hile freedom of expression is important for everybody, it is especially so for an elected representative of the people. He represents his electorate, draws attention to their preoccupations and defends their interests. Accordingly, interferences with the freedom of expression of an opposition member of parliament... call for the closest scrutiny on the part of the Court' (see *Castells v. Spain*, judgment of 23 April 1992, Series A no. 236, § 42).

See also, *Affaire Feridun Yazar et autres c. Turquie* 42713/98, ECtHR (Third Chamber) 23 September 2004, at para. 29.

said many times, there can be no democracy without pluralism. It is for that reason that freedom of expression as enshrined in Article 10 is applicable, subject to paragraph 2, not only to 'information' or 'ideas' that are favourably received or regarded as inoffensive or as a matter of indifference, but also to those that offend, shock or disturb. *The fact that their activities form part of a collective exercise of freedom of expression in itself entitles political parties to seek the protection of Articles 10 and 11 of the Convention.*[47] (emphasis added)

On the other hand, in *McGuinness*,[48] an admissibility decision, newly elected members of the British Parliament had to swear an oath that they would bear faithful and true allegiance to the Queen and her heirs. As a member of Sinn Féin, a party dedicated to the principle that the Irish people have the right to self-determination, the applicant refused to take such an oath and fought the election knowing he would not be allowed to take his seat. However, after the election the Speaker of the House of Commons ruled he could have no access to the facilities of the House, including an office, staff allowances and research facilities. He complained of violations of Articles 10 (oath contrary to his political principles), 9 (oath contrary to his religion as a Roman Catholic, since the monarch can never be a Roman Catholic), 3 of Protocol 1 (the new ruling by the Speaker prevented him properly representing his constituents), 13 (no effective remedy) and 14 (discrimination). The Court held that freedom of expression is especially important for elected representatives of the people. Nevertheless, the restriction in paragraph 2 of Article 10 relating to the 'protection of the rights of others' could extend to the protection of effective democracy:[49]

In its view, this term must equally extend to the protection of the constitutional principles which underpin a democracy. It notes that the requirement in the respondent State that elected representatives take an oath of allegiance to the monarch is incorporated in a legal rule dating back to 1866. This rule forms part of the constitutional system of the respondent State, which, it is to be observed, is based on a monarchical model of government. For the Court, the requirement that elected representatives to the House of Commons take an oath of allegiance to the reigning monarch can be reasonably viewed as an affirmation of loyalty to the constitutional principles which support, *inter alia*, the workings of representative democracy in the respondent State.... In the Court's view it must be open to the respondent State to attach such a condition, which is an integral part of its constitutional order, to membership of

[47] *Freedom and Democracy Party (ÖZDEP) v. Turkey*, 23885/94, ECtHR (Grand Chamber), 8 December 1999.

[48] 39511/98, ECtHR (Third Chamber), 8 June 1999.

[49] See *Ahmed v. United Kingdom*, ECtHR, 2 September 1998, at para. 52.

Parliament and to make access to the institution's facilities dependent on compliance with the condition.

...

The Court observes that the oath requirement and the terms of the Speaker's Statement applied to all elected representatives without distinction. While the effects of these measures may have weighed more heavily on Sinn Féin members this is to be explained in terms of that party's own official policy on the oath requirement. The Court also recalls that in the context of the applicant's complaint under Article 10 of the Convention it found that the measures at issue could be considered a proportionate response taken in furtherance of a legitimate aim. That reasoning equally serves to lead it to conclude that there is no appearance of a violation of [Art. 14] either.[50]

The entire complaint was dismissed as inadmissible as manifestly ill-founded. Much seemed to turn on the fact that the applicant was not required to swear or affirm allegiance to a particular religion, that he would be able to retain his republican views and pursue them in Parliament, and that he and his electors had known throughout that as a matter of principle he would never be allowed to sit in Parliament if elected.[51]

3. Use of Mother Tongue

Implicit in freedom of expression is the idea that the expression can be in the mother tongue of the speaker and her/his audience, an aspect of the right that is of central importance to persons belonging to minority groups. In private, this can never be an issue, but the question is how far a state must provide mother-tongue facilities in public settings. For linguistic minorities, this may be a major concern. The United Nations Human Rights Committee in *Singer v. Canada*[52] held that while a state could choose an official language, it could not impose restrictions on the use in the private sphere of other languages:

3. The author contends that Bill No. 101, as amended by Bill No. 178, is discriminatory, in that it restricts the use of English to indoor advertising and places businesses that carry out their activities in English in a disadvantageous position vis-à-vis French businesses....

12.2 Concerning the question of whether section 58 of Bill No. 101, as amended by Bill No. 178, section 1, violated Mr. Singer's right, under article 19 of the Covenant, to freedom of expression, the Committee, having concluded that a State party to the

[50] *Supra* n 48, para. 1 and 4.

[51] It seems the Court accepted that one can waive some rights to some extent. However, while Sinn Féin supporters can be assumed to have acquiesced in their loss of representation, a Member of Parliament represents all her/his constituents and those voting for other parties definitely did not agree that they should have no MP if their candidate lost.

[52] Communication No. 455/1991, UN Doc. CCPR/C/51/D/455/1991 (1994).

Covenant may choose one or more official languages, but that it may not exclude, outside the spheres of public life, the freedom to express oneself in a language of one's choice, finds that there has been a violation of article 19, paragraph 2.

However, in another communication the Committee rejected an argument that the discouragement of teaching Breton interfered with the applicant's freedom of expression.[53] The Strasbourg organs of the ECHR have been equally restrictive towards the use of mother-tongue in an educational setting. It has held that there is no right to mother-tongue education under Articles 9, 10,[54] or Article 2 of Protocol 1,[55] except in very specific circumstances. In *Cyprus v. Turkey*[56] the Commission radically held that it might be a violation in certain circumstances to deny such education even at the secondary school level. However, one has to have regard to the particular situation in northern Cyprus: the prior existence of such schools and their abolition by the Turkish authorities; an international agreement (UN Doc. S/11789, Vienna, 31 July–2 August 1975) to allow the Greek Cypriot authorities to provide such education in the north, fulfilment of which the Turkish authorities prevented; and, the denial of the right to return to northern Cyprus of Greek Cypriot children who went to the southern part of the island for their education, even though by the time of the hearing this denial was limited to males over 16.

478.... However, education in [Turkish- or English-speaking] schools does not correspond to the needs of the persons concerned *who have the legitimate wish to preserve their own ethnic and cultural identity.* While it is true that Article 2 of Protocol No. 1 guarantees access only to existing educational facilities, it must be noted that in the present case such educational facilities have in fact existed in the past and have been abolished by the Turkish Cypriot authorities.... In the Commission's opinion the total absence of appropriate secondary schools for Greek Cypriots living in northern

[53] *R.L.M. v. France*, Communication No.363/1989, UN Doc.CCPR/C/44/D/363/1989 (1992):

2.2 In the author's opinion, the Rectorate of the Academy of Nantes (Rectorat de l'Académie de Nantes) has systematically discouraged and obstructed the teaching of Breton. ...

5.2 Concerning the author's claim under article 19, paragraph 2, the Committee observes that R.L.M. has failed to substantiate how his freedom of expression was violated by the French authorities policy *vis-à-vis* the teaching of Breton. In this respect, therefore, he has failed to advance a claim within the meaning of article 2 of the Optional Protocol.

[54] *23 Inhabitants of Alsemberg and Beersel v. Belgium*, 1474/62, 26 July 1963.

[55] *Case Relating to Certain Aspects of the Laws on the Use of Languages in Education in Belgium (Merits)*, Judgment of 23 July 1968, Series A, Vol. 6. See also, *Skender v. fYROM* 62059/00, ECtHR (Third Chamber), inadmissible, 10 March 2005.

[56] *Cyprus v. Turkey* 25781/94, European Commission of Human Rights, adopted on 4 June 1999, at paras. 474–79; ECtHR (Grand Chamber), 10 May 2001.

Cyprus cannot be compensated for either by the authorities' allowing the pupils concerned to attend such schools in southern Cyprus.... In these circumstances the practice of the Turkish Cypriot authorities amounts to a denial of the substance of the right to education. (emphasis added)

The Court upheld this reasoning: 'It cannot be maintained that the provision of secondary education in the south in keeping with the linguistic tradition of the enclaved Greek Cypriots suffices to fulfil the obligation laid down in Article 2 of Protocol No. 1, having regard to the impact of that option on family life'.[57] Accepting the peculiar situation that applies in northern Cyprus, these arguments may be of relevance wherever there is a slow decline in inter-communal relations between the state and the minority, and pre-existing domestic rights are withdrawn.

The Commission also held, though, that the vetting and non-approval of a substantial proportion of mother-tongue schoolbooks supplied by the kin-state for primary schoolchildren, even where there was no possibility for Greek Cypriots in the north to challenge these actions through the courts, was not a violation of Article 2 of Protocol 1. However, it was a breach of Article 10—even where the books might give the kin-state's view of history and culture, it was still for the respondent Government:

to show that the undisputed censorship or blocking of the books was done *in accordance with law* and pursued a legitimate aim, such as the prevention of disorder. It would then be for the respondent Government to show that the censorship measures were necessary in a democratic society.[58]

Beyond education, the Strasbourg organs have not been prepared to grant a right to use one's mother-tongue before administrative bodies.[59] Even where a state recognizes the linguistic differences of its population, it may not be possible to resolve all issues. The politics of language in Belgium subsequently gave rise to *Mathieu-Mohin and Clerfayt v. Belgium* before the European Court of Human Rights.[60] The facts were complex, but the language in which the elected representative took the oath when being sworn into Parliament determined on

[57] At para. 278; see also, para. 292.

[58] At para. 459—upheld by the Court at paras. 252 and 254 of its judgment.

[59] See *Fryske Nasjonale Partij and Others v. the Netherlands*, 11100/84, 12 December 1985, para. 3

However, the Commission recalls that these provisions do not guarantee 'linguistic freedom' as such. In particular, they do not guarantee the right to use the language of one's choice in administrative matters'; see also, *Georges Clerfayt, Pierre Legros et al. v. Belgium*, 10650/83, 17 May 1985.

[60] 9267/81, Series A, Vol. 113, (1988) 10 EHRR 1.

which regional council he would sit, and which language-bloc he would vote with in Parliament. Once again, the problem arose that the substantial French-speaking minority in a nominally Dutch-speaking region could elect representatives who would either join the French language-bloc, but would not then sit on the Dutch regional council which dealt with their constituencies, or who would sit on that council, but would then not be part of the French language-bloc for important constitutional votes in Parliament. The Court saw this limitation on voters' choice as justified in that it was part of an attempt to:

achieve an equilibrium between the Kingdom's various regions and cultural communities by means of a complex pattern of checks and balances. The aim is to defuse the language disputes in the country by establishing more stable and decentralised organisational structures. This intention, which is legitimate in itself, clearly emerges from the debates in the democratic national Parliament and is borne out by the massive majorities achieved in favour [of the relevant legislation] .... In any consideration of the electoral system in issue, its general context must not be forgotten. The system does not appear unreasonable if regard is had to the intentions it reflects and to the respondent State's margin of appreciation within the Belgian parliamentary system—a margin that is all the greater as the system is incomplete and provisional.[61]

The Court is probably technically correct in its interpretation of Article 3 of Protocol 1, but its reasoning betrays the lack of a minority rights provision in the ECHR, and the concomitant result that the Court is preoccupied with individual rights. Minority rights treaties recognize the need to protect the group in regions as well as in the state overall. While each linguistic group in Belgium has its own region, pockets of the French-speaking minority in the Dutch unilingual area lack full representation. The dissenting judgment in *Mathieu-Mohin* appreciated this in coming to the view that Article 3 of Protocol 1 in conjunction with Article 14 had been breached.

In our opinion, such a situation, excluding, as it does in practice, representation of the French-speaking electorate of Halle-Vilvoorde at regional level, does not ensure 'the free expression of the opinion of the people in the choice of the legislature' as stipulated in Article 3 of Protocol No. 1, and it creates a language-based distinction contrary to Article 14 of the Convention. None of the reasons put forward to justify this incompatibility appears to us to be convincing. In the first place, it is true that the French-speakers elected in Halle-Vilvoorde could belong to the (Flemish) regional Council if they agreed to take the oath in Dutch. In that eventuality, however, the representatives concerned would lose their status as French-speakers in Parliament, and this—in addition to the psychological and moral aspect of the issue—would

[61] *Supra*, n. 60, at 18.

have important political consequences, given the role played by the parliamentary language groups.[62]

The dissenting judges have interpreted Article 14 to include principles of indirect discrimination to reach this opinion, but an express minority rights provision would obviate the need for semantic argument and allow discussion of the facts in their appropriate context. Moreover, the decision fails to pay sufficient regard to the right to freedom of expression of the French-speaking politicians—Article 3 of Protocol 1 needed to be read with Article 10 of the Convention.[63]

4. Restrictions on Freedom of Expression

Although Article 9 of the African Charter on Human and Peoples' Rights simply states that the right to express one's opinions has to be 'within the law', the Commission has made it clear that domestic law cannot trump international human rights law standards.

66. According to Article 9.2 of the Charter, dissemination of opinions may be restricted by law. This does not mean that national law can set aside the right to express and disseminate one's opinions; this would make the protection of the right to express one's opinions ineffective. To allow national law to have precedence over the international law of the Charter would defeat the purpose of the rights and freedoms enshrined in the Charter. International human rights standards must always prevail over contradictory national law. Any limitation on the rights of the Charter must be in conformity with the provisions of the Charter.

. . .

69. The reasons for possible limitations must be founded in a legitimate state interest and the evils of limitations of rights must be strictly proportionate with and absolutely necessary for the advantages which are to be obtained.

[62] *Supra*, n. 60, at 20.

[63] See *Podkolzina v. Latvia* 46726/99, ECtHR (Fourth Chamber), 9 April 2002

34. [The Court] considers that the interest of each State in ensuring that its own institutional system functions normally is incontestably legitimate. That applies all the more to the national parliament, which is vested with legislative power and plays a primordial role in a democratic State. Similarly, regard being had to the principle of respect for national characteristics enunciated above, the Court is not required to adopt a position on the choice of a national parliament's working language. That decision, which is determined by historical and political considerations specific to each country, is in principle one which the State alone has the power to make. Accordingly, regard being had to the respondent State's margin of appreciation, the Court concludes that requiring a candidate for election to the national parliament to have sufficient knowledge of the official language pursues a legitimate aim.

See also, the Committee of Ministers, Resolution ResDH(2003)124 concerning the judgment of the ECtHR of 9 April 2002 (final on 9 July 2002) in the case of *Podkolzina v. Latvia,* 22 July 2003.

70. Even more important, a limitation may never have as a consequence that the right itself becomes illusory.[64]

Those sorts of restrictions, more fully set out in other instruments, have been considered by the various treaty bodies.

Most instruments require any restriction to be prescribed by law, necessary in a democratic society, for a legitimate and proportionate aim; in the case of freedom of expression, there is also a reference to concomitant duties on persons exercising the right. They should also be applied restrictively and only after convincing evidence.[65] In *Kivenmaa v. Finland*[66] the government failed to show that it had a law in place that allowed for the freedom to be restricted. In *Ballantyne, Davidson and McIntyre v. Canada*,[67] the issue was whether the restriction was necessary for respect for the rights of others. Since displaying outdoor advertising signs for shops in the English language did not threaten the rights of francophone Québécois to use French, Canada was held to have violated Article 19 CCPR when it required all external signs only to be in the minority language. In *Ahmet Sadik v. Greece*,[68] the European Commission of Human Rights held that while maintaining peaceable relations between Christians and Moslems in North West Thrace was a legitimate aim, imposing a prison sentence on someone for calling themselves a Turk during an election campaign, a statement of their own identity as a member of a minority group, was not necessary in a democratic society.[69] Incitement to violence will ordinarily justify a restriction on freedom of expression by the state:

54. The Court stresses that the 'duties and responsibilities' which accompany the exercise of the right to freedom of expression by media professionals assume special

[64] *Media Rights Agenda, Constitutional Rights Project, Media Rights Agenda and Constitutional Rights Project v. Nigeria*, Comm. No. 105/93, 128/94,130/94, 152/96, not dated.

[65] See *Arslan*, 23462/94, ECtHR 8 July 1999, at para. 44. Which is not to say that the Strasbourg organs have always reached the right answer. See *G and E v. Norway*, 9278 & 9415/81, 35 DR 30 (1983), where mere disruption to traffic was enough to prove that there were 'public order' issues.

> 4. ... It is to be noted that the applicants had been given permission to demonstrate on 8 October 1979 from 11 to 16 o'clock (*sic*), but that they erected the tent and stayed there day and night until 11 October. Under these circumstances, the Commission finds that the interference with their right to freedom of expression can be reasonably considered to be necessary to protect the public order. A demonstration by setting up a tent for several days in an area open to public traffic must necessarily cause disorder.

[66] Communication No. 412/1990, UN Doc. CCPR/C/50/D/412/1990 (1994), para. 9.3.

[67] Communication Nos 359 and 385/1989, UN Doc. CCPR/C/47/D/359/1989 and 385/1989/Rev.1 (1993),at paras. 11.3 and 11.4.

[68] 18877/91 (46/1995/552/638), 25 October 1996, para. 53.

[69] Lack of proportionality is an element of necessity. See also, *Sener v. Turkey* 26680/95, ECtHR, 18 July 2000.

significance in situations of conflict and tension. Particular caution is called for when consideration is being given to the publication of the views of representatives of organisations which resort to violence against the State lest the media become a vehicle for the dissemination of hate speech and the promotion of violence. At the same time, where such views cannot be categorised as such, Contracting States cannot with reference to the protection of territorial integrity or national security or the prevention of crime or disorder restrict the right of the public to be informed of them by bringing the weight of the criminal law to bear on the media.[70]

Restrictions in relation to political activities are harder to justify. In *Womah Mukong v. Cameroon*,[71] the Human Rights Committee held that multiparty democracy cannot be subjugated to national unity. The European Court of Human Rights dealt with criticism of governments and freedom of expression in *Ozgür Gündem v. Turkey*:

70.... The Court is not convinced that, even against the background of serious disturbances in the region, expressions which appear to support the idea of a separate Kurdish entity must be regarded as inevitably exacerbating the situation. While several of the articles were highly critical of the authorities and attributed unlawful conduct to the security forces, sometimes in colourful and derogatory terms, the Court nonetheless finds that they cannot be reasonably regarded as advocating or inciting the use of violence. Having regard to the severity of the penalties, it concludes that the restrictions imposed on the newspaper's freedom of expression disclosed in these cases were disproportionate to the aim pursued and cannot be justified as 'necessary in a democratic society'.[72]

The one discordant note with respect to freedom of expression is to be found in *Hogefeld*.[73] The applicant was a member of the Red Army Faction who had been involved in some of the 'terrorist' activities of the RAF in the 1970s and 1980s. The RAF renounced its campaign of violence in 1992 and even issued a statement critical of its former strategy. The applicant had been arrested in 1993 and held on remand; she was sentenced to life imprisonment in 1996. During her detention on remand, a radio journalist and a film-maker had been denied access to her for the purpose of conducting an interview and making a documentary, respectively. The German courts held that although the applicant had personally renounced violence and criticized certain earlier crimes committed by the RAF, 'it had to be expected that the applicant would explain

[70] *Erdogdu and Ince v. Turkey* 25067/94, 25068/94, ECtHR (Grand Chamber), 8 July 1999. And see *Sener v. Turkey* 26680/95, 18 July 2000, at para. 45.

[71] Communication No. 458/1991, UN Doc. CCPR/C/51/D/458/1991 (1994) at para. 9.7.

[72] 23144/93, ECtHR (Grand Chamber) 16 March 2000, at paras. 60, 68, and 70.

[73] *Hogefeld v. Germany* 35402/97, ECtHR (Fourth Chamber), 20 January 2000.

and advocate ideological positions of the RAF, which would amount to a new act of participation in a terrorist organization pursuant to Section 129a of the Criminal Code'. In 1994, while on remand, she had issued a statement that was critical of the RAF, but did not challenge its philosophy:

> The fight for a humane future, for a world without government, in which people can live in liberty and self-determination, is still on the agenda. The reversal of the social developments is still a matter for which one must fight. Those who think that they have driven us into a dead-end street, should not rejoice too soon. They should know that we will fight for ourselves. There will be no return to the old strategy as a political concept, but we have our right to self-defence. I do not think that we will watch our destruction without resistance and I wish that everyone would think about our future.

The European Court of Human Rights held that such statements were ambiguous with respect to whether they supported terrorism.

> She continued to identify herself with the aims and the ideology of the RAF in general and apparently considered herself as a representative of the organization, consistently using the first person of the plural when talking about the organization. Although she admitted 'mistakes' in the strategy of the RAF, she continued to claim that 'our beginnings and our fight for a different world were at any time well-founded and justified, and that fight has to be conducted as a confrontation'. Moreover, she held that 'the reversal of the social developments is still a matter for which one must fight'.

The Court then read the statements in the light of the RAF's and her own history of terrorism and found that Germany's restriction on her freedom of expression met a pressing social need and was proportionate with respect to the legitimate aims of the German legislation. By comparison with the robust attitude of the Court in the Turkish freedom of expression cases,[74] the decision that the application in *Hogefeld* was manifestly ill-founded seems retrograde. The applicant's previous statement could not be taken as an incitement to violence, nor could it be construed as liable to incite violence.[75] No other individual's freedoms or liberties were threatened by her statement.[76] The European Court of Human Rights has expanded rapidly eastward in the 1990s, but has retained its pan-European guarantee of Convention rights without concessions, even where some new member states did not have the requisite infrastructure

[74] See *supra,* n. 18.

[75] *Sener, supra,* n. 69, at para.. 39. See also *Sürek and Özdemir, supra,* n. 18, where it was held that it had been wrong to have prosecuted the owners of a weekly magazine in which there had been an interview with the second in command of the PKK.

[76] See *Sürek (No. 1)* and *Sürek (No. 3),* both *supra,* n. 18.

properly to fulfil those standards. It is unfortunate that a concession in relation to a limitation of rights has been proffered westwards. The only positive note to draw from *Hogefeld* is that it may be possible to discern that a greater latitude is granted to opinions and views relating to minority groups.[77]

On the other hand, there are limits on freedom of speech. The Human Rights Committee held that denigrating Jews was not protected by Article 19. In *Malcolm Ross v. Canada*,[78] the Committee held that while the applicant had been dismissed from his teaching post,[79] it was justified.

> In that context, the removal of the author from a teaching position can be considered a restriction necessary to protect the right and freedom of Jewish children to have a school system free from bias, prejudice and intolerance.[80]

B. Freedom of Assembly

1. Content and Context of the Right

Freedom of assembly and freedom of expression have been held to be inextricably linked:

> 2. The Court considers that in the circumstances Article 10 is to be regarded as a *lex generalis* in relation to Article 11, a *lex specialis*, so that it is unnecessary to take it into consideration separately (see the *Ezelin v France* judgment of 26 April 1991, Series A no. 202, p. 20, § 35). On the other hand, Article 11 should also be considered in the light of Article 10, as notwithstanding the autonomous role and particular sphere of application of Article 11, the protection of personal opinions, secured by Article 10, is one of the objectives of freedom of peaceful assembly as enshrined in Article 11 . . . .[81]

Assembly and association are often part of one composite right. Nevertheless, the right to peaceful assembly has its own characteristics: the right of persons belonging to minorities to assemble together in private or in public is

[77] NB. *Hogefeld* was decided on 20 January 2000 and does not seem to have heralded any generally restrictive attitude in any subsequent case.

[78] Communication No. 736/1997, UN Doc. CCPR/C/70/D/736/1997 (2000).

[79] On dismissal amounting to an interference, see the ECtHR in *Vogt*, 17851/91, 26 September 1995.

[80] See also, *Stephen Hagan v. Australia*, Communication No. 26/2002-CERD/C/62/D/26/2002, 14 April 2003.

[81] *Rassemblement Jurassien & Unité Jurassienne v. Switzerland*, 17 DR 93 (1979):

> 2. … The allegation concerning Article 10 may be considered as subsidiary in relation to that concerning the right of peaceful assembly. The problem of freedom of expression cannot in this case be separated from that of freedom of assembly, as guaranteed by Article 11, and it is the latter freedom which is primarily involved in this issue.

fundamental to them, protecting the existence and identity of the group.[82] In *Djavit An*,[83] the applicant's complaint was not about freedom of movement across the Green Line in Cyprus, but about denial of his right to meet with other Greek Cypriots contrary to Article 11.

States parties have positive obligations to ensure that peaceful assemblies can take place. This requires them to prevent third party interference.[84] With respect to minority groups, it may require the state to take steps vis-à-vis the majority population.

2. *Restrictions on Freedom of Assembly*

As with freedom of expression, the restriction has to be prescribed by law. In *Djavit An*, Turkey could not point to any law of the TRNC that dealt with the issuance of permits to cross the green line.[85] Moreover, while freedom of assembly is essential for politicians if they are to carry out their representative functions, it cannot be used to foment violence.[86] Furthermore, Strasbourg will explicitly allow states a margin of appreciation.[87] However, where there is no violence, the Court will give those assembling a broad freedom; in the case of minority groups, even to the extent of calling for autonomy or secession.

> 97. The Court reiterates, however, that the fact that a group of persons calls for autonomy or even requests secession of part of the country's territory—thus demanding fundamental constitutional and territorial changes—cannot automatically justify a prohibition of its assemblies. Demanding territorial changes in speeches and demonstrations does not automatically amount to a threat to the country's territorial integrity and national security. Freedom of assembly and the right to express one's views through it are among the paramount values of a democratic society. The essence of democracy is its capacity to resolve problems through open debate. Sweeping measures of a preventive nature to suppress freedom of assembly and expression other than in cases of incitement to violence or rejection of democratic principles—however

[82] *Djavit An v. Turkey* 20652/92, ECtHR, 20 February 2003:

> 56. The Court observes at the outset that the right to freedom of assembly is a fundamental right in a democratic society and, like the right to freedom of expression, is one of the foundations of such a society. Thus, it should not be interpreted restrictively.... As such this right covers both private meetings and meetings in public thoroughfares as well as static meetings and public processions; in addition, it can be exercised by individuals and those organising the assembly....

[83] *Supra,* n. 82, at para. 54.

[84] See the *Plattform* case, at paras. 30–34. See also, *UMO Ilinden and Ivanov*, at para. 115. Both *supra*, n. 37.

[85] *Supra,* n. 82, at para. 66.

[86] In *Osmani v. fYROM* 50841/99, ECtHR (Second Chamber), 11 October 2001, there were riots and three people lost their lives.

[87] *Rassemblement Jurassien*, *supra*, n. 81, at paras. 8–12.

shocking and unacceptable certain views or words used may appear to the authorities, and however illegitimate the demands made may be—do a disservice to democracy and often even endanger it.[88]

C. Freedom of Association

Freedom of association is linked with freedom of expression and freedom of religion. As such, it is easy to see why it is fundamental to the enjoyment of rights by persons belonging to minority groups.

> 100. ... Freedom of thought and opinion and freedom of expression, guaranteed by Articles 9 and 10 of the Convention respectively, would thus be of very limited scope if they were not accompanied by a guarantee of being able to share one's beliefs or ideas in community with others, particularly through associations of individuals having the same beliefs, ideas or interests.[89]

It needs to be borne in mind, though, that there will be a need to balance the rights of the individual against those of the group.[90]

1. Content

Minority groups have the right to form associations,[91] even if trade unions are the only type specifically named in any of the treaties.[92] In *Sidoropoulos*,[93] the European Court of Human Rights was prepared to hold that minority groups could form associations to protect their spiritual and cultural heritage.

[88] *Stankov and United Macedonian Organisation 'ILINDEN' v. Bulgaria* 29221 and 29225/95, ECommHR, 29 June 1998, ECtHR (First Chamber), 2 October 2001, at para. 97. See also, *UMO Ilinden—PIRIN v. Bulgaria* 59489/00, ECtHR (First Chamber), 20 October 2005, at para. 59.

[89] *Chassagnou et al. v. France* 25088/94, 28331/95, 28443/95, 29 April 1999, ECtHR. See also *Socialist Party v. Turkey*, ECtHR, 20/1997/804/1007, 25 May 1998, at para. 41; *Young, James and Webster v. United Kingdom* 7601/77, 7806/77, ECtHR, 13 August 1981, at para. 57.

[90] *Lovelace v. Canada*, UNGAOR, 36th Sess., Supp.No.40, 166 (1981); 2 HRLJ 158 (1981), at para. 7.2, the HRC spoke in terms of Article 27 ICCPR requiring 'States parties to accord protection to *ethnic and linguistic minorities....*' (emphasis added). Moreover, individuals cannot enjoy their Art. 27 rights unless the minority group's own existence is preserved and promoted. Cf. *Young, James and Webster, supra,* n. 89, concurring opinion of Evrigenis J:

> When attempting to strike a fair balance, account has to be taken of the welfare of the public and of the collective interest of the trade union organisation that are at stake as well as of the individual's freedom of association.

[91] See *Noack et al. v. Germany* 46346/99, ECtHR (Fourth Chamber).

[92] *Gorzelik v. Poland* 44158/98, ECtHR (Fourth Chamber), 17 May 2001 (admissibility); 20 December 2001 (Merits) at para. 55. *Gorzelik* went to the Grand Chamber—17 February 2004. *Sidoropoulos v. Greece* (57/1997/841/1047) 10 July 1998, at para. 40. *United Communist Party of Turkey (TBKP) v. Turkey*, ECtHR, 133/1996/752/951, 30 January 1998, at para 24.

[93] *Supra,* n. 92 at para. 44.

44. The Court notes, in the first place, that the aims of the association called 'Home of Macedonian Civilisation', as set out in its memorandum of association, were exclusively to preserve and develop the traditions and folk culture of the Florina region .... Such aims appear to the Court to be perfectly clear and legitimate; the inhabitants of a region in a country are entitled to form associations in order to promote the region's special characteristics, for historical as well as economic reasons. Even supposing that the founders of an association like the one in the instant case assert a minority consciousness, the Document of the Copenhagen Meeting of the Conference on the Human Dimension of the CSCE (Section IV) of 29 June 1990 and the Charter of Paris for a New Europe of 21 November 1990—which Greece has signed—allow them to form associations to protect their cultural and spiritual heritage.

In *UMO Ilinden and Others v. Bulgaria*,[94] the European Court of Human Rights addressed the failure by the state to register a minority group under its laws of recognition, thereby denying the group the ability to hold property or seek protection via the courts. Such pre-emptive action was disproportionate and not within Article 11.2.

Exclusion from participation in the political processes of the state is contrary to the democratic principles which the Council of Europe espouses.[95]

89. The inhabitants of a region in a country are entitled to form associations in order to promote the region's special characteristics. The fact that an association asserts a minority consciousness cannot in itself justify an interference with its rights under Article 11 of the [ECHR].[96]

In the *Italian Masons* case,[97] the applicant, the Grand Order, complained that laws governing regional elections barred members of the Masons from standing; as a result, the Order was a victim of, *inter alia*, breaches of Articles 11 and 14. The Fourth Chamber found the case to be admissible, in part because in singling out Masons, Italy had discriminated between that group

[94] 59491/00, ECtHR (First Chamber), 19 January 2006, at para. 82. See also, *Affaire Fener Rum Erkek Lisesi Vakfıvc. Turquie* 34478/97, ECtHR (former Second Chamber), 9 January 2007.

[95] See *KPD v. FRG* 250/57, the *German Communist Party* case, Yb.ECHR, 1 (1957) 222, which, by analogy, must imply the right to political participation in normal circumstances. See also *United Communist Party of Turkey (TBKP) v. Turkey*, ECtHR, 133/1996/752/951, 30 January 1998, where the Court held, at para. 45, that democracy was the only form of governance contemplated in the ECHR. In similar vein, See *Socialist Party v. Turkey*, ECtHR, 20/1997/804/1007, 25 May 1998, at para. 47.

[96] *Stankov and United Macedonian Organisation 'ILINDEN' v. Bulgaria* 29221 and 29225/95, European Commission of Human Rights, 29 June 1998, ECtHR (First Chamber), 2 October 2001. See also, *UMO Ilinden—PIRIN, supra,* n. 88, at paras. 61–62.

[97] *Grande Oriente D'Italia di Palazzo Giustiniani v. Italy* 35972/97, ECtHR (Fourth Chamber), 21 October 1999 and 2 August 2001.

and other organizations.[98] The relevance of this case to minorities cannot be overestimated.

Nevertheless, Article 34 ECHR does not guarantee that groups can make a claim for a violation of human rights pertaining to their members.[99] However, they can take action within the bounds of Article 11 in order to defend their members. The Human Rights Committee deciding a case under Article 22 CCPR dealt with the right to strike.[100] The separate opinion of Higgins, Lallah, Mavrommatis, Opsahl, and Wako, though, started from the premise that Article 22 is not limited to trade unions:

> 3.... However, the exercise of this right requires that some measure of concerted activities be allowed; otherwise it could not serve its purposes. To us, this is an inherent aspect of the right granted by article 22, paragraph 1. Which activities are essential to the exercise of this right cannot be listed *a priori* and must be examined in their social context in the light of the other paragraphs of this article.

On the other hand, there seems to be no right to be consulted by the state, even on matters affecting the minority group,[101] contrary to the recommendations of the OSCE's Copenhagen Document.[102]

2. *Restrictions on Freedom of Association*

Freedom of association can be restricted, but only if the limitation is prescribed by law, necessary in a democratic society, pursues a legitimate aim, and is proportionate. Pluralism has been regularly acknowledged as a factor in European democracy by the European Court of Human Rights because there

[98] The Section went on to hold on the merits (2 August 2001) that there had been a violation of Article 11 and that there was no need to consider the complaints under Article 14.

[99] NB. Only individuals can bring complaints before the Human Rights Committee, but even where groups can be victims with a right of audience, as under the ECHR, the group itself would need to show it was a victim. See *Grande Oriente D'Italia di Palazzo Giustiniani v. Italy* 35972/97, ECtHR (Fourth Chamber), 21 October 1999 and 2 August 2001.

[100] *JB et al. v. Canada* Communication No. 118/1982, UN Doc. Supp.No.40 (A/422/40) at 151 (1986).

[101] *National Union of Belgian Police v. Belgium* 4464/70, European Court of Human Rights, 27 October 1975. Cf. The separate concurring opinion of Zekia J.

[102] *Supra*, n. 13, at paras. 33 and 35.

> (33) The participating States will protect the ethnic, cultural, linguistic and religious identity of national minorities on their territory and create conditions for the promotion of that identity. They will take the necessary measures to that effect after due consultations, including contacts with organizations or associations of such minorities, in accordance with the decisionmaking procedures of each State.
>
> (35) The participating States will respect the right of persons belonging to national minorities to effective participation in public affairs, including participation in the affairs relating to the protection and promotion of the identity of such minorities.

are so many minority groups in Europe. With respect to political parties, the European Court of Human Rights has held that Article 11.2 will be strictly interpreted.[103] Nevertheless, associations must respect the ECHR and the principles of democracy and democratic change.[104] However, governments must be subject to greater criticism.[105]

The rights and freedoms of others can justify an interference with freedom of association, an issue that might be pertinent for minorities vis-à-vis the majority and their own members.

59. In that connection, the Court further recalls that the freedom of association is not absolute and that in certain cases it has accepted that the need to protect Convention rights may lead States to restrict other rights or freedoms likewise set forth in the Convention (see, *mutatis mutandis*, the *Otto-Preminger-Institut v Austria* judgment of 20 September 1994, Series A no. 295-A, 18 and 19, §§ 47 and 50). The balancing of conflicting individual interests and rights is a difficult exercise. It may involve consideration of political and social issues on which opinions within a democratic society differ significantly.[106]

Equally, the territorial integrity of the State cannot be called into question by the association, although the Court will apply any such limitation restrictively—closing down the association before it started was disproportionate.[107] That the association in *Stankov* could call for secession shows how far associations for minority groups can go before the European Court of Human Rights will interfere. Finally, pertinently for minority groups, the right to form an association cannot be restricted because the association will undermine constitutional structures, so long as it does so democratically.[108]

27. The Court notes on the other hand that an association, including a political party, is not excluded from the protection afforded by the Convention simply because its activities are regarded by the national authorities as undermining the constitutional structures of the State and calling for the imposition of restrictions.

[103] *Socialist Party v. Turkey*, ECtHR, 20/1997/804/1007, 25 May 1998, at paras. 50 and 52.

[104] *Refah Partisi*, *supra*, n. 45, at paras. 96, 100, and 103.

103. ... A Contracting State may be justified under its positive obligations in imposing on political parties, which are bodies whose raison d'être is to accede to power and direct the work of a considerable portion of the State apparatus, the duty to respect and safeguard the rights and freedoms guaranteed by the Convention and the obligation not to put forward a political programme in contradiction with the fundamental principles of democracy.

[105] *Yazar*, *supra*, n. 43, at paras. 44 and 47.

[106] *Gorzelik*, *supra*, n. 92, at paragraph 59.

[107] *Sidoropoulos*, *supra*, n. 92, at paragraphs 39, 40 and 47.

[108] *United Communist Party of Turkey (TBKP) v Turkey*, European Court of Human Rights, 133/1996/752/951, 30 January 1998, at paragraph 27. And see *Stankov and United Macedonian Organisation "ILINDEN" v Bulgaria* 29221 and 29225/95, European Commission of Human Rights, 29 June 1998, European Court of Human Rights (First Section), 2 October 2001, at para. 97.

RELIGIOUS RIGHTS

Zdenka Machnyikova

I. Introduction

The protection provided in the international standards by the freedom of thought, conscience, and religion entails a broad range of rights that are of central importance to personal, as well as group, identity. Religion and particular beliefs are often the unique features distinguishing members of minorities from the majority. In this respect, the principle of religious pluralism protected by the freedom of religion often constitutes the foundation for the protection of religious minorities. This chapter provides an overview of the nature and scope of the minimum standards for freedom of religion and belief as regulated by the principal norms of international standards with the main focus on their interpretation through the jurisprudence of the supervisory bodies, with special attention paid to the effect of their practice on the protection of the enjoyment of the right to freedom of thought, conscience and religion by minorities.

II. International Standards on the Right to Manifest Religion or Belief

The principle of religious pluralism was first embodied in Article 18 of the Universal Declaration of Human Rights (UDHR),[1] which guaranteed the right to everyone to adopt and change his or her own religious belief without fear of government interference. The rights expressed in Article 18 of the UDHR were later articulated at the universal level in the legally binding Article 18 of the International Covenant on Civil and Political Rights (CCPR)[2] and in regional contexts in Article 12 of the American Convention on Human Rights (ACHR),[3] in Article 8 the African Charter on Human and Peoples' Rights (AfrCH),[4] in Article 9 of the European Convention for the Protection of Human Rights and Fundamental Freedoms (ECHR),[5] and Article 10 of the Charter of Fundamental Rights of the European Union.[6] In general, the principal provisions address the following aspects of protection of religious rights: first, they guarantee the right to freedom of thought, conscience and religion, generally described as *forum internum*, including the right to profess or not to profess religion or hold religious and other beliefs; second, they guarantee the right to have or change religion or belief and provide protection against coercion to change religion; third, they provide for the right to manifest religion or belief in worship, observance, practice and teaching, and in comparison with the *forum internum* the limitations can be imposed on the external freedom of

[1] UNGA, Universal Declaration of Human Rights (UDHR) (adopted on 10 December 1948), UNGA Res 217 (III) (1948), UN Doc. A/810, Art. 18 stipulates: 'Everyone has the right to freedom of thought, conscience and religion; this right includes freedom to change his religion or belief, and freedom, either alone or in community with others and in public or private, to manifest his religion or belief in teaching, practice, worship and observance.'

[2] International Covenant on Civil and Political Rights (CCPR) (adopted 16 December 1966, entered into force 23 March 1976) 999 UNTS 171.

[3] American Convention on Human Rights (ACHR) (adopted at the Inter-American Specialized Conference on Human Rights, San José, Costa Rica, 22 November 1969).

[4] The African Charter on Human and Peoples' Rights (AfrCH) (adopted 27 June 1981), OAU Doc. CAB/LEG/67/3 rev. 5, 21 I.L.M. 58 (1982), entered into force 21 October 1986.

[5] European Convention for the Protection of Human Rights and Fundamental Freedoms (ECHR), ETS 5, 1950.

[6] Charter of Fundamental Rights of the European Union, Official Journal of the European Communities, 2000, C 364/1.

expression of the religious belief; lastly, the international standards guarantee the right of parents to have their children educated in accordance with their religious and philosophical convictions.

The substantive protection guaranteed by the freedom of religion is reinforced in these instruments by non-discrimination clauses and by provisions guaranteeing equality before the law and equal protection of the law, which prohibit any discrimination on the grounds of 'religion'.[7] However, a specific connection between protection of the rights to freedom of religion and non-discrimination has been made in the United Nations Declaration on the Elimination of All Forms of Intolerance and of Discrimination Based on Religion or Belief (the UN Declaration on the Elimination of All Forms of Intolerance),[8] which distils many of the principles articulated in Article 18 of the CCPR, and in Articles 2, 3 and 4, and directly connects the anti-discrimination norms to the protection of religion and belief.

Specific provisions directed at the protection of persons belonging to national, ethnic and religious minorities were included in Article 27 of the CCPR which affirms that, '[i]n those States in which ethic, religious or linguistic minorities exist, persons belonging to such minorities shall not be denied the right, in community with other members of their group, [...] to profess and practise their own religion [...]'. While Article 27 established the basic standard in the field of minority rights, Article 3(1) of the UN Declaration on the Rights of Persons Belonging to National or Ethnic, Religious and Linguistic Minorities (the UN Declaration on Minorities)[9] has implied positive action with the use of the more positive expression 'to have the right' to profess and practise their own religion freely without interference or any form of discrimination. More specific provisions are included in Articles 7 and 8 of the Framework Convention for the Protection of National Minorities (FCNM). Article 8 of the FCNM is of special importance as it expressly provides in comparison with other international instruments for the right to establish and maintain their own religious institutions and to profess and practise their religion.

The following text attempts briefly to analyse the scope of the protection provided in these instruments from the perspective of their application in state

[7] See Art. 2(1), (26) CCPR; Art. 14 ECHR; and Protocol No. 12 to the European Convention for the Protection of Human Rights and Fundamental Freedoms, ETS 177, 2000, Art. 2.

[8] Declaration on the Elimination of All Forms of Intolerance and of Discrimination Based on Religion or Belief, UNGA Res. 36/55, 36 UN GAOR, Supp. (No. 51) at 171 (1981), UN Doc. A/36/684.

[9] UN Declaration on the Rights of Persons Belonging to National or Ethnic, Religious or Linguistic Minorities, UNGA Res. 47/135 (18 December 1992), annex 47 UN GAOR 49, 210 (1992), UN Doc. A/47/49.

practice, and in the interpretation provided in the jurisprudence of the international supervisory mechanisms. The analysis focuses on issues such as the scope, nature and other substantive aspects of the freedom of religion, inner and outer religious freedom; the expression and manifestation of the freedom and permissible limitations; as well as other forms of protection such as prohibition of discrimination, and application of the principle of full equality to persons belonging to religious minorities.

III. Analysis of Case Law

A. The Right to Freedom of Thought, Conscience, and Religion

The right to freedom of thought, conscience, and religion, referred to as to *forum internum*, provides in the international instruments a broad catalogue of rights. It includes the freedom to choose a particular religion and to maintain adherence to a religion, as well as the right to change religious belief at any time. The protection is guaranteed equally to the right to profess religion, as well as the choice not to profess religion, to have a particular religious belief, but equally the right covers the non-theistic views. Most importantly, this freedom cannot be restricted and provides protection from coercive influences. States are under an obligation to refrain from interfering with the *forum internum*. This is important from the perspective of religious minorities since states are precluded from practices aimed at forced assimilation of minorities. Individuals as well as religious communities are protected against indoctrination and other forms of coercion. Freedom from coercion by a state is specifically emphasized in the right of parents to have their children educated in conformity with their religious beliefs and their convictions, discussed later in the chapter. The African Commission on Human Rights and Peoples' Rights in *Amnesty International, Comité Loosli Bachelard, Lawyers Committee for Human Rights, Association of Members of the Episcopal Conference of East Africa v. Sudan* in absence of the state's justification confirmed that persecution of non-Muslim communities in order to cause their conversion to Islam constitutes a violation of Article 8. The applicants claimed that they suffered persecution and oppression through measures introducing restrictions on freedom of expression, harassment of clergy, arbitrary arrests, expulsions and denial of access to work and food aid and education with the aim of converting Christian adherents to Islam.[10]

[10] *Amnesty International, Comité Loosli Bachelard, Lawyers Committee for Human Rights, Association of Members of the Episcopal Conference of East Africa v. Sudan*, (Comm. No. 48/90,

Although it is widely recognized that the freedom from coercion is essentially directed against states' attempts to influence choice of religion or decisions to maintain a particular religion, the expressed right to freedom from coercion has been included during the drafting process of Article 18(2) CCPR as the reflection of fears expressed by some Muslim states seeking protection against missionary activities and proselytism. They tried to shift the emphasis in the Article away from freedom to change religion toward the freedom to maintain religion. These states raised objections, claiming that their domestic laws are based on the religious laws prohibiting conversion from Islam.[11] As a result Article 18(2) CCPR has a different formulation guaranteeing the right to have or to adopt a religion in comparison with Article 18 of the UDHR and Article 9 of the ECHR, which protect the right to change religion or belief. Despite the fact that the changes to Article 18(2) were introduced to oppose any influences directed at the change of a religion and to ensure the right to maintain a religion, the HRC has explicitly interpreted the freedom to have or to adopt a religion or belief as containing 'the freedom to choose a religion or belief, including the right to replace one's current religion or belief with another or to adopt atheistic views, as well as the right to retain one's religion or belief'.[12] In comparison with the approach of the HRC at the universal level, the ECtHR has shown readiness to accept the state's discretion in claiming responsibility to prevent private parties from proselytizing. In this respect the European jurisprudence, as discussed later in greater detail, under the scope of the right to manifest one's religion, has paradoxically invoked limited recognition of the right to teach and disseminate one's religion and to proselytize in order to protect individuals' choice of religion. In this context, it is worth noting that the ACHR in Article 12 includes both the right to maintain and to change religious belief. Moreover, with respect to proselytizing, the Article expressly protects the freedom to profess or disseminate one's religion or beliefs.

From the perspective of religious minorities, in particular those whose beliefs are less known or non-traditional, the issue of what is considered to be protected 'belief' or 'profession of religion' plays an important role. The provisions of the international standards do not define the term religion. In the practice of states, as well as the international supervisory bodies, religion and

50/91, 52/91, 89/93, not dated), paras. 74 and 76. See also *Free Legal Assistance Group, Lawyers' Committee for Human Rights, Union Interafricaine des Droits de l'Homme, Les Témoins de Jehovah v. Zaire*, (Comm. No. 25/89, 47/90, 56/91, 100/93, not dated) para. 45.

[11] See the Third Committee debates on the CCPR, UN Doc. A/C.3/5/SR. (1050-1), 288–367, UN Doc. A/C.3/15/SR (1960), 1021–6.

[12] HRC, General Comment No. 22 on Freedom of Religion, 48th session (1993), UN Doc. HRI/GEN/1Rev.1, para. 5.

belief are widely conceived. The HCR in General Comment No. 22 indicated that '[the article] protects theistic, non-theistic and atheistic beliefs, as well as the right not to profess any religion or belief. The terms belief and religion are to be broadly construed. Article 18 is not limited in its application to traditional religions or to religions and beliefs with institutional characteristics or practices analogous to those of traditional religions.'[13] The Committee specifically condemned any tendency 'to discriminate against any religion or belief for any reasons, including the fact that they are newly established, or represent religious minorities that may be the subject of hostility by a predominant religious community'.[14] The ECtHR has attempted to provide some limits to the broad notion of belief and religion and established in *Campbell and Cosans v. UK* that only 'views that attain a certain level of cogency, seriousness, cohesion and importance' are protected.[15]

B. The Right to Manifest Religion or Belief

Any person can hold any internalized belief that he or she chooses. However, freedom of religion guarantees that individuals can publicly declare their religion and that they can come together with other adherents of the faith. In practice, freedom of religion includes worshipping together with other adherents. Thus, the individual human right to freedom of religion provides the religious minority with many aspects of the rights it needs as a group in terms of the manifestation of that religion. Furthermore, whereas the CCPR allows only for complaints to be brought by individuals, under the ECHR victims of a human rights violation can seek redress as a group, with religious associations and churches having brought cases in the past.[16]

C. The Scope of the Protection given to Manifestation of Religion or Belief

The provisions of the UDHR, the CCPR, the ACHR and the ECHR guaranteeing the human right to 'manifest' one's religion, establish the scope of protection along the same lines. Individuals have the right either individually or in community with others, and in public or private, to manifest their

[13] HRC, General Comment No. 22 on Freedom of Religion , 48th session (1993), UN Doc. HRI/GEN/1Rev.1, at 35.

[14] *Ibid.*

[15] *Campbell and Cosans v. UK*, ECtHR (Appls. No. 7511/76, 7743/76, (1982)), para. 36.

[16] *Metropolitan Church of Bessarabia and Others v. Moldova*, ECtHR (Application No 45701/99, 13.12.2001, Merits and just satisfaction, 51 para. 1); *Canea Catholic Church v. Greece*, ECtHR (Application No 25528/94, 16.12, 1997, Reports 1997-VIII).

religion in worship, observance, practice and teaching. In comparison with the *forum internum,* the manifestation of one's religion or belief is not unlimited. However, any limitations must be prescribed by law, necessary in a democratic society and must pursue the interests of public safety, the protection of public order, health or morals, or the protection of the rights and freedoms of others. In comparison with the provisions of the above instruments, Article 8 of the AfrCh and Article 8 of the FCNM are more general in nature and do not mention specific forms of manifestation. However, application of these provisions by states shows that in practice the manifestation deals with the wide range of religious and other beliefs, and that these Articles cover the above recognized forms of manifestation.[17] Moreover, the systematic interpretation of Article 8 of the FCNM, as well as its guarantee to establish religious institutions, organisations and associations, suggest that the Article encompasses the specific ways of manifestation mentioned in Article 9 ECHR.[18]

What exactly constitutes 'worship', 'observance', 'practice' and 'teaching' is not defined in these provisions. An attempt to provide some guidance has been made in General Comment No. 22 on Article 18 of CCPR, which has given an indicative list of acts constituting worship, observance and practice.[19] These are mostly an expression of the ordinary exercise of faith and belief. The most detailed and comprehensive articulation of the forms of manifestation so far has been provided in Article 6 of the UN Declaration on the Elimination of All Forms of Intolerance. The manifestation includes the freedom:

(a) To worship or assemble in connection with a religion or belief, and to establish and maintain places for these purposes; (b) To establish and maintain appropriate charitable or humanitarian institutions; (c) To make, acquire and use to an adequate

[17] See, for example, FCNM Sweden State Report, ACFC/SR (2001) 003, 2001, para. 23; FCNM Finland State Report, ACFC/SR (99) 3, 1999, Arts. 7–9.

[18] Steering Committee for Human Rights (CDDH), Final Activity Report of the CDDH for the Attention of the Committee of Ministers, CDDH (93) 22, 1993, Art. 11.

[19] Comment No. 22 includes in worship 'rituals and ceremonial acts giving direct expression to belief, as well as various practices integral to such acts, including the building of places of worship, the use of ritual formulae and objects, the display of symbols, and the observance of holidays and days of rest.' Furthermore, observance and practice may also include, besides ceremonial acts, such customs as the observance of dietary regulations, the wearing of distinctive clothing or head coverings, participation in rituals associated with certain stages of life, and the use of a particular language customarily spoken by a group. Under the practice, the Comment further includes activities that are integral to the conduct by religious groups of their basic affairs, such as religious teaching, the freedom to choose their religious leaders, priests and teachers, the freedom to establish seminaries or religious schools, and the freedom to prepare and distribute religious texts or publications. HRC, General Comment No. 22 on Freedom of Religion, 48th session (1993), UN Doc. HRI/GEN/1Rev.1, para. 4, p. 146.

extent the necessary articles and materials related to the rites or customs of a religion or belief; (d) To write, issue and disseminate relevant publications in these areas; (e) To teach a religion or belief in places suitable for these purposes; (f) To solicit and receive voluntary financial and other contributions from individuals and institutions; (g) To train, appoint, elect or designate by succession appropriate leaders called for by the requirements and standards of any religion or belief; (h) To observe days of rest and to celebrate holidays and ceremonies in accordance with the precepts of one's religion or belief; (i) To establish and maintain communications with individuals and communities in matters of religion and belief at the national and international levels.

There is little point in trying to discern fine distinctions between 'worship', 'observance', 'practice' and 'teaching'. The UN Declaration on the Elimination of All Forms of Intolerance, as well as state practice shows that the emphasis is on the broad coverage of the manifestation. For instance in *Al-Nashif v. Bulgaria*,[20] when the local religious group had appointed the applicant to be a teacher of Islam, but where he had not been so registered by the state, the Court clearly stated that teaching Islam to Muslim children could self-evidently be part of the manifestation of his faith, being intimately linked to that faith. However, given the vast range of acts that can represent manifestation of religion or belief, the international jurisprudence has focused on means of clarifying what constitutes manifestation protected by the freedom of religion, as not every action based on spiritual convictions and beliefs would be considered to be a manifestation of religion or belief. This practice has been applied specifically by the European Commission on Human Rights: In *Arrowsmith v. United Kingdom* the ECommHR stated that 'manifestation' does not cover each act that is motivated or influenced by a religion or belief, and that actions which do not actually express a belief cannot be considered to be protected by Article 9 ECHR. The ECommHR established that leaflets encouraging soldiers not to serve in Northern Ireland distributed by Ms. Arrowsmith did not express pacifist views and therefore they in fact did not manifest her belief in sense of Article 9.[21] The *Arrowsmith* test requires that an expression of religion or belief must be 'closely' linked to a person's or a group's religion or belief to be considered to be 'practice'. There is an evident difference between the practice under the ECHR and the determination of the range of the protected forms of manifestation at the universal level. In contrast with the ECommHR, the HRC has not applied such a restrictive

[20] *Al-Nashif v. Bulgaria,* ECtHR (Appl. No. 50963/99, 25 January 2001) Partial Decision as to Admissibility; see also Judgment of 20 June 2002.

[21] *Arrowsmith v. United Kingdom* ECtHR (Appl. No. 7050/75, 19 Decisions and Reports 5 (1978)), para. 19.

approach requiring that the manifestation must be actual expression of the belief and necessitated by the religion or belief claimed in order to be protected.[22] Moreover, the ECtHR in *Tsarknias v. Greece* stated that whether or not a person or a group is considered to be manifesting spiritual convictions is connected with perceived external expression, which in turn is then assessed on the basis of 'objective criteria'.[23] In this respect the practice of the European supervisory bodies established a narrower scope of what could be considered the manifestation of religion or belief.

Religious traditions and customs are of fundamental importance to religious minorities and their way of life. However, the European practice established that the protection offered by the right to manifest one's religion or belief does not provide religious communities with an unrestrained right to behave in the public sphere in a way which is dictated by such belief.[24] The jurisprudence refers for instance to the cases of conscientious objections of a Quaker to participating in a tax system which subsidises the military or objections to participation in state pension schemes.[25] The Court asserted that Article 9 does not provide an individual with the right to refuse to abide by legislation on the basis of one's convictions, when the operation of that legislation is provided for by the Convention, and when it applies neutrally and generally in the public sphere, without impinging on the freedoms guaranteed by Article 9. Unfortunately in some cases the EcommHR and the ECtHR have readily accepted the neutrality principle without thorough examination of whether such rules were necessary in a democratic society, and whether such a fundamental impairment of an individual's right was proportionate to the aim pursued. This concerns, for instance, the case of *Karaduman v. Turkey*. The applicant asserted that covering her head with a headscarf was one of the observances prescribed by her religion, and that such observance was restricted by the requirement of providing an identity photograph showing her bare-headed for the purpose of a degree certificate. The ECommHR accepted the state's justifications of legitimate grounds without examination of the proportionality, and without clear substantiation it stated that Article 9 'does not always guarantee the right to behave in the public sphere in a way

22 The case law of the HRC reaffirmed that Art. 18 of the Covenant protects a wide variety of manifestations. However, it did not examine whether the belief falls under the ambit of Art. 18 or whether there is relevant connection between the belief and its manifestation. See for example, *J.B v. Canada*, HCR (Communication No. 466/1991, UN Doc. A/24/40(1994), 7 November 1991, para. 4.6.

23 *Tsarknias v. Greece,* ECtHR (Appl. No. 45629/99, 1999, Decision on Admissibility ref. 4556).

24 *C. v. United Kingdom*, ECtHR (Appl. No. 10358/83, 1983, Decisions and Reports 142), at 144.

25 *Supra*, n. 9, 142 at 147.

which is dictated by such belief'.[26] The neutrality principle warrants careful consideration, since states often follow a system of having a state church or in some areas accommodate in the public domain historically established religious denominations. In some cases the rules applied in the public domain are based on religious traditions of established religions, and their application can result in direct or indirect discrimination against adherents of minority religions. The issue of differential treatment and reasonable accommodation is discussed later in the chapter.

D. Prosyletism

Another important issue that arises with respect to religious minorities concerning the protected forms of manifestation is the issue of 'prosyletism' and 'missionary work'. There are major differences in the attitude of states towards the acceptance of prosyletism, as some states with an established state religion and with religious law being part of the state system treat a change of religion as apostasy, and are strongly opposed to any activities promoting minority religions or other alternatives to the state religion. The international supervisory bodies endorsed prosyletism as a protected form of manifestation of religion and belief. However, while imposition of the state restrictions on prosyletism was rejected at the universal level by the HRC[27], the ECtHR accepted the state's discretion to impose restrictions on the prosyletism in situations of 'improper prosyletism' to protect rights and freedom of others. The ECtHR accepted the state's legitimate aim in *Kokkinakis v. Greece* and *Larrissis and others v. Greece*, claiming the need to protect individuals from coercive means which would impair their free choice of religion. The Court stated that '[i]mproper prosyletism represents a corruption or deformation of it. It may [...] take the form of activities offering material or social advantages with a view to gaining new members for a Church or exerting improper pressure on people in distress or in need; it may even entail the use of violence or brainwashing; more generally, it is not compatible with respect for the freedom of thought, conscience and religion of others.'[28]

[26] *Karaduman v. Turkey*, ECtHR (Appl. No. 16278/90, 1993, Decisions and Reports 74), 93 at 108–9.

[27] General Comment No. 22 permits missionary work and speaks about coercion only in terms of restricting an access to education, medical care and employment. The prohibition of coercion is directed essentially at the protection of individuals against legal barriers imposed by states to a change of religion. HRC, General Comment No. 22 on Freedom of Religion , 48th session (1993), UN Doc. HRI/GEN/1Rev.1, para. 5.

[28] *Kokkinakis v. Greece*, ECtHR (Appl. No 14307/88, 25 May 1993, Merits and just satisfaction), para. 48.

Another limitation which is imposed on the manifestation of religion and belief is prohibition of any manifestation of religion or belief which amounts to propaganda for war or advocacy of national, racial, or religious hatred that constitutes discrimination, hostility, or violence. This is particularly important in situations when religious groups confront each other, or when religion serves political interests and becomes a divisive factor between minority and majority. Hate speech, as well as activities inciting ethnic hatred, can be restricted on the basis of legitimate restrictions established in freedom of religion provisions of the international instruments. In particular, the State may invoke a legitimate aim of the protection of the rights of others. However, given the history of religious wars, international law, in particular Article 20 of CCPR and Article 13(5) of the ACHR, imposes a restriction on all forms of religious expression and activities constituting advocacy of religious hatred and incitement to religious intolerance, and require the State Parties to prohibit such activities by law.

E. Individually or in Community with Others

Importantly from the perspective of religious minorities, who normally aspire to live in accordance with customs (based on their beliefs and tradition) representing their specific characteristics as a community, the extent of the protection of manifestation of their faith plays a crucial role in the enjoyment of the right to manifest religion or belief. In this respect, the recognition of the collective aspect of the right to manifest one's religion and beliefs provides minority groups with the means of preserving a group's unique characteristics and way of life. The ECtHR, in comparison with the practice of the other supervisory bodies, has handed down a number of landmark decisions providing clarifications of the state's obligations to secure the enjoyment of the right to manifestation of religious belief with other members of one's religious community.

In *X. v. United Kingdom*, when the government argued that an applicant's wish to observe Muslim worship can be satisfied by private, solitary worship, the ECommHR expressly affirmed that the right to manifest 'one's religion in community with others' is an essential part of that right, and the two alternatives 'either alone or in community with others' cannot be considered mutually exclusive or leave the authorities choice in terms of the guaranteed protection.[29] This principle was later stressed by the ECtHR in *Kokkinakis v Greece* when the ECtHR expressly stated that '[a]ccording to Article 9 (art. 9)

[29] *X. v United Kingdom*, ECtHR (Appl. No. 8160/78 (1981) Decisions and Reports 27), at 34.

freedom to manifest one's religion is not only exercisable in community with others, in "public" and within the circle of those whose faith one shares, but can also be asserted "alone" and "in private"'.[30]

The importance of the community dimension was most clearly articulated by the ECtHR in *Hasan and Chaush v. Bulgaria*, which dealt with interference in the organization and leadership of the Muslim community. The Court affirmed that participation in the life of a community is a manifestation of one's religion. More specifically, the ECtHR stated that religious communities traditionally and universally exist in the form of organized structures, and abide by rules which are often seen as being of a divine origin. In this respect, the ceremonies conducted by the ministers have a sacred value and thus the personality of ministers is of fundamental importance to the members of the community. From this perspective, participation in the life of a community falls within the ambit of the protection guaranteed by Article 9 of the ECHR.[31]

In *Cyprus v Turkey*, the ECtHR found that restrictions placed on the freedom of movement of the Greek-Cypriot population curtailed their ability to observe their religious beliefs, in particular their access to places of worship and their participation in other aspects of religious life.[32]

F. The Right to Establish Religious Institutions, Organizations and Associations

Furthermore, the protection of the collective manifestation of the religion provides a basis for a religious entity to exercise its rights under Article 9, in its own capacity, on behalf of its members. The ECtHR has reconfirmed this principle in its decision in *Metropolitan Church of Bessarabia and others v. Moldova* on the state's obligations concerning the protection of the associational dimension, stating that the believers' right to freedom of religion encompasses the expectation that the community will be allowed to function peacefully, free from arbitrary state intervention. In this respect, the Court has explicitly drawn a direct connection between Article 9 and Article 11 of the ECHR, which safeguards freedom of association. It emphasized that '[t]he right of believers to freedom of religion, which includes the right to manifest one's

[30] *Kokkinakis v. Greece*, ECtHR (Appl. No 14307/88, 25 May 1993, Merits and just satisfaction) para. 31.

[31] *Hasan and Chaush v. Bulgaria*, ECtHR (Appl. No. 30985/96, 26 November 2000, Merits and just satisfaction) para. 62.

[32] *Cyprus v. Turkey*, ECtHR (Appl. No 25781/94, 10 January 2001, Merits), para. 245.

religion collectively, presupposes that believers may associate freely, without arbitrary interference by the State. The autonomy of religious communities is in fact indispensable to pluralism in a democratic society and is thus an issue at the very heart of the protection afforded by Article 9.'[33] In this respect, religious denominations are not required to register in order to come together in worship and practice. However, many aspects of 'practice', such as owning assets often require the possession of legal personality. The Court confirmed that legal personality is a critical precondition for many activities based on collective manifestation. The ECtHR stated: '[o]ne of the ways in which right to manifest one's religion may be exercised, especially in the case of a religious community, is the opportunity to seek legal protection for the community, its members and its property.'[34] In this respect, the ECtHR stipulated that refusal by the state to register a religious denomination is an interference with the right to freedom to manifest one's religion. The Court in the specific case emphasized that the applicant Church may not pursue its activities since it is not recognized. Lacking legal personality, it cannot bring legal proceedings to protect its assets, which are indispensable for worship, the priests could not hold services, and its members may not meet to practise their religion, since it has no legal status.[35]

The decision is not only important from the perspective of confirmation of the state's obligation to guarantee the right to a legal entity status to religious institutions, organizations and associations; it has also clearly established that the right to manifestation of beliefs is connected to an individual's or a community's own choice of belief, and cannot be satisfied by other available forms of manifestation. The Court dismissed the government's argument that the refusal to recognize the Metropolitan Church of Bessarabia did not violate the right to manifestation of religion or belief since the adherents retained their freedom to manifest their belief through worship in the Metropolitan Church of Moldova, which was in their view identical.[36] In *Manoussakis v. Greece*, the ECtHR clearly excluded any discretion on the part of the state to determine whether religious beliefs, or the means used to express such beliefs, are legitimate and that the authorization (ie recognition) of a church is compatible only in so far as it is intended to allow the authorities to verify whether the

[33] *Metropolitan Church of Bessarabia and Others v. Moldova*, ECtHR (Appl. No 45701/99, 13 December 2001, Merits and just satisfaction), para. 118.

[34] *Ibid.*

[35] *Ibid.*, paras. 105 and 129.

[36] *Ibid.*, paras. 96 and 117.

formal conditions required by law have been satisfied.[37] The state is permitted to review charters of religious organizations, but only if there is no substantive assessment of the beliefs and practices involved.

The right to establish religious institutions, organizations and associations must be distinguished from the mandatory registration of religious denomination required by a state in order to practise faith or religion. The ECtHR has not dealt directly with the issue whether such requirement is compatible with Article 9, but it has provided significant guidance, such as in the above mentioned case of *Mannoussakis v. Greece*, as to the permissibility of particular requirements for registration. Interestingly, the ECtHR has sustained legal entity status even without a church complying with any formalities required for the registration of religious institutions.[38] From the perspective of religious minorities the registration requirements play an important role, as states often use the registration process to deny the right to exercise the freedom of religion to certain religious groups which do not belong to the mainstream religious denomination or are small in membership. In this respect, the numerical criteria were criticized in *Mannoussakis*, when the leaders of the dominant religion had the right to examine whether a Jehovah's Witnesses' planning application for establishing a place of worship was based on genuine religious need, and was supported by at least 50 families. The Court in the specific case found the numerical criteria incompatible with Article 9, but importantly from the perspective of discriminatory consequences to religious minorities, the Court also noted that requiring permit approval to be conditional on favourable review by clergy of another church would be clearly impermissible.[39]

G. Limitations

While *forum internum* is in principle an absolute right, the freedom to manifest one's religion or belief through worship, observance, practice and teaching can be legitimately restricted. Under Article 18(3) CCPR, Article 12(3) of ACHR and Article 9(2) of the ECHR the right to manifest one's religion can be subject to such limitations as are prescribed by law and are necessary in a democratic society in the interests of public safety, for the protection of public order, health or morals, or for the protection of the rights and freedoms of others. Comparably with the limitation clauses of other human rights, the list of the

[37] *Manoussakis and Others v. Greece*, ECtHR (Appl. No 18748/91, 26 September 1996, Merits and just satisfaction), para. 47.

[38] *Canea Catholic Church v. Greece*, ECtHR (Appl. No 25528/94, 10 January 2001, Merits and just satisfaction) paras 39–47.

[39] *Supra*, n. 18, para. 47.

legitimate grounds is far more limited. This indicates the special role that the freedom of religion plays in the lives of individuals. The ECtHR in this respect stated that '[it is] one of the most vital elements that go to make up the identity of believers and their conception of life, but it is also a precious asset for atheists, agnostics, skeptics and the unconcerned. The pluralism indissociable from a democratic society, which has been dearly won over the centuries, depends on it.'[40] The Court in this context affirmed that in democratic societies, in which several religions coexist within the same population, it may be necessary to place restrictions on this freedom in order to reconcile the interests of the various groups, and ensure that everyone's beliefs are respected. The ECtHR practice is of great importance for minority religious groups, as these groups were often subject to repression and discrimination because of their different religious beliefs. In *Manoussakis and others v. Greece* the Court stated that in determining whether a restriction on worship or observance is proportionate to the legitimate aim pursued, 'very strict scrutiny' should be applied given the nature of the manifestation in question. The Court noted that 'in delimiting the extent of the margin of appreciation in the present case, the Court must have regard to what is at stake, namely the need to secure true religious pluralism, an inherent feature of the notion of a democratic society.'[41] Therefore any limitations must be strictly interpreted and must not be discriminatory.

In the specific case, the Court had to deal with the compatibility of a prior authorization requirement to set up and operate a place of worship. The Court ruled that the criminal conviction of the Jehovah's witness for setting up a place of worship without legal authorization was the creation of the state's own delays in dealing with the application. Importantly, the Court concluded that the restriction had such a direct effect on the applicant's freedom of religion that it could not be considered to be proportionate to the legitimate aim of the law in imposing planning conditions on setting up the places of worship. The Court stated that Greece used this requirement to impose rigid, or indeed prohibitive, conditions on practice of religious beliefs by Jehovah's Witnesses which was contrary to principles of pluralism.[42]

The ECtHR's emphasis on pluralism played an important role in the development of the case law concerning permissible interference by states. In *Serif v. Greece* when the government, trying to eliminate tensions among Muslims, convicted the applicant for usurping the functions of a minister of a

[40] *Kokkinakis v. Greece,* ECtHR (Appl. No.4307/88 (1993)), para. 31.

[41] *Manoussakis v. Greece,* ECtHR (Appl. No. 18748/91 (1996)), para. 44.

[42] *Ibid.*, paras. 48–53.

'known religion', and wearing the dress of such a minister, on the grounds that there were two Muftis in Rodopi, the ECtHR stressed that even if tensions are a result of pluralism the state has a duty not to eliminate that pluralism. More specifically the Court noted that: 'The role of the authorities in such circumstances is not to remove the cause of tensions by eliminating pluralism, but to ensure that the competing groups tolerate each other.'[43]

From the perspective of minority protection and permissible limitations, careful consideration should be made with respect to legitimacy of the state's interference concerning the invoked grounds of legitimate public interest. Of special importance to religious minorities is the ground invoked for the protection of morals. In principle, there is no universally applicable common standard of public morals. In fact, the concept of public morals in countries with a state religion or traditional religion is predominantly based on the belief system of this religion. Different beliefs and traditions are the distinguishing characteristics of religious minorities, and in this respect their moral precepts can be quite different from those of the majority of the population following the state or the traditional religion. In this respect the HRC noted in General Comment No. 22 that 'limitations on the freedom to manifest a religion or belief for the purpose of protecting morals must be based on principles not deriving exclusively from a single tradition'.[44] In line with this interpretation the ECtHR in *Manoussakis and others v. Greece* rejected the claim of the Greek Government, stating that the substance of the public order should vary on account of national characteristics which include a special position of the Orthodox Church in national conscience.[45]

Another area where the state's interference in the practice of minority religion has been considered before the supervisory bodies is that of public safety. Religious convictions and practices can on occasion conflict with mandatory safety or state health care measures. In *Bhinder v. Canada* the HRC accepted as legitimate the dismissal of a Sikh from the Canadian Railway Company because of his refusal to wear official headgear during his work, invoking reasons of public safety.[46] Similarly, in *X v. United Kingdom*, the ECommHR accepted as permissible the British law requiring all motorcyclists to wear crash

[43] *Serif v. Greece*, ECtHR (Appl. No 38178/97, 14 December 1999, Merits and just satisfaction), para. 53.

[44] HRC, General Comment No. 22 on Freedom of Religion, 48th session (1993), UN Doc. HRI/GEN/1Rev.1, para. 8.

[45] *Manoussakis v. Greece*, ECtHR (Appl. No. 18748/91 (1996)), para. 39.

[46] *K. Singh Bhinder v. Canada*, HRC (Communication No. 208/1986, U.N. Doc. A/45/40 vol. 1 (1990)) paras. 3, 6(2).

helmets.[47] It has been argued by the applicant in *Bhinder v. Canada* that the distinction should be drawn between manifestation of religion or belief which may endanger the safety of other persons, and those which concern only the safety of the person in question. It is interesting to note that British law, even before the decision of the HRC, has been taken to have provided an exception to Sikhs concerning the wearing of motorcycle helmets.

Public order and the rights of others were invoked as grounds for interference with respect to manifestations concerning dress restrictions prohibiting wearing headscarves for Muslim women, wearing turbans for Sikhs or growing beards for Buddhists. The case law, in particular applications before the ECommHR, seems rather restrictive with respect to accommodating such manifestations in the public sphere, accepting states' justification of the legitimate grounds of the rights of others, or public order. For instance in *X. v Austria* the Commission accepted the argument that prohibiting a Buddhist prisoner from growing a beard, as prescribed by his religion, was necessary for the protection of public order to enable the authorities to identify him.[48] *Karaduman v. Turkey*, involved a student who chose to pursue her higher education in a secular university; the Commission accepted the government's argument that the ban on the wearing of headscarves was justified, especially in a country where the majority adheres to a particular religion. In its view, the manifestation of religious symbols, without restrictions on place or form, can constitute a pressure on students who adhere to another religion, or on those who do not practise any religion at all. The principle of pluralism latterly strongly upheld by the ECtHR is not taken into account in those decisions as the Commission accepts the government's legitimate aims without examination of whether such a measure is necessary in a democratic society, and whether such a fundamental impairment of an individual's right is proportionate to the aim pursued.[49]

H. The Right of Parents to have their Children Educated in Accordance with their Religious and Moral Convictions

One particular aspect of the freedom of religion which is extremely important for religious minorities, is the right of parents to have their children educated in accordance with their religious and moral convictions. Such education is often

[47] *X. v United Kingdom*, ECtHR (Appl. No. 8160/78 (1981) Decisions and Reports 27).

[48] *X. v. Austria*, ECtHR (Appl. No.1753/63, 15 February 1965, Inadmissibility Decision) at 174.

[49] *Karaduman v. Turkey*, ECtHR (Appl. No. 16278/90 (1993) Decisions and Reports 74) 93 at 108–9.

connected with the transmission of religious, moral and other philosophical ideas. Even in states which do not provide religious education in schools, the curriculum of the state's schools sometimes reflects convictions based on the religious or other beliefs of the majority of the population of the state. The right is guaranteed in a number of international instruments. Parents' entitlement to have their children educated according to their own religious and philosophical convictions is covered in Article 26(3) of the UDHR and Article 13(3) of the CESCR, both providing for the right of persons to choose the kind of education that they want for their children, including opting for private education. A more specific guarantee of the parental choice to have their children educated in accordance with their religious and moral convictions is guaranteed by Article 18(4) of the CCPR, Article 14(2) of the CRC, Article 12(4) of ACHR and Protocol 1 of Article 2 of the ECHR in the light of interpretation provided by the Strasburg organs.

The right does not impose positive obligations on states to provide religious education in accordance with the wishes or choices of parents, or to provide funding for private education. Although the right of parents to have their children educated in accordance with their beliefs does not guarantee state support for such education, it may be required to recognize a privately established school.[50] The scope of the protection essentially arises in relation to the content of teaching on religious or philosophical ideas within the public school curriculum, and in extra-curricular activities in schools. The obligation of the state does not constitute only the negative duty to respect the freedom of choice of parents but, as the ECtHR in *Campbell and Cosans v. United Kingdom* indicated with respect to Protocol 1 of the Article 2 of the ECHR, 'in addition to a primary negative undertaking, it implies some positive obligations on the part of the State'.[51] In this respect the ECtHR maintained, providing the states with broad discretion in establishing a curriculum, that an appropriate balance needs to be established between parental wishes and the state's obligation to provide education. In *Kjeldsen, Busk Madsen and Pedersen v. Denmark*, a case which concerned the objection of parents to mandatory sex education, the ECtHR defined the limits of the state's discretion by clarifying that '[T]he second sentence of Article 2 implies [...] that the State, in fulfilling the functions assumed by it in regard of education and teaching, must take care that information or knowledge included in this curriculum is conveyed in

[50] *Al-Nashif v. Bulgaria*, ECtHR (Appl. No. 50963/96, 20 June 2002, Merits and just satisfaction).

[51] *Campbell and Cosans v. United Kingdom*, ECtHR ((1982), Decisions and Reports 48), para. 37.

an objective, critical and pluralistic manner. The State is forbidden to pursue an aim of indoctrination that might be considered as not respecting parents' religious and philosophical convictions. This is the limit that must not be exceeded.'[52]

In respect of the state's discretion to establish general curricula, General Comment No. 22 on Article 18 CCPR has clearly stated that '[i]nstruction in a particular religion or belief is inconsistent with article 18(4) unless provision is made for non-discriminatory exemptions or alternatives that would accommodate the wishes of parents and guardians'.[53] This affirmation is extremely important for minorities, since many states provide religious education based on the dominant or majority religion in the public education system. In states where public schools have religious instruction, especially if such instruction is rooted in the religious beliefs of a dominant state religion, or the religion of the majority, parents have the right to withdraw their children from such classes. Moreover, the HRC established that where alternative education is provided such must be carried on in a neutral and objective way. More specifically, the HRC established in *Hartikainen v. Finland*, a case which considered the status of compulsory teaching of history of religion and ethics as an alternative to religious instruction for children whose parents were atheists, that mandatory public school instruction in subjects such as the general history of religions and ethics is only compatible with Article 18(4) CCPR if it is given in a neutral and objective way, and respects the convictions of parents who do not believe in any religion.[54] As both the universal and the European jurisprudence have shown, this principle applies to curriculum content overall.

From the perspective of minorities, the issue of equal treatment of minorities in education plays an essential role for enjoyment of the freedom of religion or belief of minorities. As was mentioned above, many states provide, support, or reflect within the educational curricula, specific religion or religious beliefs. In situations where states fund particular religious schools, unless there is reasonable and objective justification for the difference in treatment, such support would clearly amount to discrimination. This was confirmed in *Arieh Hollis Waldman v. Canada*, when government funding was provided to Roman Catholic schools as the only non-secular schools. A Jewish father,

[52] *Kjeldsen, Busk Madsen and Pedersen v. Denmark*, ECtHR, (Appl. 5095/71, 5920/72, 5926/72, 7 December 1976, Merits), 53.

[53] HRC, General Comment No. 22 on Freedom of Religion, 48th session (1993), UN Doc. HRI/GEN/1Rev.1, para. 45.

[54] *Hartikainen v. Finland*, HCR (Communication No. 40/1978, UN Doc. A/36/40(1981), 9 April 1981), para. 10.4 at p. 147.

who enrolled his children in a private Jewish day school in the Canadian province of Ontario, claimed that choosing only Roman Catholic schools for full state funding impaired enjoyment of the right to manifest his religion and the freedom to provide religious education for his children, in a discriminatory manner. The argument of the Canadian Government, which claimed that the distinction was based on objective and reasonable criteria since the Roman Catholic schools, based on the privileged status of the Church established in the Constitution, are incorporated as a distinct part of the public school system, was rejected by the HCR stating that 'the fact that a distinction is enshrined in the Constitution does not render it reasonable and objective'.[55] The HCR has also confirmed that arrangements in the field of religious education must be in compliance with Article 26 CCPR because non-discrimination is a fundamental component in the test under Article 18(4) CCPR.

An important case concerning education of minorities has been considered by the ECommHR: In *Cyprus v. Turkey*[56] the Turkish Cypriot authorities adopted a policy of attrition, and the Cypriot authorities in Northern Cyprus were not allowed to appoint Greek-speaking teachers in schools, which has resulted in ending mother-tongue education for Greek-speaking children. The ECommHR held that such measures resulted in the withdrawal of the educational service, and its effective abolishment in violation of Article 2 of Protocol 1. With respect to state support of religious schooling, it can be assumed that the Strasbourg bodies would come to the same conclusion in a situation where the religious schooling had been provided through the state and was subsequently withdrawn. In general, however, a state is under no obligation under the ECHR to fund a private religious school set up by parents; however, recognition of any such privately funded establishment is probably going to be incumbent upon the state. A government in such circumstances could establish conditions subjecting such schools to the state's general standards for educational establishments.

I. Non-discrimination

The protection against discrimination is one of the most important safeguards for religious minorities in the enjoyment of their religious rights. Very few states are genuinely neutral with respect to the various religious communities living

[55] *Arieh Hollis Waldman v. Canada*, HCR (Communication No. 694/1996, UN Doc. CCPR/C/67/D/1996, 30 November 1999), para. 3.

[56] *Cyprus v. Turkey*, App. No. 25781/94, Report of the EuCommHR, adopted on 4 June 1999, at paras. 474–79, esp. 478; Judgment of the ECtHR (Grand Chamber) of 10 May 2001, at paras. 278, 292.

within their country. Even states that proclaim strict separation of church and state are frequently involved in religious affairs, often providing support for the state, majority or traditional religions, or are simply involved in religious matters by facilitating free and peaceful enjoyment of the right of individuals to manifest their religion and belief. Religious minorities frequently find themselves in a disadvantageous position vis-à-vis the communities professing the state or traditionally established religion. There are several areas where discrimination against minorities occurs. With this in mind the HRC in General Comment No. 22 stated that the fact that a religion is recognized as a state religion, or that its followers comprise a majority of the population, shall not result in any privileges for this religion or discrimination against adherents to other religions or non-believers. The HRC has more specifically with respect to education stressed that non-discriminatory exemptions or alternatives must be made in public education systems where the curriculum includes instruction in a certain religion.[57] The case law concerning the discriminatory treatment of religious minorities in education has already been discussed above. Similarly, the African Commission on Human and Peoples' Rights established in *Amnesty International, Comité Loosli Bachelard, Lawyers Committee for Human Rights, Association of Members of the Episcopal Conference of East Africa v. Sudan*, that application of Shari'a law to non-adherents to the Muslim religion is unjust, and stated that tribunals that apply only Shari'a law are not competent to judge non-Muslims, and that everyone should have the right to be tried by a secular court if they wish.[58]

Another issue which was considered with respect to the privileged position of a certain religion is the requirement of public oath. In many states taking a public office requires potential office-holders to take an oath of office with references to the state religion. Such a requirement discriminates against the adherents of other religions. In this respect in *Buscarini v. San Marino*, the ECtHR held that requiring elected representatives to swear allegiance to a particular religion is not compatible with Article 9 of the ECHR.

The guarantees providing protection against discrimination, such as Article 2(1) and Article 26 of the CCPR and Article 14 and Protocol 12 of ECHR, provide religious minorities with the means for effective enjoyment of the right to freedom of thought, conscience and religion even in cases when

[57] HRC, General Comment No. 22 on Freedom of Religion, 48th session (1993), UN Doc. HRI/GEN/1Rev.1, paras. 9 and 10.

[58] *Amnesty International, Comité Loosli Bachelard, Lawyers Committee for Human Rights, Association of Members of the Episcopal Conference of East Africa v. Sudan* (Comm. No. 48/90, 50/91, 52/91, 89/93, not dated), para. 73.

the supervisory bodies have not established a violation of the substantive right. The ECtHR in determining whether the differentiation constituted discrimination established that the principle of equality of treatment is violated if the distinction has no 'objective' and 'reasonable' justification. The Court stated that the existence of such a justification must be assessed in relation to the aim and effects of the measure under consideration, and the difference of treatment in the exercise of the right must pursue a legitimate aim. Importantly, the Court established that Article 14 is also violated if there is no reasonable relationship of proportionality between the means employed and the aim sought to be realized.[59]

As was established in the jurisprudence and practice of the international supervisory bodies, the principle of full equality and non-discrimination is of specific relevance in establishing permissibility of limitations on the freedom of religion. The HRC clearly established in General Comment No. 22 that state regulation which might be covered by a legitimate ground for limitation is not permissible if the limitation has a discriminatory purpose or effect.[60] More specifically in its case law the HRC stated that 'not every differentiation of treatment will constitute discrimination, if the criteria for such differentiation are reasonable and objective and if the aim is to achieve a purpose which is legitimate under the Covenant'.[61] In *Godefriedus Maria Brinkhof v. Netherlands* the HRC, in determining whether differentiation in treatment amounts to prohibited discrimination under Article 26 CCPR and referring to its General Comment,[62] stated that the exemption of only one group of conscientious objectors, and the inapplicability of exemptions for all others, is not considered to be reasonable.[63] However, in the particular case the Committee distinguished the pacifist beliefs of Mr. Brinkhof stating that he has not shown that 'his convictions as a pacifist are incompatible with the system of substitute service in the Netherlands or that the privileged treatment accorded to Jehovah's Witnesses adversely affected his rights as a conscientious

[59] *Case Relating to Certain Aspects of the Laws on the Use of Languages in Education in Belgium v. Belgium*, ECtHR, (Appl. No 1474/62, 1677/62, 1691/62, 1769/63, 1994/63, 2126/64, 23 July 1968, Merits), para. 10.

[60] HRC, General Comment No. 22 on Freedom of Religion, 48th session (1993), UN Doc. HRI/GEN/1Rev.1, para. 8.

[61] HRC, General Comment No. 18, UN Doc. CCPR/C/21/Rev. 1./ Add.1 (1989), para. 13.

[62] The General Comment No. 22 stated that when the right is recognized by law or practice 'there shall be no differentiation among conscientious objectors on the basis of the nature of their particular beliefs'. HRC, General Comment No. 22 on Freedom of Religion, 48th session (1993), UN Doc. HRI/GEN/1Rev.1, para. 11.

[63] *Godefriedus Maria Brinkhof v. Netherlands*, HRC (Communication No. 402/1990, UN Doc. CCPR/C/48/D/402/1990 (1993), para 9.3.

objector against military service'.[64] Although the HRC in the specific case has not determined that the applicant was discriminated against it called upon the Dutch authorities to amend their legislation, which provides privileged treatment to Jehovah's Witnesses, to remove any discrimination. In a different case involving conscientious objectors, the ECtHR has similarly established that differential treatment based on non-recognition of religion has resulted in treating adherents of that religion in a discriminatory manner in comparison with the ministers of the recognized Greek Orthodox Church.[65]

The case law under the ECHR shows a shift in the consideration of the differential treatment. Although the ECommHR suggested that the differential treatment should be assessed across minority religious communities in similar situations[66], it often failed to examine the differential impact of legislation which is applied uniformly to individuals finding themselves in a different situation. The example of such an approach is clearly seen in *Konttinen v. Finland* dealing with dismissal of a Seventh Day Adventist for leaving work on Friday to observe his Sabbath beliefs. The ECommHR stated that 'the Finnish legislation on working hours provides that the weekly day of rest is usually Sunday. However, this legislation does not contain provisions which would guarantee to members of a certain religious community any absolute right to have a particular day regarded as their holy day. Assuming that the applicant could be considered to be in a situation comparable to that of members of other religious communities, the Commission therefore finds that he has not been treated differently in comparison with such members.'[67]

In comparison the ECtHR adopted a different approach, introducing a more rigorous approach to the differential treatment, distinguishing between discrimination through differential treatment and discrimination through failure to differentiate appropriately. In *Thlimmenos v. Greece* the Court reiterated that it has so far considered it a violation of the rights under the ECHR when states treat differently persons in analogous situations without providing an objective and reasonable justification. More importantly the Court established that 'the right not to be discriminated against in the enjoyment of the rights guaranteed under the Convention is also violated when States without

[64] *Ibid.*

[65] *Tsirlis and Kouloumpas v. Greece*, ECtHR (Appl. No 19233/91, 19234/91, 29 May 1997, Merits and just satisfaction), paras 59–60.

[66] *X. v United Kingdom*, ECtHR (Appl. No. 8160/78 (1981) Decisions and Reports 27) at 38.

[67] *Konttinen v. Finland,* ECtHR (Appl. No 24949/94, 3 December 1996, Admissibility Decision), para. 2.

an objective and reasonable justification fail to treat differently persons whose situations are significantly different'.[68]

Interestingly the HRC, in comparison with its position taken in General Comment No. 18 (which emphasized that the principle of equality is not synonymous with the same treatment but requires differentiation in certain circumstances)[69] in *K. Singh Bhinder v. Canada* adopted a rather more restrictive approach stating that: 'the concept of freedom of religion only comprises freedom from State interference but no positive obligation for States Parties to provide special assistance to grant waivers to members of religious groups which would enable them to practise their religion'.[70]

IV. Conclusion

The analysis of the jurisprudence concerning the violations of religious rights shows that, in comparison with the universal level, the ECtHR, which applies the concept of the margin of appreciation, accords far greater discretion to states, through, among other means, broad interpretation of limitation provisions. By contrast, no equivalent latitude has been granted in implementation of the freedom of religion to states by the HRC. From the perspective of the protection of the freedom of thought, conscience and religion of religious minorities it would appear, from the jurisprudence of the supervisory mechanisms at the universal, as well as regional, levels, that the most effective protection has been provided through upholding the non-discrimination and full equality principles in implementation of the rights guaranteed under the freedom of religion rather than the developments in interpretation of the substantive articles.

[68] *Thlimmenos v. Greece*, ECtHR (Appl. No. 34369/97, 6 April 2000), para. 44.

[69] The General Comment stipulates 'the principle of equality sometimes requires State parties to take affirmative action in order to diminish or eliminate conditions which cause or help to perpetuate discrimination prohibited by the Covenant. For example, in a State where the general conditions of a certain part of the population prevent or impair their enjoyment of human rights, the State should take specific action to correct those conditions.' HRC, General Comment No. 18, UN Doc. CCPR/C/21/Rev. 1./ Add.1 (1989), para 10.

[70] *K. Singh Bhinder v. Canada*, HRC (Communication No. 208/1986, UN Doc. A/45/40 vo. 1 (1990)), para. 4.5.

FAMILY, PRIVATE LIFE, AND CULTURAL RIGHTS

Sally Holt

I. General Introduction

The notions of family, privacy and the home, as protected under international human rights law, are at the same time separate and interconnected: the home is usually the seat of the family; it is a safe haven and sanctuary from public view; the place where private life is enjoyed. The right to privacy, however, extends beyond this limited sphere of the home and the family, thus spanning the divide between public and private. On the one hand, it means the right to be left alone, the right to a private life, the right to some kind of secrecy and seclusion. It also encompasses the right to make personal choices—eg about personal convictions, appearance or choice of name—that may be, and often are, anything but private. The right to be different not only in private, but to have that difference recognized and accounted for in public policy and legislation, is important particularly for persons belonging to minorities in terms of the maintenance and development of their own cultural identity.[1]

[1] The term 'persons belonging to minorities' is generally used throughout this chapter except where discussion relates specifically to an instrument which uses different terminology, eg 'persons

The rights to family and private life are, therefore, also closely interlinked with cultural rights. While the protection of all the rights under consideration—family, private life, and cultural rights—afforded by international instruments is to be enjoyed equally by all human beings, at the same time specific aspects of the enjoyment of these rights can be of special importance for persons belonging to minorities. Cultural rights, in particular, hold especial significance for minority groups given that it is, by definition, their very cultural difference vis-à-vis the wider society that they wish to preserve. The enjoyment of culture by such groups is bound up with education, language, the arts and the media. It may also extend more widely to the choice of a particular way of life—be it in terms of the type of home one chooses, traditional activities undertaken for economic gain (which may involve a particular use of land or other natural resources) or some other aspect.[2]

Certain aspects of the right to family and private life may also be of special relevance for minority communities. Issues that have arisen in specific contexts in relation to the enjoyment of the right to respect for family life by persons belonging to minorities include the separation of family members arising from entry, residence or expulsion decisions pertaining to one or more family members who are non-nationals of the state which is making the decision. The majority relate to immigrant or so-called 'new' minorities,[3] but the situation of persons belonging to minorities who have found themselves aliens in the state of residence as the result of state succession has also been an issue. Family separation arising from alleged discrimination against non-nationals in the (lawful) country of residence, compelling the individual to return to his/her country of origin, eg in order to earn a living, is another aspect of the respect for family life that has come for consideration before the international treaty bodies. Questions of family separation arising from the exclusion of displaced persons from their homes have also been examined with respect to the Greek Cypriot population living in northern Cyprus.

belonging to national minorities' under the Council of Europe's Framework Convention for the Protection of National Minorities, adopted on 1 February 1995, entered into force on 1 February 1998, ETS No. 157 (hereinafter FCNM).

[2] Discussion of the content of these rights is dealt with separately in this chapter in view of their different sources in the international instruments, including those elaborated specifically with a view to the protection of the cultural identities of persons belonging to minorities.

[3] While reference to 'old' and 'new' minorities is used in common parlance, it should be noted that the terminology is purely descriptive and does not reflect any accepted distinction as defined in international law cf. Opinions of the Advisory Committee of the FCNM concerning states' limitation of the scope of protection of the Convention to 'old' or 'traditional' minorities only.

The right to respect for the family life of persons belonging to minorities has also been linked to states' educational policies that in effect restrict parents' choice of schooling for their children. Parental preferences are generally influenced by the wish to have their children educated in a certain way—usually related to the language of instruction. The relevant treaty and judicial bodies have examined the way that such policies impact on family life, both in relation to the separation of family members (where children attend schools at distance from the family home), as well as in terms of the impact of educating children in a language other than their mother-tongue.

Concerning privacy rights, while the right against unsanctioned intrusion of privacy by the government, individuals or corporations, as protected by international law, is generally incorporated into national legislation, at the same time almost all states have laws which allow for breaches of individual privacy in some way eg for purposes of tax data collection and retention or the interception of communications (including wire tapping and electronic surveillance etc.). While such legislative and implementing measures may apply equally to all within the state's jurisdiction, in certain political climates ethnic and minority groups, in particular, may come under suspicion of being 'disloyal' to the state, and find themselves subject to greater interference with their private lives, which is commonly justified by the authorities on the grounds of national security. In such cases persons belonging to minorities are especially vulnerable to closer monitoring than other members of the population, eg through communications surveillance or personal and body searches, as well as to breaches of the protection of the home against intrusion eg through the seizure of property. In the most extreme instances homes have been destroyed by national security forces, resulting in forced displacement of the occupants. The European Court has had occasion to examine claims of such interference brought forward by the members of the Kurdish minority in south eastern Turkey, as well as in relation to the situation of the Greek Cypriot population living in northern Cyprus.

II. Content of the Rights

A. Family and Private Life

1. Sources of International Law

Article 17 of the International Covenant on Civil and Political Rights (hereinafter CCPR), following the wording of the Universal Declaration of Human Rights (hereinafter UDHR) Art. 12, provides *inter alia* that no one shall be subjected to arbitrary or unlawful interference with his privacy, family, home or correspondence. Specific groups such as migrants and children are afforded the same protection under specialized conventions.[4] At the regional level, the parallel provision of the European Convention on Human Rights and Fundamental Freedoms (hereinafter ECHR) Article 8, places an obligation on states to respect a similar range of personal interests including the 'private and family life', home and correspondence of the individual. Article 11 of the American Convention on Human Rights (hereinafter ACHR) likewise protects the individual's private life, family, home and correspondence against arbitrary and unlawful interference.[5] The African Charter on Human and Peoples' Rights (hereinafter AfrCh), while providing for the state's protection of the family in Article 18, has no provision relating to individual privacy. The later (1990) African Charter on the Rights and Welfare of the Child does, however, protect the child from arbitrary or unlawful interference with his or her privacy, family, home or correspondence.[6]

2. *Delineation of Content*

The meaning of the personal interests as protected by the instruments is far from self-explanatory, making it difficult to define categorically what constitutes private life, family life, home or correspondence. Their meaning is also dynamic and has the potential to encompass a widening range of matters, some of which are connected to one another and some of which overlap.[7] Given the lack of watertight distinction between the different notions protected, the interpretation of each will be influenced by that of the others. It has also been observed that, while individual rights are somewhat disparate, the fact that they are grouped together strengthens the protection given by the Article as such, since each right is reinforced by its context: the rights may be

[4] International Convention on the Protection of the Rights of All Migrant Workers and Members of Their Families (hereinafter Migrant Workers Convention), adopted by GA Res 45/158 of 18 December 1990, entered into force on 1 July 2003, Art. 14. Convention on the Rights of the Child, concluded on 20 November 1989, entered into force on 2 September 1990, GA Res 44/25 (hereinafter CRC), Article 16.

[5] According to Art. 5 of the American Declaration on the Right and Duties of Man, adopted in 1948, OAS Res. XXX, OAS Off. Rec. OEA/Ser.L/V/I.4 Rev. (1965) (hereinafter Am. Decl.): 'Every person has the right to the protection of the law against abusive attacks upon his honor, his reputation, and his private and family life.'

[6] Article 10.

[7] Ursula Kilkelly, *The Right to Respect for Family and Private Life: A Guide to the Implementation of Article 8 of the European Convention on Human Rights*, Human Rights Handbooks, No.1 (Council of Europe, 2001).

read together as guaranteeing more than the sum of their parts.[8] Some general guidance as to the content of the separate interests, and evolving interpretation of these concepts by the relevant monitoring bodies and courts taking into account social, legal and technological developments, is set out below.[9] Further elaboration is provided in Section III with respect to those aspects of the rights protected that have already proven to be—or have the potential to be—most relevant to persons belonging to minorities.

(a) Family Life

The family as the 'natural and fundamental group unit of society' is entitled to protection under Article 23 of the ICCPR which also embodies the right to found a family. This latter right is similarly protected under Article 12 of the ECHR. As indicated above, a number of universal and regional instruments protect the family or the individual's 'family life' against arbitrary interference.[10] Provisions relating specifically to family reunification are also to be found in specialized conventions such as Article 10 of the Convention on the Rights of the Child (hereinafter CRC), whereby states parties are obliged to deal with applications by a child or his or her parents for family reunification in a 'positive, humane and expeditious manner'.[11] Such provision has potential bearing on the cases relating to separation of family members in the cases discussed below under Section III. Furthermore, in the European Social Charter, Article 16, states parties undertake to promote social, legal and economic protection of family life. According to the wording of the relevant provisions, family life is located squarely within the private sphere where it is allowed to function free from arbitrary state interference.

While understanding of the term family life under the Conventions was once basically confined to life in nuclear families, this has evolved to reflect a broader and more elastic understanding of the concept of the family in modern society, extending the accepted zone of intimate relations encompassed by that term beyond formal relationships and legitimate arrangements.[12] In terms

[8] Francis G. Jacobs, *The European Convention on Human Rights* (Oxford: Clarendon Press, 1975), 126.

[9] For a more detailed discussion of the content of the rights protected see: Manfred Nowak, *U.N. Covenant on Civil and Political Rights: CCPR Commentary* (Kehl am Rhein; Strasbourg; Arlington: Engel, 1993), 294–307; and D. J. Harris, M. O'Boyle and C. Warbrick, *Law of the European Convention on Human Rights* (London; Dublin; Edinburgh: Butterworths, 1995), 305–20.

[10] The terms family and family life are understood to be synonymous. Family life is used hereinafter.

[11] Article 10.

[12] Lawrence M. Friedman & Marion Rice Kirkwood, Private Lives: Families, Individuals, and the Law. Available at: http://www.law.stanford.edu/publications/lawyer/issues/72/PrivateLives.html.

of what constitutes the family or family life, the Human Rights Committee (hereinafter HRC) has clarified that the objectives of the Covenant require that the term 'family' be given a broad interpretation to include all those comprising the family as understood in the society of the state party concerned.[13] This is necessary in light of the various understandings of the scope of the 'family' unit in different cultures.[14] The Strasbourg authorities have also maintained a flexible approach bearing in mind the evolving diversity of interpersonal relationships, as well as the implications of divorce and medical advance, and have taken a case-by-case approach to deciding whether family life is involved.[15]

According to the Strasbourg organs, ECHR Article 8 concerns not *de jure* but de facto family life.[16] The determination of the Court and Commission in a particular case, therefore, relies on the reality in practice of close personal ties between the parties.[17] While this approach means it is not always easy to enumerate exactly those relationships which constitute family life or not, an increasing number of relationships beyond the traditional conjugal family unit (mother, father and children) as recognized by many European countries in their civil legislation have been accepted as falling within the meaning of family life. These include extended family (eg near relatives such as grandparents, uncles/aunts etc.) as well as other arrangements (eg adoptive parents and children, parents and children in foster relationships, etc.).[18]

While marriages that are lawful and genuine, and the relationship with the children born within that marriage are always protected, the scope of family life extends also to the 'illegitimate' family on an equal footing with the traditional family.[19] Factors taken into account by the Strasbourg organs when deciding whether a relationship can be said to amount to 'family life', in so far as a couple are concerned, include cohabitation, length of relationship and demonstration of their commitment to each other by having children 'or any other means'.[20]

[13] Human Rights Committee General Comment No. 16, The Right to Respect of Privacy, Family, Home and Correspondence, and protection of honour and reputation (Art. 17) 08/04/88 (Twenty-third session, 1988), Compilation of General Comments and General Recommendations Adopted by Human Rights Treaty Bodies, UN Doc. HRI/GEN/1/Rev.6 at 142 (2003), para. 5.

[14] See Nowak, *CCPR Commentary*, *supra*, n. 9, 299, para 27.

[15] Harris, *Law of the ECHR*, 312 and Kilkelly, *Right to Respect, supra*, n. 7 p. 16.

[16] ECtHR, *Marckx v. Belgium*, (Appl. No 6833/74, 13 June 1979, Merits and just satisfaction), para. 31.

[17] ECtHR, *Al-Nashif v. Bulgaria*, (Appl. No 50963/96, 20 June 2002, Merits and just satisfaction), para. 112.

[18] See Kilkelly, *Right to Respect, supra*, n. 7, 18–19 for reference to relevant cases in this regard.

[19] ECtHR, *Johnston and Others v. Ireland*, (Appl. No 9697/82, 18 December 1986), para. 55. *Marckx v. Belgium*, *supra*, n. 16, para. 40.

[20] ECtHR, *Al-Nashif v. Bulgaria*, *supra*, n. 17, para. 112.

The HRC likewise looks for ties beyond blood relationships and statutory forms of establishing relations such as marriage or adoption, to expression of a regular relationship through other forms such as cohabitation.[21]

Couples who live together with their children will normally be said to enjoy family life, but family life may exist even without either cohabitation or marriage, especially in the case of parent-child relationships. The European Court has observed with regard to the latter that this tie can only be broken in exceptional circumstances,[22] and may survive beyond divorce. The HRC has likewise noted that the bond between parent and child does not depend on the continuation of the parents' marriage.[23] Nor does the bond automatically come to an end when the parties no longer live together[24] or when a child is placed in care.[25] It is the actual circumstances of the closeness of the relationship between parent and child that determine its continuing existence, rather than some formal legal status such as marriage. Parents and children born into second relationships, and those born as a result of extra-marital affairs, may also enjoy family life. Family life may exist also between those who do not have a blood link.[26]

(b) Private Life

The right to privacy finds protection in the major human rights instruments as enumerated above. While the exact terminology of the two key instruments in this regard differs somewhat, it can be assumed that 'privacy' under the CCPR and 'private life' under the ECHR enjoy essentially the same meaning.[27] It has been noted that '(...) Article 17 is one of the more enigmatic provisions of the Covenant. In particular, the term "privacy" would seem open to

[21] HRC, *Shirin Aumeeruddy-Cziffra and 19 other Mauritian Women v. Mauritius* (Communication No. 35/1978, U.N. Doc. CCPR/C/OP/1) at 67 (1984), para. 9.2(b) 2 (i) 2, discussed further below.

[22] ECtHR, *Boughanemi v. France*, (Appl. No 16/1995/522/608, 27 March 1996, Merits), para. 35.

[23] HRC, *Hendriks v. Netherlands* (Communication No 201/1985, UN Doc. Supp. No. 40 (A/43/40)) at 230 (1988), para. 10.3. See also, the Individual Opinion submitted by Messrs. Vojin Dimitrijevic and Omar El Shafei, Mrs Rosalyn Higgins and Mr. Adam Zielinski concurring that the right to the protection of the child and to a family life continues, in the parent-child relationship, beyond the termination of marriage, para. 2.

[24] ECtHR, *Berrehab v. Netherlands*, (Appl. No 10730/84, 21 June 1988, Merits and just satisfaction), para. 21.

[25] ECtHR, *Andersson v. Sweden*, (Appl. No 12963/87, 25 February 1992, Merits and just satisfaction), para. 72.

[26] ECtHR, *X, Y and Z v. United Kingdom*, (Appl. No 21830/93, 22 April 1997, Merits), para. 37.

[27] Nowak, *CCPR Commentary*, *supra*, n. 9, 294, para. 15. Consequently, the terms are used interchangeably throughout this chapter.

interpretation.'[28] In his 1993 commentary on the Covenant, Nowak confirms that the prohibition of interference with privacy in the narrow sense relating to the individual was the subject of virtually no debate during the Article's drafting, and that the case law on individual communications is of no assistance in ascertaining the meaning of the word privacy.[29] Neither does the HRC's 1988 General Comment on the Article attempt to define the notion (whereas the terms 'family' and 'home' are defined).[30] Similarly with regard to Article 8 of the ECHR: 'The Commission's practice concerning the meaning of private life has been distinguished neither by its clarity nor its discipline', while the European Court has also been 'unwilling to attempt an exhaustive definition of private life or even isolate the values it protects'.[31]

Concepts of liberty developed in the eighteenth and nineteenth centuries provide the backdrop to—and valuable guidance in understanding—the notion of privacy as manifested in the legal instruments. Central to these concepts is the idea of the autonomous individual standing alone as the master of all of his or her actions that do not interfere with the sphere of liberty of others. The idea of privacy in the sense of this isolated personal zone was further manifested in the development of institutional structures related to the protection of the home, family and secrecy of correspondence.[32]

Despite the limitations alluded to above, both the HRC and the European Commission and Court have provided some guidance as to the meaning or ambit of Articles 17 and 8 respectively, which has developed beyond the 'Anglo-American' notion of privacy described above with its emphasis on the secrecy of personal information and seclusion.[33] In this respect, they have confirmed that the scope of application of the notion of privacy extends beyond the private personal space or 'inner circle' in which the individual may live his or her own personal life as he or she chooses, to include the establishment and development of relationships with others in the 'outside world'—extending also to some professional and business relationships.[34]

[28] HRC, *Coeriel et al v. Netherlands* (Communication No. 453/1991, UN Doc. CCPR/C/52/453/1991 (1994), Individual opinion by Mr. Kurt Herndl (dissenting).

[29] Nowak, *CCPR Commentary*, *supra*, n. 9, 294, para. 15.

[30] HRC General Comment, No. 16, *supra*, n. 13.

[31] Harris, *Law of the ECHR*, *supra*, n. 9, 305.

[32] Nowak, *CCPR Commentary*, *supra*, n. 9, 288, paras. 3–4.

[33] Harris, *Law of the ECHR*, *supra*, n. 9, 305–6.

[34] See: HRC, *Coeriel et al v. Netherlands*, *supra*, n. 28: 'The Committee considers that the notion of privacy refers to the sphere of a person's life in which he or she can freely express his or her identity, be it by entering into relationships with others or alone.'; and ECtHR, *Sidabras and Dziautas v. Lithuania*, (Appl. No 55480/00, 59330/00, 27 July 2004, Merits and just satisfaction), para. 44, citing the Court's judgment in *Niemitz v.Germany*: 'Respect for private life must also comprise to

Privacy, then, is as much about an individual's relationship with society and culture as it is with one's self and, in principle, the right to respect for privacy encompasses both the individual's right to a zone of autonomy within a 'private sphere' such as the home, and also with respect to personal choices within the public sphere.[35]

As Harris et al observe, the extension of the concept of privacy to include the protection of a sphere of personal relationships beyond the 'inner circle' also raises the possibility that the effective enjoyment of a social life (involving the capacity by reason of cultural familiarity and linguistic facility to enter into social relationships with others) may also be regarded as an aspect of private life.[36] While individual members of the Commission and judges of the Court have accepted a view of private life that encompasses this possibility, the idea has yet to be developed. It could, however, have important implications for persons belonging to minorities who find themselves isolated from wider society for reasons of cultural tradition or educational opportunities.[37]

Elements of privacy encompassed by the protection of CCPR, Article 17 and ECHR, Article 8, as identified in recent commentaries,[38] include:

- individual autonomy, ie that area of individual existence that does not impinge upon the sphere of liberty and privacy of others, encompassing a right to treat one's own body as one wishes, which is closely linked to;
- personal (moral and physical) integrity, encompassing intellectual freedom as well as the inviolability of one's body and protection against inhuman and degrading treatment that does not fall within the scope of other provisions;
- personal identity, ie the capacity to determine one's individual qualities, characteristics, beliefs, etc.;
- 'intimacy' or private space free from unwelcome interferences, encompassing the secrecy and confidentiality of personal information; and
- communication, encompassing the establishment of social relationships with others.

a certain degree the right to establish and develop relationships with other human beings. There appears, furthermore, to be no reason of principle why this understanding of the notion of "private life" should be taken to exclude activities of a professional or business nature since it is, after all, in the course of their working lives that the majority of people have a significant, if not the greatest, opportunity of developing relationships with the outside world.'

[35] Nowak, *CCPR Commentary, supra*, n. 9, 289, para. 5.

[36] Harris, *Law of the ECHR, supra*, n. 9, 312.

[37] *Ibid.*

[38] For a fuller delineation of the content of these categories, see: Harris, *Law of the ECHR*, 307–312; and Nowak, *CCPR Commentary*, 294–299, *supra*, n. 9.

Of all of the above, the one perhaps of most obvious immediate relevance for persons belonging to minorities is that of personal identity. The capacity of the individual to determine his or her personal identity in all its manifestations—in terms of manner, appearance, choice of name, feelings and thoughts, as well as a confession to a belief or some other conviction, etc.—is fundamental to the right to respect for one's private life. This is not merely a right to closet identity; the individual must be free to choose how he or she is to be regarded by the state, and how to present him or herself to others.[39] Thus the right to express one's individuality, for example through a particular form of dress, can be enforced in public against arbitrary or unlawful interference (such as the imposition of a mandatory dress code, for example). It is not unlikely, therefore, that situations may arise where state measures impinge on matters relating to the identity of persons belonging to minorities. In the case of *Singh Bhinder v. Canada* considered by the HRC, for example, measures imposed to ensure individual safety conflicted with the individual's dress code in conformity with his Sikh religion, although, in this case, the Committee examined the applicant's claim only in relation to freedom of religion and the prohibition of discrimination.[40]

(c) Home

In relation to the various meanings of the concept of 'home' as protected by the instruments, the core idea is one of a private sanctuary or refuge without intrusion by public authorities.[41] Home is generally the place of residence[42] (although not necessarily the only one or on a permanent basis), but can also extend to a place where it is intended to live.[43] The HRC's General Comment on CCPR Article 17 indicates the term 'home' can also be understood to indicate the place where a person carries out his/her usual occupation.[44] In the case of *Niemietz v. Germany*, the European Court likewise extended the notion of 'home' to cover some business premises, in recognition of the difficulties in drawing distinctions between activities carried out on business premises, and those carried out in a private residence.[45]

Under Article 17 CCPR, the protection of 'home' relates to all types of accommodation regardless of legal title (ownership, rental, leasing etc.) and

[39] Harris, *Law of the ECHR*, *supra*, n. 9, 307.

[40] Communication No. 208/1986, U.N. Doc. CCPR/C/37/D/208/1986, 28 November 1989.

[41] Harris, *Law of the ECHR*, 319; Nowak, *CCPR Commentary*, 302, para. 31, *supra*, n. 9.

[42] See HRC General Comment 16, *supra*, n. 13, para. 5.

[43] See *Gillow v. UK*, (Appl. No. 9063/80, 24 November 1986, Merits), para. 46.

[44] HRC General Comment 16, *supra*, n. 13, para. 5.

[45] (Appl. No 13710/88, 16 December 1992, Merits), para. 30.

nature of use (main domicile, weekend use etc.), and would extend, eg to a mobile home or house boat.[46] Likewise, under ECHR Article 8 the Court has examined the complaints of UK Gypsies living in mobile homes alleging violation of the right to respect for their home. While Article 8 does not recognize a right to be provided with a home,[47] in general the applicants in these cases merely seek respect for their existing home—their caravans or other vehicles. As these cases also indicate, the individual's choice of lifestyle may have ramifications for the nature of the home that one wants. The concept of home is not limited to residences that have been lawfully established.[48]

Where it is established that premises are 'home', then the first protection is of a right of access and occupation, and a right not to be evicted from them. Beyond the right to occupy one's home, Article 17 CCPR and Article 8 ECHR also afford protection against intrusion by the authorities of the state through surveillance activities as well as, for example, to search, seize, inspect or arrest for the purposes of administration of criminal justice. With respect to house searches, for example, Article 17(2) would require that such action would only ensue on the basis of a specific decision by a competent state authority empowered by the law to do so for the purpose of securing evidence, and that they respect the principle of proportionality.[49] Likewise under the ECHR, the weight attached to the strong interest a person has in the sanctuary of his home puts the burden on the state to justify such interventions for legitimate public purposes.[50]

(d) Correspondence

The right to respect for one's correspondence protects the integrity and confidentiality of communications with others. The HRC's General Comment on Article 17 makes it clear that protection is afforded to all forms of communications, electronic or otherwise.[51] While developments in technology have brought new methods of communication such as the Internet and e-mail into operation and enabled more sophisticted monitoring (eg the use of closed-circuit television cameras in public places) there is no reason why these should not also be covered by the protection afforded by the instruments.[52]

The protection relates to the *agency* of communication as opposed to its content (which is ordinarily protected by the right to freedom of expression),

[46] Nowak, *CCPR Commentary*, *supra*, n. 9, 302, para. 32.

[47] *Chapman v. United Kingdom*, (Appl. No 27238/95, 18 January 2001, Merits), para. 99.

[48] *Buckley v. United Kingdom*, (Appl. No 20348/92, 25 September 1996, Merits), para. 53.

[49] Nowak, *CCPR Commentary*, *supra*, n. 9, 303. para. 35.

[50] Harris, *Law of the ECHR*, *supra*, n. 9, 319.

[51] HRC General Comment 16, *supra*, n. 13, para. 8.

[52] Harris, *Law of the ECHR*, *supra*, n. 9, 320.

although the content can be relevant in determining the limits of the state's right to interfere with a communication.[53] The most common interference is secret state surveillance for the purposes of administration of criminal justice, preventing and combating crime, or the prevention of terrorism, etc. Such activity is subject to the same constraints described above with respect to house searches.

3. State Duties

(a) The Horizontal Effect

While formulated in the essentially negative terms of non-interference, Article 17 CCPR also encompasses a positive duty on states not only to refrain from arbitrary interference themselves, but to protect against such interference by private parties. Express recognition of the state's duty in this regard was made in the drafting process,[54] and is confirmed by the HRC's General Comment on Article 17, according to which: 'The obligations imposed by this article require the state to adopt legislative and other measures to give effect to the prohibition against such interferences and attacks [from state authorities or from natural or legal persons] as well as to the protection of this right.'[55]

With respect to state responsibility for violations of the rights protected under ECHR Article 8 by private persons, the Court's judgment in *X and Y v. Netherlands* confirmed that states' positive obligations may involve the adoption of measures designed to secure respect for private life even in the sphere of the relations between individuals themselves.[56] Clearly, the state does have an obligation to provide for an effective remedy for any violation whether committed by it or a private individual.[57] Whether or not this would extend to, for example, a positive obligation on states to criminalize private surveillance or data collection impinging upon an individual's rights to private life or correspondence, even if it has an obligation to provide civil remedies, is less clear-cut.[58]

As Harris notes, the positive obligation on a state with respect to private conduct may extend even to requiring positive action from private persons: states

[53] See further, Harris, *Law of the ECHR, supra*, n. 9, 320 & 346 with regard to prisoners' correspondence.

[54] Nowak, *CCPR Commentary, supra*, n. 9, 289, para. 6.

[55] HRC General Comment 16, *supra*, n. 13, para. 1. See also para. 9.

[56] ECtHR, *X and Y v. Netherlands*, (Appl. No 8978/80, 26 March 1985), para. 23. In this case, it found that the state had failed in its obligation to provide an effective criminal remedy for the private action of an individual who had sexually assaulted a mentally handicapped girl, see para. 27.

[57] Jacobs, *The European Convention, supra*, n. 8, 12 with reference to ICCPR Art. 13.

[58] Harris, *Law of the ECHR, supra*, n. 9, 324.

might be obliged to require that private data collection firms grant access to individuals to records kept about them, for example.[59]

(b) Positive Action

Although the primary object of Article 8 ECHR is that of protecting the individual from arbitrary interference by public authorities, it does not merely compel the state to abstain from such interference. European case law confirms with respect to Article 8 that, in addition to this primarily negative undertaking, there may be positive obligations inherent in an effective respect for private and family life. Thus, under the ECHR, the state has an obligation not only to desist from undue interference in the private business of individuals that they would prefer hidden from view, but must also allow and even facilitate the establishment of open relationships between individuals.[60]

The identification of the circumstances in which the duty to respect an individual's interest involves positive action is not, however, without its difficulties.[61] As the European Court has observed:

> (...) the notion of 'respect' is not clear-cut: having regard to the diversity of practices followed and the situations obtaining in the Contracting States, the notion's requirements will vary considerably from case to case. Accordingly, this is an area in which the Contracting Parties enjoy a wide margin of appreciation in determining the steps to be taken to ensure compliance with the Convention with due regard to the needs and resources of the community and individuals.[62]

As the Court noted further in the case of *Stjerna v. Finland*: 'The boundaries between the State's positive and negative obligations under Article 8 do not lend themselves to precise definition.' The Court went on to reaffirm the importance in both contexts of striking a fair balance between the competing interests of the individual and of the community as a whole.[63]

The HRC has taken a similar approach to Strasbourg in recognizing that the varying conditions and traditions (social, economic, political and cultural) existing in different countries will dictate the legal protection or measures a society or a state can afford to the family.[64]

[59] Harris, *Law of the ECHR, supra*, n. 9, 324.
[60] *Ibdi.*, 303.
[61] *Ibid.*, 321.
[62] ECtHR, *Abdulaziz, Cabales and Balkandi v. United Kingdom* (Appl. No 9214/80, 9473/81, 28 May 1985, Merits and just satisfaction), para. 67.
[63] *Stjerna v. Finland* (Appl. No 18131/91, 25 November 1994, Merits), para. 38.
[64] ECtHR, *Mauritian Women* case, *supra* n. 21, para. 9.2.(b) 2(ii).

As Harris observes with respect to the European organs, such general observations do not take us very far. Whereas under Article 8(2) the balance to be struck is between a right already established and the interests the state is seeking to protect, in reaching the balance under Article 8(1), the Court is determining the content of the protected right. It is thus up to the individual to establish the distinctive importance of the interest to him as there is no formal weight attached to this claim as there would be for an established right which, formally at least, carries special weight.[65]

In sum, while Article 17 CCPR and Article 8 ECHR provide a framework of general standards, the lack of precision in identifying the positive obligation of the state vis-à-vis private and family life means that the great variety of situations that fall under these provisions may require as many different solutions.

4. Permissible Limitations

Article 8(1) ECHR alone confers its protection in absolute terms, listing in Article 8(2) the specific grounds on which public authorities may interfere with the exercise of the protected right.[66] It is for the state to identify the legitimate aim in pursuit of which it is interfering with an individual's right—although, it may be noted in this respect, that the interest invoked as a ground for limitation has rarely been examined critically. Interference must be 'in accordance with the law' (ie it must have a legal basis and the law in question must be sufficiently precise and contain a measure of protection against arbitrariness by public authorities). It must also be 'necessary in a democratic society' for the prescribed purposes. What is 'necessary' for the purposes of Article 8 is determined by reference to the balance achieved between the rights of the individual and the public interest, through the application of the principle of proportionality. Deciding whether the interference is proportionate to the aim which it pursues involves consideration of a number of factors including the interest to be protected from interference, the severity of the interference and the 'pressing social need' for limiting the enjoyment of the individual's right. With regard to the latter, the Court recognizes that some aspects of the various rights protected by Article 8 are more important than others.[67]

[65] Harris, *Law of the ECHR*, *supra*, n. 9, 322. For more in-depth analysis of ECHR jurisprudence in relation to states' positive obligations with respect to each of the interests protected under Art. 8 see *ibid.*, 320–35.

[66] These are in the interests of national security, public safety or the economic well-being of the country, for the prevention of disorder or crime, for the protection of health or morals or for the protection of the rights and freedoms of others.

[67] Harris, *Law of the ECHR*, *supra*, n. 9, 344.

The other instruments, including the CCPR, do not contain a legal proviso allowing for restrictions in the interest of public order or similar purposes, providing instead that no one shall be subject to 'arbitrary or unlawful interference' with the rights protected. In the absence of express provision for interference by the authorities under certain prescribed conditions, it is necessary to draw upon the purposes set down in the legal provisos found in other Articles of the Covenant in order to define more closely those legitimate purposes justifying interference with the rights protected under Article 17.[68] As Nowak points out, given the relatively far-reaching possibilities for interference provided by these provisions it is unlikely that interference with Article 17 rights for reasons beyond those prescribed there will be compatible with Article 17. Indeed, not all of the purposes provided in those provisions can be applied to Article 17. For example, interference with freedom of religion that is permissible on the grounds of public morals might seem arbitrary with respect to privacy.[69]

In any event, as the HRC has clarified, any interference with Article 17 must be envisaged by national law and such law itself must comply with the provisions, aims and objectives of the Covenant. Thus, interference provided for under national law will violate Article 17 when it is based on arbitrary (eg, discriminatory) legal footing.[70] Any interference (even if provided by law) must be 'reasonable in the particular circumstances'.[71] Assessment of whether or not this is in fact the case depends on a precise balancing of the circumstances in a given case, paying regard to the principle of proportionality.[72]

While views differ as to which formulation (ECHR or other) affords the better protection of the right, Nowak's analysis of the arguments on both sides (with reference to the *traveaux préparatoires*) comes down against the hypothesis that Article 17 CCPR permits greater interference than Article 8 ECHR.[73]

B. Cultural Rights

1. *Sources of International Law*

As Thornberry notes, present day international law still has no definition of 'culture', but prefers to regulate 'cultural rights'.[74] The main sources for these

[68] See Arts. 12(3), 18(3), 19(3), 21 and 22(2).
[69] Nowak, *CCPR Commentary*, *supra*, n. 9, 293, para. 13.
[70] *Ibid.*
[71] General Comment, No. 16, *supra*, n. 13, paras. 3–4.
[72] Nowak, *CCPR Commentary*, *supra*, n. 9, 293, para. 13.
[73] *Ibid.*, 291. para. 8.
[74] Patrick Thornberry, *International Law and the Rights of Minorities* (Clarendon Press: Oxford, 1991), 187.

rights are found in Article 27(1) UDHR which recognizes everyone's rights to participate in 'the cultural life of the community' and the International Covenant on Economic, Social and Cultural Rights (CESCR) Article 15 which protects the right of everyone to 'take part in cultural life'. Under Article 31 of the CRC states have an obligation to protect and promote the rights of the child to participate fully in cultural and artistic life. Similar provisions to those articulated at the universal level are found in regional instruments such as the American Declaration of the Rights and Duties of Man, Article 13; and the Additional Protocol to the American Convention on Human Rights in the Area of Economic, Social and Cultural Rights. In a different approach, Article 17 of the African Charter on Human and Peoples' Rights also protects the right of the individual to take part in the life of his or her community, but Article 29(7) makes it a duty to 'preserve and strengthen positive African cultural values'. The emphasis, then, is on the preservation of an existing 'African' culture, rather than on the right to cultural innovation.[75]

The wording of the provisions referred to above does not make it clear whether the cultural life referred to is that of the state as a whole (which usually reflects the culture of the dominant majority) or of the (minority) group to which one belongs. At the time of drafting, cultural life under CESCR Article 15 was considered to refer to the dominant national culture: arguments for a reference to the cultural life of communities other than the national were rejected.[76] The Committee on Economic Social and Cultural Right's 1990 revised guidelines for reporting under the Covenant, however, indicate a shift in understanding to include the cultural life of minorities and indigenous peoples within the scope of the provision.[77] The more recently drafted Article 29(1) CRC is also indicative of developments in the understanding of cultural rights in international law. Accordingly, it provides in relation to the right to education that the state must develop respect for the child's *own cultural identity* as well as for the 'national values of the country in which the child is living'.[78]

Furthermore, the rights of persons belonging to minorities to 'enjoy their own culture' are specifically protected under Article 27 of the CCPR[79] and

[75] Asbjørn Eide, 'Cultural Rights and Minorities: Essay in Honour of Erica-Irene Daes', in Gudmundur Alfredsson & Maria Stavropoulo (eds.), *Justice Pending: Indigenous Peoples and Other Good Causes* (Kluwer Law International: Netherlands, 2002), 83–97 at 86.

[76] UN Doc. A/C.3/SR. 797, *Summary record of the General Assembly*, Third Committee, Twelfth Session, 797th Meeting, 31 October 1957, 178.

[77] UN Doc. E/1991/23, Annex 4, Committee on Economic, Social and Cultural Rights, *Report of the Fifth Session, Revised Guidelines*, 1990, 110.

[78] Emphasis added.

[79] Similar provision is made in CRC Art. 30.

this right is reaffirmed in Article 2(1) of the UN Declaration of the Rights of Persons Belonging to National or Ethnic, Religious and Linguistic Minorities (UN Decl. Min.).[80] At the regional level, Article 5 of the Council of Europe's Framework Convention for the Protection of National Minorities (FCNM) similarly protects the rights of persons belonging to national minorities in relation to the maintenance and development of their own cultural identity. Article 15 of the same instrument provides for the effective participation of those persons in cultural life, while Article 17 protects their free contacts across borders with persons with whom they share a cultural identity or common cultural heritage.[81] Article 12 refers specifically to the fostering of knowledge of the culture of national minorities in the field of education. CSCE/OSCE documents likewise confirm the right of persons belonging to national minorities to freely express, preserve and develop their culture in all its aspects.[82] The Council of Europe's Charter for Regional or Minority Languages (EChRML) sets out to protect and promote language as one specific aspect of culture. It is to be noted in this regard that it is the minority languages themselves that are protected, rather than the linguistic minorities who use them, although it is recognized that the Charter will have an obvious effect on the situation of the communities concerned and their individual members.[83]

The rights of indigenous peoples with respect to their social and cultural identity, customs and traditions, and institutions are protected both by the minority standards as well as dedicated instruments which provide special protection by means of positive measures going beyond Article 27.[84] International Labour Organization Convention (No.169) concerning Indigenous and Tribal Peoples in Independent Countries represents the principle and most comprehensive source of protection in this regard.[85] The rights to freely enjoy

[80] See further below under State Duties for analysis of the different wording of these provisions.

[81] See further below under State Duties for an analysis of states' obligations in this regard.

[82] Document of the Copenhagen Meeting of the Conference on the Human Dimension of the CSCE, 1990, (hereinafter Copenhagen Document), para. 22 and CSCE Geneva Meeting of Experts on National Minorities, 1–19 July 1991 (hereinafter CSCE Geneva Report).

[83] Explanatory Report, paras. 10–11.

[84] See Nowak, *CCPR Commentary*, *supra*, n. 9, 492–4 regarding indigenous peoples as minorities.

[85] See, in particular, Art. 2(2)b. See also: the Draft Declaration on the Rights of Indigenous Peoples, UN Doc. E/CN.4/Sub.2/1994/2/Add.1 (1994) which elaborates a number of specific rights in relation to indigenous peoples' maintenance, development and control over their own particular cultural identities; and the Proposed American Declaration on the Rights of Indigenous Peoples (Approved by the Inter-American Commission on Human Rights on February 26, 1997, at its 1333rd session, 95th Regular Session), OEA/Ser/L/V/.II.95 Doc.6 (1997), at Arts. VI & VII regarding cultural integrity in particular.

and maintain their national culture and have access to the culture of the host country are also extended specifically to migrant workers.[86]

2. Delineation of Content

While it is not necessary to define the concept of 'culture' itself, it is necessary, at least in general terms, to identify the components of 'culture' or 'cultural life' as protected by the standards in order to delineate their content and associated states obligations.

It is difficult to create an inventory of pure 'cultural rights' since many of those rights in the normative catalogue themselves have cultural elements. These include freedom of expression, assembly and association (including free and peaceful contacts across frontiers), freedom of religion (since religions and cultures are closely interrelated), as well as other rights such as property. Some, such as the right to education (or at least aspects of it), can be regarded as a cultural right in themselves.[87]

Guidance as to the scope of rights encompassed by 'culture' or 'cultural life' in international legal instruments is provided by the following categorization: material heritage; artistic and scientific creation; and culture as 'the sum total of the material and spiritual activities and products of a given social group which distinguishes it from other social groups'.[88] Having initially started from a minimalist position concerning the concept of culture equivalent to material aspects such as art and literature,[89] the CESCR has broadened its interpretation of cultural life under Article 15 to mean 'a way of life', that is 'a world view representing the totality of a person's encounter with the external forces affecting his life and that of his community'.[90] This has been translated in concrete terms into a concern on the Committee's part for the rights of minorities to practise and develop their distinct cultural identity.[91] From the perspective of minorities, 'culture' or cultural life can be seen to encompass almost all aspects of the community life of the minority group with a view to the preservation and development of their cultural identity. In fact, in many

[86] Article 31 of the UN Migrant Workers Convention; CSCE Vienna Document para. 42.

[87] Asbjørn Eide, 'Cultural Rights and Minorities', *supra*, n. 75, at 87.

[88] Rodolfo Stavenhagen, 'Cultural Rights and Universal Human Rights', in Asbjørn Eide et al (eds.), *Economic, Social and Cultural Rights—A Textbook*, (Netherlands: Kluwer Academic Publishers, 1995), 63–77, at 65–7.

[89] See UN Doc.E/1992 (E.CN.4/640) *Report of the Seventh Session of the Commission on Human Rights*, 24 May 1951.

[90] Committee ESCR General Day of Discussion on Art. 15, para. 213, cited in: Roger O'Keefe, 'The Right to Take Part in Cultural Life under the ICESCR', *International and Comparative Law Quarterly*, 47, (1998), 904–23 at 917.

[91] O'Keefe, *ibid.*, citing Revised Guidelines at paras. 1(c) & (d) and concluding subpara.

ways, the enjoyment of culture is the *raison d'être* of all minority groups, since they are generally defined as such by the fact that they have cultural features that differ from those of the wider society in which they live, and which they want to preserve. This is reflected in the minority standards, which include a range of provisions that protect important aspects of cultural identity, such as those pertaining to the use of minority languages (in education, contact with public authorities and the media as well as in relation to names), for example.[92]

Thus, while some cultural rights are available to any human being, others are available only to persons belonging to minorities. As the HRC observes in its General Comment on Article 27 CCPR: 'The protection of these rights is directed to ensure the survival and continued development of the cultural (...) identity of the minorities concerned (...) these rights must be protected as such and should not be confused with other personal rights conferred on one and all under the Covenant.'[93]

The enjoyment of culture, then, is closely bound up with the arts and with language, and education, regardless of international borders. It also extends to the traditions and customs[94] of a particular group including, for example, traditional dress or attire, as well as to their particular way of life including the right to make a living in their own cultural ways.[95] Thus, with regard to the exercise of the cultural rights protected under Article 27, the HRC has observed that culture manifests itself in many forms, including *a particular way of life* associated with the use of land resources, especially in the case of indigenous peoples. That right may include such traditional activities as fishing or hunting and the right to live in reserves protected by law.[96]

(a) Underlying Principles

The wording of Article 15 CESCR, ie the right to *take part* in cultural life, indicates the importance of the principle of participation in the enjoyment of cultural rights. This encompasses both the right to have access to a cultural life and to participate in that cultural life. Regional minority-related instruments likewise provide for the effective participation of persons belonging to

[92] See, eg, FCNM, Arts. 10, 11 and 14.

[93] HRC General Comment 23, Art. 27 (Fiftieth session, 1994), UN Doc. CCPR/C/21/Rev.1/Add.5 (1994), reprinted in Compilation of General Comments and General Recommendations Adopted by Human Rights Treaty Bodies, UN Doc. HRI/GEN/1/Rev.6 at 158 (2003) para. 9.

[94] See Art. 4(2) of the UN Decl. Min.

[95] Commentary to the Declaration on the Rights of Persons Belonging to National or Ethnic, Religious and Linguistic Minorities by Asbjørn Eide, Chairperson of the Working Group on Minorities, UN Doc. E/CN.4/Sub.2/AC.5/2001/2, 2 April 2001, para. 56.

[96] HRC General Comment 23, *supra*, n. 93, para. 7, emphasis added.

national minorities in cultural life.[97] OSCE participating states have explicitly recognized in this regard that 'the preservation of the values and of the cultural heritage of national minorities requires the involvement of persons belonging to such minorities.'[98] The right to take part in cultural life also encompasses the right to shape and change culture, since cultural practices are not natural, pure, or immutable, and may in fact be contested within the community of practitioners. In this respect the right to innovate and challenge is a significant aspect of individual cultural rights. Recognition of the fact that cultures are not static is implicit in state obligations (discussed further below) to create the conditions for the promotion of the cultural identity of persons belonging to minorities as provided by UN Decl. Min. Article 1 and the preamble of the FCNM, as well as for the maintenance and development of their culture under UN Decl. Min Article 4(2), and Article 5 of the FCNM.[99] Under these provisions minorities should be given the opportunity to develop their own culture in the context of an ongoing process.[100]

Effective participation in cultural life as elaborated in the minority standards[101] encompasses two key elements: 1) participation in relevant decision-making processes (including political ones) with a view to influencing policy to represent one's own cultural interests and those of the group; and 2) the management of one's own or the group's cultural affairs. The latter element implies a degree of self-governance, including (but not exclusively) through territorial arrangements, as a tool to achieve the overall aim of maintaining and developing culture and identity.[102] Thus under Article 2(3) UN Decl. Min. persons belonging to minorities have the right to participate in 'decisions (...) concerning the minority to which they belong or the region in which they live'.[103] Paragraph 4 of the same article encompasses the right of persons belonging to minorities to establish and maintain their own institutions, including those related to their own cultural identity. The degree of self-governance will be specific to each group, depending partly on the extent of the desire of the group to maintain and develop its cultural life.

[97] See FCNM Art. 15.

[98] CSCE Geneva Report.

[99] See also CSCE Copenhagen Document para. 33 in this respect.

[100] Eide Commentary, *supra*, n. 95, para. 29.

[101] See in particular UN Decl. Min, Art. 2 and FCNM Art. 15.

[102] See CSCE Copenhagen Document, para. 35 noting efforts to protect and create the conditions for cultural identity of certain national minorities by establishing 'appropriate local or autonomous administrations corresponding to the specific historical and territorial circumstances of such minorities (...)'.

[103] Article 2(3).

A second key underlying principle is that of equality and the related standard of non-discrimination. However the duty-holder (usually the state) interprets the right to take part in cultural life, essentially there must be a meaningful freedom available to all on equal terms. This implies the availability of equal opportunities for everyone. In this respect, Article 5(e)vi of the International Convention on the Elimination of All Forms of Racial Discrimination (CERD) specifically provides for equal participation in cultural activities. The principle of non-discrimination with regard to cultural life is further embodied in the minority instruments including Article 2(1) UN Decl. Min. whereby persons belonging to minorities have the right to enjoy their own culture without any form of discrimination. Under Article 4(2) FCNM Parties undertake to promote 'full and effective equality between persons belonging to a national minority and those belonging to the majority' in all areas of cultural life.

Thus, the overlapping and changing cultural practices of diverse cultural groups should take place under conditions of equality. In this respect it should also be recalled that according to the principle of non-discrimination the treatment of like groups differently or different groups similarly can be in breach of international standards.[104]

Finally, it should be noted that while the cultural rights of persons belonging to minorities have a collective dimension, in the sense that they are to be enjoyed in community with others,[105] the subject of these rights is the individual not the community as a whole. Whether individuals may choose to identify in specific situations with specific cultural practices as 'identity markers' is a matter of personal choice, but this cannot be conceived as the exercise of a collective right.[106]

3. State Duties

Three elements of obligation with regard to the right to take part in cultural life can be identified: recognition, protection, and promotion of cultural identity.

At the most basic level, the state has an obligation to recognize (if not endorse) the existence of different cultures, and ensure the right of individuals to take part in that cultural life and the components of that right. This may require more than a policy of non-interference and inaction. If the entitlement is to be meaningful as a human right, then it is not enough merely to refrain from

[104] See CERD 1(4) and HRC General Comment 23, *supra*, n. 93, para. 6.2. with regard to the legitimacy of differential treatment.

[105] CCPR Art. 27.

[106] This point was made by several members in the CESCR's General Day of Discussion on Art. 15, 1992. See further Nowak, *CCPR Commentary*, *supra*, n. 9, 497–9 regarding the collective element in Art. 27.

hindering the enjoyment of cultural rights by persons belonging to minorities. Such possibly 'benign neglect' may mean only loss for persons desiring, but unable, to preserve their cultural identities. The state may therefore need to do more than let such persons fend for themselves in this endeavour: it may need to take action to *protect* the existence of minority cultures and the individual's enjoyment of such.

(a) Protection

While the nature of the state's obligations is expressed in negative terms in Article 27 CCPR, according to which 'minorities shall *not be denied the right*, in community with the other members of their group, to enjoy their own culture (...)',[107] the HRC's General Comment on Article 27 makes it clear that the provision goes beyond mere passive non-interference. Positive measures by states may be necessary to protect the identity of a minority, and the rights of its members to enjoy and develop their culture in community with other members of the group.[108] In accordance with this interpretation, Article 2(1) UN Decl. Min. couches the right of persons belonging to minorities to enjoy their own culture, and to participate effectively in cultural life in positive terms.[109] Article 1(1) of the same instrument also makes it clear that these cultural rights often require action, including protective measures. Under paragraph 2 of this provision, states are required to adopt 'appropriate legislative and other measures' to achieve the ends of protecting the existence and cultural identity of minorities.

States, therefore, have a minimum obligation to protect the existence of cultural groups, especially cultural minorities, from annihilation or from cultural assimilation against their will.[110] The HRC is clear that this obligation extends to taking positive measures to protect cultural groups from the actions of third parties which have assimilatory effect.[111] Article 5(2) of the FCNM likewise requires that the parties protect persons belonging to national minorities from any action aimed at assimilation. It should be noted that, according to the Explanatory Report to the FCNM, protection against involuntary assimilation under the Convention does not preclude states from taking measures in

[107] Emphasis added.

[108] HRC General Comment 23, *supra*, n. 93, para. 6.1.

[109] Article 2(1).

[110] See: UN Decl. Min, Art. 1(1) according to which 'States shall protect the existence and the (...) cultural (...) identity of minorities (...)'; and FCNM Art. 5(2).

[111] HRC General Comment 23, *supra*, n. 93, para. 6.1. See further, Nowak, *CCPR Commentary*, *supra*, n. 9, 502–4 regarding horizontal effects and the positive duty of protection under Art. 27.

pursuance of their general integration policy.[112] This provision should be read also in the context of the preamble to the instrument which acknowledges the importance of social cohesion in establishing the aim that cultural diversity be a factor not of division, but of enrichment to society.

(b) Promotion

Recognition and a basic level of protection form only a part of a state's respect for cultural rights. Article 15 International Covenant on Economic Social and Cultural Rights (CESCR), as well as relevant minority standards, also encompass the substantive ability to take part in and presumably enjoy cultural life and impose on states parties an obligation to take positive and continuing action to foster the full realization of this right.

The minority rights standards specifically require that states encourage or promote the conditions whereby persons belonging to minorities may maintain and develop their cultural identity. In other words states have a duty to create the space for cultural pluralism. Thus under Article 1(1) UN Decl. Min. states shall encourage conditions for the promotion of the cultural identity of persons belonging to minorities. Article 4(2) places an obligation on states to take measures to create 'favourable conditions' to enable persons belonging to minorities to express their characteristics and develop their culture. In the European context, the preamble to the FCNM considers that '(...) a pluralist and genuinely democratic society should not only respect the ... cultural ... identity of each person belonging to a national minority, but also create appropriate conditions enabling them to express, preserve and develop this identity (...).' Under Article 5 states parties undertake to promote the conditions necessary for persons belonging to national minorities to maintain and develop their culture and to preserve the essential elements of their identity. Article 15 FCNM subsequently obliges the state to create the conditions necessary for the effective participation of persons belonging to national minorities in cultural life and in public affairs—particularly in those affecting them.[113]

Thus, a state does not satisfy its obligation to recognize the right to take part in cultural life merely by removing any formal barriers to the equal participation of each individual in the cultural life of his or her community. If

[112] Explanantory Report to the FCNM, para. 46.

[113] The provision mirrors Copenhagen Document para. 33 according to which participating states are committed not only to protecting the cultural identity of national minorities on their territory, but to creating the conditions for the promotion of that identity. See also the CSCE Geneva Document, Chapter IV and Vienna Document, Principles, para. 19 encompassing similar commitments to protect and create conditions for the promotion of the identities of persons belonging to national minorities.

cultural rights are to be realized, then access to active participation is necessary, and this may require support and facilitative measures from the state. In this respect, the HRC's General Comment 23 clearly establishes that in order to fulfil their positive obligation with respect to the cultural rights of minorities states may, and should where necessary, take 'special measures' including affirmative action.[114] Articles 1 and 4 of the UN Decl. Min. likewise require specified, active measures by the state to ensure that persons belonging to minorities may exercise their cultural rights without discrimination. Such measures include those in the field of education, in order to encourage knowledge of the history, traditions, language and culture of the minorities.[115] Any such measures will be in conformity with the principles of equality and non-discrimination with respect to the other citizens of the participating state concerned.

In policy terms, protection and promotion of cultural identity requires not only tolerance of diversity, but also a positive attitude of cultural pluralism by the state and society as a whole.[116] This implies the elaboration of appropriate policies and probably the adoption of specific legislation facilitating programme development and resource allocation. With regard to the latter, the principle of non-discrimination would require that, in the same way as the state provides funding for the development of the culture and language of the majority, it should provide resources for similar activities of the minority. It may also be noted with regard to the enjoyment of economic, social and cultural rights, more generally, that even where resources are seriously constrained, 'the vulnerable members of society can and indeed must be protected

[114] See also, HRC General Comment 23, *supra*, n. 93, paras. 6.2 regarding positive measures and the principle of non-discrimination: 'as long as those measures are aimed at correcting conditions which prevent or impair the enjoyment of the rights guaranteed under article 27, they may constitute a legitimate differentiation under the Covenant, provided that they are based on reasonable and objective criteria.'

[115] Art. 4(4) UN Decl. Min.; Art. 12 FCNM. See also CERD Art. 7 and CRC Art. 29 regarding intercultural education.

[116] See the UNESCO Declaration on Cultural Diversity, Adopted by the 31st session of the UNESCO General Conference, Paris, 2 November 2001, as well as UN General Assembly Resolution 54/160 on Human Rights and Cultural Diversity, UN Doc. A/RES/54/160, 22 February 2000, affirming the value of cultural diversity and cultural pluralism for society in general and their contribution to peace and security. Respect for cultural diversity, social cohesion and intercultural cooperation are also enshrined in the minority-specific instruments. Thus, under FCNM Art. 6, for example, parties are obliged to encourage a spirit of tolerance and intercultural dialogue and take effective measures to promote mutual respect and understanding and cooperation among all persons living on their territory. See also para. 30 of the Copenhagen Document regarding the promotion of tolerance and diversity in the context of peaceful, stable, just and democratic states.

by the adoption of relatively low cost targeted programmes'.[117] Inaction is not therefore an option for states regardless of resource limitations.

One possibility in creating the conditions for the promotion of minority culture is for the state to accord autonomy to cultural communities in the management of their own cultural affairs. The Lund Recommendations on the Effective Participation of National Minorities in Public Life, developed by independent experts at the request of the OSCE High Commissioner on National Minorities, provide a number of alternative models in this regard.[118]

In sum, states have an obligation not only clearly to recognize cultural rights, but to take legislative, administrative and financial measures designed to protect and support the nourishment of cultural life for all on equal terms. Key spheres in this regard relate to the fields of education, use of language, media, literature and the arts, religion (to the extent the state engages in this field), and 'way of life' broadly understood (eg the nomadic lifestyle of English Gypsies as recognized by the European Court of Human Rights (see further below under Section III)).

4. Permissible Limitations

There exist important permissible limitations on cultural rights, not least of all the limitation that such rights must not violate the rights of others. In other words, neither majorities nor minorities should be allowed to assert their identity in such a way that they deny the possibility for others to do the same, or which lead to discrimination against others in the common domain. The caveat in Article 4(2) UN Decl. Min. whereby 'States shall take measures to create favourable conditions to enable persons belonging to minorities to develop their culture (...) except where specific practices are in violation of national law' raises more difficult questions. As Eide notes in his commentary on this Article, while it is clear that the state is not free to adopt whatever prohibitions against minorities' cultural practices that it wants, it is intended to respect the margin of appreciation which any state must have regarding which practices it wants to prohibit, taking into account the particular conditions prevailing in that country. As long as those prohibitions are based on reasonable and objective grounds, they must therefore be respected. Similarly, the Explanatory

[117] Committee ESCR General Comment 3 on the nature of the States Parties' Obligations (Art. 2(1) of the Covenant), (Fifth session, 1990), UN Doc. E/1991/23, annex III at 86 (1990), reprinted in Compilation of General Comments and General Recommendations Adopted by Human Rights Treaty Bodies, UN Doc. HRI/GEN/1/Rev.6 at 14 (2003), 1990, para. 12.

[118] Lund Recommendations on the Effective Participation of National Minorities in Public Life, (The Hague, September 1999).

Report to the FCNM confirms that reference to state obligations to promote conditions for the preservation of *inter alia* the 'traditions' of persons belonging to minorities as an essential element of their identity is not an endorsement or acceptance of practices contrary to national law or international standards. Accordingly, 'Traditional practices remain subject to the limitation arising from the requirements of public order'.[119]

III. Analysis of Case Law

A. Family Life and Impact on Family Life

1. Entry, Residency, and Expulsion Cases

One developing aspect of the positive obligation of the state to respect family life relates to issues of entry, residency permission, or expulsion of family members who do not have an independent right to enter or stay in a Convention state where other family members have a right to reside. Both the Strasbourg organs and the HRC have examined complaints that such measures have disrupted the family unit in violation of respect for the family life of those concerned.

In cases considered thus far, the HRC has taken the view that the common residence of husband and wife has to be considered the 'normal' behaviour of a family, and has confirmed that the exclusion of a person from a country where close members of his or her family are living can amount to an interference within the meaning of Article 17; in principle, this also applies when one of the spouses is an alien.[120] The HRC General Comment on the position of aliens under the Covenant confirms that the respect for family life has effects on the right of non-nationals to enter or reside in a particular state.[121] European Court case law also confirms that measures in the field of immigration may affect the right to respect for family life under Article 8 of the Convention where entry or deportation measures result (or threaten to) in lawfully resident persons being deprived or threatened with deprivation of the society of their spouses in Convention states. Like the HRC, the Court has recognized the centrality of spousal cohabitation to the respect for family life protected

[119] Explanatory Report to the FCNM, para. 44.

[120] ECtHR, *Mauritian Women* case, *supra*, n. 21, para. 9.2.(b) 2(i)2.

[121] (. . .) in certain circumstances an alien may enjoy the protection of the Covenant even in relation to entry or residence, for example, when considerations of (. . .) respect for family life arise. HRC, General Comment No. 15: The position of aliens under the Covenant (Twenty-seventh session, 1986), Compilation of General Comments and General Recommendations Adopted by Human Rights Treaty Bodies, UN Doc. HRI/GEN/1/Rev.6 at 140 (2003), para. 5.

by Article 8 as reinforced by the existence of Article 12, 'for it is scarcely conceivable that the right to found a family should not encompass the right to live together'.[122]

According to jurisprudence of the HRC, the protection of a family cannot vary with the sex of one or other spouse, as was established in the *Mauritian Women* case, in which the HRC was of the opinion that, while it might be justified for a state to restrict the access of aliens to their territory, and to expel them from there for security reasons, *unequal treatment* between foreign husbands and wives in this regard was discriminatory, and could not be justified by security requirements.[123] This position contrasts with the initial jurisprudence of the European organs which seemed to indicate that the place where family life is to be enjoyed is the place where the father or husband has a right to reside.[124] The Court, however, in its later consideration of such differential treatment between the sexes in terms of the place of residence, found it to be discriminatory.[125]

While the HRC's jurisprudence indicates that there may be cases in which a state party's refusal to allow one member of a family to enter/remain on its territory would involve interference in that person's family life, the fact that one member of the family is entitled to remain does not necessarily mean that refusing others entry or requiring them to leave involves such interference.[126] Similarly under the ECHR, entry refusal or deportation of one member of the relationship will constitute interference under Article 8 which will only be compatible with the Convention where it fulfils the requirements of paragraph 2. As the Court noted in *Abdulaziz, Cabales and Balkandi v. United Kingdom*, the scope of Article 8 does not, however, protect the right of married couples to live in a particular contracting state of their choice nor does the duty imposed on states by that article extend to a general obligation to accept non-national spouses for settlement.[127] While the Court has acknowledged that there may be positive obligations inherent in an effective 'respect' for family life beyond protection against arbitrary interference by the authorities, states enjoy a wide margin of appreciation in this area.[128]

[122] ECtHR, *Abdulaziz, Cabales and Balkandi v. United Kingdom*, *supra*, n. 62, para. 62.

[123] *Mauritian Women* case, *supra*, n. 21, para. 9.2. (b) 2 (ii) 3.

[124] See, the Commission in *Agee v. UK*, cited in Harris, *Law of the ECHR*, *supra*, n. 9, 331.

[125] ECtHR, *Abdulaziz, Cabales and Balkandi v. United Kingdom*, *supra*, n. 62.

[126] HRC, *Jonny Rubin Byahuranga v. Denmark* (Communication No 1222/2003, UN Doc. CCPR/C/82/D/1222/2003 (2004)), para. 11.5.

[127] ECtHR, *Abdulaziz, Cabales and Balkandi v. United Kingdom*, *supra*, n. 62, para. 68.

[128] *Ibid.*, para. 67.

The approach of both the HRC and European Court in such cases is first to establish the existence of family life. This does not follow merely from the existence of tie of kinship. An existing close relationship must be established (i.e. the state is not obliged to grant a foreign citizen entry to its territory for the purpose of establishing a new family relationship there). Thus, in the *Polish-Canadian* case, the HRC rejected the claim of a Canadian national of Polish origin, whose daughter and grandson (both Polish nationals) were refused entry to join her, that her rights had been violated under Article 17 on the grounds that after 17 years of separation 'family life' did not exist. In doing so, it confirmed that cohabitation is a significant factor in establishing the closeness of family ties, and consequent existence of family life. While the case was declared inadmissible, the formulation of the decision did indicate that the Committee was not indisposed, in principle, to recognizing a right of aliens to join family members legally residing in a Convention state.[129]

Case law under both the CCPR and ECHR indicates that spousal and parent–child relationships are those most likely to be considered to enjoy the protection of family life. Thus under ECHR Article 8, even in cases where family life has not been fully established in the country in question, lawful and genuine marriages 'may be considered to attract such respect as may be due under Article 8'.[130] The HRC's opinion in the case of *Jonny Rubin Byahuranga v. Denmark* likewise illustrates the importance attached by the Committee to the parent–child relationship. The deportation of a father of a family with two minor children, compelling the family to choose whether to accompany him or stay in the state party, was found to constitute interference with the family.[131] As the Committee's jurisprudence in the case of *Hendriks v. Netherlands* confirms, this relationship can be considered to constitute family life, even after divorce.[132]

Developments in European jurisprudence would seem to indicate, however, that the level of protection afforded to the relationships between the family unit of parents and children does not extend to wider family relationships in the type of cases under consideration here. In *Slivenko v. Latvia*, the Court, referring to its own case law related to expulsion and extradition, stated that

[129] Nowak, *CCPR Commentary*, *supra*, n. 9, 301, para. 29.

[130] ECtHR, *Abdulaziz, Cabales and Balkandi v. United Kingdom*, *supra*, n. 62, para. 62.

[131] HRC, *Jonny Rubin Byahuranga v. Denmark*, *supra*, n. 126, para. 11.5. In this case, however, no violation was found since the author had submitted the communication solely in his own right and not on behalf of his wife or children, meaning the Committee considered only whether the author's rights under Arts. 17 and 23 would be violated as a result of his removal.

[132] *Hendriks v. Netherlands*, *supra*, n. 23, para. 10.3 & Individual Opinion submitted by Messrs. Vojin Dimitrijevic and Omar El Shafei, Mrs. Rosalyn Higgins and Mr. Adam Zielenski, (...) 2.

'family life' established in the territory of a contracting state by aliens lawfully resident there has been understood as 'normally' limited to the core family.[133] The implication is that in such cases, where one party is not a national of a Convention state and has no right of residency there, then the interpretation of the scope of 'family life' will be narrower than that allowed in other cases. As argued by Judge Kovler in his separate opinion, in doing so the Court has reverted from a wider concept of 'family life' within the meaning of Article 8 as established in its own case law that includes at least ties between near relatives such as grandparents and grandchildren, to a narrow interpretation based on the conjugal family. Such a step, he argues, is out of line with European sociological trends vis-à-vis the contemporary family.[134] Such a restrictive interpretation of 'family life' has obvious implications for 'non-core' family members in such cases.

Under Article 17 CCPR, where there has been an interference with 'family life', whether the existence and application of immigration laws affecting the residence of a family member is compatible with the Covenant depends on whether such interference is either 'arbitrary or unlawful' as stated in Article 17 or conflicts in any other way with the state party's obligation under the Covenant.[135] Relevant criteria identified by the HRC for assessing whether or not the specific interference with family life could be justified in the case of *Jonny Rubin Byahuranga v. Denmark* included the degree of hardship the family and its members would encounter as a consequence of such removal.[136] In this case, the Committee conceded that the author's expulsion might well constitute a considerable hardship for his wife and children, whether they remain in Denmark, or whether they decide to avoid separation of the family by following the author to a country they do not know and whose language the children do not speak.

European jurisprudence has gone further than the HRC in elaborating the relevant factors to be taken into account when considering whether a decision is compatible with respect for private and family life. In deportation cases the extent of links which the individual enjoys with both the host state, and that to which the individual will be deported, is considered relevant. Such links include the degree of social integration of the person concerned in terms of the

133 *Slivenko v. Latvia* (Appl. No 48321/99, 9 October 2003, Merits and just satisfaction), para. 94.

134 Partly Concurring and Partly Dissenting Opinion of Judge Kovler, *Marckx v. Belgium*, *supra*, n. 16, para. 45.

135 *Mauritian Women* case, *supra*, n. 21, para. 9.2. (b) 2 (i) 2.

136 *Jonny Rubin Byahuranga v. Denmark, supra*, n. 126, para. 11.7.

length of time spent, and knowledge of the culture, in either state[137] as well as the existence of family ties and social circle in respective countries (parental ties are considered particularly important in this regard).[138] The impact on their relationship with those family members who remain behind, and any other personal circumstances such as health or psychological factors, are also considered.[139] Whether the couple were aware of problems of entry and the limited leave available when they married is also considered relevant.[140] These factors are then balanced against the reason for removal in order to determine whether the interference is proportionate to the need fulfilled.

This approach suggests that the duty to respect family life will be stronger where family life is already established in a Convention state—the more so, if it has been established for a long time. This is good news for persons belonging to minorities who face deportation from states where they are not citizens, but have long and established ties (often since birth). This was the case in *Slivenko v. Latvia* where the applicants were former Latvian residents of Russian origin who were required to leave Latvia (and then detained as illegal immigrants) as the spouse and daughter of a former Russian Officer. Their long-term (and in the daughter's case life-long) residency was an important factor in the Court's finding their removal to be an interference with their private life and home, incompatible with the Convention.

Similarly, as established by the Court in *Abdulaziz*, where it can be shown that obstacles exist to establishing the home elsewhere, in the country of the spouse or applicant's own origin or where there are any special reasons why they should not be expected to do so then their case will be stronger.[141] The strongest are those where the family members residing in the Convention state have no right in the law of the alien member state to join their spouse there or where the alien member cannot return to his home state because he is a

[137] See, for example, *Moustaquim v. Belgium* (Appl. No 12313/86, 18 February 1991, Merits and just satisfaction) where the applicant was able to demonstrate strong social and family ties with the expelling state and had had little contact with the receiving state. The opposite was the case in *Boughanemi v. France, supra*, n. 22, where the Court found it probable that the applicant retained links with his country of origin.

[138] See: *Berrehab v. Netherlands* (Appl. No. 10730/84, 21 June 1998, Merits and just satisfaction) where the Court put particular weight on the effect the applicant's deportation would have on his relationship with his daughter; and *Ciliz v. Netherlands* (Appl. No. 29192/95, 11 July 2000, Merits and just satisfaction) re the applicant's ties with his son.

[139] Kilkelly, *Rights to Respect, supra*, n. 7, 58. See further, Harris, *Law of the ECHR, supra*, n. 9, 332–4 for an account of relevant cases.

[140] ECtHR, *Abdulaziz, Cabales and Balkandi v. United Kingdom, supra*, n. 62.

[141] In *Abdulaziz, supra*, n. 62, the applicants (non-UK national women with rights of residence there) had not shown that there were obstacles to establishing family life in their own or their husbands' (non-UK nationals with no right of residence in the UK) home countries.

refugee.[142] As Harris et al note, situations where the Convention rights of the spouse would not be enjoyed in the alien member state (eg a woman's subjection to an Islamic regime against her will in her husband's home state) should also be a compelling reason against deportation.[143]

The evolving jurisprudence of the Court has seen a gradual shift in the direction of stronger protection for alien family members against expulsion. In the *Berrehab* case the Court moved away from its established position that the right to family life does not in general involve a positive obligation to allow the family to establish itself in a particular country and that the state is entitled to remove an alien for good reason under Article 8(2)—usually for the protection of public order or prevention of crime—even where the enjoyment of family life may be difficult thereafter.[144] The strength of the ties of the applicant (who lost his right to stay in The Netherlands after his divorce from his Dutch wife) was the deciding factor in finding that the state had a positive obligation to allow him to stay. This principle was extended in the *Moustaquim* case, where the applicant—a second-generation immigrant in Belgium—was able to demonstrate real and substantial ties to the host state. As Harris et al observe: 'With different degrees of enthusiasm, some members of the Commission and Court have said that the case law is tantamount to giving a second-generation alien with family ties in a state the right to stay.'[145] The Court's approach in the *Beldjoudi* case further demonstrates a shift in emphasis from the relevance of the possibility of family life being enjoyed elsewhere to an assessment of the proportionality of any proposed removal under Article 8(2).[146] The applicant's close ties to the host state combined with practical and legal obstacles to his wife accompanying him to his country of origin were considered to outweigh the aims of preventing crime or preserving public order in considering the proportionality of his proposed deportation.

2. *Family Separation Resulting from (Claimed) Violations of Other Rights*

The Committee on the Elimination of Racial Discrimination (CERD/C) has had occasion to examine whether the alleged violation of the rights of a legally resident non-national in a Convention state, leading to the return of that

142 Harris, *Law of the ECHR*, *supra*, n. 9, 332.

143 *Ibid.*

144 *Ibid.*, 351.

145 *Ibid.*, 352, referring to the concurring opinion of Judge Martens and dissenting opinion of Judge Pettiti in the *Beldjoudi* case (Appl. No. 12083/86, 26 March 1992, Merits and just satisfaction).

146 *Ibid.*, 333, 352–3.

individual to his/her country of origin and consequent family separation, may constitute a violation of the respect for family life. In *Demba Talibe Diop v. France* a Senegalese citizen living in France claimed that the rejection of his application to practise law constituted a violation not only of his right to work, but also of his right to a family life because it meant he was forced temporarily to leave his home, and take up residence and practise law in Senegal, so as to be able to provide for his family. The case was considered to be ill-founded by the CERD. The Committee's opinion was based on the programmatic nature of the rights protected by Article 5 (e) of the Convention, noting that it is not the Committee's mandate to see that the rights protected by this provision are established, but rather to monitor their progressive implementation.[147] In dismissing the claim, the Committee provided no indication of whether, in the case of the violation of a non-national's rights under Article 5 (eg of his/her civil and political rights) causing him/her to leave the country, so resulting in family separation, a violation might also be found in conjunction with Article 17.

3. Family Separation Resulting from Displacement

The European Court has recognized that Article 8 applies to enforced family separation resulting from the exclusion of displaced persons from their homes. In *Cyprus v. Turkey*, the Court considered the applicant government's complaint regarding the refusal to allow the return of any Greek-Cypriot displaced persons to their homes in northern Cyprus in the context of their allegations in respect of the living conditions of the Greek Cypriots. Severe restrictions on the freedom of movement as a matter of policy and in the absence of any legal basis—including limitations on the number and duration of family visits during the period under consideration, as well as the refusal to allow schoolchildren attending schools in the south to return permanently to the north after having attained the ages of 16 and 18 for males and females respectively, and restrictions applied to visits of those children to their parents in the north—resulted, in the Court's opinion, in the enforced separation of families and consequent denial to the Greek-Cypriot population of the possibility of leading a normal family life.[148]

4. Impact of Education Policies on Family Life

While the finding of a violation in the *Cyprus v. Turkey* case related in part to enforced separation of families resulting from serious restrictions on the choice

[147] *Demba Talibe Diop v. France* (Communication No 2/1989-CERD/C/39/D/2/1989, 10 May 1991), para 6.4.

[148] *Cyprus v. Turkey* (Appl. No. 25781/94, 10 January 2001, Merits), paras. 292–293.

of education as a matter of policy, the Strasbourg organs have also examined specifically whether measures taken in the field of education—notably relating to the language of education—can affect the right to respect for private and family life. Such matters are obviously of particular relevance and concern for persons belonging to linguistic minorities. The Commission in its consideration of the *Inhabitants of les Fourons* case confirmed the relevance of such measures, '(...) for instance, if their aim or result were to disturb private or family life in an unjustifiable manner, *inter alia*, by separating children from their parents in an arbitrary way.'[149] This might be the case, for example, if school hours were deliberately arranged in such a way as to prevent contact between children and their parents or to reduce such contact to a minimum or if, where education was compulsory, children were obliged to live in boarding schools.

Concerning the language of education, in *Inhabitants of les Fourons,* the Commission went on to find that the fact that French-speaking children living in the six townships of the Fourons area of Belgium could only obtain education in Dutch unless their parents had the resources to send them to private French-language schools did have an impact on family life. However, 'harsh though the consequences might be in individual cases, they do not involve a breach of Article 8. This provision in no way guarantees the right to be educated in the language of one's parents by the public authorities or with their aid.'[150] he European Court followed this line in the *Belgian Linguistics* case where it found that the effects on private and family life of a child being educated far away from his/her home in order to receive that education in a language of their parent's choice could not be considered interference by the authorities with their rights as protected under Article 8. The Court stressed in this regard that the decision of certain applicants to separate themselves from their children by sending them to a French-language school in Greater Brussels because French language education was either unavailable or inadequate in their districts was a

[149] *Inhabitants of les Fourons v. Belgium* (Appl. No. 2209/64, 30 May 1974, Report of the Commission, 30 March 1971 [Part 2, B, Section II, B]), para. 135. The adoption of general measures taking away the discrimination of French-speaking schools in certain regions in Belgium (by allowing French-speaking schools to receive subsidies) led to the Committee of Ministers' decision that no further action was called for in this case. See General measures adopted to prevent new violations of the European Convention on Human Rights: Stock-taking of measures reported to the Committee of Ministers in its control of execution of the judgments and decisions under the Convention (Application of former Arts. 32 and 54 and of Art. 46), Council of Europe Doc. H/Conf (2000) 7.

[150] *Inhabitants of les Fourons v. Belgium, supra*, n. 149.

result of their own choice and not imposed by legislation.[151] Thus, while under certain conditions provisions relating to the language of instruction might be considered incompatible with ECHR Article 8, this would not be due to the state's failure to respect parental wishes with regard to the language of education, but to the grave and unjustified disturbances caused to family life.[152] The approach of the Court and Commission in these cases, affirming the right of the state to determine official languages of the country which are thus the languages of instruction in public schools, demonstrates a reluctance to question the organization of the state vis-à-vis official language use and affording the state a wide margin of appreciation in this regard. In its judgment of 23 July 1968 (Series A, No. 6, para. 31), the European Court of Human Rights affirmed the right of the state to determine official languages of the country which are thus the languages of instruction in public schools, but denied that there was a right to education in a language of one's choice.

Aside from the question of the impact of the separation of family members as a result of the child having to travel to school and the hardships entailed in that 'scholastic emigration', these cases raise questions with respect to the way in which language as a marker of identity and culture relates to the enjoyment of family life and, specifically, whether for the authorities to oblige a child to receive an education in a language other than that of his/her home interferes with family life within the meaning of Article 8 of the Convention. Judge G. Maridakis in his partly dissenting opinion in the *Belgian Linguistics* case addressed the matter to some extent, as follows:

> Private and family life would be violated if the authorities intervened to force a person to shape that life in a way that departed from his traditions and thus from the spirit that by virtue of blood ties predominated in relations between parents and their children and between members of the same family in general.

He went on to argue that neither family traditions nor ties of blood in this case were disturbed by the fact that the applicants were obliged to send their children to French-language schools far from their homes. The fact of children receiving their education in a language that is not their mother tongue is not, then, considered to detract from their ability to enjoy family relations in accordance with their traditions. This is in line with the Court's observation in finding no interference in the *Inhabitants of les Fourons* case that: 'To require

[151] *Case Relating to Certain Aspects of the Laws on the Use of Languages in Education in Belgium v. Belgium* (Appl. Nno 1474/62, 1677/62, 1691/62, 1769/63, 1994/63, 2126/64, 23 July 1968, Merits) [at The Law, B] 7.

[152] Paul Sieghart, *The International Law of Human Rights* (Oxford: Clarendon Press, 1983), 317.

a child to study in depth that national language which is not his own, cannot be characterised as an act of "depersonalisation".'[153] It can be inferred from these observations that the fact that family members can continue to use their mother-tongue in their own private communications is considered sufficient in order to continue family traditions. This would seem to be confirmed by the Commission's findings in its inadmissibility decision in the case of *X. v. Belgium* that: '(...) it does not appear likely that for the youngest daughter to be taught in that language contrary to her parents wishes should in any way disturb family life, in which the Greek language is used.'[154]

B. Private Life[155]

1. Protection of the Home

At its most basic, Article 8 includes a right to have one's home protected from attacks by the state and its agents. Thus, in the case of *Hasan Ilhan*, a Turkish citizen belonging to the Kurdish minority living in south-eastern Turkey, the Court was in no doubt that the deliberate destruction of a house and property causing displacement of the applicant's family constituted a grave and unjustified interference with the respect for his private and family life and home.[156] Similar issues concerning the destruction of property and the transfer and eviction of civilians have arisen in the context of the Cyprus conflict resulting in the denial of access to their homes in the north of Cyprus to Greek Cypriots as discussed above.

2. Surveillance and Monitoring

The European Court has observed on a number of occasions that Article 8 protects the moral and physical integrity of the individual, including the right to live privately, away from unwanted attention.[157] The collection of information by officials of the state about an individual without his consent will interfere with his respect for his private life.[158] While some secret surveillance may be justified under the European Convention even though the individual

[153] *Inhabitants of Les Fourons v. Belgium, supra*, n. 149, [Part 2, B, Section II, B], para. 135.

[154] *X v. Belgium*, (Application No 4372/70, 2 February 1971, Admissibility Decision).

[155] Jurisprudence relating to the home and correspondence as protected by the instruments are considered in this section under the umbrella of 'private life'.

[156] *Hasan Ilhan v. Turkey* (Appl. No 22494/93, 9 November 2004, Merits and just satisfaction), para. 112.

[157] *Sidabras and Dziautas v. Lithuania* (Appl. No 55480/00, 59330/00, 27 July 2004, Merits and just satisfaction), para. 43.

[158] Harris, *Law of the ECHR, supra*, n. 9, 309.

is never informed about it, states must, however, have in place an adequate framework of safeguards offering minimum standards of protection in order to prevent the abuse of power by the state and the violation of Article 8 rights. Interference with an individual's Article 8(1) right by collecting information about him/her will have to be justified under Article 8(2).

In the case of *Cyprus v. Turkey*, the Court noted that the population concerned was subjected to serious restrictions on the exercise of these rights, including monitoring of its members' movements and contacts. The 'intrusive and invasive acts' effected by the authorities even extended to the physical presence of state agents in the homes of Greek Cypriots on the occasion of social or other visits paid by third parties, including family members. The Court found a violation of the right of Greek Cypriots living in northern Cyprus to respect for their private and family life and to respect for their home since 'no legal basis for these acts has been adduced, less so any justification which could attract the provisions of Article 8(2) of the Convention.'[159]

The Court further found no violation of Article 8 concerning the alleged practice of interference with the right of Greek Cypriots living in northern Cyprus to respect for their correspondence. The applicant state's claims that correspondence was intercepted or opened as a matter of administrative practice, and that there was a consistent practice of tapping telephone calls made to and from the north were not considered to be substantiated by the Court.[160]

In the Court's opinion the specific allegations of the applicant government in question were bound up with the more general allegation of the respondent state's colonisation policy on the demographic and cultural environment of the Greek Cypriots' homes. It went on to confirm the Commission's conclusion that the restrictions which beset the daily lives of the enclaved Greek Cypriots who remained in the north, and which created a feeling among them of feeling 'compelled to live in a hostile environment in which it is hardly possible to lead a normal family and private life', to be factors aggravating the violations found in relation to the respect for private and family life.[161] Clearly, then, sustained campaigns of harassment, discrimination and oppression as a matter of policy, leading either to outright expulsion or gradual deterioration in the living conditions of persons belonging to certain groups carried out with a

[159] *Cyprus v. Turkey, supra*, n. 148, paras. 294–6.
[160] *Ibid.*, paras. 297–8.
[161] *Ibid.*, paras. 300–1. Such factors, as identified by the Court, included: absence of normal means of communication, unavailability in practice of Greek-Cypriot press, insufficient numbers of priests, difficult choice with which parents and schoolchildren were faced regarding secondary education; the restrictions and formalities applied to freedom of movement (. . .).

view to removing those groups from (occupied) territory, constitute a violation under the European Convention. Having regard to its conclusion concerning the hostile environment for Greek Cypriots in northern Cyprus, the Court did not, however, consider it necessary to examine the allegations concerning the implantation of Turkish settlers in northern Cyprus separately.[162]

3. Names

The use of personal names is a matter of particular resonance for persons belonging to minorities, given their relation both to the language and the identity of the individual, as well as their indication of ties with the family and wider community.[163] Jurisprudence under both the CCPR and ECHR confirms that the right to choose and change one's own name falls under the scope of private and family life as protected by Articles 17 and 8 respectively.

In *Coeriel et al v. Netherlands*, the HRC expressed the view that:

> (...) a person's surname constitutes an important component of one's identity and that the protection against arbitrary or unlawful interference with one's privacy includes the protection against arbitrary or unlawful interference with the right to choose and change one's own name.[164]

While Article 8 does not contain any explicit reference to names, the European Court has also found nonetheless that 'since it constitutes a means of personal identification and a link to a family, an individual's name does concern his or her private and family life'.[165]

The HRC and the European Court have both indicated that an obligation imposed by the public authorities on the individual to change his/her surname against his/her will would constitute an interference with the individual's right to respect for his/her private life. According to the Committee such interference would be in contravention of Article 17.[166] Under the ECHR such interference would have to be justified under Article 8(2).[167] While the Committee has made reference specifically to the treatment of 'foreigners' in this regard, this also has implications for national minorities and official attitudes to the spelling of their names.

162 *Ibid.*, para. 302.

163 See Ferand De Varennes, 'Linguistic Identity and Language Rights' in Marc Weller, *Universal Minority Rights: A Commentary on the Jurisprudence of International Courts and Treaty Bodies*, sub-heading III.3.(b) called *Names and Topographical Indications in a Minority Language.*

164 *Coeriel et al v. Netherlands*, *supra*, n. 28, para. 10.2.

165 *Stjerna v. Finland*, *supra*, n. 63, para. 37.

166 *Coeriel et al v. Netherlands*, *supra*, n. 28, para. 10.2.

167 *Stjerna v. Finland*, *supra*, n. 63, para. 38.

Both the HRC and the European Court have also examined whether refusal of the authorities to *recognize* a change of surname is also beyond the threshold of permissible interference within the meaning of Articles 17 and 8. In this respect, they recognize that there may be a public interest in regulating name changes and choice.[168] Such public interest considerations as identified by the Court include: accurate population registration; safeguarding the means of personal identification; and linking the bearers of a given name to a family.[169] In the light of the lack of uniformity of practice with regard to the restrictions on permissible name changes and choices in contracting states, the Court affords a wide margin of appreciation in this area.

In the only case of its kind to be considered by the Strasbourg authorities so far, the Court found that the refusal of the state to allow the applicant (a Finnish national with a Swedish minority name) to register a change of surname in the official records did not constitute an interference with his right to respect for his private life under Article 8(1). The Court's reasoning in this case indicates that inconvenience suffered by the individual in relation to difficulties in pronunciation and spelling of his name, as well as susceptibility to nicknames, as reasons for changing his/her name might raise an issue of failure to respect private life under paragraph 1—although in this case they were not deemed sufficient to do so. In reaching its findings, the Court considered that the level of inconvenience suffered by the applicant was no more significant than that experienced by a large number of people in Europe today, where movement of people between countries and language areas is becoming more and more commonplace.[170] The implication here is that some degree of inconvenience because it is commonplace is acceptable. The case also indicates that the connection of the individual to his/her chosen new name needs to be more substantial than that to an ancestor who died over 200 years ago, regardless of the individual's personal feelings of attachment.[171]

[168] See *Coeriel et al v. Netherlands, supra*, n. 28, para. 6.1. concerning the Committee's admissibility decision: '(. . .) the Committee considered that the regulation of surnames and the change thereof was eminently a matter of public order (. . .).' As the Explanatory Note to the Oslo Recommendations regarding the Linguistic Rights of National Minorities, The Hague, February 1998, points out at p. 15: 'For example, public authorities would be justified in using the script of an official language of languages of the state to record the names of persons belonging to national minorities in their phonetic form. However, this must be done in accordance with the language system and tradition of the national minority in question.'

[169] *Stjerna v. Finland, supra*, n. 63, para. 39.

[170] *Ibid.*, para. 42.

[171] *Ibid.*, para. 43.

While the Court's approach in this case does not rule out the possibility of a violation in name-change cases arising in the future, the applicant would need to be able to make a more convincing argument in terms of both the inconvenience experienced, and of established links with the proposed new name. As Harris observes, while the Court uses the language of 'margin of appreciation' in this and other cases, the inquiry under Article 8(1) is not identical to that made under paragraph 2 in deciding whether an interference is in accordance with the law and necessary in a democratic society—where the balance is struck between an established right and the countervailing interests which the state is seeking to protect. In reaching the balance under Article 8(1) the Court is determining the *content* of the protected right. It is therefore incumbent on the applicant to establish the distinctive importance of the interest to him.[172]

While the HRC, like the European Court, has not interpreted the right to respect for privacy to embody an absolute right to change one's own name on request and at a whim, it did find a violation of the applicant's rights in relation to refusal of official recognition for a name change in *Coeriel et al v. Netherlands*. In this case the applicants' request to change their surnames into Hindu names in accordance with the requirements of their religion had been rejected. The Court found that the circumstances in which a change of surname will be recognized were defined so narrowly in the Dutch authorities' guidelines as to limit the authors' rights under Article 17 unreasonably. The refusal of the authors' request was therefore held to be arbitrary within the meaning of Article 17(1).[173]

In his individual dissenting opinion, Mr. Kurt Herndl considered that the Committee's position in *Coeriel* represents an expansion of Article 17 and that, in reaching its finding of a violation, it introduces a new notion of 'reasonableness'. The Committee's opinion, however, seems more to be a finding that there were no compelling state considerations for refusing the change. This is consistent with the approach taken with respect to the term 'arbitrary' in Article 9.

In a separate individual dissenting opinion, Mr. Nisuke Ando argued that the Committee may not be attaching enough importance to the social and

[172] Harris, *Law of the ECHR*, *supra*, n. 9, 322.

[173] *Coeriel et al v. Netherlands*, *supra*, n. 28, para. 10.5. In reaching this conclusion, the Committee recalled its General Comment on Article 17, in which it observed that the notion of arbitrariness 'is intended to guarantee that even interference provided for by law should be in accordance with the provisions, aims and objectives of the Covenant and should be, in any event, reasonable in the particular circumstances.'

legal functions of a surname or to the implications for others. He regarded the consideration of a family name as belonging to an individual person alone, whose privacy is protected by Article 17 as taking a 'Western' approach in treating a surname as a matter of personal identity when there are many social, historical and cultural considerations to be taken into account, particularly as a change has implications for other members of the family (cf. ECHR Article 8 which puts the rights of others as an express limit on the privacy right).

C. Cultural Rights

The HRC has considered a number of cases brought by indigenous peoples in relation to their rights to continue their traditional activities and lifestyles. These are significant from a minority perspective in view of the Committee's expansive interpretation of the concept of culture under Article 27 to include '(...) protection to a particular way of life associated with the use of land resources through economic activities, such as hunting and fishing, especially in the case of indigenous peoples.'[174] This link between economic activities and culture is further confirmed by paragraph 7 of the Committee's General Comment on Article 27 which employs similar language, while additionally observing that the exercise of cultural rights may include the right to live in reserves protected by law.[175]

The Committee's approach in addressing such cases has been, first, to establish that the economic activity constitutes an essential element in the culture of the community in question. While in cases relating to indigenous communities this relationship has generally gone undisputed,[176] the situation when it comes to ethnic, linguistic or religious minorities has been less clear-cut, raising questions with regard to the way that the culture of a minority which is protected by the Covenant is to be defined, and the role that economic activities have in that culture. Thus, in *J.G.A. Diergaardt et al v. Namibia*, although the community in question had a historically established link to the land (going back 125 years) this was not considered by the Committee to be the result of a relationship that would give rise to a particular culture.[177] Argumentation

[174] *J.G.A. Diergaardt et al v. Namibia* (Communication No 760/1997, UN Doc. CCPR/C/69/D/760/1997 (2000)), para. 10.6.

[175] HRC General Comment 23, *supra*, n. 93.

[176] See: *Anni Äärelä and Jouni Näkkäläjärvi v. Finland* (Communication No 779/1997, UN Doc. CCPR/C/73/D/779/1997, 4 February 1997), para. 7.5; *Ilmari Länsman et al. v. Finland*, (Communication No 671/1995, UN Doc. CCPR/C/58/D/671/1995, 1996), para. 9.2.; and *Apirana Mahuika et al. v. New Zealand* (Communication No 547/1993, UN Doc. CCPR/C/70/D/547/1993, 2000), para. 9.3.

[177] *J.G.A. Diergaardt et al v. Namibia*, *supra*, n. 174, para. 10.6.

leading to the same conclusion was further elaborated in an individual concurring opinion, according to which the authors' claim was essentially considered an economic rather than a cultural one as they had 'defined their culture almost solely in terms of the economic activity of grazing cattle' and could not show that they enjoyed a culture 'intimately bound up with and dependent on' the use of the lands in question.[178] Indigenous peoples, on the other hand, can very often show that their particular way of life or culture is closely bound up with particular lands in regard to not only economic, but other cultural and spiritual activities as well.[179] Thus, it would appear that the demonstration of some additional cultural element beyond the traditional pursuit of an economic activity on certain lands is necessary in order to draw the protection of Article 27. Although in the *Diergaardt* case the authors could show that they were from a community that enjoyed its own culture, as reflected in its distinctive forms of self-government (i.e. as a manifestation of their own distinctive culture), they failed to establish how their way of raising cattle constituted an essential element of this culture.

The Committee has accepted that the right to enjoy one's culture as protected by Article 27 can extend beyond traditional means of livelihood of minorities, to include those activities that have undergone some modern developments and adaptations.[180] This reflects an understanding that culture is not static, but may change and develop without losing its protected character. At the same time, it has been argued that the right to enjoy one's own culture should not be understood to imply that a traditional way of life must be preserved intact at all costs. This was the view expressed by Mr. Nisuke Ando in his Individual Opinion in the *Lubicon Lake Band* case where he observed that outright refusal by a group in a given society to change its traditional way of life may hamper the economic development of the society as a whole.[181]

Having established that the authors are members of a minority, and that the activity in question is an essential element in their culture, the Committee's approach in this regard, is to inquire whether the *extent* of the interference by the state party in that activity is such that it has failed to protect the authors' right to enjoy their culture. In doing so it examines whether the correct balance

[178] Individual Opinion of Elizabeth Evatt and Cecilia Medina Quiroga (Concurring).

[179] See, eg, *Ilmari Länsman et al v. Finland*, *supra*, n. 176, para. 9.3, where the Committee found that the area in question continued to have spiritual significance relevant to the culture of the applicants who were of Sami origin.

[180] *Ilmari Länsman et al v. Finland*, *supra*, n. 176, para. 9.3. See also, *Apirana Mahuika et al. v. New Zealand*, *supra*, n. 176, para. 9.4.

[181] Individual Opinion of Mr. Nisuke Ando in the *Lubicon Lake Band* case (Communication No 167/1984, U.N. Doc. CCPR/C/33/D/167/1984 (1990)).

has been struck between the regulation of economic activity by the state, eg in the interests of the economic development of society as a whole or for ecological reasons, and the cultural rights of those affected. In this respect, the Committee does recognize that a State may understandably wish to encourage development or allow economic activity by enterprises and has observed that: '(…) measures that have a certain limited impact on the way of life of persons belonging to a minority will not necessarily amount to a denial of the right [to enjoy culture] under Article 27.'[182]

So, for example, quarrying in an area traditionally used by reindeer herders of Sami origin was not considered by the Committee to violate the cultural rights of those persons since reindeer herding in that area did not appear to be adversely affected by such quarrying as occurred.[183] The scope and proportion of those measures impacting on the way of life of minorities is, therefore, important in deciding whether they have reasonable and objective justification and can be considered consistent with Article 27.[184] Thus, while the Committee found no violation of the rights of the authors in the *Ilmari Länsman* case, it did indicate that:

> (…) if mining activities in the Angeli area were to be approved on a large scale and significantly expanded by those companies to which exploitation permits have been issued, then this may constitute a violation of the authors' rights under article 27.[185]

Furthermore, the Committee has pointed out to states parties that, while individual activities that affect the rights under Article 27 may not in themselves constitute a violation, such activities may have a cumulative effect that serves to erode the cultural rights of those affected.[186]

A similar approach to that of the HRC has been followed by the Strasbourg organs in their consideration of claims brought by minorities that their cultural rights had been violated under Article 8, indicating that not every interference which in some limited way alters previous conditions can be regarded as a denial of cultural rights as protected by that provision. Thus, in *G. and E. v. Norway*, in finding the application inadmissible, the Commission acknowledged that the construction of a hydroelectric plant could interfere with the private life of the applicants 'as members of a minority, who move their herds

[182] *Ilmari Länsman et al v. Finland*, *supra*, n. 176, para. 9.3.

[183] *Ibid.*, para. 9.6.

[184] *Sandra Lovelace v. Canada*, Communication No. 24/1977, UN Doc. CCPR/C/OP/1 at 83 (1984), para. 16.

[185] *Ilmari Länsman et al v. Finland*, *supra*, n. 176, para. 9.8. See also *Jouni E.Länsman et al v. Finland* (Communication No 671/1995, UN Doc. CCPR/C/58/D/671/1995 (1996), para. 10.4.

[186] *Jouni E.Länsman et al v. Finland*, *ibid.*, para. 10.7.

and deer around over a considerable distance', but considered nevertheless only a comparatively small area would be lost. Similarly, in *Noack and Others v. Germany* concerning transfer of the occupants of a village, the vast majority of whom were members of the Sorbian minority. The fact that the inhabitants were to be resettled in a town within the original settlement area of the Sorbs where the protection of their rights as a member of a minority would continue under the Constitution of the Land of Brandenburg, was particularly important in the Court's consideration that the interference with their rights was not disproportionate to the legitimate aim pursued.[187]

Whether consultation with those affected has taken place is a further important factor in considering whether measures that impact on the way of life of persons belonging to minorities constitute a violation of their cultural rights. In delivering its opinion in the *Ilmari Länsman et al v. Finland* case, for example, the Committee took particular note of the fact that the authors had been consulted during the proceedings leading to the delivery of the quarrying permit in question.[188] The Committee has also recalled its General Comment on Article 27 in this regard, according to which the right to one's own culture '(...) may require positive legal measures of protection and measures to ensure the effective participation of members of minority communities in decisions which affect them'.[189] It should be noted that the latter refers to *effective* participation which may imply something more than mere consultation. In *Anni Äärelä and Jouni Näkkäläjärvi v. Finland*, for example, the Committee noted that the authors and other key stakeholder groups were consulted in the evolution of the logging plans in question and that the plans were partially altered in response to criticisms from those quarters.[190] This was one consideration taken into account by the Committee in concluding that there had been no violation under Article 27 under the Covenant.

In the absence of a parallel provision to Article 27 CCPR protecting the cultural rights of minorities in the European Convention, several cases involving the Roma have sought to claim the right to respect for their particular lifestyle as an aspect of private life, family life or home under Article 8 ECHR. While Article 8 does not make specific reference to cultural rights, the Commission, in its admissibility decision in *G. and E. v. Norway* recognized

[187] *Noack and Others v. Germany* (Appl. No 46346/99, 25 May 2000, Admissibility Decision).

[188] *Ilmari Länsman et al v. Finland, supra*, n. 176, para. 9.6.

[189] *Apirana Mahuika et al. v. New Zealand, supra*, n. 176, para. 9.5, referring to General Comment No 23 at para. 7.

[190] *Anni Äärelä and Jouni Näkkäläjärvi v. Finland, supra*, n. 176, para. 7.6.

that: 'A minority group is, in principle, entitled to claim the right to respect for a particular lifestyle it may lead as "private life", "family life" or "home".'

The approach of the Commission in *G. and E. v. Norway* was borne out in the case of *Buckley v. United Kingdom* where it held that 'the traditional lifestyle of a minority may attract the guarantees of Article 8'. The case concerned the claim of a woman of Roma ethnic origin (or Gypsy, as known in the UK) who claimed that the authorities' rejection of her planning application, whereby she and her family were prevented from living in caravans on her own land, constituted a violation of her right to respect for her private and family life and her home. She further argued that British planning policy was discriminatory in character for not taking into account the traditional travelling lifestyle of a Gypsy. In finding in favour of the applicant, the Commission submitted that Gypsies following a traditional lifestyle required special consideration in planning matters and that, although this had been recognized by the government, in the specific circumstances of the applicant's case a proper balance between the interests of the individual and those of the community as a whole had not been achieved.

The European Court's reversal of the Commission's decision, however, focused on the applicant's right to a home, rather than a particular way of life. The judgment was based on the wide margin of appreciation to be afforded to states in deciding whether a fair balance has been struck between individual and community in planning decisions: given the complexity of competing interests involved and the 'direct and continuous contact with the vital forces of their countries', the national authorities are in principle better placed than an international court to evaluate local needs and conditions, rendering the Court itself a strictly supervisory role.[191] While noting that the importance of the applicant and her family's right to respect for the 'home' must be taken into account in determining the scope of the margin of appreciation allowed to the respondent State,[192] the Court considered that, in this case, proper procedural safeguards were in place and that planning officials exercised proper discretion in weighing the interests at issue (i.e. the applicant's predicament against the interests of highway, safety, environmental and public health) and was satisfied that the reasons relied on by them were relevant and sufficient, for the purposes of Article 8, to justify the resultant interference with the applicant's right to respect for her home.[193]

[191] ECtHR, *Buckley v. United Kingdom* (Appl. No. 20348/92, 25 September 1996, Merits) Para. 75.

[192] *Ibid.*, para. 75.

[193] *Ibid.*, para. 84.

Despite this finding, the Court did imply that planning authorities, in balancing the interests at issue, should afford special consideration to Gypsies as members of a minority group with a different lifestyle from that of the majority of the population.[194] As Judge Lohmus, in his partly Dissenting Opinion, pointed out, to treat the applicant, a Gypsy, as having the same rights and duties as other members of the community would fail to take account of the particular situation of the Gypsy minority. Thus, '[i]t may not be enough to prevent discrimination so that members of a minority receive equal treatment under law. In order to establish equality in fact, different treatment may be necessary to preserve their special cultural heritage.'

Indeed, the possibility of legitimate differential treatment based on reasonable and objective criteria is a well-established general principle in international human rights law[195] which can be especially important when it comes to protecting the identity of a minority and the rights of its members to enjoy and develop their culture.[196] Where a situation of inequality exists and individuals or groups of individuals find themselves in a disadvantaged position, states have an obligation to take corrective action. With regard to minorities, in particular, 'positive measures' by states may be necessary in order to protect the identity of a minority'.[197] It may be, therefore, that in order to ensure de facto equality, criteria for ruling in individual planning applications involving Gypsies need to be materially different to those applied in other cases in order to allow for the special needs of the Gypsy minority in relation to the enjoyment and preservation of their traditional lifestyle and culture.

In this respect, both Judge Lohmus and Judge Repik in a separate Partly Dissenting Opinion, followed the approach of the Commission in recognizing that the exercise of one's right to adopt a particular lifestyle may have implications for the type of home one wants (in this case living in a caravan to facilitate periodic travelling and wishing to establish a safe and stable place to set up home in order to be sure of having somewhere to return to in the light of the inadequate provision of legal sites), and the importance of these considerations in deciding whether the correct balance has been struck between the rights of the Gypsy family and those of the community.[198]

194 *Ibid.*, paras. 80–84.

195 See Arts. 1(4) and 2(2) of the CERD; see also, HRC General Comment 18 on Non-Discrimination (Thirty-seventh session, 1989), Compilation of General Comments and General Recommendations Adopted by Human Rights Treaty Bodies, UN Doc. HRI/GEN/1/Rev.6 at 146 (2003), para. 8.

196 See, HRC General Comment 23, *supra*, n. 93, para. 6.2.

197 *Ibid.*

198 ECtHR, *Buckley v. United Kingdom*, (Appl. No 20348/92, 25 September 1996, Merits).

The question of legitimate differentiation in the treatment of different groups arose again in *Chapman v. United Kingdom*, also concerning restrictions placed upon the accommodation opportunities available to Gypsies living a nomadic lifestyle in the UK related to inadequate provision of legal sites that are both affordable, and acceptable to Gypsies. Pointing to the difficulties that would be raised under Article 14 of the Convention should a Gypsy who has unlawfully stationed a caravan site at a particular place be accorded different treatment from that accorded to non-Gypsies in the same circumstances, the Court observed that: '(. . .) belonging to a minority with a traditional lifestyle different from that of the majority does not confer an immunity from general laws intended to safeguard the assets of the community as a whole, such as the environment (. . .)'.[199] While finding no violation of Article 8, the Court did, however, go further than in *Buckley* in addressing the question of a right to a particular way of life, conceding that lifestyle may have an incidence on the manner in which such laws are to be implemented.[200] The Court thus extended its understanding of the impacts of planning enforcement to remove a caravan vis-à-vis the rights protected under Article 8 to include not only the respect for one's home, but also the right to family and private life where a traditional way of life is at stake. In this case, the Court considered the applicant's occupation of her caravan to be 'an integral part of her ethnic identity',[201] and acknowledged that, as intimated in *Buckley*, the vulnerable position of Gypsies as a minority means that some special consideration should be given to their needs and their different lifestyle both in the relevant regulatory planning framework and in reaching decisions in particular cases. It concluded that: 'To this extent, there is a *positive obligation* on Contracting States by virtue of Article 8 to *facilitate* the Gypsy way of life.'[202] In this case, the positive obligation on the UK was not sufficient to overcome the environmental land restrictions where the applicant wanted to live. This raises the question as to what such an obligation might reasonably be expected to embody in practice.

A key issue in the *Chapman* case was the extent to which European 'norms' in respect to the treatment of minorities have become established. In this respect, the Court pointed to an emerging consensus among Council of Europe States recognizing the special needs of minorities and an obligation to protect their security, identity and lifestyle.[203] The Court was not, however,

[199] ECtHR, *Chapman v. United Kingdom* (Appl. No 27238/95 18 January 2001, Merits), para 96.
[200] *Ibid.*
[201] *Ibid.*, para. 73.
[202] *Ibid.*, para. 96.
[203] *Ibid.*, para. 93.

persuaded that the consensus is 'sufficiently concrete... for it to derive any guidance as to the conduct or standards which Contracting States consider desirable in any particular situation.'[204] In this particular case the Court was not convinced, '(...) despite the undoubted progress in international law with regard to the protection of minorities (...)', that Article 8 can be interpreted to involve a positive obligation of general social policy which would demand the provision of places in authorized caravan sites to match the statistical numbers of Gypsies.[205]

The Court's assessment with regard to accepted standards for the protection of minorities in Europe is disappointing especially in the light of recent European standard setting in this area, most notably the FCNM which has been ratified by 34 states to date, the entry into force of ECHR Protocol 12 and Directive 2000/78/EC, as well as a number of important specifically Roma-related recommendations.[206] Indeed, the minority in *Chapman* in a dissenting opinion rejected the majority's assertion that the consensus is not sufficiently concrete, arguing that there is indeed an emerging consensus amongst the member states of the Council of Europe which 'includes a recognition that the protection of the rights of minorities, such as Gypsies, requires not only that Contracting States refrain from policies or practices which discriminate against them but also that, where necessary, they should take positive steps to improve their situation through, for example, legislation or specific programmes'.[207] It is to be hoped that future rulings of the Court will be informed by this range of international developments and trends pertaining to the rights of minorities with respect to its interpretation of Article 8 of the Convention.

As Clements observes, while the decision in *Chapman* reflects the view by a narrow majority (10:7) that a generally accepted standard for the treatment of minorities throughout Europe has yet to reach sufficient maturity as to dictate an adverse finding against the UK in this case, implicit in the disagreement between majority and minority is that such a standard will, at some point in the future, become sufficiently established as to enable the Court to require

[204] Emphasis added. *Ibid.*, para. 94.

[205] *Ibid.*, para. 98. The crux of the matter here was that insufficient provision of official sites had caused Gypsies to buy their own land on which to park their caravans.

[206] See, for example: ECRI Policy Recommendation No.3: Combating Racism and Intolerance Against Roma/Gypsies, 1998; and Report of the OSCE High Commissioner on National Minorities on the *Situation of Roma and Sinti in the OSCE Area* (The Hague: 2000).

[207] Joint Dissenting Opinion of Judges Pastor Ridruejo, Bonello, Tulkens, Strážnická, Lorenzen, Fischbach and Casadevall. para. 3.

states to conform to such.[208] This opens up the possibility that the Court will in time find a violation in such cases.[209]

A number of differing factors in the circumstances of particular cases may point to a more positive outcome for applicants in future. The Court's indication in *Chapman* that the availability of alternative accommodation in eviction cases is an important factor in weighing the proportionality of interference with the individual's rights under Article 8, for example, suggests that governments may have an obligation to provide alternative accommodations in such situations to those wishing to maintain their traditional lifestyle, and that the Court might find a violation where no such alternative provision existed. It also follows from the Court's observations with regard to the need for special consideration of the needs of the Gypsy minority in the relevant regulatory planning framework and decision-making process, that any flaws in the legal framework itself or any material irregularity or unfairness arising in the implementation of planning regulations will be viewed very seriously by the Court. This was indeed the situation in *Varey v. United Kingdom* where the granting of permission by a planning officer was overturned at Ministerial level. A friendly settlement was reached. This likelihood is further confirmed by the positive outcome in favour of the applicant in *Connors v. United Kingdom*—the only case concerning accommodation of UK Gypsies successfully brought before the Court to date—where the lack of a legal framework providing sufficient procedural safeguards to the individuals who were evicted from a legally occupied site was a determining factor in finding that their rights had been violated. The Court was not persuaded of the necessity for a statutory scheme which failed to provide legal security of tenure, but rather permitted the summary eviction of the applicant and his family without providing reasons liable to examination by an independent tribunal.[210] The Court was careful in this case to draw a distinction with *Chapman*, and other similar cases where matters of general planning or economic policy were at issue, concerning itself with the much narrower issue of the policy of procedural protection for a special category of persons.[211] Despite the Court's proclaimed concern only with procedure, the *Connors* judgment is, however, also significant in that the Court did delve deeper into the question of positive obligations in relation

[208] Luke Clements, *An Emerging Consensus on the Special Needs of Minorities: the Lessons of Chapman v. the UK*, available at: http://www.errc.org/cikk.php?cikk=1711.

[209] *Ibid.*

[210] ECtHR, *Connors v. United Kingdom* (Appl. No 66746/01, 27.05.2004, Merits and just satisfaction), paras. 89, 94–95.

[211] *Ibid*, para. 86.

to its examination of the government's claim that its policy exempting local authority Gypsy sites from security of tenure provisions sought to cater for the special needs of Gypsies who live a nomadic lifestyle which, they emphasized, required flexibility in the management of such sites.[212] In this respect, the Court considered whether those affected actually derived any benefit from the policies nominally in place to assist them—finding, in this instance, that they did not.[213]

IV. Conclusion

As noted at the outset, the rights under consideration are at once separate, interconnected and mutually reinforcing. Their somewhat disparate nature is reflected in the jurisprudence which is both more developed (in terms of the number of cases which affect minorities in particular) as well as more progressive (in terms of the scope and content of the protection afforded by the standards) in some areas than others.

Concerning those privacy rights which can be regarded as 'non-minority-specific', European jurisprudence relating to the destruction of homes, leading to displacement is quite clear-cut: such actions contravene international standards. Some indication of the permissible parameters of surveillance and monitoring is also provided by the Court's judgment in the *Cyprus v. Turkey* case. These findings are especially important for persons belonging to minorities given that it is they who are often the subject of such violations, including in situations where the perpetrators are deliberately engaged in a process of 'ethnic cleansing'. The Court's willingness in *Cyprus v. Turkey* to recognize Turkey's policy of deliberate displacement and extension of cultural influence as an aggravating factor in the violations of specific rights is significant in this respect.

Jurisprudence relating to immigration and the expulsion of non-nationals is another area of jurisprudence which can be of particular relevance for minorities, and where a number of cases have been considered under both the ECHR and HRC (although HRC jurisprudence in this field is more limited). In this respect, European case law shows progressive development with respect to the level of protection afforded to alien family members. This, however, is countered by retrograde steps in terms of understanding of the relationships covered by the scope of that protection.

212 *Ibid.*, para. 87.

213 *Ibid.*, para. 90.

Evolution in ECHR jurisprudence in recent years concerning what might be considered more 'minority-specific' issues pertaining to culture, including certain aspects such as language rights, but also in its widest sense as the right to pursue a certain way of life, can only be described as cautious. Clarification that the protection of Article 8 encompasses the cultural rights of persons belonging to minorities—specifically in relation to the choice of lifestyle—is a significant and positive step. The Court's findings with regard to the European consensus around minority rights is, however, disappointing and raises questions regarding the margin of appreciation afforded to states in such cases. While the HRC has had more occasion to consider alleged violations of the right to enjoy cultural rights under Article 27 these have primarily concerned the rights of indigenous peoples relating to the enjoyment of land rights and national resources. In cases concerning minorities that are not indigenous peoples it has proven more difficult to establish a link between the livelihood and economic activities at threat, and the culture of the group concerned. It remains to be seen how the HRC will approach cases of minorities who are not indigenous peoples in the future.

Cases relating specifically to minority-language education (and the impact on family life of limitations on parental choice in this respect) likewise illustrate reluctance on the part of the European organs to question the status quo in terms of states' arrangements to accommodate linguistic diversity. Similarly, with regard to name-change, under the ECHR the onus is on the individual to prove the importance of the interest to him/her and that a violation has taken place. Under the CCPR, more positively, the burden of proof is shifted to the state which needs to find a compelling reason not to allow change.

In sum, some important seeds have been sown, especially with regard to the scope and content of ECHR Article 8 concerning the cultural rights of minorities. As Åkermark notes, however, there is an important and systemic question of the coherency of minority protection in the Council of Europe—and specifically with regard to the relationship between the ECHR and FCNM.[214] Such coherency—not only within regional regimes, but also between the universal and regional monitoring and enforcement systems—will be important in the positions adopted by the relevant bodies in cases concerning minorities currently pending.

214 Sia Spiliopoulou Åkermark, 'The Limits of Pluralism—Recent Jurisprudence of the European Court of Human Rights with Regard to Minorities: Does the Prohibition of Discrimination Add Anything?', *Journal on Ethnopolitics and Minority Issues in Europe*, 3 (2002).

LINGUISTIC IDENTITY AND LANGUAGE RIGHTS

Fernand de Varennes

I. General Introduction

[T]he Imperial City has endeavoured to impose on subject nations not only her yoke, but her language, as a bond of peace . . . but how many great wars, how much slaughter and bloodshed have provided this unity.

Saint Augustine, Of Just War (circa 413 AD)[1]

It has often in recent times been assumed that the single treaty provision which dealt specifically with the language rights and linguistic identity of minorities in international law was Article 27 of the International Covenant on Civil and Political Rights,[2] followed later by regional treaties of the Council of Europe which dealt more narrowly with language or minority protection. The jurisprudence of the last 10–15 years shows otherwise.

[1] Text available at <http://www.greatbooksandfilm.com/augustine.htm>

[2] (1966), United Nations Treaty Series, Vol. 999.

As this chapter will show, there has been a two-fold development that has in recent years greatly expanded the recognition and protection of language rights and linguistic identity: first, the jurisprudence under traditional human rights—especially freedom of expression and non-discrimination, as well as to a lesser extent the right to education—is starting to be reassessed in a way that demonstrates that, contrary to widely held assumptions, many language rights are protected in traditional human rights provisions. Secondly, new regional treaties dealing directly with minority and linguistic protection have been developed, have entered into force and have started to have significant impact, offering the world community for the first time what could be described as a truly global set of standards as to what ought to be seen as standards of tolerance, acceptance and accommodation in the area of language. They provide, in other words, practical guideposts indicating how the path to pluralism can be followed in the area of language policies in democratic societies.

This seemingly unconnected duo, of individual international human rights standards and minority and linguistic protection, is in substance if not wording surprisingly similar when one examines more closely the emerging cases, opinions and views from various courts and other treaty-based bodies.

II. Content of the Rights

A. Historical and Theoretical Background

It was believed for a long time that language rights for minorities had almost vanished from international courts and treaty bodies with the demise of the so-called 'Minorities Treaties' and the League of Nations by the Second World War.[3]

Perhaps because of Hitler's abuse of these rights to buttress his aggressive manoeuvres under the guise of protecting German minorities abroad, or perhaps it was because of the desire to move away from ethno-nationalism and concentrate on the new 'individual' of the new international order after 1945—whatever the reasons, most of the international and regional treaties appearing

[3] Despite various proposals, no provisions dealing with the protection of minorities, nor for that matter human rights, were incorporated in the establishment of the League of Nations at the end of the First World War, apparently to avoid subjecting all members of the future organisation to such provisions. In fact, the main opposition to have rights protected under the League of Nations system came from western democracies, opposing for example a very limited proposal from an Asian state, Japan, to have racial discrimination prohibited. See further on this issue Fernand de Varennes, *Language, Minorities and Human Rights* (Kluwer, 1996), ch. 2.

under the UN system after the end of that war are surprisingly, even obstinately, silent on any right to linguistic identity or language rights of minorities.

There was therefore, from both a theoretical and legal point of view, a clear schism between the pre-Second World War and Second World War approaches to the rights of minorities and their languages: whereas the Minorities Treaties subjected a limited number of states to obligations that included various types of language rights and general human rights,[4] none of these were retained under the Charter of the United Nations or the Universal Declaration of Human Rights with their purely individualistic rather than communal focus. Only individuals were thought to be the legitimate holders of rights under this new international regime and, consequently, specific right to language or to linguistic identity seemed to be part of this new order. Indeed, there was apparently no reference to the Minorities Treaties at all during the discussions on human rights at United Nations Conference.[5]

B. Delineation of the Content

A frequent misconception that has not quite disappeared completely yet is that all rights involving language disappeared from international law after 1945, with perhaps one main—and quite restricted exception—under Article 27 of the International Covenant on Civil and Political Rights. A closer examination of specific treaties shows however that this was never truly the case, and that various rights pertaining to language and linguistic identity have been retained, though admittedly shrouded in the wording used for individual human rights which gained favour from the end of the Second World War onward.

Thus the Charter of the United Nations proclaims in Article 1(3) that one of the purposes of the new organisation is '[t]o achieve international co-operation . . . in promoting and encouraging respect for human rights

[4] Some of the treaties were imposed upon the defeated states of Austria, Hungary, Bulgaria, and Turkey, others covered new states born of the remains of the Ottoman Empire or whose boundaries were altered at the end of the First World War under the self-determination principle (Czechoslovakia, Greece, Poland, Romania, and Yugoslavia), while a last grouping involved special provisions relating to minorities in Åland, Danzig, the Memel Territory, and Upper Silesia and a series of five unilateral declarations made by Albania, Lithuania, Latvia, Estonia, and Iraq upon their admission to the League of Nations. Though these treaties were not all identical, most contained the right of minorities to establish and control their own institutions, a state obligation to provide equitable financial support to schools in which instruction at the primary level would be in the minority language where warranted by sufficient numbers, and the recognition of the supremacy over other statutes of laws protecting minority rights.

[5] Warwick McKean, *Equality and Discrimination under International Law* (Clarendon Press, 1983), 53.

and fundamental freedoms for all without distinction as to . . . language', and according to Article 13, the General Assembly in the exercise of its functions may initiate studies and make recommendations for the purpose of assisting in the realisation of human rights and fundamental freedoms for all without distinction as to language and other grounds. Pursuant to Article 55, the United Nations is also to promote universal respect for, and observance of, human rights and fundamental freedoms for all without distinction as to language.

For most of the next two decades, non-discrimination on grounds of language would be almost the extent of recognition of any language 'right' component to international law; on 10 December 1948, the United Nations General Assembly proclaimed the Universal Declaration of Human Rights and included Article 2(1) which provides that 'everyone is entitled to all rights and freedoms set forth in this Declaration, without distinction of any kind, such as . . . language'.[6] Similar types of provisions were included in the European Convention for the Protection of Human Rights and Fundamental Freedoms (though limited in application to the enjoyment of the rights and freedoms set forth in that Convention),[7] Article 1 of the UNESCO Convention against Discrimination in Education of 1960,[8] Articles 2(1) and 26 of the International Covenant of Civil and Political Rights,[9] Article 2(2) of the International Covenant on Economic, Social, and Cultural Rights,[10] Article 1 of the American Convention on Human Rights,[11] and Article 2 of the African Charter on Human Rights and Peoples' Rights.[12]

These are not the only individual rights which refer directly to language in these treaties. Though often acknowledged or simply lumped together under 'due process', the main human rights instruments also recognize the importance of language as part of a fair trial and the due process of law.[13] Thus, Article 14, Paragraphs 3(a) and (f) of the International Covenant on Civil and Political Rights provides that in connection with any criminal charge an accused is to be 'informed promptly and in detail in a language which he understands of the nature and cause of the charge against him' and is to have

[6] General Assembly Resolution 217 A (III), UN GAOR, 3rd Session, Resolutions, Part 1, at 71 (1948).

[7] Council of Europe, European Treaty Series, No. 5.

[8] (1960), United Nations Treaty Series, Vol. 428, at 93.

[9] (1966), United Nations Treaty Series, Vol. 999, at 171.

[10] (1966), United Nations Treaty Series, Vol. 993, at 3.

[11] (1969), Organisation of American States, Treaties Series, No. 36, 1.

[12] (1981), Organisation of African Unity, OAU Doc. CAB/LEG/67/3/Rev.5.

[13] Arts. 5(2) and 6(3)(a)of the European Convention for the Protection of Human Rights and Fundamental Freedoms; Article 8 of the American Convention on Human Rights.

'the free assistance of an interpreter if he cannot understand or speak the language used in court'.

Additionally, there are a number of treaty provisions which, contrary to what had been seen as the initial rejection of specific group protection nevertheless rather quickly reappeared at the international level after 1945. Thus, there are at the universal level provisions that deal specifically with language guarantees for national minorities (Article 27 of the CCPR and Article 5(1)(c) of the UNESCO Convention) and indigenous peoples (Articles 23 and 26 of ILO Convention No. 107, as well as 28 and 30 of ILO Convention No. 169).

Thus, pursuant to the International Labour Organization Convention (No. 169) concerning Indigenous and Tribal Peoples in Independent Countries, protected indigenous populations have the right to be taught in their mother tongue or, where this is not practicable, in the language most commonly used by the group to which they belong, to have their languages promoted and protected, and to receive where necessary materials in their language.

The UNESCO Convention also provides in Article 5(1)(c), that it is essential to 'recognise the right of members of national minorities to carry on their own educational activities, including the maintenance of schools and, depending on the educational policy of each state, the use or the teaching of their own language', provided that 'this right is not exercised in a manner which prevents the members of these minorities from understanding the culture and language of the community as a whole and from participating in its activities, or which prejudices national sovereignty'.

Finally, another highly influential provision in regard to language matters for minorities is Article 27 of the Covenant, which provides that:

> In those States in which ethnic, religious or linguistic minorities exist, persons belonging to such minorities shall not be denied the right, in community with the other members of their group, to enjoy their own culture, to profess and practise their own religion, or to use their own language.

These are the obvious international human rights that have a direct connection to language, but they are not the only ones, as the jurisprudence of international courts and treaty bodies has started to demonstrate in the last ten years or so.

Quite often 'forgotten' are freedom of expression (which protects the use of language in private expression contexts) and the right to private life (which also protects the right to the linguistic form of one's name or surname) which jurisprudence has more recently shown are very significant linguistic dimensions in practical terms for minorities.

Finally, international and regional treaties, declarations and other instruments have appeared in the last few years in which language rights and freedoms have proliferated, though not always in legally binding form. Amongst the more prominent are the UN Declaration on the Rights of Persons Belonging to National or Ethnic, Religious and Linguistic Minorities, the draft UN Declaration on the Rights of Indigenous Peoples, the Vienna Declaration on Human Rights, the Organisation on Security and Cooperation in Europe (formerly the Conference on Security and Cooperation in Europe) Document of the Copenhagen Meeting of the Conference on the Human Dimension, the European Charter for Regional and Minority Languages, the Central European Initiative Instrument for the Protection of Minority Rights, and the Framework Convention for the Protection of National Minorities.

C. Analysis of the Existence of these Rights in Different Regional and International Documents

Given their rather diffuse distribution among a number of treaty provisions, some of which have only recently begun to be interpreted and understood at the international level, it would initially seem difficult to speak of any coherent system of language rights or right to linguistic identity, except for later treaties that deal specifically with language (European Charter for Regional and Minority Languages) or minority rights (Framework Convention for the Protection of National Minorities).

There are, nevertheless, common threads that join together all of the rights with a linguistic component in different regional and international documents. As the analysis of jurisprudence shows, courts and other treaty bodies have essentially found that a state's linguistic preferences—be it for an official language or any other language—are restrained in two broad categories: firstly, there are a number of international rights that protect individuals in their private activities, including private language choices; and secondly, there are also rights that mandate the use of different languages by public authorities.

The first category of rights that impact on private language preferences is in some ways the simplest to identify. If public authorities prevent the use of any language, including a minority language, in private activities, this could potentially, depending on the type of intervention, breach a number of rights such as the right to private and family life, freedom of expression, non-discrimination, or the right of persons belonging to a linguistic minority to use their language with other members of their group.

Thus, in addition to freedom of expression which covers all private modes of expression including the private use of a particular language, most international treaties and other documents which deal with the rights of minorities or language tend to contain general provisions, often based on the wording used in Article 27 of the International Covenant on Civil and Political Rights, that 'persons belonging to minorities have the right to use their language freely, in public as well as in private'. For minorities, as well as members of a majority or for indigenous peoples, this last right and other rights linked to the enjoyment of language in the private sphere offer a range of protection in a number of specific areas, such as:

- the freedom to speak or write in a minority or other language, including in the context of private business activities and private organizations;
- the freedom to use, in private contexts, names and local designations in a minority or other language;
- the freedom to display signs in a minority or other language;
- the freedom to have private media using a minority or other language;
- the freedom to choose the language of instruction for the purpose of private education;
- the freedom to use minority and other languages in religious and cultural activities.

The second category of 'language rights'—or rights relevant to the linguistic identity of minorities—is more controversial, but seems to be increasingly accepted in the growing jurisprudence emanating at the international level. To start with in this category are the specific treaty provisions which provide an obligation for state authorities to use the language of minorities in 'appropriate circumstances' in different types of settings: first, in judicial matters where an individual may not understand the language of court proceedings or the charges brought against him or her (usually subsumed under the category of the requirements of a fair trial), and more generally where the numbers and geographic concentration of the speakers of a minority language make it a reasonable or justified arrangement. The former is found in almost all basic human rights treaties, whereas the latter is from a legal point of view expressly recognized in two treaties of the Council of Europe, the Framework Convention on the Protection of National Minorities and the European Charter for Regional or Minority Languages.

The right to have public authorities use a minority language where reasonable or justified is also referred to in an increasingly large number of resolutions, declarations and other documents of the Council of Europe, the European

Union (respect for minority rights is now part of the political criteria for admission of new states to the EU), the Organisation for Security and Co-operation in Europe, and the United Nations.

Additionally, it would seem that the use in some situations of a minority language by state authorities can be deemed required from the application of non-discrimination as to language. Though controversial, the content of the right of non-discrimination could lead to such a conclusion, as has been suggested by some jurists[14] and more recently tentatively confirmed in jurisprudence under the general non-discrimination provisions (Article 26) of the International Covenant on Civil and Political Rights.[15]

Within this last category are a number of legal standards in most international human rights treaties which recognize for individuals, including minorities, a limited entitlement to the use of their language for the sake of fairness within a state's court and administrative system. For example, every person facing criminal proceedings who does not understand the language used in these proceedings has the right to be informed promptly in a language he or she understands, of the reasons for his or her arrest, and of the nature and cause of any accusation against him or her, and to defend himself or herself in this language.

These various categories of language rights and freedoms contained in different regional and international documents are still very far from being fully fleshed out in case law. Disappointingly, many of the early decisions emanating from international courts and other treaty bodies have tended to be negative. As will be shown in the analysis of case law, more often than not courts and other international treaty bodies were asked the 'wrong questions' and presented arguments on the use of minority languages that were based on the wrong provisions. It is only in more recent years that case law has started to emerge that sets out clearly the extent and content of the various rights affecting language and linguistic identity.

III. Analysis of Case Law

[T]he state is more than a passive register of citizen preferences, and in policy deliberation state leadership and initiative are critical... Here we encounter another paradox: the state is the arbiter and broker of cultural difference, yet the state is

[14] See F. de Varennes, *Language, Minorities and Human Rights* (Martinus Nijhoff, The Hague, 1996), ch. 4 for a detailed discussion of this issue.

[15] *J.G.A. Diergaardt (late Captain of the Rehoboth Baster Community) et al. v. Namibia*, (Communication No 760/1997, UN Doc. CCPR/C/69/D/760/1997 (2000)).

unlikely to be wholly neutral in ethnic terms. In the distribution of power within their structures, states inevitably reflect the dominant groups within civil society (by class and interest, as well as ethnic derivation). As noted earlier, many states invest their national personality with the cultural attributes of the leading ethnic community.[16]

Analysing all of the case law relating to language may at times appear a daunting task given the distinct categories of provisions and types of protection they afford to linguistic identity. However, this difficulty is more apparent than real for two main reasons: it is possible to treat the various issues that arise in all of the treaties in the two broad categories already described, and thus have a framework by which to approach systematically these rather numerous provisions; and secondly there is in reality still a relatively low number of judgments, decisions and views involving clearly a language dimension which have been handed down by various courts and treaty bodies.

A. The Private Use of a Minority Language

1. Comparison in Time and between Courts

As indicated above, the private use of a language, including of a minority language, is protected through a number of provisions. At the most basic level, freedom of expression and Article 27 of the ICCPR probably offer the most comprehensive, and to some degree overlapping, protections in this area, though other legal provisions may also be involved in specific areas such as the use of names and surnames (where the right to private or family life may protect linguistic forms of a person's name).

While Article 27 specifically refers to language as part of its scope, this is not the case with freedom of expression. A number of scholars have traditionally taken for granted that language is implicitly a component of freedom of expression,[17] and that 'freedom of expression, in particular, [is] intimately linked to freedom of access to language'.[18]

Yet, whether language is an integral part of freedom of expression does not appear to have been specifically considered in the *travaux préparatoires* of

[16] Crawford Young, 'Ethnic Diversity and Public Policy: An Overview', Occasional Paper No. 8, (World Summit for Social Development, UNRISD, 1994).

[17] See Bruno de Witte, 'Droits fondamentaux et protection de la diversité linguistique', in P. Pupier and J. Woehrling (eds.), *Language and Law: Proceedings of the First Conference of the International Institute of Comparative Linguistic Law* (Wilson & Lafleur, Montréal, 1988), at 91.

[18] M. S. McDougal, H. D. Lasswell, and Lung-chu Chen, *Human Rights and World Public Order* (Yale University Press, New Haven, USA, 1980) at 726.

either the Universal Declaration of Human Rights or the CCPR,[19] and the issue was never clearly settled in cases until 1993.

Cases before 1993, mainly though not exclusively before the United Nations Human Rights Committee (HRC), may have led to the impression that international legal provisions such as freedom of expression offered no linguistic protection whatsoever.

It was in 1990 that the HRC first had the opportunity to consider the relationship between language and freedom of expression in *Dominique Guesdon v. France*.[20] The claim was that freedom of expression guaranteed the right to testify in Breton in court, with the HRC concluding that the freedom of expression argument was inadmissible:

> As to the author's claim that he had been denied his freedom of expression, the Committee observed that the fact of not having been able to speak the language of his choice before the French courts raised no issues under article 19, paragraph 2. The Committee therefore found that this aspect of the communication was inadmissible...[21]

In other similar communications (the '*Breton* cases'), the HRC preferred to declare arguments based upon freedom of expression inadmissible. In *T.K. v. France*,[22] the author submitted that the *Tribunal administratif* of Rennes had refused to consider a case that he had submitted in the Breton language, and that subsequent letters of complaint in Breton had gone unanswered:

> The Committee observes that the matter of the exclusive use of French to institute proceedings in courts is the issue to be examined at first instance by the French judicial organs and that, under the applicable laws, this can be done only by using French. In view of the fact that the author has demonstrated his proficiency in French, the Committee finds that it would not be unreasonable for him to submit his claim in French to the French courts. Further, no irreparable harm would be done to the author's substantive case by using the French language to pursue his remedy.[23]

[19] See UN Documents E/CN.4/AC.1/3/Add.1, at 126–9, 130–48; E/CN.4/21, at 48 and 67; E/CN.4/SR.62, at 14–16, and Albert Verdoodt, *Naissance et signification de la Déclaration universelle des droits de l'homme*, (Nauwelaerts, Louvain-Paris, 1963), at 183–91 for an excellent summary of the *travaux préparatoires* and freedom of expression. As for the *travaux préparatoires* surrounding the International Covenant on Civil and Political Rights, see Marc J. Bossuyt, *Guide to the Travaux Préparatoires of the International Covenant on Civil and Political Right*, (Martinus Nijhoff, The Hague, Netherlands, 1987), at 373–402.

[20] UN GAOR, Vol. II, forty-fifth session, at 61, UN Doc. A/45/40 (1990).

[21] *Ibid.*, at para. 7.2.

[22] UN GAOR, Vol. II, forty-fifth session, Appendix X at 118, UN Doc. A/45/40 (1990).

[23] *Ibid.*, at para. 8.4.

The HRC adopted a similar approach in *M.K. v. France*,[24] wherein it was submitted that the *Tribunal administratif* of Rennes had refused to consider a complaint directed against French tax authorities for having declined to write the author's address in Breton. The Committee again refused to study the substantive issue until such time as all domestic remedies had been exhausted, in French.

In *Yves Cadoret and Hervé Le Bihan v. France*,[25] the authors had appeared before the *Tribunal correctionnel* of Rennes on charges of having vandalized three road signs. Although Breton was their first language, they had not been allowed to express themselves in Breton before the tribunal, nor had three witnesses they had called on their behalf been allowed to testify in Breton.

In their communications, they contended that the refusal of the courts to allow them to present their defence in Breton was a clear and serious restriction of their freedom of expression, contrary to Article 19(2) because it signified that they would only be allowed to air their views in French when in court. The HRC rejection of this line of argument does not fully explain why there was no language 'issue' under freedom of expression:

> As to the authors' claim that they had been denied their freedom of expression, the Committee observed that the fact of not having been able to speak the language of their choice before the French courts raised no issues under article 19, paragraph 2.[26]

These early views show the high degree of uncertainty as to the relationship between language and freedom of expression pursuant to Article 19 of the International Covenant on Civil and Political Rights until 1993, when the HRC definitely considered the issue head on in the Québec commercial signs language communications.

In *Ballantyne, Davidson and McIntyre v. Canada*,[27] the authors claimed that the prohibition against using any language other than French on outdoor commercial signs or in a firm's name infringed upon their freedom of expression, guaranteed by Article 19 of the International Covenant on Civil and Political Rights.

The government of Québec argued, among other things, that freedom of expression did not include an individual's absolute right to choose the language of commercial signs. The HCR stated that Article 19(2) CCPR applies

[24] Communication No.222/1987, 8 November 1989.

[25] Communications Nos. 221/1987 and 333/1988, 11 April 1991.

[26] *Ibid.*, at para. 5.2.

[27] *John Ballantyne, Elizabeth Davidson, and Gordon McIntyre v. Canada*, (Communication No. 359/1989 and 385/1989, U.N. Doc. CCPR/C/47/D/359/1989 and 385/1989/Rev.1 (1993)).

not only to ideas and subjective opinions which can be transmitted to others, but also to any news or information, any expression, any commercial publicity or signs, and to any work of art. To restrict the private use of a language would be a restriction to a form of expression, and cannot be done under the guise of an official language policy:

> The Committee believes that it is not necessary, in order to protect the vulnerable position in Canada of the francophone group, to prohibit commercial advertising in English. This protection may be achieved in other ways that do not preclude the freedom of expression, in a language of their choice, of those engaged in such fields as trade. For example, the law could have required that advertising be in both French and English. A State may choose one or more official languages, but it may not exclude, outside the spheres of public life, the freedom to express oneself in a language of one's choice.[28]

For the first time ever, and only quite recently, an international treaty body not only clearly concluded that language was a constituent component of freedom of expression, but that it could not be restricted, contrary to the requirements of international law, because of a state's having an exclusive official language.

The early situation in the context of the European Convention for the Protection of Human Rights and Fundamental Freedoms was in many ways similarly ambiguous because no case directly addressed the position of language or linguistic identity in relation to the freedom of expression.

In *Inhabitants of Leeuw-St. Pierre v. Belgium*,[29] the European Commission on Human Rights examined the matter of a group of Belgian citizens who had unsuccessfully requested administrative documents from their municipality in French. They claimed that the municipality's refusal to provide such documents in French violated their freedom of expression under Article 10. The Commission declared that the application was inadmissible *ratione materiae* because the ECHR does not expressly guarantee 'linguistic freedom' as it relates to the right to use one's language of choice in relations with municipal authorities.

This case, though not couched in very clear words, appears to acknowledge that there may be a distinction between the right to freedom of expression in one's language outside governmental activity on the one hand, and a right to have administrative formalities completed in one's language, on the other:

> These considerations are obviously applicable without restriction to the applicants' grievances regarding the use of languages in administration. It is clear that one has to distort the usual meaning of the passages [Articles 9 and 10 of the Convention] if one

[28] See also *Allan Singer v. Canada*, para. 12.2.

[29] *Yearbook of the European Convention on Human Rights*, 8 (1965), 338.

is to transform the right to express one's thought freely in the language of one's choice into a right to complete, and insist on the completion of, all administrative formalities in that language.[30]

In another early case the European Commission on Human Rights proceeded again to reject an application involving language and freedom of expression in *X v. Ireland*.[31] The applicant was a civil servant entitled to children's allowance for each of his four children, provided he filled out a prescribed form. The form was entirely in Irish which he could apparently neither read nor write. He refused to comply with what he described as a 'language dictatorship'. The applicant maintained that the requirement to use exclusively Irish in these forms constituted a violation of his freedom of expression guaranteed under Article 10. The Commission indicated that the requirement to complete the form in the Irish language did not in any way interfere with the applicant's freedom of expression, and that the application was inadmissible.

Although not directly involving the issue of freedom of expression and language, the European Commission in *Charlent v. Belgium* implicitly acknowledged that in private affairs freedom of expression included the freedom to use one's language of choice:

> Whereas freedom of religion is not in question; whereas this is also true of the freedoms of thought, conscience and expression of the Applicants themselves, since nothing prevents them from expressing their thought freely in the language of their choice.[32]

Finally, in *Fryske Nasjonale Partij v. Netherlands*,[33] the applicants submitted that they had been prevented from standing as candidates in elections of the *Eerste Kamer der Staten-Generaal* because they had submitted their registration for election in Frisian[34] and not in Dutch. They asserted, *inter alia*, that this infringed their freedom of expression guaranteed under Article 10 ECHR. The European Commission on Human Rights indicated that freedom of expression and language preference may, in certain situations, be relevant when it stated that the 'applicants... failed to demonstrate that they were prevented from using the Frisian language for other purposes', but not in the type of situation in which they were involved in the case of election registration.[35]

[30] *Ibid.*

[31] *Yearbook of the European Convention on Human Rights*, 13 (1970), 792.

[32] *Yearbook of the European Convention on Human Rights*, 6 (1963) 445, at 454–456.

[33] (1986) Decisions and Reports 45, 240 (European Commission of Human Rights), at 243.

[34] Frisian is a Germanic language spoken in the province of Friesland (*Fryslân*) in the Netherlands, as well as in Schleswig-Holstein and Niedersachsen in Germany.

[35] (1986) Decisions and Reports 45, 240 (EuCommHR), at 243.

It is therefore some ten years after the HCR's conclusions in *Ballantyne, Davidson and McIntyre v. Canada* that the European Court on Human Rights (and the previous European Commission) can be said to have finally confirmed that language is a component of freedom of expression in the field of private activities, though this still came about rather indirectly.

In *Association Ekin v. France*,[36] a book entitled *Euskadi at War* was published in Spain in four languages—Basque, English, Spanish and French. A ministerial order was issued by the French Ministry of the Interior under legislation banning the circulation, distribution and sale of the book in France in any of its four languages on the ground that 'the circulation in France of this book, which promotes separatism and vindicates recourse to violence, is likely to constitute a threat to public order'. The association claimed this infringed their freedom of expression. Commenting on a number of issues, the European Court of Human Rights had no difficulty considering that the language of publication fell within the purview of freedom of expression, pointing out the arbitrariness of the application of the rules involved depending on the language of publication:

> 60. With regard to the scope of the rules applicable to foreign publications, the Court notes that section 14 of the Law of 1881, as amended, establishes an exception to the general law by giving the Minister of the Interior powers to impose general and absolute bans throughout France on the circulation, distribution or sale of any document written in a foreign language or any document regarded as being of foreign origin, even if written in French. The Court notes that the provision does not state the circumstances in which the power may be used. In particular, there is no definition of the concept of "foreign origin" nor any indication of the grounds on which a publication deemed to be foreign may be banned. Admittedly, those gaps have gradually been filled by the administrative courts' case-law. Nonetheless, as the applicant association pointed out, the application of those rules has, in certain cases, produced results that are at best surprising and in some cases verge on the arbitrary, depending on the language of publication or the place of origin.

The ban based on the language of publication or the place of origin, did not meet a pressing social need, and was not proportionate to the legitimate aim pursued, therefore constituting a violation of freedom of expression.[37]

Much more recently, though still rather indirectly, and this time linking the issue to a denial of freedom of association, the European Court of Human

[36] *Ekin Association v. France*, (Application No 39288/98, 17 July 2001).

[37] Para. 63.

Rights in *Ouranio Toxo and Others v. Greece*[38] reacted to the suggestion by Greek authorities that it might be permissible to ban the private use of an expression in a minority language which might be seen as provocative:

40. La Cour considère que l'invocation de la conscience d'appartenir à une minorité ainsi que la préservation et le développement de la culture d'une minorité ne sauraient passer pour constituer une menace pour la « société démocratique », même si cela peut provoquer à des tensions (voir *Sidiropoulos et autres c. Grèce,* précité, § 41). En effet, l'apparition de tensions est une conséquence inévitable du pluralisme, c'est-à-dire du libre débat sur toute idée politique. Dans ce cas, le rôle des autorités en pareilles circonstances ne consiste pas à éliminer la cause des tensions en supprimant le pluralisme, mais à veiller à ce que les groupes politiques concurrents se tolèrent les uns les autres (voir, *Plattform « Ärzte für das Leben » c. Autriche, ibid,* p. 12, § 32 ; *Serif c. Grèce,* nº 38178/97, § 53, CEDH 1999-IX).

41. En l'occurrence, la Cour constate que le parti Ouranio Toxo est un parti légalement constitué dont l'un des buts est la défense de la minorité macédonienne qui habite en Grèce. Le fait d'accrocher sur la devanture de son siège un panneau avec le nom du parti en macédonien ne saurait passer pour un acte répréhensible ni constituer en soi un danger présent et imminent pour l'ordre public. Certes, la Cour admet que l'emploi du terme *vino-zito* a certainement suscité des sentiments hostiles au sein de la population locale. De connotation ambiguë, il était susceptible de heurter le sentiment patriotique ou politique de la majorité des habitants de Florina. Toutefois, le risque d'engendrer des tensions au sein d'une communauté par l'emploi public de termes politiques ne suffit pas, à lui seul, à justifier des entraves à la liberté d'association.

These cases, based on freedom of expression, are not however the only ones which courts and treaty bodies have concluded have a direct impact on the right to use a language in private contexts. As noted earlier, in addition to being able to invoke freedom of expression, linguistic minorities could also avail themselves of the rights under Article 27 of the International Covenant on Civil and Political Rights. Though not identical in scope or wording, freedom of expression and Article 27 of the CCPR have significant overlapping when involving issues surrounding the private use of a minority language.

Most of the previous freedom of expression cases at the HRC and the European Court on Human Rights involved linguistic minorities, except for *Ballantyne, Davidson and McIntyre v. Canada* which dealt with members of the English-speaking majority in Canada. The outcome in the former cases might however also have been successful under Article 27 of the CCPR since

[38] Application No 74989/01, 20 October 2005.

jurisprudence, though scarce on the topic of language, still suggests that this provision protects widely the private use of a minority language.

In *Lovelace v. Canada,*[39] the HRC examined the situation of Mrs. Lovelace, an indigenous person and member of an ethnic and linguistic community called Maliseets which are numerically a minority in Canada. Although born a Maliseet and so registered by Canadian authorities, Mrs Lovelace lost her rights and status as an Indian in accordance with Article 12(1) (b) of the Indian Act after having married a non-Indian. In its views, the Human Rights Committee concentrates on the loss of the cultural benefits of living in an Indian community, the inability to use her language with other members of her community, and the loss of identity. It concluded:

> [I]n the opinion of the Committee the right of Sandra Lovelace to access to her native culture and language 'in community with the other members' of her group, has in fact been, and continues to be interfered with, because there is no place outside the Tobique Reserve where such a community exists.

It should be noted that the Committee in the above in no way suggests that state authorities have an obligation to use an indigenous people's language when they constitute a minority as the case is limited to the use of a minority language between individuals acting in a private capacity. The views of the HRC do however indicate clearly that, as with freedom of expression, the use of a minority language could be widely protected under Article 27 CCPR when it occurs in private contexts.

2. Analysis and Criticism, Possible Evolution of Interpretation by Courts

There was, perhaps, a view in many circles that any language right or right to linguistic identity was necessarily anchored in international law in a specific 'minority' provision such as Article 27 of the CCPR. The case law emanating from international courts and treaty bodies has slowly begun to displace this misconception, making it unambiguous that this was incorrect in respect to the private use of a language.

This evolution could be characterized as moving from initial, and rather vague, pronouncements which did not actually set out the relationship between language and basic human rights such as freedom of expression, to acceptance of language as a constituent 'medium' of expression, and therefore also protected in its private usage under this basic right. The European Court

[39] Communication 24/1977, UN Doc. A/36/40.

of Human Rights has not had as many cases dealing with the private use of a minority language as the HRC. Most of the Court's previous cases dealt with requests for the use of a language by state authorities, not any private use of language.

For this reason, the European Court of Human Rights has had fewer opportunities to comment on the provisions that might protect private language use, and it has been left to the HRC in many respects to 'fill the gap': it has pointed out in *Ballantyne, Davidson and McIntyre v. Canada* that language is a protected component of expression in the private realm, and even rejected firmly the notion in the same case that 'official language status' in, and of, itself could constitute a legitimate reason for state authorities to violate international human rights obligations, such as the right to use a particular language for private purposes, including a minority language. It also indicated that freedom of expression extends to any possible medium of expression. Because the expression of opinions, information and ideas can be conveyed orally, in writing, or in print, one cannot suppose that the state may limit the speaker's choice of medium—including language—other than by the limits provided in Article 19(3) CCPR and in Article 10(2) ECHR.

This jurisprudence sets out the general acknowledgement that the private use of a language can be protected—amongst others—by freedom of expression and Article 27 CCPR. It does not spell out all possible areas where this protection may be applicable, nor for that matter exclude other provisions as being relevant for specific situations. This is what will now be considered in the next section.

3. Application of the Rights

Provisions dealing with freedom of expression and Article 27 CCPR cover many of the same areas of application when dealing with language, though they are not completely identical (one of the main differences being that freedom of expression is applicable to any person, whereas Article 27 is limited to linguistic, religious or ethnic minorities).

(a) **Private Use of a Minority Language in Written and Oral Forms**

One obvious application of this right would involve any type of private use of a minority language in the private field, whether written or verbal. Persons who are members of a minority (and all individuals in the case of freedom of expression) have the right to use their language among themselves in private activities. If state authorities forbid or restrict the private use of a minority language, whether in written or oral form, this would be a violation of freedom of expression. It would also breach Article 27 CCPR, since individuals who are members of a linguistic minority could also claim they are entitled not to be denied the right to use their language with other members of their group. That would seem to be the clear effect of the application of the views of the HRC in a number of communications.[40] Many international treaties and other documents dealing with human rights or the rights of minorities have a provision where this right is expressly provided for.[41]

The same applies to cases regarding the written use of a minority language, or using such a language as a means of communication. Public authorities must not prevent individuals from writing in or using a minority language in private correspondence or communications, and this would include the use of a minority language in private business or commercial correspondence, by telephone, electronic means, etc.

To prevent the use of a minority language in such circumstances would violate the freedom of expression and a person's right to use his or her own language with other members of his or her own minority group in the case of a linguistic minority, as set out in provisions such as Article 27 CCPR,[42] as well as other treaty provisions which guarantee this type of protection specifically, such as Article 10 of the Framework Convention for the Protection of National Minorities.[43] This does not however exclude the possibility for a government to require that the official language also be used simultaneously with an individual's language of choice in private matters—as long as it does not interfere with an individual's ability to use his/her own language to the point where it could be an obstruction. This was also confirmed by the HRC in *Ballantyne, Davidson and McIntyre v. Canada*:

> 11.4 . . .The Committee believes that it is not necessary, in order to protect the vulnerable position in Canada of the francophone group, to prohibit commercial advertising in English. This protection may be achieved in other ways that do not preclude

[40] See *Ballantyne, Davidson and McIntyre v. Canada*, United Nations Human Rights Committee Communications Nos. 359/1989 and 385/1989, 31 March 1993 and *Lovelace v. Canada*, United Nations Human Rights Committee Communication 24/1977, UN Doc. A/36/40.

[41] These include, among others, Art. 9(1) of the Framework Convention for the Protection of National Minorities and Art. 2 of the UN Declaration on the Rights of Persons Belonging to National or Ethnic, Religious or Linguistic Minorities.

[42] In addition to the UN Human Rights Committee's views in *Ballantyne, Davidson and McIntyre v. Canada*, see the comments of the European Commission on Human Rights in *Charlent v. Belgium, only Yearbook of the European Convention on Human Rights*, 6 (1963), 445, at 454–6.

[43] The Parties undertake to recognize that every person belonging to a national minority has the right to use freely and without interference his or her minority language, in private and in public, orally and in writing.

the freedom of expression, in a language of their choice, of those engaged in such fields as trade. For example, the law could have required that advertising be in both French and English. A State may choose one or more official languages, but it may not exclude, outside the spheres of public life, the freedom to express oneself in a language of one's choice.

There are no known cases in international law or under Council of Europe treaties identifying situations in which public authorities could ban the use of a minority language in private correspondence or communication. In theory, the only situations where this might be possible is if such a restriction would be necessary in order to protect the reputation of others, or for the protection of national security, public order or public morality, or to prevent incitement to racial hatred or violence. In practice it would seem difficult to imagine a case where a ban on a minority language would fit any of these categories. Once again, the HRC appears to confirm this in *Ballantyne, Davidson and McIntyre v. Canada*, though its comments were limited to whether there was an issue involving public order or protection of the rights of others which might constitute a legitimate reason to restrict the freedom of expression of those involved:

11.4 Any restriction of the freedom of expression must cumulatively meet the following conditions: it must be provided for by law, it must address one of the aims enumerated in paragraph 3(a) and (b) of article 19, and must be necessary to achieve the legitimate purpose. While the restrictions on outdoor advertising are indeed provided for by law, the issue to be addressed is whether they are necessary for the respect of the rights of others. The rights of others could only be the rights of the francophone minority within Canada under article 27. This is the right to use their own language, which is not jeopardized by the freedom of others to advertise in other than the French language. Nor does the Committee have reason to believe that public order would be jeopardized by commercial advertising outdoors in a language other than French.

The European Court of Human Rights seemed to concur with this reasoning, although in a much more indirect way, pointing out in *Association Ekin v. France*:

60. With regard to the scope of the rules applicable to foreign publications, the Court notes that section 14 of the Law of 1881, as amended, establishes an exception to the general law by giving the Minister of the Interior powers to impose general and absolute bans throughout France on the circulation, distribution or sale of any document written in a foreign language or any document regarded as being of foreign origin, even if written in French. The Court notes that the provision does not state the circumstances in which the power may be used. In particular, there is no definition of

the concept of 'foreign origin' nor any indication of the grounds on which a publication deemed to be foreign may be banned. Admittedly, those gaps have gradually been filled by the administrative courts' case-law. Nonetheless, as the applicant association pointed out, the application of those rules has, in certain cases, produced results that are at best surprising and in some cases verge on the arbitrary, depending on the language of publication or the place of origin.

63. In the case before it, the Court, like the *Conseil d'Etat*, considers that the content of the book did not justify, in particular as regards the issues of public safety and public order, so serious an interference with the applicant association's freedom of expression as that constituted by the ban imposed by the Minister of the Interior. Ultimately, the Court considers that the ban did not meet a pressing social need and was not proportionate to the legitimate aim pursued.[44]

Though there are no specific cases dealing with the use of a minority language in private cultural or musical activities, it would seem consistent with the above cases to conclude that these would also be protected under freedom of expression and Article 27 CCPR. There are additionally a number of treaty provisions which do deal more precisely with such a type of protection.[45]

The application of these rights may also impact on the actual writing form of a minority language. A few documents make direct reference to this,[46] and in particular Article 11(2) of the Framework Convention for the Protection of National Minorities:

The Parties undertake to recognise that every person belonging to a national minority has the right to display in his or her minority language signs, inscriptions and other information of a private nature visible to the public.

As part of these rights, minorities have the right to use a particular script (such as Cyrillic, Arabic, Greek, Latin, Hebrew, etc.) in their private activities. There are however no reported cases specifically on this point, and relatively little analysis on such an application,[47] though once again it would appear consistent with the reasoning of the more general cases on freedom of expression and Article 27 CCPR that any attempt by state authorities to ban the private use of a particular script would likely be a violation of these guarantees.

[44] *Ekin Association v. France* (Application No 39288/98, 17 July 2001).

[45] Article 11 of the Framework Convention for the Protection of National Minorities; Article 12 of the European Charter for Regional or Minority Languages and Art. 2 UN Declaration on the Rights of Persons Belonging to National or Ethnic, Religious or Linguistic Minorities.

[46] Article 11 of the Framework Convention for the Protection of National Minorities.

[47] See specifically on this point F. de Varennes, *Language, Minorities*, *supra*, n. 14, Section 4.6.

Similarly, the same results should emerge in relation to the private publication of books or newspapers in a minority language. If public authorities attempted to prohibit such activities because they are undertaken in an unrecognized or banned language, this would constitute a violation of freedom of expression guaranteed under international law and in the European Convention on Human Rights. It should also be protected under Article 27 CCPR and similar provisions in the case of minorities generally. Members of a minority cannot be prevented from publishing privately in their own language. Recognition of this right is found in a fairly large number of treaties and other documents.[48]

There is nevertheless a dearth of cases on this precise point. The closest to case law dealing with it are the comments of the European Court of Human Rights in *Association Ekin v. France*, where it was implied that banning private publications on the basis of the language used in them appeared to be 'surprising' and 'arbitrary' as applied in that particular situation,[49] and *Cyprus v. Turkey* where, had it not been for the failure to find any northern Cyprus authorities preventing the circulation of Greek language books, it seems the Court could have concluded that there had been a breach of freedom of expression under Article 10.[50]

While there are no reported cases dealing with the language of private broadcasting, it would be generally guaranteed in international law and Council of Europe treaties under freedom of expression, and freedom of the press. A prohibition on the use of a minority language in private broadcasting would therefore be a violation of freedom of expression, and arguably of Article 27 of the CCPR. This has been confirmed by the United Nations Human Rights Committee in a number of comments to reports from states such as the following:

> 7. The Committee expresses its concern over the inadequate protection of the rights of ethnic, religious and linguistic minorities in the Dominican Republic. In this regard, the Committee notes that the prohibition of broadcasting in a language other than Spanish is not in conformity with article 19 [freedom of expression] of the Covenant.[51]

[48] Article 9 of the Framework Convention for the Protection of National Minorities and Art. 11(2) of the European Charter for Regional or Minority Languages. Paragraph 12(ii) of Recommendation 1134 (1990) on the Rights of Minorities, Art. 7(2) of Recommendation 1201 (1993) on an Additional Protocol on the Rights of National Minorities to the European Convention on Human Rights and Recommendation 8 of the Oslo Recommendations regarding the Linguistic Rights of National Minorities are also useful in this regard, though of a non-binding nature.

[49] *Ekin Association v. France*, (Application No 39288/98, 17 July 2001), para. 60.

[50] E.H.R.R., 35 (2002), 30, judgment of 10 May 2001 (Grand Chamber), para. 251.

[51] Comments on Dominican Republic, UN Doc. CCPR/C/79/Add.18 (1993).

Many legal and political documents also recognize this as a minority or linguistic right.[52]

(b) Names and Topographical Indications in a Minority Language

A potentially more complicated area of application is the use of names, and even topographical designations, in a minority language. While at first glance one could surmise that a prohibition from exhibiting or having an individual's name or surname in a minority language might also involve freedom of expression, and arguably Article 27 CCPR, a limited number of cases point the finger at the right to private life as the basis for such use. While not excluding the possibility of arguing the same right on the basis of the latter two international guarantees, an individual's name is, at the same time, so intimately connected to a person's private and family life that any interference with this, whether linked to its linguistic form or some other dimension, risks constituting a breach of the right to private life.[53] In one of its decisions, the United Nations Human Rights Committee made it clear that the notion of privacy includes:

> . . . the sphere of a person's life in which he or she can freely express his or her identity, be it by entering into relationships with others or alone. The Committee is of the view that a person's surname [and name] constitutes an important component of one's identity and that the protection against arbitrary or unlawful interference with one's privacy includes the protection against arbitrary or unlawful interference with the right to choose and change one's own name.[54]

Public authorities cannot interfere with this right arbitrarily or unlawfully, and the Committee has indicated that a restriction on the right to choose one's name would have to be reasonable to satisfy this requirement. Evidently, unless the prohibition or restriction of the particular linguistic form of a person's name can be shown to be reasonable, the application of this right would protect the private use of a person's name or surname in a minority language. An increasing number of international and regional treaties, and other documents

[52] Article 9 of the Framework Convention for the Protection of National Minorities; and Art. 11(3) of the European Charter for Regional or Minority Languages; Article 18 of the Central European Initiative Instrument for the Protection of Minority Rights. The following are also relevant, though non-binding: Article 7(2) of Recommendation 1201 (1993) on an Additional Protocol on the Rights of National Minorities to the European Convention on Human Rights; paragraph 7 of the Resolution on the Languages and Cultures of Regional and Ethnic Minorities; and Recommendation 8 of the Oslo Recommendations regarding the Linguistic Rights of National Minorities.

[53] *Coeriel and Aurik v. Netherlands*, United Nations Human Rights Committee, Communication No. 453/1991, UN Doc. CCPR/C/52/D/453/1991 (1994); *Burghartz v. Switzerland*, European Court of Human Rights, judgment of 22 February 1994, E.H.R.R. 18, 101.

[54] *Coeriel and Aurik v. Netherlands*, *ibid*, para. 10.2.

dealing either with national minorities, linguistic minorities or ethnic minorities have seized on this area of application and spelled out such a right as worthy of protection.[55]

However, the exact limitations to the application of the right to private life are not yet well defined in relation to its impact on a name or surname's linguistic form. Particularly when considering the case law of the European Court of Human Rights, it is not clear if a state is always obliged to officially recognize or use an individual's preferred name or surname. As long as individuals are not prevented by public authorities from using their preferred names or surnames privately, there may not be a violation of the right to private life.[56]

The Court has acknowledged in a number of decisions that the matter of a person's name or surname is inherently a private matter protected by the right to private and family life, though it has not explored the linguistic dimension of such a choice:

> ...disputes relating to individuals' surnames and forenames come within Article 8 of the Convention. Although that provision does not mention a right to a name explicitly, a person's name—as a means of personal identification and of linking to a family—nonetheless concerns his or her private and family life (see, in particular, the following judgments: *Burghartz v. Switzerland* of 22 February 1994, Series A no. 280-B, p. 28, § 24; *Stjerna v. Finland* of 25 November 1994, Series A no. 299-B, p. 60, § 37; and *Guillot v. France* of 24 October 1996, *Reports of Judgments and Decisions* 1996-V, pp. 1602-03, § 21).[57]

Even the European Community case law has recognized the fundamental importance of a person's name—and that it is protected in international law:

> 55. In addition to practical matters, which may range from the merely annoying to—in the climate of suspicion which has followed the events of 11 September 2001—the extremely serious, a person's name is a fundamental part of his or her identity and private life, the protection of which is widely recognised in national constitutions and international instruments.[58]

[55] See for example Art. 11 of the Framework Convention for the Protection of National Minorities; Article 11 of the Central European Initiative for the Protection of Minority Rights; Article 7(2) of Recommendation 1201 (1993) on an Additional Protocol on the Rights of National Minorities to the European Convention on Human Rights; and paragraph 6 of the 30 October 1987 European Parliament Resolution on the Languages and Cultures of Regional and Ethnic Minorities. Also noteworthy, though not legally, nor politically, binding, is Recommendation 1 of the Oslo Recommendations regarding the Linguistic Rights of National Minorities.

[56] See *Guillot v. France*, ECtHR, 52/1995/558/644, judgment of 24 October 1996, and *Stjerna v. Finland*, judgment of 25 November 1994, Series A no. 299-B.

[57] *Znamenskaya v. Russia*, judgment of 12 October 2005.

[58] *Standesamt Stadt Niebüll*, Case C-96/04, 30 June 2005. See also *Konstantinidis*, Case C-168/91 [1993] ECR I-1191, and *Garcia Avello*, Case C-148/02 [2003] ECR I-11613.

The main difficulty, and continuing source of uncertainty, is the precise interaction between this aspect of private and family life, and the well-established practice in many states in Europe and elsewhere to regulate a person's surname for administrative and other purposes such as to facilitate identification. In other words, while individuals may be entitled to call themselves whatever they want, states also have an interest in managing the names or surnames by which they will be known for official and administrative purposes.

On the one hand, it would seem therefore that state authorities cannot prevent an individual from using a particular name or surname in a minority language in a purely private context. On the other hand, state authorities may require that the person conform to certain administrative demands on the form of his or her name when it interacts with some type of state involvement; as would be required for example in contacts with health, police, immigration and other authorities, or even where an individual's right to private life may be restricted for reasons of morality, public safety, etc.

The latter issue of the use of a person's name or surname in a minority language by state authorities—as opposed to the prohibition of the private use of such a name—will be further examined in the following Section 2.

But the name or surname of individuals is not the only area of 'designation' where minorities may have a right to use their language. It would appear clear that state authorities cannot ban the purely private use of topographical or locality names in a minority language. Individuals have the right to designate and use privately local names and topographical designations in their own language. If state authorities were to ban such private use, this would constitute a violation of freedom of expression and Article 27 International Covenant on Civil and Political Rights. This right is additionally recognized in a number of treaties and other international or regional documents.[59] No case law on this point currently exists however, so that while the theoretical basis for such a conclusion appears rather solid based on the other judgments and views mentioned earlier for other areas, this still has to be confirmed specifically for this particular type of purpose.

Additionally, this protection of the private use of a minority language does not mean that state authorities must in all cases adopt, and officially use, local designations in minority languages. That is an issue which involves official topographical designations, and therefore belongs to the use of a minority

[59] See for example Art. 11 of the Framework Convention for the Protection of National Minorities; Article 14 of the Central European Initiative Instrument for the Protection of Minority Rights; and of a non-binding nature Recommendation 3 of the Oslo Recommendations regarding the Linguistic Rights of National Minorities.

language by state authorities—not its private use. It therefore extends beyond any issue of freedom of expression or of private life, and is therefore also considered in Section 2.

(c) Private Education and Minority Languages

The rights of minorities in the area of private education are dealt with more generally in the next chapter of this book. This section will therefore be limited to focusing on the linguistic dimension of the right to education for minorities.

As with other activities dealing with the private use of a minority language, state authorities cannot forbid the establishment or operation of private schools teaching a minority language or using a minority language as a medium of instruction.

The ancestry of this right pre-dates the creation of the United Nations. Though the case is based on a specific treaty which is no longer operative in international law, the *Minority Schools in Albania* case is still referred to as an early example of a right to a private school teaching in a minority language,[60] and indeed is even mentioned as proof of the existence of a rule of customary law that minorities are entitled to open, and operate, their own schools. What is often forgotten is that the case only dealt with a right in relation to a private minority school.

In that case the Permanent Court of International Justice examined the validity of an Albanian law aimed at abolishing all private schools in the country. It concluded that pursuant to Article 5 of the relevant treaty, the Greek-speaking minority in Albania enjoyed special rights required in order to ensure 'suitable means for the preservation of their racial peculiarities, their traditions and their national characteristics.'

The Permanent Court of International Justice reached this conclusion even though public schools using Greek as the medium of instruction did continue to exist at that time in Albania. It would seem that because they were public schools subject to direct and extensive control by the Albanian government and, for the most part, non-Greek-speaking officials, this would leave Greek-speakers with little influence on the quality and content of Greek-language instruction. In acknowledgment of these and other difficulties facing linguistic minorities in the context of public schooling, the Court appears to have adopted the position that members of a minority should always be entitled to their 'own' institutions, signifying institutions set up and controlled by the

[60] *Supra*, n. 8.

members of the minority community themselves, despite the fact that such a right may be denied to members of the majority.

> [Private educational institutions] are indispensable to enable the minority to enjoy the same treatment as the majority, not only in law but also in fact. The abolition of these institutions, which alone can satisfy the special requirements of the minority groups, and their replacement by government institutions, would destroy this equality of treatment, for its effects would be to deprive the minority of the institutions appropriate to its needs, whereas the majority would continue to have them supplied in the institutions created by the state.[61]

Though treaty-specific, the foundation for such a continued right has been maintained in more contemporary times in legal and political documents, despite some differences in the way it is formulated.[62] Additionally, there would seem to be a fairly broad consensus that such a right falls within the ambit of the protections afforded by Article 27 CCPR, even though this provision is silent on such an application.

Even what is meant by a minority's own language has not been the matter of any substantial discussion in recent jurisprudence, though it was the subject of a handful of cases in the inter-war period at the Permanent Court of International Justice. Though one must be careful once again with the treaties of the period, which dealt with the rights of a number of targeted minorities and did not concern themselves with the general right to education, they do provide interesting guidelines as to judicial views on what constitutes an individual's language, a not always self-evident point. It pointed out in one case that dialectal differences which might result in children not knowing their 'own language' did not mean that these children did not still belong to that minority and were entitled to education in their own language,[63] and suggested that while an individual could freely declare whether or not his or her child belonged to a racial, linguistic or religious minority, therefore entitling the latter to go to a minority school, such declarations did not eliminate the need for some requirement of factual backup:

[61] *Supra*, n. 8, 19–20.

[62] Article 13 of the Framework Convention for the Protection of National Minorities and Art. 16 of the Central European Initiative Instrument for the Protection of Minority Rights. Non-legal documents which clarify this right include para. 32.2 of the Document of the Copenhagen Meeting of the Conference on the Human Dimension; paragraph 11(ii) of Recommendation 1134 (1990) on the Rights of Minorities; Article 8(2) of Recommendation 1201 (1993) on an Additional Protocol on the Rights of National Minorities to the European Convention on Human Rights; and Recommendations 8 and 9 of the Hague Recommendations regarding the Education of National Minorities and Part IV of the Report of Experts on National Minorities.

[63] *Access to German Minority Schools in Upper Silesia.*

[The] declarations must set out what their author regards as the true position in regard to the point in question and that the right freely to declare what is the language of a pupil or child, though comprising, when necessary, the exercise of some discretion in the appreciation of circumstances, does not constitute an unrestricted right to choose the language in which instruction is to be imparted or the corresponding school.[64]

In other areas there is a rather glaring paucity of modern jurisprudence on the freedom to obtain private education in a minority language, partially explainable by its fairly widely accepted existence as a right in international law. While there are a number of other cases which deal with the use of a minority language as a medium of instruction, these deal not with the situation of private schools, but of state-provided education, and will thus be considered in a later section.

It should finally be noted that all of these legal and other documents usually add that state authorities may impose the obligation that all students in such private schools learn the official language up to a reasonable level of fluency.[65]

(d) Minority Language Use in Private Economic and Commercial Activities

Minorities have the right to freely use their language in private economic and commercial activities as this is, once again, linked to a private use of a language, and thus protected under provisions guaranteeing either a minority's enjoyment of their own language among themselves, such as Article 27 CCPR, or freedom of expression. State authorities cannot prevent an individual or business from using their preferred language in the economic field. Legislation or restrictions that would prevent the use of a language between an employer and his or her employees, between a business owner and a client, or in written, visual or audio form for private commercial activities, would be a violation of freedom of expression.

Once again, there is very little case law which makes this point, apart from the UNHRC views in *Ballantyne, et al. v. Canada*:

11.3 Under article 19 of the Covenant, everyone shall have the right to freedom of expression; this right may be subjected to restrictions, conditions for which are set out

[64] *Rights of Minorities in Upper Silesia (Minority Schools)*, (1928) Permanent Court of International Justice, Series A, No. 12, 46.

[65] Article 14 of the Framework Convention for the Protection of National Minorities and Art. 17 of the Central European Initiative Instrument for the Protection of Minority Rights. Though not binding, Recommendations 12 and 13 of the The Hague Recommendations regarding the Education of National Minorities and para. 34 of the Document of the Copenhagen Meeting of the Conference on the Human Dimension are also relevant.

in article 19, paragraph 3. The Government of Quebec has asserted that commercial activity such as outdoor advertising does not fall within the ambit of article 19. The Committee does not share this opinion. Article 19, paragraph 2, must be interpreted as encompassing every form of subjective ideas and opinions capable of transmission to others, which are compatible with article 20 of the Covenant, of news and information, of commercial expression and advertising, of works of art, etc.; it should not be confined to means of political, cultural or artistic expression. In the Committee's opinion, the commercial element in an expression taking the form of outdoor advertising cannot have the effect of removing this expression from the scope of protected freedom. The Committee does not agree either that any of the above forms of expression can be subjected to varying degrees of limitation, with the result that some forms of expression may suffer broader restrictions than others.[66]

Therefore, language use by minorities in economic and commercial activities also falls within the protection of freedom of expression so as to prevent state authorities from prohibiting the conduct of these activities in minority languages.

As the HRC itself admitted in the same communication, it is possible for public authorities to require that an official or some other language also be used in addition to a minority language in private economic activities if it does not exclude or hamper the use of the minority language.[67] As long as this requirement did not prevent individuals from also using freely their language of choice, or constitute too much of a burden, the need to have business documentation available in the official or national language—in addition to a minority language—would not constitute a breach of freedom of expression. This type of application of a language right for minorities in the private economic sphere also exists specifically in a few instruments.[68]

(e) Use of Minority Languages by Private Organisations; Registration of Minority Languages

Private groups or organisations, such as cultural societies, minority associations, etc., have the right to use minority languages in their activities. As indicated earlier, this is protected in international law and in Council of Europe treaties under the guarantee of either freedom of expression or specific

[66] *Ballantyne, Davidson and McIntyre v. Canada*, Communications Nos. 359/1989 and 385/1989, 31 March 1993, para. 11.3.

[67] *Ballantyne, Davidson and McIntyre v. Canada*, Communications Nos. 359/1989 and 385/1989, 31 March 1993, para. 11.4.

[68] Article 13 of the European Charter for Regional or Minority Languages, as well as the non-binding Recommendation 12 of the Oslo Recommendations regarding the Linguistic Rights of National Minorities.

provisions to this effect. It might also constitute discrimination and involve a violation of Article 27 International Covenant on Civil and Political Rights, as would also any attempt by the state to prohibit the use of a minority language during meetings or other activities of private groups or organisations. This right is included in a number of documents and at least one treaty.[69]

There is also an interaction or overlapping between freedom of association and that of expression, as for example state authorities may seek to prevent the activities of an association, even declare it illegal, because of its connection with a particular minority or its use of a minority language. Though somewhat indirectly, the European Court of Human Rights rather clearly implied that to refuse recognition of such an association or to try to prevent its use of a minority language was incompatible with the fundamental values of European democratic societies:

86. Freedom of expression constitutes one of the essential foundations of a democratic society and one of the basic conditions for its progress and for each individual's self-fulfillment. Subject to paragraph 2 of Article 10, it is applicable not only to 'information' or 'ideas' that are favourably received or regarded as inoffensive or as a matter of indifference, but also to those that offend, shock or disturb. Such are the demands of pluralism, tolerance and broadmindedness without which there is no 'democratic society' (see *Handyside v. the United Kingdom*, judgment of 7 December 1976, Series A no. 24, p. 23, § 49, and *Gerger v Turkey* [GC], no. 24919/94, § 46, 8 July 1999, unreported). Likewise, freedom of assembly as enshrined in Article 11 of the Convention protects a demonstration that may annoy or give offence to persons opposed to the ideas or claims that it is seeking to promote (see *Plattform 'Ärzte für das Leben' v. Austria*, judgment of 21 June 1988, Series A no. 139, p. 12, § 32). (...)

89. The inhabitants of a region in a country are entitled to form associations in order to promote the region's special characteristics [including presumably linguistic]. The fact that an association asserts a minority consciousness cannot in itself justify an interference with its rights under Article 11 of the Convention (see *Sidiropoulos and others*, cited above, pp. 1616-17, § 44). (...)[70]

On the basis of this and the other cases mentioned in the European Court of Human Rights, state authorities cannot prohibit the establishment or operation of private organisations because of their use or identification with a minority language, nor can they refuse the registration of such organisations when this

[69] Article 13 of the European Charter for Regional or Minority Languages and the non-binding Recommendation 6 of the Oslo Recommendations regarding the Linguistic Rights of National Minorities.

[70] *Stankov and the United Macedonian Organisation Ilinden v. Bulgaria*. See also the comments of the European Court, *supra*, in *Ouranio Toxo and Others v. Greece*.

is required by legislation. Such a refusal or prohibition would violate freedom of association, unless it is prescribed by law, in pursuit of a legitimate aim and necessary in a democratic society. This appears to have been confirmed indirectly by the European Court of Human Rights,[71] and would similarly be the case in other human rights and minority treaties.[72] In the case of a refusal by state authorities to register a minority organisation, or to interfere in its operations, this would be a violation of the Convention for the Protection of Human Rights and Fundamental Freedoms; if there is no law setting out clear criteria for registration and there are no procedural safeguards against arbitrary exercise of discretion, the interference is not one that can be prescribed by law. Although the European Court of Human Rights was referring to a violation of freedom of religion, it also indicated, *inter alia*, that the same reasoning would be applicable to freedom of association. In the case of linguistic minorities, 'if there is no law setting out clear criteria for registration and there are no procedural safeguards against arbitrary exercise of discretion', there would be a violation of Article 11(2) of the Convention in such a situation.[73]

In addition, individuals, as well as political parties or associations, have the right to use a minority language in their own affairs. Their activities are private by nature, even during times of elections. A prohibition on the use of a minority language in private political activities or during events with a political character would therefore be in violation, at the very least, of freedom of expression, Article 27 of the International Covenant on Civil and Political Rights, and non-discrimination. There are no cases specifically on such matter, though there are a handful of cases that deal with whether state authorities have the obligation to accept the use of minority languages in the course of an electoral or political process.[74] This exceeds the purely private use of a language, and therefore falls in the next area of the use or recognition of a minority language by state authorities themselves.

B. The Use of a Minority Language by State Authorities

A not uncommon point of view until recently assumed that any positive entitlement to the use of a minority language by state authorities was dependent on being granted specific language rights under a state's legislation or constitution, or under a specific treaty to that effect. It was thought—and indeed the

[71] *Sidiropoulos and Others v. Greece*, European Court of Human Rights, Judgment of 10 July 1998.

[72] See for example Recommendation 6 of the Oslo Recommendations regarding the Linguistic Rights of National Minorities.

[73] *Hasan and Chaush v. Bulgaria*, Judgment of 26 October 2000.

[74] *Charlent v. Belgium* and *Fryske Nasjonale Partij v. Netherlands*.

comments of a few of members of the HRC in *Dieergardt v. Namibia* shows how strongly this view is still held by some—that once a state has regulated linguistic matters by adopting an official language policy, this completely covers the field, since in international law there was no 'right to language', and a state may freely prohibit any or all other use of other languages which are not official.

This however suggests a profound misunderstanding of what official language status entails. Whilst a state is free to designate whatever language it prefers as official, and thus recognize its legal obligation to respond in the official language (or languages)—subject to appropriate limitations—such a designation can never entitle public authorities to violate the fundamental human rights of individuals.

Indeed, the claim still sometimes implied that an official language is somehow 'above' international human rights law is perplexing, since there is no legal basis to support it. No treaty provision anywhere in the world places an official language above basic rights such as freedom of expression or non-discrimination, any more than there is any treaty provision which places an official religion as excluding the application of freedom of religion or non-discrimination.

Nevertheless, there have been only a handful of cases, which mostly indirectly and for the most part quite recently, have started to address the questions to what extent state authorities may be obliged to use a minority language in their activities, in addition to a state's official language(s).

One notable exception where an official language has been restricted historically is in relation to the use of a minority language when required for reasons of due process or of a fair trial. Though in a sense a quite restricted right, it is still an example of the type of limits any official language policy may have when it interferes with basic international human rights: judicial authorities must provide interpretation or translation services in a minority language when faced with the situation of an accused who does not comprehend the official language.

Beyond that example, there have been very few clear pronouncements as to when and where there may be an entitlement to have state authorities use a minority language, except when this is specifically provided for in treaties such as the Framework Convention on the Protection of National Minorities and the European Charter on Regional or Minority Languages.

1. *Comparison over Time and between Courts*

With the exception of the use of a minority language when required under guarantees of due process and of a fair trial, it is only recently that international bodies have started to address more closely and comprehensively any right to have a minority language used by state authorities. Perhaps surprisingly, the relative silence of these authorities and their case law can be best understood on the basis that they were being asked to determine the issues on the basis of the wrong treaty provision: in almost all cases they were asked to find, under freedom of expression, a positive obligation for state authorities to use a minority language. And in all of these early cases, this line of argument failed—as it should.

In all the early communications which raised the issue of the use of a minority language by state authorities, the HRC tended to ignore or reject these almost out of hand.

This is what occurred in 1990 when the HRC was asked to rule on whether the right to testify in a minority language was protected under freedom of expression in *Dominique Guesdon v. France*,[75] to which the Committee concluded rather abruptly that there were 'absolutely no issues' under Article 19, paragraph 2, and added that the communication was inadmissible.[76]

In other similar communications (the '*Breton* cases' of *T.K. v. France*,[77] *M.K. v. France*,[78] and *Yves Cadoret and Hervé Le Bihan v. France*[79]), the UNHRC always indicated that arguments based upon freedom of expression in order to seek to have administrative, judicial or other authorities use a minority language were unambiguously inadmissible as having no basis, or had not been argued in any way that would permit examination by the Committee.[80]

In the 1990 and 1991 communications of *Dominique Guesdon v. France*,[81] and *Yves Cadoret and Hervé Le Bihan v. France*,[82] the HRC also had to look into a totally different line of argument that did not use freedom of expression, but rather used non-discrimination, as the legal basis under which to seek the right to have an administrative tribunal use a minority language.

The authors of those communications submitted that legislation in France making French the only language to be used before criminal courts constituted discrimination based upon language, as they were not permitted to use Breton, their primary language, before the courts. The HRC dealt with these

[75] UN GAOR, Vol. II, forty-fifth session, at 61, UN Doc. A/45/40 (1990).
[76] *Ibid.*, at para. 7.2.
[77] UN GAOR, Vol. II, forty-fifth session, Appendix X at p. 118, UN Doc. A/45/40 (1990).
[78] Communication No. 222/1987, 8 November 1989.
[79] Communications Nos. 221/1987 and 333/1988, 11 April 1991.
[80] *G.B. v. France*, para. 5.2.
[81] UN GAOR, forty-fifth session at p. 61, UN Doc. A/45/40 (1990).
[82] Communications Nos. 221/1987 and 333/1988, 11 April 1991.

communications mainly by focusing on the freedom of expression arguments, and limited its response in both cases with the same comments:

French law does not, as such, give everyone a right to speak his own language in court. Those unable to speak or understand French are provided with the services of an interpreter. This service would have been available to the author had the facts required it; as they did not, he suffered no discrimination under Article 26 on the ground of his language.

A few years later in *Ballantyne, Davidson and McIntyre v. Canada,*[83] the HRC mainly dealt with the matter using the guarantee of freedom of expression, as the Québec government tried to use its official language policy to restrict the private use of English in commercial activities in that province. Having essentially settled the matter by relying upon an infringement of the authors' freedom of expression, the HRC nevertheless added that in its view, since the law applied to all business people in the province, be they anglophones or francophones, there could be no discrimination:

11.5 The authors have claimed a violation of their right, under article 26, to equality before the law; the Government of Quebec has contended that Sections 1 and 6 of Bill 178 are general measures applicable to all those engaged in trade, regardless of their language. The Committee notes that Sections 1 and 6 of Bill 178 operate to prohibit the use of commercial advertising outdoors in other than the French language. This prohibition applies to French speakers as well as English speakers, so that a French speaking person wishing to advertise in English, in order to reach those of his or her clientele who are English speaking, may not do so. Accordingly, the Committee finds that the authors have not been discriminated against on the ground of their language, and concludes that there has been no violation of article 26 of the Covenant.

The above observations of the HRC are perplexing, since the issue under consideration was whether there was an unreasonable distinction based on language, not on an individual's linguistic or ethnic background. Nevertheless, it was not until about ten years later in *Dieergardt v. Namibia* that it would be asked more fully to consider the issue of what constitutes discrimination on the ground of language. And it is in this last communication that for the first time the HRC set out to explain, in light of its own previous views dealing with non-discrimination in other areas, whether this could be the basis for a right to have state authorities use a minority language. The answer, perhaps surprisingly for some—though not when one looks at the jurisprudence of other international bodies—was yes.

[83] Communications Nos. 359/1989 and 385/1989, 31 March 1993.

At the centre of that case was whether individuals of an Afrikaans-speaking minority in Namibia—known as Basters—were the subjects of discrimination because of the refusal of authorities to respond to telephone calls and other contacts in that language. English was the only official language recognized for use by state authorities under the Constitution of that country, and a government circular specifically prohibited the use of Afrikaans by government officials in official phone calls and correspondence.

Unfortunately, the views of the HRC are very brief on the reasons for its conclusion that this constituted a form of discrimination:

> 10.10 The authors have also claimed that the lack of language legislation in Namibia has had as a consequence that they have been denied the use of their mother tongue in administration, justice, education and public life. The Committee notes that the authors have shown that the State party has instructed civil servants not to reply to the authors' written or oral communications with the authorities in the Afrikaans language, even when they are perfectly capable of doing so. These instructions barring the use of Afrikaans do not relate merely to the issuing of public documents but even to telephone conversations. In the absence of any response from the State party the Committee must give due weight to the allegation of the authors that the circular in question is intentionally targeted against the possibility to use Afrikaans when dealing with public authorities. Consequently, the Committee finds that the authors, as Afrikaans speakers, are victims of a violation of article 26 of the Covenant.

The failure of the Namibian authorities to present any type of justification for its 'English only' policy is somewhat surprising and unique. Nevertheless, as will be shown in relation to the case law in other international bodies, it is not all that unusual as to the conclusion that in some cases for state authorities only to use one language—be it official or otherwise—can be discriminatory.

The central point that should be understood from this communication is that using only one language—even the official language—creates a distinction based on language, which can either exclude or disadvantage an individual. Once such a distinction or 'linguistic preference' is established, it is for authorities to demonstrate that such a distinction is justified—and non-discriminatory. Whether or not the threshold for such a justification is very high remains unanswered, and will undoubtedly come up in future communications as language issues are a source of much tension in many states worldwide.

Diergaardt v. Namibia is also a noteworthy communication because it is the first to directly address whether an official language is somehow 'excluded' from the application of international human rights law. As odd as it may sound, a few of the members of the HRC actually seemed to suggest that international law has no relevance once a state has determined its own official language, the official language somehow becoming 'invisible' or 'insulated' from a state's obligations under the CCPR:

7. (...) It is significant to note that it is nowhere alleged in the communication that the action of the State in declaring English as the official language and not allowing the use of other languages was directed only against the use of Afrikaans while permitting the other languages to be used. The action of the State in declaring English as the official language and not allowing the use of other languages by enacting appropriate legislation was clearly not violative of article 26 because all languages other than English were treated on the same footing and were not allowed to be used for official purposes and there was no discrimination against Afrikaans vis-à-vis other languages.[84]

This appeared to be the main difficulty encountered by the Committee members that were in dissent: Afrikaans is treated like all the other languages (except English) since all languages (except English) are prohibited, therefore there is no discrimination. Because English is official, it would seem it disappears from any consideration of human rights issues.

This logic is however untenable on closer inspection, since the Basters minority was not claiming that there was a discriminatory difference in the treatment of Afrikaans in relation with other languages: they were simply alleging that the exclusive use of English, and prohibition of the use of Afrikaans, in the circumstances were an unjustified and unreasonable distinction on the ground of language. Most of those who were in dissent actually refused to even consider that there was a distinction on the ground of language in relation to English—simply because English was official and therefore 'magically' not subject to any consideration of discriminatory difference of treatment.

Thankfully, the majority of the Committee did not agree with such an approach, probably sensing that this would open a Pandora's Box of other possible exclusions under the guise of 'official religion', 'official culture', etc. that could eventually weaken the whole structure of human rights protection in international law.

Other international bodies have not dealt with many matters on the use of a minority language by state authorities, except once again when it involved

[84] See the individual opinions of P. N. Bhagwati, Lord Colvill, Maxwell Yalden and Abdalfattah Amor. Nisuke Ando was also dissenting, but more consistent with the HRC previous views in other communications concluding that in the circumstances, even though there was a distinction based on language that disadvantaged or denied to the Basters some advantage or benefit enjoyed by others who used English, this difference of treatment and linguistic preference were reasonable and justified.

the right to due process and fair trial. The one other exception which should be noted is the European Court of Human Rights which, like the HRC, did deal with a small number of cases where it was alleged the failure of authorities to use a minority language in their affairs constituted a breach of freedom of expression.

Initial responses by the European Commission on Human Rights, such as *Inhabitants of Leeuw-St. Pierre v. Belgium*,[85] were often argued on the basis of freedom of expression, though here the parties also argued that the prohibition on distributing bilingual census forms (in French and Flemish) was also discriminatory. The Commission declared that the application was inadmissible *ratione materiae* because the Convention does not expressly guarantee 'linguistic freedom', nor did anything in the Convention guarantee the right 'to be able to use the language of their choice, or of their mother tongue or usual language, in their relations with the authorities'. Other early cases such as *X v. Ireland*,[86] *Charlent v. Belgium*,[87] and more recently *Fryske Nasjonale Partij v. Netherlands*[88] were all dismissed rather quickly as the argument that freedom of expression could be used as the premise for a right to get state authorities to use a minority language was rejected as without foundation.

The European Commission's jurisprudence is however not always consistent or easy to understand, and it would fall to the European Court of Human Rights at a later time to clarify, and address more comprehensively, whether it was possible to obtain the use of a minority language by state authorities by using the provision which prohibits discrimination. Again as with the HRC, the answer appears to be yes, though it cannot yet be said that the European Court of Human Rights has done so in a very detailed or unambiguous way.

In one of the leading post-World War II cases on the question of non-discrimination, the *Belgian Linguistics Case*,[89] the European Court of Human Rights considered whether there was a right to education in one's own language raised under Article 2 of the First Protocol of the Convention for the Protection of Human Rights and Fundamental Freedoms (involving the right to education). It was also asked whether forcing a large group of children, of the French-speaking minority in a small part of Belgium, to be educated exclusively in Dutch at local schools instead of in their own language contravened Articles 8 (right to family life) and 14 (non-discrimination provision).

[85] *Yearbook of the European Convention on Human Rights*, 8 (1965), 338.
[86] *Yearbook of the European Convention on Human Rights*, 13 (1970), 792.
[87] *Yearbook of the European Convention on Human Rights*, 6 (1963), 445, at 454–6.
[88] (1986) Decisions and Reports 45, 240 (European Commission of Human Rights), at 243.
[89] *Belgian Linguistics Case*, [1968] *Yearbook of the European Convention on Human Rights*, 1, 832.

The Court recognized that Article 2 Protocol 1 does not give an automatic right to education in a person's own language, nor did Article 14 read in conjunction with Article 2. It did however go on to say that in the case at hand there was no violation of the Convention—not because Article 2 and Article 14 together could not support a right to state-provided education in a minority language—but rather because the Belgian legislation was a justified and reasonable measure in light of the country's circumstances:

The Court...does not consider that the measures adopted in this matter by the Belgian legislature are so disproportionate to the requirements of the public interest which is being pursued as to constitute discrimination contrary to Article 14 of the Convention, read in conjunction with the first sentence of Article 2 of the Protocol...[90]

Despite some ambiguity as to the exact meaning of the Court's comment, it essentially used the same approach advanced by the HRC in *Dieergardt v. Namibia*: that a language preference by state authorities is a distinction on the ground of language that must be justified and reasonable in order not to be discriminatory. As it went on to explain on the process involved in determining what should be considered in this respect, the Court handed down what is still often seen as the classic formulation for the application of non-discrimination:

Article 14 does not prohibit distinctions in treatment which are founded on an objective assessment of essentially different factual circumstances and which, being based on the public interest, strike a fair balance between the protection of the interests of the community and respect for the rights and freedoms safeguarded by the Convention. In examining whether the legal provisions which have been attacked satisfy these criteria, the Court finds that their purpose is to achieve linguistic unity within the two large regions of Belgium in which a large majority of the population speaks only one of the two national languages. This legislation makes scarcely viable schools in which teaching is conducted solely in the national language that is not that of the majority of the inhabitants of the region. In other words, it tends to prevent, in the Dutch-unilingual region, the establishment or maintenance of schools which teach only in French. Such a measure cannot be considered arbitrary. To begin with, it is based on the objective element which the region constitutes. Furthermore it is based on a public interest, namely to ensure that all schools dependent on the state and existing in a unilingual region conduct their teaching in the language which is essentially that of the region.[91]

[90] *Ibid.*, at 886. [91] *Ibid.*, at 884–6.

In other words, to impose a single language of instruction constitutes a difference of treatment for those who have a different language, and may in some situations be discriminatory. According to the court:

> ...the legislation has instituted an educational system which, in the Dutch unilingual region, exclusively encourages teaching in Dutch, in the same way as it establishes the linguistic homogeneity of education in the French unilingual region. These differences in treatment of the two national languages in the two unilingual regions are, however compatible [with Articles 2 and 14].[92]

Presumably, not permitting education in French in state schools in the Dutch region, although a difference of treatment based upon language within the meaning of Article 14, was not discriminatory in the Belgian context because it was reasonable and justified by the general linguistic scheme adopted in the country.

The obverse of this is that in order not to be discriminatory, it may be necessary for state authorities to use a minority language in their activities where it is reasonable and justified to do so, including in the area of public education.

This approach was confirmed in *Mathieu-Mohin and Clerfayt*,[93] where the European Court of Human Rights did not simply reject out of hand a request from elected officials to be able to take a test of eligibility for the Council consisting of a parliamentary oath in French rather than Dutch. This therefore involved a request to use a minority language in state activities and fell outside the purview of freedom of expression. The applicants argued that this linguistic preference constituted a breach of Article 3 of the First Protocol of the Convention for the Protection of Human Rights and Fundamental Freedoms (free elections), or violated Article 3 when read in conjunction with Article 14 of the Convention (non-discrimination).

After indicating that nothing in Article 3 of the First Protocol suggested any sort of linguistic component, the court proceeded to the question of the alleged violation of Article 14 of the Convention taken together with Article 3 of the First Protocol. Here it did not adopt the position that since language was not a part of the substantive right under Article 3, the applicants could not avail themselves of the non-discrimination provision. On the contrary, the European Court came rather to the conclusion that Article 14 could be evoked, but that in the circumstances the measure adopted by the state was not unreasonable or disproportionate:

> The aim is to defuse the language disputes in the country by establishing more stable and decentralised organisational structures... In any consideration of the electoral system in issue, its general context must not be forgotten. The system does not appear

[92] *Ibid.*, at 884.

[93] (1987) European Convention on Human Rights, Series A, No. 113.

unreasonable if regard is had to the intentions it reflects and to the respondent state's margin of appreciation within the Belgian parliamentary system—a margin that is all the greater as the system is incomplete and provisional.[94]

Later cases in the European Court of Human Rights have tended to confirm that state authorities may have to use a minority language in their activities if the prohibition of such use is unreasonable in the circumstances. A refusal to use a minority language could therefore be a breach of non-discrimination and of the European Convention, and form the basis for the right to have such a language used by state authorities, even in the absence of a specific 'minority language' provision in the treaty.

The same conclusions were arrived at by the European Court of Justice in its jurisprudence. Once again, most treaties of the European Community have been silent on a 'right to use a minority language', but the case law has been able to push this limit, usually by reference to the principle of non-discrimination, though one should bear in mind that the reference to non-discrimination dealt with the denial of benefits among nationals of member states.

In an early noteworthy case, *Groener v. Minister for Education*,[95] the European Court of Justice considered national regulations on employment in Ireland requiring basic knowledge of the Irish language. Such knowledge was not related to the actual performance of Groener's duties as an art teacher. The court had to determine whether such a policy was discriminatory since it had the effect of excluding other European Union nationals, contrary to Article 3 of Regulation 1612/68.

The Court's approach held a great deal of deference to the emotional and symbolic ties between the Irish language and much of Irish society. Although Article 3 of the European Union regulation only permitted 'conditions relating to linguistic knowledge required by reason of the nature of the post to be filled', the court went out of its way in establishing another possible exception: there may be social and cultural considerations which are relevant in determining whether linguistic requirements are discriminatory or not. In the case of Irish, the requirement of some knowledge of that language by teachers, as part of a policy for its promotion, was justified according to the court, although the subject of the course taught by Groener was not linguistic, and teaching at the vocational school was as a general rule in English:

The EEC Treaty does not prohibit the adoption of a policy for the protection and promotion of a language of a member state which is both the national language and

[94] *Ibid.*, at 25.

[95] Case C379/87, [1990] Common Market Law Review, 1, 401.

the first official language.... The importance of education for the implementation of such a policy must be recognised. Teachers have an essential role to play, not only through the teaching which they provide but also by their participation in the daily life of the school and the privileged relationship which they have with their pupils. In those circumstances, it is not unreasonable to require them to have some knowledge of the first national language.

This case is especially relevant for its treatment of the relationship between a language requirement and non-discrimination: the Court recognized that any language imposition outside Article 3(1) of Regulation 1612/68 (linguistic knowledge related to job performance) must be applied without discrimination, meaning amongst other things, that the level of linguistic knowledge required must not be disproportionate to the object of the policy.

In another early decision, *Ministère Public v. Mutsch*,[96] a Belgian statute gave Belgian members of the German-speaking minority living in the German-speaking part of the country the right to use their language in criminal appeal proceedings. As a citizen of Luxembourg living in that area, Mutsch did not have the same right. The European Court of Justice held that the use of one's own language in court is to be considered as a 'social advantage' to which, according to the same regulation dealt with in *Groener*, Regulation 1612/68), all European Union workers are equally entitled. The court also stated that the principle of equal treatment means that European Union workers and their families have to be able to avail themselves of the same linguistic rights as the state's own citizens. Since Mutsch, as a European Union worker, did not have the same rights as other citizens, he was subject in this case to unlawful discrimination.

The decision in *Ministère Public v. Mutsch* is interesting mainly because it recognizes the use of one's primary language as a benefit—or conversely the denial of its use as a burden or disadvantage—which must be considered when determining whether or not government action or restrictions are discriminatory. Whilst *Ministère Public v. Mutsch* dealt very narrowly with the issue of differences of treatment as between citizens of the European Union, it does nevertheless suggest that the use of one language in a court of law, as in other state 'services' such as state schooling, impacts differently upon those who have a different primary language. The consequence which follows on a larger scale is that, unless otherwise justifiable, any exclusive state requirement of choice of language signals a difference of treatment, thereby denying to some a benefit enjoyed by others, more precisely the use of one's primary language.

[96] Case C137/84, (1985) ECR 2681.

This point was reinforced more recently in 1998 in *Criminal Proceedings against Otto Bickel and Ulrich Franz*,[97] where the European Court of Justice confirmed that to have a 'service' such as a court hearing in your own language is an advantage, and to be denied this advantage can be discriminatory, unless it is justified:

25. Even on the assumption that, as the Italian Government maintains, German-speaking nationals of other Member States who are resident in the Province of Bolzano may rely on the rules in issue and submit their pleadings in German—so that there is no discrimination on grounds of nationality as between residents of the region—Italian nationals are at an advantage by comparison with nationals of other Member States. The majority of Italian nationals whose language is German are in a position to demand that German be used throughout the proceedings in the Province of Bolzano, because they meet the residence requirement laid down by the rules in issue; the majority of German-speaking nationals of other Member States, on the other hand, cannot avail themselves of that right because they do not satisfy that requirement.

The treatment of any right to obtain the use of a minority language by state authorities from the case law of the Inter-American Court of Human Rights and the International Court of Justice is almost non-existent, except of course in relation to the consequences of the rights linked to due process and a fair trial which are considered in greater detail later. There are however two interesting cases which once again confirm that through the application of non-discrimination, it is possible to be entitled to the use of a minority language in appropriate circumstances where it would be unjustified and unreasonable not to use a specific language to some degree.

In the Advisory Opinion of 19 January 1984[98] on proposed amendments to the naturalisation provisions of the Constitution of Costa Rica of the Inter-American Court of Human Rights (the '*Costa Rican Naturalisation* case'), one of the amendments was to require that an applicant had to be able to speak, write and read Spanish in order to acquire citizenship. This is once again not a 'private matter', but one which dealt with receiving a service or benefit—here citizenship—that is linked to a linguistic preference by state authorities.

On the issue of imposing a language requirement in order to be eligible for citizenship, the Court had no difficulty accepting that it was not unreasonable, nor unjustified, to require proof of the ability to communicate in the

[97] *Criminal Proceedings against Horst Otto Bickel and Ulrich Franz*, (Reference for a preliminary ruling - Case C274/96, (1998) ECR I-7637, 27 November 1998).

[98] Case No. OC-4/84.

official language of the country. There were however some reservations on the literacy requirement: even if in the end the criterion was judged to be non-discriminatory, it was clear that it could in some situations constitute discrimination on the ground of language, as proscribed by Article 24 of the American Convention on Human Rights if it were:

> ...an unreasonable and disproportionate discrimination in accordance with the nature and purpose of the right to a nationality with its inclusion in the law of the Convention as a whole, and with the circumstances of the society in which it is designed to function.[99]

Acknowledging the desirability that all Costa Ricans know and are able to communicate in Spanish, as it is the official language of the country, one of the judges noted that such a context does not mean that a state can simply impose an official language requirement in complete disregard of the other languages used by its nationals, especially when the official language is not the primary tongue of a large number of individuals and indigenous peoples:

> [E]quality and non-discrimination cannot function in a vacuum nor, therefore, without the specific conditions of the society in which the people live. In this regard, my concern comes from the fact that there are among the country's own native-born people persons and substantial communities that do not know the Spanish language or that do not know it well, and that do not even speak that language as their native language: Indian communities that, although they are small and isolated, retain their ancestral languages and even resist learning or having to use the official language; and there is an important Costa Rican community of Jamaican origin that retains its language and many of whose members at least have problems in expressing themselves correctly in Spanish. Of course, the Costa Rican state, aware of the desirability and even the duty of preserving the native cultures and the rights of minorities in the country, is conducting programs of instruction and for promoting of the culture in the Indian languages and, recognising its cultural situation, has provided courts and public bureaus with official interpreters of those native or minority languages.[100]

Once again, the significance of this case is that it broadly conforms with most of the more recent case law from international bodies which all seem to acknowledge that, even in the absence of a right for the use of a minority language by state authorities in their respective treaties, it would still be possible to require in appropriate circumstances some use of another language if the refusal to do so were unreasonable, and therefore discriminatory.

[99] *Ibid.*, at para. 22. [100] *Ibid.*, at para. 23.

Finally, and even though the following comments were made by only one judge, Judge Tanaka, in dissent, it is still noteworthy since it is one of the few times the International Court of Justice made a direct reference to the issue of the language used by state authorities. Essentially, the judge concluded in *South West Africa Case (Second Phase)*[101] that having separate schools, including presumably schools using a minority language as a medium of instruction, would not necessarily be discriminatory, and in fact was highly desirable:

> [I]f there exists the necessity to treat one race differently from another, this necessity is not derived from the physical characteristics or other racial qualifications but other factors, namely religious, linguistic, educational, social, etc. which in themselves are not related to race or colour... For instance, if we consider education... we cannot deny the value of vernacular as the medium of instruction and the result thereof would be separate schooling as between children of diverse population groups... In this case separate education and schooling may be recognised as reasonable. This is justified by the nature of the matter in question.[102]

While all of the above mainly rested on the application of non-discrimination, one of the most recent—and in some ways puzzling if not controversial—cases from the European Court of Human Rights has even dispensed with the need to refer to non-discrimination, and recognized (to a minority in northern Cyprus) the right to receive instruction in their own language in state schools. The case of *Cyprus v. Turkey* will be discussed in greater detail under the heading of education, but the main point which needs to be emphasized is that clearly, in addition to the possibility of using a 'minority rights' treaty such as the Framework Convention on the Protection of National Minorities, or one dealing specifically with linguistic rights such as the European Charter for Regional or Minority Languages, there can be other rights invoked, especially, but not exclusively, non-discrimination, which can form the basis for having state authorities use to an appropriate and 'reasonable' degree a minority language.

2. *Analysis and Criticism, Possible Evolution of Interpretation by Courts*

Although by no means insignificant, there has still not been an overwhelming number of cases dealing with the possible obligations of state authorities to use a minority language.

In relation to a limited number of rights dealing with the obligation for judicial authorities to provide an interpreter or translation for an accused individual who does not understand the language of proceedings, the cases are

[101] [1966] International Court of Justice 284. [102] *Ibid.*

based on clear treaty provisions which enshrine unambiguously this entitlement, regardless of a state's official language policy. This right thus allows for a carefully circumscribed use of a minority language, and in reality does not grant any type of formal recognition or value to the minority language itself, but to the official language version.

Beyond this, no general international treaty, with the exception of treaties dealing with minority or linguistic rights, spells out a clear-cut obligation of state authorities to use any minority language. Yet, despite this apparent lacuna, jurisprudence has been mounting to the effect that while there may not be a 'right to a minority language' from state authorities, some fundamental human rights guarantees can be invoked where a particular linguistic preference by state authorities—including a preference based on the official language of the state—conflicts with international human rights law.

Thus, cases from most international bodies have gradually and increasingly suggested that provisions such as non-discrimination could be used to require the use of other languages where it would be unreasonable to only prefer, use or privilege one language (usually the official language). That was in essence the reasoning of the European Court of Human Rights in the *Belgian Linguistics Case* and of the HRC in *Diergaardt v. Namibia*, among others.

It would be simplistic however to suggest that this has been a steady and consistent development at any level, though at the same time given the rather widespread similarity of approaches one finds with all of the international bodies, it would seem the trend will be in the next decades towards consolidation and further elaboration of the application of the rights involved.

Still, there has been noteworthy resistance to this approach, though the objections have been raised largely by a small number of judges or committee members who, in the main, seem to refuse any interference with a state's 'official language' determination.

Their views are perhaps not so surprising since there had been a long-standing view that the language rights of minorities were largely unprotected in international law, except for the very limited offerings of Article 27 CCPR. Furthermore, it is not an uncommon assertion that a state's official language policies and practices are determinative and conclusive: according to this view, international human rights are silent and do not protect language preferences. Therefore, once the state has legislated on language use for official purposes, this excludes any possibility of claiming any other language right.

This 'exclusive official language fallacy' is falling by the wayside when one examines the jurisprudence from the *Belgian Linguistics Case* onwards, since it now appears fairly obvious that there are in fact quite a few human rights provisions which protect certain aspects of linguistic identity and language rights, regardless of a state's own language preferences or policies.

The 'exclusive official language fallacy' (that can still nevertheless be found in some dissenting comments such as in *Diergaardt v. Namibia*) would appear to conveniently ignore the express linguistic component of a number of treaty provisions in international law which state public authorities could not breach, such as the prohibition of discrimination on the ground of language, the right to use a language one understands in criminal proceedings, etc.

This necessarily means that an official language cannot breach these basic human rights and their linguistic dimension, nor does it somehow insulate a state from its international legal obligations. Having an official language, or an official religion for that matter, cannot be used as a basis for legislation, policies or practices that would be deemed discriminatory in international law, or in breach of any other rights guaranteed under international treaties. This is in all likelihood to be one of the main 'battlegrounds' which future case law will need to address more directly and comprehensively.

The other main area of evolution may be the extent to which non-discrimination can be used as a basis to claim the right to have a minority language used by state authorities, at least where this could be deemed justified and reasonable. Until now, most of the case law from all of the international bodies has simply acknowledged that this is a possibility. In other words, cases such as the *Belgian Linguistic Case* and *Mathieu-Mohin and Clerfayt v. Belgium*, while raising the possibility of requiring authorities to use a minority language (French), did not go so far as to do so. While the HRC did in fact make such a determination, and required that Namibia act in a non-discriminatory way and have some state authorities use Afrikaans, a minority language, this recent communication is somewhat unusual as the Namibian government had failed to make any argument for the exclusive use of English and the complete prohibition of any use of Afrikaans. Finally, and the odd one out of all of the international cases, is one of the most recent from the European Court of Human Rights, *Cyprus v. Turkey*, where the court dispensed with any need to even discuss the reasonable nature of having state education in only one language.

This last case, while on the one hand apparently quite generous for minorities which it would seem to give an automatic right to be instructed in one's language in state schools—if you started your education in your language—on the other hand is really almost completely inconsistent with the much more reasoned analysis contained in the *Belgian Linguistics Case*. The two cases cannot comfortably coexist, and future cases are necessary in order to address when exactly a minority is entitled to be educated in its own language in state schools.

Perhaps the most significant issue here is that the European Court of Human Rights case law has evolved so as not to exclude this possibility under the European Convention, while in the past many commentators had mistakenly taken it for granted that the *Belgian Linguistics Case* had once and for all prevented any right to receive public instruction in one's own language.

3. *Application of the Rights*

(a) Use of a Minority Language by State Authorities Generally

The use of a minority language by state authorities generally remains one of the great unexplored issues that still need to be addressed under existing treaties. It is true that a number of treaties and international instruments often embody the concept of a 'sliding-scale' approach as a proper response to requests for the use of the language of minorities by state authorities. The Framework Convention for the Protection of National Minorities refers in Article 10 to 'areas inhabited by persons belonging to national minorities traditionally or in substantial numbers, if those persons so request and where such a request corresponds to a real need, the Parties shall endeavour to ensure, as far as possible…' while the European Charter for Minority or Regional Languages in Article 10 talks about 'within the administrative districts…in which the number of residents…justifies the measures specified below and according to the situation of each language'. Both recognize that there is a gradation that must be respected as to the degree that state authorities must use a minority language.

Essentially, this 'sliding-scale approach' requires that where public authorities at the national, regional or local levels face a sufficiently large number of individuals who use a minority language, authorities must provide an appropriate level of service in this language.

Case law based on general human rights treaties has been of little assistance since the treaties do not contain any similar provisions. Even the CCPR, which has a minority right guarantee in Article 27, appears to be limited to the need to protect minorities in their own private activities from outside or state interference only, since 'persons belonging to [linguistic] minorities shall not be denied the right, in community with the other members of their group… to use their own language' indicates rather clearly it only protects the use of a language as between private individuals who belong to a minority. There are no communications which have concluded that Article 27 can be extended as a basis for state services or indeed financial support for activities in a minority language. Indeed, the one communication which unambiguously recognized that a minority might be entitled to active state financial support did so on the basis of non-discrimination, not Article 27 CCPR.[103]

Case law under the European Convention on Human Rights is also not very helpful on this issue because—in the absence of a specific 'right to services from state administrative services' or of a general non-discrimination clause—the few matters that have been considered on the issue of the language of administrative services were simply declared inadmissible, often because claimants were trying to assert a right to have state authorities use a particular language on the basis of freedom of expression:

> Whereas in the last analysis the Applicants are claiming the right to be able to use the language of their choice, or of their mother tongue or usual language, in their relations with the authorities;
>
> Whereas, however, it appears that the guarantee of this right lies outside the scope of the Convention, in particular of Articles 9 and 10;
>
> Whereas, in fact, there is no article in the Convention or First Protocol that expressly guarantees 'linguistic freedom' as such (see for example the decisions of 26th July 1963 on the admissibility of applications Nos. 1474/62 and 1769/73, Yearbook 6, pp. 340–342 and 454);
>
> Whereas the only clauses in the Convention that deal with the use of languages, that is to say Articles 5 (2) and 6 (3) (a) and (e), are limited in scope and irrelevant to the case in point (see for example the two decisions mentioned above, *loc. cit.*); whereas their existence would be incomprehensible if the Convention were intended to afford much wider protection to the right which the Applicants allege to have been violated.[104]

There is nevertheless a very recent communication which has looked at the substantive arguments in this area and has concluded that state authorities are obligated to use a specific minority language in administrative contacts with the public because there was no reasonable justification for refusing to do so (*Diergaardt v. Namibia*), and strong indications in the majority of more recent cases that, had the justification provided by the state not been a sufficient

[103] In *Arieh Hollis Waldman v. Canada*, (Communication N° 694/1996, UN Doc. CCPR/C/67/D/694/1996 (1999)) the HRC concluded that to only provide state financial support to Catholic schools in the province of Ontario was discriminatory for Jewish parents who were denied the same benefit for their own private schools and children. While the HRC did not actually conclude that therefore Jewish schools were entitled to the same financial support, it did indicate that the discriminatory practice had to cease, and that the government of Canada could either cease all funding to Catholic schools or choose to provide it to other private schools such as the minority Jewish schools. The government of Canada chose the latter option, so that using Art. 26 of the CCPR and non-discrimination, minorities were for the first time able to get state support for their educational activities, and not through the use of Art. 27.

[104] *Inhabitants of Leeuw-St. Pierre v. Belgium*. See also *X. v. Ireland*.

and reasonable justification, it would have concluded that there was a breach of non-discrimination in not permitting the use of a minority language in a variety of fields involving state administrative services (*Belgian Linguistics Case, Mathieu-Mohin and Clerfayt v. Belgium*, and *Costa Rican Naturalisation Case*).

It would seem possible therefore that in general in administrative and other state activities, that not to provide a reasonable, i.e. 'sliding-scale', response could constitute a form of discrimination as to language. In situations where it is relatively simple for state authorities to accommodate to some degree the language of a minority, such as in *Diergaardt v. Namibia* where a minority was substantial, concentrated territorially, and where many state officials already spoke the minority language, not to use their language as is 'appropriate' in the circumstances could be deemed to be unreasonable or arbitrary in light of the disadvantages caused, and therefore discriminatory:

> 10.10 The authors have also claimed that the lack of language legislation in Namibia has had as a consequence that they have been denied the use of their mother tongue in administration, justice, education and public life. The Committee notes that the authors have shown that the State party has instructed civil servants not to reply to the authors' written or oral communications with the authorities in the Afrikaans language, even when they are perfectly capable of doing so. These instructions barring the use of Afrikaans do not relate merely to the issuing of public documents but even to telephone conversations. In the absence of any response from the State party the Committee must give due weight to the allegation of the authors that the circular in question is intentionally targeted against the possibility to use Afrikaans when dealing with public authorities. Consequently, the Committee finds that the authors, as Afrikaans speakers, are victims of a violation of article 26 of the Covenant.

What the jurisprudence is clearly consistent and unambiguous about, despite some resistance, is that an official language policy in and of itself does not constitute a sufficient and reasonable justification to prohibit all use of a minority language by state authorities.

(b) Use of a Minority Language under Due Process and Fair Trial Guarantees

Most international treaties dealing with civil and political rights[105] have provisions recognizing that when an accused faces proceedings in a language which s/he does not understand, s/he shall have the right to the assistance of an

[105] Article 14 of the International Covenant on Civil and Political Rights, Art. 5 of the European Convention for the Protection of Human Rights and Fundamental Freedoms, and Art. 8 of the American Convention on Human Rights.

interpreter, most often free of charge. If a person is being charged with a criminal offence, s/he must also be informed of the nature of the charge in a language which s/he understands. Since it is a right which is available to everyone, it has the effect of requiring some accommodation for individuals who are not fluent in the language used as part of the criminal court process, and means that in some cases translation and interpretation for minority languages must be provided. In this sense, in addition to being a fundamental right linked to concepts of due process and fair trial, it simultaneously could be described as an admittedly rather limited 'linguistic' right available to members of a linguistic minority, as well as any other individuals. Judicial authorities must use a minority language where an individual does not understand the language used by state officials in criminal charges and procedures, regardless of a state's official language policy, though only as far as is required in order to translate it into the language used in court.

Because of the highly prejudicial consequences of a criminal offence and the importance of court proceedings involved, a state is never entitled to set aside these guarantees, nor are these related to the status of a particular language or the number of individuals who speak a particular language in a state. As the fairness and legitimacy of the legal system are at stake, as well as the defendant's interests, the state must adopt what is perceived to be a reasonable measure in the circumstances: at minimum, it must provide free interpretation of court proceedings, as well as inform any individual being charged of the nature and cause of his or her offence, in a language which he or she understands.

The provisions which recognize this right make quite clear that it only applies to criminal matters, and not civil or other type of proceedings.[106] In *Isop v. Austria*,[107] an applicant sought the right to use Slovene in civil court proceedings by invoking Article 6 (right to a fair hearing) and Article 14 (non-discrimination on the basis of language or national association) of the Convention for the Protection of Human Rights and Fundamental Freedoms.

The European Commission on Human Rights made two relevant observations: first that these provisions, used in conjunction, do not guarantee a right to have a minority language used in the civil court system, but were limited to criminal matters, and secondly that the applicant's own knowledge of the German language made the use of an interpreter unnecessary.

[106] *X. and Y. v. Belgium*, where the case claiming a right to civil proceedings to be held in French instead of Dutch was declared inadmissible since the due process provisions of the European Convention on Human Rights (Arts. 5.2 and 6.3) only applied to criminal proceedings.

[107] Application 808/60, *Yearbook of the European Convention on Human Rights*, 5, 108.

Other international decisions confirm this latter limit. In *Dominique Guesdon v. France*,[108] the Human Rights Committee noted that the notion of a fair trial, within the meaning of Article 14 of the International Covenant on Civil and Political Rights, does not have the effect of entitling an accused in criminal proceedings to express himself in his language of preference:

The Committee observes, as it has done on a previous occasion, that Article 14 is concerned with procedural equality; it enshrines, *inter alia*, the principle of equality of arms in criminal proceedings. The provision for the use of one official court language by states parties to the Covenant does not, in the Committee's opinion, violate Article 14. Nor does the requirement of a fair hearing mandate states parties to make available to a citizen whose mother tongue differs from the official court language, the services of an interpreter, if this citizen is capable of expressing himself adequately in the official language. Only if the accused or the defence witnesses have difficulties in understanding or in expressing themselves in the court language, must the services of an interpreter be made available.[109]

These comments indicate that individuals having pronounced difficulty with the language of proceedings suffer from a severe disadvantage which, whilst not requiring that the language of the accused necessarily be used in the criminal proceedings themselves, renders obligatory as a minimum the free use of an interpreter.[110]

[108] Communication No. 219/1986.

[109] *Ibid.*, at para. 10.2. See also similar conclusions in *Hervé Barzhig v. France* and from the European Commission on Human Rights in *K. v. France*, (1984) Decisions and Reports 35, 203, and *Bideault v. France*, (1986) Decisions and Reports 48, 232.

[110] In another case, the Human Rights Committee declared a communication inadmissible because the author had refused to exhaust local remedies in the language of administrative proceedings, claiming that he should be entitled to proceed with the assistance of an interpreter. In *M.K. v. France*, Communication No. 222/1987, UN Document A/45/40, the *Tribunal administratif* of Rennes had refused to consider a complaint which the author had submitted in Breton after French tax authorities had refused to indicate his address in Breton. The *Tribunal* subsequently ruled that the document had to be submitted in French if it were to be considered by the court. The author contended that the right to the assistance of an interpreter pursuant to Art. 14(3)(f) of the International Covenant on Civil and Political Rights was being continuously violated in France. The Human Rights Committee declared the communication inadmissible as the author had not exhausted all domestic remedies. It also noted that the author was not being criminally prosecuted—under Art. 14, the right to an interpreter only applies in criminal proceedings—but rather was seeking to initiate proceedings before an administrative court in order to establish that he had been denied rights protected by the Covenant. The Human Rights Committee concluded that even if the matter of the exclusive use of French in court proceedings was the issue complained of by the author, and that it would be examined in the first instance by French judicial organs using French, this was not an unreasonable route, as the author was proficient in French and no irreparable harm would be done to his substantive case by using the French language to pursue his remedy.

The European Court of Human Rights arrived at a similar conclusion in *Kamasinski v. Austria*.[111] This case is also more detailed and provides a wider sense of the actual extent to which a minority language may be used for purposes of translation and interpretation. The accused had little knowledge of the German language and, though he was given the assistance of an interpreter, was unhappy with the quality of the translation as well as objecting to not having received a translation of court documents which he intended to use on appeal. The European Court stated that the Article 6(3)(e) guarantees should be interpreted generously:

> The right to the free assistance of an interpreter applies not only to oral statements made at the trial hearing but also to documentary material and the pre-trial proceedings. Paragraph 3(e) signifies that a person "charged with a criminal offence" who cannot understand or speak the language used in court has the right to free assistance of an interpreter for the translation or interpretation of all those documents or statements in the proceedings instituted against him which is necessary for him to understand or to have rendered into the court's language in order to have the benefit of a fair trial.[112]

However, the Court emphasized that the provision does not go so far as to require a written translation of all of the items of evidence and official documents in a procedure, but rather a translation such that the defendant has full and sufficient knowledge of the case against him and is able to defend himself.

It added that:

> [T]he obligation of the competent authorities is not limited to the appointment of an interpreter but, if they are put on notice in the particular circumstances, may also extend to a degree of subsequent control over the adequacy of the interpretation provided.[113]

In essence, there would be a violation of Article 6 if a translation were inadequate or otherwise affected the defendant's ability to defend himself or his right to a fair trial. It would obviously be impossible to attain absolute equality between a defendant who understands the language of the court and one who does not, as this would be an extremely long and costly process if every single document and every single utterance were to be translated.

This is why the European Court held that the requirements of Article 6 do not require the full-scale use of the accused's language in criminal proceedings,

[111] Judgment of 19 December 1989, ECtHR.
[112] *Ibid.*, at para. 74.
[113] *Ibid.*

but only the use of what is required for an accused's defence in order for him to understand the nature of the charges being brought against him, and for him to be able to properly appreciate the evidence being presented and the testimony of witnesses during the proceedings, and finally for him to effectively present his own evidence and testimony.[114] The language used during translation should also be simple and non-technical so as to ensure that an accused truly understands:

> 50. As to the merits, the Court reiterates that paragraph 2 of Article 5 contains the elementary safeguard that any person arrested should know why he is being deprived of his liberty. This provision is an integral part of the scheme of protection afforded by Article 5: by virtue of paragraph 2 any person arrested must be told, in simple, non-technical language that he can understand, the essential legal and factual grounds for his arrest, so as to be able, if he sees fit, to apply to a court to challenge its lawfulness in accordance with paragraph 4.... Whilst this information must be conveyed "promptly" (in French: '*dans le plus court délai*'), it need not be related in its entirety by the arresting officer at the very moment of the arrest. Whether the content and promptness of the information conveyed were sufficient is to be assessed in each case according to its special features (see, *mutatis mutandis*, *Murray v. the United Kingdom*, Series A no. 300-A, p. 31, § 72). (...)[115]

As for the extent of the right to be informed promptly of the nature and cause of a criminal accusation, this was also described in *Brozicek v. Italy*.[116] On the subject of Article 6(3)(a), the European Court stated that any document constituting an 'accusation' within the meaning of Article 6 should be provided to the applicant in a language which he understands. Since the competent judicial authorities had been informed of the accused's lack of knowledge of Italian, it was their duty to ensure the observance of the requirements of Article 6(3)(a) unless they could in fact establish that the applicant had sufficient knowledge of Italian to understand the purport of the communication.[117]

Similarly, in *Dominique Guesdon v. France*, the Human Rights Committee clearly indicated that the right to an interpreter is not limited to situations where an individual has absolutely no knowledge of the language of proceedings, but arises whenever an 'accused or the defence witnesses have difficulties in understanding, or in expressing themselves in the court language'.

There are also possibilities for being entitled to use a minority language in court proceedings that go far beyond what may be provided for by the

[114] *Supra*, at para. 79.
[115] *Conka v. Belgium*
[116] (1989) European Convention on Human Rights, Series A, No. 167.
[117] *Ibid.*, at paras. 38–41.

principles of due process or of a fair trial. For example, as pointed out clearly by the European Court of Justice, if court proceedings can already be held in a minority language in a member state, then all citizens of member states must be entitled to access to these proceedings in this minority language, regardless as to whether they may be able to understand the language of proceedings in another language under the application of non-discrimination under Community law. Two cases have confirmed this, the first in a general way,[118] and the second rejecting the idea that because the possibility to use a minority language was deemed to be for the protection of a specific minority (the German-speaking minority of Süd Tirol/Alto Adige), it could only be made available to members of that community:

17. Although, generally speaking, criminal legislation and the rules of criminal procedure—such as the national rules in issue, which govern the language of the proceedings—are matters for which the Member States are responsible, the Court has consistently held that Community law sets certain limits to their power in that respect. Such legislative provisions may not discriminate against persons to whom Community law gives the right to equal treatment or restrict the fundamental freedoms guaranteed by Community law (...)

24. In those circumstances, it appears that German-speaking nationals of other Member States travelling or staying in the Province of Bolzano are at a disadvantage by comparison with Italian nationals resident there whose language is German. Whereas a member of the latter group may, if charged with an offence in the Province of Bolzano, have the proceedings conducted in German, a German-speaking national from another Member State, travelling in that province, is denied that right.

26. Consequently, rules such as those in issue in the main proceedings, which make the right, in a defined area, to have criminal proceedings conducted in the language of the person concerned conditional on that person being resident in that area, favour nationals of the host State by comparison with nationals of other Member States exercising their right to freedom of movement and therefore run counter to the principle of non-discrimination laid down in Article 6 of the Treaty.

27. A residence requirement of that kind can be justified only if it is based on objective considerations independent of the nationality of the persons concerned and is proportionate to the legitimate aim of the national provisions (see, to that effect, Case C-15/96 *Schöning-Kougebetopoulou* [1998] ECR I-47, paragraph 21).

28. However, it is clear from the order for reference that this is not the position in the case of the rules in issue.[119]

[118] *Criminal Proceedings against Robert Heinrich Maria Mutsch.*
[119] *Criminal Proceedings against Otto Bickel and Ulrich Franz.*

(c) State-provided Education and Minority Languages

It is undoubtedly true that a mother tongue is not merely a linguistic system which can, with impunity, be replaced by another language. A child's mother tongue is the language which allows him to impose a structure on the universe. It is associated with his thought processes, his sense of identity and his solidarity with his family and environment. As he matures, his mother tongue may become a symbol of regional or national pride, a means of gaining access to knowledge and wisdom. And it will usually be associated with feelings of warmth, intimacy, spontaneity.[120]

The right to education being covered in a separate chapter in this book, this section will restrict itself to the narrow issue of the language aspect to this right.

Contrary to what is sometimes presented, there is (from a legal point of view strictly speaking) no unqualified 'right to be educated in one's own language' which anyone could invoke at any time without any restrictions. However, and what is also contrary to what may at times be suggested, jurisprudence has been showing that this does not necessarily mean that there is absolutely no right to be educated in a minority language in general international law. As with other areas of state-provided services or facilities, arguments that the refusal to use a minority language constituted a breach of freedom of expression have been readily dismissed as unfounded.[121]

Case law on the language component of the right to education itself—as opposed to claims founded on freedom of expression—is still relatively limited, however, because even though the right to education is widely enshrined in many general international treaties on human rights, these same treaties are either silent or ambiguous as to the language of instruction. It is still clear that an initial examination of the international instruments recognizing a right to education show that these have consistently excluded a parent's automatic right to choose the language in which his or her child receives a state's educational services.[122] In almost all of these provisions it would seem the language of instruction in state schools is left to the state's determination—as long as no human rights are breached in the process.

The European Court of Human Rights came to the same conclusion in a highly influential judgment—and indeed still to this day the single most

[120] Chris Kennedy (ed.), *Language Planning and Language Education*, (1983) (Unwin Publishers, London, 1983), at 165.

[121] *R.L.M. v. France*, para. 5.2.

[122] Article 13 of the International Covenant on Economic, Social and Cultural Rights; Article 2 of Protocol No. 1 to the Convention for the Protection of Human Rights and Fundamental Freedoms; Article 13 of the Additional Protocol to the American Convention on Human Rights in the Area of Economic, Social and Cultural Rights; Article 5(e)(v) of the Racial Discrimination Convention; Article 28(1) of the Convention on the Rights of the Child.

comprehensive case specifically on this issue—where it addressed itself directly to the *travaux préparatoires* and the context of Article 2 of the Protocol 1 of the Convention for the Protection of Human Rights and Fundamental Freedoms dealing with the right to education:

> ... the first sentence of Article 2 does not specify the language in which education must be conducted in order that the right to education should be respected. It does not contain precise provisions similar to those which appear in Articles 5(2) and 6(3) (a) and (e). However, the right to education would be meaningless if it did not imply in favour of its beneficiaries, the right to be educated in the national language or in one of the national languages, as the case may be.[123]

Although Article 2 is, *a priori*, 'language neutral', it must of necessity include the right to learn at least one national language. The court further adds, on dealing with the second sentence of this provision on the religious and philosophical preferences of parents:

> This provision does not require of states that they should, in the sphere of education or teaching, respect parents' linguistic preferences, but only their religious and philosophical convictions... Moreover the 'preparatory work' confirms that the object of the second sentence of Article 2 was in no way to secure respect by the state of a right for parents to have education conducted in a language other than that of the country in question: indeed in June 1951 the Committee of Experts which had the task of drafting the Protocol set aside a proposal put forward in this sense. Several members of the Committee believed that it concerned an aspect of the problem of ethnic minorities and that it consequently fell outside the scope of the Convention.[124]

The European Court here is unambiguous: the right to education does not guarantee a 'right to education in one's own language', at least in state schools. Nor does the non-discrimination provision in combination with the right to education guarantee an individual's unrestricted freedom of choice as to the language of instruction to be used in state-provided education:

> Article 14, even when read in conjunction with Article 2 of the Protocol, does not have the effect of guaranteeing to a child or to his parents the right to obtain instruction in a language of his choice. The object of these two Articles, read in conjunction, is more limited: it is to ensure that the right to education shall be secured by each contracting

[123] *Belgian Linguistic Case*, [1968] *Yearbook of the European Convention on Human Rights*, 1, 832, at 858. In an earlier matter prior to the entry into force of Protocol 1 and the right to education, the European Commission on Human Rights ruled inadmissible a case where the applicants, also French-speaking Belgians, asserted that there was a right to education in their own language in state schools based on the right to private life (Art. 8) or freedom of thought (Art. 9), in conjunction with the prohibition of discrimination under Art. 14 (*X and others v. Belgium*)

[124] *Ibid.*, at 861 and 862.

party to everyone within its jurisdiction without discrimination on the ground, for instance, of language. This is the natural and ordinary meaning of Article 14 read in conjunction with Article 2. Furthermore, to interpret the two provisions as conferring on everyone within the jurisdiction of a state a right to obtain education in the language of his own choice would lead to absurd results, for it would be open to anyone to claim any language of instruction in any of the territories of the contracting parties... The Court notes that, where the contracting parties intended to confer upon everyone within their jurisdiction specific rights with respect to the use or understanding of a language, as in Article 5(2) and Article 6(3)(a)(e) of the Convention, they did so in clear terms. It must be concluded that if they had intended to create for everyone within their jurisdiction a specific right with respect to the language of instruction, they would have done so in express terms in Article 2 of the Protocol. For this reason also, the Court cannot attribute to Article 14, when read in conjunction with Article 2 of the Protocol, a meaning which would secure to everyone within the jurisdiction of a contracting party a right to education conducted in a language of his own choice.[125]

While the European Court of Human Rights was very clear that the French-speaking minority did not automatically have a right to be educated in French in state schools in the Dutch-speaking part of Belgium, it then indicated that had the legislation which prevented them from being instructed in their language been 'so disproportionate to the requirements of the public interest which is being pursued as to constitute a discrimination contrary to Article 14 of the Convention, read in conjunction with the first sentence of Article 2 of the Protocol',[126] then they would have been entitled to education in their own language.

This is the aspect of the significance of the *Belgian Linguistic Case* which is often overlooked: it actually does stand for a right for education in a minority language where such a refusal would be a 'disproportionate' response to the circumstances, and thus discrimination prohibited by Article 14 of the Convention in conjunction with Article 2 of the Protocol.

The same reasoning was followed in a number of other cases involving the right to education in French in Belgium, *Roger Vanden Berghe v. Belgium*, *X v. Ireland* and *Inhabitants of Les Fourons v. Belgium*. As indicated by the Commission in the first matter:

Whereas however this difference is based on objective and reasonable criteria and the means employed are not out of proportion to the end pursued; whereas it is clear that a French-speaking child will find it easier to follow teaching given in French and a Flemish child will find it easier to follow teaching given in Dutch so that to this extent

[125] *Ibid.*, at 866–8. [126] *Ibid.*, at 886.

the system operates in favour of such children; whereas on the other hand the presence of Flemish children in considerable numbers in a French class—and vice versa—would be likely to disturb the teaching; whereas in this connection it is irrelevant to point out that these arguments were not taken into consideration by the legislature when it organized the use of languages in the unilingual areas, in which there are a number of minorities which use another national language; whereas it follows that there is no appearance of a violation of Article 14, taken in conjunction with Article 8 of the Convention in the legislation applicable to the Brussels capital area.

The question left unanswered in the *Belgian Linguistic Case, Roger Vanden Berghe v. Belgium* and *Inhabitants of Les Fourons v. Belgium* which has not yet been addressed in later cases is what exactly are the criteria to apply in order to determine whether a refusal to provide education in a minority language is a 'disproportionate response' to the point of constituting a discrimination on the basis of language under Articles 14 of the Convention and 2 of the Protocol.

The answer is possibly what has been emerging as the European 'standard' in other treaties in the last 20 years, since two legally binding treaties have given a perhaps more definite form and structure to this right: Article 14 of the Framework Convention for the Protection of National Minorities and Article 8 of the European Charter for Regional or Minority Languages. Both indicate that 'in appropriate circumstances' states must make available in schools the teaching of or in a minority language. For Article 14 of the Framework Convention this involves 'areas inhabited by persons belonging to national minorities traditionally or in substantial numbers, if there is sufficient demand' while the European Charter in Article 8 speaks of within the territory of use of each language and 'according to the situation of each language' to determine the exact extent of the use of a minority language for purposes of state education.

They both seem to suggest that the numbers of pupils necessary for the purpose of demanding education in their own language must be 'sufficient'. This therefore suggests, as the European Court of Human Rights stated in the *Belgian Linguistic Case* in respect of the right to education and the prohibition of discrimination, that the mere presence of one or a handful of pupils in a district would not automatically give rise to a right to be taught in a minority language in a state school.

However, in the light of the many international and European instruments which generally refer to a state's obligation to protect and promote the language (and culture) of minorities, it would seem that what is 'sufficient' should be interpreted in a generous and flexible way, and that the number of pupils required in order to be able to claim the right to be taught in the minority language should be quite small if a state's resources make it reasonably practical to accommodate them.

This may eventually provide for the broad principles to be applied for determining what is a 'disproportionate' response to the circumstances and the conditions where states would need to ensure a minority has access to state education in their own language.

In the same vein, there are numerous political and other pronouncements which together create an impressive foundation acknowledging the validity of providing education in a minority language. Amongst the more prominent are of course the UN Declaration on the Rights of Persons Belonging to National or Ethnic, Religious and Linguistic Minorities, the draft UN Declaration on the Rights of Indigenous Peoples, the Organization for Security and Cooperation in Europe's Document of the Copenhagen Meeting of the Conference on the Human Dimension, the The Hague Recommendations regarding the Education Rights of National Minorities, as well as a very large number of resolutions from bodies such as the European Parliament.

Curiously, the European Court of Human Rights had an opportunity recently in *Cyprus v. Turkey* to clarify this right but failed to do so. As indicated earlier, the case does seem at one level to give rise to a right to be educated in a minority language, but hardly makes any reference to its previous jurisprudence and avoids explaining how it could reach its conclusions in light of its own previous cases.[127]

[127] This is particularly striking as at almost the same time, in the case of *Skender v. The Former Yugoslav Republic of Macedonia*, it was again reiterated that Art. 2 of Protocol 1 did not guarantee instruction in a minority language: '2. (...) The Court recalls that Art. 2 of Protocol No. 1 does not guarantee education in a particular language in accordance with the parents' preferences (see the judgment in the "Belgian Linguistic Case" of 23 July 1968, Series A No. 6, p. 32, § 3) (...) 3. (...) The Court points out that a right to education in a particular language or a right to obtain from the State the creation of a particular kind of educational establishment cannot be derived from Art. 2 of Protocol No. 1. This provision does not require of States that they should, in the sphere of education or teaching, respect parents' linguistic preferences, but only their religious and philosophical convictions. To interpret the terms "religious" and "philosophical" as covering linguistic preferences would amount to a distortion of their ordinary and usual meaning and to read into the Convention something which is not there. Moreover, the Court recalls that the "drafting history of that Article" confirms that the object of the second sentence of Art. 2 was in no way to secure respect by the State of a right for parents to have education conducted in a language other than that of the country in question; indeed in 1951 the Committee which drafted Protocol No. 1 to the Convention set aside a proposal put forward in this sense, several of its members having believed that it concerned an aspect of the problem of ethnic minorities and that it thus fell outside the scope of the Convention (see the above-cited judgment in the "Belgian Linguistic Case", p. 32, § 6).'

In *Cyprus v. Turkey*, the linguistic policies of northern Cyprus authorities in the area of public education were essentially described as so inadequate in view of the circumstances as to constitute a violation of Article 2 Protocol 1 which deals with the right to education. The Court noted that children of Greek-Cypriot parents in northern Cyprus wishing to pursue a secondary education through the medium of the Greek language were obliged to transfer to schools in the south, though children could continue their education at a Turkish or English-language school in the north.

On the basis of the court's previous reasoning in the *Belgian Linguistic Case*, many expected the Court to reject the parents' claims. It did not and instead concluded that there was a right to be educated in one's language for the following reasons:

277. The Court notes that children of Greek-Cypriot parents in northern Cyprus wishing to pursue a secondary education through the medium of the Greek language are obliged to transfer to schools in the south, this facility being unavailable in the 'TRNC' ever since the decision of the Turkish-Cypriot authorities to abolish it. Admittedly, it is open to children, on reaching the age of 12, to continue their education at a Turkish or English-language school in the north. In the strict sense, accordingly, there is no denial of the right to education, which is the primary obligation devolving on a Contracting Party under the first sentence of Article 2 of Protocol No. 1 (see the *Kjeldsen, Busk Madsen and Pedersen v. Denmark* judgment of 7 December 1976, Series A no. 23, pp. 25–26 § 52). Moreover, this provision does not specify the language in which education must be conducted in order that the right to education be respected (see... the *Belgian Linguistic* judgment, pp. 30-31).

278. However, in the Court's opinion, the option available to Greek-Cypriot parents to continue their children's education in the north is unrealistic in view of the fact that the children in question have already received their primary education in a Greek-Cypriot school there. The authorities must no doubt be aware that it is the wish of Greek-Cypriot parents that the schooling of their children be completed through the medium of the Greek language. Having assumed responsibility for the provision of Greek-language primary schooling, the failure of the 'TRNC' authorities to make continuing provision for it at the secondary-school level must be considered in effect to be a denial of the substance of the right at issue. It cannot be maintained that the provision of secondary education in the south in keeping with the linguistic tradition of the enclaved Greek Cypriots suffices to fulfil the obligation laid down in Article 2 of Protocol No. 1, having regard to the impact of that option on family life...

280. Having regard to the above considerations, the Court concludes that there has been a violation of Article 2 of Protocol No. 1 in respect of Greek Cypriots living in northern Cyprus in so far as no appropriate secondary-school facilities were available to them.

The logic used by the European Court is rather perplexing, to say the least. It admits on the one hand that Article 2 of Protocol No. 1 is devoid of a linguistic component, but then says there is a linguistic component for secondary education because authorities in Northern Cyprus provided Greek-language primary education, and therefore to stop offering it at the end of primary level schooling 'negated' the right to education.

Perhaps what the European Court is trying to say is that since the students had already received their primary education in Greek, they would be completely incapable of using the Turkish language with the degree of fluency required at secondary school level, this constituting in effect 'a denial of the substance of the right [to education]' since they would, to all intent and purposes, be unable to receive any real education because of their inability to understand Turkish. It would therefore constitute an obstacle to their access to education since the students would have been unable to understand the language used as the medium of instruction.

This case is significant and cannot be discounted because it represents a clear pronouncement that the *Belgian Linguistic Case* does not preclude future development and recognition of the possibility to have a right to education in one's own language in state schools.

Finally, in a very rare instance of a judge of the International Court of Justice commenting on language issues, Judge Tanaka in *South West Africa Cases (Second Phase)*, indicated that the existence of separate schools operating along linguistic lines was not objectionable at all, but rather would be required in some situations in order to truly conform with the requirements of equality:

> For instance, if we consider education...we cannot deny the value of vernacular as the medium of instruction and the result thereof would be separate schooling as between children of diverse population groups... In this case separate education and schooling may be recognised as reasonable. This is justified by the nature of the matter in question.[128]

As the judge intimates, to have separate schools teaching in the vernacular is not objectionable per se: on the contrary, it may indeed be a reasonable adaptation required by the principle of equality and non-discrimination.

(d) Official Recognition and Use of Minority Languages in Names, Surnames and Toponomy

As discussed previously, a state which prohibits the private use of a person's name or surname because of its linguistic form breaches the right to private

[128] *Supra*, n. 62.

and family life. Prima facie then, based on the consistent jurisprudence of both the UNHRC and the European Court of Human Rights, a person can freely express his or her identity through their surname—and name—under the notion of private life.[129]

However, a state may through its authorities refuse to recognize or use a person's name nor surname for official purposes as long as such a refusal is neither arbitrary nor unlawful, since treaties such as the International Covenant on Civil and Political Rights and the European Convention on Human Rights both only permit those restrictions to the right to private and family life that satisfy both requirements.

Thus, the right to private and family life does not automatically oblige state authorities to use or officially recognize an individual's name or surname in a minority language, as long as such refusal is neither an arbitrary nor unlawful interference. For the UNHRC, it suggested that a policy to change all of the surnames of foreigners, which presumably would possibly all be in foreign languages, would without any doubt 'constitute interference in contravention of article 17.'[130]

Most cases dealt with requests to change a person's name or surname and not directly with the issue of the language used in a person's name.[131] The one exception—almost—actually involved the European Court of Justice which considered the case of a surname which had to be transcribed—for official purposes—into a script different from the one used in the language of origin.

In *Christos Konstantinidis v. Stadt Altensteig Standesamt and Landratsamt Calw—Ordnungsamt*, a member of the Greek-speaking minority in Germany objected to the way authorities in that country transcribed his name into Roman characters in the registers of civil status. Ruling on the application of whether or not the transliteration of his name could be seen as discriminatory since it arguably placed 'him at a disadvantage in law or in fact, in comparison with the way in which a national of that Member State would be treated in the same circumstances' in the exercise of freedom of the right of establishment,[132] the European Court of Justice concluded:

> 17. It should therefore be stated in reply to the national court that Article 52 of the Treaty must be interpreted as meaning that it is contrary to that provision for a Greek national to be obliged, under the applicable national legislation, to use, in the pursuit

[129] *Coeriel and Aurik v. Netherlands*, para. 10.2, *Burghartz v. Switzerland,* para. 24 .

[130] *Coeriel and Aurik v. Netherlands*, para. 10.2.

[131] Such as in the case of *Sterna v. Finland.*

[132] Para.13.

of his occupation, a spelling of his name whereby its pronunciation is modified and the resulting distortion exposes him to the risk that potential clients may confuse him with other persons.

Overall, based on this limited jurisprudence, it would seem that as far as is possible state authorities should always use a person's chosen name or surname. There would seem to be few arguments to support a policy wording to which state authorities would simply refuse to recognize or use an individual's name or surname because it is in a minority (or foreign) language.[133] A number of treaties and other documents specifically make reference to this right.[134]

As for a 'right' to have state authorities use a minority language for naming geographical places, even street or road names, in a national minority language—while there are both legal and political international documents which recognize that it is 'reasonable' for states to accommodate in this way the language of where they are territorially concentrated in sufficient numbers,[135] and it may be possible that in those circumstances not to have bilingual signs is to unreasonably deny to individuals a benefit enjoyed by some (in the form of a state service in one's own language), there is no case law to that effect based on general international human rights treaties, although it should be noted that it is possible to construct an argument to that effect by using a general non-discrimination clause such as Article 26 CCPR or Protocol 12 of the European Convention on Human Rights.

There was one communication where the issue was raised, but there was no actual discussion of the substance of the claim since that communication was ruled inadmissible because the complainant had failed to present any argument as to how her rights had been denied under the International Covenant of Civil and Political Rights:

5.2 The Committee has considered the material placed before it by the parties. As to the claims under articles 19, paragraph 2, 25 (c) and 26 of the Covenant, it considers that the author has failed to substantiate, for purposes of admissibility, how she was denied her freedom of expression, how she was denied her right of access, under general terms of equality, to public service, and how she was discriminated against on the ground of language. The Committee observes that the defacing of road signs does not raise issues under article 19 and notes that the material before it shows that G. B. was

133 *Coeriel and Aurik v. Netherlands*, para. 10.2.

134 See for example Art. 11 of the Framework Convention for the Protection of National Minorities.

135 Including Art. 14 of the Central European Initiative Instrument for the Protection of Minority Rights, Art. 11 of the Framework Convention for the Protection of National Minorities, and Article 10(2) (g) of the European Charter for Regional or Minority Languages.

able to express herself freely throughout the proceedings, that she chose to express herself in French, a language she did not claim not to understand, and that such sanctions as were imposed on her by the postal administration of Rennes were suspended and did not affect her employment in public service.[136]

(e) Use of Minority Languages and Political and Public Participation

As with other activities by state authorities, elections of local or national representatives and the proceedings in a state's parliament can all be regulated in terms of the language to be used daily or even in order to accede to elected positions. While there is no 'right to use of a minority language' in general human rights treaties, the jurisprudence shows both at the level of the International Covenant on Civil and Political Rights and the European Convention on Human Rights that while mandating the use of any particular language, state authorities must always comply with basic human rights, and especially non-discrimination on the ground of language, in these matters, and that it is possible that in some situations this may require the use of another language in addition to the official language.

In *Mathieu-Mohin and Clerfayt*,[137] the European Court of Human Rights reviewed the principles embodied in Article 3 of the First Protocol of the Convention for the Protection of Human Rights and Fundamental Freedoms. The applicants had been elected respectively to the Belgian Senate and House of Representatives from the bilingual electoral district of Brussels, but also in an administrative district which came under the Dutch-language Council in respect to certain matters. They had to submit to a test of eligibility for the Council consisting of a parliamentary oath in Dutch. The applicants, being francophones, took their oath in French instead and were denied the right to sit on the Council, despite the fact that their administrative district came under the Dutch-language Council in respect of important matters for their voters. This, they claimed, either violated Article 3, First Protocol of the Convention, or violated Article 3 when read in conjunction with Article 14 of the Convention.

Article 3 of the First Protocol provides that states undertake to hold elections by secret ballot, under conditions which will ensure the free expression of the opinion of the people in the choice of legislature. There is linguistic component in this provision. The Court indicated that the French-speaking electors exercised their right to vote and the right to stand for election on the

136 *G.B. v. France*, Communication No. 348/1989.
137 (1987) European Convention on Human Rights, Series A, No. 113.

same legal footing as Dutch-speaking electors and were therefore not deprived of their Article 3 rights sufficiently in this case as to thwart the 'free expression of the opinion of the people in the choice of the legislature'.[138]

More precisely on the language issue and whether the requirement in the circumstances was discriminatory under Article 14 of the Convention taken together with Article 3 of the First Protocol, it concluded that in the circumstances the measure adopted by the state was neither unreasonable nor disproportionate:

> The aim is to defuse the language disputes in the country by establishing more stable and decentralised organisational structures... In any consideration of the electoral system in issue, its general context must not be forgotten. The system does not appear unreasonable if regard is had to the intentions it reflects and to the respondent state's margin of appreciation within the Belgian parliamentary system—a margin that is all the greater as the system is incomplete and provisional.[139]

The reasoning here follows a similar path to the Court's approach in the *Belgian Linguistics Case*, as well as for that matter the approach adopted by the HRC in *Diergaardt v. Namibia*: while the preference for the exclusive use of the official language in the circumstances was not unreasonable nor disproportionate (as in *Belgian Linguistics Case* and *Mathieu-Mohin and Clerfayt*) with the result that it is not discriminatory and therefore not necessary to use the minority language, if the preference for the exclusive use of a language is unreasonable or disproportionate (as in the case of *Diergaardt v. Namibia* where the state failed to present any evidence to this effect), then there must be a use of the minority language appropriate to the circumstances.

Thus, while the individuals in *Mathieu-Mohin and Clerfayt* were in fact allowed to run for office, win an election and—eventually—sit in their respective positions, the HRC found that a language requirement which automatically excluded an individual from even running for office was prima facie unreasonable and disproportionate in *Antonina Ignatane v. Latvia*. The complainant was prevented from being a candidate in municipal elections under the motive that she did not have a sufficiently high level of proficiency in that country's official language.

> 7.3 According to the State party participation in public affairs requires a high level of proficiency in the State language and a language requirement for standing as a candidate in elections is hence reasonable and objective. The Committee notes that article 25 secures to every citizen the right and the opportunity to be elected at genuine

[138] *Ibid*., at 25. [139] *Ibid*., at 25.

periodic elections without any of the distinctions mentioned in article 2, including language.

7.5 The Committee concludes that Mrs. Ignatane has suffered specific injury in being prevented from standing for the local elections in the city of Riga in 1997, because of having been struck off the list of candidates on the basis of insufficient proficiency in the official language. The Human Rights Committee considers that the author is a victim of a violation of article 25, in conjunction with article 2 of the Covenant.

While the result of this communication was also due to the somewhat arbitrary nature of the requirement for the candidate to have a 'very high' level of fluency to run for office, when Latvian law itself did not provide for separate levels of proficiency in the official language in order to stand for election, and the behaviour of the 'language review' in the circumstances seemed to be less than transparent and fair, the communication provides a rather clear indication that to prevent an individual from voting, running for office, holding office or any other function linked to political participation processes through an official language requirement can be discriminatory.

The European Court of Human Rights also had to deal with a case involving an applicant who was prevented from standing as a candidate in parliamentary elections because she did not demonstrate a sufficient command of the official language.

While the Court concluded in *Podkolzina v. Lettonie (Latvia)* that there was a violation of Article 3 of Protocol 1, it did so not on the basis that the Latvian language requirement was discriminatory. The Court had indicated that a requirement of fluency in the official language was prima facie a legitimate objective and that the means employed in pursuit of this aim must not be disproportionate, but it did not pursue this matter as to whether the requirement of a high level of fluency in Latvian in the circumstances was necessarily proportionate.[140] Instead, it focused on the behaviour of officials in determining the applicant's degree of fluency, and then excluding her from the list of candidates in a way which the Court deemed arbitrary and a breach of Article 3 of Protocol 1:

36. (…) The Court observes that the State Language Centre decided to subject the applicant to a new language examination even though she had a valid, lawful certificate. It notes, however, that of the twenty-one candidates who had to provide certificates attesting to knowledge of the State language only nine, including the applicant, were required to sit a second examination. The Court has grave doubts about the legal basis

[140] Para. 33.

for that distinction, and the Government has not supplied any explanation on the point. In any event, and even supposing that the legal basis for the additional verification was section 13(3) of the Parliamentary Elections Act, the Court notes that the procedure followed differed fundamentally from the normal procedure for certification of linguistic competence, which is governed by the above-mentioned regulation of 25 May 1992. In particular, the additional verification which the applicant was subjected to was carried out by one examiner instead of a board of experts and the examiner was not required to observe the procedural safeguards and assessment criteria laid down in the regulation. Thus the full responsibility for assessing the applicant's linguistic knowledge was left to a single civil servant, who had exorbitant power in the matter. Moreover, the Court can only express its surprise over the fact—related by the applicant and not disputed by the Government—that during the examination the applicant was questioned mainly about the reasons for her political orientation, a subject which quite clearly had nothing to do with the requirement that she should have a good knowledge of Latvian.

It is also interesting to reconsider with hindsight the mistake made in some earlier cases where, instead of arguing that being excluded from the political process was discriminatory, an attempt was made to argue that not to use a minority language breached freedom of expression. As mentioned earlier, the applicants in *Fryske Nasjonale Partij v. Netherlands*[141] had been prevented from standing as candidates in elections of the *Eerste Kamer der Staten-Generaal*[142] because they had submitted their registration for election in Frisian and not in Dutch. Their argument that this infringed Article 3 of Protocol 1 which guarantees the right to vote and to stand as a candidate in legislative elections failed for the following reasons:

The Commission notes that the applicants were not as such prevented from standing as candidates, but that problems arose concerning the language in which their registration for election should take place. However, the Commission finds that nothing prevented the applicants from submitting a translation into Dutch of their request for registration of the name of the party and the list of candidates respectively. Moreover, neither Article 3 of Protocol No. 1 to the Convention, nor any other provision of the Convention guarantees the right to use a particular language for electoral purposes. Consequently, the Commission is of opinion that the applicants may not claim that their right to stand as a candidate for election was limited by the requirement that registration could only take place in Dutch.

It would have been preferable to argue that the refusal to register the applicants was "unreasonable and disproportionate" given the status and history

[141] (1986) Decisions and Reports, 45, 240 (European Commission of Human Rights), at 243.

[142] The 'First Chamber of the States General' essentially functions as a senate.

and usage of the Frisian language in the Netherlands, and relatively simple to accommodate, and therefore discriminatory and a breach of Article 3, First Protocol of the Convention, in conjunction with Article 14 of the Convention (or of Article 25 of the CCPR in conjunction with Article 2 of the same treaty; or even of Protocol 12 of the European Convention which now contains a general prohibition of discrimination).

While the outcome cannot be second guessed, international and European standards involving the use of a minority language would seem to suggest that it would be not only reasonable, but highly desirable to ensure that political institutions be flexible in taking measures to permit the use of a minority language in order to ensure their effective participation in public affairs. [143]

(f) Citizenship Naturalization Requirements and Minority Languages

This is what I order you to do, my son: Take care of your foreigners, esteem and support them. They should favour your country to others. Keep in mind, everybody has been born as a free human being.

Stephen the Great, King of Hungary (11th Century)[144]

Though the granting of citizenship is clearly and primarily a prerogative of the state, once it has initiated a naturalization process in the granting of citizenship, a government must respect fundamental human rights in the process. This most obviously suggests that the right of non-discrimination in particular may limit a state's conduct in the determination of who is entitled to become a citizen. This conclusion is indeed clearly stated in a general comment on the application of the prohibition of discrimination to non-citizens:

13. [States are to] ensure that particular groups of non-citizens are not discriminated against with regard to access to citizenship or naturalization, and to pay due attention to possible barriers to naturalization that may exist for long-term or permanent residents;[145]

The European Court of Human Rights has also concluded that the acquisition of citizenship is not insulated from the purview of international law, noting that it may be subjected to human rights standards such as the prohibition of discrimination. This meant that naturalisation criteria may be set aside

[143] See Art. 10(2)(e) & (f) of the European Charter for Regional or Minority Languages, and para. 35 of the Copenhagen Meeting of the Conference on the Human Dimension.

[144] From King Stephen's advice to his son in *Scriptores rerum Hungaricum Tempore ducum regumque stripis Arpadianae gestarum*, Emericus Szentpétery, Budapest, 1938.

[145] General Recommendation No. 30: Discrimination Against Non Citizens: 01/10/2004. Committee on the Elimination of Racial Discrimination.

under Article 14 of the Convention for the Protection of Human Rights and Fundamental Freedoms if a difference of treatment:

'. . . has no objective and reasonable justification', that is, if it does not pursue a 'legitimate aim' or if there is not a reasonable 'relationship of proportionality between the means employed and the aim sought to be realised'.[146]

It is in the same way possible for a state to exclude or make it more difficult for individuals from a minority to be naturalized by using an official or prescribed language requirement. Members of a minority who are less or not fluent in the official language may not be able to surmount the disadvantage imposed by the naturalization regulations in order to become citizens.

It is therefore possible to have linguistic naturalization requirements that are 'unreasonable', and therefore discriminatory. This can be significant for minorities, since it may suggest that citizenship should perhaps be made available to individuals who are not fluent in the official language, but where it may be justified to permit naturalization where someone is fluent in a particular minority language for a number of reasons.

As seen earlier, the Inter-American Court of Human Rights' Advisory Opinion of 19 January 1984 (*Costa Rican Naturalisation* case)[147] examined amendments which required that an applicant have the ability to speak, write and read Spanish in order to acquire citizenship. While admitting that states have a wide margin of appreciation in determining the naturalization policy appropriate for their specific cultural, social and political context,[148] it indicated that the imposition of a language requirement was a difference of treatment of individuals that could in some circumstances be considered discriminatory. The majority of judges did not feel that the Spanish language requirements in the proposed amendment were too unreasonable, in the

[146] Case of *Abdulaziz, Cabales and Balkandali v. United Kingdom*, Application no. 9214/80; 9473/81; 9474/81, 28 May 1985, para. 72.

[147] Case No. OC-4/84.

[148] *Ibid.* at para. 36: 'Since it is the state that offers the possibility of acquiring its nationality to persons who were originally aliens, it is natural that the conditions and procedures for its acquisition should be governed primarily by the domestic law of the state. As long as such rules do not conflict with superior norms, it is the state conferring nationality which is best able to judge what conditions to impose to ensure that an effective link exists between the applicant for naturalisation and the systems of values and interests of the society with which he seeks to fully associate himself. That state is also able to decide whether these conditions have been complied with. Within these same limits, it is equally logical that the perceived needs of each state should determine the decision whether to facilitate naturalisation to a greater or less degree; and since a state's perceived needs do not remain static, it is quite natural that the conditions for naturalisation might be liberalised or restricted with the changed circumstances.'

context of that country, and concluded that they fell within the state's margin of appreciation:

Consistent with its clearly restrictive approach, the proposed amendment also provides for new conditions which must be complied with by those applying for naturalisation. Draft Article 15 requires, among other things, proof of the ability to 'speak, write and read' the Spanish language; it also prescribes a 'comprehensive examination on the history of the country and its values'. These conditions can be deemed, prima facie, to fall within the margin of appreciation reserved to the state as far as concerns the enactment and assessment of the requirements designed to ensure the existence of real and effective links upon which to base the acquisition of the new nationality. So viewed, it cannot be said to be unreasonable and unjustified to require proof of the ability to communicate in the language of the country or, although this is less clear, to require the applicant to 'speak, write and read' the language.[149]

One judge provided a more detailed view on this issue, pointing out that there were many in Costa Rica, even 'substantial communities', including indigenous peoples, who were not fluent in Spanish, and in particular could not write it. He suggested in his comments that a reasonable and non-discriminatory naturalization policy must reflect the 'specific conditions' of society in Costa Rica, including its population and linguistic make-up: it cannot simply operate in a vacuum in complete disregard of the languages in actual use in the country.[150]

From the above, it would seem that the jurisprudence which is now emerging is beginning to cast aside the mistaken view that naturalization laws could completely disregard any limitations imposed by international human rights standards, especially in the area of language. The opinion of the Inter-American Court is just such a case and very narrow in the insights it provides as to the relationship between the right of non-discrimination and language requirements for the purposes of naturalization. However, other international treaty bodies have issued comments which tend to buttress the position that unreasonable or unjustified linguistic conditions which constitute a difficult obstacle for the acquisition of citizenship would be a breach of international law:

9. The Committee notes the information provided in the sixteenth report on the complex provisions of the Icelandic Naturalization Act and other relevant legislation. It welcomes the 1998 amendment to address the unequal rights of men and women with regard to the naturalization of their children, and the elimination of the requirement to adopt an Icelandic patronym as a condition for naturalization.[151]

[149] *Ibid.* at para. 63. [150] Para. 23.

[151] Concluding Observations of the Committee on the Elimination of Racial Discrimination: Iceland. 27 April 2001. CERD/C/304/Add.111.

Similarly, the UN Human Rights Committee and the UN Committee on the Elimination of Racial Discrimination have on a number of occasions referred to the 'stringency of language criterion' and other similar criteria as issues of concern where it resulted in the inability of a large number of members of a minority of obtaining citizenship.[152]

IV. Conclusion

Does not the sun shine equally for the whole world? Do we not all equally breathe the air? Do you not feel shame at authorizing only three languages and condemning other people to blindness and deafness? Tell me, do you think that God is helpless and cannot bestow equality, or that he is envious and will not give it?

Saint Constantine (Cyril)[153]

A number of preconceptions as to the nature and extent of 'language rights' in international law seem to have been discreetly cast aside in the last two decades. The jurisprudence which has emerged from bodies such as the UN Human Rights Committee and the European Court of Human Rights has begun to dispel the view that anything regarding language or minority rights belongs either to a new generation of cultural or minority specific rights, or is limited to rather weak provisions such as Article 27 of the International Covenant on Civil and Political Rights, or to regional treaties that are minority or language specific such as the European Charter for Regional or Minority Languages and the Framework Convention on the Protection of National Minorities.

The latter instruments are becoming increasingly important in light of the conclusions which emanate from their interpretation which serve to clarify concrete and detailed areas of significance to address areas of language concerns for minorities—just as there are treaties that deal with areas of concern for the rights of women, children, migrants and other vulnerable segments of society.

Nevertheless, it is at the same time rather surprising to discover the extent to which some fundamental individual human rights can be used for the protection of language rights when one focuses directly on the case law and

[152] Concluding Observations of the Human Rights Committee : Estonia. 9 November 1995. CCPR/C/79/Add.59 and Concluding Observations of the Committee on the Elimination of Racial Discrimination: Latvia. 12 April 2001. CERD/C/304/Add.79, among others.

[153] Quoted in *Readings in the Sociology of Language*, Joshua A. Fishman (ed.), (Mouton and Co. N.V., The Hague, 1968), at 589.

views of treaty-based bodies. Almost unnoticed have gone the views of the Human Rights Committee which, by linking language as one of the facets of freedom of expression protected in international law, have acknowledged that any private use of a language, for minorities and others, is automatically protected from being prohibited. This conclusion, even though premised on an individual right long established in human rights law, is also a recognized 'language right' specific to minorities as enshrined in treaties such as the Framework Convention on the Protection of National Minorities. The same new appreciation for the effects of individual rights and freedoms in language matters could be said to be emerging in light of recent jurisprudence affecting the issues of names and surnames (relevant for the application of the right to private and family life) and state-provided services and other state activities, including political participation and citizenship (involving the prohibition of discrimination). Even the right to education which it had almost universally been assumed to be 'linguistically neutral' will need to be re-examined since the European Court of Human Rights seems to have seriously changed its previous position in the *Belgian Linguistics Case* and now recognizes a possibility for minorities to have a right to education in their own language—in still rather undefined circumstances.

The advent of two regional treaties with the Council of Europe—one which focuses on minority rights where language figures in many provisions (the Framework Convention on the Protection of National Minorities) and the other which creates no rights per se but instead imposes state obligations to protect and promote certain European languages (the Charter for Regional or Minority Languages)—is beginning to provide richer and deeper sources from which it is increasingly possible to draw in order to provide more clearly outlines of the rights of minorities that are taking shape in matters of language and identity. Despite the relative recentness of these two treaties and the differences in their objectives, emphasis and provisions, the conclusions of the advisory committees of experts under both treaties are, broadly speaking, showing a high degree of resonance where they have provisions dealing with a similar subject-matter.

EDUCATION

Patrick Thornberry

I. General Introduction

State policies towards minorities have ranged from attempts to eliminate groups by physical means or forced assimilation, through neglect—benign or otherwise—discrimination, and forcible segregation,[1] to positive attempts at integration, protection, and promotion and even celebration of minority identity.[2] Following a post-1945 period of relative neglect of minority issues

[1] The best-known examples of which concern the system of *Apartheid* in South Africa and the segregation of African-Americans in southern states of the USA. For contemporary European examples, consult: OSCE High Commissioner on National Minorities, Report on the Situation of Roma and Sinti in the OSCE Area (The Hague, 2000) (hereinafter 'OSCE Roma Report').

[2] Patrick Thornberry, *International Law and the Rights of Minorities* (Oxford, 1991), ch. 1. Compare the statement made in the Commentary to the UN Declaration on the Rights of Persons belonging to Minorities: 'The relationship between the State and its minorities has in the past taken five different forms: elimination, assimilation, toleration, protection and promotion', Commentary of the Working Group on Minorities to the United Nations Declaration on the Rights of Persons

in terms of recognition and endorsement of group presence, international law now robustly insists that minorities have rights to exist and maintain their identity. They also have the right to be free from discrimination, and are deemed to enjoy general human rights including those with a cultural aspect, and those specifically directed to them. The contemporary formulation of rights is individualist though there are collective rights such as self-determination, and collective exercise of individual rights is generally recognized—the overall collective imprint being heavier in instruments on indigenous peoples.[3] International law recognizes various categories of right-holder, of which members of minorities are only one, producing an interconnected family of instruments and principles. Processes of text reading are complex in that particular minority rights are only imperfectly understood without a wider frame of reference to other texts in the human rights 'family'.[4] Even in the limited framework of the League of Nations, the treaties and declarations integrated rights of inhabitants and nationals with those of nationals belonging to 'racial, religious or linguistic minorities'.[5] Those who ignore such complexity can fall into 'the Brownlie trap', laid for those 'super-specialists' with 'super tunnel vision', when: 'it does not seem to occur to them that their subject of special interest belongs to a much wider world of normative development'.[6] It may also be noted that the more specific norms can also lend content to the general

Belonging to National or Ethnic, Religious and Linguistic Minorities, E/CN.4/Sub.2/AC.5/2005/2, 4 April 2005 (hereinafter 'Commentary on the UN Declaration on Minorities'), para. 21.

[3] See, for example, the 1989 ILO Convention concerning Indigenous and Tribal Peoples in Independent Countries (ILO No. 169), *ILO Official Bull.*, 72, 59, entered into force 5 September 1991. For lengthy reflection on collective rights and related issues, see Patrick Thornberry, *Indigenous Peoples and Human Rights* (Manchester, 2002). See also Miodrag Jovanovic, 'Recognizing Minority Identities through Collective Rights', *Human Rights Quarterly*, 27 (2005), 625–51; Peter Jones, 'Human Rights, Group Rights, and Peoples' Rights', *Human Rights Quarterly*, 21 (1999), 80–107.

[4] The Commentary on the UN Declaration on Minorities, *supra*, n. 2, makes a similar point: 'The Declaration builds on and adds to the rights contained in the International Bill of Rights and other human rights instruments by strengthening and clarifying those rights which make it possible for persons belonging to minorities to preserve and develop their group identity. The human rights set out in the Universal Declaration of Human Rights must at all times be respected in the process, including the principle of non-discrimination… The State is obliged to respect and to ensure to every person within its territory and subject to its jurisdiction, without discrimination on any ground, including race, ethnicity, religion or national origin, the rights contained in the instruments to which that State is a party'—para. 4.

[5] Thornberry, *International Law*, *supra*, n. 2, Ch. 3.

[6] Ian Brownlie, 'Indigenous Peoples: A Relevant Concept?' in F. M. Brookfield (ed.), *Treaties and Indigenous Peoples* (Oxford, 1992), 55–75 at 63.

instruments, especially where the latter make little more than passing reference to the right in question.[7]

In the present chapter, emphasis is placed on the development of norms through jurisprudence. However, it may be noted that, with some treaty bodies,[8] the contribution of case-based jurisprudence is limited, so recourse will be had to snapshots of the concluding observations of such bodies. Secondly, despite demands made on monitoring bodies to achieve an integrated approach to human rights, in practice a treaty body will commence norm interpretation from within the four corners of 'its own' treaty, so that convergence of norms may represent an ideal rather than describe reality. The complexity of the legal canon has led to initiatives endeavouring to synthesize minority law and practice such as the Hague, Oslo, and Lund Recommendations on minority education, language, and effective participation in public life, respectively.[9] It is also necessary to allow the possibility that some instruments respect the education rights of minorities better than others, and that aspects of the rights remain unelaborated, so that any 'synthesis' in the present chapter will be of limited scope. Finally, while it may seem to state the obvious, the chapter is intended to underscore education as *a human right*.[10] UN Special rapporteurs on education are among those[11] who have expressed concern that the

[7] CERD for example makes only brief reference to education in Art. 5 and 7. These limited provisions have nonetheless spawned a considerable array of recommendations on bilingual education and many other aspects of minority-relevant education and to education for indigenous peoples bearing in mind also that the Convention makes no mention of either 'minority' or 'indigenous people'. General recommendations on the Roma—General Recommendation XXVII, A/55/18, Annex V C (2000) and indigenous peoples—General Recommendation XXIII, UN Doc. /52/18, Annex II V (1997), draw heavily on specific texts of minority and indigenous rights. See Patrick Thornberry, 'Confronting Racial Discrimination: A CERD Perspective', *Human Rights Law Review*, 5 (2005), 239–69.

[8] The term is used here in the generic sense of human rights bodies set up by treaty and thus includes courts as well as 'committees' and 'commissions', etc.

[9] The Hague Recommendations regarding the Education Rights of National Minorities (The Hague: Foundation on Inter-Ethnic Relations, 1996) (hereinafter 'the Hague Recommendations'); The Oslo Recommendations regarding the Linguistic Rights of National Minorities (The Hague: Foundation on Inter-Ethnic Relations, 1998) (hereinafter 'the Oslo Recommendations'); The Lund Recommendations on the Effective Participation of National Minorities in Public Life (The Hague: Foundation on Inter-Ethnic Relations, 1999) (hereinafter 'the Lund Recommendations'). The Recommendations were prepared by groups of internationally recognized independent experts under the auspices of the Foundation on Inter-Ethnic Relations, at the request of the OSCE High Commissioner on National Minorities. While their status is essentially that of expert group reflection on human rights principles, they attempt to subsume, elaborate, and re-present relevant principles of international law from a range of sources.

[10] Present author's emphasis.

[11] See Klaus Dieter Beiter, *The Protection of the Right to Education by International Law* (Leiden and Boston, 2005).

concept of education as a human right has been under challenge from some governments and institutions inclined to regard it as no more than a service or economic good subject to the 'laws' of supply and demand.[12] From one perspective, education is even more than that, and is, as the UN Committee on Economic, Social and Cultural Rights puts it, 'both a human right in itself and an indispensable means of realizing other human rights'.[13] In similar vein, commentary has distinguished between 'primordial' and 'instrumental' aspects of the right.[14]

II. Content of the Right

A. Historical and Theoretical Background

From the time of the League of Nations, the education component of the treaties and declarations was prominent in sundry stipulations on schools, institutions, and minority language education; the education rights provisions were the subject of controversy and contestation.[15] Contemporary—UN-era—instruments on minority rights almost inevitably include an education component, as do those on indigenous peoples. The formative role of the education system in the maintenance of identity is widely understood, as well as its role as an agency of socialization for democratic citizenship. Education can also be a formidable engine of assimilation, and draconian strategies of

[12] 'Following up on the work initiated by his predecessor, the Special Rapporteur intends to continue strengthening the human rights dimension of education by encouraging the shift from education policies that address education as an economic good to the right to education, which States have an obligation to implement and which is justiciable': Comments of the UN Special Rapporteur on the right to education, Mr. Vernor Muñoz Villalobos, in Report on The Right to Education, E/CN.4/2005/50, 17 December 2004, 2.

[13] Committee on Economic, Social and Cultural Rights General Comment No. 13, The Right to Education, E/C.12/1999/10, para. 1.

[14] With reference to the aims of education, the Commentary on Education by the Advisory Committee on the Framework Convention for the Protection of National Minorities, ACFC/25DOC(2006)002 (hereinafter 'Advisory Committee Commentary on Education') remarks that 'some...aims, such as the development of the linguistic capabilities of a child, are understood as primarily instrumental. In these cases, education is seen as a tool for the achievement of other goals...Other aims of education are perceived as primordial in that they are....important per se...This is the case with the development of respect for the child's identity'. *ibid.*, section 1.3. The Commentary goes on to state (*ibid.*) that 'the distinction between instrumental and primordial aims is to some extent artificial. Respect for a child's linguistic identity is, for instance, a precondition for additive bilingualism and plurilingualism, i.e. one which develops and strengthens the cognitive and emotional capabilities of the child, and the different languages reinforce each other and the linguistic identity is then both instrumental and a goal in itself.'

[15] Thornberry, *International Law, supra*, n. 2, Ch. 3.

forcible assimilation have been visited upon the Roma[16] and other groups.[17] Such policies are outlawed by contemporary standards of human rights which prefer the principle that education should contribute to the integration of minorities into general society, whilst ruling out policies of assimilation against the will of those who belong to minorities. Assimilation essentially involves the disappearance of a culture through absorption in another—usually larger and more dominant—group. Assimilation per se is not forbidden by international norms which, on the contrary, allow individuals a choice of whether they wish or do not wish to embrace minority rights.[18] On the other hand, if assimilation is not to be against the will of individuals, conditions in the state, including the institutions of education, should be adequate to facilitate the maintenance of minority distinctiveness.[19] Contemporary commentary focuses increasingly on the active or proactive state in the field of minority rights.[20]

Key terms in debates on educating mixed populations are: 'multiculturalism' and 'interculturalism'. 'Multiculturalism' refers to the coexistence of cultures in the same society and is often understood as a programme or policy to recognize cultural differences, expressed in the education system and elsewhere. 'Interculturalism' is used in, for example, the Council of Europe's European Charter for Regional or Minority Languages (hereinafter 'the

[16] Claude Cahn et al., 'Roma in the Educational Systems of Central and Eastern Europe', *Roma Rights*, Summer 1998.

[17] John Milloy, *A National Crime: The Canadian Government and the Residential School System, 1879–1986* (Winnipeg, 1999).

[18] See Article 3(1) of the Framework Convention, which protects the right of persons belonging to a minority to choose to be treated, or not to be treated, as such. The choice is expressed as one belonging to those already 'belonging' to minorities. Paragraph 32 of the 1990 Conference on Security and Cooperation in Europe (CSCE, now OSCE) Document of the Copenhagen Meeting of the Conference on the Human Dimension (hereinafter, 'the Copenhagen Document'), bites deeper in that it visualizes choice as governing the initial question of belonging to a group.

[19] 'The Declaration is based on the consideration that forced assimilation is unacceptable. While a degree of integration is required in every national society in order to make it possible for the State to respect and ensure human rights to every person within its territory without discrimination, the protection of minorities is intended to ensure that integration does not become unwanted assimilation or undermine the group identity of persons living on the territory of the State': Commentary on the UN Declaration on Minorities, *supra*, n. 2, para. 21. See also the case of Estonia, where the Advisory Committee under the Framework Convention, commented, in relation to reforms involving reduction of instruction in Russian, that 'the implementation of the reform must be carried out in a manner that contributes to the integration of persons belonging to national minorities but not their assimilation': ACFC/INF/OP/1 (2002) 005, para. 50.

[20] 'The Framework Convention presupposes that States actively pursue the goals embodied in the Convention. A passive attitude may amount to a violation of the obligations provided for under the Convention': Advisory Committee Commentary on Education, *supra*, n. 14, section 1.4.

European Language Charter')[21] and denotes reciprocity of respect between cultures. The terms were explained with minorities specifically in mind in a UN-sponsored seminar: 'multicultural education involves educational policies which meet the separate educational needs of groups in society which belong to different cultural traditions . . . Intercultural education involves educational policies and practices by which the members of the different cultures . . . learn to interact constructively with each other'.[22] Whatever the nuance, international standards tend to insist on the relevance of both notions to minority education.

'Multiculturalism' has become a loaded term in recent discourse in a number of countries, including European countries, fuelled in part by perceptions of increased immigration.[23] Debates in the United Kingdom have been given added impetus by speeches critical of the concept or its uses by the head of the Commission for Racial Equality.[24] A 2005 debate on multiculturalism within the UN Committee on the Elimination of Racial Discrimination (hereinafter CERD/C) disclosed considerable variation of views. One member of the Committee recalled the duty of CERD/C in the matter of non-discrimination and argued that some CERD/C recommendations have not served the cause of non-discrimination but may have served, on the contrary, to exacerbate societal differences. The member also suggested that ambitious models of minority rights 'made in Europe' may not be suitable for Africa and the Americas including, for example, practice in the field of multilingual education.[25] One

[21] ETS No. 148, 1992, entered into force 1 March 1998. See the preamble which stresses the value of interculturalism and multilingualism. The Explanatory Report on the Charter on Regional or Minority Languages (Strasbourg: Council of Europe, 1993) (hereinafter 'Explanatory Report on the European Language Charter') does not define the term 'interculturalism' but provides some illumination in its observation in para. 14 that the approach 'corresponds fully to the values traditionally upheld by the Council of Europe and its efforts to promote closer relations between peoples, increased European cooperation and a better understanding between different population groups within the State on an intercultural basis'. Elsewhere (para. 29) the Report notes that the Charter 'by no means seeks to foster any kind of partitioning off of linguistic groups . . . none of the Charter's provisions should be interpreted as . . . raising obstacles to the knowledge of official languages'.

[22] Report of the Seminar on Multicultural and Intercultural Education, E/CN.4/Sub.2/AC.5/1997/WP.5, 23 May 1997; the Commentary on the UN Declaration on Minorities, *supra*, n. 2, para. 66, uses the same language.

[23] See, *inter alia*, Dominic McGoldrick, 'Multiculturalism and its Discontents', in Nazila Ghanea-Hercock and Alexandra Xanthaki (eds.), *Minorities, Peoples and Self-Determination: Essays in Honour of Patrick Thornberry* (Leiden/Boston, 2005), 211–35.

[24] See the span of authors in 'What now for Multiculturalism?' *Connections*, Winter 2004/5 (London, house journal of the Commission for Racial Equality).

[25] 'by applying the European model to Africa or Latin America, the Committee only served to foster fragmentation in countries which had been struggling to create unity'—Lindgren Alves, SR.1724 at para. 3.

member challenged the notion that nation building was hindered by policies respecting cultural diversity, and distinguished, as did other members, the policy of the Convention (hereinafter CERD)[26] from programmes of assimilation.[27] There was broad support for the treatment of minority issues, including language, on a case-by-case basis, with necessary flexibility.[28] Criticism of 'the European model' of minority rights was partly based on a perception that European standards envisaged the teaching of all minority languages in the state to the same extent regardless of circumstances—something of a straw man in view of the many qualifying clauses in European instruments which incorporate the relevant rights.[29] Emerging from the debates is a mixed understanding of multiculturalism, ranging from a necessary expression of the reality of cultural diversity to a recipe for segregation and social fragmentation. The polemics surrounding multiculturalism have implications for the scope and purpose of education systems.

B. Delineation of the Content

1. Right to Education

The right to education was one of the first fruits of the modern human rights movement. Article 26 of the Universal Declaration of Human Rights (hereinafter 'UDHR') provides that everyone has the right to education, which shall be free, 'at least in the elementary and fundamental stages', and that elementary education shall be compulsory. Furthermore, 'education shall be directed to the full development of the human personality and to the strengthening of respect for human rights and fundamental freedoms. It shall promote understanding, tolerance and friendship among all nations, racial or religious groups, and shall further the activities of the United Nations for the maintenance of peace.' The article provides that parents 'have a prior right to choose the kind of education that shall be given to their children'. No linguistic medium of education is specified, but there is a content and purpose for education in the encouragement of mutual understanding, tolerance, and friendship between nations, religions, and races.[30] Converting the premises of the Declaration

[26] The International Convention on the Elimination of All Forms of Racial Discrimination, concluded on 7 March 1966, entered into force on 4 January 1969, 660 UNTS 195.

[27] Pillai, SR. 1724, paras. 17–19; Valencia Rodriguez, SR. 1694 at paras. 25–26.

[28] For example Sicilianos, SR.1724, para. 12.

[29] For the approach of CERD/C in general, see *The Practice of the Committee on the Elimination of Racial Discrimination with respect to Multiculturalism*, CERD/C/67/Misc. 5, 3 August 2005.

[30] For observations on the drafting of the article, see Johannes Morsink, *The Universal Declaration of Human Rights: Origins, Drafting and Intent* (Philadelphia, 1999), 212–17.

into a binding treaty, Article 13 of the International Covenant on Economic, Social and Cultural Rights (hereinafter CESCR) reiterates Article 26 of the UDHR on the purposes of education, adding that 'education shall enable all persons to participate effectively in a free society'.[31] The commitment of the international community to raising the general level of education in society is evidenced by the references in Article 13 to the provision of free and compulsory primary education for all,[32] to making secondary and higher education equally accessible to all, and the progressive introduction of free secondary education and higher education.[33] Article 13.3. refers to the liberty of parents, etc., to choose schools other than those established by the public authorities, to ensure 'the religious and moral education of their children in conformity with their own convictions'.

At the regional level, the African Charter on Human and Peoples' Rights[34] includes the briefly stated principle that 'Every individual shall have the right to education'.[35] The Inter-American Declaration of the Rights and Duties of Man sets out a principle of non-discrimination and also addresses education rights;[36] in the case of the American Convention on Human Rights, the question of education rights is addressed in a separate protocol (the Protocol of San Salvador).[37] The European Convention on Human Rights and Fundamental Freedoms (hereinafter, ECHR) refers to the right to education in Article 2 of Protocol 1: 'No person shall be denied the right to education. In the exercise of any functions which it assumes in relation to education and to teaching, the

[31] Article 13(1).

[32] A softer commitment is included in the Protocol of San Salvador, requiring that 'Primary education *should* be compulsory and accessible to all without cost' (present author's emphasis).

[33] Article 13(2). Compare Art. 13(3) (b) and (c) of the Protocol of San Salvador.

[34] African Charter on Human and Peoples' Rights (hereinafter African Charter, or AfrCh), concluded on 26 June 1981, entered into force on 21 October 1986, O.A.U. Doc. CAB/LEG/67/3 Rev.5.

[35] *Ibid.*, Art. 17(1).

[36] American Declaration of the Rights and Duties of Man (hereinafter Am Decl or American Declaration), adopted in 1948, O.A.S. Res. XXX, O.A.S. Off. Rec. OEA/Ser.L/V/I.4 Rec. (1965), Art. II (non-discrimination), and Art. XII (education) which commences with 'Every person has the right to an education, which should be based on the principles of liberty, morality and human solidarity.'

[37] Additional Protocol to the American Convention on Human Rights in the Area of Economic, Social and Cultural Rights, adopted on 14 November 1988, entered into force on 16 November 1999, OAS Treaty Series 69, Article 13 (hereinafter, Protocol of San Salvador). The Protocol does not make specific reference to particular groups such as the indigenous peoples—so important in the American context—but provides that education 'ought to enable everyone to participate effectively in a democratic and pluralistic society and achieve a decent existence and should foster understanding, tolerance and friendship among all nations and all racial, ethnic or religious groups and promote activities for the maintenance of peace.'

State shall respect the right of parents to ensure such education and teaching in conformity with their own religious and philosophical convictions.'[38]

Provisions on education also appear in general instruments on religious rights, which include religious minorities. In their elaboration of the principles of Article 18 of the CCPR (on freedom of thought, conscience, or religion), the Human Rights Committee noted that public school instruction in religion and ethics should be given in a neutral and objective manner, and that it was imperative to make provision for non-discriminatory exemptions from or alternatives to such instruction.[39] The UN Declaration on the Elimination of All Forms of Intolerance and of Discrimination Based on Religion or Belief[40] refers to the right of parents or guardians to organize family life for the moral education of the child (Art. 5(1)); and safeguards access to religious education and freedom from compulsion in religion, guided by the principle of the best interests of the child (Art. 5(2)). Article 6 of the Declaration elaborates on the content of freedom of religion, including in this freedom scope to establish institutions, to write, issue, and disseminate publications, and to teach a religion or belief—all of which impact on the education process.[41]

2. *Discrimination*

All international standards on education are buttressed by the principle of non-discrimination. According to Article 2 of the UDHR,[42] the right to education and other rights and freedoms 'set forth in this Declaration' must be accorded 'without distinction of any kind, such as race, colour, sex, language, religion, political or other opinion, national or social origin, property, birth or other status'. Similar non-discrimination formulae are found elsewhere. Article 26 of the CCPR combines equality with non-discrimination in a broad prescription.[43] According to the Human Rights Committee, the article 'prohibits discrimination in law or in

[38] 4 November 1950, ETS No. 5.

[39] UN Human Rights Committee, General Comment No. 22 on Article 18 (forty-eighth session, 1993), UN Doc. CCPR/C/21/Rev.1/Add.4, 27 September 1993, para. 6. Cf. Article 9 of the ECHR.

[40] Declaration on the Elimination of All Forms of Intolerance and of Discrimination Based on Religion or Belief, UN Doc. A/36/684 (1981).

[41] The Vienna Concluding Document of the OSCE (1989) makes specific reference (para. 16.6.) to respecting 'the right of everyone to give and receive religious education in the language of his choice, whether individually or in association with others.'

[42] Adopted by the UNGA on 10 December 1948.

[43] 'All persons are equal before the law and are entitled without any discrimination to the equal protection of the law. In this respect, the law shall prohibit any discrimination and guarantee to all persons equal and effective protection against discrimination.' The Covenant also includes a general, narrower reference to non-discrimination in Art. 2(1) as well as references specific to certain rights.

fact in any field regulated and protected by public authorities'.[44] The Committee adds that when any 'legislation is adopted by a State party, it must comply with the requirement of Article 26 that its content must not be discriminatory'[45]—including legislation in the sphere of education.

Dealing with discrimination on specific grounds, CERD includes in Article 5(e)(v) the right to education and training among the rights to be protected against discrimination; and Article 7 of the Convention calls in essence for anti-racist education.[46] The Convention's principles on non-discrimination include provision in Articles 1(4) and 2(2) for special measures. The International Convention on the Elimination of All Forms of Discrimination against Women (hereinafter CEDAW) also provides for special measures,[47] and includes education among the specific fields where discrimination is prohibited,[48] with a list of areas where principles of equality are to operate, including curricula, access to educational programmes, resources, and educational information. The CEDAW, in Article 10(c), also calls for the elimination of stereotyping through encouraging co-education and revision of textbooks and teaching methods. In the 1960 UNESCO Convention against Discrimination in Education,[49] discrimination is described as including: depriving any person or group of persons of access to education or limiting them to education of an inferior standard. On the other hand, 'when permitted in a State', separate systems set up 'for religious or linguistic reasons'[50] are not discriminatory providing that attendance at such institutions is optional and that they conform to standards for comparable levels of education.

At the regional level, the Inter-American instruments, as noted,[51] include provisions on non-discrimination. The African Charter provides for

[44] UN Human Rights Committee, General Comment No. 18 on non-discrimination (thirty-seventh session, 1989), 10 November 1989, in *Manual of Human Rights Reporting* (New York: United Nations, 1991), 117–19, para. 12.

[45] *Ibid.*

[46] 'States parties undertake to adopt immediate and effective measures, particularly in the fields of teaching, education, culture and information, with a view to combating prejudices which lead to racial discrimination and to promoting understanding, tolerance and friendship among nations and racial or ethnical groups.'

[47] 1979 Convention on the Elimination of All Forms of Discrimination against Women, UN Doc. A/34/46, entered into force 3 September 1981, Art. 4.

[48] *Ibid.*, Art. 10.

[49] 1960 Convention against Discrimination in Education, adopted on 14 December 1960, entered into force on 22 May 1962, 429 UNTS 93.

[50] *Ibid.*, Art. 2(b).

[51] Article 2, American Declaration of the Rights and Duties of Man; Article 3, Additional Protocol to the American Convention on Human Rights in the Area of Economic, Social and Cultural Rights; Article 1, American Convention on Human Rights.

non-discrimination (more precisely, 'without distinction of any kind') on grounds 'such as race, ethnic group, colour, sex, language, religion, political or other opinion, national and social origin, fortune, birth or other status'.[52] The non-discrimination requirement in Article 14 of the ECHR includes 'association with a national minority' among the prohibited grounds of discrimination. Article 14 is not open-ended like Article 26 of the CCPR,[53] although other articles do not have to be breached independently before the non-discrimination clause becomes applicable.

3. *Minority Rights*

Many texts on minority rights are comparatively recent, and the drafting processes almost inevitably have incorporated reflections on the existing body of human rights law: in any case, the application of standards must be consistent with the body of human rights law.[54] Article 27 of the CCPR functions as a minimum global treaty standard: 'In those States in which ethnic, religious or linguistic minorities exist, persons belonging to such minorities shall not be denied the right, in community with the other members of their group, to enjoy their own culture, to profess and practise their own religion, or to use their own language.' There is no express mention of education in Article 27, which may best be regarded as a framework to condition general educational policy as it affects minorities.[55] The underlying right to identity is crucial, and the state educational system must be arranged to facilitate the retention and promotion of the minority's identity.

There are now many other texts, global and regional, on minority rights, including notably the Declaration on the Rights of Persons Belonging to Minorities[56] and the Framework Convention, both of which address the issue

[52] AfrCh, Art. 2.

[53] John Merrills and A. H. Robertson, *Human Rights in Europe: A Study of the European Convention on Human Rights* (Manchester, 2001), 198–205. Protocol No. 12 to the Convention for the Protection of Human Rights and Fundamental Freedoms, ETS No. 177, opened for signature on 4 October 2000, entered into force on 1 April 2005, provides for a general prohibition against discrimination. Article 1 of the Protocol provides that 'The enjoyment of any right set forth by law shall be secured without discrimination on any ground such as sex, race, colour, language, religion, political or other opinion, national or social origin, association with a national minority, property, birth or other status.'

[54] UN General Assembly resolution 'Setting international standards in the field of human rights' (adopted at the 97th plenary meeting), UN Doc. A/Res/41/120, 4 December 1986. See also Commentary on the UN Declaration on Minorities, *supra*, n. 2, paras. 4 and 5.

[55] Neither is there express mention of education in General Comment (No. 23) of the Human Rights Committee on Article 27: CCPR/C/21/Rev.1/Add.5 (fiftieth Session, 1994).

[56] Declaration on the Rights of Persons belonging to National or Ethnic, Religious and Linguistic Minorities (hereinafter UN Declaration on Minorities or UN Decl. Min.), adopted by the UN GA on 18 December 1992, GA Res. 47/135.

of education. The texts on minority rights supplement the basic right to education on a non-discriminatory basis with innovations on the overlapping issues of curriculum content where Article 4(5) of the UN Declaration on Minorities sets the basic global standard;[57] minority input into determinations of educational policy (the texts are rarely specific on this aspect, though the European Language Charter is one exception);[58] language in education,[59] access to education,[60] and institutions underpinning minority education.[61]

C. Analysis of the Existence of this Right in Different Regional/International Documents

The present section draws out some elements in the interpretations of the standards set out above. It outlines developments of key notions advanced by

[57] 'States should, where appropriate, take measures in the field of education in order to encourage knowledge of the history, traditions, language and culture of the minorities existing within their territory. Persons belonging to minorities should have adequate opportunities to gain knowledge of the society as a whole.' The Framework Convention introduces in Art. 6 the notion of intercultural dialogue and seeks to encourage mutual respect and understanding and cooperation among all persons living on state territory. The basic education and minority cultures provision in the Framework Convention is Art. 12, whereby the Parties: 'shall, where appropriate, take measures in the fields of education and research to foster knowledge of the culture, history, language and religion of their national minorities and of the majority.' The OSCE Canon also addresses this issue: Paragraphs 34 and 40.4, of 'the Copenhagen Document', *supra*, n. 18.

[58] Article 7(4) provides that 'In determining their policy with regard to regional or minority languages, the Parties shall take into consideration the needs and wishes expressed by the groups which use such languages. They are encouraged to establish bodies, if necessary, for the purpose of advising the authorities on all matters pertaining to regional or minority languages.'

[59] General rights instruments are deficient in making provision for language in education—the UNESCO Convention against Discrimination in Education is exceptional. Article 4(3) of the UN Declaration on Minorities provides that States 'should take appropriate measures so that, wherever possible, persons belonging to minorities have adequate opportunities to learn their mother tongue or to have instruction in their mother tongue'. The provision appears to offer study *of* the minority language and study *in* the language as alternatives, although the language is not particularly well chosen—the phrase 'have instruction in' appears rather ambiguous if the intention is to convey the right to be taught *through the medium of* one's mother tongue. See the Commentary on the UN Declaration on Minorities, *supra*, n. 2, paras. 59–64. The provision in the Declaration may be compared with the Framework Convention. Article 14(1) of the latter stresses that 'every person belonging to a national minority has the right to learn his or her minority language'; Article 14(2) provides further that: 'In areas inhabited by persons belonging to national minorities traditionally or in substantial numbers, if there is sufficient demand the parties shall endeavour to ensure, as far as possible and within the framework of their education systems, that persons belonging to those minorities have adequate opportunities for being taught in the minority language or for receiving instruction in this language.' This latter provision is to be implemented 'without prejudice to the learning of the official language or the teaching in this language.' (Art. 14(3))

[60] For example, in Art. 12(3) of the Framework Convention, the parties 'undertake to promote equal opportunities for access to education at all levels for persons belonging to national minorities'.

[61] See below.

the human rights bodies and integrates with the preceding section and the later material on jurisprudence.

1. *Right to Education*

Article 13 of the CESCR is the subject of an extensive General Comment by the Committee on Economic, Social and Cultural Rights (General Comment No. 13).[62] An outstanding feature of the Comment is the extent to which it draws on and integrates various domains of discourse among human rights principles, including minority and indigenous rights. According to the Comment, 'education in all its forms and at all levels shall exhibit the following interrelated and essential features'[63]—those of availability, accessibility (which incorporates overlapping dimensions of non-discrimination, physical accessibility and economic accessibility), acceptability, and adaptability.[64] Of these essential features, some have specific significance for minority groups—notably the emphasis on non-discrimination in access to education, and the notion of acceptability. On the former, the Comment draws on principles from, *inter alia*, the CERD, the UNESCO Convention against Discrimination in Education, the Convention on the Rights of the Child (hereinafter CRC)[65] and the ILO Indigenous and Tribal Peoples Convention. In particular, the Comment affirms Article 2 of the UNESCO Convention regarding the validity of separate systems of education under particular circumstances. On 'acceptability', the Comment explains that education must be 'relevant, culturally appropriate and of good quality'.[66] It is asserted further that in the appropriate application of these interrelated and essential features, 'the best interests of the student shall be a primary consideration'.[67] Concerning the purposes of education (CESCR Art. 13(1)), the Comment states that, among educational objectives, 'perhaps the most fundamental is that "education shall be directed to the full development of the human personality" '.[68] Additionally, various purposes of education set out in related texts—including the final Declaration of the World Conference on Human Rights[69] and the CRC—are deemed to be 'implicit in, and reflect a contemporary interpretation of Article

[62] General Comment No. 13, The Right to Education, E/C.12/1999/10, 8 December 1999.

[63] *Ibid.*, para. 6.

[64] The '4-A scheme'.

[65] Concluded on 20 November 1989, entered into force on 2 September 1990, GA Res. 44/25.

[66] General Comment No. 13, para. 33.

[67] *Ibid.* Cf. 'the best interests of the child' in Art. 3(1) of the CRC.

[68] General Comment No. 13, para. 4.

[69] Vienna Declaration and Programme of Action, adopted by the World Conference on Human Rights on 25 June 1993, UN Doc. A/CONF.157/24 (Part I).

13.1.'[70]—a claim which, like much else in the Comment, evokes systemic connections between expressions of rights. The Comment notes that while the instruments cited contain elements not explicitly found in Article 13 (such as gender equality and respect for the environment as educational aims), they nonetheless inform its interpretation. If this is the case, elements of minority rights may also be deemed intrinsic to readings of the text. Evidence for this approach is found in the Comment's reading of Article 13(2): 'States have obligations to respect, protect and fulfil each of the "essential features" (availability, accessibility, acceptability and adaptability) of the right to education. By way of illustration, a State must respect the availability of education by not closing private schools... fulfil (facilitate) the acceptability of education by taking positive measures to ensure that education is culturally appropriate for minorities and indigenous peoples, and of good quality for all.'[71] This is an important validation of the contemporary sensitivity of international law to cultural diversity.[72] Instruments on minority rights are not rendered redundant by this affirmation of culturally appropriate education; while binding in their own right, the specific instruments supply essential guidance to the content of the Covenant.[73]

2. *Non-Discrimination*

On the core notion of discrimination, CERD/C General Recommendation XIV observes that 'differentiation of treatment will not constitute discrimination if the criteria for such differentiation, judged against the objectives and purposes of the Convention, are legitimate';[74] in this and on other occasions, CERD/C has adopted a normative register similar to that of the ECHR in appraising discrimination.[75] The European Court of Human Rights has pronounced on many occasions that a difference in treatment is discriminatory

[70] *Ibid.*, para. 5.

[71] General Comment No. 13, para. 50.

[72] See also the UNESCO Universal Declaration on Cultural Diversity, adopted by the General Conference on 2 November 2001; UNESCO Convention on the Protection and Promotion of the Diversity of Cultural Expressions, adopted by the General Conference on 20 October 2005.

[73] This is true of other instruments. For example, General Recommendation 23 of CERD/C on the rights of indigenous peoples uses language which echoes the UN Draft Declaration on the Rights of Indigenous Peoples and texts on minority rights. See Thornberry, 'Confronting Racial Discrimination', *supra*, n. 7, 260–62.

[74] A/48/18, Chapter VIII B.

[75] For example in concluding observations on Australia in 2005—CERD/C/AUS/CO/14, para.24. See also *Sefic v. Denmark*, Communication No. 32/2003, A/60/18, annex III A, para. 7(2).

if it has no objective and reasonable justification, that is, if it does not pursue a legitimate aim or if there is not a reasonable relationship of proportionality between the means employed and the aim sought to be realized.[76] The principle of non-discrimination does not demand uniformity of treatment: like cases are to be treated alike, and unlike cases according to the extent of the 'unlikeness'. A 'version' of this principle appears in the European Court of Human Rights' judgment in *Thlimmenos v. Greece*:

> The right . . . not to be discriminated against is violated when States treat differently persons in analogous situations without providing an objective and reasonable justification . . . The right not to be discriminated against . . . is also violated when States without an objective and reasonable justification *fail to treat differently persons whose situations are significantly different*.[77]

This nuance may be lost in appraising discrimination, but it is essential to retain it in responding to critics who argue the tendency of the equality principle to carry with it notions of homogeneity or reproduction of cultural sameness. It may be added that international standards against discrimination are not limited to purposive or intentional discrimination, but include discrimination in effect (and indirect discrimination) as well as aim.[78] The recognition in the canon of non-discrimination of temporary special measures may be misunderstood in the context of minority rights, respect for which will demand more than temporary measures.[79] The same is true for indigenous rights.[80] Indigenous groups and minorities enjoy their own rights in international law which stand independently of the case for special measures, though some state policies for such groups may be brought within this framework. Accurate appraisal of the situation of minority and indigenous groups is indispensable for the fulfilment of international obligations on special measures

[76] Among many possible citations, see *Abdulaziz, Cabales and Balkandali v. United Kingdom*, (Application No. 9214/80, 9473/81, 9474/81, 28 May 1985, Merits and just satisfaction), para. 72; *Case relating to Certain Aspects of the Laws on the Use of Languages in Education in Belgium*, (Application No. 1474/62, 1677/62, 1691/62, 1769/63, 1994/63, 2126/64, 23 July 1968, Merits), at The Law B, 10. What counts as a permissible or impermissible distinction will also relate to the principle that the Convention is a living instrument to be interpreted in light of present-day conditions—see among many expressions of this view for the ECHR, *Mazurek v. France*, (Application No. 34406/97, 1 February 2000), para. 49 (further case citations therein).

[77] Application No. 34369/97, 6 April 2000, para. 44 (emphasis added).

[78] For a detailed reading of current practice, see Wouter Vandenhole, *Non-Discrimination and Equality in the View of the UN Human Rights Treaty Bodies* (Antwerp, 2005).

[79] Compare the reference to temporary special measures in Art. 4 of CEDAW.

[80] Kristian Myntti, 'The Prevention of Discrimination v. Protection of Minorities—With Particular Reference to "Special Measures"', *Baltic Yearbook of International Law*, 2 (2002), 199–226.

and minority rights, and highlights the importance of collecting disaggregated data.[81]

3. Specific Minority Rights

(a) **Curriculum Content**

Recurring elements in curriculum standards for and about minorities include the following: First, the *multicultural* essence of education for minorities is the provision of means by which the groups can protect and promote their identity. The Commentary on the UN Declaration on Minorities recognizes that in the protection of the identity of minorities, the 'language and educational policies of the State are crucial'; further, to deny to minorities 'the possibility of learning their own language and of receiving instruction in their own language, or excluding from their education the transmission of knowledge about their own culture, history, tradition and language, would be a violation of the obligation to protect their identity.'[82] Promotion of identity requires 'special measures to facilitate the maintenance, reproduction and further development of their culture'.[83] Secondly, Article 4.4. of the UN Declaration on Minorities is interpreted in the commentary by the UN Working Group on Minorities to call for *intercultural* education, 'by encouraging knowledge in the society as a whole of the history, tradition and culture of the minorities living there.'[84] The education of the population at large is to be complemented by education for members of minorities—'the complementary duty to ensure that persons belonging to minorities gain knowledge of the society as a whole',[85] within the overall purpose of ensuring 'egalitarian integration based on non-discrimination and respect for each of the cultural, linguistic or religious groups which together form the national society'.[86]

[81] 'In addition to the requirement of clear and coherent legislative and institutional guarantees, the existence of basic data in the field of education is a precondition for any active educational policy ... all State parties need to have adequate data on the different groups living within their countries as well as their needs and aspirations in the field of education': Advisory Committee Commentary on Education, *supra*, n. 14, section 1.4. Reporting guidelines for UN treaty bodies—see Compilation of Guidelines on the Form and Content of Reports to be Submitted by States Parties to the International Human Rights Treaties, UN Doc. HRI/GEN/2/Rev.3, 8 May 2006.

[82] Commentary on the UN Declaration on Minorities, *supra*, n. 2, para. 28.

[83] *Ibid.*, para. 29.

[84] *Ibid.*, para. 67. The paragraph continues: 'Cultures and languages of minorities should be made accessible to the majorities as a means of encouraging interaction and conflict prevention in pluri-ethnic societies.'

[85] *Ibid.*, para. 68.

[86] *Ibid.*, para. 69.

A similar spirit informs Article 7 of CERD; accordingly, CERD/C has made many recommendations to the effect that state parties ensure that school curricula foster understanding, tolerance, and friendship among nations and ethnic groups,[87] the overall message being one of the inherent dignity and equality of human beings.[88] The intercultural element is complemented by recommendations for 'multicultural' programmes in relation to opportunities for learning minority and indigenous languages, etc. The lack of provision in educational curricula for indigenous or minority languages has been a matter of regular concern.[89] Other UN treaty bodies have made similar recommendations—the CRC/C for example has insisted on the importance of adapting school curricula to suit the particularities of local communities;[90] CESCR/C recommended Greece to ensure adequate staffing with teachers specialized in multicultural education.[91]

The Framework Convention's account of intercultural education implies that the general population should be aware of minority presence, history, culture, etc.; and equally that minorities should not retreat into psychological ghettos where they take no interest in fellow citizens.[92] The Advisory Committee has taken the view that history taught in schools should reflect a country's ethnic diversity,[93] and that education materials which contain negative stereotypes of minorities should be revised.[94] Since history teaching is a natural forum for evoking national memories,[95] texts should be drafted with

[87] For example, the 2005 Concluding Observations on Turkmenistan, A/60/18, para. 326.

[88] The point is made explicit by CERD/C in the context of descent-based communities in General Recommendation XXIX, paras. uu and vv: A/57/18, Annex 11 F.

[89] See, among recent concluding observations of CERD/C, those on Albania, A/58/18, para. 310; Armenia, A/57/18, para. 280; Mauritania, A/59/18, paras. 347, 349; Turkmenistan, A/60/18, para. 321. Language issues figure strongly in the 2006 report of CERD/C, A/61/18: see comments on Botswana, para. 64; Guyana, para. 148; Lithuania, para. 176; Uzbekistan, para. 228; Mongolia, para. 311; South Africa, para. 398; and Ukraine, para. 426.

[90] CRC/C/15/Add. 237, para. 63(f)—concluding observations on Myanmar.

[91] E/C/12/1/Add. 97.

[92] The work of the Council of Europe in the field of Minorities is appraised in Patrick Thornberry and Maria Amor Martin Estebanez, *Minority Rights in Europe: A Review of the Work and Standards of the Council of Europe* (Strasbourg, 2004), including a specific chapter on the Roma/Gypsies by Dr Alexandra Xanthaki.

[93] Opinion on Finland, ACFC/INF/OP/1 (2001) 002, para. 36; on Norway, ACFC/INF/OP/1 (2003) 003, para. 53; on Romania, ACFC/INF/OP/1 (2002) 001, para. 54.

[94] Opinion on Albania, ACFC/INF/OP/1 (2003) 004, para. 57; on Croatia, ACFC/INF/OP/1 (2002) 003, para. 47. Compare CERD/C general recommendation XXIX on descent-based communities referring to the need to review 'all language in textbooks which conveys stereotyped or demeaning images, references, names or opinions concerning' these communities—para. 48.

[95] Or contributing to the construction of a national identity through the selection of events, personalities, and principles.

special sensitivity to the historical role of minorities. *Inter alia*, UNESCO has also paid attention to questions surrounding the teaching of history which focuses too narrowly on national aspects of history 'to the detriment of giving due account of periods of peaceful coexistence, cooperation and cultural exchange, of mutual enrichment between different groups as well as between nations'.[96] General principles to be applied in curriculum development are set out in Recommendation 19 of the Hague Recommendations.[97]

A third element not to be neglected in the curriculum area is the imparting to members of minorities of the *necessary knowledge and skills* to enhance possibilities of succeeding in the wider society. This requirement pertains to education rights—including the issue of adequate knowledge of the state or official language—as well as to rights of effective participation of minorities in 'cultural, religious, social, economic and public life',[98] and participation in development.[99] Hence the widespread approval by treaty bodies of bilingual education.

(b) Participation

In many countries, decisions on syllabuses are taken at central government level. The texts on minority rights mandate or encourage participatory processes, so that there is a bottom-up as well as a top-down element in educational decision-making. Participation principles are widely recognized in international law.[100] The principles go beyond general participation in public life to participation in national and local *decisions* which affect minorities.[101] Education 'decisions' may have a profound effect on minority communities and are clearly within the

[96] From UNESCO, *Disarming History*, Conclusions and Recommendations of the International Conference on Combating Stereotypes and Prejudice in History Textbooks of South-East Europe, Visby, Gotland, 23–25 September 1999.

[97] 'In view of the importance and value that international instruments attach to intercultural education and the highlighting of minority histories, culture and traditions, State educational authorities should ensure that the general compulsory curriculum includes the teaching of the histories, cultures and traditions of their respective national minorities.'

[98] Article 2.2. of the UN Declaration on Minorities—see Commentary on the UN Declaration on Minorities, *supra*, n. 2, paras. 35–37.

[99] Article 4.5. and Art. 5 of the UN Declaration on Minorities—see Commentary on the UN Declaration on Minorities, *supra*, n. 2, paras. 71–74.

[100] The Lund Recommendations, *supra*, n. 9, do not specifically focus on education, but their general principles are applicable to a range of educational issues—including access, structures, policy input, etc. The Framework Convention deals with participation tersely in Art. 15. The elaboration of the norm in para. 80 of the Explanatory Report on the Framework Convention draws heavily on OSCE practice—particularly the Geneva Meeting of Experts on National Minorities, 1991. See also the general provision in para. 35 of the OSCE Copenhagen Document, *supra*, n. 18.

[101] See, eg, Art. 2(3) of the UN Declaration on Minorities.

language of the texts.[102] The Hague Recommendations put the matter simply: 'The curriculum content related to minorities should be developed with the active participation of bodies representative of the minorities in question'.[103] The message is reinforced by the Lund Recommendations.[104] *Inter alia*, Lund Recommendation 17 identifies education as among areas particularly appropriate for institutions of self-governance.[105] The message is further elaborated through sundry recommendations of treaty bodies. CERD/C has called specifically for the participation of minorities in the elaboration of educational and cultural policies.[106]

Besides political and decisional aspects of participation in education, questions of non-attendance, school exclusions, etc., are also to be considered in the context of both participation and access. Participation in the school system means that groups should not be effectively excluded, and that drop-out rates should be reduced. School exclusions are also an aspect of the participation nexus. All of these aspects may be directly linked to discrimination, whether direct or indirect. CERD/C is only one among many treaty bodies to be greatly exercised by discrimination against the Roma, issuing a general recommendation on this group in 2000.[107] Paragraph 17 of the Recommendation recommends that states parties 'support the inclusion in the school system of all children of Roma origin and . . . act to reduce drop-out rates, in particular among Roma girls, and, for these purposes, . . . cooperate actively with Roma parents, associations and local communities.' Among many

[102] For example, in the context of the Roma, the Committee of Ministers of the Council of Europe has recommended that 'involvement of all parties concerned (ministry of education, school authorities, Roma families and organizations) in the design, implementation and monitoring of education policies for Roma/Gypsies should be promoted by the State': Committee of Ministers Recommendation No. R (2000) 4, para. 19. Such advice could usefully be extended to other minority groups.

[103] Hague Recommendation 20, *supra*, n. 9.

[104] Lund Recommendation 12, *supra*, n. 9, suggests that 'States should establish advisory or consultative bodies within appropriate institutional frameworks to serve as channels for dialogue between governmental authorities and national minorities. Such bodies might also include special purpose committees for addressing such issues as . . . education, language, and culture. The composition of such bodies should reflect their purpose and contribute to more effective communication and advancement of minority interests.'

[105] For general commentaries on participation rights, see Marc Weller, 'Creating the Conditions necessary for the Effective Participation of Persons belonging to National Minorities', *International Journal of Minority and Group Rights* 10 (2003), 265–90; and vol. 12/2 (2005) of the same journal devoted to commentaries on the Lund Recommendations, *supra*, n. 9.

[106] An extensive recommendation was made in the case of Azerbaijan, commencing with: 'The Committee invites the State party to facilitate the participation of ethnic minorities in the elaboration of cultural and educational policies'—A/60/18, para. 62.

[107] General Recommendation XXVII, A/55/18, Annex V C.

deprivations recorded or alleged, the question of so-called 'special schools' has aroused widespread concern: specifically, the practice of placing Roma pupils in schools or special remedial classes for mentally handicapped children. Principles such as avoiding segregation while keeping open the possibility of mother-tongue education are recalled by the Committee, and among remedies suggested are recruitment of more Roma teachers, and 'sensitization of teachers and other education professionals to the social fabric and world views of Roma children'.[108] This suggests a point that the roots of the discrimination lie in divergent cultural assumptions concerning the role of education in the larger and smaller community, and the nature of the educational structures. Following its earlier comments, CERD/C issued a particularly robust observation in 2007 on the special schools phenomenon in the Czech Republic:

> The Committee... notes with particular concern that a disproportionately large number of Roma children attend 'special schools'. While noting the views of the State party that this results from the vulnerable situation of the Roma and the need to adopt special measures to respond to their needs... the Committee remains concerned that this situation also seems to result from discriminatory practices and lack of sensitivity on the part of the authorities to the cultural identity and specific difficulties faced by the Roma... The State party should increase its efforts to assess the situation of the Roma in the field of education. It should develop effective programmes specifically aimed at putting an end to the segregation of Roma in this area, and ensure that Roma children are not deprived of their right... to education of any type or any level. The Committee, in particular, recommends that the State party review the methodological tools used to determine the cases in which children are to be enrolled in special schools so as to avoid indirect discrimination against Roma children on the basis of their cultural identity.[109]

The Advisory Committee regards the 'special schools' phenomenon as incompatible with the Framework Convention. Such placements may only occur when absolutely necessary and always on the basis of consistent, objective, and

[108] Concluding observations on the Czech Republic, A/58/18, para. 386. Compare the statements on Roma issues made in the Durban Declaration and Programme of Action of the World Conference on Racism, etc. convened at Durban from 31 August to 8 September 2001 (A/CONF./189/12), which include a call upon states 'to ensure that Roma/Gypsy/Sinti/Traveller children and youth, especially girls, are given equal access to education and that educational curricula at all levels, including complementary programmes on intercultural education, which might, *inter alia*, include opportunities for them to learn the official languages in the pre-school period and to recruit Roma/Gypsy/Sinti/Traveller teachers and classroom assistants in order for such children and youth to learn their mother tongue, are sensitive and responsive to their needs': Programme of Action, para. 39; and, *ibid.*, paras 40–42.

[109] CERD/C/CZE/CO/7, para. 17.

comprehensive tests.[110] The Committee's commentary on education refers to various 'methods and structures' designed to cater for the needs of specific groups, observing that 'Some of these structures are legitimate, while others are unacceptable, especially if they impose segregated education and have discriminatory effects, as is often the case for the Roma.'[111] At the time of writing, the European Court of Human Rights appears to be the only major institution to stand back from the developing consensus on the incompatibility of the Czech system with anti-discrimination norms.[112]

Participation and exclusion are also linked to the idea of *access*. Equality of access can be denied directly, or indirectly when an individual belonging to a minority is frustrated by an apparently 'objective' condition for entry to an educational institution which *in fact* weighs particularly against that person. This reading can be expressed in the language of non-discrimination and positive minority rights with essentially the same result. CESCR/C General Comment No. 13 interprets accessibility to include not only non-discrimination, but also physical accessibility (by convenient geographic location or modern distance learning technology) and economic accessibility (affordability).[113] The concept of physical accessibility is particularly relevant to dispersed minorities; that of economic accessibility is relevant to all members of society. By Article 12 of the Framework Convention, the parties 'undertake to promote equal opportunities for access to education at all levels for persons belonging to minorities'. The reference to 'all levels' should be given its ordinary meaning.[114] One

[110] See opinion on Hungary, ACFC/INF/OP/1 (2001) 004, para. 41; on Croatia, ACFC/INF/OP/1 (2002) 003, para. 49; on Czech Republic, ACFC/INF/OP/1 (2002) 002, para. 61; on Finland, ACFFC/INF/OP/1 (2001) 002, para. 37; on Albania, ACFC/INF/OP/1 (2003) 004, para. 39. The Committee, while respecting principles of parental choice, urges states to find ways and means of combating such de facto segregation.

[111] Commentary on Education, Section 2.1. The Commentary examples 'So-called "special classes" or even "special schools" (which are sometimes meant for mentally disabled pupils but have often been used disproportionately for Roma children due to an erroneously generalized perception of their inability to follow instruction in the "regular" school system)'.

[112] In *D.H. and Others v. the Czech Republic*, a chamber of the Court decided by a 6–1 majority that the system did not breach Art. 14 of the Convention in conjunction with Art. 2 of Protocol 1, reasoning, *inter alia*, that statistics in themselves were not sufficient to establish indirect discrimination, that the tests were administered by professional psychologists and it was not for the Court to go beyond the facts of the case and require the government to show that individual psychologists had not adopted a discriminatory approach. Among many comments, see Morag Goodwin, 'D.H. and Others v Czech Republic: a Major Set-back for the Development of Non-discrimination Norms in Europe', *German Law Journal*, 7/4 (2006), 421–31. The case is currently being examined by the Grand Chamber of the Court.

[113] General Comment No. 13, para. 6.

[114] In practice, the Advisory Committee appears to consider any under-representation of minorities in institutions of higher education to be contrary to the right to equal opportunities in access

point to be made is that ensuring the survival of minorities means, *inter alia*, that they will need their professionals and intellectuals, so that third-level education is a clear desideratum, and educational possibilities should not be constrained on account of membership of a minority.[115]

(c) Minority Languages in Education

Regarding the UN Declaration on Minorities, the Commentary on the UN Declaration on Minorities has advanced the view that the provision on 'learning' and 'having instruction' in mother tongue implies a distinction between the depth of commitment required on behalf of the state, with the latter ('instruction') requiring steps beyond 'learning'.[116] Steps required are asserted to depend on variables such as the size of groups, the density of settlement, and whether the minority is long established or a newer arrival.[117] The matter is regarded as easier with compact traditionally settled groups, where the state should ensure the preservation of linguistic identity to the maximum of their resources, so that mother-tongue education is envisaged for pre-school and primary stages, followed by a gradual introduction of the state or official language through later stages.[118] Even with dispersed groups, the possibility of learning mother tongue should always be present, though the state/official language may be introduced into education earlier.[119] On new groups, the comment stresses the necessity of learning the language of the host country; where immigrants live compactly, there is no reason to treat them differently from old minorities.[120]

The Commentary makes explicit reference to European instruments in the field, citing the European Language Charter and the Hague Recommendations—the latter's account of the 'stages of education' is broadly similar to that in the Commentary and appears to have influenced it. The balance between the empowerment derived from learning the state or official language and the cultural self-confidence derived from education through

to education at all levels as set out in Art. 12(3)—Opinion on the UK, ACFC/INF/OP/1 (2002) 006 para. 85.

[115] P. Thornberry, in M. Weller, (ed.) *The Rights of Minorities in Europe*, (Oxford University Press, Oxford 2005), 384–86.

[116] Commentary, *supra*, n. 2, para. 59: Although the language of the Declaration is ambiguous in this respect, the Commentary's 'resolution' of the ambiguity may prove persuasive.

[117] *Ibid.*, para. 60.

[118] *Ibid.*, para. 61.

[119] For further, nuanced reflection on the understandings of 'minority language' and 'mother tongue', see the Advisory Committee Commentary on Education, *supra*, n. 14, section 2.3.

[120] Commentary, *supra*, n. 2, para. 64—though see also paras. 10 and 11. Compare this with section 2.3. of the Advisory Committee Commentary on Education, *supra*, n. 14.

mother tongue is an issue of the highest sensitivity. So, on the one hand, the Framework Convention's Advisory Committee has made it clear that adequate resources must be devoted by the state to the teaching of the state language for national minorities,[121] while criticizing states that do not set out clear 'demand' thresholds to trigger the introduction of minority language education.[122] In cases such as the UK, where there is less demand from the large immigrant community, the Committee has encouraged a more proactive approach to minority language education particularly in areas where there are substantial numbers of ethnic minorities.[123]

(d) Institutions

The right of a minority to set up private educational institutions is a basic understanding in human rights law, reflected in the UNESCO Convention against Discrimination in Education and the Covenant on Economic, Social and Cultural Rights in broadly similar terms. The former instrument is more explicit as regards minorities,[124] Article 5(1)c providing that 'It is essential to recognize the right of members of national minorities to carry on their own educational activities, including the maintenance of schools and, depending on the educational policy of each State, the use or the teaching of their own language . . . '.[125] Such general provisions have influenced the concerns of treaty bodies including those expressed by CERD/C in relation to Mauritania where state policies were directed to ensuring that the curricula in private institutions were identical to those for the public schools. The Committee, taking account of the state party's desire to monitor the quality of private education, nevertheless

[121] Opinion on Armenia, ACFC/INF/OP/1 (2003) 001, para. 71.

[122] Opinion on Croatia, ACFC/INF/OP/1 (2002) 003, para. 51; Opinion on Armenia, para. 71.

[123] Opinion on the UK, AFC/INF/OP/1 (2002) 006, para. 91.

[124] The right of persons belonging to minorities to establish and maintain their own associations in Art. 2.5. of the UN Declaration on Minorities draws the comment from the Working Group on Minorities that 'Persons belonging to minorities are entitled, in the same way as other members of society, to set up any association they may want, including educational or religious institutions, but their right to association is not limited to concerns relating to their cultural, religious or linguistic identity': E/CN.4/Sub.2/A.C.5/2005/2, para. 51; it follows that any limitation must only be those which could also apply to 'associations of majorities'—*ibid.*

[125] 'Provided however (i) That this right is not exercised in a manner which prevents the members of these minorities from understanding the culture and language of the community as a whole and from participating in its activities, or which prejudices national sovereignty; (ii) That the standard of education is not lower than the general standard laid down or approved by the competent authorities; and (iii) That attendance at such schools is optional.' The language in the Convention, including the reference to sovereignty, reflects the more cautious approach to minority rights prevalent in the decades immediately following the establishment of the United Nations.

expressed 'doubts whether such control over private schools is conducive to the teaching of the languages and cultures of minority groups'.[126]

Among European instruments, the OSCE Copenhagen Document includes a right of members of minorities 'to establish and maintain their own educational, cultural and religious *institutions, organizations or associations*, which can seek voluntary financial and other contributions as well as public assistance in conformity with national legislation'.[127] Article 13 of the Framework Convention translates the 'own institutions' point into one on public and private education, providing for the right to set up and manage private educational establishments—stating that 'the exercise of this right shall not entail any financial obligation for the Parties'.[128] It is clear that the non-discrimination principle should be kept in mind in making assessments of what resources are to be allocated to minority education for particular groups.[129] Too generous an allocation of resources to particular groups at the expense of others may raise issues of discrimination.[130] The Hague Recommendations raise two further pertinent points: (i) the setting up of private schools should not be inhibited by unduly burdensome regulations (Recommendation 9); and (ii) minority education institutions (or promoters) are entitled to seek funding from the state or elsewhere (Recommendation 10). In any case, international conventions should be interpreted in such a manner as to make their standards available in practice. This principle is relevant to all minority educational provision, not just private educational facilities.[131] Thus, even in the case of resource constraints, or where obligations require 'only' progressive implementation of standards, states should be diligent in focusing available resources for social objectives. The provisions in Article 12(2) of the Framework Convention are a further call on resources, in mandating that the parties 'provide adequate

[126] A/59/18, para. 348. Accordingly, CERD/C recommended that 'the State party respect parents' freedom to choose the type of education they wish for their children and to choose for their children private schools that offer programmes meeting their expectations in terms of culture and language'.

[127] The Copenhagen Document, *supra*, n. 18, para. 32.2. (present author's emphasis).

[128] Thornberry, *supra*, n. 115, 395–406.

[129] The Framework Convention contains its own anti-discrimination provision in Art. 4. The Advisory Committee has encouraged states that subsidize the schools of some minorities to expand the practice to include other groups—Opinion on Germany, ACFC/INF/OP/1 (2002) 008, para. 56.

[130] Human Rights Committee, *Waldman v. Canada*, Communication 694/1996, 3 Nov 1999, CCPR/C/67/D/694/1996, http://www.bayefsky.com/./html/162_canada694vws.php.

[131] 'States should approach minority education rights in a proactive manner. Where required, special measures should be adopted by States to actively implement minority language education rights to the maximum of their available resources, individually and through international assistance and co-operation, especially economic and technical'—Recommendation 4 of the Hague Recommendations, *supra*, n. 9.

opportunities for teacher training and access to textbooks, and facilitate contacts among students and teachers of different communities'.[132] This is reinforced by Article 17 regarding the legitimacy of free and peaceful cross-border contacts.

D. State Duties

The duties of states in the above regard stem from the mix of instruments. Obligations of states in the general field of economic, social, and cultural rights are set out in General Comment No. 3 of the CESCR/C; the inscription of education in human rights texts is not a recipe for indefinite postponement of action; on the contrary, steps must be taken towards the achievement of rights objectives which are 'deliberate, concrete and targeted'.[133] Additionally, certain rights are ripe for immediate implementation such as the right to primary education.[134] The principle of effective interpretation of treaties also implies that rights are available in practice and not merely on paper—the search for evidence of implementation in practice is a standard aspect of the work of treaty bodies in education as for other human rights.[135] Further, it is imperative for discrimination to be eliminated and special measures taken where necessary as in many circumstances they will be.[136] Overall, the state needs to keep a balance between participation and inclusion rights for members of minorities and the specific identity rights demanded by them. The education system should endeavour to respect the diversity of society through diversity of curricula, and reciprocal learning among population groups, while avoiding the creation of educational ghettoes. The notion of the 'national interest' in education policy may be calibrated not in terms of simple majoritarianism

[132] Thornberry, *supra*, n. 115, 381–4.

[133] CESCR/C General Comment No. 3, The Nature of States Parties Obligations, E/1991/23, para. 2.

[134] CESCR/C General Comment No. 11, Plans of Action for Primary Education, E/C.12/1999/4, paras. 6 and 7. This comment observes in para. 2 that the right to education 'has been variously classified as an economic right, a social right and a cultural right. It is all of these. *It is also, in many ways, a civil and a political right*, since it is central to the full and effective realization of these rights as well. In this respect, the right to education epitomizes the indivisibility and interdependence of all human rights' (present author's emphasis).

[135] See also General Comment No. 31 of the Human Rights Committee on the Nature of the General Legal Obligation Imposed on States Parties to the Covenant, CCPR/21/Rev.1/Add.13, 26 May 2004.

[136] Recommendation 4 of the Hague Recommendations, *supra*, n. 9, summarizes this obligation that: 'States should approach minority education rights in a proactive manner. Where required, special measures should be adopted by States to actively implement minority language education rights to the maximum of their available resources, individually and through international assistance and cooperation, especially economic and technical.'

but through an inclusive approach incorporating minority as well as majority perspectives.

III. Analysis of Case Law

A. Comparison over Time between Courts

Litigation before the Permanent Court of International Justice was instrumental in the development of minority rights: the League of Nations regime was based on the notion of 'perfect equality' between members of minorities and other nationals of the state, and on ensuring that conditions for minorities gave them the means to preserve their characteristics and traditions.[137] The cases did little to expound detailed principles of education rights, though they contributed to establishing the validity of principles relating to minority rights, including the significance of declarations of appurtenance to a minority, and use of a minority language in the determination of minority identity.[138] In the UN era the contribution of international case law in the area of minority education (and education rights in general) is limited compared to other aspects of minority rights. The significance of the cases should not be overrated compared to other work of treaty bodies, including the concluding observations and general comments and recommendations. The absence of a protocol to the CESCR allowing for individual claims has limited the development of norms at the UN level. CERD/C has also not been forthcoming on education issues in the context of its communications procedure under Article 14 of CERD. The few cases of significance under the first Optional Protocol to the CCPR leave many education issues untouched, though they perhaps point to questions likely to be litigated in future. *Waldman v. Canada*[139] utilized the equality principle under Article 26 to address a claim by the author of the communication that, while Roman Catholic schools in Ontario were publicly funded, those of other denominations, including that of the author, who

[137] Further, 'these two requirements are indeed closely interlocked, for there would be no true equality between a majority and a minority if the latter were deprived of its own institutions, and were consequently compelled to renounce that which constitutes the very essence of its being as a minority': *Minority Schools in Albania*, P.C.I.J. Series A. /B, No. 64, 17, Advisory Opinion of 6 April 1935.

[138] *Access to German Minority Schools in Upper Silesia*, P.C.I.J. Series A/B No. 40, Advisory Opinion of 15 May 1931; *Rights of Minorities in Upper Silesia (Minority Schools)* P.C.I.J. Series A No. 15, Judgment of 26 April 1928.

[139] Communication No. 694/1996, UN Doc. CCPR/C/67/D/694/1996 (1999); compare *Tadman v. Canada*, Communication No. 816/1998, UN Doc. CCPR/C/67/D/816/1998 (1999).

was of the Jewish faith, were not. The Human Rights Committee averred that the Covenant 'does not oblige States parties to fund schools which are established on a religious basis. However, if a State party chooses to provide public funding to religious schools, it should make this funding available without discrimination.'[140] *Hudoyberganova v. Uzbekistan*[141] is a case that, while not specifically concerning a minority, has implications for minority religious rights in other contexts. Here, the Human Rights Committee found a violation of Article 18 following the refusal by the state party to allow the wearing of religious attire in a state educational institution, eventually debarring the author of the communication who chose to wear a hijab. The relevant law provided, *inter alia*, that 'Citizens of the Republic of Uzbekistan (except religious organizations' ministers) cannot appear in public places in religious attire'. The finding of a violation by the Committee is contextual[142] and it may not be entirely appropriate to draw wider inferences, though it stands in contrast to the approach of the European Court of Human Rights in the *Leyla*

[140] *Waldman*, para. 10.6. In a concurring individual opinion, Committee member Scheinin pointed out that the existence of Roman Catholic schools in Ontario was related to a historical arrangement and should have been addressed under Art. 18 (freedom of religion) and Art. 27 (minority rights) in addition to Art. 26. He continued: 'Article 27 imposes positive obligations for States to promote religious instruction in minority religions, and... providing that such education as an optional arrangement within the public education system is one permissible arrangement to that end. Providing for publicly funded education in minority languages for those who wish to receive such education is not as such discriminatory, though care must of course be taken that possible distinctions between different minority languages are based on objective and reasonable grounds. The same rule applies in relation to religious education in minority religions.' In the circumstance, in the light of principle and the disproportionate levels of funding to Roman Catholic schools as opposed to others, he agreed that the system prevailing in Ontario was discriminatory.

[141] Communication No. 931/2000, UN Doc. CCPR/C/82/D/931/2000 (2005).

[142] The dispositive relevant paragraph of the Views (para. 6.2.) states: 'The Committee has noted the author's claim that her right to freedom of thought, conscience and religion was violated as she was excluded from University because she refused to remove the headscarf that she wore in accordance with her beliefs. The Committee considers that the freedom to manifest one's religion encompasses the right to wear clothes or attire in public which is in conformity with the individual's faith or religion. Furthermore, it considers that to prevent a person from wearing religious clothing in public or private may constitute a violation of article 18, paragraph 2, which prohibits any coercion that would impair the individual's freedom to have or adopt a religion... policies or practices that have the same intention or effect as direct coercion, such as those restricting access to education, are inconsistent with article 18, paragraph 2. It recalls, however, that the freedom to manifest one's religion or beliefs is not absolute and may be subject to limitations... In the present case, the author's exclusion... was based on the provisions of the Institute's new regulations. The Committee notes that the State party has not invoked any specific ground for which the restriction imposed on the author... Neither the author nor the State party have specified what precise kind of attire the author wore and which was referred to as "hijab" by both parties. In the particular circumstances of the present case, and without either prejudging the right of a State party to limit expressions of religion and belief in the context of article 18... and duly taking into account the specifics of the context... the Committee is led to conclude... that there has been a violation of article 18, paragraph 2.'

Sahin case.[143] Besides narrow legal considerations, the difference in approach may reflect the wider range of state parties to UN instruments as opposed to Council of Europe or other regional conventions.

The most substantial body of case law emanates from the European Convention of Human Rights, some of which makes only a limited contribution to the development of standards of minority rights. As noted, the ECHR includes 'association with a national minority' among the prohibited grounds of discrimination in Article 14, and an education provision in Article 2 of Protocol 1. On the general purpose of education, in *Kjeldsen, Busk Madsen and Pedersen v. Denmark*,[144] the European Court of Human Rights emphasized the role played by education in a democratic society, observing that the First Protocol 'aims . . . at safeguarding the possibility of pluralism in education . . . essential for the preservation of the "democratic society" as conceived by the Convention . . . '.[145] This implies that the state must take care that 'information or knowledge included in the curriculum is conveyed in an objective, critical and pluralistic manner'.[146] The state is forbidden to pursue an aim of indoctrination—which might be considered as not respecting parents' religious and philosophical convictions.[147]

Article 14 is not open-ended like Article 26 of the CCPR,[148] although other articles do not have to be breached independently before the non-discrimination clause becomes applicable. Analogously to the *Waldman* case before the Human Rights Committee, an issue can be raised when a private school using a minority language is set up in pursuance of a right to education, as to whether the state might be obliged to subsidise such a school to make the right a reality, and to ensure that there is no discrimination when compared to similar schools subsidised elsewhere. This is possible even in the absence of

[143] *Leyla Sahin v. Turkey*, (Appl. 44774/98, judgment of 10 Nov, 2005), ECHR (also see n. 180).

[144] *Kjeldsen, Busk Madsen and Pedersen v. Denmark*, (Application No. 5095/71, 5920/72, 5926/72, 07 December 1976, Merits).

[145] *Ibid.*, para. 50.

[146] *Ibid.*, para. 53.

[147] See also *Efstratiou v. Greece*, (Application No. 24095/94, 18 December 1996); *Valsamis v. Greece*, (Application No. 21787/93, 18 December 1996).

[148] However, Protocol No. 12 to the Convention for the Protection of Human Rights and Fundamental Freedoms, ETS No. 177, provides for a general prohibition against discrimination. Article 1 of the Protocol provides that 'The enjoyment of any right set forth by law shall be secured without discrimination on any ground such as sex, race, colour, language, religion, political or other opinion, national or social origin, association with a national minority, property, birth or other status.'

a Convention right for private schools to a subsidy or any explicit Convention demand on states to provide mother-tongue instruction.[149]

In European Convention jurisprudence, the *Belgian Linguistics* case of 1968[150] retains much of its interest in the area of minority rights. According to legislation of 1963, the national territory of Belgium was divided into four linguistic regions: the Flemish, the French, the German, and Greater Brussels. The regime incorporated rules mandating teaching in the regional language in public schools, with no subsidies offered to private schools which used another language. Parents who did not want to use the regional language were free to teach at home or send their children to an unsubsidised school. They could also send children across the linguistic border or to Greater Brussels where the language of instruction would be in Dutch or French according to the child's home language. There were additional problems with school certificates which did not conform to the language regime—the state would refuse to homologate the certificates which were important for access to certain careers and professions. A regime deviating from the territorial principle existed in six communes on the outskirts of Brussels. Here, French classes were restricted to children whose parents resided in the communes; on the other hand, the Dutch classes accepted children from outside. The case was brought by French-speaking applicants residing in the Dutch unilingual region who asserted that the principles of territorial unilingualism violated Articles 8 (the right to family life) and 14 (non-discrimination) of the ECHR, and Article 2 (the right to education) of the First Protocol to the ECHR.[151]

The Commission found the Belgian system incompatible with Article 2 of Protocol 1 because of the draconian nature of the subsidy issue. They also found a violation of Article 2 of Protocol 1 in conjunction with Article 14 in relation to the limitations on access to the French language schools in the special status communes, as well as a violation in regard to the school certificates. The Court disagreed in that it did not find a violation on the subsidy and school certificate regulations, and held that the ECHR did not recognize a right to be

[149] The argument is developed in Christian Hillgruber and Matthias Jestaedt, *The European Convention on Human Rights and the Protection of National Minorities* (Koln, 1994), 34–6. See also Peter van Dijk and Fried van Hoof, *Theory and Practice of the European Convention on Human Rights* (The Hague, 2nd edn, 1990) 473.

[150] *Case relating to Certain Aspects of the Laws on the Use of Language in Belgium*, (Application No. 1474/62 et al, 23 July 1968 Merits). See also *Inhabitants of Les Fourons v. Belgium*, (Resolution DH (74) I, relating to Application No. 2209/64, 30 May 1974, 231st meeting of the Ministers' deputies); *Roger Vanden Berghe v. Belgium*, (Application No. 2924/26, 16 December 1969, Admissibility decision); *X v. Belgium*, (Application No. 4372/70, 2 February 1971, Admissibility decision).

[151] ETS No. 9, entered into force 18 May 1954.

educated through a particular language: Article 2 of Protocol 1 did not specify the language in which instruction had to be provided. Equally, the judgment did not impugn the pursuit of linguistic unity within the regions, a project which implicated the public education system. The Court did, however, find a violation of Article 2 of Protocol 1 in conjunction with Article 14 on the question of access to education in the special communes. The law prevented children, solely on the basis of residence of their parents, from having access to the French schools in the six communes. The violation was found on the ground of residence in relation to language (a prohibited ground of discrimination), not on the specific ground of association with a national minority.[152] Not all distinctions are prohibited by Article 14 but:

> the principle of equality of treatment is violated if the distinction has no reasonable or objective justification. The existence of such a justification must be assessed in relation to the aim and effects of the measure under consideration, regard being had to the principles which normally prevail in democratic societies. A difference in treatment... must not only pursue a legitimate aim: Article 14 is likewise violated when it is clearly established that there is no reasonable relationship between the means employed and the aim sought to be realized.[153]

While the Court's exposition of the non-discrimination principle represented a significant determination of that norm, the judgment is limiting and ambivalent on other issues. The content and scope of the right to education in Article 2 of Protocol 1 were interpreted restrictively.[154] According to the Court, the states parties are not obliged by Article 2 to establish at their own expense, or to subsidize, education of any particular type or at any particular level. Rather, the case safeguards the question of access to schools once established.[155] One authority comments on this that 'the exercise of the right to education, even if understood in this way, requires by implication the existence and the maintenance of a minimum of education provided by the State, since otherwise the right would be illusory, in particular for those who have

[152] The complaint on the ground of Art 8—that families were compelled to split up in consequence of the legislation—was rejected: such separations were not compelled by law, but resulted from the free choice of parents.

[153] ECtHR, Judgment, section I B, para. 10. The Court concluded that the means employed by the Belgian legislation pursuant to its linguistic policy objectives were not disproportionate.

[154] The Court did, however, establish that despite the negative wording of Art. 2 of Protocol 1 ('no person shall be denied the right to education'), the article does enshrine a right: The Law 1B. 3. It may be suggested that it would be extraordinary if it did not!

[155] Summary in Francis G. Jacobs and Robin C. A. White, *The European Convention on Human Rights* (Oxford, 1996), 262.

insufficient means'.[156] In any case, the parties to the ECHR will also be parties to the CESCR, where the right to education is spelled out in more definitive explicit terms.

Overall, the Commission and the Court read the import of the Belgian legislation differently. For the Commission the Belgian policy amounted to the assimilation of minorities against their will into the regional language bloc. For the Court, the Belgian legislation was in the defensible realm of pursuing the public interest through the attainment of linguistic unity in order to stabilize the structure of the state. One important point for minority protection emerging from the case is that language maintenance and development constitute legitimate aims within the ECHR, consistent with Article 14; on the other hand, the refusal to interpret the right to education to include the right to education in one's own language is limiting. A 'positive' for minorities is the understanding that official recognition of diplomas, etc. attained is indispensable to the completion of the education process,[157] otherwise there would be only limited economic benefit to be derived from establishing private schools.[158] Finally, as the case indicates, non-discrimination does not mean completely identical treatment for all groups: what is prohibited are those distinctions which have no objective merit, and which have the effect or purpose of nullifying or impairing the enjoyment or exercise of human rights.

In terms of the substance of the education right in Protocol 1, the term 'philosophical convictions'—dismissed as irrelevant to the issue of language teaching in the *Belgian Linguistics* case—was explained by the European Court of Human Rights in *Campbell and Cosans v. United Kingdom*[159] as relating to 'such convictions as are worthy of respect in a democratic society . . . and are not incompatible with human dignity'.[160] The views of the applicant on the practice of corporal punishment in schools related to 'a weighty and substantial aspect of human life and behaviour'.[161] On the basis of the reading of philosophical convictions in *Campbell and Cosans*, one author comments that

[156] Van Dijk and van Hoof, *supra*, n. 149, 467.

[157] The laws did not block this access to careers, etc., but only made access dependent on a further examination.

[158] The Hague Recommendations, *supra*, n. 9, do not deal explicitly with the certificates issue. However, Recommendation 9 states that in the matter of private schools, states may not hinder the enjoyment of the right 'by imposing unduly burdensome legal and administrative requirements regulating the establishment and management of such schools'.

[159] *Campbell and Cosans v. United Kingdom*, (Application No. 7511/76, 7743/76, 25 February 1982).

[160] *Ibid.*, para. 36.

[161] *Ibid.*

'the desire of parents, based on cultural and linguistic association with an ethnic group, to have their children educated in their "mother tongue" also has to be recognized as such a conviction'.[162] This approach has been doubted in the admissibility decision in *Skender v. the Former Yugoslav Republic of Macedonia*,[163] where the Third Chamber of the Court revisited the *Belgian Linguistics* case, and stated that to interpret 'religious' and 'philosophical' as covering linguistic preferences 'would amount to a distortion of their ordinary and usual meaning and read into the Convention something which is not there';[164] the Court prayed in aid the drafting history of the Convention,[165] an approach which, it may be observed, is less cogent than it might be otherwise in view of the development of minority rights universally, and their lack of development in 1951 when the Convention was being drafted. The use of the term 'preferences' as opposed to 'convictions' also sends a signal that the language education aspect was regarded as less 'weighty' than a 'genuine conviction', an approach with which many would disagree.

Nevertheless, there is potential in the ECHR to address education issues afresh, especially in the light of contemporary perceptions of the fundamental importance of cultural and linguistic identity in the constitution of the post-modern self. Equally, it would be inappropriate if the existence of the newer texts on minority rights such as the Framework Convention were to act as a reason for not developing ECHR jurisprudence further.[166] The decision of the European Commission and the judgment of the Court of Human Rights in the case of *Cyprus v. Turkey*[167] illustrate the further potential of the ECHR. On schools in northern Cyprus which offered teaching in English or Turkish, but were also open to Greek Cypriots, the Commission observed that:

> education in such schools does not correspond to the needs of the persons concerned who have the legitimate wish to preserve their own ethnic and cultural identity. While

[162] Blum, cited in C. Hillgruber and M. Jestaedt, *The European Convention on Human Rights and the Protection of National Minorities* (Köln, Verlag Wissenschaft and Politik, 1994), 26, n. 64.

[163] Application 62059/00, 22 November 2001, Admissibility decision.

[164] *Ibid.*, para. 3.

[165] *Skender*, para. 3.

[166] In this respect, one is not entirely encouraged by the remarks in *Beard v. the United Kingdom*, where the Court observed that: 'there may be said to be an emerging international consensus... recognising the special needs of minorities and the obligation to protect their security, identity and lifestyle... However the Court is not persuaded that the consensus is sufficiently concrete for it to derive any guidance as to the conduct or standards which contracting States consider desirable in any particular situation' (Application No. 24882/94, 18 January 2001, Merits), paras. 104–5. On the face of it, this seems a remarkably limiting approach to the interpretation of a body of norms which is by now reasonably well established in general international law.

[167] *Cyprus v. Turkey*, (App. No. 25781/94), Report of the EuCommHR, adopted on 4 June 1999.

it is true that Article 2 of Protocol No. 1 guarantees access only to existing educational facilities, it must be noted that . . . such educational facilities have in fact existed in the past and have been abolished by the Turkish Cypriot authorities . . . In the Commission's opinion, the total absence of appropriate secondary schools for Greek Cypriots living in northern Cyprus cannot be compensated for either by the authorities' allowing the pupils concerned to attend such schools in southern Cyprus . . . In these circumstances the practice of the Turkish authorities amounts to a denial of the substance of the right to education.[168]

For the Court,[169] the situation meant that the option to continue education in the north of Cyprus at a Turkish or English-language school meant that: 'In the strict sense, there is no denial of the right to education . . . moreover [Article 2 of Protocol 1] does not specify the language in which education must be conducted in order that the right to education be respected.' The Court continued: 'However . . . the option available to Greek-Cypriot parents to continue their children's education in the north is unrealistic . . . It cannot be maintained that the provision of secondary education in the south in keeping with the linguistic tradition of enclaved Greek-Cypriots suffices to fulfil the obligation [in the Protocol] having regard to the impact of that option on family life.'[170]

1. Religious Convictions and Education

Although not specifically concerning minorities, the case of *Leyla Sahin v. Turkey*[171] has clear implications for the broader field of minority education bearing in mind that immigrant populations in many countries will often hold, and manifest, religious beliefs, and possess ethnic/cultural characteristics different from majority populations in their host countries.[172] The applicant complained under Article 9 that she had been prohibited from wearing the Islamic headscarf at university, of an unjustified interference with her right to education within the meaning of Article 2 of Protocol No. 1, and of a violation of Article 14, taken together with Article 9, arguing that the prohibition on wearing the Islamic headscarf obliged students to choose between

[168] *Ibid.*, para. 478.

[169] *Cyprus v. Turkey*, (Application No. 25781/94, 10 January 2001 Merits).

[170] *Ibid.*, para. 278. The Court also found a violation of Art. 10 of the Convention (freedom of expression) for excessive censorship of school textbooks: paras. 250–54.

[171] Application No. 44774/98, Grand Chamber, 10 November 2005; the Grand Chamber judgment was preceded by a lower Chamber judgment of 29 June 2004; cf. *Zeynep Tekin v. Turkey*, (Application No. 41556/98, Chamber judgment of 29 June 2004). References in the present text are to the judgment of the Grand Chamber.

[172] The account of the case given here is in summary form.

education and religion and discriminated between believers and non-believers. Lastly, she relied on Articles 8 and 10. The Court found no violation of any of these articles. Concerning Article 9, the Court considered that interference primarily pursued the legitimate aims of protecting the rights and freedoms of others and of protecting public order, and, as to whether the interference was necessary, that it was based on principles of secularism and equality. The Grand Chamber considered the notion of secularism to be consistent with the values underpinning the Convention so that upholding that principle could be considered necessary to protect the democratic system in Turkey. *Inter alia*, the Court noted the emphasis in the Turkish constitutional system on the protection of the rights of women, and considered further that, when examining the question of the Islamic headscarf in the Turkish context, there had to be borne in mind the impact which wearing such a symbol may have on those who chose not to wear it.[173] In those circumstances, and having regard to the contracting states' margin of appreciation, the Court found that the interference at issue was justified in principle and proportionate to the aims pursued, and could therefore be considered to have been 'necessary in a democratic society'.[174] Concerning Article 2 of Protocol No. 1, the Court reiterated that it was of crucial importance that the Convention was interpreted and applied in a manner which rendered its rights practical and effective, not theoretical and illusory. While the first sentence of Article 2 essentially established access to primary and secondary education, there was no watertight division separating higher education from other forms of education; consequently, it would be hard to imagine that institutions of higher education existing at a given time did not come within the scope of the first sentence of Article 2 of Protocol No. 1. Consequently, the Court considered that any institutions of higher education existing at a given time came within the scope of the first sentence of Article 2 of Protocol No. 1.[175] In the case before it, by analogy with its reasoning under Article 9, the Court accepted that the regulations on the basis of which the applicant had been refused access to various lectures and examinations for wearing the Islamic headscarf constituted a restriction on her right to education. As with Article 9, the restriction was foreseeable and pursued legitimate aims and the means used were proportionate. The measures

[173] *Sahin*, para. 115. See paras. 115 and 116 for gender aspects of the decision; in her dissenting opinion, Judge Tulkens (para. 12 of her opinion) remarked: 'I fail to see how the principle of sexual equality can justify prohibiting a woman from following a practice which, in the absence of proof to the contrary, she must be taken to have freely adopted.'

[174] *Ibid.*, paras. 104–23.

[175] *Sahin*, paras. 134–42.

in question manifestly did not hinder the students in performing the duties imposed by the habitual forms of religious observance. Secondly, the decision-making process for applying the internal regulations satisfied, so far as was possible, the requirement to weigh up the various interests at stake. Lastly, the process appeared to have been accompanied by safeguards—the rule requiring conformity with statute and judicial review—that were apt to protect the students' interests. Further, the applicant could reasonably have foreseen that she ran the risk of being refused access to lectures and examinations if, as subsequently happened, she continued to wear the Islamic headscarf. In these circumstances, the ban on wearing the Islamic headscarf had not impaired the very essence of the applicant's right to education.[176] Neither did it conflict with other rights enshrined in the Convention or its Protocols.[177]

B. Analysis and Criticism, Possible Evolution of Interpretation by Courts

The various aspects of the right to education have been litigated in a patchwork fashion, with mixed results. The element of discrimination in education is tolerably well understood and is underpinned by a panoply of texts.[178] The substance of the education right itself is becoming better understood, as much through comment by UN treaty bodies as through litigation. In the particular context of the ECHR, the case of *Cyprus v. Turkey* appears to offer some possibilities for minorities and to move in substance beyond previous rather negative positions in the field of language in education. The result of the case is heavily conditioned by the facts, including the previous existence of schools, latterly abolished. The decision brings to mind the principle that human rights instruments should be interpreted as far as possible to preserve and augment the existing stock of international and domestic rights. In the light of the case, it will be interesting to see if the observations can be generalized by the Court

[176] Judge Tulkens disagreed with this proposition, asserting on the contrary that the applicant 'was de facto deprived of the right of access to the University and, consequently, of her right to education'—*dissenting opinion*, para. 15; and *ibid.*, para. 18: 'The question ... arises whether such an infringement of the right to education does not, ultimately, amount to an implicit acceptance of discrimination against the applicant on grounds of religion. In its Resolution No. 1464 (2005) of 4 October 2005, the Parliamentary Assembly of the Council of Europe reminded ... member States that it was important to "fully protect all women living in their country against violations of their rights based on or attributed to religion".'

[177] *Ibid.*, paras. 152–62. Cf. *Dahlab v. Switzerland*, (Application No. 42393/98, 15 February 2001).

[178] In the context of the ECHR, see for example *Nachova and Others v. Bulgaria*, (Application No. 43577/98, 26 February 2004, Merits). For an overall critique of the ECHR's approach to discrimination, see Luzius Wildhaber, 'Protection against Discrimination under the European Convention on Human Rights: A Second-Class Guarantee', *Baltic Yearbook of International Law*, 2 (2002), 71–82.

in cases which do not reflect a set of special circumstances. In terms of the intersection between manifestation of religion and education, and prospects for religious minorities to manifest their identity in the educational context, the approach of UN bodies is broadly reassuring as regards respect for beliefs and practices. On the other hand, in the present author's view, the current stance of the European Court of Human Rights, as evidenced by the *Sahin* case, may be a cause of concern, in particular through allowing very wide scope for 'the margin of appreciation' to the detriment of European supervision, in situations where the degree of restriction imposed on religious symbols is stricter than for European states in general.[179] The position in such cases may be even more delicate and legally contestable when essential minority rights to existence and identity are at issue. In general terms, it may be suggested that the ECHR has some way to travel to recognize adequately the claims of religious and other minorities. This is one area where the various treaty bodies may not speak with one voice, and send out inconsistent signals to governments. There is a clear need for further integration of principle, allowing scope for the embedding or mainstreaming of minority rights standards across the full spectrum of human rights.

C. Application of the Right (Enforcement by States)

The application of minority rights to education has made considerable progress in many countries, and such progress is not confined to European states. However, there is still a considerable distance to travel regarding the various elements of the rights. The work of the UN treaty bodies has been broadly consistent in stressing that all countries are in essence multicultural, and that there are rights issues to be addressed, including in the sphere of education and training. While the number of states claiming they have no minorities, or that there is no problem or discrimination against them, is diminishing; residual resistance to rights or failure to acknowledge the existence of minorities as such, means that public provision for minority education may be lacking. Challenges to 'multiculturalism' may have substantially the same negative

[179] See paras. 55–65 of the *Sahin* judgment, setting out the position in 'comparative law'. Judge Tulkens pointed to 'the diversity of practice on the issue of regulating the wearing of religious symbols in educational institutions and, thus, the lack of a European consensus in this sphere'—Sahin, *Dissenting opinion*, para. 3; she added, *ibid.*, that 'in none of the member States has the ban on wearing religious symbols extended to university education, which is intended for young adults, who are less amenable to pressure'. See also The European Commission against Racism and Intolerance (ECRI) General Policy Recommendation no. 5, Combating Intolerance and Discrimination against Muslims, CRI (2000) 21, 27 April 2000; EC Council Directives 2000/78/EC3 and 2000/43/EC4.

effect. Rigid adherence to 'uniformity' models of equality or undifferentiated egalitarian citizenship is another obstacle to addressing underlying issues, though conceptual questions of how to adapt general standards to a kaleidoscopic variety of situations always arise. Flexible and nuanced approaches to norm-application have increasing appeal, perhaps especially through reporting procedures. Where possible, such flexibility ought to benefit the beneficiaries of rights and victims of discrimination rather than provide platforms for the possible erosion of rights. A further problem is the gap between theory and practice in that model laws may remain without substantial implementation. Human rights bodies are rightly vigilant on this issue, and insist on the practical implementation of rights. Issues of asymmetrical treatment of minority groups in the field of education are also of concern: the reciprocity of intercultural learning demanded by the instruments is not always met in practice. The Advisory Committee under the Framework Convention has highlighted questions of resources. The problematic issue of Roma education continues to trouble and perplex.

IV. Conclusion

The above presentation reveals a complex and multifaceted picture. The emergence of principles in different instruments at different times also creates conceptual distance between them, which requires resolution creatively and in good faith. The general right to education is reasonably elaborate as concerns levels of education, parental choice, the curriculum, participation, and resources. There is evidence of increased sensitivity to minority issues in the implementation of general norms—the General Comment on the Right to Education under the CESCR is an example. Comparable data can be extracted from recent practice under, for example, CERD/C under CERD. The principle of non-discrimination remains a fundamental norm in the architecture of human rights. Apart from other virtues, the principle reminds us that specific minority rights should not stray beyond what is reasonable under the circumstances, and proportional to the aims which are sought to be realized. Minority rights should be interpreted as far as possible to add to the sum of social virtues, and not as a zero sum game wherein the gains of some are a loss to others. Provisions regarding the identity of minority groups are as important as the other norms. The development of minority rights instruments itself suggests that new or rediscovered sets of values are at work in the world, new 'philosophical convictions' which refresh the goals of democratic societies. The corpus of rights carries the assumption that the best way of facilitating rights to existence and identity is to promote the social integration of minorities, while taking care to avoid cultural constriction in the integration process.

Current international standards favour real choices for minorities in curricula and institutions, and are anti-fundamentalist in tone. While knowledge of one's own culture and language constitute crucial contributions to personal evaluations of identity, the lives of others are assumed to have equal value. The texts contain both multicultural and intercultural elements: individuals and groups shape their identity in relation to others.[180] Sentimental stories about others may be the beginning of transcultural solidarity.[181] Mutual knowledge conveyed without stereotyping may serve to reinforce that empathy, that solidarity, leading ultimately to mutual respect. Edward Said has observed that all cultures are involved in one another; none is single and pure, all are hybrid and heterogeneous.[182] Monocultural and monolingual approaches to education are perceived through the corpus of international standards as having questionable merit, even as questions continue to be asked. Human communities will not always agree on ultimate values, on ultimate questions of what education is *for*. Value consensus looks increasingly difficult in the face of the erosion of the grand narratives of enlightenment and progress in a postmodern world, and the reality of cultural diversity and its corollary, cultural divergence.[183] International standards suggest that what is required in the matter of education rights is good faith, the keeping of promises, and ongoing dialogue between all groups concerned. Human rights agreements serve to channel and partially codify that sentimental education to which Rorty draws our attention, and without which our humanity is incomplete.

180 Charles Taylor, *The Ethics of Authenticity* (Cambridge, Mass. and London, 1991).

181 Richard Rorty, 'Human Rights, Rationality and Sentimentality', in Stephen Shute and Susan Hurley (eds.), *On Human Rights: The Oxford Amnesty Lectures* (New York, 1993), 111–34.

182 Edward W. Said, *Culture and Imperialism* (London, 1994).

183 See UNESCO Declaration on Cultural Diversity, adopted by the General Conference of UNESCO at its 31st session on 2 November 2001.

PHYSICAL INTEGRITY, DUE PROCESS AND THE ADMINISTRATION OF JUSTICE

Rainer Hofmann and Halida Nasic

Racial violence is a particular affront to human dignity and, in view of its perilous consequences, requires from the authorities special vigilance and a vigorous reaction. It is for this reason that the authorities must use all available means to combat racism and racist violence, thereby reinforcing democracy's vision of a society in which diversity is not perceived as a threat but as a source of its enrichment.

European Court of Human Rights, *Nachova and Others v. Bulgaria*, 6 July 2005, para. 145

I. Introduction

Under contemporary international law, and in any consideration of the rights of minorities, the right to existence is by necessity a precondition for the enjoyment of any other rights. Beyond physical existence, the *existence* of a minority group also occurs through the shared consciousness of its members, manifested perhaps through language, culture, or religion, a shared sense of history, a common destiny. Without this notion of 'existence' it is possible to say that individuals live but the group does not: it has been replaced by something other than itself, perhaps a new group, larger or smaller.[1] However, in this first part of the chapter, the focus will be on the more limited notion of 'physical' existence of individual persons belonging to minorities, specifically their right to life, and freedom from torture, inhuman and degrading treatment.

The importance of ensuring that there are effective structures and procedures for the administration of justice by the judiciary, law enforcement agencies and other relevant state organs is increasingly recognized by the bodies responsible for monitoring the implementation of major international human rights instruments. For example, both the European Court of Human Rights (ECtHR) and the Inter-American Court of Human Rights (IACHR) have repeatedly held that an effective and independent investigation of allegations of the breach of the right to life or the right to be protected from torture or inhuman or degrading treatment or punishment is an essential requirement for any legal order respecting these most fundamental human rights.[2] The second part of the chapter will analyse the jurisprudence relevant to questions of ensuring due process as a critical element of minority protection, including issues such as the right to an effective remedy and to be entitled to a hearing in a language one understands.

The three parts of this chapter are structured in such a way as to provide, first, an overview of each respective right, followed, second, by an assessment of the contents of the respective right in the different international human rights documents with global or regional applicability, based on a general analysis of the pertinent case law with a particular emphasis on the emerging jurisprudence relevant to minority protection.

[1] Patrick Thornberry, *International Law and the Rights of Minorities* (Oxford University Press, Oxford, 1991), 57.

[2] See, eg, ECtHR, *Salman v. Turkey*, (Appl. No 21986/93, 27 June 2000, Merits) RJD 2000-VII, paras. 97 ff.; and IACHR, *Velásquez-Rodriguez v. Honduras* (Judgment, Ser. C No 4, 29 June 1988), para. 176 ff.

II. Physical Integrity and Existence

A. The Right to Life

The right to life is one of the most fundamental, yet controversial rights. It has been characterized by, *inter alia*, the United Nations Human Rights Committee (HRC) as the supreme human right, because without effective guarantee of this right, all the other rights of the human being would be devoid of meaning.[3]

1. International Instruments and the Right to Life

The right to life is protected in all major international human rights instruments: Article 3 of the Universal Declaration of Human Rights (UDHR) stipulates that '[e]veryone has the right to life, liberty and security of person'. In Article 6 (1) of the International Covenant on Civil and Political Rights (CCPR)[4] it is stated that '[e]very human being has the inherent right to life. This right shall be protected by law. No one shall be arbitrarily deprived of his life.' Relevant to those jurisdictions where the death penalty remains in practice, Article 6 (2) imposes the obligation that '... sentence of death may be imposed only for the most serious crimes in accordance with the law in force at the time of the commission of the crime and not contrary to the provisions of the present Covenant and to the Convention on the Prevention and Punishment of the Crime of Genocide. This penalty can only be carried out pursuant to a final judgment rendered by a competent court.' Article 6(3) states '[w]hen deprivation of life constitutes the crime of genocide, it is understood that nothing in this article shall authorize any State Party to the present Covenant to derogate in any way from any obligation assumed under the provisions of the Convention on the Prevention and Punishment of the Crime of Genocide'. The United Nations special procedure mandates present regular reports on situations of enforced or involuntary disappearances and arbitrary and extra-judicial executions around the world.[5] In 1984, the Human

[3] Manfred Nowak, *U.N. Covenant on Civil and Political Rights: CCPR Commentary*, 2nd edn, (N. P. Engel, Kehl, 2005), 121.

[4] On the ICCPR see, in addition to the Commentary by Manfred Nowak (*supra*, n. 3), Alex Conte, Scott Davidson, and Richard Burchill, *Defining Civil and Political Rights. The Jurisprudence of the United Nations Human Rights Committee* (Ashgate, London, 2004) and Sarah Joseph, Jenny Schultz, and Melissa Castan, *The International Covenant on Civil and Political Rights* (Oxford University Press, Oxford, 2000).

[5] For information on the work of the UN Working Group on enforced or involuntary disappearances, and the UN Special Rapporteur on arbitrary and extra-judicial executions see www.ohchr.org/english/issues/executions/index.htm.

Rights Committee adopted General Comment No. 14, on the right to life and Article 6, in which it confirmed that no derogation is permitted to the right to life, even in time of public emergency.[6] Furthermore, several international instruments aimed at the abolition of the death penalty have been adopted, among them the 1989 Second Optional Protocol to the CCPR, Protocols 6 and 13 of 1983 and 2002, respectively, to the European Convention for the Protection of Human Rights and Fundamental Freedoms (ECHR), and the 1990 Protocol to the American Convention on Human Rights (ACHR) to abolish the Death Penalty.

On the regional level, Article 2(1) ECHR[7] stipulates that: 'Everyone's right to life shall be protected by law. No one shall be deprived of his life intentionally save in the execution of a sentence of a court following his conviction of a crime for which this penalty is provided by law.' Furthermore, Article 2(2) states that '[d]eprivation of life shall not be regarded as inflicted in contravention of this article when it results from the use of force which is no more than absolutely necessary: a) in defence of any person from unlawful violence; b) in order to effect a lawful arrest or to prevent the escape of a person lawfully detained; and c) in action lawfully taken for the purpose of quelling a riot or insurrection'. Article 4 ACHR[8] states that 'Every person has the right to have his life respected. This Right shall be protected by law and, in general, from the moment of conception. No one shall be arbitrarily deprived of his life (...).'

[6] In its General Comment No. 6 [16] adopted at its 378th meeting on 27 July 1982, the Human Rights Committee observed that the right to life enunciated in Art. 6(1) of the ICCPR is the supreme right from which no derogation is permitted even in time of public emergency. See General Comment No. 6 of the Human Rights Committee in UN Doc. HRI/GEN/1/Rev.7, *Compilation of General Comments and General Recommendations adopted by Human Rights Treaty Bodies*, 128 (hereinafter referred to as *United Nations Compilation of General Comments*).

[7] On the ECHR see, eg, Pieter van Dijk and G. J. H. van Hoof, *Theory and Practice of the European Convention on Human Rights*, 4th edn, (Intersentia, Antwerp, 2006); Jochen Abr. Frowein and Wolfgang Peukert, *Europäische Menschenrechtskonvention,* 2nd edn, (N. P. Engel, Kehl, 1996); Christian Grabenwarter, *Europäische Menschenrechtskonvention,* 2nd edn, (Beck, München, 2005); David Harris, Michael O'Boyle, and Colin Warbrick, *Law of the European Convention on Human Rights* (Butterworth, London, 1995); Jens Meyer-Ladewig, *Konvention zum Schutz der Menschenrechte und Grundfreiheiten* (Nomos, Baden-Baden, 2003); Louis-Edmond Pettiti, Emmanuel Decaux, and Pierre-Henri Imbert, *La Convention Européenne des Droits de l'Homme,* 2nd edn, (Economica, Paris, 1999); and Mark Eugen Villiger, *Handbuch zur Europäischen Menschenrechtskonvention*, 2nd edn, (Schulthess, Zürich, 1999).

[8] On the ACHR see, eg, Thomas Burgenthal and Dinah Shelton, *Protecting Human Rights in the Americas*, 4th edn, (N. P. Engel, Kehl, 1995); Sergio García Ramirez, *La jurisprudencia de la Corte Interamericana de Derechos Humanos* (UNAM, Mexico, 2001); and Jo Pasqualucci, *The Practice and Procedure of Inter-American Court of Human Rights* (Cambridge University Press, Cambridge, 2003).

Article 4 African Charter on Human and Peoples' Rights (AfrCh)[9] stipulates that '[h]uman beings are inviolable. Every human being shall be entitled to respect for his life and the integrity of his person. No one may be arbitrarily deprived of this right.'

The first and most obvious element of the state's obligation is to refrain from deliberate, unjustified killings committed by its agents. Article 2 ECHR for instance provided for both positive and negative obligations of states.[10] The negative obligation implies that no person should be intentionally deprived of his or her life by state agents, whereas the positive obligation relates to measures adopted by states to safeguard that right. From the jurisprudence of the ECtHR emerges that the state's obligation to safeguard life consists of three main aspects: (i) the duty to refrain from unlawful killing by state agents; (ii) the duty to investigate suspicious deaths; (iii) and in certain circumstances, a positive obligation to take steps to prevent the avoidable loss of life.[11]

The HRC in its General Comment No. 6 also states that states parties should take measures not only to prevent and punish deprivation of life by criminal acts, but also to prevent intentional killing by their own security forces. This HRC General Comment No. 6 further establishes the obligations of states to take specific and effective measures to prevent the disappearances of individuals and establish effective facilities and procedures to investigate thoroughly cases of missing and disappeared persons.[12] In addition, the HRC has found that mandatory death sentences are a breach of Article 6 CCPR. This Article has also been applied in cases concerning the extradition of a person to a state

[9] On the AfrCh see, eg, Malcolm Evans, *The African Charter on Human and Peoples' Rights* (Cambridge University Press, Cambridge, 2002); Mutoy Mubiola, *Le système africain de protection des droits de l'homme* (Bruylant, Bruxelles, 2005); and U. Oji Umozurike, *The African Charter on Human and Peoples' Rights* (Nijhoff, The Hague, 1997).

[10] The ECtHR has consistently held that Art. 2 which safeguards the right to life, ranks as one of the most fundamental provisions in the ECHR. Together with Art. 3, it also enshrines one of the basic values of the democratic societies making up the Council of Europe. The object and purpose of the ECHR as an instrument for the protection of individual human beings also requires that Art. 2 be interpreted and applied so as to make its safeguards practical and effective (see, eg ECtHR, *McCann and Others v. United Kingdom,* 27 September 1995, Series A 324 para. 146–147; ECtHR, *Velikova v. Bulgaria*, 18 May 2000, RJD 2000-VI, para. 80; ECtHR, *Pretty v. United Kingdom*, 29 April 2002, RJD 2002-III, para. 37; and ECtHR, *Anguelova v. Bulgaria*, 13 June 2002, RJD 2002-IV, para. 110).

[11] For example, in the *McCann* case (*supra*, n. 10) the ECtHR found that the killings violated Art. 2 of the ECHR, and that it had not been necessary to use lethal force. The case concerned three Irish Republican Army terrorists killed by members of the British security forces in Gibraltar. The ECtHR found violation of Art. 2 stating that the identities of three members of the terrorist squad were known to the British authorities, and it would have been possible to arrest them as they entered Gibraltar and before there was any risk of them having prepared and placed a car bomb.

[12] See HRC General Comment 6, paras. 3–4.

where he or she may face capital punishment; the HRC now disallows such extraditions, at least in cases where the extraditing state has abolished the death penalty.[13]

1. Analysis of the Case Law on the Right to Life

(a) Jurisprudence of the European Court of Human Right (ECtHR)

While the ECtHR has developed significant case law on state obligations under the respective articles, the explicit link in its jurisprudence to 'minorities' is less established.[14] In the absence of a specific provision on the rights of persons belonging to national minorities and still awaiting the effect of the recent entry-into-force of Protocol 12 establishing a general, non-accessory right to non-discrimination as in Article 26 CCPR, the relevant case law is derived from the non-discrimination provision in Article 14 of the ECHR which, as an accessory right, needs to be read in conjunction with another Article of the ECHR.

In the 1998 case of *Kaya v. Turkey*,[15] the applicant, a Turkish national of Kurdish ethnicity, alleged the violation of Articles 2, 6 and 13 ECHR in conjunction with Article 14.[16] He claimed that his rights, and the rights of his deceased brother under Articles 2, 6 and 13 ECHR, had been violated in conjunction with Article 14 ECHR on grounds of their ethnic origin. The applicant submitted that the lives of his deceased brother, as well as those of the Kurdish civilian population in general in south-east Turkey, were protected to a lesser extent than the lives of persons of non-Kurdish origin. He argued that the Kurdish population was most adversely affected by military operations conducted in the region and that the security forces failed to take adequate measures to minimize risk to civilian lives. Furthermore, the attitude of the security forces was to treat the Kurdish civilian population as in some way involved with the PKK. No distinction was made between terrorists and ordinary civilians. Thus, although his deceased brother was dressed as a

[13] See HRC, *Judge v. Canada*, (Communication No. 829/1998), § 10.3.

[14] Cf. Geoff Gilbert, 'The Burgeoning Minority Rights Jurisprudence of the European Court of Human Rights', *Human Rights Quarterly* 24 (2002), 736–80. This authoritative and comprehensive account of developments is notably absent with references to the rights addressed in this chapter. See also Rainer Hofmann, 'Nationale Minderheiten und der Europäische Gerichtshof für Menschenrechte', in Jürgen Bröhmer et al. (eds.), *Internationale Gerichtsbarkeit und Menschenrechte. Festschrift für Georg Ress* (Heymann, Köln, 2005), 1011–26.

[15] ECtHR, *Kaya v. Turkey*, 19 February 1998, RJD 1998-I.

[16] Article 14 ECHR reads: 'The enjoyment of the rights and freedoms set forth in [the] Convention shall be secured without discrimination on any ground such as sex, race, colour, language, religion, political or other opinion, national or social origin, association with a national minority, property, birth or other status.'

typical villager, he was automatically presumed by the security forces and by the prosecutor to be a PKK terrorist. The Government did not address the allegation other than to deny the factual basis of the applicant's allegations under Article 2 ECHR and to assert the availability of remedies at the domestic level to redress his grievances. The European Commission on Human Rights had concluded that the evidence submitted to it did not substantiate the applicant's complaint under Article 14 ECHR in so far as this related to the breaches which it had found to be established. In its assessment, the Court agreed with the conclusion reached by the Commission, that the applicant had not produced evidence to establish a violation under this head of the complaint.

In the 1999 ECtHR case of *Çakici v. Turkey*, the applicant argued that his brother, a person of Kurdish ethnicity, had been taken into custody by the Turkish security forces and not been seen since.[17] The applicant brought a claim against Turkey under Articles 2, 3, 5, 13, 14 in conjunction with Article 2, and 18 ECHR. The ECtHR did find violations of Articles 2, 3 (in relation to his brother), 5, and 13 ECHR. However, the ECtHR did not find a violation of Article 14 in conjunction with Article 2 ECHR. The applicant had submitted that the disappearance of his brother illustrated the discriminatory policy pursued by the authorities against Kurds and the existence of an authorized practice, in violation of Articles 14 and 18 ECHR respectively.[18] However, the ECtHR did not, on the basis of the facts as established by the Commission, find a violation of these provisions.

In the 2001 case of *Denizci and Others v. Cyprus*, the ECtHR recalled that the first sentence of Article 2(1) ECHR enjoins the state not only to refrain from the intentional and unlawful taking of life, but also to take appropriate steps to safeguard the lives of those within its jurisdiction.[19] The state's obligation in this respect extends beyond its primary duty to secure the right to life by putting in place effective criminal-law provisions to deter the commission of offences against any person, backed up by law enforcement machinery for the prevention, suppression and sanctioning of breaches of such provisions.[20] However, such an obligation must be interpreted in a way which does not impose an impossible or disproportionate burden on the authorities. Where there is an allegation that the authorities have violated their positive obligation to protect the right to life with regard to their above-mentioned duty to prevent and

[17] ECtHR, *Çakici v. Turkey*, 08 July 1999, RJD 1999-IV.

[18] *Ibid.*, para. 115.

[19] ECtHR, *Denizci and Others v. Cyprus*, 23 May 2001, RJD 2001-V, para. 375.

[20] Here the Court referred to its judgment in the case *Osman v. United Kingdom*, 28 October 1998, RJD 1998-VIII, para. 115.

suppress offences against a person, it must be established that the authorities knew, or ought to have known at the time, of the existence of a real and immediate risk to the life of an identified individual from the criminal acts of a third party, and that they failed to take measures within the scope of their powers which, judged reasonably, might have been expected to avoid that risk.[21]

In the 2001 case of *Cyprus v. Turkey*, the ECtHR found a continuing violation of Article 2 ECHR on account of the failure of the Turkish authorities to conduct an effective investigation aimed at clarifying the whereabouts and fate of Greek-Cypriot missing persons who disappeared in life-threatening circumstances.[22] Concerning Article 14 (as well as Articles 3, 6, 8, 13, and 17) ECHR, the ECtHR observed that, at the merits stage of the proceedings before the Commission, the applicant government had submitted that the facts of the case disclosed violations of the above-mentioned Articles.[23] The Commission had concluded that these complaints were outside the scope of its admissibility decision and on that account could not be examined. Furthermore, the Court held that there had been no violation of Article 2 ECHR as a result of the Turkish Republic of northern Cyprus (TRNC) authorities' refusal to afford Greek Cypriots and Maronites living in Northern Cyprus access to medical care in another part of the island. It noted, however, that the Commission was unable to establish on the evidence that the TRNC authorities deliberately withheld medical treatment from the population concerned or adopted a practice of delaying the processing of requests of patients to receive medical treatment in the south. It observed that during the period under consideration medical visits were indeed hampered on account of restrictions imposed by the TRNC authorities on the movement of the populations concerned and that in certain cases delays did occur. However, it had not been established that the lives of any patients were put in danger on account of delay in individual cases. It also observed that neither the Greek-Cypriot nor Maronite populations had been prevented from availing themselves of medical services including hospitals in the north.[24]

[21] *Ibid.*, para. 116.

[22] ECtHR, *Cyprus v. Turkey*, 10 May 2001, RJD 2001-IV.

[23] *Ibid.*, para. 152.

[24] In his partly dissenting opinion, Judge Marcus-Helmon said that at a time when freedom of movement is regarded as essential, especially when it comes to obtaining optimal medical care, a denial of such freedom by the State amounts to a serious breach of its obligations towards those within its jurisdiction. He considered that this is something which may amount to a violation of the state's undertaking under Art. 2 of the Convention to protect everyone's right to life by law. In order for this 'fourth generation of human rights' to be taken into account so that human dignity is protected against possible abuse by scientific progress, he suggested the Court could issue a reminder that under Art. 2 of the ECHR the states undertook to protect everyone's right to life by law.

In the 2002 case of *Anguelova v. Bulgaria*, the ECtHR recalled that where an individual is taken into police custody in good health but later dies, it is incumbent on the State to provide a plausible explanation of the events leading to his death.[25] In this case, the ECtHR found that the behaviour of police officers between 3 a.m. and 5 a.m. on 29 January 1996, and the lack of any reaction by the authorities, constituted a violation of the state's obligation to protect the lives of persons in custody. However, the ECtHR found that it had not been established 'beyond reasonable doubt' that in the death of the seventeen-year-old Roma, Angel Zabchekov, as a consequence of the injuries inflicted on him by police officers, his ethnicity was 'a determining factor' with those police officers who killed him.[26] In this case the Court did find a violation of Articles 2, 3, 5 and 13, but did not find a violation of Article 14 ECHR. The applicant's mother had considered it 'striking that some of the police officers had been unable to refrain from referring to Mr Zabchekov as the Gypsy, even in their official statements'. She had further considered that the 'reference to her son's ethnic origin and the acts of the police and the investigation authorities had to be seen against the broader context of systematic racism and hostility which law-enforcement bodies in Bulgaria had repeatedly displayed with regard to Roma. This attitude had been widely documented by intergovernmental and human rights organizations.'[27] In light of this submission, the Court repeated that proof 'beyond reasonable doubt' may follow from the coexistence of sufficiently strong, clear and concordant inferences or of similar unrebutted presumptions of fact.[28] It also stated the need to assess all the relevant facts, including any inferences that may be drawn from the general information adduced by the applicant about the alleged existence of discriminatory attitudes.[29] It further recalled that in *Velikova v. Bulgaria* it had examined a very similar complaint, and had held in that judgment:

> [t]he Court observes that the applicant's complaint under Article 14 ECHR is grounded on a number of serious arguments. It also notes that the respondent State failed to

[25] Insofar the Court referred to its judgment in ECtHR, *Selmouni v. France* [GC], 28 July 1999, RJD 1999-V, para. 87.

[26] ECtHR, *Anguelova v. Bulgaria*, 13 June 2002, RJD 2002-IV.

[27] *Ibid.*, para.164.

[28] See *ibid.*, paras. 66 and 111, and the case law cited there: 'In assessing evidence, the Court adopts the standard of proof "beyond reasonable doubt" (see ECtHR, *Ireland v. United Kingdom*, Series A No 25, 64–5, § 161, 18 January 1978, Merits and Just Satisfaction). Where the events in issue lie wholly, or in large part, within the exclusive knowledge of the authorities, as in the case of persons within their control in custody, strong presumptions of fact will arise in respect of injuries and death occurring during that detention. Indeed, the burden of proof may be regarded as resting on the authorities to provide a satisfactory and convincing explanation.'

[29] *Ibid.*, para.167.

provide a plausible explanation as to the circumstances of Mr Tsonchev's death and as to the reasons why the investigation omitted certain fundamental and indispensable steps which could have shed light on the events . . . The Court recalls, however, that the standard of proof required under the Convention is 'proof beyond reasonable doubt'. The material before it does not enable the Court to conclude beyond reasonable doubt that Mr Tsonchev's killing and the lack of a meaningful investigation into it were motivated by racial prejudice, as claimed by the applicant.[30]

In his partly dissenting opinion in the judgment in the *Anguelova* case, Judge Bonello considered it 'particularly disturbing that the Court, in over fifty years of pertinacious judicial scrutiny, has not, to date, found one single instance of violation of the right to life (Article 2) or the right not to be subjected to torture or other degrading or inhuman treatment or punishment (Article 3) induced by the race, colour or place of origin of the victim'.[31] Judge Bonello continued to note that the Court's 'inability to establish a link between physical abuse and ethnicity comes notwithstanding that the red light about the special treatment of Roma by the Bulgarian police in breach of Articles 2 and 3 has been flashing insistently and alarmingly'. Judge Bonello also observed that 'frequently and regularly the Court acknowledges that members of vulnerable minorities are deprived of life or subjected to torture or other degrading or inhuman treatment or punishment in violation of Article 3; but not once has the Court found that this happens to be linked to their ethnicity. Kurds, coloureds, Islamics, Roma and others are again and again killed, tortured or maimed, but the Court is not persuaded that their race, colour, nationality or place of origin has anything to do with it.'[32] On a related note, a comparative overview in 2005 of racist violence and responses to it in 15 of the member states of the European Union noted that, traditionally, the criminal law in

[30] *Ibid.*, para. 94.; see ECtHR, *Velikova v. Bulgaria*, 18 May 2000, RJD 2000-VI.

[31] ECtHR, *Anguelova v. Bulgaria*, 13 June 2002, RJD 2002-IV, Partly Dissenting Opinion of Judge Bonello (2).

[32] Judge Bonello referred to the statement of the European Commission on Human Rights in the *East African Asians* case where it had stated that 'differential treatment of a group of persons on the basis of race might therefore be capable of constituting degrading treatment when different treatment on some other ground would raise no such question' – *East African Asians v. UK*, 3 EHRR 76 (15 December 1973). Judge Bonello also wrote that 'Leafing through the annals of the Court, an uninformed observer would be justified to conclude that, for over fifty years democratic Europe has been exempted from any suspicion of racism, intolerance or xenophobia. The Europe projected by the Court's case law is that of an exemplary haven of ethnic fraternity, in which peoples of the most diverse origin coalesce without distress, prejudice or recrimination. The present case energizes that delusion.' Judge Bonello makes reference to the judgments in the cases ECtHR, *Assenov and Others v. Bulgaria*, 28 October 1998, RJD 1998-VIII and ECtHR, *Velikova v. Bulgaria*, 18 May 2000, RJD 2000-VI.

most of the jurisdictions had not focused on the motivation behind acts of violence; this tradition is slowly changing as laws have begun to recognize crimes as 'racially motivated'.[33]

It was only in 2004, in the case of *Nachova and Others v. Bulgaria*, that the ECtHR (for the first time) found a violation of Article 14 of the ECHR in conjunction with Article 2, acknowledging that the violation was linked to the ethnicity of the victim. The case concerned Bulgarian nationals of Roma origin, who alleged that their relatives had been deprived of their lives in violation of Article 2 and the right to life of the ECHR, as a result of deficient law and practice which permitted the use of lethal force without absolute necessity. The Court noted that any use of force must be no more than 'absolutely necessary' for the achievement of one or more of the purposes set out in sub-paragraphs (a) to (c). The term 'absolutely necessary' indicates that a stricter and more compelling test of necessity must be employed than that normally applicable when determining whether State action is 'necessary in a democratic society' under paragraphs 2 of Articles 8 to 11 of the Convention. Consequently, the force used must be strictly proportionate to the achievement of the permitted aims. The Court considered that it can in no circumstances be 'absolutely necessary' to use such firearms to arrest a person suspected of a non-violent offence who is known not to pose a threat to life or limb, even where a failure to do so may result in the opportunity to arrest the fugitive being lost.[34]

[33] In April 2005 the European Monitoring Centre on Racism and Xenophobia published a comparative overview on racist violence and responses to it in fifteen of the Member States of the European Union. It noted, *inter alia*, that, traditionally, criminal law in most of the jurisdictions surveyed did not specifically refer to 'racist violence', the focus not being on the motivation behind acts of violence. However, that tradition was slowly changing as laws began to recognize crime as 'racially motivated'. In particular, racist motivation was increasingly being considered as an aggravating factor for sentencing purposes under the legislation of some Member States. The relevant legislation in the following countries specifically provided for that possibility: Austria, Belgium, Denmark, Finland, France, Italy, Portugal, Spain, Sweden and the United Kingdom. In particular, Article 132–76 of the French Penal Code, which was introduced in February 2003, provides in its second paragraph for an 'objective' definition of racism as an aggravating circumstance leading to an increase in sentence: 'The penalties incurred for a crime or major offence shall be increased where the offence is committed on account of the victim's actual or supposed membership or non-membership of a particular ethnic group, nation, race or religion'. See *Racist Violence in 15 EU Member States: A Comparative Overview of Findings from the RAXEN National Focal Points Reports 2001–2004*: http://eumc.europa.eu/eumc/material/pub/comparativestudy/CS-RV-05-SUM.pdf.

[34] ECtHR, *Nachova and Others v. Bulgaria*, (Appl. No. 43577/98 and 43579/98, 26 February 2004, final judgment 6 July 2005, Merits and just satisfaction), paras. 93–106. See below the following cases in which the use of firearms was found to have been justified. The cases concern situations where the state agents acted in the belief that there was a threat of violence or in order to apprehend fugitives suspected of violent offences: ECommHR, *W. v. Germany* (Appl. No. 11257/84, Commission decision of 6 October 1986, DR 49), p. 213; ECommHR, *Kelly v. United Kingdom* (Appl. No. 17579/90, Commission decision of 13 January 1993); ECommHR, *M.D. v. Turkey* (Appl. No.

The applicants also held that the authorities had failed to conduct an effective investigation into the deaths, in violation of Article 2 and Article 13 (effective remedy). The applicants alleged that prejudice and hostile attitudes towards persons of Roma origin had played a decisive role in the events leading up to the shootings, and the fact that no meaningful investigation was carried out, relying on Article 14 (prohibition of discrimination) in conjunction with Article 2 ECHR. The Court found a violation of Article 2 in regard of the deaths and the lack of an effective investigation, and it was also held that Article 14 had been violated in conjunction with Article 2 ECHR.

The path leading to this finding was the ECtHR's important decision to shift the burden of proof, as to the question whether discrimination had occurred, to the respondent party. The Chamber noted that in cases of deprivation of life Articles 2 and 14 ECHR combined imposed a duty on State authorities to conduct an effective investigation irrespective of the victim's racial or ethnic origin. It also considered that the authorities had the additional duty to take all reasonable steps to unmask any racist motive in an incident involving the use of force by law-enforcement agents. The ECtHR continued by saying:

> [c]onsidering that the particular evidentiary difficulties involved in proving discrimination called for a specific approach to the issue of proof, the Chamber held that in cases where the authorities had not pursued lines of inquiry that had been clearly warranted in their investigation into acts of violence by State agents and had disregarded evidence of possible discrimination, the Court might, when examining complaints under Article 14 of the Convention, draw negative inferences or shift the burden of proof to the respondent Government.[35]

Applied to the facts of the case under consideration, the Chamber 'considered that the conduct of the investigating authorities—which had omitted to refer to a number of disquieting facts such as the excessive nature of the force used by Major G. and the evidence that he had uttered a racist slur—warranted a shift of the burden of proof. It thus fell to the respondent Government to satisfy the Court, on the basis of additional evidence or a convincing explanation of the facts that the events complained of had not been shaped by discrimination on the part of State agents'. The Chamber concluded that '[a]s the Government had not offered a convincing explanation, and noting that there had been

28518/95, Commission decision of 30 June 1997, unreported); ECommHR, *Laginha de Matos v. Portugal* (Appl. No. 28955/95, Commission decision of 7 April 1997, DR 89), p. 98; see also ECtHR, *McCann and Others*, (*supra*, n. 10), paras. 146–50 and paras. 192–214; see also ECtHR, *Streletz, Kessler and Krenz v. Germany* [GC], 22 March 2001, paras. 87, 96 and 97, RJD 2001-II).

[35] *Ibid.*, paras. 128–130.

previous cases in which the Court had found that law enforcement officers in Bulgaria had subjected Roma to violence resulting in death, the Chamber concluded that there had also been a violation of the substantive aspect of Article 14 taken together with Article 2 of the Convention'.[36] However, in addressing the appeal, the Grand Chamber, departing from the Chamber's approach, did not consider that the alleged failure of the authorities to carry out an effective investigation into the alleged racist motive for the killing in this particular case should shift the burden of proof to the respondent government with regard to the alleged violation of Article 14 in conjunction with the substantive aspect of Article 2 of the ECHR. The Grand Chamber continued to assess the procedural obligation of the respondent state to investigate possible racist motives. The Grand Chamber established the 'additional duty' of public authorities to take all reasonable steps to unmask any racist motive, and to establish whether or not ethnic hatred or prejudice may have played a role in the events. It noted that: '[f]ailing to do so and treating racially induced violence and brutality on an equal footing with cases that have no racist overtones would be to turn a blind eye to the specific nature of acts that are particularly destructive of fundamental rights. A failure to make a distinction in the way in which situations that are essentially different are handled may constitute unjustified treatment irreconcilable with Article 14 of the Convention', with a *mutatis mutandis* reference made to the *Thlimmenos v. Greece* case establishing this important principle in the ECtHR's jurisprudence.[37] In sum, the Grand Chamber found that the authorities failed in their duty under Article 14 taken together with Article 2 to take all possible steps to investigate whether or not discrimination may have played a role in the events, and concluded that there had been a violation of Article 14 taken together with Article 2 in its procedural aspect.[38]

(b) African Commission on Human and Peoples' Rights (AfrCommHPR)

In the case *Amnesty International et al. v. Sudan* before the African Commission on Human and Peoples' Rights (AfrCommHPR), the Commission stated regarding the thousands of executions in Sudan that '[e]ven if these are not all the work of forces of the government, the government has a responsibility to protect all people residing under its jurisdiction'. Notwithstanding the

[36] *Ibid.*, para. 156.

[37] ECtHR, *Thlimmenos v. Greece*, 6 June 2000, RJD 2000-IV, para. 44.

[38] ECtHR, *Nachova and Others v. Bulgaria*, (Appl. Nos. 43577/98 and 43579/98, 26 February 2004, final judgment 6 July 2005, Merits and just satisfaction), para. 168.

ongoing turmoil and civil war, 'civilians in areas of strife are especially vulnerable and the state must take all possible measures to ensure that they are treated in accordance with international humanitarian law'.[39] The AfrCommHPR continued to note that the scope and depth of the investigations undertaken by the government 'fall short of what is required to prevent and punish extra-judicial executions'. It observed that the 1987 Commission of Enquiry, set up by the Governor of South Darfur, overlooked the possibility that police and security forces may be implicated in the very massacres they are charged to investigate, and that the commission, by its very composition, does not provide the required guarantees of impartiality and independence. In reiterating the AfrCommHPR's 'long-standing practice, in cases of human rights violations, the burden of proof rests on the government (See, AfrCommHPR/59/91, AfrCommHPR/60/91, AfrCommHPR/64/91, AfrCommHPR/87/93, AfrCommHPR/101/93)'. If the government provides no evidence contradicting an allegation of human rights violations made against it, the AfrCommHPR will take it as proven, or at the least probable or plausible. On the information available, the AfrCommHPR considered that there was a violation of Article 4 AfrCh.

In the case of *Organisation Mondiale Contre La Torture v. Rwanda*, the AfrCommHPR stated that the 'massacre of a large number of Rwandan villagers by the Rwandan armed forces and the many reported extra-judicial executions for reasons of their membership of a particular ethnic group is a violation of Article 4 AfrCH'.[40]

In the case of *The Social and Economic Rights Action Center for Economic and Social Rights v. Nigeria* before the AfrCommHPR, the complainants alleged that the Nigerian government had violated Article 4 of the Charter with regard to Ogoni community and land. The complainants argued that security forces and private actors (whether Government supported or not) were engaged in wide spread 'terrorisations and killings' of the Ogoni, and that the government was directly involved in threatening the survival of the Ogonis, also by means of pollution and environmental degradation affecting the community's lands and farms. The AfrCommHPR conducted a mission to Nigeria, and witnessed

[39] AfrCommHPR, *Amnesty International, Comité Loosli Bachelard, Lawyers Committee for Human Rights, Association of Members of the Episcopal Conference of East Africa v. Sudan*, (Comm. No. 48/90, 50/91, 52/91, 89/93, not dated), para. 50. Reference also to: AfrCommHPR7491: 93, *Union des Jeunes Avocats v. Chad*.

[40] AfrCommHPR, *Organisation Mondiale Contre La Torture v. Rwanda, (Comm. No. 27/89, 46/91,99/93,* at para. 24.

that the deplorable situation in the Ogoni land including environmental degradation is real.[41]

In the case of *Commission Nationale des Droits de l'Homme et des Libertés v. Chad*, the AfrCommHPR reiterated the effect of Article 1 AfrCh that if a state neglects to ensure the rights in the African Charter, this can constitute a violation, even if the state or its agents are not the immediate cause of the violation. In the case in question, 'Chad has failed to provide security and stability in the country, thereby allowing serious and massive violations of human rights. The national armed forces are participants in the civil war and there have been several instances in which the Government has failed to intervene to prevent the assassination and killing of specific individuals. Even where it cannot be proved that violations were committed by government agents, the government had a responsibility to secure the safety and the liberty of its citizens, and to conduct investigations into murders. Chad therefore is responsible for the violations of the African Charter.'[42]

B. Prohibition of Torture, Inhuman and Degrading Treatment and Punishment

International human rights law contains no more basic prohibition than the absolute, unconditional ban on torture, cruel, inhuman, or degrading treatment.[43] Even the right to life acknowledges some exceptions, such as the killing of combatants allowed in wartime. The universal rejection of torture has, however, not been able to prevent 'the persistent phenomenon of State arbitrariness from experiencing a dubious renaissance in the second half of the 20th century and the beginning of the twenty-first, a period by some characterized as the age of torture'.[44] This development is all the more disturbing because it presents a direct attack on the core of human dignity, and the fact

[41] AfrCommHPR, *The Social and Economic Rights Action Center for Economic and Social Rights v. Nigeria*, (Comm. No. 155/96, 6 June 2001).

[42] AfrCommHPR, *Commission Nationale des Droits de l'Homme et des Libertés v Chad* (Comm. No. 74/92, 10/95).

[43] Every act of torture is a crime under international law. If torture is committed in an armed conflict, it constitutes the war crime of torture. If torture is committed as part of a systematic or a widespread pattern of similar acts, then it constitutes the crime against humanity of torture. The Convention against Torture, for instance, prohibits torture as an independent crime, as a war crime, and as a crime against humanity, absolutely and in all circumstances. Furthermore, the Geneva Conventions prohibit the war crime of torture in both international wars and internal conflicts such as civil wars or rebellions. The Rome Statute of the International Criminal Court prohibits torture when it constitutes genocide, a crime against humanity or a war crime.

[44] Manfred Nowak, *supra*, n. 3, 158.

that torture is practised—often systematically—in all regions of the world.[45] This has pressed states to provide additional protection to the right to personal integrity by way of specialized conventions both at international and regional levels with specific instruments and mechanisms for monitoring implementation. In addition to the numerous treaty law provisions (listed below), the prohibition of torture has a special status in international law as it is part also of customary international law, which means it is binding on all states, whether or not they have ratified any of the international human rights treaties. The prohibition on torture is also a 'peremptory norm' (*jus cogens*) which means that it cannot be overruled by any other law or by local custom.

1. International Instruments and Standards

Freedom from subjection to torture and to cruel, inhuman or degrading treatment is provided in Article 5 UDHR which states '[n]o one shall be subjected to torture or to cruel, inhuman or degrading treatment or punishment'. The wording of Article 7 CCPR corresponds literally to the formulation of Article 5 UDHR and states '[n]o one shall be subjected to torture or to cruel, inhuman or degrading treatment or punishment. In particular, no one shall be subjected without his free consent to medical or scientific experimentation.' Further, the 1984 Convention against Torture and Other Cruel, Inhuman or Degrading treatment or Punishment (CAT) is aimed at the abolition of all forms of torture and other cruel, inhuman or degrading treatment, and led to the establishment of the treaty-monitoring Committee against Torture (CAT/C). In 1985, the UN Commission on Human Rights established a Special Rapporteur with a broad mandate to investigate allegations of torture in all countries of the world.[46] In 2002, the General Assembly adopted an Optional Protocol to CAT which establishes a system of regular and preventive visits to all places of detention (similar to the system applied since 1987 in Europe, see below).[47] Article 1 of the Optional Protocol states that 'the objective of the present protocol is to establish a system of regular visits undertaken by independent international and national bodies to places where people are

[45] *Ibid.*

[46] The current Special Rapporteur on the Freedom from Torture is Mr. Manfred Novak, Professor of International Law at Vienna University. For more information of the work of the Special Rapporteur, see http://www.ohchr.org/english/issues/torture/rapporteur/.

[47] On 9 December 1988, the United Nations General Assembly adopted the Body of Principles for the Protection of all Persons under Any Form of Detention or Imprisonment, and in December 1990 the Basic Principles for the Treatment of Prisoners (1990). In 1992 the UN General Assembly adopted Declaration on the Protection of All Persons from Enforced Disappearances.

deprived of their liberty, in order to prevent torture and other cruel, inhuman or degrading treatment or punishment'.

As concerns Europe, freedom from torture is guaranteed by the European Convention for the Prevention of Torture (ECPT) of June 1987, (based on Article 3 of the European Convention for the Protection of Human Rights and Fundamental Freedoms (ECHR) from 1950); Article 3 of the ECHR imposes an obligation upon states to prohibit torture, inhuman and degrading treatment or punishment. This obligation does not only encompass a duty to simply prohibit acts of torture or inhuman or degrading treatment or punishment; the ECtHR and the EcommHR have extended a positive duty incumbent upon states to protect individuals from these forms of abuses. The exact nature of a state's obligation to protect individuals against violations of this right has been examined extensively also in respect of expulsion and extradition cases. No state may extradite a person to a country where she or he might face torture. The European system of protecting individuals against torture is completed by the 1987 ECPT which—with its two Additional Protocols—provides for a preventive system of unannounced, confidential visits to prisons and other facilities by the European Committee for the Prevention of Torture.[48]

2. Distinctions between 'Torture', 'Inhuman Treatment', and 'Degrading Treatment'

In Article 1 CAT 'torture' is defined as 'any act by which severe pain or suffering, whether physical or mental, is intentionally inflicted on a person for such purposes as a) obtaining from him or a third person information or a confession, b) punishing him for an act he or a third person has committed or is suspected of having committed, or c) intimidating or coercing him or a third person, or for any other reason based on discrimination of any kind when such pain or suffering is inflicted by or at the instigation of or with the consent or acquiescence of a public official or other person acting in an official capacity'. Article 2 of this Convention states that: 'No exceptional circumstances whatsoever, whether a state of war or a threat of war, internal political instability or any other public emergency may be invoked as a justification of torture.' Article 3 contains an obligation incumbent upon states parties: 'No state shall expel, return ('*refouler*') or extradite a person to another state where there are

[48] Protocol No. 1 to the European Convention for the Prevention of Torture and Inhuman or Degrading Treatment or Punishment (1993), Protocol No. 2 to the European Convention for the Prevention of Torture and Inhuman or Degrading Treatment or Punishment.

substantial grounds for believing that he would be in danger of being subjected to torture.'

The ECHR (and other instruments) indicates the relationship between the three elements that are prohibited in Article 3 ECHR (and other instruments) namely, torture, inhuman treatment and degrading treatment. Torture and inhuman treatment are considered to be deliberate, inhuman treatment causing very serious and cruel suffering. Degrading treatment requires the presence of gross humiliation or being driven to act against will or conscience. In every case the determination of whether there has been torture, inhuman or degrading treatment must be decided in the light of all the circumstances, and the principle of proportionality of the case, taking into account all the factors relevant to such a determination as evidence in decisions of the ECtHR.[49] The assessment of seriousness will be relative. In different judgments, the ECtHR noted that ill-treatment must attain a minimum level of severity if it is to fall within the scope of Article 3 ECHR.[50] The assessment of this minimum is relative: it depends on all the circumstances of the case, such as the duration of the treatment, its physical and/or mental effects and, in some cases, the sex, age and state of health of the victim. The ECtHR considered also that burning, destruction of home and deprivation of shelter and support cause anguish and stress that are sufficiently severe to be categorized as inhuman treatment within the meaning of Article 3 ECHR.[51]

Degrading treatment is the weakest level of a violation of Article 3 ECHR. With regard to degrading treatment the circumstances and the principle of proportionality are pivotal points.[52] The defining feature of degrading treatment is the element of humiliation or debasement; the threshold of severity would appear to require that humiliation is 'gross'. In *Cyprus v. Turkey* the ECtHR found that Greek Cypriots living in the Karpas region of northern Cyprus had been subjected to discriminatory treatment which attained a level of severity which amounted to degrading treatment.[53] The European Commission of Human Rights had stated in 1973 that 'as generally recognised, a special importance should be attached to discrimination based on race; that publicly to single out a group of persons for differential treatment on

[49] Mark Kelly, 'Prohibition of torture and of inhuman and degrading treatment or punishment' in *European Convention on Human Rights*, 2nd edn, (New York, Oxford, 1996), 60–89.

[50] ECtHR, *Hasan Ilhan v. Turkey (*Appl. No 22494/93) 23 July 2004, Merits and Just Satisfaction).

[51] See *Selçuk and Asker v. Turkey,* 24 April 1998, RJD 1998-II, paras. 77–78.

[52] Manfred Nowak, *supra*, n. 3, 165.

[53] Mark Kelly, *supra*, n. 49, 60–89.

the basis of race might, in certain circumstances, constitute a special form of affront to human dignity; and that differential treatment of a group of persons on the basis of race might therefore be capable of constituting degrading treatment when different treatment on some other ground would raise no such question'.[54]

3. Positive Obligations of States

The right to be protected against torture, inhuman or degrading treatment or punishment has also been of considerable importance in cases of expulsion and extradition which often affect persons belonging to minority, 'new minority' and migrant communities. The major lines of this jurisprudence were first developed by the ECtHR in the *Soering* case in which the US demanded from the United Kingdom the extradition of Mr Soering, a German national who had previously resided in the US, on a charge of murder.[55] The applicant claimed that the United Kingdom would violate, *inter alia*, Article 3 ECHR, if it allowed the extradition to take place. Whilst the ECHR does not prohibit the imposition of the death penalty per se, nor does it consider it to be a form of torture, it was claimed that a violation would arise because the conditions on death row amounted to a breach of Article 3 ECHR. As regards the duty to protect individuals, the ECtHR held that the United Kingdom would violate Art 3 ECHR if Mr Soering were to be extradited because he would be exposed to a 'real risk' of being subjected to inhuman or degrading treatment. In other words, the finding of a violation was not attached to the receiving state for what it might do, but to the returning state for exposing the individual to the real risk of ill-treatment. Thus, a state owes individuals a duty to ensure that they are not going to be exposed to ill-treatment upon extradition or expulsion.

The reasoning in *Soering v. UK* has been revisited in subsequent cases, and an expansive jurisprudence on this issue has arisen. One of the most influential and much cited cases in this body of jurisprudence is *Cruz Varas and Others v. Sweden*.[56] This case involved the potential expulsion of two Chilean applicants for political asylum on the grounds that they had not invoked sufficiently strong political reasons to be considered refugees. The applicants claimed that if they were expelled to Chile, where they claimed to have been tortured previously, they faced a real risk of being tortured again. The Court held that it must be shown that there are 'substantial grounds' for believing

[54] Report on 31 Applications Lodged by East African Asians against the United Kingdom, *East African Asians v. UK*, 3 EHRR 76 (1973); see P. Thornberry, *supra*, n. 1, 303.

[55] ECtHR, *Soering v. United Kingdom*, 07 July 1989, Series A 161.

[56] ECtHR, *Cruz Varas and Others v. Sweden*, 20 March 1991, Series 201.

in the existence of a real risk of treatment contrary to Article 3 ECHR. The Court stated that this would be assessed primarily with reference to those facts which were known or ought to have been known at the time of the expulsion, although this would not preclude the Court from considering other information which comes to light subsequent to the expulsion. In this instance, the Court concluded that there were no substantial grounds for believing in the existence of a real risk. The yardstick for assessing the 'level of risk' was later upheld in the case of *Vilvarajah v. United Kingdom* where it was noted that: 'the Court's examination of the existence of a risk of ill-treatment . . . at the relevant time must necessarily be a rigorous one in view of the absolute character of this provision and the fact that it enshrines one of the fundamental values of democratic societies'.[57]

On a related and relevant theme, much debated is the practice of interrogation techniques and detention by states engaged in the 'war on terrorism', with attempts to circumvent or limit the application of existing standards. In this context, the landmark case of *Chahal v. United Kingdom* is of particular relevance. The applicant was to be expelled to India because he was suspected of being involved in acts of terrorism in India. Whilst the ECtHR stated that it was aware of the difficulties facing states in protecting communities against acts of terrorism, it confirmed, nevertheless, that Article 3 ECHR prohibits, in absolute terms, torture (and inhuman or degrading treatment or punishment) irrespective of the victim's conduct. Accordingly, national security interests could not override the interests of the individual where substantial grounds have been shown for believing that he would be subjected to ill-treatment if expelled.[58]

This also opens the critical question of state responsibility vis-à-vis non-state actors. Traditionally, the ECtHR (and the Commission) have confined themselves to considering allegations of risks emanating from the state's authorities. However, recently the Court has confirmed that the absolute nature of the prohibition, and the duty to protect individuals, can engage a state's responsibility even where the risk emanates from sources other than the state's authorities. One of the most notable cases to examine this issue was *H.L.R. v. France*. In this instance, H.L.R. was a Colombian national, who had been imprisoned for a drugs offence, and was the subject of an order for deportation from France back to Colombia. He claimed that if he were to be deported back to Colombia he would be exposed to acts of vengeance from drug traffickers who had recruited

[57] ECtHR, *Vilvarajah and Others v. United Kingdom*, 30 October 1991, Series A 215.

[58] ECtHR, *Chahal v. United Kingdom*, 15 November 1996, RJD 1996-V.

him. Therefore, it was claimed that France would be in violation of Article 3 ECHR by virtue of the positive obligations incumbent on states to protect individuals. Whilst the source of the risk of ill-treatment to H.L.R. emanated from private actors and not the state authorities themselves, the ECtHR nevertheless held that: '[o]wing to the absolute character of the right guaranteed, the Court does not rule out the possibility that Article 3 of the Convention may apply where danger emanates from persons or groups of persons who are not public officials.'[59]

There are also several cases which hold that a state's responsibility under Article 3 ECHR can be engaged by its failure to provide methods under which incidents of torture, inhuman and degrading treatment can be verified and protection against these violations can be ensured. These obligations apply regardless of whether the conduct in question is that of state agents or private persons. In *Aksoy v. Turkey*, the ECtHR said: Given the fundamental importance of the prohibition of torture and the especially vulnerable position of torture victims, Article 13 imposes, without prejudice to any other remedy available under the domestic system, an obligation on States to carry out a thorough and effective investigation of incidents of torture'.[60]

4. Analysis of the Case Law on the Prohibition of Torture

The jurisprudence on the prohibition of torture is limited when it comes to expressly addressing situations faced by persons belonging to 'minorities', although they are likely to be exposed in a disproportionate way to this practice when in detention in many countries.

(a) European Court of Human Rights (ECtHR)

In the 1997 case of *Çakici v. Turkey*,[61] the ECtHR noted that the evidence provided by Mr. Mustafa Engin, a person of Kurdish origin, to the delegates was judged to be reliable and credible. This witness was detained in the same room as Mr Ahmet Çakici for a period of 16–17 days and had the opportunity to see and talk to him. His evidence was that he saw bloodstains on Mr Çakici's

[59] ECtHR, *H.L.R. v. France*, 29 April 1997, RJD 1997-III; see also ECtHR, *Z and Others v. UK* (Appl. No. 35980/97, 07 May 2005, Merits and Just Satisfaction), a case of ill-treatment of four children by their parents, and *A v. UK* (54), the case about ill-treatment by his stepfather, where the the ECtHR considered 'that the obligation on High Contracting Parties under Art. 1 of the Convention to secure to everyone within their jurisdiction the rights and freedoms defined in the Convention, taken together with Art. 3, requires States to take measures designed to ensure that individuals within their jurisdiction are not subjected to torture or inhuman or degrading treatment or punishment, including such ill-treatment administrated by private persons.'

[60] *Aksoy v. Turkey*, 18 December 1996, RJD 1996-VI, para. 98.

[61] ECtHR, *Çakici v. Turkey* (*supra*, n. 17).

clothing, and that he was in a very poor physical condition. Mr Çakici told him that he had been beaten, that one of his ribs had been broken and his head split open. He was taken from the room in which they were held together and informed Mr Engin on his return that he had twice been given electric shocks, which treatment Mr Engin also stated that he received during interrogation. The Court shared the Commission's opinion that this evidence supports a finding to the required standard of proof, i.e. beyond reasonable doubt, that Mr Çakici was tortured during his detention. There had, consequently, been a violation of Article 3 of the ECHR in respect of the applicant's brother, Mr Ahmet Çakici. However, no reference to Article 14 ECHR was made.

In the case of *Assenov and Others v. Bulgaria*, the ECtHR observed that unlike most of the substantive clauses of the ECHR and of Protocols Nos. 1 and 4, Article 3 makes no provision for exception, and no derogation from it is permissible under Article 15 ECHR even in the event of a public emergency threatening the life of the nation.[62] In view of the lack of a thorough and effective investigation into the applicant's arguable claim that he had been beaten by police officers, the Court found that there had been a violation of Article 3 of the ECHR. However, again no reference was made to Article 14 ECHR.

5. Analysis of the Case Law on Inhuman and Degrading Treatment

(a) United Nations Committee against Torture (CAT/C)

In its decision of 21 November 2002, the CAT/C examined (under the Optional Protocol to this Convention) the communication of *Hajrizi Dzemajl and others against Yugoslavia* and found that a mob action by non-Roma residents of Danilovgrad, Montenegro, during which a Roma settlement was destroyed on 14 April 1995 in the presence of police officers, was 'committed with a significant level of racial motivation'. The burning and destruction of homes was held to constitute cruel, inhumane, and degrading treatment and, thus, a violation of Article 16(1) CAT. Two expert members of the CAT/C went further and stated that:

> the illegal incidents for which the Yugoslav state is responsible constitute 'torture' within the meaning of Article 1, paragraph 1, of the Convention, not merely 'cruel, inhuman or degrading treatment' as covered by Article 16. The failure of the state authorities to react to violent evictions, forced displacement and the destruction of homes and property by individuals amounts to unlawful acquiescence which, in our judgement, violates Article 1, paragraph 1 ... All the inhabitants who were violently displaced belong to the Romani ethnic group, which is known to be especially

[62] ECtHR, *Assenov and Others v. Bulgaria*, 28 October 1998, RJD 1998-VIII.

vulnerable in many parts of Europe. In view of this, states must afford them greater protection.[63]

(b) Committee on the Elimination of Racial Discrimination (CERD/C)

Concerning the protection offered on degrading treatment by the UN Committee on the Elimination of Racial Discrimination (CERD), CERD/C held in its decision in the 2000 complaint of *Anna Koptova v. Slovakia* that municipal regulation banning Roma in two Slovak villages violated Article 5(d)(i) CERD guaranteeing freedom of movement and residence. The applicant held that two resolutions may apply to her (as, indeed, to all Roma in Slovakia). The author was seeking to be able to be free to visit the two municipalities, Nagov and Rokytovce, for instance in order to further the work of her organization. However, she had not entered either municipality since the resolutions were adopted, in part because she feared that they could be enforced against her. The applicant believed that, by publicly and formally using the term 'Roma' to refer to certain unspecified persons and by singling out such persons for special and invidious treatment, the resolutions subjected her, as a person of Romany ethnicity, to degrading treatment.[64] The CERD/C, however, limited itself to find a violation of the freedom of movement.

(c) European Court of Human Rights (ECtHR)

Turning further to the opportunities offered by the EctHR, and specifically Article 14 in conjunction with Article 3 ECHR regarding situations of inhuman and degrading treatment facing persons belonging to minorities, the experience has been similar to the jurisprudence on other Articles of the ECHR: (i) the ECtHR has often not found it necessary to consider Article 14 in conjunction with another Article if a violation of a separate Article had already been established, and by (ii) not making explicit reference to ethnic belonging. For instance, in the case *Hasan Ilhan v. Turkey*, the ECtHR noted[65] that the burning of the applicant's home deprived him and his Kurdish family of shelter and support, and obliged them to leave the place where they and their friends had been living. Therefore, the ECtHR concluded that destruction of the applicant's home and possessions, as well as the anguish and distress suffered by members of his family, must have caused him suffering of sufficient

[63] CAT/C, *Hajrizi Dzemajl et al. v. Yugoslavia*, (2002), Complaint No. 161/2000: Yugoslavia, CAT, 29th Sess., online: Office of the High Commissioner for Human Rights. See http://www.hri.ca/fortherecordCanada/vol_app/appendix1.htm#ComTort.

[64] CERD/C, *Anna Koptova v. Slovak Republic*, (Communication No. 13/1998, UN Doc. CERD/C/57/D/13/1998 (2000)).

[65] ECtHR, *Hasan Ilhan v. Turkey* (*supra*, n. 50), para. 108.

severity for the acts of the security forces to be categorized as inhuman treatment within the meaning of Article 3 ECHR, without making any reference to ethnic belonging.

However, Article 3 ECHR has, interestingly, been found to hold a 'discriminatory' element in its own right. This became clear in the very pertinent case of *Cyprus v. Turkey*.[66] The applicant government alleged that, as a matter of practice, Greek Cypriots living in the Karpas area of northern Cyprus were subjected to discriminatory treatment amounting to inhuman and degrading treatment. The applicant government pleaded a violation of Article 3 since, in their view, treatment especially singling out categories of persons on racial and ethnic grounds, subjecting them to severe hardship, denying them or interfering with their Convention rights, and doing so specifically and publicly, amounted to conduct which was an affront to human dignity to the point of being inhuman treatment. The Commission did not accept the respondent government's argument that it was prevented from examining whether the totality of the measures impugned by the applicant government, including those in respect of which it found no breach of the Convention, provided proof of the pursuit of a policy of racial discrimination amounting to a breach of Article 3 ECHR.[67] Having regard to the fact that it found the Convention to be violated in several respects, the Commission noted that all the established interferences concerned exclusively Greek Cypriots living in northern Cyprus and were imposed on them for the very reason that they belonged to this class of persons. In the Commission's conclusion, the treatment complained of was clearly discriminatory against them on the basis of their 'ethnic origin, race and religion'. Regardless of recent improvements in their situation, the hardships to which the enclaved Greek Cypriots were subjected during the period under consideration still affected their daily lives, and attained a level of severity which constituted an affront to their human dignity. However, having found a violation within the meaning of Article 3 ECHR, the Commission considered it unnecessary to examine whether the discrimination at issue also constituted inhuman or degrading treatment within the meaning of Article 3 ECHR, having regard to its finding under Article 14 ECHR.

In its examination of the *Cyprus v. Turkey* case, the Court also recalled the *Abdulaziz, Cabales and Balkandali v. United Kingdom* judgment of 28 May 1985, where it had accepted the applicants' argument that, irrespective of the

[66] ECommHR, *Cyprus v. Turkey* (*supra*, n. 22), para. 305.

[67] The Commission had particular regard in this connection to its report under former Art. 31 in the *East African Asians v. United Kingdom* case adopted on 14 December 1973 (Decisions and Reports 78-A, p. 62).

relevance of Article 14, a complaint of discriminatory treatment could give rise to a separate issue under Article 3.[68] It concluded on the merits that the difference of treatment complained of in that case did not denote any contempt or lack of respect for the personality of the applicants and that it was not designed to, and did not, humiliate or debase them. The Court further recalled that the Commission, in its decision in the *East African Asians* case, had observed, with respect to an allegation of racial discrimination, that a special importance should be attached to discrimination based on race, and that publicly to single out a group of persons for differential treatment on the basis of race might, in certain circumstances, constitute a special affront to human dignity.[69] In the Commission's opinion, differential treatment of a group of persons on the basis of race might therefore be capable of constituting degrading treatment when differential treatment on some other ground would raise no such question. In the *Cyprus v. Turkey* case, the ECtHR went on to observe that the United Nations Secretary-General, in his progress report of 10 December 1995 on the 'Karpas Brief', had stated that the review carried out by United Nations Peacekeeping Force in Cyprus (UNFICYP) of the living conditions of the Karpas Greek Cypriots confirmed that they were the object of very severe restrictions which curtailed the exercise of basic freedoms and had the effect of ensuring that, inexorably, with the passage of time, the community would cease to exist. The ECtHR recalled that the matters raised by the United Nations Secretary-General in his progress report, from the perspective of the ECtHR's analysis, led it to conclude that there had been violations of the enclaved Greek Cypriots' Convention rights. For the ECtHR it was an inescapable conclusion that the interferences at issue were directed at the Karpas Greek-Cypriot community for the very reason that they belonged to this class of persons. The treatment to which they were subjected during the period under consideration could only be explained in terms of the features which distinguish them from the Turkish-Cypriot population, namely their ethnic origin, race and religion. In the Court's opinion, and with reference to the period under consideration, the discriminatory treatment attained a level of severity which amounted to degrading treatment; therefore, the ECtHR

[68] In the case of *Abdulaziz, Cabales and Balkandali v. United Kingdom*, 28 May 1985, Series A No. 94, paras. 90–92, the ECtHR stated that the difference of treatment complained of did not denote any contempt or lack of respect for the personality of the applicants and that it was not designed to, and did not, humiliate or debase but was intended solely to achieve the aims referred to, and could therefore not be regarded as 'degrading'.

[69] ECommHR, *East African Asians v. United Kingdom*, 14 December 1973 (Decisions and Reports 78-A), para. 207.

concluded that there had been a violation of Article 3 ECHR as concerns the situation of the Greek Cypriots living in the Karpas area of northern Cyprus.

However, the applicant government in *Cyprus v. Turkey* had stated that, notwithstanding the Commission's conclusion on their complaint under Article 3, the Court should give separate examination to the discriminatory measures imposed on, and exclusively on, Greek Cypriots living in northern Cyprus from the standpoint of compliance with Article 14 ECHR. The applicant government had submitted that, since the enclaved Greek Cypriots were victims of unreasonable and unjustified differences in treatment based on racial and religious grounds, the fundamental principle underlying Article 14 was violated as a matter of practice. They had contended that the elements of discrimination included the pattern of restrictions and pressures which constituted the policy of ethnic cleansing in the Karpas region; the respondent state's policy of demographic homogeneity; the continuing violations of Greek-Cypriots' property rights as a consequence of the systematic implantation of settlers; the restrictions on the movement of displaced Greek Cypriots as a facet of ethnic exclusiveness; the transfer of possession of the property of displaced Greek Cypriots forced to leave the Karpas region to Turkish settlers; and the continued deprivation of possessions of Greek Cypriots located within the Turkish-occupied area. The Commission, for its part, had not found it necessary, in view of its finding on the applicant government's Article 3 ECHR complaint, to consider the instant complaints also in the context of the respondent state's obligations under Article 14 ECHR, and the Court agreed with the Commission's conclusion. Having regard to the reasoning underpinning its own finding of a violation of Article 3 ECHR it considered that there was no need to pronounce separately on what is in reality a restatement of a complaint which is substantially addressed in that finding. The ECtHR concluded therefore that, in view of its finding under Article 3 ECHR, it was not necessary to examine whether during the period under consideration there has been a violation of Article 14 ECHR taken in conjunction with Article 3 in respect of Greek Cypriots living in northern Cyprus.

In the 2005 case *Bekos and Koutropoulos v. Greece*[70], the applicants, two Greek nationals belonging to the Roma ethnic group, complained that during their arrest and subsequent detention they were subjected to acts of police brutality which inflicted on them great physical and mental suffering amounting to torture, inhuman and/or degrading treatment or punishment. They also complained that the Greek investigative and prosecuting authorities had failed

[70] ECtHR, *Bekos and Koutropoulos v. Greece* (Application no. 15250/02, 13 December 2005).

to carry out a prompt and effective official investigation into the incident. They argued that there had been a breach of Article 3 ECHR and further held that the ill-treatment they had suffered, along with the subsequent lack of an effective investigation into the incident, were in part due to their Roma ethnic origin and alleged a violation of Article 14 ECHR. The applicants claimed that the nature of the incident itself, the racist language used by the police, and the continuous failure of the domestic authorities to sanction anti-Roma police brutality, clearly demonstrated a compelling case of racially motivated abuse and dereliction of responsibility. The ECtHR stated that the serious physical harm suffered by the applicants at the hands of the police, as well as the feelings of fear, anguish and inferiority which the impugned treatment had produced in them, must have caused the applicants suffering of sufficient severity for the acts of the police to be categorized as inhuman and degrading treatment within the meaning of Article 3 ECHR. The Court concluded that there had been a breach of Article 3 ECHR in this regard.

Continuing to assess the claim of a breach of Article 14 in conjunction with Article 3 ECHR, the ECtHR restated much of the reasoning of the above-mentioned *Nachova v. Bulgaria* case. It reiterated that it had not excluded the possibility that in certain cases of alleged discrimination, it may require the respondent government to disprove an arguable allegation of discrimination and—if they fail to do so—find a violation of Article 14 ECHR on that basis. However, where it is alleged—as in the present case—that a violent act was motivated by racial prejudice, such an approach would amount to requiring the respondent government to prove the absence of a particular subjective attitude on the part of the person concerned. While in the legal systems of many countries proof of the discriminatory effect of a policy or decision will dispense with the need to prove intent in respect of alleged discrimination in employment or the provision of services, that approach is difficult to transpose to a case where it is alleged that an act of violence was racially motivated.[71] Therefore, turning to the facts of the present case, the ECtHR considered that whilst the police officers' conduct during the applicants' detention calls for serious criticism, that behaviour was of itself an insufficient basis for concluding that the treatment inflicted on the applicants by the police was racially motivated. In all, the ECtHR did not consider that the failure of the authorities to carry out an effective investigation into the alleged racist motive for the incident should shift the burden of proof to the respondent government with regard to the alleged violation of Article 14 in conjunction with the

[71] ECtHR, *Nachova and Others v. Bulgaria*, *supra*, n. 34, para. 157.

substantive aspect of Article 3 ECHR. The ECtHR did not consider that it had been established beyond reasonable doubt that racist attitudes played a role in the applicants' treatment by the police. Therefore, it found that there had been no violation of Article 14 ECHR taken together with Article 3 in its substantive aspect.

However, the ECtHR considered that the question of the authorities' compliance with their procedural obligation, namely whether the respondent state had complied with its obligation to investigate possible racist motives, was a separate issue. It held that the Greek authorities had violated Article 3 ECHR in that they had failed duly to investigate the existence of a possible link between racist attitudes and an act of violence as an important aspect of their procedural obligations arising under Article 3 ECHR, namely to conduct an effective investigation. It might also be seen as implicit in their responsibilities under Article 14 ECHR to secure the fundamental value enshrined in Article 3 without discrimination. Owing to the interplay of the two provisions, issues such as those in the present case might fall to be examined under one of the two provisions only, with no separate issue arising under the other, or might require examination under both Articles. This was a question to be decided in each case on its facts and depending on the nature of the allegations made.[72] The Court was informed in its assessment by a joint open letter of the applicants and Greek Helsinki Monitor and the Greek Minority Rights Group protesting about the ill-treatment of the applicants, which they qualified as police brutality against Roma by the Greek police, and referring to some 30 oral testimonies concerning similar incidents of ill-treatment of members of the Roma community. The letter concluded by urging that precise and detailed instructions should be given to all police stations in the country regarding the treatment of Roma by the police. The ECtHR considered that these statements, when combined with the reports of international organisations on alleged discrimination by the police in Greece against Roma and similar groups, including physical abuse and the excessive use of force, called for verification. In its view, where evidence comes to light of racist verbal abuse being uttered by law enforcement agents in connection with the alleged ill-treatment of detained persons from an ethnic or other minority, a thorough examination of all the facts should be undertaken in order to discover any possible racial motives.[73] In the present case, despite the plausible information available to the authorities that the alleged assaults had

[72] See *mutatis mutandis*, ECtHR, *Nachova and Others v. Bulgaria, ibid.*, para. 161.

[73] See, *mutatis mutandis*, ECtHR, *Nachova and Others v. Bulgaria, ibid.*, para. 164.

been racially motivated, there was no evidence that they carried out any examination into this question. In particular, nothing was done to verify the statements of the first applicant that they had been racially verbally abused or the other statements referred to in the open letter alleging similar ill-treatment of Roma; nor do any inquiries appear to have been made as to whether the police officer accused of such acts had previously been involved in similar incidents or whether he had ever been accused in the past of displaying anti-Roma sentiment; nor, further, did any investigation appear to have been conducted into how the other officers of the Mesolonghi police station were carrying out their duties when dealing with ethnic minority groups. Moreover, the Court noted that, even though the Greek Helsinki Monitor gave evidence before the trial court in the applicants' case, and that the possible racial motives for the incident could not therefore have escaped the attention of the court, no specific regard appears to have been paid to this aspect, the court treating the case in the same way as one which had no racial overtones. In all, the ECtHR found that the Greek authorities had failed in their duty under Article 14 ECHR taken together with Article 3 to take all possible steps to investigate whether or not discrimination might have played a role in the events. It follows that there had been a violation of Article 14 ECHR taken together with Article 3 in its procedural aspect.

(d) African Commission for Human and Peoples' Rights (AfrCommHPR)

Also to note is the existence of pertinent jurisprudence from the case law of the AfrCommHPR, for example in the case of *International Pen, Constitutional Rights Project, Interights on behalf of Ken Saro-Wiwa Jr. and Civil Liberties Organisation v. Nigeria*,[74] where it is reiterated that Article 5 AfrCh prohibits not only torture, but also cruel, inhuman or degrading treatment. This includes not only actions which cause serious physical or psychological suffering, but which humiliate the individual or force him or her to act against his will or conscience. In communication 154/96 it had been alleged that the actual reason for the trial, and the ultimate death sentences, was the peaceful expression of views by the accused persons. The victims in the case were disseminating information and opinions on the rights of the people who live in the oil producing area of Ogoniland, through an organization, Movement for the Survival of Ogoni People (MOSOP) and specifically a rally. These allegations were not contradicted by the government, which had already been shown to be highly

[74] Decision of 31 October 1998 on Communications No 137/94, 139/94, 154/96 and 161/97.

prejudiced against MOSOP, without giving concrete justifications. MOSOP was founded specifically for the expression of views of the people who live in the oil producing areas, and the rally was organized with this in view. The government's actions were found to be inconsistent with Art. 9(2) AfrCh implicit when it violated Arts. 10(1) and 11 AfrCh.

III. Due Process and the Administration of Justice

Procedural justice is an umbrella term for the administration of justice and legal proceedings in a procedurally fair and transparent manner, and encompasses the related terms due process, fundamental justice, procedural fairness and natural justice, as defined in different jurisdictions. 'Procedural justice' concerns the fairness of the processes by which decisions are made, and may be contrasted with the 'distributive justice' (fairness in the distribution of rights or resources), and 'corrective justice' (fairness in the rectification of wrongdoings). Some theories of procedural justice hold that fair procedure leads to equitable outcomes, even if the requirements of distributive or corrective justice are not met. The term is also synonymous with hearing all parties before a decision is made. The most relevant standards in this regard include Articles 2(3)(a), 14 and 26 CCPR, Articles 6, 13 and 14 ECHR, Articles 8 and 25 ACHR and Article 7 AfrCh.

A. Effective Remedy and Investigation

Everyone whose rights and freedoms as set forth in this Convention are violated shall have an effective remedy before a national authority notwithstanding that the violation has been committed by persons acting in an official capacity.

ECHR, Article 13

Article 13 ECHR provides the right to an effective remedy, similar to that of Article 2(3)(a) CCPR. Article 13 ECHR guarantees the availability at national level of a remedy to enforce the substance of the Convention rights and freedoms in whatever form they might happen to be secured in the domestic legal order. The effect of Article 13 ECHR is thus to require the provision of a domestic remedy to deal with the substance of an 'arguable complaint' under the Convention and to grant appropriate relief, although contracting states are afforded some discretion as to the manner in which they conform to their Convention obligations under this provision. The scope of the obligation under Article 13 ECHR varies depending on the nature of the applicant's complaint under the Convention. Nevertheless, the remedy required by Article 13 ECHR must be 'effective' in practice as well as in law.[75]

1. Jurisprudence of the UN Treaty-monitoring Bodies

In *Rodríguez v. Uruguay*,[76] the HRC rejected the state party's argument that it had no obligation to investigate violations of Covenant rights by a prior régime, especially when these include crimes as serious as torture. Article 2(3)(a) CCPR clearly stipulates that each state party undertakes 'to ensure that any person whose rights or freedoms as herein recognized are violated shall have an effective remedy, notwithstanding that the violation has been committed by persons acting in an official capacity'. The HRC noted that 'amnesties are generally incompatible with the duty of states to investigate such acts; to guarantee freedom from such acts within their jurisdiction; and to ensure that they do not occur in the future'. States may not deprive individuals of the right to an effective remedy, including compensation and such full rehabilitation as may be possible. 'The State party has suggested that the author may still conduct private investigations into his torture. The Committee finds that the responsibility for investigations falls under the State party's obligation to grant an effective remedy. Having examined the specific circumstances of this case, the Committee finds that the author has not had an effective remedy.'

The CERD/C has issued several opinions relevant to the issue of effective remedy under Article 5(f) CERD. In *Kashif Ahmad v. Denmark*, the CERD/C recommended to the state party to ensure that the police and the public prosecutors properly investigate accusations and complaints related to acts of racial discrimination which should be punishable by law according to Article 4 CERD.[77] In *M. B. v. Denmark*, the specific circumstances in this case meant that the police could not accomplish a complete and in-depth investigation of the case. Therefore, the Committee had no elements at its disposal which would allow it to conclude that a violation by the state party of the provisions of the Convention had indeed taken place. However, the CERD/C emphasized the importance it attaches to the duty of the state party and, for that matter, of all states parties, to remain vigilant, in particular by prompt and effective police investigations of complaints, that the right is enjoyed without

[75] See, *inter alia*, ECtHR, *Anguelova v. Bulgaria*, *supra*, n. 26, para. 161.

[76] HRC, *Hugo Rodriguez v Uruguay* (Comm. No. 322/1988), §§ 12–14.

[77] CERD/C, *Ahmad v. Denmark* (Communication No 16/1999, Opinion adopted on 13 March 2000).

discrimination by all persons, nationals or foreigners, under the jurisdiction of the state party.[78]

In the case of *Yilmaz Dogan v. Netherlands*, the Committee examined whether Articles 4 and 6 CERD impose on states parties an obligation to initiate criminal proceedings in cases of alleged racial discrimination and to provide for an appeal mechanism in cases of such discrimination. The CERD/C observed that the freedom to prosecute criminal offences, commonly known as the expediency principle, is governed by considerations of public policy and noted that the Convention cannot be interpreted as challenging the *raison d'être* of that principle. Notwithstanding, it should be applied in each case of alleged racial discrimination, in the light of the guarantees laid down in the Convention. As to the case, it concluded that the prosecutor acted in accordance with these criteria. Furthermore, the state party had shown that the application of the expediency principle is subject to, and has indeed in the present case been subjected to, judicial review, since a decision not to prosecute may be, and was in this case reviewed by the Court of Appeal, pursuant to Article 12 of the Netherlands Code of Criminal Procedure. In the Committee's opinion, this mechanism of judicial review is compatible with Article 4 CERD; contrary to the petitioner's affirmation, it does not render meaningless the protection afforded by the applicable sections of the Netherlands Penal Code. Concerning the petitioner's inability to have the Sub-district Court's decision pronouncing the termination of her employment contract reviewed by a higher tribunal, the CERD/C observed that the terms of Article 6 CERD do not impose upon states parties the duty to institute a mechanism of sequential remedies, up to and including the Supreme Court level, in cases of alleged racial discrimination.[79]

In the case of *Ziad Ben Ahmed Habassi v. Denmark*, the CERD/C found that it is appropriate to initiate a proper investigation into the real reasons behind a bank's loan policy vis-à-vis foreign residents, in order to ascertain whether or not criteria involving racial discrimination, within the meaning of Article 1 CERD, are being applied. It noted that the author of the petition, considering the incident an offence under the Danish Act against Discrimination, had reported it to the police. First the police and subsequently the State Prosecutor in Viborg had accepted the explanations provided by a representative of the bank and decided not to investigate the case further. In the Committee's

[78] CERD/C, *M.B. v. Denmark* (Communication No. 20/2000, Opinion adopted on 13 March 2002).

[79] CERD/C, *Dogan v. Netherlands* (Communication No. 1/1984, Opinion adopted on 10 August 1988).

opinion, however, the steps taken by the police and the State Prosecutor were insufficient to determine whether or not an act of racial discrimination had taken place. It further recommended that the State party provide the applicant with reparation or satisfaction commensurate with any damage he has suffered.[80] In the case of *B.J. v. Denmark*, it considered that the conviction and punishment of the perpetrator of a criminal act, and the order to pay economic compensation to the victim, are legal sanctions with different functions and purposes. The victim is not necessarily entitled to compensation in addition to the criminal sanction of the perpetrator under all circumstances. However, in accordance with Article 6 CERD, the CERD/C stressed that the victim's claim for compensation had to be considered in every case, including those cases where no bodily harm had been inflicted, but where the victim had suffered humiliation, defamation or other attack against his/her reputation and self-esteem. Being refused access to a place of service intended for the use of the general public solely on the ground of a person's national or ethnic background is a humiliating experience which, in the opinion of the Committee, may merit economic compensation and cannot always be adequately repaired or satisfied by merely imposing a criminal sanction on the perpetrator. While the CERD/C considered that the facts described in the present communication disclose no violation of Article 6 CERD by the state party, it recommended that the state party take the measures necessary to ensure that the victims of racial discrimination seeking just and adequate reparation or satisfaction in accordance with Article 6 CERD including economic compensation, will have their claims considered with due respect for situations where the discrimination has not resulted in any physical damage but humiliation or similar suffering.[81]

In the case of *Miroslav Lacko v. Slovakia*, counsel claimed that the petitioner was denied equality before the law in that he and his Romany companion suffered discrimination in access to service in the restaurant, on grounds of race and/or ethnicity. The counsel claimed that by being refused service in the restaurant, and told to leave solely for racial reasons, and then being told that only 'polite' Roma would be admitted, the petitioner was subjected to policies of racial segregation. Counsel considered that the state party's failure to provide any remedies, and the absence of any legal norm expressly prohibiting non-discrimination in access to public accommodations, constitute

80 CERD/C, *Habassi v. Denmark* (Communication No. 10/1997, Opinion adopted on 17 March 1999).

81 CERD/C, *B.J. v. Denmark* (Communication No. 17/1999, Opinion adopted on 17 March 2000).

failure to comply with its obligation under Article 3 CERD. The CERD/C recommended to the state party that it complete its legislation in order to guarantee the right of access to public places in conformity with Article 5(f) CERD, and to condemn the refusal of access to such places for reason of racial discrimination. It also recommended the state party to take the necessary measures to ensure that the procedure for the investigation of violations is not unduly prolonged.[82]

The case of *C.P. v. Denmark* concerned the issue of exhaustion of domestic remedies concerning the petitioner's claim of having been unlawfully dismissed by the Technical School of Roskilde. The author of the petition affirmed that he did convey to his lawyer in time that he wanted to appeal this judgment, and he blamed the lawyer for having acted negligently by failing to file the appeal within statutory deadlines. The CERD/C noted that the file before it revealed that the author's lawyer was privately retained. In such circumstances, this lawyer's inaction or negligence cannot be attributed to the state party. Although the state party's judicial authorities did provide the author with relevant information on how to file his appeal in a timely manner, it was questionable whether, given the fact that the author alleged to have been the victim of racial harassment, the authorities had really exhausted all means to ensure that the author could enjoy effectively his rights in accordance with Article 6 CERD. However, since the author did not provide prima facie evidence that the judicial authorities were tainted by racially discriminatory considerations, and since it was the author's own responsibility to pursue the domestic remedies, the Committee concluded that the requirements of a violation of Article 14(7)(a) CERD were not met.[83]

In the case of *Kamal Quereshi v. Denmark*, the CERD/C noted that this case was to be distinguished from previous cases where, on the facts, it had on occasion considered that an investigation into the alleged acts of racial discrimination that had taken place had been insufficient for the purposes of Article 6 CERD.[84] In each of these previous cases, in fact, the investigation had been in respect of the individual(s) directly committing the alleged act of racial discrimination, rather than a third party, with the result that no person had been held criminally responsible for the acts in question. In the present case, on the other hand, criminal complaints had been lodged against those

82 CERD/C, *Miroslav Lacko v. Slovakia* (Communication No. 11 /1998, Opinion adopted on 09 August 2000).

83 CERD/C, *C.P. v. Denmark*

84 See, for example, *Ahmad v. Denmark* (*supra*, n. 77), and *Habassi v. Denmark* (*supra*, n. 80).

directly responsible. Therefore, it could not be considered that there was no effective action taken in response to the acts in question. As to the review of the decisions not to prosecute in the present case, the CERD/C referred to its jurisprudence that 'the terms of article 6 do not impose upon States parties the duty to institute a mechanism of sequential remedies' in cases of alleged racial discrimination.[85] Accordingly, even if Article 6 CERD might be interpreted to require the possibility of judicial review of a decision not to bring a criminal prosecution in a particular case alleging racial discrimination, the CERD/C referred to the state party's statement that it is open, under national law, judicially to challenge a prosecutor's decision.[86]

In the case of *Ahmad Najaati Sadic v. Denmark*, the petitioner brought a complaint against his former employer alleging racial discrimination. The petitioner had made criminal charges, which had not been pursued, and questioned the effectiveness of remedies sought under defamatory statements. The CERD/C observed that the notion of 'effective remedy', within the meaning of Article 6 CERD, was not limited to criminal proceedings based on provisions which specifically, expressly and exclusively penalize acts of racial discrimination. In particular, it did not consider it contrary to Articles 2(1)(d) and 6 CERD if the provisions of criminal law specifically adopted to outlaw acts of racial discrimination are supplemented by a general provision criminalizing defamatory statements and being applicable to racist statements, even if they are not covered by specific legislation. The Committee therefore noted that it did not appear that the Danish authorities' decision to discontinue proceedings on the ground of lack of evidence as to whether the employer's statements were made publicly or with the intention of wider dissemination had prejudiced a request by the petitioner to institute criminal proceedings under the applicable provisions of the Danish Criminal Code. The CERD/C therefore considered that the institution of such proceedings can be regarded as an effective remedy which the petitioner failed to exhaust. As to the question of damages, it recalled the state party's argument that the petitioner did not institute civil proceedings against his former employer, and therefore did not exhaust domestic remedies. With regard to the petitioner's arguments that a previous decision of a Danish Appellate Court had held that an incident of racial discrimination did not in itself constitute a violation of the honour and reputation of a person, the CERD/C considered that mere doubts about the effectiveness of

[85] CERD/C, *Dogan v. Netherlands* (*supra*, n. 79), at 9.4 (finding no violation of Art. 6 CERD).
[86] CERD/C, *Qureshi v. Denmark* (Communication No. 27/2002, adopted on 19 August 2003).

available civil remedies do not absolve a petitioner from pursuing them.[87] However, the Committee invited the state party to reconsider its legislation, since the restrictive condition of 'broad publicity' or 'wider dissemination' required by the pertinent provision of the Danish Criminal Code for the criminalization of racial insults did not appear to be fully in conformity with the requirements of Articles 4 and 6 CERD.[88]

2. *Jurisprudence of the European Court of Human Rights*

In the case of *Abdulaziz, Cabales and Balkandali v. United Kingdom,*[89] the Court found that the discrimination on the ground of sex of which the applicants were victims was the result of norms that were in this respect incompatible with the Convention. In this regard, since the United Kingdom has not incorporated the Convention into its domestic law, there could be no 'effective remedy' as required by Article 13 ECHR.[90]

In the case of *Al-Nashif v. Bulgaria,*[91] the Court noted that the 'effectiveness' of a 'remedy' within the meaning of Article 13 ECHR does not depend on the certainty of a favourable outcome for the applicant. Nor does the 'authority' referred to in that provision necessarily have to be a judicial 'authority'.[92] It further stated that where national security considerations are involved certain limitations on the type of remedies available to the individual may be justified. As regards secret surveillance and the use of secret information for screening job candidates who would have access to sensitive information, Article 13 ECHR requires a remedy 'as effective as it can be' having regard to the fact that it is inherent in any system of secret surveillance or secret checks that there would be a restricted scope for recourse.[93]

In the above mentioned case *Anguelova v. Bulgaria*[94] it is reiterated that in cases of suspicious deaths, given the fundamental importance of the right to

[87] CERD/C, See *Mostafa v. Denmark* (Communication 19/2000, Decision adopted on 10 August 2001), para. 7.4.

[88] CERD/C, *Sadic v. Denmark* (Communication No. 25/2002, Decision adopted on March 2003), para 6.2–6.8.

[89] ECtHR, *Abdulaziz, Cabales and Balkandali v. United Kingdom*, 28 May 1985, Series A No. 94.

[90] See also the *Silver and Others v. United Kingdom* judgment of 25 March 1983, Series A No. 61, paras. 111–119; and the *Campbell and Fell v. United Kingdom* judgment of 28 June 1984, Series A No. 80, para. 127.

[91] ECtHR, *Al-Nashif v. Bulgaria* (Appl. No 50963/96, 20.06.2002).

[92] Here the ECtHR referred to its judgments in, *inter alia*, *Kudla v. Poland* [GC], 26.10.2000, RJD 2000-XI, para. 152, and in *T.P. and K.M. v. United Kingdom* [GC], 10.05.2001, 2001-V, para. 107.

[93] Here the ECtHR referred to its judgments in *Klass and Others v. Germany*, judgment of 6 September 1978, Series A No. 28, para. 69, and in *Leander v. Sweden*, judgment of 26 March 1987, Series A No. 116, para. 78.

[94] ECtHR, *Anguelova v. Bulgaria* (*supra*, n. 26).

the protection of life, Article 13 ECHR requires, in addition to the payment of compensation where appropriate, a thorough and effective investigation capable of leading to the identification and punishment of those responsible for the deprivation of life, including effective access for the complainant to the investigation procedure.[95] Also, in the mentioned case *Assenov and Others v. Bulgaria,*[96] where an individual had an arguable claim that he had been ill-treated in breach of Article 3 ECHR, the notion of an effective remedy entails, in addition to a thorough and effective investigation of the kind also required by Article 3, effective access for the complainant to the investigatory procedure, and the payment of compensation where appropriate. The ECtHR referred to its findings that the applicant had an arguable claim that he had been ill-treated by agents of the State, and that the domestic investigation of this claim was not sufficiently thorough and effective.

In the case of *Çakici v. Turkey,*[97] the ECtHR reiterated that, given the fundamental importance of the rights in issue, the right to protection of life and freedom from torture and ill-treatment, Article 13 ECHR imposes, without prejudice to any other remedy available under the domestic system, an obligation on states to carry out a thorough and effective investigation apt to lead to those responsible being identified and punished, and in which the complainant has effective access to the investigation proceedings. The ECtHR found in the instant case that the authorities had an obligation to carry out an effective investigation into the disappearance of the applicant's brother. It also found that Turkey had failed to comply with this obligation, which failure undermined the effectiveness of any other remedies which might have existed.

In the above mentioned case of *Cyprus v. Turkey,*[98] the applicant government had requested the ECtHR to rule that the respondent state, as a matter of law and practice, had violated Article 13 ECHR by reason of its failure to provide an effective remedy before a national authority to the Gypsy community and political opponents of Turkey's policy in Cyprus. The ECtHR considered that the applicant government had not succeeded in refuting the respondent government's submissions in the proceedings before the Commission that remedies were available to aggrieved individuals within the TRNC legal system. The evidence before the ECtHR in this connection could not be said to prove beyond reasonable doubt the existence of any such practice, and the

[95] Here the ECtHR referred to its judgments in, *inter alia*, *Kaya v. Turkey* (*supra*, n. 15), para.107; and in *Velikova v. Bulgaria* (*supra*, n. 30), para. 89.

[96] ECtHR, *Assenov and Others v. Bulgaria* (*supra*, n. 62).

[97] ECtHR, *Çakici v. Turkey* (*supra*, n. 17).

[98] ECtHR, *Cyprus v. Turkey* (*supra*, n. 22).

ECtHR concluded accordingly that no violation of Article 13 ECHR had been established by reason of a failure as a matter of administrative practice to secure effective remedies to Turkish Cypriots living in northern Cyprus.

In his partly dissenting opinion Judge Costa noted, as regards the Turkish Cypriots of Gypsy origin, that the Court merely relied on the fact that the victims did not exercise any remedies before the local courts. He continued to state that surely a distinction should be drawn between the infringement of the victims' rights and freedoms, which is undisputed, and the fact that, rightly or wrongly, the victims did not believe an action in the courts feasible or effective. He asked further whether their failure to bring an action should be equated to a lack of evidence of an administrative practice, something which is in any event very difficult to prove and had been only rarely accepted as substantiated in the Court's decisions.

In her partly dissenting opinion Judge Palm (joined by Judges Jungwiert, Levits, Pantîru, Kovler and Marcus-Helmons) stressed that the Court had found that this population is the victim of discriminatory and degrading treatment based on ethnic origin, race and religion and that its members are compelled to live 'isolated, restricted in their movements, controlled and with no prospect of renewing or developing their community'. She continued by stating that, when one stands away from the legal detail supporting these conclusions, the Court accepts the general picture of a dwindling and aged community that has been subjected to a substantial reduction of the Convention rights of its members under a policy of ethnic separation. She questioned whether in such a context, it is realistic to say that the members of this community have access to the courts in respect of their civil claims, and whether it is a credible proposition that there exists a haven of juridical relief ready and able to defend the rights of this beleaguered population notwithstanding the existence of an official policy of containment and oppression. Judge Palm also noted that experience and common sense teach that the courts are generally powerless in such a situation. She continued by stating that it must also be borne in mind that the inhabitants during the period under consideration were not permitted to travel more than three miles from their homes—a fact which is hardly conducive to a desire to have recourse to the courts to settle disputes. It is thus a perfectly natural and predictable state of affairs that this population makes no real use of the court system. Judge Palm considers, therefore, that the Court ought to have found a violation of this provision as an inevitable consequence of its general appraisal of the plight of this community, and left open all issues concerning the legal system of the TRNC. Furthermore, with regard to the complaints concerning Turkish-Cypriot political opponents and 'gypsies',

Judge Palm noted that under the Convention authorities are strictly liable for the conduct of their subordinates, and they are under a duty to impose their will on subordinates, and cannot shelter behind their inability to ensure that it is respected. When the Court accepted the Commission's conclusions that the facts did not support the claims of such a general and widespread interference with the rights of the members of these groups, it could not be said that the first limb of one of the constituent elements of administrative practice—namely a repetition of acts—was present. Having reached this conclusion, Judge Palm argues it is unnecessary to go further and decide that members of these groups did not have recourse to remedies as the Court had done. Furthermore, considering the political situation obtaining in the TRNC, Judge Palm declared herself 'not at all convinced' that the court system is capable of affording or would be permitted to afford remedies to political dissidents who call into question the policy of ethnic separation on which the entity is constructed or to impoverished Gypsies living on the margins of civil society. Accordingly, Judge Palm concluded that the problem of remedies could also have been avoided in this context either by finding that it was not necessary to examine Article 13 or, in the alternative, finding that there was also a violation of that provision on the basis of the ineffectiveness of remedies—while leaving open the question of their legality. In all, Judge Palm considered it 'unwise' of the ECtHR to follow the Commission in elaborating a general theory concerning the validity and effectiveness of remedies in the TRNC, and 'unnecessary to decide the issues presented in this case'. She concluded by pointing out that in 'such a political area' the ECtHR should have allowed itself to be guided by the firm—and unrelenting—approach followed up to the present day by the international community, and adopted a measure of caution and judicial restraint.[99]

In the case of *Hasan and Chaush v. Bulgaria*,[100] the ECtHR, like the Commission, took the view that Article 13 ECHR cannot be seen as requiring a possibility for every believer, such as the second applicant, to institute in his individual capacity formal proceedings challenging a decision concerning the registration of his religious community's leadership. Individual believers' interests in this respect can be safeguarded by their turning to their leaders, and supporting any legal action which the latter may initiate. The ECtHR thus found that in such a case the state's obligation under Article 13 ECHR

[99] Judge Palm refers explicitly to the *Loizidou* judgment of the ECtHR, *Loizidou v. Turkey*, 18 December 1996, RJD 1996-VI.

[100] ECtHR, *Hasan and Chaush v. Bulgaria*, 26 November 2000; RJD 2000-XI, para. 96.

may well be discharged by the provision of remedies which are only accessible to representatives of the religious community aggrieved by a state interference with its internal organisation. It found, therefore, that the leadership of the faction led by the first applicant were unable to mount an effective challenge to the unlawful state interference in the internal affairs of the religious community and to assert their right to organizational autonomy, as protected by Article 9 ECHR.[101]

In the case of *Lacko and Others v. Slovakia*,[102] the ECHR recalled that a decision or measure favourable to the applicant is not in principle sufficient to deprive the applicant of his or her status as a 'victim' unless the national authorities have afforded redress for the breach of the Convention.[103] Subsequently, the government had made available the sum of 3,300,000 Slovakian korunas with a view to resolving the housing problem of the Romani citizens which apparently had been at the origin of the contested municipal resolutions. A housing facility had been purchased and rebuilt for that purpose, and the persons concerned had been provided with accommodation in it. Having regard to the particular circumstances of the case, the ECtHR was satisfied that in doing so the domestic authorities had provided the applicants with adequate redress for the breach of their rights under Article 2 of Protocol 4 and under Article 14 ECHR.

In the case of *Metropolitan Church of Bessarabia and Others v. Moldova*,[104] the ECtHR observed that the applicants' complaint that the refusal to recognize the applicant Church had infringed their right to the freedom of religion guaranteed by Article 9 ECHR was undoubtedly arguable. The applicants were therefore entitled to an effective domestic remedy within the meaning of Article 13 ECHR. The Court noted that in its judgment of 9 December 1997 the Moldovan Supreme Court of Justice had held that the government's refusal to reply to the application for recognition lodged by the applicant Church

[101] The ECtHR referred to its judgment of 18 December 1996 in the case *Efstratiou v. Greece* (RJD 1996-IV, para. 47) and recalled that Art. 13 ECHR secures to anyone claiming on arguable grounds to be the victim of a violation of his rights and freedoms as protected in the Convention an effective remedy before a national authority in order both to have his claim decided and, if appropriate, to obtain redress. In the end, the ECtHR found that the applicants did not have an effective remedy before a national authority. See also ECtHR, *Holy Monasteries v. Greece,* 9 December 1994, Series A No. 301 and ECtHR, *Kelly and Others v. United Kingdom* (Appl. 30054/96, 04 May 2001).

[102] ECtHR, *Lacko and Others v. Slovakia*, (Appl. No 47237/99, 02 July 2002, Admissibility Decision).

[103] The ECtHR referred to its judgment in *Amuur v France* of 25 June 1996, RJD 1996-III, para. 36 and *Dalban v Romania* [GC], 28 September 1999, RJD 1999-VI, para. 39.

[104] ECtHR, *Metropolitan Church of Bessarabia and Others v. Moldova*, 13 December 2001, RJD 1999-XII.

had not been unlawful, nor had it been in breach of Article 9 ECHR since the applicants could manifest their religion within the Metropolitan Church of Moldova. However, in doing so the Moldovan Supreme Court of Justice had not replied to the applicants' main complaints, namely their wish to join together and manifest their religion collectively within a Church distinct from the Metropolitan Church of Moldova, and to have the right of access to a court to defend their rights and protect their assets, given that only denominations recognized by the State enjoyed legal protection. Consequently, not being recognised by the State, the Metropolitan Church of Bessarabia had no rights it could assert in the Moldovan Supreme Court of Justice. Accordingly, the appeal to this court was not effective. Moreover, the ECtHR noted that although the applicable Religious Denominations Act made the activity of a religious denomination conditional upon government recognition, and the obligation to comply with the laws of the Republic, it did not contain any specific provision governing the recognition procedure and making remedies available in the event of a dispute. The government did not mention any other remedy of which the applicants could have made use. Consequently, the ECtHR considered that the applicants were unable to obtain redress from a national authority in respect of their complaint relating to their right to the freedom of religion.

In the above mentioned case of *Nachova and Others v. Bulgaria*,[105] the ECtHR reiterated that it regards as particularly serious cases where indispensable and obvious investigative steps that could have elucidated acts of deprivation of life by state agents were not taken, and the respondent government failed to provide a plausible explanation about the reasons why that was not done. The ECtHR considered that such conduct on the part of the authorities—which had already been remarked on by the Court in previous cases against Bulgaria[106]—was a matter of particular concern, as it cast serious doubts on the objectivity and impartiality of the investigators and prosecutors involved. The ECtHR also recalled that acts motivated by ethnic hatred that lead to deprivation of life undermine the foundations of societies and require particular vigilance and an effective response by the authorities.

In the case of *Valsamis v. Greece*,[107] the ECtHR noted that, in that case, it had not been possible to apply to the administrative courts for judicial review. The applicants had argued, not being able to obtain a judicial decision,

[105] ECtHR, *Nachova and Others v. Bulgaria* (*supra*, n. 34), paras. 116–119.

[106] The ECtHR referred to its judgments in the cases *Anguelova* (*supra*, n. 26) and *Velikova* (*supra*, n. 30).

[107] See ECtHR, *Valsamis v. Greece*, 18 December 1996, RJD 1996-VI, paras. 46–49 and 89–90.

that the disciplinary measure of suspension from a school was unlawful. In Greece, such a decision, however, is a prerequisite for submitting a claim for compensation. The actions for damages referred to in the applicable legislation were therefore of no avail to them. As to the other remedies relied on, the government had cited no instance of their use similar to the present case, and their effectiveness had accordingly not been established. Like the Commission, the ECtHR found, therefore, that the applicants did not have an effective remedy before a national authority in order to raise their complaints.

In the above mentioned case of *Velikova v. Bulgaria*,[108] the ECtHR noted that given the fundamental importance of the right to protection of life, Article 13 ECHR imposes, without prejudice to any other remedy available under the domestic system, an obligation on states to carry out a thorough and effective investigation likely to lead to those responsible being identified and punished, and in which the complainant has effective access to the investigation proceedings. In the instant case, the Court found that the respondent state had failed to comply with its obligation to carry out such an effective investigation. This failure undermined the effectiveness of any other remedies which might have existed. Therefore, the question about the applicant's status in the criminal investigation does not call for a separate examination.

3. *Jurisprudence of the Inter-American Court of Human Rights (InterAmCHR)*

In the case of *Mayagna (Sumo) Awas Tingni Community v. Nicaragua*,[109] the (InterAmCHR) noted that Article 25 ACHR established, in broad terms, the obligation of states to offer, to all persons under their jurisdiction, effective legal remedy against acts that violate their fundamental rights. It also establishes that the rights protected therein apply not only to rights included in the Convention but also to those recognized by the Constitution or by the law of the state concerned. The (InterAmCHR) also recalled that the right of every person to a simple and rapid remedy or to any other effective remedy before the competent judges or courts, to protect them against acts that violate their fundamental rights 'is one of the basic mainstays, not only of the American Convention, but also of the Rule of Law in a democratic society, in the sense set forth in the Convention'.

[108] ECtHR, *Velikova v. Bulgaria* (*supra*, n. 30), para. 89.

[109] InterAmCHR, *Mayagna (Sumo) Awas Tingni Community v. Nicaragua* (Judgment, Ser. C No. 79, 31 August 2001), para.111.

B. Positive Measures by States to Provide an Effective Remedy and Effective Investigation

Building upon the jurisprudence under section 3.1, this section aims to address specifically the positive measures by states to meet their obligations to provide for an effective remedy and effective investigation.

1. Jurisprudence of the Committee on the Elimination of Racial Discrimination (CERD/C)

In the case of *L.K. v. Netherlands*,[110] CERD/C stated that when threats of racial violence are made, and especially when they are made in public and by a group, it is incumbent upon the state to investigate with due diligence and expedition. In the instant case, the state party failed to do this. The Committee found that in view of the inadequate response to the incidents, the police and judicial proceedings in this case did not afford the applicant effective protection and remedies within the meaning of Article 6 CERD. The Committee recommended that the state party review its policy and procedures concerning the decision to prosecute in cases of alleged racial discrimination, in the light of its obligations under Article 4 CERD. The Committee further recommended that the state party provide the applicant with relief commensurate with the moral damage he had suffered.

2. Jurisprudence of the European Court of Human Rights (ECtHR)

In the above mentioned case of *Anguelova v. Bulgaria*,[111] the ECtHR recalled that the obligation to protect the right to life under Article 2 ECHR, read in conjunction with the state's general duty under Article 1 ECHR to 'secure to everyone within [its] jurisdiction the rights and freedoms defined in [the] Convention', requires by implication that there should be some form of effective official investigation when individuals have been killed as a result of the use of force. The Court elaborated upon assessing the effectiveness of an investigation, and noted that this cannot be gauged on the basis of the number of reports made, witnesses questioned or other investigative measures taken. The essential purpose of such an investigation is to secure the effective implementation of the domestic laws which protect the right to life and, in those cases involving state agents or bodies, to ensure their accountability for deaths occurring

[110] CERD, *L.K. v. Netherlands*, paras 6.6–7.

[111] ECtHR, *Anguelova v. Bulgaria* (Appl. No 38361/97, 13 June 2002, Merits and just satisfaction), paras 9.2–9.4 (*supra*, n. 26).

under their responsibility.[112] For an investigation into alleged unlawful killing by state agents to be effective, it may generally be regarded as necessary for the persons responsible for and carrying out the investigation to be independent from those implicated in the events.[113] This means not only a lack of hierarchical or institutional connection but also a practical independence. The investigation must also be effective in the sense that it is capable of leading to the identification and punishment of those responsible. This is not an obligation of result, but of means. The authorities must have taken the reasonable steps available to them to secure the evidence concerning the incident, including, *inter alia*, eyewitness testimony, forensic evidence and, where appropriate, an autopsy which provides a complete and accurate record of injury and an objective analysis of clinical findings, including the cause of death. Any deficiency in the investigation which undermines its ability to establish the cause of death or the person responsible will risk falling foul of this standard. There must be a sufficient element of public scrutiny of the investigation or its results to secure accountability in practice as well as in theory, maintain public confidence in the authorities' adherence to the rule of law and prevent any appearance of collusion in or tolerance of unlawful acts. The degree of public scrutiny required may well vary from case to case. In all cases, however, the next of kin of the victim must be involved in the procedure to the extent necessary to safeguard his or her legitimate interests.[114]

In the above-mentioned case of *Nachova and Others v. Bulgaria,*[115] the ECtHR considered that states have a general obligation under Article 2 ECHR to conduct an effective investigation in cases of deprivation of life. Compliance with the state's positive obligations under Article 2 ECHR requires that the domestic legal system must demonstrate its capacity to enforce criminal law against those who unlawfully took the life of another, irrespective of the victim's racial or ethnic origin. The ECtHR considered it highly relevant that this was not the first case against Bulgaria in which it had found that law

[112] See, eg, *mutatis mutandis*, ECtHR, *Ilhan v. Turkey* [GC] (Appl. No. 22277/93, 27 June 2000, RJD 2000-VII, § 63).

[113] See, eg, *The Güleç v. Turkey* judgment of 27 July 1998, Reports 1998-IV, §§ 81–82 and *Özgur v. Turkey* [GC], no. 21954/93, ECHR 1999-III, §§ 91–92.

[114] See the *Güleç* judgment, p. 1733, § 82, where the father of the victim was not informed of the decisions not to prosecute; *Ögur*, § 92, where the family of the victim had no access to the investigation and court documents and *Gül*, § 93 (all *supra*, n. 113); for a full summary of the relevant case law see *McKerr v. United Kingdom*, no. 28883/95, §§ 111–115, ECHR 2001-III.

[115] ECtHR, *Nachova and Others v. Bulgaria*, (Appl. No 43577/98, 43579/98, 26 February 2004, Merits and just satisfaction), paras 131, 140 and 156–174.

enforcement officers had subjected Roma to violence resulting in death. In its *Velikova* and *Anguelova* judgments, the ECtHR had noted that the complaints of racial motivation in the killing of two Roma in police custody in separate incidents were based on 'serious arguments', and had found a violation of Bulgaria's obligation under Article 2 ECHR to conduct an effective investigation into the deaths.[116]

In the above mentioned case of *Assenov and Others v. Bulgaria*,[117] the ECtHR addressed the issue of effective investigation of serious ill-treatment on the basis of Article 3 ECHR. Although this incident had taken place in public view at a bus station, and although, according to the statements of the police officers concerned, it was seen by approximately 15–20 Roma and 20 bus drivers, no attempt appeared to have been made to ascertain the truth through contacting and questioning these witnesses in the immediate aftermath of the incident, when memories would have been fresh. Instead, at that time a statement was taken from only one independent witness, who was unable to recall the events. Against this background, in view of the lack of a thorough and effective investigation into the applicant's arguable claim that he had been beaten by police officers, the ECtHR found that there had been a violation of Article 3 ECHR.

In the above mentioned case of *Cyprus v. Turkey*,[118] the ECtHR also recalled that there should be some form of effective official investigation when individuals have been killed as a result of the use of force by agents of the state. In the absence of any information about their fate, the relatives of persons who went missing during the events of July and August 1974 were condemned to live in a prolonged state of acute anxiety which cannot be said to have been erased with the passage of time. That the missing persons in this case had disappeared could not be denied, and the ECtHR noted that the authorities of the respondent state had never undertaken any investigation into the claims made by the relatives of the missing persons that the latter had disappeared after being detained in circumstances in which there was real cause to fear for their welfare. The ECtHR noted also that there had been no attempt made to identify the names of the persons who had been reportedly released from Turkish custody into the hands of Turkish-Cypriot paramilitaries or to

[116] ECtHR, *Velikova v. Bulgaria* (Application No 41488/98, 18 May 2000, Merits and just satisfaction).

[117] ECtHR, *Assenov and Others v. Bulgaria* (Appl. No 24760/94, 28 October 1998), paras. 102–106.

[118] ECtHR, *Cyprus v. Turkey* (Appl. No 25781/94, 10 January 2001, Merits), paras. 131–136 and 147–157.

inquire into the whereabouts of the places where the bodies had been disposed of. It did not appear either that any official inquiry was made into the claim that Greek-Cypriot prisoners were transferred to Turkey. Having regard to the above considerations, the ECtHR concluded that there had been a continuing violation of Article 2 ECHR on account of the failure of the authorities of the respondent state to conduct an effective investigation aimed at clarifying the whereabouts and fate of Greek-Cypriot missing persons who disappeared in life-threatening circumstances. The ECtHR stated that Article 5 ECHR must be seen as requiring the authorities to take effective measures to safeguard persons against the risk of disappearance, and to conduct a prompt and effective investigation into an arguable claim that a person had been taken into custody and had not been seen since. The Court concluded that, during the period under consideration, there had been a continuing violation of Article 5 ECHR by virtue of the failure of the authorities of the respondent state to conduct an effective investigation into the whereabouts and fate of the missing Greek-Cypriot persons in respect of whom there was an arguable claim that they were in custody at the time they disappeared. As noted above in section 2.1, the ECtHR considered that the silence of the authorities of the respondent state in the face of the real concerns of the relatives of the missing persons attained a level of severity categorized as inhuman treatment within the meaning of Article 3 ECHR. In his partly dissenting opinion, Judge Fuad stated that neither the Commission nor the Court found sufficient evidence to hold that the missing persons were still in the custody of the Turkish authorities at the relevant time. In his opinion, it could not be right to treat the Convention obligation which arises in certain circumstances to conduct a prompt and effective investigation as having persisted for 15 years after the events which required investigation so that, when Turkey did become bound by the ECHR, her alleged failure to date to conduct appropriate investigations could be regarded as a violation of the ECHR. Judge Fuad concluded that the concept of continuing violations cannot be prayed in aid to reach such a result, and that such an approach would be to apply an obligation imposed by the Convention retrospectively, and to divest the time limitation in the declaration of its effect.

In the case of *Hugh Jordan v. United Kingdom*,[119] the ECtHR, while addressing the requirement of promptness and reasonable expedition, considered that it must be accepted that there may be obstacles or difficulties which prevent progress in an investigation in a particular situation. However, a prompt

[119] ECtHR, *Hugh Jordan v. United Kingdom* (Appl. No 24746/94, 4 May 2001, Merits and just satisfaction), paras. 105–197 and 115.

response by the authorities in investigating a use of lethal force may generally be regarded as essential in maintaining public confidence in their adherence to the rule of law, and in preventing any appearance of collusion in or tolerance of unlawful acts. Conversely, as regards the government's argument that the availability of civil proceedings provided the applicant with a remedy which he had yet to exhaust as regards Article 35(1) ECHR and, therefore, that no further examination of the case was required under Article 2 ECHR, the ECtHR recalled that the obligations of the state under Article 2 ECHR cannot be satisfied merely by awarding damages. The investigations required under Articles 2 and 13 ECHR must be able to lead to the identification and punishment of those responsible. In the case of *McKerr v. United Kingdom*,[120] the ECtHR similarly recalled that the obligations of the state under Article 2 ECHR cannot be satisfied merely by awarding damages.

In the case of *Ozgür Gündem v. Turkey*,[121] the ECHR noted the government's submissions concerning its strongly held conviction that Özgür Gündem and its staff supported the PKK and acted as its propaganda tool. This did not, even if true, provide a justification for failing to take steps effectively to investigate and, where necessary, provide protection against unlawful acts involving violence. The ECtHR concluded that the respondent state had failed to take adequate protective and investigative measures to protect Özgür Gündem's exercise of its freedom of expression and that it had imposed measures on the newspaper, through the search-and-arrest operation of 10 December 1993, and through numerous prosecutions and convictions in respect of issues of the newspaper, which were disproportionate and unjustified in the pursuit of any legitimate aim. As a result of these cumulative factors, the newspaper ceased publication.

In the case of *Tepe v. Turkey*,[122] the ECtHR also pointed out that the positive obligation imposed on the contracting states by Article 2 (1) ECHR requires that the right to life be protected by law. The state is obliged to provide a framework of law which generally prohibits the taking of life and to ensure the necessary structures to enforce these prohibitions, including the provision of a police

[120] ECtHR, *McKerr v. United Kingdom* (Appl. No 28883/95, 4 March 2001, Merits and just satisfaction), paras. 109, 121. See also *Salman v. Turkey* [GC], no. 21986/93, § 100, ECHR 2000-VII; and also *Çakici v. Turkey* [GC], no. 23657/94, § 85, ECHR 1999-IV; *Ertak v. Turkey*, no. 20764/92, § 32, ECHR 2000-V; and *Timurtas v. Turkey*, no. 23531/94, § 82, ECHR 2000-VI.

[121] ECtHR, *Ozgür Gündem v. Turkey* (Appl. No 23144/93, 16 March 2000, Merits and just satisfaction), para. 45.

[122] ECtHR, *Tepe v. Turkey* (Application No 27244/95, 9 May 2003, Merits and just satisfaction).

force with responsibility for investigating and suppressing infringements.[123] That positive obligation, however, does not impose a requirement that a state must necessarily succeed in locating and prosecuting perpetrators of fatal attacks. Therefore, the ECtHR held that the national authorities had failed to carry out an adequate and effective investigation into the circumstances surrounding the death of the applicant's son. It concluded therefore that there had been a violation of Article 2 ECHR under its procedural limb.

C. Equal Protection of and before the Law

The principle of elementary justice is proclaimed in Article 7 UDHR which states that: 'All are equal before the law and are entitled without any discrimination to equal protection of the law. All are entitled to equal protection against any discrimination in violation of this declaration and against any incitement to such discrimination'. The CCPR contains a similar provision in Article 26 which states: 'All persons are equal before the law and are entitled without any discrimination to the equal protection of the law…'. Similar provisions on the right to the equal protection of the law without discrimination are also contained in Article 5 CERD and in the regional instruments, namely in Articles 1 and 14 ECHR, Articles 1 and 24 ACHR, and Articles 2 and 3 AfrCh.

1. Jurisprudence under the Committee on the Elimination of Racial Discrimination (CERD/C)

In the case of *Kashif Ahmad v. Denmark,* CERD/C observed that owing to the failure of the police to continue their investigations, and the final decision of the public prosecutor against which there was no right of appeal, the author was denied any opportunity to establish whether his rights under CERD had been violated. From this it was concluded that the author has been denied effective protection against racial discrimination and remedies by the state party.[124]

In the case of *Yilmaz Dogan v. Netherlands*, the main issues were whether the state party had failed to meet its obligation, under Article 5(e)(i) CERD, to guarantee equality before the law in respect of the right to work and protection against unemployment. The CERD/C concluded that the outcome of the judicial proceedings upholding the dismissal of the applicant was a result of the

[123] ECtHR, See *Osman v. United Kingdom*, Judgment of 28 October 1998, Reports 1998-VIII, p. 3159, § 115.

[124] CERD/C, *Ahmad v. Denmark* (*supra*, n. 77), para. 6.4.

failure to take into account all the circumstances of the case. Consequently, there had been a violation of her right under Article 5(e)(i) CERD.[125]

In the case of *Michael L. Narrainen v. Norway*, CERD/C considered the principal issue before it whether the proceedings against the applicant had respected his right, under Article 5(a) CERD, to equal treatment before the tribunals, without distinction as to race, colour or national or ethnic origin.[126] In light of the facts the CERD/C came to the conclusion that the remarks made by a juror about the applicant were tainted with racial prejudice, and could be regarded as sufficient to disqualify the juror. However, the CERD/C held that it was not within its competences to decide whether such a disqualification had been mandatory under Norwegian law and came, therefore, to the conclusion that there was no violation of Article 5(a) CERD.

2. Jurisprudence under the African Commission on Human and Peoples' Rights (AfrCommHPR)

In the case of *Organisation Mondiale Contre La Torture v. Rwanda,* it was stated that the arrests and detentions of the Rwandan government based on grounds of ethnic origin alone, in light of Article 2 AfrCh in particular, constituted arbitrary deprivation of the liberty of an individual. The AfrCommHPR concluded that these acts were clear evidence of a violation of Article 6 AfrCh.[127]

3. Jurisprudence under the European Court of Human Rights (ECtHR)

In the case of *Cyprus v. Turkey* the ECtHR deduced from the evidence submitted to the Commission that there is a functioning court system in the TRNC for the settlement of disputes relating to civil rights and obligations defined in 'domestic law', and which is available to the Greek-Cypriot population.[128] In its opinion, having regard to the fact that it is the 'TRNC domestic law' which defines the substance of those rights and obligations for the benefit of the population as a whole, it must follow that the domestic courts, set up by the 'law' of the 'TRNC', are the fora for their enforcement. For the ECtHR, and for the purposes of adjudicating on 'civil rights and obligations', the local courts can be considered to be 'established by law' with reference to the 'constitutional and legal basis' on which they operate. The ECtHR was of the opinion that any

[125] CERD/C, *Dogan v. The Netherlands* (*supra*, n. 79) para. 9.2.

[126] CERD/C, *Narrainen v. Norway* (Communication No. 3/1991, Opinion adopted on 15 March 1994), para. 9.2.

[127] AfrCommHPR, *Organisation Mondiale Contre La Torture vs. Rwanda* (Communication Nos. 27/89, 46/91, 49/91, 99/93 (1996)) para. 28.

[128] ECtHR, *Cyprus v. Turkey,* (*supra*, n. 22), para. 237.

other conclusion would be to the detriment of the Greek-Cypriot community and would result in a denial of opportunity to individuals from that community to have an adjudication on a cause of action against a private or public body. It is to be noted in this connection that the evidence confirmed that Greek Cypriots had taken successful court actions in defence of their civil rights.

In the case of *Tsirlis and Kouloumpas v. Greece*, the ECtHR stated that detention will in principle be lawful if it is carried out pursuant to a court order.[129] A subsequent finding that the court erred under domestic law in making the order will not necessarily retrospectively affect the validity of the intervening period of detention. The ECtHR noted that the provision of the applicable legislation by operation of which the applicants had been detained referred to ministers of all 'known religions'. As early as 1975, the Greek Supreme Administrative Court had acknowledged that the Jehovah's Witnesses were to be considered as such, and this case law could unquestionably be regarded as established by 1990. It was not disputed throughout the domestic proceedings that the applicants were ministers of that religion. However, in deciding on the issue of the applicants' criminal liability, and thus on the lawfulness of their detention, the military authorities had blatantly ignored this case law. As a result, the applicants had spent 13 and 12 months in detention respectively. Furthermore, the relevant authorities' persistent refusal not to recognize Jehovah's Witnesses as a 'known religion', and the disregard of the applicants' right to liberty that followed, were of a discriminatory nature when contrasted with the way in which ministers of the Greek Orthodox Church obtain exemption. Therefore, the ECtHR stated that the applicants' detention following their conviction on charges of insubordination had no basis under domestic law and was arbitrary. The Court stated further that it cannot accordingly be considered to have been 'lawful' for the purposes of Article 5 (1) ECHR.

D. Positive Measures by States to Promote Effective Equality

1. Jurisprudence under the Committee on the Elimination of Racial Discrimination (CERD/C)

In the case of *F.A. v. Norway*, CERD/C urged the state party to take effective measures to ensure that housing agencies refrain from engaging in discriminatory practices and do not accept submissions from private landlords which would discriminate on racial grounds.[130]

[129] ECtHR, *Tsirlis and Kouloumpas v. Greece*, 29 May 1997, RJD 1997-III, para. 58.

[130] CERD/C *F.A. v. Norway* (Communication No 18/2000-CEDR/C/58/D/18/2000, 17 April 2001), para. 8.

In the case of *POEM and FASM v. Denmark,* CERD/C called the state party's attention to the content of Paragraph 115 of the Programme of Action adopted by the World Conference against Racism, Racial Discrimination, Xenophobia and Related Intolerance in Durban (South Africa) on 8 September 2001, which 'underlines the key role that politicians and political parties can play in combating racism, racial discrimination, xenophobia and related intolerance and encourages political parties to take concrete steps to promote equality, solidarity and non-discrimination in society, *inter alia* by developing voluntary codes of conduct which include internal disciplinary measures for violations thereof, so their members refrain from public statements and actions that encourage or incite racism, racial discrimination, xenophobia and related intolerance'.[131]

In the case of *Ziad Ben Ahmed Habassi v. Denmark,* CERD/C recommended that the state party take measures to counteract racial discrimination in the loan market.[132]

E. Language Use in Court

In the determination of any criminal charge against him, everyone shall be entitled to the following minimum guarantees, in full equality: To be informed promptly and in detail in a language which he understands of the nature and cause of the charge against him. . .To have the free assistance of an interpreter if he cannot understand or speak the language used in court.

CCPR, Art 14(3)

Article 14 CCPR concerns procedural equality. It enshrines elements of the principle of equality of arms in criminal proceedings, including through the right of free assistance of an interpreter to the accused if he or she cannot understand or speak the language of the court. The HRC stated in its General Comment on Article 14 that this right is independent of the outcome of the proceedings, and must be available to both aliens and nationals.[133] The importance of this right is particularly clear in cases where the difficulty in understanding the language used in the court could amount to a serious obstacle to the right of defence. However, this provision does not prevent a state from using *one* official court language. Also, a state is not obliged to provide an interpreter for an individual whose mother tongue differs from the

[131] *POEM and FASM v. Denmark* (Communication No. 22/2002, Opinion adopted on 19 March 2003), para. 7.

[132] *Habassi v. Denmark* (*supra*, n. 80).

[133] General Comment 13/21 of 12 April 1984, para.13.

official language. The state is obliged to provide an interpreter if the accused or the defence witnesses have difficulty understanding or expressing themselves in the court language. Similar provisions are available under the regional instruments, namely in Article 6(3) ECHR and Article 8(2) ACHR; notably enough, it is absent in the AfrCh. Finally, mention must be made of the fact that the European Court of Justice handed down several judgments dealing with this issue.

1. *Jurisprudence under CCPR*

Four cases involving France exemplify the approach the HRC has taken in interpreting Article 14(3)(f) CCPR. In the case of *Dominique Guesdon v. France*, a French citizen whose mother tongue was Breton was charged with defacing road signs in French, and tried in a French court. The court denied the request of the accused for an interpreter and his preference to speak in Breton, and conducted the trial in French. The accused alleged that denying him, and the witnesses called on his behalf, the right to express themselves in their mother tongue violated his right to a fair trial. The HRC concluded that denying the accused the right to speak in Breton, when he understood and spoke French, did not violate his right to a fair trial or his rights under Article 14(3)(f) CCPR. French law does not, as such, give everyone a right to speak his own language in court; those unable to speak or understand French are provided with the services of an interpreter. This service would have been available to the author had the facts required it; as they did not, he suffered no discrimination under Article 26 CCPR on the ground of his language.[134] In the case of *Hervé Barzhig v. France*, the HRC similarly considered that the French courts had complied with their obligations under Article 14 CCPR. The author had failed to show that he and the witness called on his behalf were unable to understand, and to express themselves adequately in, French before the Tribunal Correctionnel of Rennes. In this context, the HRC recalled that the notion of a fair trial in Article 14 (3(f) CCPR does not imply that the accused be afforded the opportunity to express himself or herself in the language that he or she normally speaks or speaks with a maximum of ease. If the court is certain, as it follows from the decision of the Tribunal Correctionnel of Rennes, that the accused is sufficiently proficient in the court language, it need not take into account whether it would be preferable for the accused to

[134] *Dominique Guesdon v. France* (Communication No 219/1986, UN Doc A/45/40, vol. 2 at 61 (1990)) ; see also *Cadoret and Le Bihan v. France* (Communication Nos. 221/1987 and 323/1988, UN Doc. A/46/40 at 219 (1991)). *Barzhig v. France* (Communication No. 327/1988, UN Doc. A/46/40 at 262 (1991)).

express himself in a language other than the court language. The service of an interpreter would have been available to the author, had the facts required it; as the facts did not, he suffered no discrimination under Article 26 on account of his language.[135] In *G.B. v. France*, the HRC also observed that the material before it showed that G.B. was perfectly capable of expressing herself in French, a language she did not claim not to understand, and found no violation of the CCPR on this ground.[136] In the case of *T.K. v. France*, in assessing the issue of whether it was a violation of the applicant's right to an available and effective remedy under the CCPR to have to use French, rather than Breton, in legal proceedings, the HRC observed the exclusive use of French to institute proceedings in courts. With the author having demonstrated his proficiency in French, the HCR found that it would not be unreasonable for him to submit his claim in French to the French courts. Further, no irreparable harm would be done to the author's substantive case by using the French language to pursue his remedy.[137]

In the case of *J.G.A. Diergaardt et al. v. Namibia,* the applicants claimed that the lack of language legislation in Namibia has had as a consequence that they have been denied the use of their mother tongue in administration, justice, education and public life. Consequently, the HRC found that the authors, as Afrikaans speakers, are victims of a violation of Article 26 CCPR.[138]

2. Jurisprudence under the European Court of Human Rights (ECtHR)

In the case of *Bideault v. France*,[139] the applicant was arrested because he failed to appear at the national service office, and was later prosecuted. For the trial, the applicant's defence council called several witnesses, some of whom asked for permission to give evidence in Breton through an interpreter, which was rejected by the court. The applicant complained and relied on Articles 6(3)(d) and 14 ECHR. The ECtHR noted that Article 6(3)(d) ECHR does not guarantee the right of witnesses to speak in a language of their choice. The ECtHR considered that these provisions were not violated if the judge refuses to hear witnesses in a language other than the official court language, and the witnesses have not claimed that they are unable to give evidence in the official language. The ECtHR therefore declared the application as inadmissible. In

[135] See *Hervé Barzhig v. France* (Communication No 327/1988, UN Doc. A/46/40 (1991) at 262), paras. 5.3–5.4.

[136] *G.B. v. France* (Communication No 348/1989), para.5.2.

[137] *T.K. v. France* (Communication No 220/1987), para. 8.4.

[138] *J.G.A. Diergaardt et al. v Namibia* (Communication No 760/1997), para 10.10.

[139] ECtHR, *Bideault v. France* (Appl. No 11261/84, 6 October 1986, Admissibility Decision).

addition, it examined whether the French courts, in not allowing the witnesses to speak Breton, breached the right to a fair hearing guaranteed by Article 6(1) ECHR. The ECtHR did not consider that this was the case, since the witnesses called by the defence had not claimed that they were unable to speak French. For these reasons, no violation of Article 14 of the ECHR was disclosed in this case.

In the case of *Conka v. Belgium*,[140] the ECtHR recalled that Article 5 (2) ECHR contains the elementary safeguard that any person arrested should know why he is being deprived of his liberty. This should be done in simple, non-technical language so that he can understand the essential legal and factual grounds for his arrest, so as to be able, if he sees fit, to apply to a court to challenge its lawfulness. Whilst this information must be conveyed 'promptly', it need not be related in its entirety by the arresting officer at the very moment of the arrest. Whether the content and promptness of the information conveyed were sufficient is to be assessed in each case according to its special features.[141] The Court has already noted that when the applicants were arrested at the police station a Slovakian-speaking interpreter was present, notably for the purposes of informing the aliens of the content of the verbal and written communications which they received, in particular, the document ordering their arrest. Even though in the present case those measures by themselves were not in practice sufficient to allow the applicants to lodge an appeal with the competent authority, the information thus furnished to them nonetheless satisfied the requirements of Article 5(2) ECHR. Consequently, the ECtHR found that there had been no violation of that provision.

In the case of *Isop v. Austria*,[142] the Commission considered whether the decisions of the court of Rosegg of 18 November 1959 and of the court of Klagenfurt of 12 January 1960, rejecting the applicant's complaint written in the Slovenian language, constitute a violation of the rights guaranteed to him in Articles 6(1) and 14 ECHR, namely, that the applicant was entitled to a fair hearing without any discrimination on the basis of language or association with a national minority. The relevant Austrian legislation did not recognize the Slovenian language as an official language in court in the district of Rosegg. It considered the question of whether, on other legal grounds, the Slovenian language ought to be recognized as an official language for court purposes, and whether this might, in view of the decision of the Court of Appeal of

[140] *Conka v. Belgium*, 5 February 2002, RJD 1992-I.

[141] See, *mutatis mutandis*, *Murray v. United Kingdom*, 28 October 1994, Series A no. 300-A, para. 72.

[142] ECtHR, *Isop v. Austria* (Appl. No 808/60, 8 March 1962, Admissibility Decision).

Graz of 1 October 1959, give rise to doubts as to the actual legal situation in Austria. The question to be answered was whether the applicant, with the assistance of his lawyer, had sufficient linguistic knowledge to permit him to lodge his complaint in the German language. The Commission found that the refusals by the Courts of Rosegg and Klagenfurt to accept his complaint in the Slovenian language, and the expiry of the time-limit for introducing a similar complaint in the German language, which occurred during the proceedings concerning his right to use the Slovenian language, did not constitute a violation of the applicant's right under Article 6(1) ECHR.

In the case of *X. and Y. v. Belgium*,[143] where the applicants had requested certain court hearings to be held in French (and not in Flemish), the ECtHR noted that neither the ECHR nor the First Protocol expressly provides for 'linguistic freedom'. It observed that the only clauses in the ECHR which deal with the use of languages, Articles 5(2) and 6(3) (a) and (e), are limited in scope and are not relevant to the present case, since the applicants had not been arrested or charged with a criminal offence. The Court noted that 'it is nevertheless conceivable that violation of that right may, in certain cases, result in indirect violation of one of the rights and freedoms defined in the Convention and the Protocol 1, especially the right of everyone "to a fair hearing (...) by a tribunal (...) in the determination",' as in the present case, 'of his civil rights and obligations'. In finding no violation, the ECtHR noted that the Correctional Court and the Court of Appeal of Brussels followed the Belgian law on the use of languages in judicial matters, since the accused was Dutch-speaking; whereas, moreover, the applicants had the services of a bilingual barrister.

In the case of *Zana v. Turkey*,[144] the ECtHR observed that, contrary to the government's contention, the fact that the applicant raised procedural objections or wished to address the court in Kurdish, as he did at the hearing in the Aydin Assize Court, in no way signified that he implicitly waived his right to defend himself and to appear before the Diyarbakir National Security Court. The ECtHR concluded that waiver of the exercise of a right guaranteed by the Convention must be established in an unequivocal manner.

3. *Jurisprudence under the European Court of Justice (ECJ)*

In the 1985 case of *Ministère Public v. Mutsch*[145] the ECJ considered whether a Luxembourg national had the right to use German in criminal proceedings in

[143] ECtHR, *X v. Belgium* (Appl. No 4372/70, 2 February 1971, Admissibility Decision).

[144] ECtHR, see *Zana v. Turkey*, 25 November 1997, RJD 1997-VII, para. 70.

[145] ECJ, Case 137/84 *Ministère Public v. Mutsch* [1985] ECR 2681.

a German-speaking municipality of Belgium where Belgian law granted that right to Belgian nationals residing in that municipality. The Court based its conclusion that he was entitled to use German on the ground that a migrant worker's right to use his own language in court proceedings on the same terms as national workers was important in ensuring his and his family's integration into the host country. The ECJ thus clarified the principle of free movement of workers in this regard, as laid down in Article 48 TEC and more particularly in Regulation no. 1612/68 of the Council. The ECJ stated that a worker who is a national of one member state and habitually resides in another member state should be entitled to require that criminal proceedings against him take place in a language other than the language normally used in proceedings before the court which tries him if workers who are nationals of the host member state have that right in the same circumstances.

In the 1998 case of *Otto Bickel and Ulrich Franz*,[146] the national court was uncertain whether the rules of procedure applicable to the citizens of the Province of Bolzano must, under Community law, be extended to nationals of other member states visiting the province. It therefore decided to stay proceedings pending a preliminary ruling from the ECJ on the following question:

> 'Do the principle of non-discrimination as laid down in the first paragraph of Article 6, the right of movement and residence for citizens of the Union as laid down in Article 8a and the freedom to provide services as laid down in Article 59 of the Treaty require that a citizen of the Union who is a national of one Member State but is in another Member State be granted the right to have criminal proceedings against him conducted in another language where nationals of the host State enjoy that right in the same circumstances?'

The ECJ observed that in the context of a Community based on the principles of freedom of movement for persons and freedom of establishment, the protection of the linguistic rights and privileges of individuals is of particular importance. The ECJ continued to note that German-speaking nationals of other member states travelling or staying in the autonomous Province of Bolzano in Italy are at a disadvantage by comparison with Italian nationals residing there whose language is German. Whereas a member of the latter group may, if charged with an offence in the Province of Bolzano, have the proceedings conducted in German, a German-speaking national from another member state, travelling in that province, is denied that right. The

[146] ECJ, Case 274/96 *Bickel and Franz* [1998] ECR 7637.

Italian government noted that German-speaking nationals of other member states who are residents in the Province of Bolzano may rely on the rules in issue and submit their pleadings in German, and argued that there is no discrimination on grounds of nationality as between residents of the region. The majority of Italian nationals whose language is German are in a position to demand that German be used throughout the proceedings in the Province of Bolzano, because they meet the residence requirement laid down by the rules in issue; the majority of German-speaking nationals of other member states, on the other hand, cannot avail themselves of that right because they do not satisfy that requirement. The ECJ held that rules such as those in issue in the main proceedings, which make the right, in a defined area, to have criminal proceedings conducted in the language of the person concerned conditional on that person being resident in that area, favour nationals of the host state by comparison with nationals of other member states exercising their right to freedom of movement, and therefore run counter to the principle of non-discrimination laid down in Article 6 TEC. Furthermore, the ECJ recalled that the applicants had pointed out at the hearing, without being contradicted, that the courts concerned are in a position to conduct proceedings in German without additional complications or costs. Consequently, the ECJ held that Article 6 TEC precludes national rules which, in respect of a particular language other than the principal language of the member state concerned, confer on citizens whose language is that particular language and who are resident in a defined area the right to require that criminal proceedings be conducted in that language, without conferring the same right on nationals of other member states travelling or staying in that area, whose language is the same.

With this ruling, the ECJ followed the proposal made in his opinion on that case by Advocate General *Sir Francis Jacobs* who had noted, first, that it would be wholly disproportionate to let the accused opt for the use of their native language with a view to safeguarding the rights of defence since such rights were safeguarded by other means, such as the right to a free interpreter, in accordance with the relevant provisions of the ECHR and the CCPR. On the latter point the Italian government had referred to a recent judgment of the Corte Costituzionale in which it had been held that the scope of the rules on the protection of linguistic minorities is different from the scope of the rules on rights of defence. The latter rules, in relation to languages, aim to ensure that a defendant is capable of understanding the proceedings, which is assumed not to be the case if he does not perfectly master the official language. The former rules, by contrast, amount to a special form of constitutional protection, corresponding to the cultural heritage of a specific ethnic group, and thus take no account of whether a person belonging to such a group masters the official language.[147] The Italian government had drawn the conclusion, with respect to the present case, that the right of residents of the province of Bolzano to opt for the use of German did not depend on whether they are incapable of using Italian. In cases where a defendant is so incapable, Italian law thus deals with the problem by different means.

Advocate General Jacobs continued to note that the right to opt for the use of German is not conferred on all Italian citizens, but only on residents of the province of Bolzano, and observed that the Italian rule works to the particular disadvantage of German-speaking visitors to Bolzano from Germany and Austria (who will be predominantly German and Austrian nationals) because the latter are all, without exception, prevented from choosing German for the conduct of criminal proceedings whereas most Italian residents being prosecuted in Bolzano who wish to use German are able to do so. Advocate General Jacobs further observed the difficulty in advancing any administrative justification if, as appears to be the case here, local criminal courts are set up to conduct proceedings largely in German, but are obliged to hear cases against German-speaking visitors in Italian. At the hearing, counsel for Mr Bickel and Mr Franz, a German-speaker, had stated that their case had been heard by German-speaking judges, and that the public prosecutor was German-speaking. While advocate General Jacobs argued that it would be unduly onerous to require a state to provide for the conduct of criminal proceedings in every community language, he stated that no such justification could be advanced where, as here, the local courts commonly function in the language of the visitor. According to counsel for Mr Bickel and Mr Franz, the requirement to use Italian would in their cases, if anything, lead to extra costs because the accused would then be entitled to a free interpreter. In the absence, therefore, of any administrative impediment some other justification must be sought. Accordingly, advocate General Jacobs concluded by proposing to the ECJ to answer the question referred it by the Bolzano court as follows: 'Where a Member State grants residents in part of its territory the right to use a language other than its official language in criminal proceedings against them, Article 6 of the EC Treaty must be interpreted as requiring it to afford the same right to nationals of other Member States visiting that territory if those nationals have that other language as their mother tongue.'

[147] Judgment No. 15 of 29 January 1996, GURI, special series, 7 February 1996, No 6.

F. Right of Access to Court

1. International Standards in Access to Justice and Discrimination

The right of (equal) access to justice is one of cornerstones of any legal system based on the rule of law. It is enshrined in Article 14(1) CCPR and, on the regional level, in Article 6(1) ECHR, Article 8(1) ACHR and may be read into Article 7 AfrCh. It obliges states parties to set up independent, impartial courts, and to give them such an institutional and financial framework that they are able to conduct a fair trial in all types of civil and criminal matters, and to accord to all accused persons the minimum rights guaranteed to them in the pertinent provisions. This means, in particular, that it must guarantee that the rights provided for in the respective instrument are not rights that are theoretical and illusory, but rights that are practical and effective. Excessive court fees and cost burdens may effectively prevent persons from resorting to the courts and may, thereby, violate their right of equal access to courts. This means that states are not only under a legal obligation to provide for free legal aid in criminal cases as explicitly provided for as concerns criminal charges in Article 14 (3) (d) CCPR, Article 6(3)(c) ECHR and Article 8(2)(8d) ACHR but it may be convincingly argued that such an obligation could be read into the notion of 'fair hearing', and thus be applicable also to suits at law concerning civil rights. In this context, it is important to ensure that such free legal aid is accorded without any discrimination, both direct and indirect. For example, data from a survey undertaken by the Bulgarian Helsinki Committee suggests that although Bulgarian legal provisions relating to legal aid are neutral on their face, they might have been applied in a discriminatory manner.[148] Furthermore, the extent to which free legal assistance is withheld from indigent defendants may have a disproportionate, adverse impact on the Romani minority. Although there is little statistical information about the impact on racial and ethnic minorities stemming from the deficiencies in the legal aid systems in Central and Eastern European countries, informal inquiries among lawyers indicate that the situation in other countries of the region may be similar.[149]

[148] In 1999, the Bulgarian Helsinki Committee conducted a survey among 1000 accused and convicted persons detained in prisons in Bulgaria. The purpose of this survey was to determine the rough percentage of defendants convicted without a lawyer and to collect other information about the deficiencies of the current system. The results of the survey reveal that 64% of Romani defendants had no lawyer during the preliminary investigation, while the corresponding figure for ethnic Bulgarians was 48%. Similarly, during the trial procedure, 48% of Romani defendants had no lawyer, which was true for only 35% of the Bulgarians.

[149] As part of the Access to Justice Project, and in cooperation with the Association of the Bar of the City of New York, the Public Interest Law Initiative in Transitional Societies maintains a website

2. Jurisprudence from European Court of Human Rights (ECtHR)

In the case of *Canea Catholic Church v. Greece*,[150] the ECtHR recalled that Article 6(1) ECHR embodies the 'right to a court', of which the right of access, that is the right to institute proceedings before courts in civil matters, constitutes one aspect. The right is not, however, an absolute one; since, by its very nature, it calls for regulation by the state, it may be subject to limitations, although these must not restrict or reduce access in such a way or to such an extent that the very essence of the right is impaired. Similarly, in the case of *Devenney v. United Kingdom*,[151] the ECtHR recalled that the right in Article 6(1) ECHR is not absolute, but may be subject to limitations; these are permitted by implication since the right of access by its very nature calls for regulation by the state. In this respect, the contracting states enjoy a certain margin of appreciation, although the final decision as to the observance of the Convention's requirements rests with the ECtHR. A limitation will not be compatible with Article 6(1) ECHR if it does not pursue a legitimate aim and if there is not a reasonable relationship of proportionality between the means employed and the aim sought to be achieved.[152] On the procedural issue of length of time of proceedings, the case of *Ekin Association v. France*[153] provides an example, with proceedings that took more than nine years at two levels of jurisdiction. None of the procedural steps taken by the applicant association revealed any dilatory conduct on its part. The slowness of the proceedings was mainly due to the conduct of the courts before which the case was brought. The ECtHR recalled that it is for the contracting states to organize their legal systems in such a way that their courts can guarantee to everyone the right to a final decision determining his or her civil rights and obligations within a

containing a large variety of information and resources relating to public interest law in Central and Eastern Europe, including a Library on Access to Justice, http://www. Pili.org.

150 ECtHR, *Canea Catholic Church v. Greece* (Appl. No 25528/94, 10 January 2001, Merits and just satisfaction), para. 38. See ECtHR, *Golder v. United Kingdom* judgment of 21 February 1975 and the ECtHR, *Ashingdane v. the United Kingdom* judgment of 28 May 1985, Series A no. 18, p. 18, § 36, and no. 93, pp. 24–25, § 57.

151 ECtHR, *Devenney v. United Kingdom* (Appl. No 24265/94, 19 March 2002, Merits and just satisfaction), para. 23.

152 See among other authoritive judgments in this regard, *Stubbings and Others v. United Kingdom* judgment of 22 October 1996, Reports 1996-IV, p.1502, § 50.

153 ECtHR, *Ekin Association v. France* (Appl. No 39288/98, 20 February 2003, Merits and just satisfaction), para. 72. The ECtHR observed that the administrative court took over two years to decide which court had jurisdiction. There was also a period of some two and a half years between 9 January 1991, when the President of the Judicial Division of the Conseil d'Etat decided to remit the case to the Pau Administrative Court, and 1 June 1993, when the latter passed judgment. It also noted that the proceedings before the Conseil d'Etat took nearly four years.

reasonable time. It considered that the overall length of the proceedings, more than nine years, cannot be considered 'reasonable', when what was at stake in the litigation was of particular importance, and thus found a violation of Article 6(1) ECHR.

In the case of *Holy Monasteries v. Greece,*[154] the ECtHR noted that Greek legislation had vested the applicant monasteries with legal personality in public law in their legal relations in order to afford them greater protection. It noted, moreover, that the monasteries had capacity to take legal proceedings. By depriving them of any further possibility of bringing before the appropriate courts any complaint they might make against the Greek state, third parties or the Greek church itself in relation to their rights of property, or even of intervening in such proceedings, the applicable Greek legislation impaired the very essence of their 'right to a court'.[155]

G. Right to Fair Trial

The right to a fair trial is an indispensable element among the procedural guarantees, provided in several international instruments, including Article 10 UDHR, Article 14 CCPR and Article 5 CERD. Aspects of this right are also found in Articles 9, 14 and 15 CCPR. This right is also recognized in the regional instruments, including Articles 5 and 6 ECHR and Article 8 ACHR; some of its aspects are protected in Article 7 AfrCh.

1. Jurisprudence under the Committee on the Elimination of Racial Discrimination (CERD/C)

In the case of *Michael L. Narrainen v. Norway,*[156] CERD/C considered whether the proceedings against Mr. Narrainen had respected his right, under Article 5 (a) CERD, to equal treatment before the tribunals, without distinction as to race, colour or national or ethnic origin. CERD/C noted that the rule laid down in Article 5(a) CERD applies to all types of judicial proceedings, including trial by jury. If members of a jury are suspected of displaying or voicing racial bias against the accused, it is incumbent upon the national judicial authorities to investigate the issue and to disqualify the juror if there is a suspicion that the juror might be biased. In the present case, the inimical remarks made by one had been brought to the attention of the competent

[154] *Holy Monasteries v. Greece* (Appl. No 13092/87, 13984/88, 9 December 1994, Merits and just satisfaction), para. 80.

[155] See the *Philis v. Greece,* Judgment of 27 August 1991, Series A no. 209, p. 23, para. 65; and the *Fayed v. United Kingdom,* Judgment of 21 September 1994, Series A no. 294-B, pp. 49–50, para. 65.

[156] CERD, *Michel L. Narrainen v. Norway,* paras. 9.2–9.5, 10.

High Court, which duly suspended the proceedings, investigated the issue and heard testimony about the allegedly inimical statement. In the view of the CERD/C, the statement in question may be seen as an indication of racial prejudice and, in the light of the provision of Article 5(a) CERD, the CERD/C was of the opinion that this remark might have been regarded as sufficient to disqualify the juror. However, the competent judicial bodies of Norway had examined the nature of the contested remarks, and their potential implications for the course of the trial. Taking into account that it is neither the function of the Committee to interpret the Norwegian rules on criminal procedure concerning the disqualification of jurors, nor to decide as to whether the juror had to be disqualified on that basis, the CERD/C was unable to conclude, on the basis of the information before it, that a breach of the Convention has occurred. However, the CERD/C recommended to the state party that every effort should be made to prevent any form of racial bias from entering into judicial proceedings which might result in adversely affecting the administration of justice on the basis of equality and non-discrimination. Consequently, the Committee recommends that in criminal cases like the one it has examined due attention be given to the impartiality of juries, in line with the principles underlying Article 5(a) CERD.

2. *Jurisprudence under the European Court of Human Rights (ECtHR)*

In the case of *Al-Nashif v. Bulgaria,*[157] the ECtHR recalled that everyone who is deprived of his liberty is entitled to a review of the lawfulness of his detention by a court, regardless of the length of confinement, to provide safeguards against arbitrariness. The person concerned should have access to a court and the opportunity to be heard either in person or through some form of representation. In the present case, the detention order itself had stated no reasons. Moreover, Mr Al-Nashif had been detained practically incommunicado, and had not been allowed to meet a lawyer to discuss any possible legal challenge to the measures against him. The ECtHR held that this situation was incompatible with Article 5(4) ECHR since national authorities cannot do away with effective control of lawfulness of detention by the domestic courts whenever they choose to assert that national security and terrorism are involved.[158]

In the above mentioned case of *Bideault v. France,*[159] the Commission had examined whether the French courts, in not allowing the witnesses to speak

[157] ECtHR, *Al-Nashif v. Bulgaria* (Appl. No 50963/96, 20 June 2002, Merits and just satisfaction), paras. 92–94.

[158] See the *Chahal v. United Kingdom,* Judgment of 15 November 1996, Reports 1996-V.

[159] ECtHR, *Bideault v. France* (Appl. No 11261/84, 6 October 1986, Admissibility Decision).

Breton, breached the right to a fair hearing guaranteed by Article 6(1) ECHR. The Commission did not consider that this was the case, since the witnesses called by the defence had not claimed that they were unable to speak French.

In the also previously referred to case of *Cyprus v. Turkey*,[160] in his partly dissenting opinion, Judge Marcus-Helmons stated: 'It is quite unrealistic to consider that the courts established in the territories occupied by the Turkish forces in northern Cyprus could administer independent and impartial justice, especially to Greek Cypriots, but also to Turkish Cypriots, in matters that are manifestly contrary to the rules established under the Turkish military occupation. Even though those courts could hear and determine disputes between members of the local population, they would *never* dare take an impartial decision in a case relating to an event resulting from the military occupation.'

In the case of *Zana v. Turkey*,[161] the applicant had been sentenced to months' imprisonment. The ECtHR held that the National Security Court could not, if the trial was to be fair, give judgment without a direct assessment of the applicant's evidence given in person.[162] If the applicant had been present at the hearing, he would have had an opportunity, in particular, to say what his intentions had been when he had made his statement, and in what circumstances the interview in question had taken place, to summon journalists as witnesses or to seek production of the recording which constituted the grounds he was tried for. The ECtHR noted that neither the 'indirect' hearing by the Aydin Assize Court nor the presence of the applicant's lawyers at the hearing before the Diyarbakir National Security Court could compensate for the absence of the accused. The ECtHR accordingly considered that such an interference with the rights of the defence cannot be justified: regard being had to the prominent place held in a democratic society by the right to a fair trial within the meaning of the Convention.

In the case of *Gerger v. Turkey*,[163] the ECtHR noted that the status of military judges sitting as members of National Security Courts did provide some guarantees of independence and impartiality.[164] On the other hand, the ECtHR found that certain aspects of these judges' status made their independence and

[160] ECtHR (Appl. No 25781/94, 10 January 2001, Merits), paras. 231, 235–240.

[161] ECtHR, *Zana v. Turkey* (Application No 18954/91, 25 November 1997), paras. 71–73.

[162] See, *mutatis mutandis*, the *Botten v. Norway* judgment of 19 February 1996, RJD 1996-I, para. 53.

[163] ECtHR, *Gerger v. Turkey* (Appl. No 24919/94, 8 July 1999, Merits and just satisfaction), paras. 60–68.

[164] See ECtHR, *Incal v. Turkey*, 41/1997/825/1031 p. 1571, § 65, Judgment of 9 June 1998, *Ciraklar v. Turkey*, 70/1997/854/106, § 38, Judgment of 28 October 1998.

impartiality questionable: for example, the fact that they are servicemen who still belong to the army, which in turn takes its orders from the executive; the fact that they remain subject to military discipline; and the fact that decisions pertaining to their appointment are to a great extent taken by the administrative authorities and the army. As in its *Incal* judgment, the ECtHR considered that its task was not to determine *in abstracto* the necessity for the establishment of National Security Courts in the light of the justifications advanced by the government. Its task was to ascertain whether the manner in which the Ankara National Security Court functioned, had infringed the applicant's right to a fair trial, in particular whether, viewed objectively, he had had a legitimate reason to fear that the court which tried him lacked independence and impartiality. As to that question, the Court saw no reason to reach a conclusion different from that in the cases of *Incal* and *Çiraklar*, both of whom, like the applicant in the present case were civilians. The ECtHR found it understandable that the applicant—prosecuted in a National Security Court of disseminating propaganda aimed at undermining the territorial integrity of the state and national unity—should be apprehensive about being tried by a bench which included a regular army officer, who was a member of the Military Legal Service. On that account he could legitimately fear that the Ankara National Security Court might allow itself to be unduly influenced by considerations which had nothing to do with the nature of the case. Therefore, the ECtHR held that the applicant's fears as to that court's lack of independence and impartiality could be regarded as objectively justified. The same conclusion was reached in the almost identical case of *Okçuoglu v. Turkey.*[165]

In the case of *Gregory v. United Kingdom,*[166] the ECtHR recalled that it had constantly stressed that a tribunal, including a jury, must be impartial from a subjective as well as an objective point of view.

The case concerned the question of how a trial judge should deal with a situation in which a juror seemed to share racial prejudices. The trial judge had chosen to deal with the allegation by means of a firmly worded redirection to the jury having had the benefit of submissions from both counsels. He sought to impress on the jury that their sworn duty was to try the case on the evidence alone, and that they must not allow any other factor to influence their decision. The meaning of such words must have been clear, in particular to any juror whose conduct may have given rise to the allegation of racial

[165] ECtHR *Okçuoglu v. Turkey* (Appl. No 24246/94, 8 July 1999, Merits and just satisfaction), paras. 57.

[166] ECtHR, *Gregory v. United Kingdom* (Appl. No 22299/93, 25 February 1997, Merits), para. 43.

overtones. In the opinion of the ECtHR, it was significant that on no subsequent occasion was there any further suggestion of racial comment. The judge could reasonably consider therefore that the jury had complied with the terms of his redirection, and that any risk of prejudice had been effectively neutralized. The ECtHR further observed that the facts in issue are to be distinguished from those which led it to find a violation in the *Remli* case. In that case, the trial judges had failed to react to an allegation that an identifiable juror had been overheard to say that he was a racist. In the present case, the judge was faced with an allegation of jury racism which, although vague and imprecise, could not be said to be devoid of substance. In the circumstances, he took sufficient steps to check that the court was established as an impartial tribunal within the meaning of Article 6(1) ECHR, and he offered sufficient guarantees to dispel any doubts in this regard. In his dissenting opinion, Judge Foighel stressed that it is of the utmost importance that remedies should be in place to enable a trial judge to ensure that the decision of the jury is not tainted with any objective suspicion of bias. This is especially true when, as in the instant case, the suspicion of bias is brought directly to the attention of the judge. Judge Foighel took the view that a speech from a judge—a redirection—cannot dispel racial prejudice within a jury, if such prejudice exists. The only safeguard which could have been offered by the trial judge in this case was to discharge part or the whole of the jury, or at least to have conducted a more probing enquiry into the effect of the note on the jury's deliberations and decision making by asking the jury in open court whether they were still capable of continuing and returning a verdict in the circumstances.

In the case of *48 Kalderas Gipsies v. the Federal Republic of Germany and Netherlands,*[167] the Commission observed that no right to free legal aid in civil proceedings is as such included among the rights and freedoms guaranteed by the Convention.[168] Nevertheless, the question was raised, whether the denial of free legal aid did prevent the children from going before the courts, and thereby amount to a failure by the courts to secure without discrimination for the children a fair trial as guaranteed under Articles 6 (1) and Article 14 ECHR.

[167] ECtHR *48 Kalderas Gipsies v. the Federal Republic of Germany and the Netherlands* (Appl. No 7823/77, 7824/77, 6 July 1977, Admissibility Decision), paras. 63–64.

[168] Cf., eg, ECtHR *X. v. Switzerland* (Appl. No. 6958/75, Decisions and Reports No. 3).

In the case of *Sander v. United Kingdom*,[169] there had been clear and precise allegations that racist comments had been made by jurors called upon to try an Asian accused. The ECtHR considered this to be a very serious matter given that, in today's multicultural European societies, the eradication of racism has become a common priority goal for all contracting states. The Court noted that the allegations in question led the applicant to the conclusion that he was tried by a racially prejudiced jury. The applicant's complaint was, therefore, that there was subjective bias on the part of some jurors.

In view of the facts, the ECtHR considered that it was established that at least one juror had made comments that could be understood as jokes about Asians. In the Court's view, this did not on its own amount to evidence that the juror in question was actually biased against the applicant. Moreover, the Court noted that it was not possible for the trial judge to question the jurors about the true nature of these comments and the exact context in which they had been made. Therefore, the ECtHR concluded that it had not been established that the court that tried the applicant was lacking in impartiality from a subjective point of view. The ECtHR accepted that, although discharging the jury may not always be the only means to achieve a fair trial, there are certain circumstances where this is required by Art. 6(1) ECHR. In the present case the judge was faced with a serious allegation that the applicant risked being condemned because of his ethnic origin. Moreover, one of the jurors indirectly admitted to making racist comments. Given the importance attached by all contracting states to the need to combat racism, the ECtHR considered that the judge should have reacted in a more robust manner than merely seeking vague assurances that the jurors could set aside their prejudices and try the case solely on the evidence. By failing to do so, the judge did not provide sufficient guarantees to exclude any objectively justified or legitimate doubts as to the impartiality of the court. Therefore, the ECtHR concluded that the court that condemned the applicant was not impartial from an objective point of view.

H. Right to Public Trial

The basic principle of equality for all in the administration of justice, including the right to a fair and public trial, is set out in Article 10 UDHR: 'Everyone is entitled in full equality to a fair and public hearing by an independent and impartial tribunal, in the determination of his rights and obligations and of any criminal charge against him.' It is further elaborated in Article 14(1) CCPR

[169] See ECtHR *Sander v. United Kingdom* (Appl. No 34129/96, 9 May 2000, Merits), paras. 22–26, 34.

which stipulates that: '. . . everyone shall be entitled to a fair and public hearing by a competent, independent and impartial tribunal established by law.' This principle refers not only to criminal cases, but also to civil disputes where one person sues another. The right is also provided in Article 5 CERD.

On the regional level, this right is guaranteed in Article 6(1) ECHR and Article 8(5) ACHR. In contrast thereto, Article 7 AfrCh does not contain any express provision on a right to public trial. Nonetheless, the AfrCommHPR stated in the case of *Media Rights Agenda v. Nigeria,*[170] that it considered itself to be empowered by Articles 60 and 61 AfrCH to draw inspiration from international law on human and peoples' rights, and to take into consideration as subsidiary measures other general or special international conventions, customs generally accepted as law, general principles of law recognized by African states as well as legal precedents and doctrine. The AfrCommHPR referred to HCR General Comment 13 on the right to a fair trial from which it derived that a court hearing must in general be open to the public, including members of the press, and must not be limited only to a particular category of persons.

IV. Conclusion

One of the aims of the Commentary of which this chapter is a part, is to consolidate practice that has arisen within universal and regional treaty bodies and courts in relation to minority rights. The analysis of the above compilation of the jurisprudence of these courts and treaty bodies shows, as concerns the rights dealt with in this chapter, namely physical integrity, due process and administration of justice, that there seem to be very few differences between the pertinent legal and factual situation of persons belonging to (national) minorities as compared to persons belonging to the 'majority population'. This result might come as a surprise—but on a second thought it seems much less surprising: after all, the rights dealt with all constitute most basic elements of any legal order based on the rule of law and should, therefore, be accorded to every person irrespective of his or her belonging to a national minority. Another reason might be that the enjoyment and exercise of the rights dealt with in this chapter are not of *specific* relevance for persons belonging to a minority such as eg, linguistic, educational, religious, or media rights, which are essential for the protection and promotion of the distinct identity of such minorities. So, states which would not be prepared to accept the existence

[170] AfrCommHPR, *Media Rights Agenda v. Nigeria,* para. 51.

of national minorities on their territory would probably first resort to limiting such rights essential for the preservation of the distinct identity of the group, whereas political activities by a majority population directed against a minority which would violate the rights to physical identity, due process or the administration of justice would probably only be resorted to as a kind of last instance measure.

This assessment applies, in particular, to the right to life and freedom from torture. As concerns the right to life, cases involving persons belonging to a national minority mostly seem to originate from areas stricken by internal strife or even civil war: A large proportion of the cases examined in this chapter is constituted by applications against Turkey, and lodged by persons of Kurdish ethnicity. The same applies with regard to freedom from torture. In addition thereto, there is a frightening number of cases where persons belonging to a national minority, most frequently Roma, have been victims of severe ill-treatment by state agents, in particular police officers, based on obvious racist attitudes; in some instances, such action even resulted in the death of the victims. It seems, however, that the motives behind such aggressive acts are not so much that persons belonging to such groups are considered to constitute a 'threat' to the majority population, but are victims of general discrimination which results in the recourse to excessive physical force. Nonetheless, it is quite disconcerting to see the reluctance of, in particular, the ECtHR to find a violation of the relevant provisions, i.e. Article 14 in conjunction with either Article 2 or Article 3 ECHR.

Similarly, with regard to due process and the administration of justice, there were very few, if any, cases where the enjoyment of the corresponding rights was withheld from persons because of their belonging to a minority. The only exception might be the right to use one's language before courts of law as a most important aspect of the linguistic identity of any person. On the other hand, it must be stressed that the cases reported did not concern persons who could not understand or speak the court language, but simply preferred to use another language, the language of the minority to which they belong; in such a situation, however, it would be difficult to maintain that such an attitude of insisting on the use of the official court language would amount to the violation of the right to a fair trial or hearing. An apparently important aspect of these judicial rights is the right to have equal access to court and it seems that, due to widespread patterns of indirect discrimination, persons belonging to minorities might encounter more problems in obtaining free legal aid than persons belonging to the majority.

SOCIO-ECONOMIC RIGHTS AS MINORITY RIGHTS

*Margot E. Salomon**

I. Introduction

This chapter covers international jurisprudential developments relating to minorities as regards socio-economic rights.[1] On the one hand it considers cases that deal with discrimination against minorities in access to socio-economic rights and opportunities, but its focus lies beyond these concerns.[2] As a direct result of the absence of any instrument explicitly addressing rights to housing, land, natural resources, food, health, and a healthy environment from a minority perspective, the recent history of minority jurisprudence in this area is reflective of a gap in our international system of protection, and the resultant innovative and purposive evolution of it.

* I am grateful to Fergus MacKay and Virginia Mantouvalou for their very helpful comments on a draft of this text and to Lala Stone for her valuable research assistance.

[1] This volume includes a dedicated chapter by Patrick Thornberry on the right to education and is thus omitted from consideration herein.

[2] For detailed coverage see the chapter in this volume by Kristin Henrard on non-discrimination and full and effective equality.

The effective protection of their socio-economic rights for minorities becomes tantamount to the protection of minority rights. That is, the exercise of socio-economic rights serves to protect their culture and particular ways of life: the elements of their collective identity that make them distinct. Yet, given the absence of any adjudicating mechanisms for the consideration of socio-economic rights internationally[3] and only partial protection provided regionally,[4] traditional civil rights—such as the right to privacy and the right to property, as well as the right to life—have begun to fill jurisprudential voids.

Thus much of the coverage in this chapter highlights a complex interplay among the human rights standards. Where explicit minority rights exist, notably collective cultural, religious, and linguistic rights under Article 27 of the International Covenant on Civil and Political Rights (ie individual rights exercised in community with others), we see economic rights read as part of minority culture. Where standards exist along with a mechanism for the adjudication of socio-economic rights, such as under the African Charter on Human and Peoples' Rights, and under the collective complaints procedure of the revised European Social Charter, the socio-economic rights have been applied also to minority groups (and in the case of the former to

[3] Notably, in 2003 the UN established a Working Group to consider options regarding the elaboration of an optional protocol allowing for petitions under the International Covenant on Economic, Social and Cultural Rights: CHR Resolution 2003/18, Question of the Realization in All Countries of the Economic, Social and Cultural Rights, pursuant to Economic and Social Council decision 2002/254.

[4] Under the Additional Protocol to the American Convention on Human Rights in the Area of Economic, Social and Cultural Rights (Protocol of San Salvador) only the right to education and the right to organize can be the subject of petitions before the Inter-American Court of Human Rights (submitted to the Court by the Commission): the Inter-American Commission on Human Rights can consider petitions for violations of the American Declaration on the Rights and Duties of Man which contains socio-economic rights. In Europe, socio-economic rights are protected under the revised European Social Charter, with a complaints procedure effective as of 1998. The African Charter on Human and Peoples' Rights entrenches socio-economic and developmental rights and has a complaints procedure. There is no regional human rights mechanism in Asia. Among these mechanisms expressly authorized to consider alleged violations of economic, social, and cultural rights none, bar the Inter-American Court (and then only in relation to a very limited range of social rights), can issue binding judgments or order reparations and award compensation. On the authority of quasi-judicial bodies to grant reparations, see, for example, European Committee of Social Rights, *The European Roma Rights Centre v. Greece*, Complaint No. 15/2003, Decision on the Merits of 8 December 2004, para. 54. In response to the complainant organizations' request to have the Committee direct Greece to reimburse legal expenses the Committee noted that 'the Protocol does not regulate the issue of compensation ... However it does consider that a consequence of the quasi-judicial nature of the proceedings under the Protocol is where there has been a finding of a violation of the Charter, the defending State should meet some of the costs incurred'.

indigenous communities). From the European Court of Human Rights and the Inter-American Court of Human Rights, we see a 'tag team' solution to the protection of minority rights emerging whereby civil rights are framed as socio-economic rights and as socio-economic rights they are interpreted as minority rights. This is not quite reflective of the method that has come to be known as an 'integrated approach' to the interpretation of human rights treaties[5] whereby it is recognized that the enjoyment of civil and political rights requires the exercise of certain socio-economic rights, that is, there may be socio-economic dimensions to the 'real and practical' exercise of civil and political rights,[6] (or vice versa). Rather it is more aligned with what one commentator referred to as 'permeability'—'the openness of a treaty dealing with one category of human rights to having its norms used as a vehicle for the direct or indirect protection of norms of another treaty dealing with a different category of human rights'.[7] Yet in our consideration of socio-economic rights as minority rights we diverge from one objective of the 'permeability' thesis which like the integrated approach offers a legal method for giving effect to the notion of the interdependence of rights.[8] For us, socio-economic rights are not merely being considered in their instrumental capacity to contribute to the realization of minority rights (eg adequate housing facilitates the ability of minorities to enjoy their culture), nor solely as intrinsically valuable to minorities (eg everyone wants a decent and appropriate place to live),[9] rather, in many instances,

[5] Martin Scheinin, 'Economic and Social Rights as Legal Rights', in Asbjørn Eide, Catarina Krause, and Allan Rosas (eds.), *Economic, Social and Cultural Rights* (Martinus Nijhoff, 2001), 29–54, at 32–42.

[6] ECtHR, *Airey v. Ireland*, Appl. 6289/73, Judgment of 9 October 1979, Series A, No. 32, 11, paras. 20–28.

[7] Craig Scott, 'The Interdependence and Permeability of Human Rights Norms: Towards a Partial Fusion of the International Covenants on Human Rights', *Osgoode Hall Law Journal*, 27 (1989), 769–878, at 771. This is essentially the approach taken by the Indian Supreme Court when it interprets the right to life as for example the right to adequate nutrition, clothing, and shelter. To name one among many, see *Francis Coralie Mullin v. The Administrator, Union Territory of Delhi, SCR*, 2 (1981) 516; see also, the landmark '*Limbuela*' case in which the UK House of Lords found that the government's practice of refusing accommodation or food to asylum-seekers who failed to claim asylum promptly on arrival in the country constitutes inhuman and degrading treatment in breach of the ECHR, *Regina v. Secretary of State for the Home Department (Appellant) ex parte Limbuela (FC) (Respondent) and Ors (Conjoined Appeals)* [2005] UKHL 66. In developing the aforementioned 'integrated approach' Scheinin also touches on this 'social interpretation' of rights found in treaties addressing civil and political rights. Scheinin, *supra*, n. 5, 29–54, at 40–1.

[8] Scott, *supra*, n. 7, 769–878, at 771.

[9] For an interesting consideration of the integrated approach, including distinguishing the instrumental from the substantive aspects, see Virginia Mantouvalou, 'Work and Private Life: Sidabras and Dziautas v Lithuania', *European Law Review*, 30(4) (2005), 573–85.

they quite simply *are* minority rights. When cast in this way they are revealed as serving a primary purpose of protecting difference, of securing norms essential to the cultural survival, dignity, and well-being of minorities, and of indigenous peoples. In applying socio-economic norms to minorities comes the expansion of the body of minority law.

We begin by looking at the case law under the only binding international provision providing for the rights of persons belonging to minorities. The UN Human Rights Committee in its consideration of communications under Article 27 of the CCPR has developed quite a rich jurisprudence equating traditional economic activities as essential elements of minority (indigenous) culture. Article 27 protects the right of persons belonging to minorities in community with other members of their group, to enjoy their own culture, to profess and practise their own religion, or to use their own language,[10] and it has been through cultural rights claims that the particular economic rights of minorities have been advanced.

At the regional level minorities have sought protection of their traditional housing rights through Article 8 of the European Convention on Human Rights—a convention largely dedicated to civil and political rights—providing for the right to private life, family life, and home, as well as through claims related to key issues of access, free movement, and exclusion under Article 1 of Protocol 1 on the right to property. Significantly, the state's positive obligation to provide a minimum level of acceptable living conditions has also been developed through its case law. The Inter-American Court on Human Rights has been particularly progressive in its consideration of the right to property as applied to minority (indigenous) peoples reading it as a right to communal use and ownership of land and fundamental to cultural as well as physical integrity. Under the African Charter on Human and Peoples' Rights, we have seen the beginning of important jurisprudential developments detailing the scope of state obligations in the areas of a healthy environment, food, water, property, housing, and the communities' right to use and benefit from natural resources. The interrelated and interdependent nature of, for example, health and housing that we find developed by the African Commission on Human and Peoples' Rights, surfaces also in the case law of the European Court. While the African Commission has only dealt with a small number of cases

[10] Article 27 CCPR: 'In those States in which ethnic, religious or linguistic minorities exist, persons belonging to such minorities shall not be denied the right, in community with the other members of their group, to enjoy their own culture, to profess and practise their own religion, or to use their own language.' The same article only referring to indigenous as well as minority children is found in Article 30 of the UN Convention on the Rights of the Child.

pertaining to economic, social, and cultural rights—and they have involved widespread and grave violations of Charter rights—it is hoped that the future will see greater consideration of the economic, social, cultural, developmental, and environmental rights under the Charter, including through the eventual cases brought to the forthcoming African Court on Human and Peoples' Rights.[11] Indeed, the Commission made clear in the famous *Ogoni* case that 'there is no right in the African Charter that cannot be made effective'.[12]

Despite the absence so far of a petition mechanism under the International Covenant on Economic, Social and Cultural Rights, the UN Committee on Economic, Social and Cultural Rights is playing a prominent role in refining the contours and substance of the rights found in the Covenant through its General Comments. Its elaboration of the multi-tiered system for determining the content of both the negative and positive aspects of obligations under the Covenant, as we will see, has proved influential to legal developments in the area of minority rights beyond the United Nations. Detailed consideration of the components of Article 11 CESCR on the right to an adequate standard of living, including adequate food, clothing, and housing; the concept and parameters of a minimum essential level of each of the rights and the corresponding core obligations that trump progressive realization; and some delineation of the content of the obligations of international assistance and cooperation and of what constitutes maximum available resources, all have something significant to offer the emerging legal thinking and jurisprudence related to the socio-economic rights of minorities.[13]

The exclusion of minorities and indigenous peoples from the exercise of their socio-economic rights, as for all people, serves to keep them poor, politically marginalized, and powerless, but it also erodes their ability to preserve their way of life—as noted by the European Committee of Social Rights, solidarity,

[11] Protocol to the African Charter on Human and Peoples' Rights on the Establishment of an African Court on Human and Peoples' Rights, entry into force 1998, OAU Doc. OAU/LEG/EXP/AFCHPR/PROT (III).

[12] AfrCommHPR, *Social and Economic Rights Action Center and Center for Economic and Social Rights v. Nigeria*, (Communication No. 155/96, 30th Ordinary Session, October 2001), para. 68. (hereinafter the *Ogoni* case).

[13] Article 2(1) CESCR: 'Each State Party to the present Covenant undertakes to take steps, individually and through international assistance and co-operation, especially economic and technical, to the maximum of its available resources, with a view to achieving progressively the full realization of the rights recognized in the present Covenant by all appropriate means, including particularly the adoption of legislative measures.'

social inclusion, and respect for difference lie at the heart of socio-economic rights and nowhere more so than when applied to minorities.[14]

II. Economic Rights as Cultural Rights

Article 27 of the CCPR offers a certain protection of the economic rights of minorities. The rights of a minority community to 'enjoy their own culture' under Article 27 include economic activities that are 'an essential element of the culture of the ethnic community',[15] such as reindeer husbandry among the Saami[16] and the use and control of fisheries among the Maori.[17] In finding that Canada had violated Article 27 in the *Lubicon Lake Band* case, the Human Rights Committee recognized 'that the rights protected by Article 27, include the rights of persons, in community with others, to engage in economic and social activities which are part of the culture of the community to which they belong'.[18] The Committee further observed that it was not merely *recent* developments that 'threaten the way of life and culture of the Lubicon Lake Band', but 'historical inequities' which also 'constitute a violation of Article 27 as long as they continue'.[19] In its General Comment of 1994 on the rights of minorities the Committee provides that 'culture manifests itself in many forms, including in a particular way of life associated with the use of land resources, especially in the case of indigenous peoples. That right may include such traditional activities as fishing or hunting and the right to live in a reserve protected by law'.[20] Moreover, economic activities that form part of

[14] 'One of the underlying purposes of the social rights protected in the [European Social] Charter is to express solidarity and promote social inclusion. It follows that States must respect difference and ensure that social arrangements are not such as would effectively lead to or enforce social exclusion.' European Committee of Social Rights, *The European Roma Rights Centre v. Greece, supra*, n. 4, para. 19.

[15] HRC, Communication No. 197/1985, *Kitok v. Sweden*, (27 July 1988), UN Doc. Supp. No. 40 (A/43/40) at 221, para. 9.2; HRC, Communication No. 511/1992, *Länsman et al. v. Finland*, UN Doc. CCPR/C/52/D/511/1992 (1994) para. 9.2; HRC, Communication No. 547/1993, *Apirana Mahuika et al. v. New Zealand*, UN Doc. CCPR/C/70/D/547/1993 (2000), para. 9.3; HRC, Communication No. 1023/2001, *Jouni Länsman et al. v. Finland*, UN Doc. CCPR/C/83/D/1023/2001 (2005), para. 10.1.

[16] *Kitok v. Sweden, supra*, n. 15; *Länsman et al. v. Finland* (1994); *Jouni Länsman et al. v. Finland*, (2005), *supra*, n. 15.

[17] *Apirana Mahuika et al. v. New Zealand, supra*, n. 15.

[18] HRC, Communication No. 167/1984, *Chief Bernard Ominayak and the Lubicon Lake Band v. Canada*, (26 March 1990), UN Doc. Supp. No. 40 (A/45/40), para. 32.2.

[19] *Ibid.*, para. 33.

[20] HRC, General Comment No. 23 (Article 27) on The Rights of Minorities, UN Doc. CCPR/C/21/Rev.1/Add.4 (1994), para. 7.

minority culture might reflect the adaptation of traditional means of livelihood to modern methods of production, such as through the use of technology, but this does not deprive minorities of the protection afforded under Article 27, as the Committee reaffirmed in *Mahuika et al. v. New Zealand* with regard to the commercial and non-commercial control and use of tribal fisheries.[21]

In the case of *Diergaardt (late Captain of the Rehoboth Baster Community) et al. v. Namibia*, the Human Rights Committee found no violation of Article 27 based on the conclusion that the link of the Rehoboth community, made up of descendants of Afrikaaner and Khoi communities, to the lands in question—while dating back some 125 years and the basis of the communities' economic livelihood through cattle farming—'is not the result of a distinctive culture'.[22] Committee members Evatt and Quiroga concurring drew attention to the distinction the Committee made between defining culture in terms of an economic activity, in this case cattle grazing, and 'a distinct culture which is ultimately bound up with or dependent on the use of... particular lands...'.[23] They went on to explain that the nature of the claim was economic rather than cultural and as such does not draw the protection of Article 27. In so doing, they acknowledged that defining the role that economic activities associated with land play in culture is often more readily resolved with regard to indigenous communities than non-indigenous minority groups.[24]

In determining the threshold for finding a violation of Article 27 the Committee has drawn a distinction between measures that amount to a denial of the right to culture and those that merely have 'a certain limited impact on the way of life of persons belonging to minorities'. On this basis, no violation

[21] *Apirana Mahuika et al. v. New Zealand, supra*, n. 15 para. 9.4; *Länsman et al. v. Finland* (1994), *supra*, n. 15 para. 9.3: 'The right to enjoy one's culture cannot be determined in abstracto but has to be placed in context. In this connection, the Committee observes that article 27 does not only protect traditional means of livelihood of national minorities, as indicated in the State party's submission. Therefore, that the authors may have adapted their methods of reindeer herding over the years and practise it with the help of modern technology does not prevent them from invoking article 27 of the Covenant.' Thornberry and Estébanez remark on the 'mutable' nature of culture and identity recognized in international instruments through the use of terms such as 'express, preserve and develop'. Referring in particular to the Council of Europe's Framework Convention for the Protection of National Minorities the commentators conclude that: 'There is no question within its terms of locking-in minorities to an unchangeable corpus of traditional lifestyles and practices before allowing access to the norms of international law.' Patrick Thornberry and María Amor Martín Estébanez, *Minority Rights in Europe: A Review of the Work and Standards of the Council of Europe* (Council of Europe Publishing, 2004), 102–3.

[22] HRC, Communication No. 760/1997, *J.G.A. Diergaard (late Captain of the Rehoboth Baster Community) et al. v. Namibia*, UN Doc. CCPR/C/69/D/760/1997 (2000), para. 10.6.

[23] *J.G.A. Diergaardt et al. v. Namibia*, Individual opinion of Elizabeth Evatt and Cecilia Medina Quiroga (concurring), para. 1

[24] *Ibid.*

of Article 27 was found regarding the impact on Saami reindeer herding as a result of stone-quarrying on their traditional lands as was at issue in the 1994 case of *Ilmari Lansman et al. v. Finland*[25] or as a result of logging as in *Jouni Lansman et al. v. Finland* (1996)[26] and *Lansman et al. v. Finland* of 2005.[27] The Committee looks also to the scale of the approved plans for future years in the area in question and hence potential interference with the cultural rights of the 'authors' (ie petitioners), or the potential seriousness of their effects in determining the limited nature of the foreseen impact,[28] and the extent to which the alleged victims were consulted about and meaningfully participated in decision-making.[29] As a former member of the Committee explains, the Article 27 case law reflects a combined test of participation by the affected community and the traditional economy remaining sustainable.[30] And the standard of proof on the latter aspect is not that there is merely an impairment of a minority way of life, but rather that there is a serious deprivation of cultural life.[31]

The judicial determination of economic, social, and cultural rights is one that requires weighing competing interests, at times between the pursuit by the state of national economic development, against the culture and livelihood of the communities, between traditional ways of life and claims of general interest. In deciding the scope of a state's freedom to act, the Human Rights Committee focuses not on the margin of appreciation afforded the state, for example, in encouraging private enterprise, but on whether the measures amount to a *denial* of Article 27 rights. The ability of the community to continue exercising its rights provides the test.[32] Under the relevant minority case

[25] *Länsman et al. v. Finland* (1994), *supra*, n. 15 para. 9.4.

[26] HRC, Communication No. 671/1995, *Jouni E. Länsman et al. v. Finland*, UN Doc. CCPR/C/58/D/671/1995 (1996), para. 10.3.

[27] *Jouni Länsman et al. v. Finland* (2005), *supra*, n. 15 para. 10.1.

[28] *Jouni E. Länsman et al. v. Finland* (1996), *supra*, n. 26 para. 10.7; *Jouni Länsman et al. v. Finland* (2005), *supra*, n. 15 para. 10.2.

[29] *Jouni E. Länsman et al. v. Finland* (1996), *supra*, n. 26 para. 10.4; and notably, *Apirana Mahuika et al. v. New Zealand*, *supra*, n. 15 para. 9.6, see below.

[30] Martin Scheinin, 'New Trends in the Law on Indigenous Peoples' Rights: Reflections based on the work by the UN Human Rights Committee and the proposed Nordic Saami Rights Treaty', 72nd International Law Association Conference, Toronto 4–8 June 2006. Notes on file with author.

[31] See Dinah Shelton, 'The UN Human Rights Committee Decisions', *Human Rights Dialogue: Cultural Rights*, Carnegie Council on Ethics and International Affairs, Spring 2005, at www.cceia.org.

[32] While the Committee's Art. 27 case law reflects the consideration of whether interferences with a minority's rights has a 'reasonable and objective justification and are consistent with the other provisions of the Covenant read as a whole' (and necessary for the continued viability of the welfare of the minority as a whole ie not determined 'in abstracto'), this test is applied in cases that pit the right of an individual member of the community, against the rights of the minority community

law of the European Court (notably cases with social and economic policy implications, brought under Articles with express limitations), quite a wide margin of appreciation is afforded the state, yet, any interference with human rights must be in response to a pressing social need and be proportionate to the legitimate aim being pursued in that it strikes a fair balance between the individual interest and the collective interest, and does not impose a disproportionate and excessive burden on individuals or on a particular sector of the population.[33]

Thus the specific obligations imposed on states parties under Article 27 are 'directed towards ensuring the survival and continued development of the cultural, religious and social identity of the minorities concerned'.[34] The rights of minorities (including indigenous rights), as for most human rights, are not absolute and may have to be balanced against competing interests, including the state's wish to encourage economic development and to allow economic activity by the private sector.[35] However, under the CCPR, the scope of the state's freedom to do so 'is not to be assessed by reference to a margin of appreciation, but by reference to the obligations it has undertaken in Article 27 . . . that a member of a minority shall not be denied his right to enjoy his culture'.[36] In order to comply with Article 27, the state's economic activities must be carried out in a way that ensures the affected minority can continue to benefit from his/her traditional way of life.[37]

As noted, an essential element in the protection of Article 27 rights requires giving effect to the procedural aspect of participation. The acceptability of measures that affect or interfere with the culturally significant economic activities of a minority depends on whether the affected community participated in decision-making processes, and whether it will continue to benefit from its

as a whole (or members of it). See, the *ratio dicendi* in HRC, Communication No. R.6/24, *Sandra Lovelace v. Canada*, UN Doc. Supp. No. 40 (A/36/40) at 166 (1981), para. 16; *Kitok v. Sweden*, *supra*, n. 15, para. 9.8.

33 Taking the lead from the ECtHR on limitation clauses generally, interference by authorities with the rights protected in a treaty would need to be prescribed by law, pursue a legitimate aim, and be proportionate to that legitimate aim sought, eg '*necessary* in a democratic society'. For CESCR's application of a similar three-part test under CESCR Art. 4 see CESCR, General Comment No. 14 (Article 12) on the Right to the Highest Attainable Standard of Health, UN Doc. E/C.12/2000/4 (2000) paras. 28–9.

34 HRC, General Comment No. 23, *supra*, n. 20, para. 9.

35 Although not explicitly provided in the text, restrictions on the exercise of Art. 27 'must be considered justified to the extent that they are necessary in a democratic society in view of public interests of vital importance or for the protection of the rights and freedoms of others'. *Kitok v. Sweden*, *supra*, n. 15, para. 4.3.

36 *Kitok v. Sweden, supra*, n. 15; *Länsman et al. v. Finland* (1994), *supra*, n. 15, para. 9.4.

37 *Länsman et al. v. Finland* (1994), *supra*, n. 15, para. 9.8.

traditional economy.[38] Meeting this standard requires positive measures on the part of the state.[39]

Over the years we have seen a more stringent test of what constitutes participation being applied by the Human Rights Committee. So while the standard 'to ensure the effective participation of members of minority communities in decisions which affect them'[40] in the 1994 case of *Ilmari Lansmann et al.* was met when the community was 'consulted' and their 'interests were considered' by the state,[41] by *Mahuika v. New Zealand* in 2000, the scope of participation which was central to the finding of no violation was that 'the State party undertook a complicated process of consultation in order to secure broad Maori support... and [that] their proposals affect[ed] the design of the arrangement'.[42] The Inter-American Court of Human Rights in *The Mayagna (Sumo) Indigenous Community of Awas Tingni v. Nicaragua* also ruled on the importance of consent and the implied need for prior participation in decision-making regarding indigenous peoples and their land.[43] International Labour Organization Convention No. 169 on Indigenous and Tribal Peoples refers to 'free and informed consent' in respect of relocation as a result of the removal of indigenous peoples from the lands which they occupy,[44] and the General Recommendation on Indigenous Rights adopted by the UN Committee on the Elimination of Racial Discrimination requires 'that no decision directly relating to their rights and interests are taken without their informed consent'.[45] Focused on minorities rather than indigenous peoples more specifically, the UN Declaration on the Rights of Persons Belonging to National or Ethnic, Religious and Linguistic Minorities, and the European Framework Convention for the Protection of National Minorities both

[38] *Apirana Mahuika et al. v. New Zealand, supra*, n. 15, para. 9.5.

[39] HRC, General Comment No. 23, *supra*, n. 20, para.7.

[40] *Ibid.*

[41] *Länsman et al. v. Finland* (1994), *supra*, n. 15, para. 9.6.

[42] *Apirana Mahuika et al. v. New Zealand, supra*, n. 15, para. 9.6.

[43] Inter-AmCtHR, *The Mayagna (Sumo) Indigenous Community of Awas Tingni v. the Republic of Nicaragua*, Judgment of 31 August 2001, Series C, No. 79, para. 142.

[44] ILO Convention No. 169, Art. 16(2).

[45] CERD, General Recommendation No. 23 on Indigenous Peoples, (1997) para. 4 (d), and para. 5 (regarding restitution for lands taken without the informed consent of the community). But see Australia's objection to the doctrine: Comments by the Government of Australia on the Concluding Observations of the Committee on the Elimination of Racial Discrimination, UN Doc. CERD/C/AUS/CO/14/Add.1 (2006), paras. 20 and 23. On free, prior, and informed consent see further, Antoanella-Iulia Motoc and the Tebtebba Foundation, *Preliminary working paper on the principle of free, prior and informed consent of indigenous peoples in relation to development affecting their lands and natural resources that would serve as a framework for the drafting of a legal commentary by the UN Working Group on Indigenous Populations*, UN Doc. E/CN.4/Sub.2/AC.4/2004/4.

provide provisions related to minority participation in decisions which affect them.[46] While perhaps less rigorous than the participation standard applied to indigenous peoples, particularly as it pertains to their lands and natural resources, the rights of minorities to participate go beyond the general human rights related to political participation, encompassing wide areas of public and social life.[47] And while the rights of minorities and indigenous peoples are read into the African Charter, the failure of a respondent government to involve the communities in socio-economic decisions that affect them has informed the Commissions findings of a violation.[48]

Where there are explicit grounds for limiting rights as in Article 8(2) of the European Convention on Human Rights,[49] we saw in the early case of *G. and E. v. Norway* before the European Commission of Human Rights, which addressed cultural rights of the Lapps minority, that the loss of a comparatively small area of land upon which the applicants carried out their particular way of life of herding deer and fishing, to allow for the construction of a hydro-electric plant, constituted a permissible interference with their enjoyment of the right to respect for their private life since it did not render the applicants unable 'to continue their life as reindeer herder and a fisherman respectively'.[50] Although the case was declared inadmissible, the Commission observed that a (indigenous) minority group is 'entitled to claim the right to respect for the

[46] Article 15 FCNM: 'The Parties shall create the conditions necessary for the effective participation of persons belonging to national minorities in cultural, social and economic life and in public affairs, in particular those affecting them'; Art. 2(2) UNDM: 'Persons belonging to minorities have the right to participate effectively in cultural, religious, social, economic and public life'; Art. 2(3) UNDM: 'Persons belonging to minorities have the right to participate effectively in decisions on the national and, where appropriate, regional level concerning the minority to which they belong or the regions in which they live, in a manner not incompatible with national legislation.'

[47] Thornberry and Estébanez, *supra*, n. 21, 109, drawing on the work of the FCNM Advisory Committee.

[48] *Ogoni* case, *supra*, n. 12, para. 55.

[49] Article 8 ECHR: '1. Everyone has the right to respect for his private and family life, his home and his correspondence. 2. There shall be no interference by a public authority with the exercise of this right except such as is in accordance with the law and is necessary in a democratic society in the interests of national security, public safety or the economic well-being of the country, for the prevention of disorder or crime, for the protection of health or morals, or for the protection of the rights and freedoms of others.'

[50] ECommHR, *G. and E. v. Norway*, Appl. 9278/1981 and 9415/1981 (joined) Decisions and Reports 35, para. 2. On the latter point see similarly *Noack v. Germany* in which a decisive factor in the Court's decision in declaring the application inadmissible was its determination that the minority Sorb identity would continue to be protected even though they would be displaced by a mining venture. ECtHR, *Noack and Others v. Germany*, Appl. 46346/99, admissibility decision, 2000, Fourth Chamber. See further, Geoff Gilbert, 'Article 5', in Marc Weller (ed.), *A Commentary for the European Framework Convention for the Protection of National Minorities* (Oxford University Press, 2005), 153–75, at 167.

particular life style it may lead as being "private life", "family life" or "home." '[51] However, under the terms of Article 8(2), the Commission stressed, interference with Article 8(1) of the Convention '. . . is permissible if it is in accordance with the law and necessary in a democratic society for one of the purposes enumerated, *inter alia*, the economic well-being of the country'.[52]

There is an inherent danger in weighing minority rights against the economic well-being of a country. Economic development and growth in national wealth tell us nothing about whether the most marginalized groups within the country—often minorities and indigenous peoples—will benefit. Minorities are potentially twice harmed from the outcomes of this formulation—first through the interference with their rights, and second, often by being excluded from the aggregate benefits that the application of the utilitarian concept of 'economic well-being of the country' affords.

III. Housing Rights as Minority Rights

Under the European Convention on Human Rights, the Court sitting as Grand Chamber recognized in *Chapman v. United Kingdom* that a minority's particular way of life is, in principle, entitled to the protection guaranteed for an individual's private life, family life, and home as provided for in Article 8.[53] And while Article 8 does not currently confer a right to be provided with a home,[54] it does entail positive obligations for the state 'to facilitate the minority way of life'.[55] While the Court considered developments within Europe

[51] *G. and E. v. Norway, supra*, n. 50, para. 2.

[52] *Ibid.*

[53] ECtHR, *Chapman v. United Kingdom*, Appl. 27238/95, Judgment of 18 January 2001, para. 73. The Court accepting that the impact of such evictions materially interferes with 'family life' and not just 'home', suggests that any such evictions will engage Art. 8, because the existence of family ties are independent of the length of time of any particular encampment. Luke Clements, 'An Emerging Consensus on the Special Needs of Minorities: the Lessons of Chapman v. UK', European Roma Rights Centre, at www.errc.org. On the former point, see also, *G. and E. v. Norway, supra*, n. 50, para. 35.

[54] ECtHR, *Beard v. United Kingdom*, Appl. 24882/94, Judgment of 18 January 2001, para. 110.

[55] '[A]lthough the fact of belonging to a minority with a traditional lifestyle different from that of the majority does not confer an immunity from general laws intended to safeguard the assets of the community as a whole, such as the environment, it may have an incidence on the manner in which such laws are to be implemented. As intimated in *Buckley*, the vulnerable position of Gypsies as a minority means that some special consideration should be given to their needs and their different lifestyle both in the relevant regulatory planning framework and in reaching decisions in particular cases. To this extent, there is thus a positive obligation imposed on the Contracting States by virtue of Article 8 to facilitate the Gypsy way of life.' *Chapman v. United Kingdom, supra*, n. 53, para. 96. See also, Kristin Henrard, 'Ever-Increasing Synergy towards a Stronger Level of Minority

to protect the rights of minorities generally, and the vulnerable Roma/Gypsy population specifically,[56] on the facts of *Chapman* it was satisfied with the procedural safeguards the state had in place to secure the Article 8 rights of the applicant, and with the consideration given by the authorities to the competing interests.[57] Thus a majority of ten judges found no violation of Article 8 which would have allowed the applicant (and eventually many others in similar situations) to remain on her land, living in her caravan. The ruling incurred a vociferous dissenting opinion issued by the seven minority judges. The opinion challenged the Court's decision on a range of grounds regarding Article 8, including: the effectiveness of procedural safeguards which indicated 'a general presumption against inappropriate [Gypsy] development in the Green Belt... [which] was [not] able to give anything more than marginal or token weight to the applicant's interests or to the associated public interest in preserving cultural diversity through the protection of traditional ethnic lifestyles';[58] and a failure to demonstrate that the interference with the rights of the applicant constituted a ' "pressing social need" when compared with what was at stake for the applicant', and that to take steps to evict the Roma/Gypsy family 'from their home on their own land in circumstances where there has not been shown to be any other lawful alternative site reasonably open to them' is disproportionate.[59]

There has been a series of other cases with the Court sitting as Grand Chamber brought by Roma/Gypsies against the United Kingdom which addressed the same issues of the stationing of caravans on the land owned by the applicants without planning permission, followed by unsuccessful

Protection between Minority Specific and Non-Minority Specific Instruments', *European Yearbook of Minority Issues,* 3 (2003–4), 15–41, at 31.

[56] Reference is made to the Framework Convention for the Protection of National Minorities and developments under the auspices of the European Union and Organisation for Security and Cooperation in Europe.

[57] In considering whether the interference with the applicant's Art. 8 rights 'pursued a legitimate aim' as per Art. 8.2, the Court found that the measures pursued the legitimate aim of protecting the 'rights of others' through the preservation of the environment. *Chapman v. United Kingdom*, *supra*, n. 53, para. 82.

[58] *Chapman v. United Kingdom*, Joint Dissenting Opinion of Judges Pastor, Ridruejo, Bonello, Tulkens, Strážnická, Lorenzen, Fischbach, and Casadevall, para. 4: 'The Court observes that there may be an emerging international consensus among the Contracting States of the Council of Europe recognising the special needs of minorities and an obligation to protect their security, identity and lifestyle, not only for the purpose of safeguarding the interests of the minorities themselves but to preserve a cultural diversity of value to the whole community.' *Ibid.*, para. 93.

[59] *Ibid.*, paras. 4–5.

planning appeals and some prosecutions.[60] In all cases the Court found the contracting state not to have violated Article 8, but with the same large number of minority judges and a reaffirmation of the joint dissenting opinion found in *Chapman*. In *Buckley v. United Kingdom*, the first case before the Court concerning a member of the Roma/Gypsy minority, and pertaining also to the issue of parking a caravan on the applicant's own land without planning permission, a finding of a violation of Article 8 by the Commission linked not solely to the applicant's right to a home but to a particular way of life,[61] was subsequently reversed by the Court inviting several dissenting opinions.[62] In his partly dissenting opinion, Judge Repik remarked that '[i]n the present case the national authorities did not properly assess whether the aim pursued was proportionate to the applicant's right to respect for her home and to the seriousness of the infringement of that right'. Addressing the wide margin of appreciation afforded the respondent state and elaborating on the function of the Strasbourg Court he continued: 'the Court, in order to fulfil its supervisory role, ought itself to have considered whether the interference was proportionate to the right in issue and to its importance to the applicant, all the more so as where a fundamental right of a member of a minority is concerned, especially a minority as vulnerable as the Gypsies, the Court has an obligation to subject any such interference to particularly close scrutiny.'[63] In his dissenting opinion, Judge Petiti took the position that the case gave rise to issues pertaining to the free movement of persons by forcing them to live in a designated area, and to the use of property within the meaning of Article 1 Protocol 1 on account of the systematic refusal to convert retrospective planning permission into permanent permission to park the caravans.[64]

[60] ECtHR, *Chapman v. United Kingdom*, *supra*, n. 53; *Beard v. United Kingdom*, *supra*, n. 54; *Coster v. United Kingdom*, Appl. 24876/94; *Lee v. United Kingdom*, Appl. 25289/94; *Jane Smith v. United Kingdom*, Appl. 25154/94, Judgments of 18 January 2001.

[61] See further, Geoff Gilbert, 'The Burgeoning Minority Rights Jurisprudence of the European Court of Human Rights', *Human Rights Quarterly*, 24 (2002), 736–80, at 778.

[62] ECtHR, *Buckley v. United Kingdom*, Judgment of 25 September 1996, Reports 1996-IV, 1291, 1292, para. 74

[63] *Buckley v. United Kingdom*, partly dissenting opinion of Judge Repik. See also, the partly dissenting opinion of Judge Lohmus advancing the theorem that the question of minority rights is not simply one of rights and duties as per all other members of society but 'in order to establish equality in fact, different treatment may be necessary to preserve their special heritage'.

[64] *Buckley v. United Kingdom*, dissenting opinion of Judge Petiti. All the applicants in the subsequent cases as noted above, save for the Beard family, alleged violations also of Art. 1 of Protocol 1 (peaceful enjoyment of their land) although no violations of the article were found by the Court.

In a unanimous decision in favour of a Gypsy/Roma applicant in a case in which a violation of Article 8 was found (on facts different from those described above), the Court addressed the significance of applying a narrow margin of appreciation under Article 8 since it 'concerns rights of central importance to the individual's identity, self-determination, physical and moral integrity, maintenance of relationships with others and a settled and secure place in the community'.[65] However, there is potential for tension in light of the Court's subsequent reference in the same case to its continued support for a wide margin of appreciation in Article 8 cases dealing with social and economic policy[66] (eg *Buckley v. United Kingdom*); where the implications for cultural identity and self-determination cannot be divorced from policy choices these two approaches to applying the margin of appreciation stand in conflict. While the Court is sensitive to changing conditions and emerging consensus among member states of the Council of Europe, it notes that 'in the interest of legal certainty, foreseeability and equality before the law [...] it should not depart without good reason, from precedents laid down in previous cases'.[67] Yet, questions have been raised as to whether cultural arguments under the provisions on respect for private and family life, home, and ways of life 'have been treated as having sufficient weight. Lifestyle in the Roma/Gypsy and Saami cases is not the best description for cultural characteristics. It suggests that individuals choose a way of life, and does not adequately address those who were born into the folkways of specific communities. The fact of being a member of such a community is a result of choice only in a very limited sense—perhaps to stay or leave, though the latter could do considerable violence to a sense of self-nurture within a particular peoples.'[68]

Housing rights jurisprudence has been creatively developed through a number of different avenues resulting in protection for violations perpetrated against minorities. In *Koptova v. Slovakia* Romani families had found themselves without housing after the closure of an agricultural cooperative which had provided employees with places to live. Anti-Romani racism saw the families exposed to years of homelessness and insecure housing arrangements culminating in the adoption of municipal resolutions prohibiting Roma from

[65] ECtHR, *Connors v. United Kingdom,* Appl. 66746/01, judgment of 27 May 2004, para. 82.

[66] *Ibid.*, para. 86.

[67] *Chapman v. United Kingdom, supra*, n. 53, para. 70. And as Thornberry and Estébanez point out, while the narrowness of the vote and the strength of the dissent may suggest future decisions on these minority issues will take a different form, other very similar applications by Roma/Gypsies in the UK since these 2001 cases have been declared inadmissible. Thornberry and Estébanez, *supra,* n. 21, 86, n. 278.

[68] Thornberry and Estébanez, *supra*, n. 21, 70.

entering and settling in two municipalities on the basis of their ethnicity. The UN Committee on the Elimination of Racial Discrimination found a violation of the International Convention on the Elimination of All Forms of Racial Discrimination Article 5(d)(i) on the right of everyone without distinction as to race, colour, descent, or national or ethnic origin to freedom of movement and residence within the border of the state, and thus the equal right of Roma to settle in the municipalities.[69] Moreover, the author of the communication alleged that merely as a person of Romani origin, she was a victim under the Convention, since the resolutions may be reasonably understood to apply to her (as indeed to all Roma in Slovakia). The Committee agreed with the author and in declaring the communication admissible noted that individuals are entitled to claim 'victim status' should the law itself violate their right, even if they have not been personally affected by the measures.[70] Notably, this was in contrast with the European Court of Human Rights' subsequent inadmissability decision in a case concerning the same facts but submitted by different people.[71] The offending resolutions were rescinded prior to the Committee's views being adopted.[72]

In the case of *Moldovan and Ors v. Romania (No. 2)* the European Court of Human Rights addressed a range of issues stemming from the burning and wholesale destruction of houses and property belonging to Roma by other villagers and the police, including in relation to the alleged violation of Article 8. Having to flee, the victims subsequently spent more than ten years in overcrowded and unsanitary living conditions as they attempted to seek justice. While the Court was barred *ratione temporis* from examining, *inter alia*, the actual burning of the applicants' houses since Romania had not yet ratified the Convention at that time, the Court could, and did, assess the subsequent acts of state agents in response to the destruction due to the direct repercussions the acts had on the applicants' rights. The Court thereby 'considered the Government's responsibility [is] engaged as regards the applicants' subsequent living conditions and that . . . the question of the applicants' living conditions

[69] CERD, Communication No. 13/1998, *Anna Koptova v. Slovak Republic*, UN Doc. CERD/C/57/D/13/1998 (2000), para. 10.1

[70] *Ibid.*, para. 6.5.

[71] ECtHR, *Ján Lacko and Ors v. Slovakia,* Appl. 47237/99, Admissibility decision 2 July 2002, para. 13.

[72] The quashing of the resolution by a unanimous vote of the municipal council, its admission that it was contrary to human rights and the provision of government funding towards resolving the housing problem was tantamount, in the Court's view, to acknowledgement of a violation of the rights of the Romani families affected by the resolution and led the Court to declare this part of the application inadmissible. *Ibid.*, para. 13.

fall within the scope of their right to respect for family and private life, as well as their homes. Article 8 is thus clearly applicable to these complaints.'[73]

This case demonstrates that the ECHR provides a certain minimum level of protection against unacceptable living conditions when the state is at fault for having caused an individual to fall below that level.[74] The Court reaffirmed the general principle that giving effect to private or family life and the home is not limited to negative duties of non-interference but may entail positive obligations including the adoption of measures designed to secure respect for these rights also within relations between individuals.[75] The Court concluded that hindrances on the part of the authorities in a range of areas[76] and the failure of the national authorities to put a stop to the breaches of the applicants' rights 'amount to a serious violation of Article 8 of a continuing nature'.[77] It held unanimously that there had been a violation of Article 8, as well as a violation of Article 14 prohibiting discrimination, in conjunction with Article 8.[78]

In the *Ogoni* case before the African Commission on Human and Peoples' Rights, the then military government of Nigeria was found to have violated a range of rights under the African Charter linked to the production of oil through the state oil company, as well as due to the state's indirect role in condoning and facilitating violations by private oil companies in the Ogoniland—home to the indigenous Ogoni minority—by placing the legal and military powers of the state at the disposal of the oil companies. While various aspects of the case will be considered below, here we draw attention to the Commission's findings of a violation of the right to housing or shelter. While the African Charter on Human and Peoples' Rights provides no explicit reference to a right to housing it was read into the Charter as a corollary of the combined provisions

[73] ECtHR, *Moldovan and Ors v. Romania (No. 2)*, Appl. 41138/98 and 64320/01, Judgment of 12 July 2005, paras. 104–5 (hereinafter *Hadareni* case).

[74] See, Antoine Buyse, 'Destruction of Housing and Discrimination against Roma—Development at the ECtHR', *Housing and ESC Rights Quarterly*, 3 (2006), 5–6, at 5.

[75] *Hadareni* case, *supra*, n. 73, para. 93.

[76] For example, their failure to institute criminal proceedings, the awarding of only partial damages and after a prolonged period of time, discrimination before the courts and failure to rebuild some of the houses and the construction of uninhabitable houses for others.

[77] *Hadareni* case, *supra*, n. 73, para. 109. For similar cases dealing with the destruction of homes constituting a violation of Art. 8, see, ECtHR, *Akdivar and Ors v. Turkey*, Appl. 21893/93, Judgment of 30 August 1996 and ECtHR, *Mentes and Ors v. Turkey*, Appl. 23186/94, Judgment of 28 November 1997.

While the claims were brought by Kurdish minorities in Turkey, consistent with the Commission's findings in the latter cases, the Court, however, did not uphold a claim under the non-discrimination provision of Art. 14 that the destruction was ethnically motivated.

[78] *Hadareni* case, *supra*, n. 73, para. 140.

protecting the right to health (Article 16), the right to property (Article 14) and the right to family life (Article 18(1)).[79] In addition to the 'very minimum' negative obligations prohibiting the destruction of housing and interference with the rebuilding by individuals or the communities of their homes,[80] and the right to protection against forced evictions,[81] the Commission elaborated on the core content of positive obligations. Drawing on the multi-tiered nature of obligations adopted by the UN Committee on Economic, Social and Cultural Rights,[82] the African Commission concluded that the actions by the government of Nigeria constituted 'massive violations' of the two minimum obligations to respect and protect Charter rights,[83] and provided that '[the state parties] obligations to protect obliges it to prevent the violation of any individual's right to housing by another individual or non-state actor... and where such infringements occur, it should act to preclude further deprivations as well as access to legal remedies. The right to shelter even goes further than a roof over one's head. It extends to embody the individual's right to be let alone and to live in peace whether under a roof or not.'[84]

In the case of *Moldovan and Ors v. Romania (No. 2)* the European Court of Human Rights also drew clear links between inadequate housing and health and well-being. The Court being influenced by the length of time during which the applicants had to endure such sub-standard conditions combined with the racially discriminatory attitude of the authorities, found that the applicants' mental suffering eroded their human dignity and amounted to 'degrading treatment' in violation of Article 3 prohibiting torture or inhuman or degrading treatment or punishment.[85] In a case against Yugoslavia, the UN Committee against Torture had similarly found that violence perpetrated by non-state actors (a mob of non-Roma) resulting in the burning and destruction of homes and property belonging to Roma, carried out with the acquiescence of the police, constituted cruel, inhuman, or degrading treatment or

[79] *Ogoni* case, *supra,* n. 12, para. 60.

[80] *Ibid.*, para. 61.

[81] *Ibid.*, para. 63. The Commission refers explicitly to the prohibition against forced evictions under CESCR, General Comment No. 4 (Article 11(1) on the Right to Adequate Housing, UN Doc. E/1992/23 (1991).

[82] See *Ogoni case, supra*, n. 12, para. 44 where the Commission refers to the 'internationally accepted ideas of the various obligations engendered by human rights'—duties to respect, protect, promote, and fulfil.

[83] *Ibid.*, para. 62

[84] *Ibid.*, para. 61. See also, para. 62. See similarly, CESCR, General Comment No. 7 (Article 11(1)) on Forced Evictions, U.N. Doc. E/1998/22, Annex IV (1997), para. 7.

[85] *Hadareni* case, *supra,* n. 73, paras. 110 and 113.

punishment.[86] The Committee pointed out aggravating factors to include, the presence of older residents within the buildings and the fact that the acts were committed with a significant level of racial motivation.[87] In an individual opinion two Committee members considered that the acts amounted to 'torture' due to the severity of the suffering inflicted upon the victims, including the destruction of their settlement, homes, and basic necessities.[88]

The right of everyone to an adequate standard of living including adequate housing and the continuous improvement of living conditions under Article 11(1) of the International Covenant on Economic, Social and Cultural Rights means more than basic shelter; it means the right to live in peace, security, and dignity,[89] in accordance, of course, with the right not to be subject to any form of discrimination.[90] These factors have particular resonance with minority communities who are disproportionately affected by forced evictions.[91] As CESCR has elaborated, the concept of 'adequacy' includes: legal security of land tenure which guarantees legal protection against forced eviction and harassment; subsidized housing for those unable to obtain affordable accommodation; habitability that serves to protect occupants from the elements and other health threats; access to adequate housing resources by disadvantaged groups must be accorded and should constitute a central policy goal; and policies must appropriately enable the expression of cultural identity.[92] In a complaint which found discrimination against Roma in Italy in relation to their access to suitable accommodation as well as protection from evictions, the European Committee of Social Rights made clear the requirement placed on states when it noted that 'equal treatment implies Italy should take measures appropriate to Roma's particular circumstances to safeguard their right to housing and prevent them, as a vulnerable group, from becoming homeless'.[93]

[86] CAT, Communication No. 161/2000, *Hajrizi Dzemajl et al. v. Federal Republic of Yugoslavia*, (2002), paras. 9.2 and 10.

[87] *Ibid.*, para. 9.2.

[88] *Hajrizi Dzemajl et al. v. Federal Republic of Yugoslavia*, Individual opinion by Committee members Fernando Marino and Alejandro Gonzáles Poblete concerning the devastation of human settlements. *Ibid.*

[89] CESCR, General Comment No. 4, *supra*, n. 81, para. 7.

[90] See, eg *ibid.*, para. 6.

[91] Miloon Kothari, *Report of the Special Rapporteur on Adequate Housing as a Component of the Right to an Adequate Standard of Living*, UN Doc. E/CN.4/2004/48 (2004), paras. 64–5; CESCR, General Comment No. 7, *supra*, n. 84, para. 10; see further, Iain Byrne, 'Housing Rights', in Margot E. Salomon (ed.), *Economic, Social and Cultural Rights: A Guide for Minorities and Indigenous Peoples* (Minority Rights Group International, 2005), 29–39, at 32.

[92] CESCR, General Comment No. 4, *supra*, n. 81, para. 8.

[93] European Committee of Social Rights, *The European Roma Rights Centre v. Italy*, Complaint No. 27/2004, 7 December 2005, Merits, para. 21.

IV. Property Rights as Minority Rights

The right to property and enjoyment of possessions[94] has an autonomous meaning in international law not limited to ownership of physical goods,[95] or to private property as defined by domestic laws.[96] While forced eviction, destruction, and encroachment on land belonging to minorities may constitute also an interference with the right to property, the right to property is characterized in particular by the economic interest and value of the possession.[97] However, where the right is applied to minorities, including indigenous peoples, there is often a convergence between its civil rights dimensions and those reflecting economic, social, and cultural rights.

The judicial application of the right to property (including the peaceful enjoyment of possessions) has developed to provide protection to minority and indigenous communities, most notably in relation to land rights. *The Mayagna (Sumo) Indigenous Community of Awas Tingni v. Nicaragua* was the first case before the Inter-American Court of Human Rights to address the territorial rights of indigenous peoples, and the Court found Nicaragua to have violated the right to property of the Awas Tingni indigenous community by its failure to delimit, demarcate, and title indigenous lands communally occupied by them. Without effective measures to ensure the property rights of the community, they were afforded no protection against interference by the state resulting from its granting of logging concessions to a private company. Through an 'evolutionary interpretation' of international instruments, the Court read Article 21 under the American Convention on Human Rights protecting the right to property 'in a sense which includes, among others, the rights of members of the indigenous communities within the framework of communal property....'[98] The Court noted moreover that as a result of customary practices,

[94] The European Convention refers to 'the right to peaceful enjoyment of [his] possessions'; the African Charter refers to 'the right to property'; and the American Convention refers to 'the right to use and enjoyment of property'.

[95] ECtHR, *Dogan and Others v. Turkey,* Appl. 8803–8811/02, 8813/02 and 8815–8819/02, Judgment of 10 November 2004, para. 138.

[96] *The Mayagna (Sumo) Awas Tingni Community v. Nicaragua, supra*, n. 43, paras. 145–6.

[97] *Dogan and Others v. Turkey, supra*, n. 95, paras. 137 and 139.

[98] *The Mayagna (Sumo) Awas Tingni Community v. Nicaragua, supra*, n. 43, para. 148. Consistent with a judicial consensus generally, at para. 146 the Court refers to human rights treaties as 'live instruments whose interpretation must adapt to the evolution of the times and, specifically, to current living conditions'. See ECtHR, *Tyrer v. the United Kingdom*, Appl. 5856/72, Judgment of 25 April 1978, Series A, No. 26 (1978).

and in the absence of formal title to property, possession of land should suffice for indigenous communities to obtain official recognition of that property.[99]

In this, its first case on indigenous land rights, the Court was afforded an opportunity to elaborate on the concept of property in indigenous matters. After remarking on the tradition among indigenous peoples that has land belonging to the collective rather than centring on individual ownership it went on to explain that:

Indigenous groups, by the fact of their very existence, have the right to live freely in their own territory; the close ties of indigenous peoples with the land must be recognized and understood as the fundamental basis of their cultures, their spiritual life, their integrity, and their economic survival. For indigenous communities, relations to the land are not merely a matter of possession and production but a material and spiritual element which they must fully enjoy, even to preserve their cultural legacy and transmit it to future generations.[100]

[99] *The Mayagna (Sumo) Awas Tingni Community v. Nicaragua, supra*, n. 43, para. 151. The same findings by the Inter-American Court are provided regarding non-indigenous tribal communities who possess an 'all-encompassing relationship' whereby their traditional lands, and their concept of ownership regarding that territory is not centred on the individual, but rather on the community as a whole. Inter-AmCtHR, *Moiwana Village v. Suriname,* Judgment of 15 June 2005, Series C, No. 124, paras. 130–1.

In considering an alleged violation of the right to peaceful enjoyment of the possessions (although not linked to the protection of minority rights per se) resulting from the forced eviction of the applicants (Kurdish minorities in Turkey) from their lands and homes by state security forces, the ECtHR found a violation of Art. 1, Protocol 1 despite the fact that the applicants held no formal title to the land in question: 'Although they did not have registered property, they either had their own houses constructed on the lands of their ascendants or lived in the houses owned by their fathers and cultivated the land belonging to the latter. The Court further notes that the applicants had unchallenged rights over the common lands in the village, such as the pasture, grazing and the forest land, and that they earned their living from stockbreeding and tree-felling. Accordingly, in the Court's opinion, all these economic resources and the revenue that the applicants derived from them may qualify as 'possessions' for the purposes of Article 1.' *Dogan and Others v. Turkey*, paras. 139 and 156.

[100] *The Mayagna (Sumo) Awas Tingni Community v. Nicaragua, supra*, n. 43, para. 149. See also, Inter-AmCtHR, *Yakye Axa v. Paraguay*, Judgment of 17 June 2005, Series C, No. 125 (Spanish only–English language case summary in *Interights Bulletin,* 15 (2006), 131–2) in which the Court elaborated on indigenous rights associated with the right to property: '[C]ommunal property of indigenous communities closely relates to indigenous traditions and expressions, customs and rituals, values and arts, and relationship with nature'. *Washington College of Law Human Rights Brief, Yakye Axa v. Paraguay,* 1 (2005), 28. See also, the Commission's Report on the *Maya Indigenous Communities of the Toledo District/Belize* in which it found a violation, *inter alia*, of the right to property under the American Declaration on Human Rights because the state failed 'to take effective measures to delimit, demarcate, and officially recognise the communal property right to the lands that they have traditionally occupied and used, and by granting logging and oil concessions to third parties to utilize the property and resources that could fall within the lands which must be delimited, demarcated and titled, without consultation with and the informed consent of the Maya people'. Inter-AmCommHR, Case 12.053, Merits 12 October 2004, Report No 40/04, para. 5.

In the 2005 case of the *Yakye Axa Indigenous Community v. Paraguay*, the Inter-American Court held that Paraguay was in breach of Article 21 in particular due to the fact that the ancestral land of which the Yakye Axa were deprived was the basis of their cultural identity, spiritual life, integrity, and economic survival. In its interpretation of the right to property the Court took into account, *inter alia*, Article 13 of ILO Convention No. 169 on the Rights of Indigenous and Tribal Peoples to which Paraguay is party, which requires that governments '... respect the special importance for the cultures and spiritual values of the peoples concerned of their relationship with the lands or territories... which they occupy or otherwise use, and in particular the collective aspects of this relationship'.[101] When the collective right to ancestral land conflicted with the right to private property of individuals as was the case, the state in so far as possible should give priority to the rights of indigenous peoples to their land, while awarding just compensation to the injured party (Article 21(2)); when due to concrete and justified reasons it is not possible to return the ancestral land to the indigenous people, the compensation given to them must be in the form of either alternative territory or payment of compensation or both.[102] Whatever compensation is awarded must be agreed with the indigenous people, and here the Court interpreted Article 21 in conjunction with Article 16(4) of ILO Convention No. 169 which details the right to compensation for the removal of indigenous or tribal peoples from their lands.[103]

The Inter-American Commission on Human Rights and the Inter-American Court of Human Rights have paid much attention to the interdependency of cultural rights and territorial rights and have generally highlighted the importance of taking into account the customs of the indigenous and tribal peoples of the Americas for purposes of applying the Convention, including in relation to reparations.[104] Significantly, orders

[101] *Yakye Axa v. Paraguay, supra*, n. 100, 131–2.

[102] *Ibid.*

[103] Article 16(4) ILO Convention 169: 'When such return is not possible, as determined by agreement or, in the absence of such agreement, through appropriate procedures, these peoples shall be provided in all possible cases with lands of quality and legal status at least equal to that of the lands previously occupied by them, suitable to provide for their present needs and future development. Where the peoples concerned express a preference for compensation in money or in kind, they shall be so compensated under appropriate guarantees.'

[104] Fergus Mackay, 'Cultural Rights', in Salomon (ed.), *Economic, Social and Cultural Rights*, 83–93, at 85. On reparations see, Inter-AmCtHR: *Aloeboetoe et al. v. Suriname*, (Reparations) Judgment of 10 September 1993, Series C, No. 15, para. 62; *Bámaca Velásquez v. Guatemala*, (Merits) judgment of 25 November 2000, Series C, No. 70 and notably the Separate Opinion of Judge A.A. Cançado Trindade, para. 4; *The Mayagna (Sumo) Awas Tingni Community v. Nicaragua, supra*, n. 43, para. 149.

have provided remedies of a collective nature when the harm is experienced by the collective.[105]

As noted above in consideration of the *Diergaardt* case before the Human Rights Committee, land rights are more readily linked to the protection of the rights of indigenous peoples than to those of other minorities.[106] However, jurisprudential developments reflect that where the non-indigenous minority community has a relationship to traditional land which is of vital spiritual, cultural, and material importance to the preservation of the group's traditional way of life, it is not essential that the relationship be traced to pre-colonial invasion and as far back as time immemorial.[107] In the case of *Moiwana Village v. Suriname,* the Inter-American Court considered the state's obligations regarding a range of rights associated with the subsequent denial of justice, and displacement—stemming from a massacre in 1986 of N'djuka Maroons who are the descendants of African slaves—from their 'ancestral lands' acquired in 1760 through negotiated peace treaties.[108]

This same logic informs the approach taken by the International Labour Organization. By applying both the terms 'indigenous' and 'tribal peoples'—as can be seen for example in Convention No. 169—the designated recipients of particular rights shift from being determined on the basis of chronological precedence in a given area to a particular form of social organization.[109] The recently established Working Group of Experts on Indigenous Populations/

[105] Its first ruling to this effect is found in: Inter-AmCtHR *Plan de Sánchez Massacre v. Gautemala,* (Reparations), Judgment of 19 November 2004, Series C, No. 116, para. 86. See further, Fergus MacKay, 'From Sacred Commitment to Justiciable Norms: Indigenous Peoples' Rights in the Inter-American System' in Margot E. Salomon, Arne Tostensen, and Wouter Vandenhole (eds.), *Casting the Net Wider: Human Rights, Development and New Duty-Bearers* (Intersentia, 2007), 371.

[106] Similarly, the World Bank has policies on indigenous peoples that seek to ensure good practice in all investment projects in which indigenous people are present, or have collective attachment to the project area, but none on safeguarding the rights of minorities. Likewise, the UNDP has a Policy on Engagement with Indigenous Peoples but none, as of yet, for minorities generally. On land issues as they pertain to minorities in Europe see, Alan Phillips, 'The Framework Convention for the Protection of National Minorities and the Protection of the Economic Rights of Minorities', *European Yearbook of Minority Issues* (2003–4), 287–306, at 299–300.

[107] *Moiwana Village v. Suriname, supra,* n. 99, para. 86(6); 'The Moiwana community members are not indigenous to the region; according to the proven facts, Moiwana Village was settled by N'djuka clans late in the 19th century. Nevertheless, from that time until the 1986 attack, the community members lived in the area in strict adherence to N'djuka custom.' (para. 132).

[108] *Ibid.,* para. 124. On the N'djuka history and culture see paras. 86(1)-86(11). The Court found violations of, *inter alia,* the right to property (Art. 21) and freedom of movement and residence (Art. 22), in relation to Art. 1(1) (non-discrimination).

[109] Lee Swepston, 'Labour Rights', in Salomon (ed.), *Economic, Social and Cultural Rights,* 69–81, at n. 1.

Communities of the African Commission on Human and Peoples' Rights is advancing a similar approach in an effort to carve out a meaningful concept of indigenousness among the multitude of African peoples native to the continent. The Working Group's inaugural report states:

> We should put much less emphasis on the early definitions focusing on aboriginality, as indeed it is difficult and [often] not very constructive... to the debate in the African context. The focus should be more on the recent approaches focusing on self-definition as indigenous and distinctly different from other groups within a state; on special attachment to and use of their traditional land whereby their ancestral land and territory has a fundamental importance for their collective physical and cultural survival as peoples; on an experience of subjugation, marginalization, dispossession, exclusion or discrimination because these peoples have different cultures, ways of life or modes of production than the national hegemonic and dominant model.[110]

Consistent with the key UN studies on the topic, the report also acknowledges that while there may not always be a clear-cut distinction between indigenous peoples and minorities, the types of rights ascribed to indigenous peoples and minorities respectively in international law differ considerably, with resultant implications, the most significant difference being that minority rights are formulated as individual rights whereas indigenous rights are collective or group rights.[111] While international human rights law, generally, still reflects its individualistic bias borne of Western liberal political philosophy, there is a growing appreciation that both dimensions are necessary for the rights of minorities (including indigenous peoples) to be given full effect.[112] The challenges are to understand individual rights and group rights not as discrete but as mutually reinforcing,[113] to reconcile competing claims between the individual and the group where they exist (the reconciliation of competing interests being a familiar centrepiece of the human rights legal regime), and to recognize any claim

[110] *Report of the African Commission on Human and Peoples' Rights' Working Group of Experts on Indigenous Populations/Communities* (2005), 92–3. See also, Samia Slimane, *Recognizing Minorities in Africa* (Minority Rights Group International, 2003).

[111] *Ibid.*, 95–7; Asbjørn Eide and Erika-Irene Daes, *Working Paper on the Relationship and Distinction between the Rights of Persons Belonging to Minorities and those of Indigenous Peoples*, UN Doc. E/CN.4/Sub.2/2000/10.

[112] Peter Leuprecht, 'Minority Rights Revisited: New Glimpses of an Old Issue' in Philip Alston (ed.), *Peoples' Rights* (Oxford University Press, 2001), 111–25; see also, Margot E. Salomon and Arjun Sengupta, *The Right to Development: Obligations of States and the Rights of Minorities and Indigenous Peoples* (Minority Rights Group International, 2003).

[113] Margot E. Salomon, 'Collective Rights in International Law', Contribution to the UK Foreign and Commonwealth Office Roundtable on Collective Rights for Indigenous People, November 2002 (Minority Rights Group International, 2002).

made for group rights as valid only in so far as it extends, rather then deprecates other human rights.[114] In actual fact minority rights are both individual rights and collective rights simultaneously: when exercised by the individual, including as against the group, preservation of the group identity provides the underlying rationale.[115] And when rights are exercised collectively, the individual is nonetheless the ultimate beneficiary.

In the case of *Malawi African Association and Others v. Mauritania* in which a range of charges was brought against the Arab Mauritanian government in relation to the abuses meted out largely against black Mauritanians between 1986 and 1992,[116] the African Commission on Human and Peoples' Rights found the right to property to have been violated as a result of the eviction, confiscation, looting, expropriation, and destruction of the property of black ethnic Mauritanians.[117] In elaborating on the essential principle of non-discrimination and its goal of eliminating all forms of discrimination and ensuring equality among all human beings, the Commission drew attention to the objectives underpinning the UN Declaration on the Rights of Persons Belonging to National or Ethnic, Religious and Linguistic Minorities.[118] Citing Article 1(1) of the UNDM which provides that: 'States shall protect the existence and the national or ethnic, cultural, religious and linguistic identity of minorities within their respective territories and shall encourage conditions for the promotion of that identity', the Commission castigated the Mauritanian state for subjecting 'its own indigenes to discriminatory treatment because of the colour of their skin'.[119] It was in these *Mauritania* cases that for the first

[114] Leslye A. Obiora, 'Beyond the Rhetoric of a Right to Development', *Law and Policy,* 18 (3&4) (July/October 1996), 366–418, at 392, n. 81.

[115] See, eg: *Sandra Lovelace v. Canada, supra*, n. 32.

[116] Soninke, Wolofs, Hal-Pulaar, as well as, Haratines and Moors. AfrCommHPR, *Malawi African Association and Others v. Mauritania,* (Communication Nos. 54/91, 61/91, 98/93, 164/97–196/97, 210/98, 13th Annual Activity Report (2000)), paras. 1–2.

[117] *Ibid.*, paras. 127–8. Destruction of property will clearly constitute a deprivation of property under the European Convention on Human Rights. See, Clare Ovey and Robin White: *Jacobs and Whites The European Convention on Human Rights*, 4th edn (Oxford University Press, 2006) 344—75, at 359, on the series of cases against Turkey related to the destruction of property stemming from clashes between the security forces and sympathisers of the Kurdistan Workers Party (PKK).

[118] Articles 60–61 of the African Charter explicitly call on the Commission to 'draw inspiration from international law' and 'to take into consideration, as subsidiary measures to determine the principles of law, other general or special international conventions . . . '.

[119] *Malawi African Association and Others v. Mauritania, supra*, n. 116, para. 131.

time in its decision making, the Commission outlined elaborate requests for specific remedial measures.[120]

In the *Ogoni case* described earlier, the Commission addressed the negative duties of 'the state and all its organs' to respect the right to property (entailing the right to housing) from '...infringing the freedom [of the individual] to use [...] material or other resources available to them in a way they find most appropriate to satisfy individual, family, household or community housing needs'.[121] Developing the scope of positive obligations, the Commission held also that in preventing violations of the (implied) right to housing, the state had a duty to protect individuals from 'state and non-state actors like landlords, property developers, and landowners [... and] to act to preclude further deprivations as well as guarantee access to legal remedies'.[122] Qualifying the right to property under the African Charter are limitations 'in the interest of public need or in the general interest of the community and in accordance with the provisions of appropriate laws'.[123] Similar to the general principle of proportionality now familiar in the adjudication of qualified human rights more broadly, the Commission has also established that 'the justification of limitations must be strictly proportionate with, and absolutely necessary for, the advantages which follow'.[124]

In the case of *Chassagnou et al. v. France*, we see the European Court reaffirm its position that the state may enjoy a wide margin of appreciation in striking a fair balance between the general interest of the community and the individual's fundamental rights in relation to the right to property.[125]

[120] Chidi Anselm Odinkalu, 'African Commission on Human and Peoples' Rights: Recent Cases', *Human Rights Law Review*, 1 (2001), 97–109, at 109. But, on the uphill battle for enforcing the remedies, see, Morné van der Linde and Lirette Louw, 'Considering the Interpretation and Implementation of Article 24 of the African Charter on Human and Peoples' Rights in light of the SERAC Communication', *African Human Rights Law Journal*, 3 (2003), 167–87, at 180–6.

[121] *Ogoni* case, *supra*, n. 12, para. 61.

[122] *Ibid.*

[123] ACHPR, Art. 14.

[124] AfrCommHPR, *Constitutional Rights Project, Civil Liberties Organisation and Media Rights Agenda v. Nigeria*, Communication Nos. 140/94, 141/94, 145/95, (1999), paras. 42 and 52 (on the Commission's conclusion that Decrees which allow property to be invaded or encroached upon 'cannot be said to be "appropriate" or in the interest of the public or the community in general [as per Art. 14].'

[125] ECtHR, *Chassagnou and Others v. France*, Appl. 25088/94, 28331/95 and 28443/95, Judgment of 29 April 1999, Reports 1999-III, p. 50, para. 75. The right to property (in addition to involving the application of social or economic planning policies where the margin of appreciation tends to be wide) is less central, according to the Court, to ensuring the 'individual's identity, self-determination and maintenance of relationships with others' than rights provided for under Art. 8 of the Convention (where consequently the margin of appreciation may be narrower): ECtHR, *Connors v. United Kingdom, supra*, n. 65, para. 82. As the case law under the Inter-American system most notably reflects, however, the right to property can be interpreted to address concerns of critical importance to minority identity, moral integrity, and the preservation of a community.

However, in restating its established case law that the second paragraph of Article 1 Protocol 1 must be construed in light of the first sentence of the Article in which the right is affirmed,[126] it has been observed that the Court places greater emphasis than in earlier case law on the need to secure a fair balance between the competing interests.[127] In relation to what is necessary in a democratic society (in its consideration of justifications for the interferences with freedom of association) the Court held that 'a balance must be achieved which ensures the fair and proper treatment of minorities and avoids any abuse of a dominant position'.[128]

Reflecting further on the right to property for minorities under the European Convention, in the complex and multifaceted case of *Loizidou v. Turkey* the Grand Chamber of the European Court considered a claim by a Greek Cypriot national who alleged a continuing violation of her right to the peaceful enjoyment of possessions as a result of being prevented by Turkish forces on the divided island from returning from Nicosia where she lived with her husband, to northern Cyprus where she had owned land prior to 1974.[129] It was then that a military intervention by Turkey established Turkish Cypriot control over the northern part of the island. In finding a violation of Article 1 of Protocol 1 of the ECHR, the Court held that by being refused access to her land since 1974, she had lost all control over and possibilities to use and enjoy her property. The continuous denial of access was held to be an interference

[126] In guaranteeing the right to property generally the Court speaks of three rules derived from the Article: the first rule is set out in the first sentence of the first paragraph of Art. 1 Protocol 1 and enunciates the principle of the peaceful enjoyment of property; the second rule, which is contained in the second sentence of the first paragraph covers deprivation of possessions and subjects it to certain conditions; and the third rule, stated in the second paragraph, recognizes that contracting states are entitled, amongst other things, to control the use of property in accordance with the general interest. The second and third rules are concerned with particular instances of interference and should be construed in light of the general principle provided in the first rule. ECtHR, *Agosi v. the United Kingdom*, Appl. 9118/80, Judgment of 24 October 1986, para. 48.

[127] Ovey and White, *supra*, n. 117, 344–75, at 372 also refer to this recent emphasis as illustrative of the Court's 'modern approach' to assessing the conditions for interference. *Chassagnou et al. v. France, supra*, n. 125, para. 75.

[128] *Chassagnou et al. v. France, supra*, n. 125, para. 112. The Court found, *inter alia*, a violation of Art. 1 Protocol 1, both taken alone or read in conjunction with Art. 14.

[129] Here the term 'minority' is used to mean a non-dominant ethnic group requiring protection of its distinct ethnic identity and discriminated against or marginalized on that basis. As the Advisory Committee to the Framework Convention for National Minorities noted in its opinion on Cyprus, the provisions of the Convention are applied to all ethnic groups making up the population of Cyprus including the Greek Cypriot numerical majority (under Turkish occupation). Advisory Committee Opinion on Cyprus, ACFC/SR (1999) 002 rev, Part II, Art. 3(2).

with the peaceful enjoyment of her possessions.[130] As it had established in earlier case law, the Court observed that 'a hindrance can amount to a violation of the Convention just like a legal impediment'.[131] Though not expressly stated, it follows from the Court's findings of a continuous violation of Article 1 Protocol 1 that a state has a positive obligation to ensure that the owner of property has access to it so that it can be enjoyed.[132] Regarding the right to property more generally under the European Convention, the Court will test both positive and negative obligations by seeking to determine whether the state action or omission called into question can be justified.[133]

Ruling that the questions raised by Cyprus in its application engaged the responsibility of Turkey under the European Convention, the Grand Chamber, reaffirming its reasoning and conclusion in the Loizidou judgment (merits), found a violation of Article 1 Protocol 1 in *Cyprus v. Turkey* by virtue of the fact that the Greek Cypriot owners of property in northern Cyprus were being denied 'access to and control, use and enjoyment of their property as well as any

[130] ECtHR, *Loizidou v. Turkey*, (Preliminary Objections) Judgment of 23 March 1995, Series A, No. 310, para. 63. The Court also required the applicant to have remained the legal owner of the land for a continuous violation to be shown (para. 62), ie in order to dismiss the objection *ratione temporis* by Turkey that the jurisdiction of the Court applies to matters which occur only subsequent to her recognition of its compulsory jurisdiction.

[131] *Ibid.* para. 63. *Mutatis mutandis, Airey v. Ireland, supra*, n. 6, para. 25 in which the Court concludes: '. . . In the first place, hindrance in fact can contravene the Convention just like a legal impediment. Furthermore, fulfilment of a duty under the Convention on occasion necessitates some positive action on the part of the State; in such circumstances, the State cannot simply remain passive . . .'.

[132] Ovey and White, *supra*, n. 117, 344–75, at 348.

Further, denial of access to property and peaceful enjoyment of possessions is broader than limitations on freedom of movement (*Loizidou v. Turkey, supra*, n. 130, paras. 60–1), just as limits on the freedom of movement of an applicant prevented him from gaining access to the southern part of Cyprus to meet bi-communally with Greek-Cypriots affecting his rights to freedom of assembly and association contrary to Art. 11 of the ECHR (ECtHR, *Djavit An v. Turkey*, Appl. 20652/92, Judgment of 20 February 2003, Reports 2003-III 286, paras. 54–5). In his dissenting opinion, Judge Golcuklu took the view that the case was in fact about freedom of movement (ie: Art. 2 of Protocol 4 which Turkey had not ratified) and the limitations on the right stemmed not from an individual act directed against the applicant, but from the consequences of the establishment of the 1974 borderline dividing Cyprus and the continued closure (referring to the Dissenting opinion of Judges Bernhardt and Lopes Rocha in *Loizidou v. Turkey* case (Merits)). Citing the Commission's conclusions *mutatis mutandis* in *Loizidou v. Turkey*, he supports the view that '. . . limitations on freedom of movement . . . may indirectly affect other matters, such as access to property. But that does not mean that deprivation of liberty, or restriction of access to a certain area, interferes directly with the right protected by Article 1 of Protocol No. 1. In other words, the right to peaceful enjoyment of one's possessions does not include as a corollary, the right to freedom of movement.' Dissenting opinion, Judge Golcuklu, *Djavit An v. Turkey*, paras. 15–16.

[133] Ovey and White, *supra*, n. 117, 344–75, at 347.

compensation for the interference with their property rights....'[134] The fact that the rights of Greek Cypriots to the peaceful enjoyment of their possessions was not secured in the case of their permanent departure from that territory,[135] and given that the inheritance rights of persons living in southern Cyprus in connection with the property in northern Cyprus of deceased Greek Cypriot relatives were not recognized, provided other aspects of a breach of Article 1 Protocol 1.[136]

The findings in this case more generally, including those arising out of the alleged violations pertaining to the living conditions of Greek-Cypriots in northern Cyprus (notably, violations of freedom of religion, expression, right to education, respect for private and family life,[137] and of the prohibition on degrading treatment as a result of severe racial discrimination,[138] and the right to a remedy[139]) demonstrate the Court's concern with the impact the circumstances would have on the ability of the community to maintain its identity and indeed its existence.[140] Reflecting on a report of the UN Secretary-General on the Karpas Greek Cypriots,[141] the Court remarked that:

> ... [T]he living conditions of the Karpas Greek Cypriots confirmed that they were the object of very severe restrictions which curtailed the exercise of basic freedoms and had the effect of ensuring that, inexorably, with the passage of time, the community would cease to exist... the Karpas Greek Cypriots were not permitted by the authorities to bequeath immovable property to a relative, even the next-of-kin, unless the latter also lived in the north; there were no secondary-school facilities in the north and Greek-Cypriot children who opted to attend secondary schools in the south were

[134] ECtHR, *Cyprus v. Turkey*, Appl. 25781/94, Judgment of 10 May 2001, para. 189. The Court found also a continuing violation of Art. 8 of the Convention 'by reason of the refusal to allow the return of any Greek-Cypriot displaced persons to their homes in northern Cyprus...' *Ibid.*, para. 175.

[135] *Ibid.*, para. 269.

[136] *Ibid.*, para. 270.

[137] The Court pointed out that restrictions on the community's freedom of movement impacted on their enjoyment of private and family life and on their right to practise their religion. *Ibid.*, para. 308.

[138] *Ibid.*, para. 310.

[139] *Ibid.*, para. 194. Failure to provide remedies under Art. 13 to displaced persons to contest interferences with their rights under Art. 8 and Art. 1 of Protocol 1.

[140] See also, Art. 1(1) of the UN Declaration on the Rights of Persons Belonging to National or Ethnic, Religious and Linguistic Minorities (1992) which states: 'States shall protect the existence and the national or ethnic, cultural, religious and linguistic identity of minorities within their respective territories and shall encourage conditions for the promotion of that identity.' UN Doc. E/CN.4/1992/48 & Corr. 1 (1992) at 16–19.

[141] Greek Cypriots living in the Karpas region of Northern Cyprus.

denied the right to reside in the north once they reached the age of 16 in the case of males and 18 in the case of females.[142] . . . For the Court it is an inescapable conclusion that the interferences at issue were directed at the Karpas Greek-Cypriot community for the very reason that they belonged to this class of persons. The treatment to which they were subjected during the period under consideration can only be explained in terms of the features which distinguish them from the Turkish-Cypriot population, namely their ethnic origin, race and religion . . . .[143]

A number of international bodies have addressed the particular issue of discrimination in relation to property and housing rights generally. In *F.A. v. Norway*, the Committee on the Elimination of Racial Discrimination recommended that Norway give full effect to its obligations under Article 5(e)(iii) of the Convention when it 'urge[d] the State party to take effective measures to ensure that housing agencies refrain from engaging in discriminatory practices and do not accept submissions from private landlords which would discriminate on racial grounds'.[144] Although property rights are as such not protected under the CCPR, the Human Rights Committee considers communications related to property right laws that may violate Covenant Article 2 on non-discrimination and Article 26 on equality before the law if they are discriminatory in character, as was made clear in *Drobek v. Slovakia*.[145] The Permanent Court of International Justice in considering property contracts belonging to ethnic Germans in Poland, similarly held in 1923 that the Minorities Treaty of 1919 provides 'that all Polish nationals shall be equal before the law and shall enjoy the same civil and political rights without distinction as to race, language or religion . . . . [the Treaty] guarantees to racial minorities the same treatment and security "in law and in fact" as to other Polish nationals'.[146]

[142] *Cyprus v. Turkey*, *supra*, n. 134, para. 307.

[143] *Ibid.*, para. 309.

[144] CERD, Communication No. 18/2000, *F. A. v. Norway*, UN Doc. CERD/C/58/D/18/2000 (2001), para. 8. On a point of procedure the communication was determined to be inadmissible.

[145] The Committee affirms this view in *Peter Drobek v. Slovakia* even though on the facts it declares the communication inadmissible. HRC, Communication No. 643/1995, *Peter Drobek v. Slovakia*, (31 May 1994), CCPR/C/60/D/643/1995, para. 6.3. See also, HRC, Communication No. 328/1988, *Blancov v. Nicaragua*, UN Doc. CCPR/C/51/D/328/1988 (1994), para. 10.1: 'With regard to the author's allegation concerning the confiscation of his property, the Committee recalls that the Covenant does not protect the right of property, as such. However, an issue under the Covenant may arise if a confiscation or expropriation is based on discriminatory grounds prohibited in article 26 of the Covenant.'

[146] PCIJ Advisory Opinion, *Questions relating to settlers of German origin in the territory ceded by Germany to Poland, (1923)* Series B, No. 6

V. Minorities and Rights over Natural Resources and to Food, Health, and a Healthy Environment

Like its sister provision providing for the self-determination of peoples, that all peoples may 'for their own ends, dispose freely of their natural wealth and resources... [and] in no case [may] be deprived of its own means of subsistence'[147] today applies to groups within countries, despite its origins as a right pertaining to states. While finding Nigeria had violated the rights of the *Ogoni* peoples to dispose freely of their wealth and natural resources (Article 21 of the Charter), the African Commission remarked that: 'The origin of this provision may be traced to colonialism... The drafters of the Charter obviously wanted to remind African governments of the continent's painful legacy....'[148]

The African Commission—with its remit of collective rights provided for in the Charter and its provision on the use of natural resources separate from that of self-determination—has, unique among international (quasi-) judicial human rights bodies with petition mechanisms, ruled on this right.[149] The state's negative duty to 'respect the free use of resources... for the purposes of rights-related needs', includes resources belonging to 'a collective group... as it has to use the same resources to satisfy its needs'.[150] In finding a violation, for the first time, of Article 21 providing for the right of peoples to dispose freely of their natural wealth and resources the African Commission remarked on the 'destructive and selfish role played by oil development in Ogoniland,... the

[147] CCPR/CESCR, common Art. 1(2): 'In no case may a people be deprived of its own means of subsistence.'

[148] *Ogoni* case, *supra*, n. 12, para. 56.

[149] The Human Rights Committee does not (as yet) consider claims under its individual petition mechanism for violations of peoples' rights to self-determination and to use of natural resources provided for in Art. 1 of the CCPR (*Chief Bernard Ominayak and the Lubicon Lake Band v. Canada*, *supra*, n. 18, para. 32.1). Increasingly, however, the Committee is amenable to applying Art. 1 in the interpretation of other rights, particularly the minority rights of Art. 27 (*Apirana Mahuika et al. v. New Zealand*, *supra*, n. 15, para. 9.2). Through the general interpretation of international human rights instruments we see the right of indigenous peoples over natural resources affirmed (see CERD, General Recommendation No. 23 on Indigenous Peoples, (1997), para. 5), and there are strong arguments that recognition and protection of indigenous peoples' land and resource rights constitute a norm of customary international law. See, S. James Anaya and Robert A. Williams Jr, 'The Protection of Indigenous Peoples' Rights over Lands and Natural Resources under the Inter-American Human Rights System', *Harvard Human Rights Journal*, 14 (2001), 33–86, at 55. In the *Mary Dann* case, the Inter-American Commission on Human Rights affirmed the recognition of the individual and collective interest that indigenous peoples have in the occupation and use of their traditional lands and resources when concluding that there had been a failure to ensure the Danns' right to property under conditions of equality contrary to the Declaration on the Rights and Duties of Man. Inter-AmCtHR, *Mary and Carrie Dann v. United States,* Report No. 75/02, Case No. 11/140, (2002) paras. 131 and 171–2.

[150] *Ogoni* case, *supra*, n. 12, para. 45.

repressive tactics of the Nigerian Government, and the lack of material benefits accruing to the local population . . .'.[151] Citing cases from the Inter-American Court and the European Court, the Commission affirmed the responsibility of states to provide protection from damaging acts perpetrated by private parties.[152]

Reading the right to food into the African Charter as implicit in the right to life (Article 4), the right to health (Article 16) and the right to economic, social, and cultural development (Article 22),[153] the African Commission charged the state party with violating 'all three minimum duties of the right to food'.[154] Drawing on international minimum core obligations of the right to food elaborated by the UN Committee on Economic, Social and Cultural Rights,[155] the Commission has the state's duty entail that it not destroy or contaminate food sources, not allow private parties (oil companies) to destroy or contaminate food sources, and not prevent peoples' efforts to feed themselves'.[156]

In finding violations of the right to the best attainable state of physical and mental health (Article 16) and the right of all peoples to a satisfactory environment favourable to their development (Article 24), the Commission expanded for the first time on the meaning, interpretation, and scope of the right to a satisfactory environment[157] and drew explicitly on the interrelated and interdependent nature of the rights to health and to a healthy

[151] *Ogoni* case, *supra*, n. 12, para. 55.

[152] *Ibid.*, paras. 57–8.

[153] *Ibid.*, para. 64. The complainants did not allege a violation of Art. 22, nor did the Commission rule on it. In the ongoing case of the *Centre for Minority Rights Development (CEMIRIDE on behalf of the Enderois Community) v. Republic of Kenya* the complainants have alleged a violation of the right to development. AfrCommHPR, *Centre for Minority Rights Development (CEMIRIDE on behalf of the Enderois Community) v. Republic of Kenya,* Communication 276/2003.

[154] *Ogoni* case, *supra*, n. 12, para. 65.

[155] See, CESCR, General Comment No. 12 (Article 11) on the Right to Adequate Food, U.N. Doc. E/C.12/1999/5.

[156] *Ogoni* case, *supra,* n. 12, paras. 65 and 66. It is widely accepted that people should not be inhibited from providing for themselves (CCPR/CESCR, common Art. 1(2): 'In no case may a people be deprived of its own means of subsistence') and that the right to adequate food entails also a right to food security, and to cultural acceptability (CESCR, General Comment No. 12, *supra*, n. 155, paras. 6, 7, and 11). Regarding physical accessibility to adequate food, CESCR has noted that 'a particular vulnerability is that of many indigenous population groups whose access to their ancestral lands may be threatened' (para. 13). Of course, any discrimination in access to food, as well as to means and entitlements for its procurement constitutes a violation of the Covenant (para. 18).

[157] Kaniye S.A. Ebeku, 'The Right to a Satisfactory Environment and the African Commission', *African Human Rights Law Journal*, 3 (2003), 149–66, at 161 *passim*.

environment.[158] In addition to abstaining from 'directly threatening the health and environment of their citizens' the state is required to 'take reasonable and other measures to prevent pollution and ecological degradation, to promote conservation, and to secure an ecologically sustainable development of natural resources'.[159] 'Government compliance with the spirit of articles 16 and 24 of the African Charter must also include ordering or at least permitting independent scientific monitoring of threatened environments, requiring and publicising environmental and social impact studies prior to any major industrial development, undertaking appropriate monitoring and providing information to those communities exposed to hazardous materials and activities and providing meaningful opportunities for individuals to be heard and to participate in the development decisions affecting their communities.'[160]

The Commission's elaboration—although short of pronouncing itself on the core content and minimum obligation of Article 24[161]—offers a welcome departure from its earlier communication of *Free Legal Assistance Group and Others v. Zaire*. In this case against Zaire it found a violation of the right to health given the government's failure to provide basic services such as safe drinking water and due to shortages of medicine, but offered no further consideration linked to the procedural or substantive aspects of the right, nor regarding the allegations of financial mismanagement that gave rise to the claims,[162] nor on the role and potential contribution of international human

[158] Both aspects of which are found in Art. 12 of the CESCR and in the Additional Protocol to the American Convention on Human Rights in the Area of Economic, Social and Cultural Rights. Under instruments where there is no explicit reference to the right to live in a healthy environment, it has been linked to the right to health, see, Inter-AmCommHR, *Case of the Yanomami Indians*, Case 7615 (Brazil), OEA/Ser.L/V/II.66 doc 10 rev.1 at 6 (1985). Under the European Court of Human Rights the impact of environmental pollution on human well-being has been linked to violations of the effective enjoyment of the right to respect for home and private life (Art. 8). See also, European Committee of Social Rights, *Marangopoulos Foundation for Human Rights v. Greece*, Complaint No. 30/2005, Decision on Admissability, Merits pending of 10 October 2005.

[159] *Ogoni* case, *supra*, n. 12, para. 52.

[160] *Ibid.*, para. 53. For the Committee's pronouncement on the procedural and substantive obligations pertaining to the right to health (and healthy environmental conditions) under the Covenant including as applied to minorities and indigenous peoples, see, CESCR, General Comment No. 14 *Supra*, n. 33, (Art. 12).

[161] Commentators lament this disappointing aspect of the Commission's consideration of Art. 24. van der Linde and Louw, *Supra*, n. 120, 179.

[162] Notably, in 2002 the UN Committee on Economic Social and Cultural Rights adopted its General Comment on the Right to Water in which it provided that: 'A State which is unwilling to use the maximum of its available resources for the realization of the right to water is in violation of its obligations under the Covenant. If resource constraints render it impossible for a State party to

rights bodies in considering complaints related to socio-economic rights.[163] An advance on these earlier omissions can be found in the Commission's Resolution on Economic, Social and Cultural Rights in Africa which systematically sets out the current domestic, regional, and international constraints on the exercise of economic, social, and cultural rights and details the content of the particular rights and duties under the Charter.[164]

While the facts of the *Ogoni* case saw the exploitation of oil reserves by the state oil companies and by private companies with the state's complicity, the Commission did not deny the right of the government to produce oil. However, this right is contingent on the income generated by the extraction being used to fulfil the economic and social rights of the country's people, and undertaken with the care that would have protected the victims from having their human rights violated.[165] In finding that the government had also violated Article 4 of the Charter which guarantees the right to life and respect for the integrity of the person, the Commission was influenced by the 'humanly unacceptable' degree of environmental pollution and degradation. Interpreting the right to life as significant for the preservation of both the individual and group, the Commission explained that the environmental impact threatened the physical survival of the Ogoni people who depend on their lands and farms for sustenance, and affected the collective life of the Ogoni community as a whole.[166] 'International law and human rights must be responsive to African circumstances', the Commission proclaimed in this landmark case, '[c]learly, collective rights, environmental rights, and social and economic rights are

comply fully with its Covenant obligations it has the burden of justifying that every effort has nevertheless been made to use all available resources at its disposal in order to satisfy, as a matter of priority [its] obligations.' The Committee went on to offer a non-exhaustive list of violations which includes 'insufficient expenditure or misallocation of public resources which results in the non-enjoyment of the right to water by individuals or groups, particularly the vulnerable or marginalized'. CESCR, General Comment No. 15 (Articles 11 and 12) on the Right to Water, UN Doc. E/C.12/2002/11 (2002), paras. 41 and 44 (c)(ii).

163 AfrCommHPR, Communication Nos. 25/89, 47/90, 56/91, 100/93, *Free Legal Assistance Group, Lawyers' Committee for Human Rights, Union Interafricaine des Droits de L'Homme, Les Témoins de Jehovah v. Zaire,* 9th Annual Activity Report 1995–96.

164 ACHPR Resolution, *Resolution on Economic, Social and Cultural Rights in Africa*, 2004, ACHPR/Res.73(XXXVI)04. The Resolution also establishes a Working Group, composed of members of the African Commission and non-governmental organizations, who are currently drafting Guidelines on the interpretation of Economic, Social and Cultural and Developmental Rights in the African Charter on Human and Peoples' Rights, as well as state reporting guidelines.

165 *Ogoni* case, *supra*, n. 12, para. 54.

166 *Ibid.*, para. 67.

essential elements of human rights in Africa'.[167] However, a case that has been widely admired for developing meaningful regional human rights jurisprudence as well as for positively promoting the profile of the Commission, suffers from institutional weaknesses that see unsatisfactory enforcement of the Commission's recommendations.[168]

The underlying principle of 'respect for the inherent dignity of the person'—and as such the right to life and physical integrity—was recognized by the Inter-American Commission on Human Rights in its Report on Ecuador as a key right at issue where the environment, survival, culture, and development intersect.[169] The Commission concluded in relation to the indigenous Huaorani of Ecuador that 'the norms of the Inter-American system neither prevent nor discourage development; rather, they require that development take place under conditions that respect and ensure the human rights of the individuals concerned'.[170] In the concluding recommendations on indigenous issues in its 1999 Report of the State of Human Rights in Colombia, the Inter-American Commission remarked that it expected the state to ensure that processes of development did not 'cause irreparable harm to the religious, economic or cultural identity and rights of indigenous communities'.[171] The

[167] *Ibid.*, para. 68.

[168] Notably, Art 21(2) explicitly provides that: 'In that case of spoliation the dispossessed people shall have the right to lawful recovery of its property as well as to an adequate compensation.' Reports on the human rights violations of the Ogoni and other minorities in the Niger Delta continue. See, Julia Maxted, 'Africa', in *State of the World's Minorities 2004–2005* (Minority Rights Group International, 2006), 50–67, at 61. Criticizing the Commission's weak enforcement in the *Ogoni* case see, Justice C. Nwobike, 'The African Commission on Human and Peoples' Rights and the Demystification of Second and Third Generation Rights under the African Charter; Social and Economic Rights Action Center and the Center for Economic and Social Rights v Nigeria', *African Journal of Legal Studies*, 2 (2005), 129–46, at 145. There are also considerable delays in providing declarations of admissibility and in reaching decisions. See Odinkalu, *Supra*, n. 120, 109.

[169] InterAmComm HR, *Report on the Situation of Human Rights in Ecuador*, Doc. OEA/Ser.L/V/II.96.Doc.10 rev.1, Ch. VIII, (1997). The Commission recalls the instruments to which Ecuador is party or has supported which recognize 'the critical connection between the sustenance of human life and the environment', including: the Additional Protocol to the American Convention in the Area of Economic, Social and Cultural Rights, the CCPR, and the CESCR, the Stockholm Declaration, the Treaty for Amazonian Cooperation, the Amazon Declaration, the World Charter for Nature, the Convention on Nature Protection and Wildlife Preservation in the Western Hemisphere, the Rio Declaration on Environment and Development, and the Convention on Biological Diversity. These conclusions can be seen as part of a broader trend towards victims of environmental damage invoking human rights doctrine for protection and redress. Ebeku, *Supra*, n. 157, 155.

[170] InterAmComm HR, *Report on the Situation of Human Rights in Ecuador*, *Supra*, n. 169.

[171] InterAmComm HR, *Report of the State of Human Rights in Colombia*, OEA/SER.L/V/II.102 Doc.9 rev.1, Ch. X, section J, Rec. 5, (1999).

connection between the physical environment and, *inter alia*, the rights to health, life, and culture of the Inuit form the basis of a petition filed with the Inter-American Commission against the United States—as the world's largest emitter of greenhouse gases—for the impact of global warming and climate change on the exercise of their fundamental rights.[172]

Interpreting the right to life beyond the deprivation of life itself to include quality of life in terms of satisfying basic needs essential to a life of dignity, and the elements essential to a particular way of life was addressed in the IACtHR case of *Yakye Axa v. Paraguay* mentioned earlier.[173] The Court found that Paraguay had violated the right to life of members of the indigenous community by failing to meet its obligation to create the minimum conditions under which a dignified existence is possible, and to avoid the creation of obstacles towards a dignified existence. While Paraguay was held not to be directly responsible for the death of the sixteen members who—dispossessed of their land—had died of, *inter alia*, malnutrition and disease, it was responsible for not allowing access to minimum conditions under which a state of human dignity was possible. In particular, the state authorities had not guaranteed the Yakye Axa Community access to its ancestral lands when medical care and nutritional assistance provided for them while not on their land had been insufficient; the state had not complied with its obligations to ensure that the circumstances did not affect the development and future of the children of the indigenous community; and it had failed to attend to the needs of the elders who were vital for the transmission of the community's culture.[174]

[172] Other rights for which the petitioners seek relief are rights to residence and movement and inviolability of the home, means of subsistence (as inherent in the rights to property, health, life, and culture in the context of indigenous peoples), and to property (lands, as well as intellectual property). *Petition to the Inter-American Commission of Human Rights seeking relief from violations resulting from global warming caused by acts and omissions of the United States*, submitted by Sheila Watt-Cloutier with the support of the Inuit Circumpolar Conference, on behalf of all Inuit of the Arctic regions of the United States and Canada, 7 December 2005.

[173] Dignity is increasingly presenting itself as the measure against which the fulfilment of positive obligations for the socio-economic rights of vulnerable groups are determined. In establishing the minimum core duty relevant to the socio-economic rights of people suffering from HIV/AIDS and homelessness respectively, the South African Constitutional Court noted that: 'This minimum core might not be easy to define, but includes at least the minimum decencies of life consistent with human dignity.' South African Constitutional Court, *Minister of Health v. Treatment Action Campaign*, judgment of 5 July 2002, para. 28; and South African Constitutional Court, *The Government of the Republic of South Africa v. Grootboom*, judgment of 4 October 2000, paras. 44 and 83.

[174] *Yakye Axa v. Paraguay*—English language case summary in *Interights Bulletin*, 15, (2006) 131–2.

VI. Minorities and Economic Opportunities

The Committee on the Elimination of Racial Discrimination has dealt with several cases related to the right to work and labour rights. In the case of *A. Yilmaz Dogan v. Netherlands*, CERD found the state to have violated the author's right to equality before the law in respect of the right to work and protection against unemployment when a Subdistrict Court failed to address the element of alleged discrimination in an employer's letter requesting the termination of the petitioner's employment contract.[175] The state party was called upon to provide a remedy in the form of secure alternative employment for the petitioner and/or another form of equitable relief.[176] In the case of *B.M.S v. Australia*, no violation of CERD Article 5(e)(i) was found since a quota system and exam requirements were applied to all overseas-trained doctors irrespective of race or national origin, and there was no basis for the conclusion that the system was working to the detriment of persons of a particular race or national origin.[177] No violation of Article 5(e)(i) was found by CERD in the early case of *Demba Talibe Diop v. France,* since the domestic law which the petitioner claimed discriminated against him operated to provide a preference or distinction between citizens and non-citizens, thereby falling within the meaning of Article 1(2) of the Convention, which allows for said distinctions or exclusions.[178] In the case of *Ziad Ben Ahmed Habassi v. Denmark*, the legitimacy of distinguishing between Danish and non-Danish nationals was queried by the Committee when a Tunisian national, permanently resident in Denmark and meeting all other criteria that would suggest his willingness and capacity to repay a loan, was refused access to the credit market by a Danish Bank on the sole ground of his non-Danish nationality.[179] Notably, the Committee's recent recommendations on the rights of non-citizens under the Convention focus explicitly on the requirement that differential treatment based on citizenship or immigration, in order not to fall foul of the Convention, pursue a legitimate aim and is proportional to the objectives sought.[180]

[175] CERD, Communication No. 1/1984, *A. Yilmaz Dogan v. the Netherlands,* UN Doc. CERD/C/36/D/1/1984, para. 9.3.

[176] *Ibid.*, para. 10.

[177] CERD, Communication No. 8/1996, *B.M.S v. Australia,* UN Doc. CERD/C/54/D/8/1996 (1999), para. 9.2.

[178] CERD, Communication No. 2/1989, *Demba Talibe Diop v. France,* UN Doc. CERD/C/39/D/2/1989 (1991), paras. 6.2, 6.5, and 6.6.

[179] CERD, Communication No. 10/1997, *Ziad Ben Ahmed Habassi v. Denmark*, UN Doc. CERD/C/54/D/10/1997 (1999), para. 9.3.

[180] CERD, General Recommendation No. 30 on Discrimination Against Non-Citizens (2004), para. 4.

In assessing the effective participation of persons belonging to minorities in economic life under the European Framework Convention for the Protection of National Minorities, the Advisory Committee has acknowledged that urban development may pose challenges to generating equal economic opportunities for people in rural areas (regions often inhabited by persons belonging to minorities).[181] While requesting that governments endeavour to develop measures capable of limiting the effects of such structural differences,[182] and noting the importance of economic and quality of life surveys in designing effective governmental action plans designed to remedy inequalities,[183] conclusions suggest that overall there has been insufficient data available, inhibiting assessment by the Committee of the situation related to economic opportunities afforded minorities.[184] A former member of the Advisory Committee nonetheless lauds the Convention's focus on economic, social, and cultural rights and its equal emphasis on policy as on national legislation.[185] Like CERD's Article 2(2) which allows for special measures—that is, affirmative action—to ensure the adequate development and protection of certain ethnic groups or individuals belonging to them, the Framework Convention at Article 4(2) encourages states parties to adopt where necessary adequate measures to redress structural discrimination in all areas of economic, social, political, and cultural life in the achievement of full and effective equality between minority and majority persons. Article 4(5) of the UN Minorities Declaration also recognizes

[181] Advisory Committee Opinion on Switzerland, ACFC/INF/OP/I (2003) 007, para. 75.

[182] *Ibid.*, para. 103.

[183] See Marc Weller, 'Article 15', in Marc Weller (ed.), *A Commentary on the European Framework Convention for the Protection of National Minorities* (Oxford University Press, 2005), 429–61, at 454–5.

[184] *Ibid.*, 429–61, at 454. The importance of disaggregated data to the formulation of suitable policies that contribute to the fulfilment of the economic, social, and cultural rights of minorities and indigenous peoples has been repeatedly voiced by treaty bodies. See, for example, CRC, Concluding Observations: Gabon, UN Doc. CRC/C/15/Add.171, (2002), para. 15. 'The Committee recommends that the State party: (a) Develop a system of data collection and indicators consistent with the Convention disaggregated by gender, age, indigenous and minority groups, and urban and rural areas. This system should cover all children up to the age of 18 years, with specific emphasis on those who are particularly vulnerable including... Pygmy children; and other children in need of special protection'; CEDAW, Concluding Observations: Japan, UN Doc. A/58/38 (2003), para. 366: 'The Committee requests the State party to provide, in its next report, comprehensive information, including disaggregated data, on the situation of minority women in Japan, especially with regard to their educational, employment and health status and exposure to violence'; European Committee of Social Rights, *The European Roma Rights Centre v. Italy*, *Supra*, n. 93, para. 23: 'The Committee recalls that when it is generally acknowledged that a particular group is or could be discriminated against, the state authorities have a responsibility for collecting data on the text of the problem. The gathering and analysis of such data... is indispensable to the formulation of rational policy.'

[185] Phillips, *Supra*, n. 106, 305.

the importance of 'appropriate measures so that persons belonging to minorities may participate fully in the economic progress and development in their country.'

The Protocol to the revised European Social Charter, since its entry into force in 1998, provides for a system of collective complaints by organizations, against those states that have accepted to be bound (via its à la carte system). It may be early yet to gauge its potential contribution to furthering the socio-economic rights of minorities, but given the Charter's coverage of labour rights, as well as rights to equal opportunity and treatment, the right to health, rights of migrant workers, the right to housing, and the right to protection against poverty and social exclusion, there may be some meaningful potential.[186]

In its promotion of fundamental rights and principles at work, the International Labour Organization pays particular attention to socially or economically disadvantaged groups, and thus the protection of ethnic minorities in the world of work, and of indigenous and tribal peoples has been a key ILO concern.[187] While the ILO has received representations under Article 24 of the ILO Constitution by trade unions alleging a violation of Convention No. 169, the bulk of supervision of ILO conventions takes place through the examination of state reports by a Committee of Experts.[188]

In its recent elaboration of the content of the right to work, the UN Committee on Economic, Social and Cultural Rights reaffirmed in its General Comment that an essential element of the right to work as provided for under Article 6 of the Covenant is that it meets the requirement of 'accessibility'. This would include that labour markets be open to everyone under the jurisdiction of the state party, that there be no discrimination (on the grounds of race, colour, religion etc.) in access to or maintenance of employment, and, as has been previously affirmed by the Committee, 'even in times of severe resource constraints, disadvantaged and marginalized individuals and groups must be protected by the adoption of relatively low-cost targeted programmes'.[189]

[186] The European Committee of Social Rights has adopted decisions in two cases concerning minorities to date, both having dealt with the rights of the Roma in the field of housing. European Committee of Social Rights, *The European Roma Rights Centre v. Greece*, *supra*, n. 4; European Committee of Social Rights, *The European Roma Rights Centre v. Italy*, *supra*, n. 93, para. 23. See generally, Robin R. Churchill and Urfan Khaliq, 'The Collective Complaints System of the European Social Charter: An Effective Mechanism for Ensuring Compliance with Economic and Social Rights?', *European Journal of International* Law, 3 (2004), 417–56.

[187] Swepston, *supra*, n. 109, 70.

[188] *Ibid.*, 69–81, at 75–6.

[189] CESCR, General Comment No. 18 (Article 6) on The Right to Work, UN Doc. E/C.12/GC/18 (2005), para. 12 (b); CESCR, General Comment No. 3 (Article 2.1) on the Nature of States Parties' Obligations, UN Doc. E/1991/23, Annex III (1990), para. 12.

Specific legal obligations to respect the right to work include prohibiting forced or compulsory labour and denying equal access to decent work for all, especially marginalized individuals and groups such as members of minorities and migrant workers.[190] The Committee has also highlighted the importance—drawing attention to standards provided for in the International Convention on the Protection of all Migrant Workers and Members of their Families—of giving effect through national plans of action and other appropriate measures to the principle of non-discrimination as it applies to this category of vulnerable group.[191]

While the Covenant allows for the progressive realization of rights, the guarantee that all rights will be exercised without *de jure* or de facto discrimination imposes an obligation of immediate effect, as does the obligation on states parties 'to take steps' (CESCR Article 2(1)) towards the full realization of the Covenant rights. The nature of states parties' obligations requires that 'such steps be deliberate, concrete and targeted' towards realizing Covenant rights, including the right to work,[192] and that states parties 'move as expeditiously and effectively as possible' towards fully implementing the provisions.[193] Should retrogressive measures be taken with regard to the right to work, or any other right under the Covenant, that impact negatively on the ability of minorities to exercise their rights, the burden of proof that the measures introduced are duly justified (and there is a strong presumption that retrogressive measures are not permissible)[194] rests with the state. The standard of proof to be met is that they have been introduced 'after consideration of all alternatives' and that they are 'justified by reference to the totality of the rights provided for in the Covenant in the context of the full use of the States parties' maximum available resources'.[195] Maximum available resources include those available from the international community in fulfilment of the obligation 'to take steps, individually and through international assistance and cooperation' (Article 2(1)).[196]

[190] CESCR, General Comment No. 18, *supra*, n. 189, para. 23.

[191] *Ibid.*, para. 18.

[192] *Ibid.*, para. 19; CESCR, General Comment No. 3, *supra*, n. 189, para. 2.

[193] CESCR, General Comment No. 18, *supra*, n. 189, para. 20; CESCR, General Comment No. 3, *supra*, n. 189, para. 9.

[194] *Ibid.*, para. 34.

[195] *Ibid.*, para. 21; CESCR, General Comment No. 3, *supra*, n. 189, para. 9.

[196] CESCR, General Comment No. 3, *supra*, n. 189, para. 13; CESCR, General Comment No. 18, *supra*, n. 189, paras. 29–30 (International obligations); see further Margot E. Salomon, 'Introduction', in Salomon (ed.), *Economic, Social and Cultural Rights*, 5–15, at 9–11; on the emerging parameters of obligations of international cooperation for socio-economic rights, see, Margot E. Salomon, 'International Human Rights Obligations in Context: Structural Obstacles and the

Securing socio-economic rights in a global economy is another aspect of the obligation of international cooperation. The right to an adequate standard of living including social security as provided for in CESCR and the relevant instruments of the ILO, today necessitates the creation of social safety nets to fulfil the rights of those excluded from achieving minimum standards of well-being and human dignity. Ethnic minorities and indigenous peoples are among the poorest groups in most parts of the world[197] and will be among those to face the greatest hardship from the effects of external economic shocks and adjustment programmes. The economic, social, and cultural rights found in the UN Convention on the Rights of the Child have compelled the Committee on the Rights of the Child to concern itself with whether social safety nets have been put in place to protect members of society from times of economic shock and recession, including those most vulnerable in times of national economic hardship.[198] Likewise, CESCR recognizes the need to determine whether debt burdens and fiscal adjustment measures are being assessed for their differential impact on the enjoyment of economic, social, and cultural rights of all people in a country.[199] The UN Minorities Declaration calls on all specialized agencies of the United Nations—this would include the World Bank and International Monetary Fund, organizations that influence significantly the socio-economic policies of partner countries—to contribute to the full realization of the rights of persons belonging to minorities.[200]

Undoubtedly, the ability of developing states to provide the essential level of protection and support engages the multilateral trade and development institutions that play a critical role in national efforts to facilitate and sustain such measures.[201] CESCR has repeatedly remarked on the scope of the obligation

Demands of Global Justice', in Bard-Anders Andreassen and Stephen P. Marks (eds.), *Development as a Human Right: Legal, Political and Economic Dimensions* (Harvard School of Public Health, Harvard University Press, 2006), 96.

[197] UNDP Human Development Report, *Cultural Liberty in Today's Diverse World*, UNDP (2004), 65; see also Gay McDougall, *Report of the UN Independent Expert on Minority Issues*, UN Doc. E/CN.4/2006/74 and generally the range of reports by Rodolfo Stavenhagen the UN Special Rapporteur on the Situation of Human Rights and Fundamental Freedoms of Indigenous Peoples.

[198] CRC, General Comment No. 5 (Arts 4, 42, 46(6)) on general measures of implementation of the Convention on the Rights of the Child, UN Doc. CRC/GC/2003/5 (2003), para. 51.

[199] CESCR, General Comment No. 2 (Arts 22) on International Technical Assistance Measures, UN Doc. E/1990/23, Annex III (1990), para. 9.

[200] UNDM, Art. 9.

[201] *Report of the UN High-Level Task Force on the Implementation of the Right to Development*, 1st session, UN Doc. E/CN.4/2005/WG.18.2, paras. 24 and 39.

of international cooperation with regard to Covenant rights, most recently in its General Comment on the Right to Work:

In negotiations with international financial institutions, states parties should ensure protection of the right to work of their population. States parties that are members of international financial institutions, in particular the International Monetary Fund, the World Bank and regional development banks, should pay greater attention to the protection of the right to work in influencing the lending policies, credit agreements, structural adjustment programmes and international measures of these institutions. The strategies, programmes and policies adopted by States parties under structural adjustment programmes should not interfere with their core obligations in relation to the right to work and impact negatively on the right to work of women, young persons and the disadvantaged and marginalized individuals and groups.[202]

That states' human rights responsibilities continue even after the transfer of competences to international organizations—as reflected in the ECtHR cases of *Matthews v. United Kingdom*[203] and *Bosphorus Airways v. Ireland*—[204] represent important nascent legal developments. And the thorny matter of the direct accountability of these IGOs as subjects of international law, gives rise to legal debates that have invited considerable attention and will no doubt continue to do so.[205]

Export processing zones,[206] the activities of multinational corporations, and privatization measures all need to be justly and effectively regulated in order not

[202] CESCR General Comment No. 18, *supra*, n. 189, paras. 30 and 53.

[203] ECtHR, *Matthews v. United Kingdom*, Appl. 24833/94, Judgment of 18 February 1999, paras. 29 and 32–4.

[204] ECtHR, *Bosphorus Airways v. Ireland*, Appl. 45036/98, Judgment of 30 June 2005, paras. 152–6.

[205] See François Gianviti, 'Economic, Social and Cultural Rights and the IMF', in Philip Alston (ed.), *Non-State Actors and Human Rights* (Oxford University Press, 2005) 113; Jean Zeigler, *Report of the Special Rapporteur on the Right to Food*, UN Doc. A/60/350 (2005); Mac Darrow, *Between Light and Shadow: The World Bank, The International Monetary Fund and International Human Rights Law* (Hart Publishing, 2003); Sigrun Skogly, *The Human Rights Obligations of the World Bank and the IMF* (Cavendish Publishing, 2001).

[206] The ILO defines EPZs as 'industrial zones with special incentives set up to attract foreign investors, in which imported materials undergo some degree of processing before being re-exported', at www.ilo.org/public/english/dialogue/sector/themes/epz.htm. While EPZs may generate employment, the ILO Committee of Experts continues to raise concerns over non-compliance with core labour rights in the EPZs. See, for example, the recent observations on Mauritius: 'The Committee notes that according to the International Confederation of Free Trade Unions, trade unions and collective bargaining in the expert processing zones are non-existent due to the repeated violation of fundamental principles and rights of workers by the employers and the lack of adequate legislative protection against acts of both anti-union discrimination and interference by the employers.' ILO Committee of Experts on the Application of Conventions and Recommendations: Individual

to reduce the social protection of workers, to ensure investment is consistent with the rights of local communities, and to guarantee availability and access, including among the most marginalized, to public goods such as water, education, essential healthcare, and a clean environment. The protection of minority cultures, traditional ways of life and means of production and subsistence, as well as indigenous knowledge, all implicate the international system.[207] The point is that today the exercise of fundamental human rights is intimately bound up in the actions and structural arrangements of the international community, and this conditions the nature of contemporary human rights obligations.[208]

VII. Conclusion

The codification and elaboration of minority rights is testament to universal recognition that a qualitatively different form of protection is required from that of human rights generally, and the non-discrimination–equality framework.[209] As the case law and related judicial recommendations suggest, the international human rights system acknowledges in no small measure that minorities require particular consideration given their entrenched socio-economic and political marginalization and the essential importance of preserving their identity as distinct communities. Yet, international jurisprudence in the area of socio-economic rights for minorities is largely a story of the creative interpretation of standards (the right to a home to protect a traditional way of life under the ECHR; the right to property as a right to communal land use under the ACHR); the use of somewhat maladjusted mechanisms (no standing for 'groups' under the Human Rights Committee's petition mechanism only complaints by 'individuals similarly affected';[210] a protocol to the American

Observation concerning Convention No. 98, Right to Organise and Collective Bargaining, Mauritius (2003); and the Committee on the Elimination of Discrimination against Women is 'deeply concerned' at the situation of women working in the free-trade zones, see CEDAW, Concluding Observations: Dominican Republic, UN Doc. A/59/38 part II (2004), para. 306.

207 See, CESCR, General Comment No. 17 (Article 15(1)(c)) on the right of everyone to benefit from the protection of the moral and material interests resulting from any scientific, literary or artistic production of which he or she is the author, UN Doc. E/C.12/GC/17 (2005).

208 Salomon, International Human Rights Obligations in Context, *supra*, n. 196, 96, at 99, in Andreassen and Marks (eds.), *Development as a Human Right*, 96, at 99; see, two among many, CESCR, General Comment No. 18, *supra*, n. 189, para. 4; CESCR, General Comment No. 14, *supra*, n. 33, para. 5.

209 See Thornberry's explanation of the development of minority protection in the early years of the UN. Patrick Thornberry, *International Law and the Rights of Minorities* (Oxford University Press, 1991), 122–3.

210 *Chief Bernard Ominayak and the Lubicon Lake Band v. Canada, supra*, n. 18, para. 32.1.

Convention entrenching economic, social and cultural rights that for the most part does not provide for their justiciability). And where the justiciability of socio-economic rights pose no ideological obstacle (nor do group rights), as in the African human rights system, enforcement is to date especially weak.[211]

The absence of an international minorities convention along with a complaints system and the lack of any explicit provision on the rights of minorities (or indigenous peoples) in the main regional instruments, invites the possibility to see limitations to effective protection everywhere. We might question whether we are left to make do with a deficient system conceived to meet very different needs[212] or rather whether we are witnessing the manifest potential of the notion of 'living instruments'. Should we marvel at an approach which sees the resourceful use of civil rights to further economic, social, and cultural rights or recognize instead the need to rely on international procedures constituted to assess civil and political rights in order to secure socio-economic rights reflective of a gap in the international system for their adjudication.[213] While we may appreciate the furtherance of socio-economic rights via traditional civil and political rights mechanisms, case-by-case judicial consideration of elements central to determining the scope of socio-economic rights and the nature of obligations consequently remain underdeveloped: distinguishing obligations of conduct from obligations of result, determining what constitutes a state's 'maximum available resources', and considering the specific content of the often essential, yet inchoate, duty of international assistance and cooperation under CESCR.

With these limitations acknowledged, and while debates over the practicability of international judicial determination of socio-economic rights continue,[214] jurisprudence at the international and regional levels are serving to inform the scope, content, and any necessary limitations of these rights on

[211] This is a problem it is hoped will be addressed with the establishment of the African Court on Human and Peoples' Rights.

[212] Illustrated by the point that the drafting of minority rights provisions was influenced mainly by the European experience and is therefore profoundly Eurocentric, with the drafting of indigenous rights having been influenced mainly by developments in the Americas and Pacific and thereby reflecting an 'America-centrism'. Eide and Daes, *Working Paper, supra*, n. 111, para. 25.

[213] See Claude Cahn, 'The Justiciability of ESC Rights at the International Level', European Roma Rights Centre, presentation to the open-ended Working-Group to consider options regarding the elaboration of an optional protocol to CESCR, 2nd Session, 2005, at www.errc.org.

[214] Michael J. Dennis and David P. Stewart, 'Justiciability of Economic, Social and Cultural Rights: Should There Be an International Complaints Mechanism to Adjudicate the Rights to Food, Water, Housing, and Health?', *American Journal of International Law*, 3 (2004), 462–515 ('Formalistic demands that economic, social and cultural rights must be treated the same as civil and political rights, and must therefore be 'justiciable' in the same sense, are... flawed. That case has not been made.'), at 465; Churchill and Khaliq, ('It is important to note... that there is nothing

a case-by-case basis, as well as guide state policy. Moreover, considered in light of the objectives of minority rights and the paucity of explicit international and regional provisions providing for their protection and promotion, socio-economic provisions read as minority rights have begun to fill a lacuna.

International and regional judicial and quasi-judicial mechanisms are now sensitive to the rights and aspirations of the most vulnerable and excluded among us. And they are responding to the primal need for the distinct cultures of minorities to be preserved and for the safeguarding of that which enriches us all. Judge Repik in his well-known dissent in the *Buckley* case before the European Court may have best articulated this appreciation. Disagreeing with the Court's finding that the interference with a minority's way of life was deemed necessary, he remarked ruefully: 'I am concerned about how the Court's first judgment on this subject will be interpreted and how it will be received by the Gypsy minority.'[215] As our universal human rights system continues to advance the rights of minorities, like Judge Repik, we will know best its successes by the way in which affected individuals and communities in turn judge our willingness and ability to place at their service international law for the protection and promotion of all fundamental human rights.

inherent in economic and social rights that prevents the judicial determination of their content'), *supra*, n. 186, 420.

215 *Buckley v. United Kingdom*, partly dissenting opinion of Judge Repik, *supra*, n. 62.

EFFECTIVE PARTICIPATION OF MINORITIES IN PUBLIC LIFE

Marc Weller

I. Introduction

In democratic states, public policy is determined by majority decision. This applies in particular to parliamentary decision-making establishing the legal environment within the state. This legal framework generated by majority decision will in turn determine, shape, or colour most subordinate aspects of public decision-making. This fact poses obvious risks for minorities. For, if such decisions are taken by the electorate, or parliamentarians representing them, according to national, ethnic, cultural, or religious identity, rather than according to shifting interests, minorities may face structural exclusion from the state. Indeed, where issue politics is replaced by identity politics, certain groups may suffer from structural discrimination in addition to exclusion.

Generally, state design will attempt to counter this possibility in various ways.[1] These include:

- anti-discrimination provisions;
- provisions ensuring full equality in law and in fact;
- minority rights;
- guarantees of a right to effective representation at the political level;
- provisions for executive representation;
- granting of territorial or cultural autonomy;
- provision of mechanisms to integrate autonomy structures with the state.

Anti-discrimination ensures that the state's power is not arbitrarily applied against individuals or groups by virtue of their appurtenance to a minority. Anti-discrimination is obviously firmly established in general international law and in regional human rights systems. First, there must not be discrimination of any kind in the enjoyment of human rights on account of factors such as race, colour, sex, language, religion, political or other opinion, national or social origin, property, birth or other status. Second, there is the duty of the state to ensure that no one is subject to discrimination of any kind in general, even outside of the ambit of the specific protection of other human rights. Finally, all persons are to be treated equally before the law, and they are entitled to equal protection by the law, notwithstanding the flavour of majority opinion at any one time.

The negative obligation of anti-discrimination is matched by the positive duty on the part of the state to ensure that all persons have equal access to the enjoyment of their rights. This is key in order to assure that equality does not remain only aspirational, and that members of minorities do not feel excluded from opportunities open to others. Accordingly, it may be necessary to take special measures or adopt positive action to provide genuine full and effective equality to communities that suffer from structural disadvantages. This may include special educational provision, accelerated training, and recruiting campaigns for members of minorities seeking opportunities in the private or public sector and other steps. Such steps are not considered discriminatory in relation to members of the majority, given the objective reasons for their application.

A third way of engaging with non-dominant groups within the state is minority rights. Minority rights go beyond simple anti-discrimination. Instead,

[1] See J. Frohwein and R. Bank, *The Participation of Minorities in Decision-Making* (Strasbourg, DH-MIN(2001)I, 2001); Y. Ghai, *Public Participation of Minorities, Minority Rights Group International* (London, 2001); Annelies Verstichel, 'Recent Developments in the UN Human Rights Committee's Approach to Minorities, with a Focus on Effective Participation', *International Journal on Minority and Group Rights*, 12 (2005), 25–42.

it is recognized that minorities require special protection and support, due to their cultural and ethnic distinctiveness. Hence, in addition to preventing an erosion of this distinctive identity through assimilation, the state is bound to provide the minority with the space and the resources necessary to experience, transmit, and develop their minority identity. More recently, the right to political participation has been emphasized in this context. According to this doctrine, minorities must gain access to points of decision-making within the state if they are to feel a sense of genuine co-ownership thereof.

One mechanism of ensuring minority access to decision-making relates to electoral representation, for instance, the facilitation of minority representatives' access to elected bodies at the local, regional, or state level. This can include the provision of guaranteed seats for minority representatives, relieving minority parties from the need to register throughout the state if the minority is only present in a particular area, waiving minimum clauses for electoral representation in parliament (often five per cent of the vote or seats in parliament), etc. Once in parliament, minority parties may also be offered special privileges, such as guaranteed seats on key committees, posts of chair or vice-chair of certain bodies, waiving of numerical thresholds for the formation of parliamentary groups, and several other steps.

Where direct representation in a decision-making body may not be possible, for instance, due to the small number of persons belonging to minorities, other mechanisms gain importance. These include minority consultative bodies. These bodies may offer all minorities a forum of engagement with the government and legislature and early input into important decisions of relevance to them. Or, minority contract points may be established in specific ministries of concern to minorities or in areas where minorities live, in order to generate opportunities for consultation and participation.

A further way of enhancing political participation of minorities is to ensure that persons belonging to minorities are fully represented in the executive. At the level of top-level government, this can include, for instance, guaranteed ministerial or deputy ministerial posts for minority representatives, or the establishment of a department or ministry for minorities. At the level of the administration, the state will seek to ensure that members of minorities are fairly represented throughout the public service. This would ordinarily include also the sensitive areas of policing, justice, and security. If minorities are not represented in these areas, they may suffer from a profound sense of exclusion, and even a sense of menace, where these emanations of state power are concerned.

In addition to the right to fully participate in the government of the state overall, the right to full and effective participation also includes the opportunity of minorities to make public decisions in relation to issues of special concern to them, or in relation to territorial units principally inhabited by their members. The former approach is often referred to as functional or cultural autonomy or minority self-governance. Even territorially dispersed minorities, for instance, may form minority representative organizations with certain authority in relation to cultural affairs, education, and language issues. Where minorities live in territorially compact areas, some states have found it convenient to grant autonomy to local municipalities or to entire regions.

Where territorial autonomy has been granted, or where a state has been organized as a federation in order to accommodate ethnic diversity, it is important to establish strong incentives for the autonomous unit to continually contribute to the state as a whole. Beyond access to central points of decision-making of the state, a clear system for the division and transfer of fiscal and economic resources, and effective mechanisms for dispute settlement in cases of clashes of competence between the centre and the autonomous entity have proven vital in this regard.

II. Standards

While these systems for political participation of minorities are well understood in theory and practice, their anchoring in legal commitments is a different matter. In the Euro-Atlantic context, the Lund Recommendations on Effective Participation of National Minorities in Public Life of the OSCE High Commissioner on National Minorities represent the most detailed catalogue of mechanisms of this kind.[2] While these recommendations have proven to be very influential on state practice, they are not legally binding. Nevertheless, in the area of application of the European Framework Convention for the Protection of National Minorities, there is an increasing trend toward recognition of the legal obligation of the state to ensure mechanisms for the effective participation of minorities in public life. Article 15 of the Framework Convention indicates that the parties:

> ...shall create the conditions necessary for the effective participation of persons belonging to national minorities in cultural, social and economic life and in public affairs, in particular those affecting them.[3]

[2] OSCE High Commissioner on National Minorities, Lund Recommendations on Effective Participation of National Minorities in Public Life, (The Hague, Foundation on Inter-Ethnic Relations, 1999).

[3] Framework Convention for the Protection of National Minorities, adopted on 1 February 1998, ETS No. 157.

Implementation practice under this article has crystallized the view that the state may be entitled to choose which of the above mechanisms for effective political participation it wishes to employ. But while states may be entitled to dine à la carte from the menu provided in the Lund Recommendations, according to the Framework Convention they are obliged to ensure a result, namely the guarantee of adequate involvement of minorities in decision-making. The state may choose the individual courses, but there must be a complete dinner at the end, providing for a range of effective participation mechanisms.[4]

At the universal level, the right to effective participation is not yet established to this extent. First of all, there does not exist a binding universal treaty specifically on minority rights. The only legally binding specialist provision can be found in Article 27 of the International Covenant on Civil and Political Rights (CCPR):

> In those States in which ethnic, religious or linguistic minorities exist, persons belonging to such minorities shall not be denied the right, in community with the other members of their group, to enjoy their own culture, to profess and practise their own religion, or to use their own language.

While Article 27 itself does not refer to political participation, the UN Human Rights Committee, the Treaty body best placed to offer an authentic interpretation of this provision, has included effective political participation of minorities in its authoritative General Comment on this provision.[5] This advancing interpretation of the Covenant, which after all dates back to 1966, is in line with international practice. This is also reflected in the 1992 United Nations General Assembly Declaration on the Rights of Persons Belonging to National or Ethnic, Religious and Linguistic Minorities. The declaration expressly confirms the right of persons belonging to minorities to participate effectively in cultural, religious, social, economic, and public life.[6] The Declaration adds that states should consider appropriate measures to enable persons belonging to minorities to participate fully in the economic progress and development of their country.[7]

More generally, all aspects of political participation are, of course, linked with the right of self-determination as reflected in Article 1 of the CCPR.

[4] M. Weller, 'Article 15', in M. Weller (ed.), *The Rights of Minorities* (Oxford, 2005), 428ff.

[5] HRC, General Comment 23, Compilation of General Comments and General Recommendations Adopted by Human Rights Treaty Bodies, UN Doc. HRI/GEN/1/Rev.1 at 38,1994, para. 7.

[6] Resolution 47/135 of 18 December 1992, Article 2.2.

[7] *Ibid.*, Article 4.5.

According to this right, all peoples freely determine their political status and political system. While the Human Rights Committee does not address individual petitions under this article in this present context, the African Commission has considered grave interferences with the right to democratic governance, for instance through a coup, violations of the right to self-determination.[8] Generally, however, universal human rights instruments and the relevant implementation bodies cover political participation in more specific terms. For instance, the CCPR guarantees the right:

(a) to take part in the conduct of public affairs, directly or through freely chosen representatives;
(b) to vote and to be elected at genuine periodic elections which shall be by universal and equal suffrage and shall be held by secret ballot, guaranteeing the free expression of the will of the electors;
(c) to have access, on general terms of equality, to public service in this country.[9]

In the exercise of their right of participation, members of minorities are protected from discrimination on any ground such as race, colour, language, religion, or national origin.[10] This is derived from the general prohibition of discrimination taken on its own, and/or when applied in conjunction with one of the substantive standards under universal human rights law (Article 25 CCPR, for instance) or regional provisions. This is also reflected in specialist conventions, such as the International Convention on the Elimination of all Forms of Racial Discrimination. According to the Convention state parties undertake to eliminate discrimination in all its forms and to guarantee the right of everyone, without distinction as to race, colour, or national or ethnic origin, to equality before the law, notably also in the enjoyment of the following rights:[11]

(c) . . . the rights to participate in election—to vote and to stand for election—on the basis of universal and equal suffrage, to take part in the Government as well as in the conduct of public affairs at any level and to have equal access to public service.

These three elements of the general right to take part in the public affairs of the state and to participate in government are also reflected in Inter-American

[8] AfrCommHR, No. 147/95 and 149/96, *Sir Dawda K Jawara v. The Gambia*, decision of May 2000, para. 73.

[9] Article 25, International Covenant on Civil and Political Rights, adopted on 16 December 1966, entered into force on 23 March 1976, 999 UNTS 171.

[10] *Ibid.*, Art 26.

[11] Article 5(c) International Convention on the Elimination of All Forms of Racial Discrimination, concluded on 7 March 1966, entered into force on 4 January 1969, 993 UNTS 195.

and African regional standards. In fact, both regional standards reflect the wording chosen in the International Covenant on Civil and Political Rights in similar terms.[12] Article 23 of the Inter-American Convention on Human Rights adds that these rights and opportunities may be regulated by the law, but only on the basis of age, nationality, residence, language, education, civil and mental capacity, or sentencing by a competent court in criminal proceedings.

The European Convention on Human Rights and Fundamental Freedoms, which preceded the adoption of the CCPR by a significant period, does not offer all three elements of participation granted in Article 25 of the Covenant.[13] In Article 3 of Protocol I, it only addresses the right to hold free elections and to stand for elected office. Broader participation issues are addressed mainly through the rights to free association, free speech, and non-discrimination.

The Human Rights Committee, the African Commission, the Inter-American and the European Courts of Human Rights have all emphasized the foundational and essential nature of the right to democratic representation and participation. In the words of the Inter-American Court, 'the right to govern rests with the people, who alone are empowered to decide their own and immediate destiny and their legitimate representatives'.[14]

While the European Convention focuses only on electoral representation, it has taken a broad view of the definition of the electoral bodies to which the right to democratic participation applies. In addition to the state parliament, electoral representation encompasses regional assemblies or the parliaments of constituent republics of a federation:

> The Commission recalls that Article (3) [of Protocol I to the European Convention] applies to the election of the 'legislature'. This word does not necessarily mean only the national parliament, but has to be interpreted in the light of the constitutional structure of the State in question.... The Commission finds that, in accordance with the federal structure of the German State, the diets of the German Länder are 'legislature'; within the meaning of Article 3.[15]

[12] Article 23 American Convention on Human Rights, concluded on 22 November 1969, entered into force on 18 July 1978, O.A.S.T.S. No. 36, 1114 UNTS 123; Article 13 African Charter on Human and Peoples' Rights, concluded on 26 June 1981, entered into force on 21 October 1986, O.A.U. Doc. CAB/LEG/24.9/49 (1990).

[13] International Covenant on Civil and Political Rights adopted on 16 December 1966, entered into force on 23 March 1976, 999 UNTS 171.

[14] Inter-AmCtHR, *Walter Humberto Vasquez Vejararno v. Peru*, Case 11.166, judgment of 13 April 2000, Report No. 48/00, para. 93.

[15] ECommHR, *Timke v. Germany*, (App. 27311/95, Decision of 11 September 1995); also ECommHR, *X v. Austria*, (Appl. 7008/95, Decision of 12 July 1976); ECtHR, *Py v. France*, (Appl. 66289/01, Judgment of 6 June 2005), Reports 2005-I, para. 36.

Similarly, the European Court of Human Rights confirms that the right to participate in the electoral process to legislatures also extends to elections to the European Parliament.[16] On the other hand, with respect to Article 3 of Protocol No. 1 to the European Convention on Human Rights and Fundamental Freedoms, which requires the parties to 'hold free elections at reasonable intervals by secret ballot, under conditions which will ensure the free expression of the opinion of the people in the choice of the legislature', the Court found that this provision only concerns the choice of legislature, not other elected offices. This would exclude, for instance, the office of state president, given that there are no legislative powers associated with it.[17] In a subsequent decision, the Court qualified this finding, adding that presidential elections might after all be covered, if the President's office has a 'role in the overall legislative process'.[18] Accordingly, the Court has given a slightly more restrictive reading to the right to democratic participation in the European context as would be the case, for instance, under Article 25 of the CCPR, or in the other regional systems.

Generally, however, one may conclude that according to general human rights standards all persons, or in some respects citizens of voting age, have at least three types of rights firmly established in universal and regional human rights law:

- the right to vote and be elected in genuine periodic elections;
- the right of access to the public service;
- and the right to take part in the conduct of public affairs directly or indirectly.

The state is under a positive obligation to 'guarantee' these rights and to ensure that they can be 'fully and effectively' exercised without discrimination of any kind. These entitlements are increasingly consolidated in the right to full and effective participation of persons belonging to minorities in public life—a right firmly established within the European Human Rights system through the Framework Convention and gradually emerging at the universal level.

[16] ECtHR, *Matthews v. the United Kingdom*, (Appl. 24833/94, Judgment of 18 February 1999), para. 43.

[17] ECommHR, *Carl-Ludwig and Lorenz Habsburg-Lothringen v Austria*, (Appl. 15344/89, Decision of 21 December 1989), para. 3.3; followed by ECommHR, *Liucija Baskauskaite v. Lithuania*, (Appl. 41090/98, Decision of 21 October 1998), para. 2.1.

[18] ECtHR, *Boskoski v. Former Yugoslav Republic of Macedonia*, (Appl. 11676/04, Judgment of 2 September 2004), para. III 1.

III. Democratic Electoral Systems, the Right to Vote and to Stand for Election

A. Democratic Electoral Systems

The Inter-American Commission has confirmed that its jurisprudence is based on the assumption that:

> Participation by citizens in government...forms the basis and underpinning of democracy, which cannot exist without it, because the right to govern rests with the people, who alone are empowered to decide their own and immediate destiny and to designate their legitimate representatives.[19]

At the European regional level, the European Court of Human Rights has confirmed tirelessly that '[d]emocracy is without doubt a fundamental feature of the European public order'.[20] In fact, it has claimed that pluralism, tolerance and multi-party democracy is the 'only political model contemplated by the European Convention on Human Rights'.[21] European practice has also pronounced itself on the question of elections to be held at 'reasonable intervals':

> The Commission finds that the question whether elections are held at reasonable intervals must be determined by reference to the purpose of parliamentary elections. The purpose is to ensure that fundamental changes in prevailing public opinion are reflected in the opinions of the representatives of the people. Parliament must in principle be in a position to develop and execute its legislative intentions—including longer-term legislative plans. Too short an interval between elections may impede political planning for the implementation of the will of the electorate; too long an interval can lead to the petrification of political groups in Parliament which may no longer bear any resemblance to the prevailing will of the electorate. In the light of these considerations, it cannot be said that a five-year interval between elections does not ensure the free expression of the opinion of the people in the choice of the legislature.[22]

The Commission also held that elections must be held under conditions which will ensure the free expression of the will of the people in the choice of

[19] Int-AmCommHR, Case No. 11.166, *Walter Humberto Vasques Vejarano v. Peru*, Report No. 48/00, para. 93, relying on an analysis of the Commission of its own practice and jurisprudence over the preceeding years.

[20] ECtHR, *Loizidou v. Turkey*, Judgment of 18 December 1996, Reports 1996-IV, para. 75.

[21] ECtHR, *Gorzelik and Others v. Poland*, (Appl. 44158/98, Judgment of 17 February 2004), para. 89; ECtHR *United Communist Party of Turkey and Others v. Turkey*, Judgment of 30 January 1998, Reports 1998-I, paras. 43–45; ECtHR, *Refah Partisi (the Welfare party) and Others v. Turkey*, Judgment of 13 February 2003, Reports 2003-II, para. 86–89.

[22] ECommHR, *Timke v. Gremany*, (Appl. 27311/95, Decision of 11 September 1995).

the legislature. However, this does not exclude the right of the state 'to attach certain limitations to the right to vote and to stand as a candidate as long as they are not arbitrary and do not infringe the free expression of the opinion of the people'.[23] The requirement of 200 signatures in support of a candidate as a condition to stand in an election was considered a permissible limitation.

Indeed, in general terms, the European Court of Human Rights has found that states enjoy a wide margin of appreciation in determining the electoral system. While there are no clawback clauses in Article 3 of Protocol I of the European Convention, the Court has found that there are implied limitations, which also permit the imposition of conditions on the right to vote and to stand in elections.[24] The limitations are broader than those specifically enumerated as grounds for restrictions of the rights enumerated in Articles 8 to 11 of the Convention, covering, for instance, freedom of expression or association.[25] Moreover, one would need to bear in mind the evolution of the political system in question. 'Features that would be unacceptable in the context of one system may accordingly be justified in the context of another. . .'.[26] However, once an electoral system has been adopted, the right to limit democratic entitlements so granted is not unlimited. Restrictions must not curtail the right to vote to such an extent as to impair its very essence and deprive it of effectiveness.[27] Restrictions must pursue a legitimate aim and the means employed must not be disproportionate, such as to 'thwart' the free expression of the electoral will.[28] Applied to the context of minorities, the Court has found, for instance, that a voting system effectively requiring linguistic minorities to vote for candidates willing and able to use the language of their region was not unreasonable, falling within the state's margin of appreciation.[29]

While acknowledging 'implied' limitations on the rights in question, allowing the state to regulate the right to vote and stand in elections, the Court has taken a somewhat more restrictive view with regard to democratic issues in conjunction with other rights, in particular, the rights to assembly and

[23] ECommHR, *X v. Austria*, (Appl. 7008/75, Decision of 12 July 1976); also ECtHR, *Py v. France*, (Appl. 66289/01, judgment of 6 June 2005), para. 45.

[24] ECtHR, *Py v. France* (Appl. 66289/01, Judgment of 6 June 2005), para. 46; ECtHR, *Zdanoka v. Latvia*, (Appl. 58278/00, Judgment of 17 June 2004), para. 82.

[25] ECtHR, *Zdanoka v. Latvia*, (Appl. 58278/00, Judgment of 16 March 2006), para. 115.

[26] ECtHR, *Mathieu-Mohin and Clerfayt v. Belgium*, (Appl. 9267/81, Judgment of 2 March 1987), para. 54.

[27] ECtHR, *Py v. France*, (Appl. 66289/01, Judgment of 6 June 2005), para. 47.

[28] ECtHR, *Matthews v. the United Kingdom*, (Appl. 24833/94, Judgment of 18 February 1999), para. 63.

[29] ECtHR, *Mathieu-Mohin and Clerfayt v. Belgium*, (Appl. 9267/81, Judgment of 2 March 1987), para. 57.

expression.[30] In view of the overriding importance of the precept of democratic governance, the Court has determined that restrictions on rights essential for the effective implementation of free association in a political context, are to be constructed strictly. That is to say, 'only convincing and compelling reasons can justify restrictions . . . '.[31] In this context, states have 'only a limited margin of appreciation' when determining which restrictions may be legally necessary.[32]

With respect to minorities, the Court has confirmed that a 'balance must be achieved which ensures the fair and proper treatment of minorities and avoids any abuse of a dominant position'.[33] The consequences of this finding were spelt out in a case concerning the electoral system in Northern Ireland. While in the rest of the United Kingdom a 'first past the post' system applies, proportional representation was introduced in that region. The aim was to ensure that non-dominant communities that would not normally have the outright majority in any voting districts would still be represented. The Court was invited to consider whether this constituted an interference with the rights of members of the majority, whose vote would be treated differently than in the rest of the UK. The Court found:

1. A simple proportional representation will lead to the minority being represented in situations where people vote generally on ethnic or religious lines and one group is in a clear minority throughout electoral districts . . . a system taking into account the specific situation as to majority and minority existing in Northern Ireland must be seen as making it easier for the people to express its opinions freely. . . .
2. . . . the United Kingdom has specific reasons for applying a different electoral system in one part of the country, namely the protection of the rights of a minority. The electoral system complained of is, therefore, based on reasonable and objective criteria which justify the differentiation applied. Moreover, it does not appear that there is no reasonable relationship of proportionality between the means employed and the aim sought to be realized.[34]

While this provision might not support the view that there must be a system of proportional representation in areas where minorities live, it confirms that

[30] ECtHR, *Mathieu-Mohin and Clerfayt v. Belgium*, (Appl. 9267/81, Judgment of 2 March 1987), para. 52.

[31] ECtHR, *United Communist Party or Turkey and Others v. Turkey*, Judgment of 30 August 1998, Reports 1998-I, para. 46.

[32] *Ibid.*

[33] ECtHR, *Gorzelik and Others v. Poland*, (Appl. 44158/98, Judgment of 17 February 2004), para. 90.

[34] EcommHR, *Lindsay and Others v. the United Kingdom*, (Appl. 8364/78, Decision of 8 March 1979), para. III 1.

altering the electoral system to their benefit is a legitimate and proportionate means that does not amount to discrimination in relation to members of the majority.

B. The Right to Vote

In a number of instances, the respective governments placed conditions on the right to vote. At the universal level, the Human Rights Committee has confirmed that the right to vote 'is not an absolute right and that restrictions may be imposed on it provided they are not discriminatory'.[35] The African Commission has found generally that Article 13(1) of the African Charter is extended to 'every citizen' and its denial can only be justified by reason of legal incapacity, i.e. the individual is not a citizen of a particular state. Such 'legal incapacity,' as a justification for denying the right under Article 13(1) can only come into play by invoking provisions of the law that conform to internationally acceptable norms and standards. These, according to the African Commission, should be based on objective and reasonable criteria established by law, as is provided by Human Rights Committee General Comment 25 in relation to the corresponding provision of Article 25 of the CCPR.[36]

Voter registration has been considered by the European Commission and Court of Human Rights in some detail. With respect to elections to the Regional Council of the Trentino-Aldige Region, it was found reasonable to require voters to reside in that region for at least four years before registration.[37] This was necessary in order to acquire a thorough understanding of the regional context such that their vote would reflect the concern for the protection of linguistic minorities. Similarly, in the unique case of New Caledonia, a very extensive ten-year period of residence, spanning two full electoral cycles was considered acceptable. This was due to the nature of the underlying nature of the self-determination conflict in that region, recently settled in an agreement. In that context, it had been particularly important to ensure that only residents with long-standing ties with the territory would be entitled to vote.[38] This view of the European Court was amplified by the Human Rights Committee. The

[35] HRC, Communication No. 932/2000, *Marie-Hélène Gillot v. France*, views of 15 July 2002, UN Doc. A/57/40 at 270, para. 12.2.

[36] AfrCommHPR, *Purohit and Moore v. The Gambia*, 15–29 May 2003, 241/2001, 33rd Sess, para. 74.

[37] ECtHR, *Hilbe v. Liechtenstein*, (Appl. 31981/96), Reports 1999-VI; EcommHR, *Polacco and Garofalo v. Italy*, (Appl. 23450/94, Decision of 15 September 1997), DR 90-A, p. 5.

[38] ECtHR, *Py v. France*, (Appl. 66289/01, Judgment of 6 June 2005), para. 64.

requirement of prolonged residence or of family ties to New Caledonia as a condition for voting in the 1998 referendum was not found to be discriminatory. Instead, it treated differently an objectively different situation of individuals in relation to their ties with that territory.[39] This difference in treatment was intended to ensure primarily that the local (in effect indigenous) population would be able to make a genuine choice as to its future. Here, a distinction that was at least indirectly based on racial or ethnic criteria (family ties) was not discriminatory, given its aim of protecting an indigenous group in the exercise of its right to self-determination.

In *Aziz v. Cyprus*, a member of the Turkish Cypriot community was denied registration in the Greek Cypriot electoral role. Separate electoral roles were kept, according to the Cypriot Supreme Court, to ensure communal checks and balances and separate elections of the representatives of each community, with 70 per cent of seats in the parliament having been allotted to the Greek community, and 30 per cent for the Turkish community. However, due to the anomaly of the situation after the Turkish occupation of the North of the island, the Turkish list no longer operated. Accordingly, Turkish inhabitants of the South could not vote. While the previous quota system might have been justified in the light of the special inter-ethnic circumstances applying in Cyprus, it was found that the very essence of the applicants' right to vote, as guaranteed in Article 3 of Protocol No. 1 of the European Convention, was impaired.[40] Moreover, the Court found that the distinction in treatment was not justified on reasonable and objective grounds. Hence, there was also a violation of Article 14 in conjunction with that provision. Cyprus immediately changed its legislation, offering registration for voting and also the right to stand in elections to members of the Turkish Cypriot community habitually resident in the 'free territory' of the Republic.[41]

C. The Right to Stand in Elections

The right to stand as a candidate in an election is 'inherent in the concept of a truly democratic regime'.[42] This right applies to local, regional, and state-wide elections. For instance, the Inter-American Court of Human Rights has considered whether the refusal to register independent candidates in local

[39] HRC, Communication No. 932/2000, *Marie-Hélène Gillot v. France*, views of 15 July 2002, UN Doc. A/57/40 at 270, paras. 13.12f.

[40] ECtHR, *Aziz v. Cyprus,* (Appl. 69949/01, Judgment of 22 June 2004), para. 30.

[41] Resolution CM/ResDH(2007)77.

[42] ECtHR, *Podkolzina v. Latvia*, Judgment of 9 April 2002, Reports 2002-II, para. 35.

elections for mayor might amount to an infringement of the right to political participation and declared admissible a case alleging such conduct.[43]

The African Commission adopted an interesting view in relation to the right of candidates from a minority group to stand for elections. An attempt by the government of Zambia to restrict the right to stand to persons of demonstrable descent from Zambian parents would allegedly have excluded some 35 per cent of citizens of immigrant or minority descent from the highest office of the state. The Commission found that depriving an individual of the right to stand for President would not only violate his or her right under Article 13 of the African Charter:

> The pain in such an instance is caused not just to the citizen who suffers discrimination by reason of place of origin but that the rights of the citizens of Zambia to 'freely choose' political representatives of their choice, is violated.[44]

Interference with what otherwise would be the individual right to stand in elections was therefore also seen as an interference in a collective right of the population as such. Furthermore, the African Commission has opposed the imposition of a ban on former Ministers and members of parliament as a contravention of their rights to participate freely in the government of their country provided for under Article 13(1) of the Charter.[45] Moreover, it dealt with the manipulation of citizenship requirements by the government as a means to deprive an individual of the right to stand. By denying citizenship, and later offering citizenship only through 'registration' action, the government of Botswana had interfered with the right to participation of the claimant, who was seeking the office of the President. This action 'gravely deprived him of one of his most cherished fundamental rights, to freely participate in the government of his country, either directly or through elected representatives'.[46] The Commission has also addressed restriction of candidacy in one-party states:

> ... the author, a leading figure of a political party in opposition to the former President, has been prevented from participating in the general election campaign as well as

[43] Inter-AmCtHR, Petition 2570–02, *Nasry Javier Ictech Guifarrao v. Honduras*, Report No. 30/06, para. 35.

[44] AfrCommHPR, *Legal Resources Foundation v. Zambia*, 23 April—7 May, AHG/229(XXXVII) 29th session.

[45] AfrCommHPR, Communication No. 147/95 and 146/96, *Sir Dawda Jawda Jaware v. the Gambia*, cited in AfrCommHPR, Communication No. 251/2002, *Lawyers for Human Rights v Swaziland*, 37th Sess., 27 April–11 May 2005, para. 62; also HRC, Communication No. R.8/34, *Silva v. Uruguay*, (34/1978), CCPR, A/36/40 (8 April 1981) paras. 8f.

[46] AfrCommHPR, Communication No. 97/93, *Modise v Botswana*, 28th Sess., 23 October–6 November 2000.

from preparing his candidacy for this party. This amounts to an unreasonable restriction on the author's right to 'take part in the conduct of public affairs' which the state party has failed to explain or justify. In particular, it has failed to explain the requisite conditions for participation in the elections. Accordingly, it must be assumed that Mr Bwalya was detained and denied the right to run for a parliamentary seat in the Constituency of Chifubu merely on account of his membership in a political party other than that officially recognized; in this context, the Committee observes that restrictions on political activity outside the only recognized political party amount to an unreasonable restriction of the right to participate in the conduct of public affairs.[47]

The Inter-American Commission and Court on Human Rights have considered cases where an entire party list of candidates was refused registration by the relevant electoral commissions. In *Yatama v. Nicaragua*, the Inter-American Court of Human Rights determined that the failure of the government to register a party list of candidates from indigenous regional groups for elections was in violation of the right to political participation. In that instance, the group had attempted to register in alliance with two other groups which also failed, in the end, to qualify under the electoral rules. Its urgent request to register independently instead had been wrongfully denied, leaving the relevant indigenous community without sufficient chance of electoral representation.[48]

The failure to register a list of candidates was also deemed a violation of the rights of the individuals to participation on that list in the case of *Susana Higuchi Miyagawa v. Peru*.[49] The list had originally been published by the state authorities and was subsequently declared invalid by the Election Board, purportedly on technical grounds. That decision was not subject to judicial review. The Inter-American Commission considered the refusal to register arbitrary and a violation of Article 23 of the Convention. Moreover, the failure to offer judicial review in relation to a decision of this kind also amounted to a violation of the right to political participation in itself.[50]

However, the Grand Chamber of the European Court of Human Rights has indicated that the state is entitled to greater latitude when restricting the

[47] AfrCommHPR, Communication No. 314/1988, *Peter Chiiko Bwalya v. Zambia*, views adopted on 14 July 1993 UN doc. GAOR, A/48/40 (vol. II) para. 6.6.

[48] Inter-AmCtHR, Informe No. 125/01, *Yatama v. Nicaragua*, Case 12.338, Report No. 125/01, judgment of 3 December 2001, paras. 218ff.

[49] Inter-AmCommHR, *Susana Higuchi Miyagawa v. Peru*, Case 11,428/99, Report No. 119/99, decision of 6 October 1999.

[50] *Ibid.*, para. 57.

right to stand in elections (the passive element), as opposed to the right to vote in elections (the 'active' element):

> ...stricter requirements may be imposed on eligibility to stand for election to Parliament than is the case for eligibility to vote. In fact, while the test relating to the 'active' aspect of Article 3 of Protocol No. 1 has usually included a wider assessment of the proportionality of the statutory provisions disqualifying a person or a certain group of persons from the right to vote, the Court's test in relation to the 'passive' aspect of the above provision has been limited largely to a check on the absence of arbitrariness in the domestic procedures leading to disqualification of an individual from standing as a candidate... .[51]

The failure to present candidates to register in their own (minority) language was considered in the case of *Fryske Nasjonale Partij and Others v. the Netherlands*.[52] The European Commission noted that the applicants were not prevented from standing as candidates as such. Nothing, it argued, would have prevented the candidates from submitting a translation in the state language of their request for registration of the name of the party and its list of candidates. In view of the Court, neither Article 3 of Protocol No. 1 to the Convention, nor any other provision of the Convention guarantees the right to use a particular language for electoral purposes.

The reverse phenomenon, the conditioning of the right to stand as a candidate on certain language requirements, has been considered repeatedly. At the universal level, the UN Human Rights Committee, for instance, addressed the case of Ms Ignatane, a teacher of Russian origin in Riga. She was denied the right to stand in local elections due to her failure to demonstrate higher proficiency in the Latvian state language required by the Law on Elections to Town Councils and Municipal Councils. In that case, the Human Rights Committee did not question the existence of the language requirement as such. Rather it found that the way in which Ms Ignatane's linguistic competence had been determined led to her 'being prevented from exercising her right to participate in public life in conformity with Article 25 of the Covenant'.[53]

The European Court on Human Rights considered a similar case. A member of the Russian-speaking minority in Latvia had been struck off the

[51] ECtHR, *Zdanoka v. Latvia*, (Appl. 58278/00, Judgment of 16 March 2006), para. 115.

[52] ECommHR, *Fryske Nasjonale Partij and Others v. the Netherlands*, (Appl. 11100/84, Decision of 12 December 1985), para. 2.

[53] HRC, Communication No. 884/1999, *Antonina Ignatane v. Lativa*, views of 25 July 2001, UN Doc. CCPR/C/72/D/884/1999 (2001), para. 7.4.

list of candidates put forward by the National Harmony Party. Previously, that candidate had certified compliance with electoral requirements, including the capability to speak Latvian. Subsequently, a language inspector visited the candidate while at work and conducted an ad hoc examination, concluding that the candidate's command of the language was inadequate. The Court went out of its way to confirm that every state would have a wide margin of appreciation in establishing its own institutional and parliamentary system, including eligibility requirements. It noted that the choice of national parliaments' working languages would be determined by historical and political considerations specific to each country. Accordingly, there would only have been a violation if the state had arbitrarily deprived the candidate of her rights under Article 3 of Protocol No. 1 to the Convention. In view of the ad hoc nature of the examination, which created a presumption against its objectivity, this was found to be the case:

The right to stand as a candidate in an election, which is guaranteed by Article 3 of Protocol No 1 and is inherent in the concept of a truly democratic regime, would only be illusory if one could be arbitrarily deprived of it at any moment. Consequently, while it is true that States have a wide margin of appreciation when establishing eligibility conditions in the abstract, the principle that rights must be effective requires the finding that this or that candidate has failed to satisfy them to comply with a number of criteria framed to prevent arbitrary decisions. In particular, such a finding must be reached by a body which can provide a minimum of guarantees of its impartiality. Similarly, the discretion enjoyed by the body concerned must not be exorbitantly wide; it must be circumscribed, with sufficient precision, by the provisions of domestic law. Lastly, the procedure for ruling a candidate ineligible must be such as to guarantee a fair and objective decision and prevent any abuse of power on the part of the relevant authority.[54]

In the case of another member of the Russian minority in Latvia, the Chamber of the Court once again confirmed that:

the state enjoys considerable latitude in establishing constitutional rules on the status of members of parliament, including the criteria for declaring them ineligible. Although they have a common origin in the need to ensure both the independence of elected representatives and the freedom of electors, these criteria vary in accordance with the historical and political factors specific to each state; the multiplicity of situations provided for in the constitutions and electoral legislation of numerous member states of the Council of Europe shows the diversity of possible approaches in this area. For the purposes of applying Article 3, any legislation must be assessed in the light

[54] ECtHR, *Podkolzina v. Latvia*, (Appl. 46726/99, Judgment of 9 July 2002), para. 3.

of the political evolution of the country concerned. However, the State's margin of appreciation in this regard is limited by the obligation to respect the fundamental principle of Article 3, namely 'the free expression of the opinion of the people in the choice of the legislature'....[55]

In a number of instances, it was asserted that candidates might be subject to particular duties of loyalty toward the state, analogous to the requirements that may be imposed upon public servants. However, in contrast to the civil service, where the state might require political neutrality and objectivity in the exercise of public functions, a 'duty of loyalty' toward the state, if it existed at all, would need to be framed in a different way.[56] This applies both to the national and local elected assemblies:

...the Court points out that the criteria established by its case-law with regard to those persons' loyalty cannot as such be applied to the members of a national parliament.... The Court finds no cause to arrive at a different conclusion with regard to members of local councils, who are also elected by the people in accordance with the principles of pluralist democracy and are likewise responsible for taking political decisions. In summary, the second sentence of Article 11(2) of the Convention authorizing 'lawful restrictions' with regard to 'members of the armed forces, of the police or of the administration of the state' does not apply to members of parliament or to members of the elected bodies of local authorities.[57]

While the individual concerned had been debarred from running in elections by virtue of her association with the Communist Party at the time of the independence of the state, the Chamber and Grand Chamber of the Court also addressed issues relevant to minorities. It found:

With regard...to the ideas advocated by the applicant concerning the Russian-speaking minority in Latvia and the legislation on language matters, the Court discerns no evidence of anti-democratic leanings or incompatibility with the fundamental values of the Convention. ... The same conclusion is inescapable as regards the means used by the applicant to attain her political objectives. In particular, she has never been accused of having been secretly active within the CPL after the latter's dissolution, let alone of having sought to re-establish that party in its totalitarian form. ... In sum, the Government have not supplied information about any specific act by the applicant capable of endangering the Latvian State, its national security or its democratic order.[58]

[55] ECtHR, *Zdanoka v. Latvia*, (Appl. 58278/00, Judgment of 17 June 2004), para. 83.
[56] *Ibid.*, para. 85.
[57] *Ibid.*, para. 108, and Judgment of the Grand Chamber, 16 May 2006, para. 117.
[58] *Ibid.*

This ruling confirms that the state may not take account of the minority background when considering action against political parties or their candidates. Instead, the evaluation of what is necessary in order to protect a democratic society is based on the question of whether or not the programme of the party is inconsistent with democracy itself, or whether the means utilized are unlawful. In this instance, however, the Grand Chamber overruled the Chamber of the European Court of Human Rights in another respect. The Chamber had found a violation of Article 3, in view of the fact that there did not appear to be any active danger to the democratic state emanating from the applicant. The Grand Chamber, on the other hand, found that the former position of the claimant in the Communist Party and her role during the days of the Latvian transition to independence warranted her exclusion from parliament even a decade later.[59] While in other states, such measures might not be warranted, the political and historical situation in Latvia was different. Only the local authorities were best placed to judge whether such measures were still necessary to prevent a 'resurgence of ideas which, if allowed to gain ground, might appear capable of restoring the former regime'.[60]

D. Party Registration

The African Commission has found that 'political parties are one means through which citizens can participate in government either directly or through elected representatives of their choice'. Prohibiting political parties, in this case in Swaziland, 'seriously undermined the ability of the Swaziland people to participate in the government of their country and thus violated Article 13 of the Charter'.[61] In addition to a violation of Article 13, the African Commission has established a close connection with the right to free association that tends to be affected when the freedom to establish or maintain parties is concerned:

> It is worthy of note that the freedom of expression and the right to association are closely linked because the protection of opinions and the right to express them freely constitute one of the objectives of the right of association. And this amalgamation of the two norms is even clearer in the case of political parties, considering their essential role of the maintenance of pluralism and the proper functioning of democracy. [62]

[59] *Ibid.*, Grand Chamber, para. 122.

[60] *Ibid.*, para. 133.

[61] AfrCommHPR, Communication No. 251/2002, *Lawyers for Human Rights v. Swaziland*, 37th Sess., 27 April–11 May 2005, para. 63.

[62] AfrCommHPR, Communication No. 242/2001, *Interights and Institute for Human Rights and Development in Africa, and Association Mauritanienne des Droits de l'Homme v. Islamic Republic of Mauretania*, 34th Sess., 6–20 November 2003, para. 80.

Accordingly, the Commission considered disproportionate the dissolution of a political party by the Government of Morocco, given the availability of milder means to maintain public order. Similarly, In *Sir Dawda K Jaware v. The Gambia*, the Court confirmed that banning political parties was a direct violation of the right to association.[63]

The Inter-American Commission has similarly confirmed that:

Modern democracy may be said to be founded on political parties. . . . At each election the parties choose the candidates from among whom the voter must choose when he casts his ballot. In this way they impose order on public opinion, for if citizens were to vote directly without this advance work of party assurances, elections would be reduced to chaos and anarchy, votes would be dispersed in disorder, and those elected would receive so few votes as to have no representativity whatever. [64]

However, the Commission also confirmed that the state is entitled to regulate the right to elect and be elected as a party candidate, provided that there exist electoral or judicial remedies for adverse decisions. In the instance of Mr. Harris H. Whitbeck Pinol, the Commission found a violation as a candidate for Vice President had been struck from the list of candidates by virtue of the disqualification of the candidate for President, with whom he shared an electoral slate.[65]

The European Court of Human Rights has also confirmed that 'political parties are a form of association essential to the proper functioning of democracy'.[66] Indeed, the Court confirmed repeatedly the 'primordial role played in a democratic regime by political parties enjoying the freedoms and rights enshrined in Article 11 and also in Article 10 of the Convention'.[67] It was added that:[68]

In the political sphere that responsibility means that the State is under the obligation, among others, to hold, in accordance with Article 3 of Protocol No. 1, free elections at reasonable intervals by secret ballot under conditions which will ensure the free

[63] AfrCommHPR, Communication No. 251/2002, *Lawyers for Human Rights v Swaziland*, 37th Sess., 27 April–11 May 2005, para. 62.

[64] Inter-AmCommHR, Petition No. 10109, *Rios Brito v. Argentina*, Resolution No. 26/88, para. 10.

[65] Inter-AmCtHR, Case 10.804 (b), *Whitbeck Pionol v. Guatemala*, Report No. 21.94 of 22 September 1994.

[66] ECtHR, *United Communist Party of Turkey and Others v. Turkey*, (Appl. 19392/92, Judgment of 30 January 1998), para. 25.

[67] ECtHR, *Refah Partisi (The Welfare Party) and Other v. Turkey*, (Appl. 41340/98,41342/98,41343/98, Grand Chamber, Judgment of 13 February 2003), para. 87.

[68] ECtHR, *United Communist Party of Turkey and Others v. Turkey*, (Appl. 19392/92, Judgment of 30 January 1998), para. 44.

expression of the opinion of the people in the choice of the legislature. Such expression is inconceivable without the participation of a plurality of political parties representing the different shades of opinion to be found within a country's population. By relaying this range of opinion, not only within political institutions but also—with the help of the media—at all levels of social life, political parties make an irreplaceable contribution to political debate, which is at the very core of the concept of a democratic society....

Nevertheless, party registration is perhaps the most contested issue regarding political participation of minorities. In this respect the European Court of Human Rights has identified a close link between Article 3 of Protocol 1 and Article 10 on freedom of expression and Article 11 on freedom of association of the European Convention where political parties are concerned: 'Accordingly, the fact that their [the Parties] activities form part of a collective exercise of freedom of expression also entitles political parties to seek the protection of Article 10 of the Convention.... As the Court has often reiterated, the protection of opinions and the freedom to express them is one of the objectives of the freedom of association as enshrined in Article 11.'[69]

While the European Court of Human Rights has granted to states a wide margin of appreciation in relation to the determination of the specific form of the democratic system, it has taken a significantly more restrictive attitude where inhibition of the activities of political parties is concerned. 'In view of the essential nature of freedom of association and its close relationship with democracy there must be convincing and compelling reasons to justify such interference with this freedom.'[70] The Court has confirmed that this relates not only to a duty on the part of the state to refrain from interfering with this freedom:

...it is incumbent upon public authorities to guarantee the proper functioning of an association or political party, even when they annoy or give offence to persons opposed to the lawful ideas or claims that they are seeking to promote. Their members must be able to hold meetings without having to fear that they will be subjected to physical violence by their opponents. [71]

Party registration issues tend to collide with two types of state concerns. The first relates to the very fact that a minority might seek representation through a party focused on the representation of its interests. This may be challenged

[69] ECtHR, *Ouranio Toxo and Others v. Greece*, (Appl. 74989/01, Judgment of 20 October 2005), para. 35.

[70] *Ibid.*, para. 36.

[71] *Ibid.*, para. 37.

because the existence of the minority that seeks representation through a party is questioned by the state altogether. Or, the existence of the minority may be accepted, but the right to form a party may be denied on grounds of general principle. At times, it is argued, ethnic representation is inconsistent with the rule of full and effective equality of all, and with the ideology of a state of citizens, instead of a state of ethnic peoples. There may also be instances where a state discourages ethnically based parties indirectly, without directly prohibiting them. This was the case of *Yatama v. Nicaragua*, where a party seeking to represent the Yatama movement of indigenous peoples of Nicaragua's Atlantic coast sought registration. Given the geographic location of the population in question, the Yatama movement could not command support outside of that region. According to Nicaraguan law, however, parties seeking to register had to demonstrate support throughout the state. In order to register, nevertheless, the movement had affiliated with another party. However, that party, too, failed to comply with the requirement of widespread representation. The Nicaraguan authorities accordingly denied registration to the Yatama movement both individually and in combination with its proposed ally. The Inter-American Court of Human Rights found that this practice constituted a violation of the right to political participation of candidates and potential voters for the party as it did not take sufficient account of the particularities of political organization in the region concerned. Moreover, this practice effectively prevented the indigenous people represented by the Yatama movement from exercising their rights to participation.[72]

A second issue concerns the allegation that a party seeking to represent minority interests might espouse unlawful aims or conduct unlawful activities. That is to say, there is no denial of the right of members of the minority to form a party in principle. However, the state may claim that the party in question can be denied registration, or must be dissolved, due to its specific aims. These might include, for instance, secessionist aims, an espousal of political violence or, more controversially, political aims that appear illegitimate to the government, such as the pursuit of governance based on religious precept.

1. Denial of Party Registration Due to Inherent Factors

The state may deny that the group in question exists as an entity that can be eligible for registration in the party register. In that respect, the issue is closely linked to the freedom of association. Generally, a minority that has been denied

[72] Inter-AmCtHR, Informe No. 125/01, *Yatama v. Nicaragua*, Case 12.338, Report No. 125/01, judgment of 3 December 2001, para. 218.

'recognition' by the territorial state will be precluded from registering a minority representative (cultural) organization, not to speak of a political party.

As the European Court found: 'It is only natural that, where a civil society functions in a healthy manner, the participation of citizens in the democratic process is to a large extent achieved through membership in associations in which they may integrate with each other and pursue common objectives collectively.'[73] This, according to the Court, also extends to political parties and other associations, including also those protecting the cultural or spiritual heritage, seeking an ethnic identity or asserting a minority consciousness.[74] However, as we have seen in Chapter 4 of this Commentary, even the freedom of association is at times contested where minority representative civil society organizations are concerned. There is an even greater reluctance in the case of the registration of minority political parties. As noted above, a number of states will discourage such practices, either because they deny the existence of the minority in question, or because they argue that minorities should integrate with society and seek representation through mainstream parties. In their view the formation of national or ethnic parties might pose a risk to the identity of the state as a whole.

This view was perhaps confirmed indirectly, when the European Court of Human Rights followed the European Commission concerning the dissolution of the United Communist Party of Turkey (TBKP) by the Turkish authorities. According to the Court, 'it was not that the TBKP was a terrorist organization or one sponsoring terrorism, but it could be regarded as openly pursuing the creation of a separate Kurdish nation and consequently a redistribution of the territory of the Turkish States'.[75] Referring to the distinction between Turks and Kurds drawn in the party programme, the Court found that the state at least had the legitimate aim of safeguarding its territorial integrity from the perceived threat to its national security. In a later passage addressing the proportionality of the measure to the risk posed, the Court noted that the party in question did not describe the Kurdish people as a 'minority', nor did it make any claim other than the recognition of their existence for them to enjoy special treatment or rights.[76]

[73] ECtHR, *Ouranio Toxo and Others v. Greece*, (Appl. 74989/01, Judgment of 20 October 2005), para. 92

[74] *Ibid.*, para. 92.

[75] ECtHR, *United Communist Party of Turkey and Others v. Turkey*, (Appl. 19392/92, Judgment of 30 January 1998), para. 44.

[76] *Ibid.*, para. 56.

The judgment might be misunderstood. It appears to suggest that the measure might be considered proportionate if indeed the party in question had described the Kurdish people as a 'minority' or had made claims for the recognition of their existence for them to enjoy special treatment or rights. This, of course, would be inconsistent with basic tenets of minority rights law, which itself is part of human rights. However, one may presume that such an interpretation would mean misreading the intention of the Court. In fact, the Court found that there can be 'no justification for hindering a political group solely because it seeks to debate in public the situation of part of the State's population and to take part in the nation's political life....'[77] It therefore determined that the dissolution of the TBKP was disproportionate to the aim pursued and consequently unnecessary in a democratic society. Rather than wishing to suggest that minorities are to be treated as threats to the state as such, the Court was engaging with the peculiar view of Turkey relating to the criteria for recognition of minorities within its jurisdiction. According to Turkey, minorities are only those referred to in the treaty of Lausanne and associated documents. The Court was apparently taking the view that even if one were to accept Turkey's position, still there would have been no grounds for disbanding the party.

The Court returned to this issue in the case of the *Socialist Party and Others v. Turkey*. The Turkish constitutional Court had noted that by distinguishing the Kurdish and Turkish nation, the party had advanced the creation of minorities within Turkey and ultimately, the establishment of a Kurdish-Turkish Federation, to the detriment of the unity of the Turkish nation and the territorial integrity of the state. The Court rejected this approach. Again, it emphasized that:

The Court notes that, read together, the statements put forward a political programme with the essential aim being the establishment, in accordance with democratic rules, of a federal system in which Turks and Kurds would be represented on an equal footing and on a voluntary basis. Admittedly, reference is made to the right to self-determination of the 'Kurdish nation' and its right to 'secede'; however, read in their context, the statements using these words do not encourage secession from Turkey but seek rather to stress that the proposed federal system could not come about without the Kurds' freely given consent, which should be expressed through a referendum.

In the Court's view, the fact that such a political programme is considered incompatible with the current principles and structures of the Turkish state does not make it incompatible with the rules of democracy. It is of the essence of democracy to allow

[77] *Ibid.*, para. 57.

diverse political programmes to be proposed and debated, even those that call into question the way a State is currently organized, provided that they do not harm democracy itself.[78]

This finding might still be seen as somewhat restrictive, given that it takes note of the fact that the party in question did not actually propose secession. This might imply that, had it made such a proposal it could have been prohibited. However, the actual test of whether or not there were legitimate grounds for such a prohibition was not whether the party advocated secession, but whether it called for violence, an uprising or another form of rejection of democratic principles.[79] Moreover, in the *Ilinden* case, which will be addressed in detail later, the Court found that even a secessionist programme would not necessarily render a party subject to non-registration or dissolution.[80]

In a further case concerning the situation of the Kurds in Turkey, and the representation of their interests through political parties, the European Court of Human Rights found:

The Court accepts that the principles supported by the HEP [the party in question], such as the right to self-determination and recognition of language rights, are not in themselves contrary to the fundamental principles of democracy. It likewise agrees with the Commission's reasoning that if merely by advocating those principles a political group were held to be supporting acts of terrorism, that would reduce the possibility of dealing with related issues in the context of a democratic debate and would allow armed movements to monopolize support for the principles in question. That in turn would be strongly at variance with the spirit of Article 11 and the democratic principles on which it is based.[81]

The freedom of association and the possible formation of a political party dedicated to minority representation were also interlinked in the *Gorzelik* case before the European Court of Human Rights. In that case, authorities in Poland had refused to register the 'Union of People of Silesian Nationality'. The Court of Appeal in Poland, and in a later phase, the Supreme Court, noted that there might exist an ethnic identity of Silesians

[78] ECtHR, *Socialist Party and Others v. Turkey*, (Appl. 20/1997/804/1007, Judgment of 25 May 1998), para. 47.

[79] ECtHR, *Freedom and Democratic Party (OEZDEP) v. Turkey*, (Appl. 23885/94, Judgment of 8 December 1999), para. 41, see also section 2, Denial Due to Unlawful Activities.

[80] ECtHR, *Stankov and the United Macedonian Organization Ilinden v. Bulgaria*, (Appl. 29221/95 and 29225/95, Judgment of 2 October 2001).

[81] ECtHR, *Yazar and Others v. Turkey*, (Appl. 22723/93, 22724/93, 22725/93, Judgment of 9 April 2002), para. 57.

in Poland, but denied that this group constituted a nation and hence a national minority that might be represented through the organization in question.[82] This in itself would have been a rather controversial act in relation to Article 11 of the European Convention. However, the European Court of Human Right further refined the issue. Poland argued that it was entitled to refuse registration, in view of the potential of the Union of People of Silesian Nationality to seek to participate in elections. According to the 1993 electoral law, parties representing national minorities could be granted an exemption of the five per cent threshold for representation in parliament. Once registered as an association, the government argued, the Union would be able to transform itself into a political party and claim this privilege without the opportunity of any further review by the Polish authorities. The Court, rather controversially, confirmed this view. It found that Poland was entitled to safeguard against the 'risk' of formation of a political party on the part of the Silesians, by denying registration as an association. Such a denial would be the last point in a chain of events leading to the granting of a five per cent exemption where the government could still intervene. While this might constitute an interference with Article 11 of the European Convention, this could be justified by a pressing social need. This decision was unanimous.

Again, a superficial reading of the decision might lead to its misinterpretation. The Court did not endorse the view that a state should have the right to determine only according to its own interests whether a group constitutes a minority and can accordingly be eligible for political representation. Rather, in this instance, the Court appears to have focused on the automaticity between registration of the organization and the possibility of claiming exemption from certain voting requirements that apply to minority parties. The state, it appears, should have been entitled at least to investigate whether the association would be eligible to such benefits, granted to minority parties. Nevertheless, the decision appears somewhat odd, as it would be for the state to ensure through its own legislation that registration as a civil society organization would not automatically trigger such a result. The consequences of this failure were attributed to the minority representative organization. The group was denied registration as a result. Moreover, the Court did not explain why the Silesian group should not automatically partake of the electoral benefits obtained by the parties of other minorities.

[82] ECtHR, *Gorzelik and Others v. Poland*, (Appl. 44156/98, Judgment of 17 February 2004), para. 32.

2. *Denial Due to Unlawful Activities*

The first part of this section has addressed cases in which party registration was denied or withdrawn simply because the party in question sought to represent a minority. A second ground for the denial of registration relates to the actual activities of the party in question. The state may claim that registration must be denied, or a party dissolved, because its programme or activities collide with the existing legal order of the state. The European Court of Human Rights has defended the right of the state to deny the existence of parties aiming to destroy pluralist democracy:

> No one must be authorized to rely on the Convention's provisions in order to weaken or destroy the ideals and values of a democratic society. Pluralism and democracy are based on a compromise that requires various concessions by individuals or groups of individuals, who must sometimes agree to limit some of the freedoms they enjoy in order to guarantee greater stability of the country as a whole.[83]

With respect to religious communities, the European Court of Human Rights found that a party programme of the Welfare Party in Turkey dedicated to implementing a religiously based system of governance based on sharia law was incompatible with democracy. Coupled with other factors, it was therefore a permissible interference with Article 11 of the Convention and other provisions to prohibit such a religiously inspired party, even if it commanded widespread support.[84]

On the other hand, it is not sufficient for the state to *suspect* that a group or party seeks to engage in undermining constitutional structures. Instead, this must be assessed objectively in the light of the programme and actual activities of the party.[85] With respect to groups seeking to assert a minority identity, it was accordingly found that one could not presume the intent to pursue aims justifying a restriction on the party. Instead, it again needs to be ascertained through the relevant party programme and the organization's actions and positions. In principle, the state's margin of appreciation decreases when the interference with the right to political organization is concerned:

> An essential factor to be taken into consideration is the question whether there has been a call for the use of violence, an uprising or any other form of rejection of

[83] ECtHR, *Refah Partisi (The Welfare Party) and Other v. Turkey*, (Appl. 41340/98,41342/98,41343/98, Grand Chamber, Judgment of 13 February 2003 or Judgment of 31 July 2001) para. 99.

[84] *Ibid.*, para. 135.

[85] ECtHR, *Grande Oriente D'Italia di Palazzo Giustiniani v. Italy*, (Appl. 35972/97, Judgment of 2 August 2001), para. 15.

democratic principles. ... Where there has been incitement to violence against an individual or a public official or a sector of the population, the State authorities enjoy a wider margin of appreciation when examining the need for an interference with freedom of expression ....[86]

In *Ouranio Toxo and Others v. Greece*, a political party's aims had included the protection of the Macedonian minority in Greece. As a consequence it had been subjected to attack by the public, incited by the local government combined with a failure on the part of the authorities to afford it protection. The government referred to the disruption of peace as evidence of the need to repress the party, rather than as confirmation of its duty to take action against those attacking it. First, with respect to the right of existence of a party dedicated to protecting a minority the existence of which has been denied by the Greek authorities, the European Court of Human Rights determined:

The Court considers that mention of the consciousness of belonging to a minority and the preservation and development of a minority's culture cannot be said to constitute a threat to democratic society, even though it may provoke tensions.... The emergence of tensions is one of the unavoidable consequences of pluralism, that is to say the free discussion of all political ideas. Accordingly, the role of the authorities in such circumstances is not to remove the cause of tension by eliminating pluralism, but to ensure that the competing political groups tolerate each other....[87]

Second, the Court found that the state had a positive obligation to protect the party from foreseeable violence when able to do so. Moreover, the authorities would need to undertake in good faith an investigation of violent incidents liable to inhibit the operation of the party. Accordingly, Greece was found to be in breach of Article 11.[88]

E. Exercise of Elected Mandates

The right to vote and to stand in elections includes the right, 'once elected, to sit as a member of parliament'.[89] As mentioned, in the controversial decision in the *Welfare Party* case, the European Court endorsed the prohibition of an entire political party that enjoyed widespread political support and even

[86] ECtHR, *Stankov and the United Macedonian Organization Ilinden v. Bulgaria*, (Appl. 29221/95 and 29225/95, Judgment of 2 October 2001), para. 90.

[87] ECtHR, *Ouranio Toxo and Others v. Greece*, (Appl. 74989/01, Judgment of 20 October 2005), para. 40.

[88] *Ibid.*, para. 43.

[89] ECtHR, *Selim Sadak and Others v. Turkey*, (Appl. 25144/94, 26149/95 to 26154/95, 27100/95, 2710195, Judgment 11 June 2002), para. 33.

significant representation in parliament. This was a major interference with the existing political order in that the party had already achieved democratic legitimization through its significant electoral success. It was the largest party in Turkey, holding 158 out of 450 seats in the national parliament. Accordingly, there had not only been a prohibition of a political party, but also an interference in a popular mandate that had already been granted in full accordance with the electoral system of Turkey. In fact, it was predicted that the Welfare Party would most likely achieve an outright victory in the next popular elections. The Court went against the verdict of a large segment of the popular sovereign in depriving it of the outcome of its democratic choice, purportedly in order to protect the democratic process.[90] This was directly based on an assessment of the religious motivation of the party, which was found to be incompatible with democratic pluralism. This rationale, one presumes, might also find application in relation to minority communities that wish to implement religiously inspired governance in relation to the areas where they live, for instance, at the local or regional level.

In another instance, the European Court of Human Rights found inadmissible an application of an ethnic Albanian mayor in Macedonia. He had been convicted and given a prison sentence, due to the decision to fly Turkish and Albanian flags next to the Macedonian state flag on public buildings. He had organized the 'defence' of the flag, including popular resistance to the state authorities seeking to implement a Court decision requiring the removal of the flags. The Court affirmed that:

> ... while freedom or peaceful assembly, and freedom of expression, is important for everybody, it is especially so for an elected representative of the people. He represents his electorate, draws attention to their preoccupations and defends their interests. Accordingly, interference with the freedom of peaceful assembly and freedom of expression of an elected representative calls for the closest scrutiny on the part of the Court ... .[91]

In this instance, however, the Court determined that the mayor had contributed to the risk of violence and failed to execute the constitutional and legal order of Macedonia. Accordingly, the criminal sanction by the state of his conduct could be justified as necessary and proportionate.

The Court has confirmed, nevertheless, in several instances the importance of the freedom of expression of elected representatives in representing their

[90] *Ibid.*

[91] ECtHR, *Osmani and Others v. the Former Yugoslav Republic of Macedonia*, (Appl. 50841/9, Final decision as to the admissibility of 6 April 2000), para. 17.

electorate.[92] It added that 'interferences with the freedom of expression of an opposition member of parliament ... call for the closest scrutiny on the part of the Court'.[93] It also found that '... the limits of permissible criticism [of public policy] are wider with regard to the government than in relation to a private citizen. In a democratic system the actions or omissions of the government must be subject to the close scrutiny not only of the legislative and judicial authorities but also of the press and public opinion'.[94]

With respect to parliamentary representation of certain groups, the Court found that '... it would be contradictory to make the exercise of a mandate intended to represent different views of society within Parliament subject to a declaration of commitment to a particular set of beliefs'.[95] However, when it came to the requirement of giving the parliamentary oath in the UK as a condition of occupying a parliamentary seat, the Court found that this requirement had been well known to the electorate in advance. As the Court determined that this requirement was in itself a reasonable one, and it applied equally to all members of parliament, its application did not deprive the voters of a certain party of their right to vote.[96]

Members of elected bodies do not enjoy, on the basis of the Convention alone, a right to use the minority language of their choice for the purpose of speaking and voting in an assembly.[97]

IV. Access to Public Service

There is, as yet, not a great deal of practice concerning access to public service of persons belonging to minorities. There are a significant number of cases from the Human Rights Committee or regional bodies addressing instances in which civil servants were removed from their positions due to political

[92] ECtHR, *Ahmet v. Greece*, (Appl. 18877/91, Judgment of 4 April 1995), para. 51; citing, ECtHR, *Castells v. Spain*, (Appl. 11798/85, Judgment of 23 April 1992), Series A, No. 236, para. 42l, and ECtHR, *McGuinness v. the UK*, (Appl. 39511/98, Admissibility decision of 8 June 1999), para. 1.

[93] ECtHR, *Castells v. Spain*, (Appl. 11798/85, Judgment of 23 April 1992), Series A, No. 236, para. 42, and ECtHR, *Sadak and Others v. Turkey*, (Appl. 25144/94, 26149/95 to 26154/95, 27100/95, 2710195, Judgment of 11 June 2002), para. 34.

[94] ECtHR, *Yazar and Others v. Turkey*, (Appl. 22723/93, 22724/93, 22725/93, Judgment of 9 April 2002), para. 59.

[95] ECtHR, *McGuinness v. the UK*, (Appl. 39511/98, Admissibility decision of 8 June 1999), para. 1.

[96] *Ibid.*

[97] ECtHR, *Georges Clerfayt, Pierre Legros et al v. Belgium*, (Appl. 10650/83, Decision of 17 May 1985), para. III 7.

motivations. Generally speaking, however, these motives were not connected with minority identity. There is also little practice relating to a positive right of gaining access to the public service, due to the need to include minorities in the administration of the state. At the universal level, the Human Rights Committee has confirmed the application of the principle of full equality also in this context, however:

> ... under Article 25 (c) of the Covenant, every citizen shall have the right and opportunity, without any of the distinctions mentioned in Article 2 and without unreasonable restrictions, to have access, on general terms of equality, to public service in his or her country. In order to ensure access on general terms of equality, the criteria and processes for appointment must be objective and reasonable.[98]

Of course, Article 25 of the CCPR does not guarantee public employment to everyone. Instead, it only grants access, or opportunities on general terms of equality.[99] Once in office, there may exist higher thresholds for the removal from a public post. This applies especially in relation to judicial appointments. When Alberto Fujimori, President of the Republic of Peru, removed 13 members of the Supreme Court per decree, the Inter-American Court addressed the situation. It found that this process had not only violated basic precepts of democratic governance incompatible with the division of power within the state, but also that it violated Article 23 of the Inter-American Convention on political participation. The Commission asserted that the right to form part of the judiciary of a state party to the Convention, under conditions of equality is a right protected by the Article.[100] In another Inter-American case, this time against Panama, the wrongful dismissal of certain Circuit Judges after they refused to give in to an attempt to interfere with the impartial administration of justice, was considered a violation of Article 23.[101]

[98] ECtHR, *G.B. v. France*, (Appl. 44069/98, Judgment of 2 October 2001), para. 9.3.

[99] HRC, Report to the General Assembly, A/52/40, *Kall v. Poland*, Vol. II of 14 July 1997, para. 13.2.

[100] Inter-AmCtHR, *Walter Humberto Vasquez Vejarano v. Peru*, Case 11.166, Report No. 48/00 of 13 April 2000, para. 997. However, in the Constitutional Court Case (*Aguirre Roca, Rey Terry and Revoredo Marsano v. Peru*, judgment of 31 January 2001) the Inter-American Court addressed impeachment of other members of the Constitutional Court who had been appointed after the constitutional 'coup' in Peru as a matter of due process, rather than equal access to public service, para. 103.

[101] Inter-AmCtHR, *de Chiriqui v. Panama*, Case 10.026, Report No. 28/94, Judgment of 30 September 1994, para. 26.

V. General Participation

As was noted at the outset, the right to vote and stand in an election and to be equally represented in public service in human rights law is matched by the more general requirement that minorities must be afforded effective participation in decisions that affect them.[102]

A. Consultation

There have emerged a significant number of cases involving the right to consultation; most of these concern indigenous communities. According to the ILO Convention No. 169 concerning Indigenous and Tribal Peoples in Independent Countries, indigenous peoples do enjoy a particularly strong right of consultation. One might therefore argue that this practice is misleading in that it might not apply to minorities in general. On the other hand, the decisions discussed here were adopted in relation to the relevant articles of the CCPR and the European Convention, without reference to the ILO Convention. One might thus presume that the findings below, regarding indigenous peoples, are also of relevance to other minorities, at least where such minorities boast comparable characteristics, such as a long-standing and culturally relevant relationship with the territory in which they live, or a particular and culturally relevant dependency on traditional economic pursuits.

In *Diergaardt*, the Baster community in Namibia claimed the heritage of some 125 years of collective identity and a previous tradition of regional self-governance.[103] It argued that its rights under Article 25 of CCPR had been violated by the termination of their right to self-governance and the splitting up of their region into two parts which were amalgamated in turn with larger regions. The Court took a very narrow view of the entitlement of public participation. It argued that the rights claimed were individual rights only, which had not been affected by the measures taken by the Namibian government. After all, the members of the community could still participate on equal terms in public life of Namibia. Underpinning this rather cursory finding, which did not give consideration to a community's right to self-governance, may have been doubts as to the character of this particular community. The Committee had denied the existence of a distinctive culture, even after 125 years had elapsed.

[102] HRC, General Comment 23, Art. 27, Compilation of General Comments and General Recommendations Adopted by Human Rights Treaty Bodies, UN Doc. HRI/GEN/1/Rev.1 at 38, 1994.

[103] HRC, Communication No. 760/1997, *J.G.A. Diergaardt, (late Captain of the Rehoboth Baster Community), et al v. Namibia*, UN Doc. CCPR/C/69/D/7601997, 2000.

In an individual opinion, Martin Scheinin, a much respected expert on minority law, opposed what he termed the unnecessary emphasis on the individual nature of the rights of participation under Article 25:

In my view there are situations where Article 25 calls for special arrangements for rights of participation to be enjoyed by members of minorities and, in particular, indigenous peoples. When such a situation arises, it is not sufficient under Article 25 to afford individual members of such communities the individual right to vote in general elections. Some forms of local, regional or cultural autonomy may be called for in order to comply with the requirement of effective rights of participation. [104]

Professor Sheinin added that Article 25 would also have to be interpreted in connection with Article 1 of the Covenant, addressing the right of self-determination.

The right to participation through consultation was found to pertain to issues in relation to which 'minorities or indigenous groups have a right to the protection of traditional activities'. In particular, the Human Rights Committee applied the test of whether 'the impact of [the proposed action] ... is so substantial that it does effectively deny to the authors the right to enjoy their cultural rights in that region'.[105] This was found not to be the case where quarrying on a certain mountain slope was concerned, as it did not constitute a denial of the right to enjoy their own culture under Article 27. Reindeer herding, their traditional activity, had not actually been affected. Moreover, it was noted that the quarrying had been preceded by consultation with the relevant groups, and that their interests had been taken account of. As the Human Rights Committee emphasized in the context of indigenous rights:

... the enjoyment of the right to one's own culture may require positive legal measures of protection by a state party and measures to ensure the effective participation of members of minority communities in decisions which affect them. In its case law under the Optional Protocol, the committee has emphasized that the acceptability of measures that affect or interfere with the culturally significant economic activities of a minority depends on whether the members of the minority in question have had the opportunity to participate in the decision-making process in relation to these measures and whether they will continue to benefit from their traditional economy.[106]

[104] *Ibid.*, Individual Opinion by Matin Sheinin (concurring).

[105] HRC, Communication No. 511/1992, *Ilmari Laensman et al v. Finland*, UN Doc. CCPR/C/52/D/511/1992, para. 9.5.

[106] HRC, Communication No. 547/1993, *Apirana Mahuika et al v. New Zealand*, UN Doc. CCPR/C/70/D/547/1993, para. 9.6.

It is clear, therefore, that consultation must take place when the special interests or rights of minorities are affected. However, this does apparently not amount to a requirement to gain agreement of the affected groups:

...It is uncontested that the Muotkatunturi Herdsmen's Committee ... was consulted in the process of drawing up the logging plans and in the consultation, the Muotkatunturi Herdsmen's Committee did not react negatively to the plans for logging. That this consultation was unsatisfactory to the authors and was capable of greater interaction does not alter the Committee's assessment. It transpires that the State party's authorities did go through the process of weighing the author's interests and the general economic interests in the area specified in the complaint when deciding on the most appropriate measures of forestry management, i.e., logging methods, choice of logging areas and construction of roads in these areas.[107]

A further problem arises in cases of a government's acceptance of a right of co-decision on certain matters by minorities. Where there is not one single minority representative organization, or a body representing all such organizations, the question arises who is entitled to fulfil that function on behalf of the minority. The Human Rights Committee has confirmed that it cannot be all individual groups purporting to represent a minority (or in that case, individual tribal groups forming one or more indigenous peoples). In the case of *Grand Chief Donald Marshall*, the Mikmak people complained of exclusion from a consultative process that had led to the establishment of constitutional legislation relating to indigenous peoples in Canada. The Canadian government involved instead four umbrella organizations purporting to represent some 600 groups. The Mikmak asserted that they had not given a mandate to the relevant umbrella organization to represent them, and at any rate, their attempts to influence the position of that group had borne no fruit. Accordingly, there had been no genuine consultative process in relation to them. The Human Rights Committee found that:

It must be beyond dispute that the conduct of public affairs in a democratic state is the task of representatives of the people, elected for that purpose. Invariably, the conduct of public affairs affects the interest of large segments of the population or even the population as a whole, while in other instances it affects more directly the interest of more specific groups of society. Although prior consultations, such as public hearings or consultations with the most interested groups may often be envisaged by law or have evolved as public policy in the conduct of public affairs, Article 25(a) of the Covenant cannot be understood as meaning that any directly affected group, large

[107] HRC, Communication No. 671/1995, *Jouni E. Laensman et al v. Finland*, CCPR/C/58/D/671/1995, para. 10.5.

or small, has the unconditional right to choose the modalities of participation in the conduct of public affairs. In fact, that would be an extrapolation of the right to direct participation by the citizens, far beyond the scope of Article 25(a).[108]

Accordingly, the Committee confirmed that the failure of the state party to invite representatives of the Mikmak tribe to the constitutional conferences on aboriginal matters, which constituted conduct of public affairs, did not infringe their right to political participation.[109]

In another instance concerning the Maori groups in New Zealand, the Committee found that this indigenous group did have a right of consultation in relation to the matter at issue (fisheries), that New Zealand had engaged in a broad process of consultation and that the legislative project in question had been changed in consequence. Maori representatives themselves had given assurances of the comprehensive nature of the consultative process. In this circumstance, it was held that New Zealand had taken steps sufficient to ensure compliance with the Covenant. However, given its limited ambit it is noteworthy that the Committee considered the issue under Article 27.[110] This would support the inclusion of the requirement of participation in the Article envisaged in the General Comment No. 23.

B. Other General Issues

In *Sankov and the United Macedonian Organization Ilinden v. Bulgaria*, the European Court of Human Rights noted that the failure by the state to register an organization could not in itself lead to a prohibition of meetings and manifestations of the unregistered entity.[111] The right to expression and assembly for political purposes therefore does not depend on previous registration.

Through the application of Articles 10 and 11 of the European Convention, the European Court of Human Rights also extended protection to the rights of unofficial political workers. In that case, the authorities in Northern Cyprus had excluded a member of the Movement for an Independent and Federal Cyprus from entry. He was aiming to hold inter-ethnic consultations in the hope of fostering a climate for the peaceful solution of the Cyprus issue. As this exclusion appeared to lack a legal basis, it was found incompatible with Article 11.[112]

108 HRC, Communication No. 205/1986, *Marshall v. Canada*, CCPR/C/43/D/205/1986, para. 5.5.

109 *Ibid.*, para. 6.

110 HRC, Communication No. 547/1993, *Apirana Mahuika et al v. New Zealand*, UN Doc. CCPR/C/70/D/547/1993, para. 9.6.

111 ECtHR, *Stankov and the United Macedonian Organization Ilinden v. Bulgaria*, (Appl. 29221/95 and 29225/95, Judgment of 2 October 2001), para. 81.

112 ECtHR, *Djavit An v. Turkey*, (Appl. 20652/92, Judgment of 10 February 2003), para. 69.

VI. Expression of Minority Identity

Contrary to the presumption in the case of the Silesians in Poland, minority representative associations will not necessarily seek parliamentary representation. In many instances, minority representative associations will form themselves to advance the identity of their group, and to campaign for it, without seeking electoral representation by forming a political party. This, too, is part of the right to full and effective participation and covered by the freedoms of expression and association. The European Court of Human Rights has confirmed that association and expression constitute essential foundations of a democratic society and of the basic conditions for its progress and for each individual's self-fulfillment.[113] This applies also to minority groups:

> ... there can be no justification for hindering a group solely because it seeks to debate in public the situation of part of the State's population and to find, according to democratic rules, solutions capable of satisfying everyone concerned ....
>
> 89. The inhabitants of a region in a country are entitled to form associations in order to promote the region's special characteristics. The fact that an association asserts a minority consciousness cannot in itself justify an interference with its rights under Article 11 of the Conventions ....[114]

It was already noted above that restrictions on the freedom of assembly and expression may be subject to a wider margin of appreciation where the organization in question espouses violence. The question arises whether, in addition to violence, the mere fact of harbouring 'separatist views' and having 'a political agenda that included the notion of autonomy' for a certain region or even secession justifies interference with the right to assembly.[115] The Court clearly denied such a view:

> The Court reiterates, however, that the fact that a group of persons calls for autonomy or even requests secession of part of the country's territory—thus demanding fundamental constitutional and territorial changes—cannot automatically justify a prohibition of its assemblies. Demanding territorial changes in speeches and demonstrations does not automatically amount to a threat to the country's territorial integrity and national security.... The essence of democracy is its capacity to resolve problems through open debate. Sweeping measures of a preventive nature to suppress freedom of assembly and expression other than in cases of incitement to violence or rejection

[113] ECtHR, *Stankov and the United Macedonian Organization Ilinden v. Bulgaria*, (Appl. 29221/95 and 29225/95, Judgment of 2 October 2001), paras. 86, 92.

[114] *Ibid.*, para. 88.

[115] *Ibid.*, para. 96.

of democratic principles—however shocking and unacceptable certain views or words used may appear to the authorities, and however illegitimate the demands may be—do a disservice to democracy and often even endanger it.

In a democratic society based on the rule of law, political ideas which challenge the existing order and whose realization is advocated by peaceful means must be afforded a proper opportunity of expression through the exercise of the right of assembly as well as by other lawful means.

98. The court finds, therefore, that the probability that separatist declaration would be made at meetings organized by Illinden could not justify a ban on such meetings.[116]

In *Sidiropoulos*, the Greek authorities had determined that an association of members of the Macedonian minority in Northern Greece was tantamount to undermining Greece's territorial integrity, national security, or public order. However, the European Court of Human Rights confirmed again that 'mention of the consciousness of belonging to a minority and the preservation and development of a minority's culture could not be said to constitute a threat to democratic society'.[117] The Court added that:

. . . the aims of the association called 'Home of Macedonian Civilization' as set out in its memorandum of association, were exclusively to preserve and develop the traditions and folk culture of the Florina regions . . . . Such aims appear to the Court to be perfectly clear and legitimate; the inhabitants of a region in a country are entitled to form an association in order to promote the region's special characteristics, for historical as well as economic reasons. Even supposing that the founders of an association like the one in the instant case assert a minority consciousness, the Document of the Copenhagen Meeting of the Conference on the Human Dimension of the CSCE (Section IV) of 29 June 1990 and the Charter of Paris for a New Europe of 21 November 1990—which Greece has signed—allow them to form associations to protect their cultural and spiritual heritage.[118]

Neither did representation of the actual or purported minority at international fora, especially the then CSCE, to which Greece itself had subscribed, furnish a ground for its repression.[119]

VII. Conclusion

The right to democratic governance is surprisingly well entrenched in the jurisprudence of international implementation bodies, including human rights

[116] *Ibid.*, at 97.

[117] ECtHR, *Sidiropoulos and Others v. Greece*, (Appl. 57/19997/841/1047, Judgment of 10 July 1998), para. 41.

[118] *Ibid.* [119] *Ibid.*

courts. This extends not only to the European system with its long tradition of practice fostered by the Council of Europe. Instead, democratic entitlements have also been addressed and defended at the universal level. This includes the entitlement to vote and to stand as a candidate in genuine and periodic elections, and to a lesser extent the right to executive participation in governance and general entitlements of participation.

It is also clearly established that members of minorities must be given full and equal opportunities to benefit from these entitlements. Certainly, appurtenance to a minority does not furnish a ground for restricting rights of participation. The question arises whether there are also additional entitlements that go beyond non-discrimination and equal rights.

At the European regional level, Article 15 of the Framework Convention has fostered a great deal of implementation practice. That practice has clearly confirmed an increasingly high standard for measures to be taken by the state in order to ensure full and effective participation of minorities. In this way, implementation practice has substantiated the general provisions offered by the Framework Convention, despite the fact that the instrument was deliberately kept beyond the jurisdictional reach of the European Court of Human Rights.

At the universal level, the situation is more complex in the absence of a binding legal standard on political participation of minorities as such. The limited scope of Article 27 of the CCPR has, however, been broadened by the Human Rights Committee, which has included political participation in its General Comment on the Article. Moreover, the implementation practice of the Human Rights Committee has begun to address this issue in relation to minorities, although often in the specific context of indigenous rights.

The gradual introduction of the doctrine of full and effective participation at the universal level is certainly supported by regional jurisprudence. Both the African Commission and the Inter-American Commission and Court on Human Rights have developed significant jurisprudence in this area, which belies the assumption that the implementation of democratic commitments and effective participation of minorities is an issue of exclusive or principal relevance to Europe. Regrettably, of course, there is no Asian regional practice that can be reviewed in this respect.

In the absence of a specialist regional standard on minorities, practice has focused on the general right to democratic participation and the rights to expression, association, and assembly. This has also allowed the European Court of Human Rights to address the issue. While the Framework Convention is not subject to review by the European Court, the Court has nevertheless been able to develop a significant body of jurisprudence of relevance to minorities. This has been possible due to its own emphasis on the rights to expression and association in the context of political parties, and the application of Article 3 of Protocol 1, both by itself, and in conjunction with Article 14 and considerations of discrimination. Accordingly, all three regional systems have generated a growing and fairly consistent jurisprudence on the subject.

The substance of the right to participation in its three aspects provided in Article 25 CCPR and regional standards has been developed accordingly. The right to vote and to be a candidate in elections has been addressed in a minority context, as has the right to establish minority representative parties and to seek executive representation. In addition, the Human Rights Committee and the European Court and Commission have had repeated occasion to consider and clarify the issue of minority consultative mechanisms.

This jurisprudence has confirmed the existence of the rights to participation of minorities in the three aspects covered by Article 25 CCPR and corresponding regional commitments. However, perhaps the greatest value of this jurisprudence lies not in establishing or confirming the rights in question as far as Article 25 CCPR and its regional shadows go—in a way this has not been controversial. Instead the true value of this jurisprudence lies in the fact that it addresses the restrictions to the exercise of these rights that are sometimes applied by states.

Interestingly enough, the oldest of the implementation bodies, the European Commission and Court, have been the most cautious. When considering political participation issues, either generally or in the context of minorities, the Court has been at great pains to emphasize the freedom of each state to provide for its own system of democratic governance. The international bodies do not wish to give the impression that they claim a right to define how democratic governance should be organized in a particular state. Accordingly, the state has been found to exercise a wide margin of appreciation when establishing its constitutional and electoral system.

In the European context this wide margin of state discretion extends to the regulation of the right of passive voting, which is generally challenged when it has been denied 'arbitrarily', thus denying the free expression of the opinion of the people. In other regions, the protection of the right to stand for election appears to be somewhat more advanced, matching the wider assessment of the proportionality of restrictive measure taken by the state before the European Commission and Court in the context of active voting. In any event, it is clear that minority identity, or the fact that a candidate stands for minority interests, cannot in itself preclude the right to stand in elections. This applies even where the existence of the minority identity claimed by the candidate in question is denied by the state, or where the candidate is committed to advancing the cause of the minority despite resistance by the state.

There is also a confluence of practice in relation to party registration. This issue has been addressed both in the context of the right to democratic participation, and the rights to association, assembly, and expression. The regional Courts have found that the democratic impact in relation to decisions on party registration requires a particularly rigorous assessment of state action in this respect. Such restrictions can be justified only by compelling reasons. Again, minority identity of party members or supporters, or a party programme dedicated towards enhancing minority interests, may not in themselves be considered such reasons. To the contrary, minority representation through parties is immediately protected by the relevant provisions. This applies even to minority parties advocating self-determination and perhaps secession. The situation differs, however, when the party concerned calls for the application of violence or for the imposition of a non-democratic system of governance. If violence is called for in a party programme, in the statements of its leaders, or through its actions, the margin of appreciation of the state increases.

With respect to association outside of the context of political parties, similar considerations apply. Minority representative organizations do have the right to form and to exhibit minority culture and to work towards the enhancement of the status of the relevant group. Restrictions should only apply where the association is dedicated to violence or the overthrow of democratic government.

Participation through democratic practices, therefore, is strongly defended through the human rights system, also and especially in relation to minorities. On the other hand, the absence of a great deal of judicial precedent on the other forms of political participation, outlined at the beginning of this chapter, is not entirely surprising. Due to the absence of binding legal standards outside of Article 15 of the Framework Convention, these issues tend not to be justiciable before universal or regional bodies. Nevertheless, by exploiting the special position of indigenous groups, and other creative uses of the international treaty bodies, a number of new elements, already well known at the European level, are gradually being introduced universally. However, it will still be some time until the full panopoly of mechanisms to ensure full and effective participation of minorities in public life will find a firm legal basis in general human rights law.

Index